THIRD EDITION

Psychology and the Legal System

THIRD EDITION

Psychology and the Legal System

Lawrence S. Wrightsman
University of Kansas

Michael T. Nietzel
University of Kentucky

William H. Fortune
University of Kentucky

BROOKS/COLE PUBLISHING COMPANY
PACIFIC GROVE, CALIFORNIA

Sponsoring Editor: *Marianne Taflinger*
Editorial Associate: *Virge Perelli-Minetti*
Production Coordinator: *Fiorella Ljunggren*
Manuscript Editor: *Micky Lawler*
Permissions Editor: *Karen Wootten*
Interior and Cover Design: *Susan Haberkorn*
Photo Coordinator: *Larry Molmud*
Typesetting: *Weimer Graphics, Inc.*
Cover Printing: *Phoenix Color Corporation*
Printing and Binding: *Arcata Graphics/Fairfield*
(Credits continue on p. 523.)

Library of Congress Cataloging-in-Publication Data

Wrightsman, Lawrence S.
    Psychology and the legal system / Lawrence S. Wrightsman, Michael
T. Nietzel, William H. Fortune. — 3rd ed.
        p.   cm.
    Includes bibliographical references and index.
    ISBN 0-534-17514-7 :
    1. Justice, Administration of—United States—Psychological
aspects.   2. Criminal justice, Administration of—United States–
–Psychological aspects.   3. Practice of law—United States–
–Psychological aspects.   4. Psychology, Forensic.   I. Nietzel,
Michael T.   II. Fortune, William H.   III. Title.
KF8700.W75   1993
347.73'001—dc20
[347.30701]   92-46588
                                             CIP

Dedicated to Franz Joseph Haydn, who wrote: "Since God gave me a joyful heart, He will forgive me for having served him joyfully."

Contents

Preface

The legal system has, for centuries, exerted an immense influence on everyday activities of all citizens. But in the last half of this century the legal system has become a focus of interest for laypersons and scholars alike. From the Supreme Court's school desegregation decision of 1954 through the recent controversial trials of prominent persons such as Mike Tyson and William Kennedy Smith, as well as recent court rulings on abortion rights, the last five decades have seen an increasing ambivalence about the law. Attorneys are distrusted; yet their numbers increase, and they continue to be consulted when people face decisions or respond to emergencies. Citizens of the United States are reminded that their country is "a nation of laws, not of men" (sic); yet they are also told (by some, at least) that social change will not result from new regulations alone.

This pervasiveness of the law demands analysis, and in the last 20 years especially, scholars from a wealth of disciplines have applied their concepts to the legal system. As one of these perspectives, psychology has much to offer. The purpose of this book is to examine the legal system through the use of psychological concepts, methods, and research results. The primary audience for the book is those students taking a course in psychology and the law or the criminal justice system, as well as others who seek to know more about the law as a profession. This book may also be used as a supplement in those psychology courses that emphasize applied social psychology, social issues, or policy analysis. In addition, it offers coverage of a number of topics relevant to law school courses that introduce law students to social science findings and applications.

Organization

This book is organized around four basic conflicts that pervade a psychological analysis of the law. These conflicts generate dilemmas that persist and recur, whether the topic is the training of lawyers, the punishment prescribed by judges, or the rights of the mentally ill. Society demands responses to these conflicts, and psychology provides methods and empirical results that bear on their resolution. Chapter 1, by introducing these conflicts and dilemmas, provides an organizing structure for the rest of the book. Chapter 2 identifies four roles for psychologists in response to the dilemmas in Chapter 1; much of the material in this chapter is not found in other psychology-and-law texts.

Textbooks on psychology and the law are mostly a product of the last 15 years, and fewer than a dozen have appeared. The field is still taking shape, but certain changes are apparent. Most earlier texts focused on the courts; others limited their coverage to the criminal justice system; some acknowledged that they were selective for other reasons. This book aspires to be comprehensive in its coverage of relevant issues. The criminal justice system is not slighted; a chronological treatment of this process is provided, with chapters on theories of crime, the police, criminal investigations, bail setting and plea bargaining, the trial process, and sentencing. But psychology has much more to offer. For example, the socialization and training of lawyers have generated empirical inquiry in recent years, in studies summarized in Chapter 4. The appellate process, neglected in most other books, also is a subject for chapter-length coverage. Conceptions of morality and legality that form a cornerstone of responses to the four conflicts are analyzed in Chapter 3 and then utilized in subsequent chapters of the book. Children's rights, a topic receiving renewed attention in our society today, are discussed at length in an expanded chapter on the rights of special groups. An entire chapter is devoted to the psychological analysis of rape.

Other, more specialized topics that receive extended coverage (often for the first time in such a book) include recent views on the hereditary explanations for criminal behavior, the use by jurors of confessions as evidence, entrapment, death-qualified jurors, and alternative dispute resolution.

This text offers a variety of devices to aid students in their learning. Each chapter begins with a chapter outline and ends with a detailed summary. Throughout the book, examples from actual cases and trials—often in the form of interest boxes—are used to illustrate concepts and to stimulate thought. Frequently used concepts are cross-referenced. A glossary of terms, prepared by Dr. Nancy W. Perry of Creighton University with the assistance of Angela Kraybill, has been supplemented with new terms for the third edition by Michael T. Nietzel and William Fortune. A separate instructor's manual is available from the publisher.

A recent survey of instructors of psychology-and-law courses by Professor Marsha B. Liss, published in the August 1992 issue of *Law and Human Behavior* (Vol. 16, No. 4, pp. 463–471), indicates that this book is the most frequently assigned textbook for undergraduate courses (Table 2, p. 467). In commenting on the second edition in her article, Professor Liss notes that its coverage, although strong on the social psychology of legal procedures, could benefit from greater recognition of clinical applications and issues of mental health law.

This third edition seeks to redress this imbalance. Two coauthors have been added: Michael R. Nietzel is a clinical psychologist who has written several texts, including ones on psychological consultation in the courtroom and theories of criminal behavior; William Fortune is a practicing attorney and a professor of law who specializes in criminal procedure and legal ethics. A completely new chapter on Competence in the Legal System (Chapter 11) has been added; this chapter contains material on various criminal competencies, particularly competence to stand trial. It also discusses the special questions surrounding the competence of children as participants in the justice system.

Mental health issues receive extended coverage in other parts of this edition. For example, additional material on mental illness and the law, the prediction of dangerousness, and the insanity defense has been included, especially in Chapters 16 and 17. At several points throughout this edition, aspects of expert forensic testimony are discussed. New material, including the latest empirical studies, has been added to several chapters dealing with the psychology of law enforcement. Forensic uses of hypnosis, analysis of eyewitness identification and lineup procedures, police selection, and intervention by police in crises are examples of topics that have been expanded. An entirely new section describes and evaluates the techniques used in criminal profiling.

The addition of an attorney as one of the three authors of the third edition has resulted in an expanded discussion of legal assumptions and important case law as well as an increased sophistication of the book's legal analyses. More material on civil case law and civil procedures has been included, in order to complement the already extensive coverage of the criminal justice system.

Discussion of alternative dispute resolution—a wave of the future in civil disputes—has been increased. New material on the death penalty, on theories of crime, and on jury selection has been provided, as well as a completely new section on pretrial publicity and resulting changes in venue. The references section, with well over 1000 entries, reflects our expanded and updated coverage.

The responsibility of textbook authors does not end with the preparation of the manuscript; any publication is only a step in the never-ending search for understanding. We continue our quest, and we earnestly hope that the third edition of *Psychology and the Legal System* will aid in yours.

Acknowledgments

Our preparation of this third edition was aided by the thoughtful comments of several colleagues who read initial drafts of the manuscript and provided detailed suggestions that contributed immensely to the quality of the book. We want to thank Lieutenant Fran Root of the Lexington Fayette County Division of Police and David Berry and Richard Milich of the University of Kentucky for their careful examination of portions of the initial draft.

Along with these evaluations, the book received extremely conscientious, well-informed prepublication reviews from a team of law and psychology scholars commissioned by the publisher. In each case these reviewers supplied lengthy evaluations of the manuscript that were both fair and pointed. We owe a considerable intellectual debt to the following people who took the time to provide a set of reviews that challenged us to improve our manuscript in important ways: Brian Cutler of Florida International University, Valerie Hans of the University of Delaware, Robert Mauro of the University of Oregon, Gary Melton of the University of Nebraska, Gary Moran of Florida International University, Steve Penrod of the University of Minnesota, and Gary L. Wells of Iowa State University. We hope they recognize their impact on the final version of the book.

Our editor at Brooks/Cole, Marianne Taflinger, was extremely helpful in coordinating the project and guiding it to completion. She provided just the right combination of support and gentle pressure to help us maintain our schedule. Once again, Fiorella Ljunggren coordinated the production with dedication and skill. And Susan Haberkorn contributed her talent and creativity to the design and cover of the book. To all of them our sincere thanks.

We received invaluable assistance from several staff members at the University of Kentucky. Cheryl Jones and Carol Parris of the University of Kentucky College of Law Library helped locate important legal materials. Finally, Shirley Jacobs of the Department of Psychology masterminded the final preparation of our manuscript while simultaneously providing editorial assistance, solving our technical word processing problems, coordinating the correspondence among three authors separated by half a continent, updating the entire bibliography, and generally keeping us on track to the final destination. Although we have become accustomed to this level of efficiency from Shirley, we never quite understand how she manages it. We cannot thank her strongly enough.

Lawrence S. Wrightsman
Michael T. Nietzel
William H. Fortune

THIRD EDITION

Psychology and the Legal System

1

Psychology and the Law: Impossible Choices

It's "one of those semesters." Over the last couple of months, you have suffered several problems. First, your "little" sister has called. Actually, she's not so little anymore. She's a junior in high school, and she's just discovered she's pregnant. She's mortified; what should she do? Although abortions are still legal in her state, she questions whether abortion is the proper choice for her. However, she seriously doubts whether having a baby would be a good idea.

Next, your bank mails you an official notice, informing you that a check has bounced. The bank claims that you wrote a check for $90; you know you didn't. But the bank, frustrated by a wave of "hot" checks by students, is considering prosecuting you. Actually, you lost your checkbook several weeks ago, and now someone apparently has forged your name. You are innocent of any criminal intent or action. But are you liable for the overdraft?

Distraught by these events, and hence distracted, you drive your car through a crosswalk and gently bump a pedestrian. As far as you can tell, he is outraged but not seriously injured. However, he copies down your name, address, and license number, and he angrily tells you to expect a call from his lawyer. Certainly these events are distressing. And we hope they do not happen to you. But they are frequent in the United States. Close to half the pregnancies in this country occur outside of wedlock, and about one-third of all pregnancies now end in abortion, at a rate of 1.6 million per year or more than 4000 a day. Although your "hot check" was beyond your control, someone has committed fraud and the bank is entitled to legal redress. And the nudging of a pedestrian by your car's fender caused no real harm, but there are close to 800,000 attorneys in the United States—most of whom stay quite busy—and more than a few of them would be willing to assist the aggrieved party in bringing suit against you.

THE IMPORTANCE OF LAWS

To outsiders, the incidents just described may seem commonplace, but they are urgently important to the people involved. Taken together, they illustrate the pervasiveness of the law in our society. But just how *does* the law work? The purpose of this book is to help you understand how the legal system operates, by applying psychological concepts, findings, and methods to its study.

The Extensiveness of Laws

Laws are everywhere. They entwine us; they bear on—often intrude on—everything from birth to death (Post, 1963). Laws regulate our private lives and our public actions. Laws dictate how long we must stay in school, how fast we can drive, when (and, to some extent, whom) we can marry, and whether we are allowed to enjoy many individualistic pleasures, such as playing our stereo at full volume or letting our dog romp through the neighbors' yards and gardens. Some say our society has too many laws, but almost all people agree that a system of laws is necessary. Social life without law as a means of social control would result in anarchy, and anarchy—for most of us—carries costs that far outweigh its freedoms.

Laws as Human Creations

Given that the body of laws is so wide in its impact, we might expect that the law is a part of nature, that it was originally discovered by a set of archaeologists or explorers. Perhaps we summon the image of Moses carrying the Ten Commandments down from the mountain. But our laws are not chiseled in stone. Rather, laws are human creations that evolve out of the need to resolve human conflicts. Any complex society generates differences in behavior and hence disagreements among people. When disagreements occur, society must have mechanisms to resolve them. So societies develop laws and other regulations as conflict-resolution mechanisms (for an example, see Box 1-1).

Laws and the Resolution of Conflict

Conflict—that is, disagreement, argument, and dispute—is not necessarily bad; nor is it always good. Mainly, conflict is inevitable. It cannot be avoided, any more than you can avoid sneezing when the urge to sneeze begins. But society can establish procedures to control your behavior when your sneezing intrudes on another's rights. We recognize the need for mechanisms—laws, rules, habits—to discourage a person from sneezing in people's faces or on their food. Customs and rules of etiquette evolve partly to deal with the conflict between one person's impulses and others' rights; hence we cover our face with a handkerchief when a sneeze is coming on, or we apologize if the act can't be constrained. Similarly, laws are developed to try to untangle and resolve conflicts that cannot be prevented.

The Changing of Laws

Because our society is so technologically developed, it also is constantly changing. As society changes, so does our day-to-day existence. The basic raw material for the construction and the revision of laws is human experience. Laws need to be developed, interpreted, reinterpreted, and modified to keep up with the rapid changes in our lives. As George Will (1984) expressed it, "Fitting the law to a technologically dynamic society often is like fitting trousers to a 10-year-old: Adjustments are constantly needed." For example, back in 1973, when the U.S. Congress passed the 55-mile-per-hour speed limit, the law made sense because of the urgent need to conserve gasoline. A decade later, with gasoline more abundant and, temporarily, less costly, the federal government allowed states to return speed limits to 65 miles per hour. Critics of the 55-mile-per-hour limit acknowledged that it conserved fuel and saved lives, but they also argued that it resulted "in a

---

Box **1-1** | A "Boom" for 50 Bucks

States have passed laws restricting the "boom car," or the playing of a car stereo at a very high volume. Effective at the beginning of 1990, California made it illegal to operate a car sound system that can be heard 50 feet away (Bishop, 1990). Convicted violators must pay a $50 fine for the first offense and increased fines for any subsequent violations.

Although California was the first state to pass such a law, other states have enacted even more severe penalties, including the confiscation of such sound systems. And many cities and municipalities have passed local ordinances that require drivers to turn down the volume.

One driver who may be affected by "boom" laws is Pat Brister, of Arlington Heights, Illinois, winner of the "Thunder on Wheels" competition for two consecutive years. His 1987 Thunderbird has a 15-speaker system with 890 watts of sound, leaving enough space for "a passenger and maybe a folding toothbrush" (Bishop, 1990, p. 10).

tremendous loss of time—and time has an economic value, just as fuel and lives have economic value" (Kilpatrick, 1985).

Certainly the framers of the U.S. Constitution, and even the lawmakers of 20 years ago, never anticipated that the possibility of surrogate motherhood would lead to a conflict between the natural mother of an infant and a couple contracting for her services. Yet this is what happened in the "Baby M" case. After agreeing to be artificially inseminated and receiving payment from a couple named Stern, Ms. Mary Beth Whitehead decided that she wanted to keep the child. The Sterns filed a lawsuit against her to gain custody of Baby M and establish their legal parental rights; a New Jersey judge ruled in their favor, although Ms. Whitehead was awarded visitation privileges. Concerned with the ethical implications of "baby selling," several states have since made it illegal to pay a surrogate mother more than her out-of-pocket expenses in connection with the pregnancy and birth.

Finally, no one could have anticipated in the early 1980s the spread of a disease like AIDS to the point that, by 1991, the U.S. Senate would vote to require mandatory AIDS testing for some health-care workers and to further require these workers, if HIV-infected, to inform their patients of the infection.

Consider again the examples at the beginning of this chapter. Each reveals how, in our complex and advanced society, basic values come into conflict. Should a woman have the legal right to have her own pregnancy aborted? Although that question has been controversial for centuries, only recently have legally tolerated and medically safe abortions become frequent in the United States. The U.S. Supreme Court, in its 1973 *Roe* v. *Wade* decision, gave virtual sanction to abortion on demand during the first trimester of pregnancy. Almost two decades later, in the case of *Rust* v. *Sullivan*

(1991), this same court ruled that federally funded family-planning clinics could be barred from even discussing abortion as an option with their clients.

These controversial rulings force us to reexamine our basic values and beliefs about the foundations of morality. Citizens of the United States are divided on this issue: On one side are women who have availed themselves of legal abortion, various organizations that advocate for its availability, and many citizens who believe that the right to an abortion is part of a fundamental right to privacy. On the other side are protesters who urge the overthrow of the *Roe* v. *Wade* decision, legislators attempting to change the ruling, and people who believe that abortion is the killing of an unborn child and is morally justified only in the rarest circumstances. Which do we value more: an ethic that endorses freedom, especially the right of individual women to control their own bodies, or a principle of interdependence that emphasizes the state's obligations to others, including the unborn (Woodward & Uehling, 1985)? The 1992 Supreme Court decision of *Planned Parenthood* v. *Casey*, in which the Court upheld its basic ruling of *Roe* v. *Wade* but allowed the states to add some restrictions on the availability of abortion, shows that the Court itself is balanced (perhaps unsteadily) between the conflicting sides of this issue.

Likewise, the ease with which checks can be forged or credit cards misused reflects a conflict in modern society. A materially abundant society must develop some system that can substitute for carrying large amounts of cash on your person. Security is an important value; you want your money to be protected. But access is also vital; when you have a reason to spend some of your hard-earned money, you want to do so right away. Bank checks and credit cards seem like a good trade-off, and ideally they work. But occasionally the system breaks down.

Current laws function as a guide for resolving controversies between affected parties. Clearly the person who forges another's name to a check and cashes it or the person who uses a stolen credit card to make purchases has violated the regulations of our society. But in cases like this, laws must help resolve disputes between other affected parties—the bank versus the owner of the checking account, the store versus the credit-card owner.

Car accidents—even minor ones—cause conflicts over basic rights. The technological development of the automobile produced several new adversaries, including pedestrians versus car drivers, and hence new laws. Consider a driver whose car strikes and injures a pedestrian. Does this driver bear a legal requirement to report the incident to the police? Yes, of course. But look again. Doesn't this requirement violate the U.S. Constitution's Fifth Amendment, which safeguards each of us against self-incrimination, against bearing witness in conflict with our own best interests?

Shortly after motor cars became popular in the first two decades of this century, a certain Edward Rosenheimer was charged with violating the newly necessary hit-and-run regulation. He did not contest the charge that he had caused an accident that injured another person, but he claimed that the law requiring him to report it to the police was unconstitutional because it forced him to incriminate himself. Therefore, he argued, that law should be removed from the books, and he should be freed of the charge of leaving the scene of an accident. Surprisingly, the Court of General Sessions in New York State agreed with him and released him from custody.

Authorities in New York were, of course, unhappy with a court decision that permitted a person who caused an injury to avoid being apprehended, and so they appealed the decision to a higher court, the New York Court of Appeals. This court, recognizing that the Constitution and the recent law clashed with each other, ruled in favor of the state and overturned the previous decision. This appeals court concluded that rights to "constitutional privilege"—that is, to avoid self-incrimination—must give way to the competing principle of the right of injured persons to seek redress for their sufferings (Post, 1963). The U.S. Supreme Court, in its *California* v. *Byers* (1971) decision, reaffirmed this principle, holding that a California statute requiring motorists involved in accidents to stop and identify themselves did not violate the self-incrimination clause. Of course the Court did not hold that the statute took precedence over the self-incrimination clause, because constitutional provisions are the supreme law of the land. Instead the Court reconciled the statute with the self-incrimination clause, by first referring to the distinction between compelled disclosure of one's thoughts (which the self-incrimination clause protects against) and compelled disclosure of physical characteristics such as hair samples (which the self-incrimination clause does not protect against). The Court then held that requiring motorists to stop and reveal identity falls on the physical characteristics (or, as the Court put it, "non-testimonial") side of the line. Through such constructive interpretations, constitutional provisions enacted 200 years ago are made consistent with the requirements of a modern industrial society.

This example illustrates once more that the law is an evolving human creation, designed to arbitrate between values that are in opposition to each other. Before the advent of automobiles, hit-and-run accidents seldom occurred. However, once cars became a part of society, many new laws had to be established, and the courts obliged by holding the new laws to be constitutional.

Most of us learned at an early age that it is

illegal for a driver to leave the scene of an accident before information has been exchanged and authorities have been contacted. But other conflicts remain between the rights of individual drivers and society's need to be protected from dangerous forces. For example, if the police stop an automobile and charge the driver with drunk driving, does the driver have a right to have an attorney present before submitting to a "breathalyzer" test? We know that, when police read suspects their "*Miranda* rights," the suspects are told they may have a lawyer present before answering any questions. (See Chapter 9 for a description of *Miranda* rights.) In a general way, the Sixth Amendment to the U.S. Constitution provides the right to counsel for persons accused of crimes. Does this right extend to a decision about participating in a chemical breath test that measures one's blood alcohol content? As recently as 1984, the supreme court of one state (Kansas) resolved this question by concluding that people arrested for drunk driving have no constitutional right to talk to a lawyer before deciding whether to take a breath test (Toplikar, 1984). The court concluded that "it is not until after the test has been administered that the state commits itself to the criminal prosecution"; that is, the Sixth Amendment right to consult one's attorney applies only after the prosecution phase has been initiated, so ruled this court.

But even this decision does not close the matter. Persons who refuse a breathalyzer test risk having their driver's license suspended (usually from three months to a year). In addition, the fact that they declined can be used as evidence against them if the authorities still decide to prosecute them. The Supreme Court (in *South Dakota* v. *Neville*, 1983) held that these requirements did not violate defendants' Fifth Amendment privilege against incriminating themselves. So the decision not to take the breathalyzer test can be a potent one, and

it would seem appropriate that the driver's attorney be consulted. Although the Fifth and Sixth Amendments to the Constitution do not require states to allow those stopped for driving under the influence to call their lawyers, states could pass laws establishing such a requirement. A state passing such a law would be resolving the conflict in favor of the motorist; a state refusing to pass such a law would be treating the safety of the public as paramount.

DIFFERENT APPROACHES TO THE STUDY OF THE LAW

A system as necessary and pervasive as the law demands study. Scholars from different perspectives have applied their disciplines' concepts and methods to understand the legal system. These different approaches may, at first glance, seem at odds, but they are simply different kinds of explanations, different ways to account for the facts (Black, 1976).

Consider an arrest. Why did it occur? Do we explain a particular arrest as a decision by an individual police officer (that is, a psychological approach) or as a fulfillment of the officer's role expectations (a sociological approach)? The law also can be studied from a historical perspective; for example, at what points in time and for what historical reasons were children given some of the protections accorded adults under the law? Or economists may study the impact of antitrust legislation on the growth of industry. Some scholars draw on several different disciplines to study the law; their use of a multidisciplinary framework is known as *sociolegal studies*. Several distinct scholarly approaches are summarized in the following sections.

The Anthropological Approach

Anthropologists compare laws (and mechanisms for instituting and altering laws) in different societies and relate them to other characteristics of these societies. They may be interested in the incidence of rape in different types of societies and its relationship to other factors, such as the amount of violence among people in each society, the extent of separation of the sexes during childhood, or the degree to which males dominate females (Sanday, 1981). An anthropological approach also questions why certain crimes are more frequent in certain societies. Aspects of this approach are examined more fully in Chapter 15.

The Sociological Approach

Sociologists, in contrast, usually study a specific society and examine its institutions (such as the family, the church, or the subculture) to determine their role in developing adherence to the law. The sociologist might ask questions like "What role does social class play in criminal behavior in the United States today?" or "Is the development of a gang the product of racial hostility?" Sociologists use concepts such as "social control" to explain deviant behavior and measure its seriousness. In fact, some sociologists define law as governmental social control (Black, 1972). Their approach tries to predict and explain social behavior without regard to the individual as such. Sociological theories of crime are reviewed in Chapter 5.

The Philosophical Approach

Philosophers seek to understand the nature of justice. They question whether differences exist between what is legal and what is moral. In doing so, they examine the purpose, the value, and the impact of law. For instance, is it just for a wealthy injury victim to receive more compensation than a poor injury victim? Should a man who rapes a 7-year-old child receive more severe punishment than a man who rapes a prostitute? Does a person suffering a painful terminal illness have the right to take her own life? Chapter 3 evaluates conceptions of justice and distinctions between morality and legality; analyses by philosophers are helpful in understanding these distinctions.

The Psychological Approach

A psychological approach to the law emphasizes its human determinants. So do sociology and anthropology—but the focus in the psychological approach is on the individual as the unit of analysis. Individuals are seen as responsible for their own conduct and as contributing to its causation. Psychology looks at the impact of the police officer, the victim, the juror, the expert witness, the lawyer, the judge, the defendant, the prison guard, and the parole officer on the legal system. Psychology assumes that characteristics of participants in the legal system affect how the system operates. By "characteristics," we mean these persons' abilities, their perspectives, their values, their experience—all the factors that influence their behavior. Will a police officer arrest a traffic violator or let her go with a reprimand? Will a defendant and his attorney accept a plea bargain, or will they go to trial? Will a Hispanic juror be more sympathetic toward a Hispanic person on trial than toward a non-Hispanic defendant? Will one type of prison inmate respond better than another to rehabilitative efforts?

The behavior of participants in the legal system is a result not only of their personal, internal qualities but also of the setting in which they operate. Kurt Lewin, a founder of social psychology, proposed the equation $B = f(p, e)$; that is, behavior is a function of the person *and* the environment. Qualities of the external environment and pressures from the situation affect an individual's behavior. A prosecuting attorney may recommend a harsher sentence for a convicted felon if the case has been highly publicized, the community is outraged over the crime, and the prosecutor happens to be waging a reelection campaign. A juror holding out for a guilty verdict may yield if all the other jurors passionately proclaim the defendant's innocence.

This book concentrates on the behavior of participants in the legal system. As the examples at the beginning of this chapter indicated, we are all active participants in the system even if we do not work in occupations directly tied to the administration of justice. We all face choices daily that are colored by the law—whether to speed through a school zone because we are late to class, or whether to report the person who removes someone else's book bag from a table at the library. Hence this book will devote some coverage to the determinants of our conceptions of justice and the moral dilemmas we all face. But more concentrated attention will be given to central participants in the legal system: parties and witnesses, civil and criminal lawyers, judges and juries, convicts and parole boards. In addition, we will also focus on the activities of *forensic psychologists*, whose specialty includes the psychological evaluation and treatment of persons under court jurisdiction, provision of expert testimony on a range of psychological topics, consultation with litigators, and research on the application of psychology to the legal system (Otto, Heilbrun, & Grisso, 1990).

BASIC CHOICES IN THE PSYCHOLOGICAL STUDY OF THE LAW

Just as each of us has to make decisions, society must decide which values it wants its laws to reflect. Choices lead to conflict, and often the resulting dilemmas are unresolvable. Should the laws uphold the rights of specific individuals or protect society in general? For example, which should take precedence—your right to run a loud floor waxer at 3:00 A.M. or the right of everyone else in your apartment building to get a decent night's sleep? Is it better for ten guilty persons to go free than for one innocent person to be sentenced to death? The law incessantly changes as it struggles to provide and ensure rights that, individually, are desirable but that, in combination, are incompatible.

What kind of a society do we want? What laws will best achieve our society's goals? What functions should the legal system serve in our society? How do we learn how well the system is working? These questions highlight four basic choices that pervade the law in the United States and Canada, as it applies to each of us. Each choice creates a dilemma. No decision about these choices will be completely satisfactory because no decision can simultaneously attain two incompatible goals both of which our society values. Nevertheless, most modifications of the law represent efforts to be fair and responsive to whichever of these values has recently been neglected. These four dilemmas are so basic that they surface time and again throughout this book.

A dialectic analysis may help us to understand how these dilemmas evolve and change. *Dialectic analysis* is an approach that studies the state of tension existing between competing values. Each value exerts a pull toward it, and society yields to the pull by creating mechanisms to achieve goals consistent with that value. But these changes may create a new tension, or imbalance, so that society now devotes its efforts more to the advocacy of a second value that is equally desirable but is in competition with the first.

For example, our society champions both

freedom and equality, but it is hard to achieve both at the same time. A small-town civic organization that has always had a "males only" policy at its Friday-night dinners also is a vehicle by which prominent citizens transact a lot of their business. The men enjoy the "freedom" to act like "good ol' boys" in the company of their own gender. But what if a woman starts a new insurance agency in the town? Doesn't she have the right to "equality"—to full and equal participation in the civic organization that is influential in the success of any business in this community? It is hard to see how a resolution of this conflict could fully meet each of the goals. So the balance in such cases often shifts from one value to another, emphasizing the fulfillment of first one and then the other.

The First Dilemma: Rights of Individuals versus the Common Good

Consider the following:

- By 1990, most states required automobile riders to wear seatbelts. What if you do not want to be confined by a seatbelt, even if you acknowledge that you are running a risk by going without one? What right does society have to tell you that you must wear a seatbelt for your own protection? Do some protections enforced by and for society predominate over the right to control your own behavior, even in situations that seemingly affect only you and no one else?
- In most states, first cousins cannot marry each other. What if two young people in a small town grow up together and fall in love? On what grounds does society base its regulations that prevent them from marrying if they are first cousins?

- In California, a federal court held that Vincent Chalk, a teacher of handicapped students in the public schools, who had recently been diagnosed as having AIDS, had a right to remain in the classroom over the objections of the school board and some of the parents. What if a majority of parents, concerned over the risk of AIDS transmission to their children, wanted Mr. Chalk out of the classroom? Why shouldn't the parents' rights trump Mr. Chalk's right? After all, the school board didn't fire Mr. Chalk but merely relegated him to a desk job. (It is worth noting, however, that not all parents felt this way; the mothers of five students greeted him with hugs and homemade gifts on his return to the classroom.)
- The U.S. Supreme Court in the case of *Bowers* v. *Hardwick* (1986) upheld a Georgia law that had classified homosexual relations (specifically, sodomy) as illegal. Which takes precedence: the right to individual privacy in sexual matters or a state's interest in defining moral behavior?

Values in Conflict

The preceding vignettes share a common theme. On the one hand, individuals possess rights, and one function of the law is to ensure that these rights are attainable. The United States is perhaps the most individualistic society in the world. People can deviate from the norm or "do their own thing" to a greater degree here than virtually anywhere else. Freedom is one of our most deeply desired values; "the right to liberty" is a key term in the U.S. Constitution.

On the other hand, society has expectations too. People need to feel secure. They need to believe that potential lawbreakers are discouraged from breaking laws because they know they will be punished. All of us have rights to a peaceful, safe existence. Likewise, society claims a vested interest in restricting those who take risks that may injure themselves or others, because these actions can create burdens on society. First cousins are not allowed to marry, in part because their offspring are likely to inherit recessive genes that can produce some mental or physical inferiority. Any children from such marriages may require treatment and maintenance by the state.

What justification exists for requiring use of seatbelts when failure to buckle up might cause death or injury only to the driver and no one else? "No man is an island," wrote John Donne, and all of us bear some cost when others lose their lives or are permanently injured through an accident. In the United States, there are approximately 20 million motor vehicle accidents annually, and about 50,000 people die in auto accidents each year. Use of seatbelts reduces rates of injury and death. Without them,

costs to society are increased, including lost wages and taxes, higher medical insurance premiums, and welfare payments to dependents of the deceased. It is estimated that motor vehicle accidents result in a total economic cost of about 90 billion dollars per year (U.S. Bureau of the Census, 1990).

It is clear that two sets of rights and two goals for the law are often in conflict. The tension between what rights each individual possesses and what constraints society may place on the individual for its collective welfare will always be with us. Sometimes, in trying to address a grievance, new statutes go too far in one direction or the other. The "California walkman" case (Box 1-2) shows that some state laws, developed to protect society, extract too great a sacrifice of basic human freedoms. On other occasions, the rights of individuals are elevated to such a degree that those who have clearly violated the law go free.

Box 1-2 | The California Walkman: Should He Be Allowed to Walk Alone?

Edward Lawson is a black man with shoulder-length hair who likes to walk. He was stopped by police more than 15 times over a two-year period while walking through white neighborhoods in San Diego. The police officer, on these occasions, would ask for identification. Lawson would refuse to provide any. On five of these occasions he was arrested, and once he was convicted of loitering and spent several weeks in jail.

Lawson had no criminal record. He simply valued his freedom and

Edward Lawson

didn't think he had to explain to anyone who he was, as long as he was obeying the law. But a state

law in California at that time made it a crime for a citizen to fail to provide "credible and reliable" identification when a police officer requested it.

Lawson objected to the law, and in 1983 the U.S. Supreme Court struck it down. Justice Sandra Day O'Connor wrote the 7–1 majority opinion, stating that the California law was unconstitutionally vague in that it gave police officers unbridled discretion to decide whether identification was "credible and reliable."

The Warren Court versus the Burger/Rehnquist Court

The tension between these two values is clearly reflected in the back-and-forth Supreme Court decisions over the last 30 years with respect to the rights of criminal suspects and defendants versus the rights of crime victims and the power of the police. As will be detailed in Chapter 9, the Supreme Court in the 1960s, headed by Chief Justice Earl Warren, established a number of principles that provided explicit rights for those suspected of breaking the law. The "*Miranda* Rule" was established in 1966. About the same time, the courts required that criminal defendants, in all cases in which incarceration is a possible consequence, have the right to an attorney, even if they can't pay for one themselves. These and other rights were established in an effort to redress a perceived imbalance in responding to basic values.

The Supreme Court under Chief Justice Warren Burger, from 1969 to 1986, and Chief Justice William Rehnquist, from 1986 to the present, has trimmed the rights established by the Warren Court by frequently ruling in favor of the police. For example, in the 1991 case of *California* v. *Acevedo,* the Supreme Court ruled that the police did not need a search warrant to search a suitcase or other container in a car if they had probable cause to believe it contained drugs or contraband. This shift toward expanding the powers of the government while reducing individual rights has accelerated in the last few years with the appointments of several politically conservative justices (such as Antonin Scalia, Anthony Kennedy, David Souter, and Clarence Thomas) to the Supreme Court. However, this shift may turn out to be less dramatic than first envisioned, because not all the appointees have been as conservative as hoped by the presidents who appointed them.

As we discuss in Chapter 19, Supreme Court justices' legal decisions cannot always be predicted by political orientation. Appointment to the Supreme Court sometimes changes an appointee's view of the legal dilemmas that frame this book.

Two Models of the Criminal Justice System

The conflict between the rights of individuals and the rights of society is related to a distinction between two models of the criminal justice system. This distinction is between the *due-process* model and the *crime-control* model (Packer, 1964).

The due-process model places primary value on the protection of innocent citizens—even if they are criminal suspects—from possible abuses of the police and the law enforcement system generally. The due-process model assumes the innocence of suspects. It subscribes to the maxim that "it is better that many guilty [persons] shall go free than one innocent [person] should suffer," a remark made by President John Adams. So the due-process model emphasizes the rights of individuals, especially those suspected of crimes, over the temptation by society to assume suspects are guilty even before a trial.

In contrast, the crime-control model seeks the punishment of lawbreakers. It emphasizes the efficient detection of suspects and effective prosecution of defendants, so that society can assume that criminal activity is being contained or reduced. The crime-control model is exemplified by a statement by the then-Attorney General of the United States, William P. Barr, that, with regard to career criminals, the goal is "incapacitation through incarceration" (Barr, 1992). When the crime-control model is dominant in society, laws may be passed that in other times would be seen as unacceptable violations of individual rights. The Racketeer Influenced and Corrupt Organizations laws (called "RICO"), passed by Congress in 1970, are an example. Although the original purpose of the RICO laws was to combat the growing influence of organized crime on legitimate business (Vise, 1989), they have been used to prosecute Wall Street executives for stock-fraud and tax-evasion charges, going beyond the usual definition of "racketeer." Further, one RICO statute permits the federal government to freeze large sums of defendants' assets before trial, thus preventing defendants from hiring the attorneys they want. Recent anticrime legislation considered by Congress reflects the crime-control model; it includes increasing the length of the mandatory prison term for use of a semiautomatic weapon in a crime, adding new agents to the Federal Bureau of Investigation, building new federal prisons, and increasing the number of crimes punishable by execution.

Psychology, as an approach to the law, provides methods for assessing public opinion about the desirability of these two models. In a nationwide telephone survey of about 1000 U.S. adults, 50% responded "true" to the following: "In a criminal trial, it is up to the person who is accused of the crime to prove his innocence." This is an *incorrect* statement—the accused doesn't even have to offer a defense, other than to plead "not guilty"—but half the respondents answered wrongly, implicitly advocating the crime-control view.

Their error does not mean that the crime-control model is wrong. The values underlying each of the contrasting models are legitimate ones, and the goal of our society is to achieve a balance between them. As you will see throughout this book, our government constantly struggles to offer a mix of laws that reasonably honors each set of values.

The Second Dilemma: Equality versus Discretion

Television evangelist Jim Bakker was originally sentenced to 45 years in prison for defrauding members of his religious flock (on appeal, Bakker's sentence was reduced to 8 years); convicted murderers receive an average prison sentence of about 20 years. Some people find no inconsistency in the severity of these punishments, believing that each case should be judged on its own merits. However, psychology analyzes these decisions by viewing them within a dilemma between the goals of equality and discretion.

What should be the underlying principle in response to persons accused of violating the law? Again we discover that two equally desirable values are often incompatible and hence create conflict. And again psychology provides concepts through which this conflict can be studied and better understood.

Fundamental to our legal system is the assumption of the founders of the American republic that "all men are created equal." This statement is frequently interpreted to mean that no one should receive special treatment by the courts simply because he or she is rich, influential, or otherwise advantaged. We cherish the belief that, in the United States, politically powerful or affluent people are brought before the courts and, if guilty, convicted and punished just like anyone else who commits similar offenses. Even though Patricia Hearst was the heiress to the Hearst publishing fortune, that didn't prevent a jury from finding her guilty of assisting in an armed robbery of a bank. Spiro Agnew, while vice president of the United States, resigned from office as part of an implicit acknowledgment that he had received financial payoffs that he had not reported on his income tax. But this value of equality before the law is not always implemented.

The principle of *equality* means the same treatment for all people who commit the same crime. In keeping with this laudable goal, the Supreme Court has, on occasion, applied a *principle of proportionality*; that is, the punishment should be consistently related to the magnitude of the offense. More serious crimes should earn more severe penalties. If a relatively minor crime leads to a harsh punishment, then the fundamental value of equality has been violated.

In 1983 the Supreme Court agreed to hear the appeal of Jerry Helm, who had been convicted of writing a check for $100 when he had no bank account. A judge in South Dakota had sentenced Helm to life in prison without parole. That sentence sounds severe for just writing a "hot check." But South Dakota had a "recidivists law" that permitted giving a sentence of life imprisonment without parole to any offender who had three previous felony convictions. Mr. Helm had six prior convictions: three for burglary, one for obtaining money under false pretenses, one for driving while intoxicated, and one for grand larceny. The U.S. Supreme Court decided, by a 5-to-4 vote, that the sentence given Helm by the South Dakota judge violated the Eighth Amendment of the U.S. Constitution, because it constituted a "cruel and unusual punishment." However, in less than a decade, the Supreme Court's requirement of proportional sentencing has been modified by the recent decision of *Harmelin* v. *Michigan* (1991), which endorses a state's right to impose mandatory, disproportionate sentences for some crimes. The *Harmelin* case (Box 1-3) illustrates a decisive swing in sentencing values toward longer, mandatory punishments.

Although equality often remains an overriding principle, society also believes that *discretion* is appropriate. By "discretion," we mean the use of judgments about the circumstances of certain offenses that lead to *variations* in how the system responds to these offenses. In judging guilt and punishment, according to the principle of discretion, a judge or jury weighs the specific circumstances that surround a crime. A police officer may decide not to arrest a juvenile who has been caught speeding because the legally prescribed punishment would result in the loss of the juvenile's license. In regard to more serious offenses, one murder may be very different from another, with respect to its motivations, its brutality, and the relationship of the murdered and the murderer. Even two murders of husbands by their wives can reflect very different circumstances. One may be the result of a woman impulsively wanting freedom from an unhappy relationship; the other may be a desperate, defensive reaction to 20 years of physical abuse.

But how do the values of equality and discretion interact? How nearly equal must two sets of facts be to apply the same judgments to them? There are no easy answers to these questions—only hard choices. Two examples illustrate the problems.

Early in the morning of July 19, 1983, Joan Hodges fired a shotgun and deliberately killed her husband, Harvey, as he lay in bed. This 51-year-old mother and grandmother was found by a jury of her peers to be guilty of voluntary manslaughter. To no avail were her claims that she had been savagely beaten by her husband ever since they had married in 1950, that she had required hospital treatment for some of the injuries, and that, as she testified, "I was terrified; he told me he was going to kill me." She even reported that the shooting occurred after he attacked her for no reason, banging her head some 20 times against a door jamb with such force that she lost control of her bowels. Her claim that she had acted out of self-defense was rejected by the jury.

In another case, which gained national attention through the showing of the television movie *The Burning Bed*, a mother of three who killed her abusive husband was found not guilty by reason of insanity. Yet the general circumstances seemed similar to those of the Hodges case. On March 9, 1977, Francine Hughes poured gasoline around her ex-husband's bed as he lay sleeping, ignited it, and drove off as the house went up in flames. Ms. Hughes claimed she had been beaten repeatedly by her husband for more than ten years.

Is this equality? At a crude level, it appears not. In one case, the taking of a life was punished; under similar circumstances, the act was considered to be a result of temporary mental disturbance and no punishment was extended.

But there may be enough subtle differences between the two cases to illustrate the healthy place of discretion in jury decisions. The jurors in Joan Hodges's trial felt sympathy for her, but they also doubted the urgency of her situation, especially the claim that her life was in danger. Her believability was also brought into question by records indicating that she had incorrectly reported some of her comings and goings during the fateful weekend.

In effect, the jury in Joan Hodges's trial opted for a compromise; it rejected the district attorney's charge of second-degree murder, but it refused to find her blameless. The eventual verdict—that she was guilty of voluntary man-

---

Box 1-3

Mandatory or Discretionary Guidelines: The Case of Ronald Harmelin

"I'm not saying I didn't know there was cocaine in the bag," Ronald Harmelin told the *Detroit News* after the police found 673 grams of cocaine and $2900 in cash in a gym bag in the trunk of his car. "But I wasn't selling anything other than the little half and quarter grams ($50 and $25 in street value). I wasn't no drug kingpin. I was doing a favor for a friend."

Harmelin was convicted of possession of cocaine and sentenced to life without parole under Michigan's tough antidrug law. He appealed to the Supreme Court of the United States, arguing that life without parole for a first-time offender constitutes cruel and unusual punishment under the Eighth Amendment to the Constitution.

Based on the earlier *Helm* case, Harmelin argued that the punishment was significantly disproportionate to the crime committed and that statutes imposing severe mandatory punishments are unconstitutional because they deny judges the power to consider mitigating circumstances.

By a 5–4 vote, the Supreme Court rejected Harmelin's appeal. Justice Kennedy wrote the crucial opinion. He noted that "competing theories of mandatory and discretionary sentencing have been in varying degrees of ascendancy or decline since the beginning of the Republic," which produces substantial state-to-state variation in the length of prison terms. Only at the extreme (for example, a life sentence for shoplifting), said Jus-

tice Kennedy, is the Court warranted to find a sentence "cruel and unusual" under the Eighth Amendment.

In upholding Michigan's statute, Justice Kennedy relied on statistics supplied by the state: in Detroit in 1988, 51% of male arrestees and 71% of female arrestees tested positive for cocaine; 60% of Detroit homicides were drug related. Looking at the correlation between cocaine and crime, Justice Kennedy held that it was rational for Michigan to enact harsh antidrug laws that make no allowance for mitigating factors. Clearly, the *Harmelin* case illustrates a rather extreme move away from the value of individualized discretion in sentencing offenders.

slaughter—was a middle ground. In contrast, in the "burning-bed" case, the jury concluded that Francine Hughes had been driven to an irrational act by an impulse fueled by her domestic problems.

As a basic influence within the legal system, the value of discretion is manifested much more widely than just in the decisions of juries. Throughout the legal process, there are efforts to make what is considered the most "appropriate" disposition for a particular individual (Teplin, 1984a). Police officers show discretion when they fail to charge someone who technically has broken the law. The police acknowledge that, if they stop someone who is speeding by 5 to 10 miles per hour, their decision to issue a citation or just a warning is determined primarily by the driver's degree of cooperation.

The sentences administered by judges to convicted criminals also reflect discretion. Community standards differ from one part of the country to another; hence, exactly the same crime will carry a stiffer sentence in one jurisdiction than in another. During the height of protest against the war in Vietnam in the late 1960s and early 1970s, young men who resisted the draft were brought to trial and, if found guilty, were given either a prison sentence or probation. In Oregon, of 33 convicted draft evaders, 18 were put on probation and 15 were sent to prison, but none of those 15 were given a term over three years. Compare those punishments with the outcomes in the southern district of Texas, a region that bristled with strong patriotic sentiments: of 16 violators, none were put on probation, and 14 of the 16 were given the five-year maximum prison sentence allowable by law. In the southern district of Mississippi, every defendant was convicted and each one was given the maximum of five years. Because draft resistance is a federal crime, we would assume that it would be judged

by the same standards throughout the country (Gaylin, 1974). Yet the United States has a strong tradition that criminal justice is administered by the local jurisdiction; consequently, many people understand and accept that judges in different areas give harsher penalties for the same crime.

From what we know about the similarity of the cases, all these men were not treated fairly by the law. This is an example of *sentencing disparity*, or the tendency of different judges to administer a variety of penalties for the same crime (see Chapter 18). For several years society has urged that judges' sentencing procedures move toward the pole of equality; in the *Helm* case referred to earlier, one of the issues in the majority decision of the Supreme Court was whether a given crime received the same sentence in different states. The Court was opting for the standard of equality, by favoring the equivalence of punishments throughout the country.

To counteract sentencing disparity, in the last 15 years many states have implemented what is known as *determinate sentencing*; the offense determines the sentence, and courts and parole commissions have little discretion. Furthermore, the U.S. Sentencing Commission has established strict guidelines for the sentences to be meted out for federal crimes (Box 1-4). Although equality is the value now in vogue, we should not forget that discretion, as a value, still has its merits. Community standards have a legitimate place in deciding punishments, and often mitigating circumstances in specific cases cry out for mercy as well as justice. Community preferences for discretion are also revealed in trials in which juries refuse to convict a defendant even though the evidence for the defendant's factual guilt is clear. This preference to acquit legally guilty, but morally blameless, defendants is known as *jury nullification*; it is discussed more fully in Chapter 12. Psychology can play a role not only in identifying what the community standards are, but in determining the degree of public discontent (if any) over sentencing and verdict disparities.

The Third Dilemma: To Discover the Truth or to Resolve Conflicts

In one of the most sensational criminal trials of the last two decades, Jean Harris, the bright, ambitious headmistress of an exclusive girls' school near Washington, DC, was charged with the murder of Dr. Herman Tarnower, the well-known "diet doctor" who had authored the best-selling *Complete Scarsdale Medical Diet.* Ms. Harris and Dr. Tarnower had been lovers for almost 15 years; at the time of Tarnower's death, it appeared that he was abandoning her for a younger woman. Ms. Harris claimed later that she had intended to commit suicide—she even had drawn up a will and had it witnessed and notarized, and she had written the doctor a suicide note. But she decided to say farewell to him in person before killing herself. So, on the evening of March 10, 1980, she loaded a gun, placed it on the car seat beside her, and drove from Washington, DC, to Purchase, New York, where she confronted Dr. Tarnower in his bedroom. There was a struggle, the gun was fired

---

Box **1-4** | *Federal Sentencing Guidelines*

In federal courts, sentences are determined by the Federal Sentencing Guidelines, which went into effect in November 1987. For every crime, the guidelines assign a "Base Offense Level," which is adjusted up or down (usually up) on the basis of certain factors in the case (for example, serious injury to the victim). The guidelines do not attempt, however, to take into account all the circumstances of cases, because to do so would prove "unworkable and seriously compromise the certainty of punishment and its deterrent effect. A bank robber with (or without) a gun, which the robber kept hidden (or brandished), might have frightened (or merely warned), injured seriously (or less seriously), tied up (or simply pushed) a guard, a teller or a customer, at night (or at noon), for a bad (or arguably less bad) motive, in an effort to obtain money for other crimes (or for other purposes), in the company of a few (or many) other robbers, for the first (or fourth) time that day, while sober (or under the influence of drugs or alcohol), and so forth" (U.S. Sentencing Commission, *Sentencing Guidelines for United States Courts,* 52 Fed. Reg. 18046; May 13, 1987).

Federal judges are required to sentence from a table (resembling any table combining two variables) on which the offense level is lined up with the defendant's criminal history to yield the sentencing range. For example, the sentencing range for a defendant with no prior offenses committing armed bank robbery would be 46 to 57 months.

Some judges resent their inability to consider all factors relating to the offense. One federal judge resigned his appointment in protest over mandatory sentencing rules. In resigning from the federal bench, Judge J. Lawrence Irving of San Diego said "It's an unfair system that has been dehumanized. There are rarely two cases that are identical. Judges should always have discretion. That's why we're judges. But now we're being made to be robots. I cannot in good conscience play this game any longer."

five times, and Dr. Tarnower died as a result of three bullet wounds. Ms. Harris claimed that the death was an accident, part of the struggle for the gun; the state maintained that Jean Harris killed Herman Tarnower in a jealous rage. Jean Harris was charged with second-degree murder and brought to trial.

What is the purpose of a trial? Your first reaction may be: to find out the truth, of course! Determining the truth means learning the facts of the case, including events, intentions, actions, and outcomes. All this assumes that "what really happened" between two parties can be ascertained. Finding out the truth is a desirable goal, but it may be a lofty, unattainable one.

Consider the few minutes of the Harris/ Tarnower confrontation. Can witnesses perceive, remember, and report occurrences completely and accurately? Psychological evidence (reviewed in Chapter 7) leads to skepticism. Only two witnesses were present. One is dead and cannot testify from the grave; the other, even if she sincerely tries to reconstruct a rapid series of events, is probably an inaccurate reporter. (At the trial, Ms. Harris testified that she remembered firing only three shots, not five.) Most experimental psychologists doubt that the brain acts like a camera to record brief and sudden events. Complex events, like a struggle or a series of gunshots, are difficult to perceive. If we are thrust into the middle of an emergency without warning—a gas explosion, an earthquake, a car wreck—we do not perceive all that is happening around us with a high level of accuracy. Even our perception of time is often very distorted. In fast-moving crises, most witnesses overestimate how much time elapses in the emergency, to the point of sometimes "seeing" the events unfold almost in slow motion. And if we are emotionally involved in the happenings—as Ms. Harris was—our memo-

ries are revised and reinterpreted, often in order to paint a self-justifying picture of our own behavior.

Whether Ms. Harris's memories were changed is impossible to say, but few of us could maintain precisely accurate memories given such crushing pressures. In her trial, Ms. Harris testified that she did not remember all the gunshots. Certainly the truth is difficult to uncover in such matters. Anne Bernays has written: "The real Jean Harris lies in pieces under layers of self-doubt, anger, conflicting feelings, rectitude, frustration, and just plain years. To expect that a trial can peel away these layers and reveal a whole and consistent woman is as foolish as to expect that any one writer can do it" (1983, p. 13).

In some cases, however, careful analysis of the crime scene can later lead to an accurate reconstruction of the events; the location of the bullets, their pathway through the body, and the pattern of blood splatters all may provide clues. And through the use of psychological procedures including hypnosis, witnesses can sometimes recall more at a later date than they do right after the crime. Recently, psychologists have begun to study crime scenes and other evidence in order to sketch psychological profiles of the type of offender who might commit certain crimes. This technique, known as *criminal profiling*, is described more fully in Chapter 8.

On February 25, 1981, the jury found Jean Harris guilty of second-degree murder, and the judge sentenced her to 15 years to life in prison. The jurors believed that the evidence presented by the prosecution was sufficiently convincing that they could accept "beyond a reasonable doubt" that the prosecution's version was what had actually happened. From her cell in the Bedford Hills Correctional Facility, Jean Harris continued for several years to appeal the outcome. Just before New Year's Day of 1993, Governor Mario Cuomo of New York granted her clemency.

The Jury's Task: Providing Stability?

In a trial, jurors are often presented with two versions of the truth—two sets of facts or at least two interpretations of the same event. Our adversary system of justice forces them to choose, or to compromise by finding that the truth lies between the competing versions of the event. If they are jurors in a criminal case, the judge tells them that their task is to determine whether the government has met its burden of proving every element of the crime beyond a reasonable doubt. In civil cases, the jury must believe that a "preponderance of the evidence" favors the plaintiff's version of the facts in order for the plaintiff to win; otherwise the jury should find for the defendant. But, by a jury's verdict, one version of the "truth" assumes the appearance of "correctness"; the other must inevitably, therefore, be "wrong." Given that it is difficult for even well-meaning people to ascertain the true facts in some cases, some observers have proposed that a trial's real purpose is to provide social stability by resolving conflict. Supreme Court Justice Louis Brandeis once wrote that "it is more important that the applicable rule of law be settled than it be settled right" (in *Burnet* v. *Coronado Oil and Gas Co.*, 1932). And Kenneth Boulding has written that "legal and political procedures, such as trials and elections, are essentially social rituals designed to minimize the costs and conflicts" (1975). In other words, there is a shift from viewing the trial's purpose as doing justice toward "creating a sense that justice is being done" (Miller & Boster, 1977, p. 34). Supporters of this viewpoint emphasize the importance of rituals in our society. These rituals provide continuity and stability, as well as, in

this instance, maintenance of "the shared perception that our legal system provides an efficient means for resolving conflict peacefully" (Miller & Boster, 1977, p. 34). Moreover, these peaceful means replace earlier methods of resolving conflicts that used force and violence, like shootouts or duels. But some of these peaceful procedures may have lost their original, truth-seeking purpose. For example, in Chapter 10 we will examine whether the grand jury has become a vehicle for "rubber-stamping" prosecutors' recommendations, rather than serving as an independent fact-finding body.

Attorneys' Opinions about the Purpose of a Trial

Truth is elusive, some advocates say, and so the most important priority of a trial is to provide a setting in which all interested parties have their "day in court." Justice for all parties replaces truth as the predominant goal. The attorneys representing the opposing parties in the case do not necessarily seek "the truth." Nor do they represent themselves as "objective." They reflect a different value—the importance of giving all sides the best representation possible, within the limits of the law. The Code of Ethics of the American Bar Association even instructs attorneys to defend their clients "zealously." So lawyers believe the purpose of a trial is to win disputes; they present arguments supporting their client's perspective and support their arguments with the best available evidence.

Some psychologists note that an argument in favor of the adversary system, in which a different attorney represents each party, is that it encourages the attorneys to discover and introduce every bit of evidence that might encourage the jury to react favorably to their client's case. When both sides believe that their representatives have revealed all the relevant facts in the trial, participants in the trial are more likely to feel they have been treated fairly by the system, and the system is considered to be an effective one.

"Conflict resolution" and "truth," as goals, are not always incompatible. When each participant sees to it that his or her concerns and supporting documentation are presented in court, the goal of knowing the truth becomes more attainable. Although truth may be too elusive ever to be known fully in all cases, it is dangerous to give up its quest. Jurors take an oath to pursue the truth, and they need to search for it even if it is not completely knowable.

Even though attainment of both values is not incompatible, a tension between the two usually exists. When conflict resolution is sought at the sacrifice of truth, the outcome can often be unsatisfactory. However, in other instances, such as the issue discussed in Box 1-5, the satisfactory resolution of a conflict may be socially and morally preferable to discovering an objectively established truth.

Truth versus Conflict Resolution in Plea Bargaining and Settlement Negotiation

The quest for truth is threatened at other points during the criminal justice process. The legal system is a massive bureaucracy, and in every bureaucracy a temptation exists to value pragmatic efficiency rather than correct or just outcomes. The huge reliance on plea bargaining is often criticized because it appears to give priority to conflict resolution over truth seeking. From 80% to 95% of defendants never go to trial; they accept the offer of the prosecutor to plead guilty to a lesser charge. Even some innocent persons plea-bargain after being convinced that the evidence against them is overwhelming. However, plea bargaining remains an integral part of the criminal justice system.

The state benefits by avoiding the expense and trouble of trial, by eliminating the possibility of an acquittal, and often by obtaining the testimony of the accused against others involved in the crime. The defendant benefits by receiving some kind of reduction in the penalty imposed. Many would argue that, in addition to these pragmatic benefits, justice is furthered by a system that rewards a show of contrition (which usually accompanies a guilty plea) and enables the prosecutor and defense counsel, often in concert with the judge, to negotiate a resolution appropriate to the degree of wrongdoing (Kamisar, LaFave, & Israel, 1986). Nonetheless, the process illustrates how the goal of maintaining stability and efficiency in the system is achieved at some sacrifice of the public's opportunity to determine the complete truth.

In civil cases, a procedure that parallels plea bargaining resolves about 90% of conflicts between a plaintiff and a defendant. *Settlement negotiation* involves a sometimes lengthy pretrial process of give-and-take, offer-and-demand that ultimately ends with a plaintiff agreeing to accept what a defendant is willing to offer to end their legal disagreement.

The Fourth Dilemma: Science versus the Law as a Source of Decisions

When one discipline (in our case, psychology) seeks to understand another (the law), a dilemma is likely because each approaches knowledge in a different way. When asked "How do you know whether that decision is the right one?" each relies on different methods, even though both share a general goal of understanding human experience. As you will see on several occasions in this book, in its recent decisions the U.S. Supreme Court has often considered data and conclusions presented by psychologists and other social scientists. In several cases in the last ten years, the American Psychological Association has prepared a supporting brief, called an *amicus curiae* (or "friend of the court") brief, for an appellant whose appeal was considered by the Court.* In many of these decisions the Court has disregarded the social science data, but in others it has incorporated the findings into its decision. Such decisions reflect how the justices often use

*Although the term *amicus curiae* refers to a "friend of the court," such briefs are prepared by individuals or organizations that have an interest in the outcome of the appeal; they serve as advice to the judges.

different procedures and concepts from those of social science in forming their judicial opinions (Grisso & Saks, 1991), a matter we discuss further in Chapter 19.

Beyond the use of different procedures, each profession may use idiosyncratic, or unique, concepts to describe the same phenomenon. An attorney and a social scientist will see the same event through different perspectives. Neither is more accurate than the other; the differences are the results of exposure to and training in different points of view. Subsequent paragraphs of this section illustrate the differences in more detail.

Box 1-5   The Agent Orange Controversy: Search for Truth or Resolution of a Social Problem?

Agent Orange (a potent herbicide that contains dioxin) was widely used by the American military during the early stages of the Vietnam War to defoliate the hiding places of the Vietcong. Following a report on the adverse effects of dioxin on laboratory animals, Agent Orange spraying was discontinued in 1970. By that time thousands of soldiers and civilians had been exposed to it.

In 1977 Paul Rutershan contracted abdominal cancer. As a helicopter pilot in Vietnam, he had flown through clouds of Agent Orange, and he believed his cancer was caused by exposure to dioxin. Rutershan (who was soon to die of the cancer) persuaded an attorney to sue the chemical companies that produced Agent Orange, and Rutershan's case eventually became a "class action" to litigate

the claims of all military personnel suffering from illnesses they believed were caused by Agent Orange. Included in the class action were the claims of wives who miscarried and children born with birth defects because of the alleged effect of dioxin on the sperm of their husbands and fathers.

This huge lawsuit, potentially involving hundreds of thousands of claims, wound up in the court of United States District Judge Jack Weinstein, who ultimately concluded that Agent Orange did not cause the deaths, illnesses, and birth defects complained of. He cited studies showing that soldiers who handled Agent Orange in Vietnam were as healthy as the general population of the United States, and he believed that the veterans lacked reliable evidence on the crucial question of causation.

Judge Weinstein did not, however, throw the claims of the veterans out of court. Instead, he pressured both sides to settle, using special assistants, called "masters," to produce a settlement that would provide a fund for sick veterans and their families—whatever the "true" cause of their illnesses—in part to make up for the nation's failure to discharge its obligation to those who served. He established an early and firm trial date, knowing that lawyers have a tendency to settle "on the courthouse steps"— that is, on the eve of trial. To the chemical companies, among them industry giants Dow and Monsanto, he pointed out the enormous risk involved in litigating the question of causation before a jury that would naturally sympathize with the veterans and their families. To the plaintiffs, he pointed out the

Law Is Doctrinal; Psychology Is Empirical

Psychology, in contrast to the law, is generally committed to the idea that there is an objectifiable world of experience that can best be understood by unwavering adherence to the rules of science—systematic testing of hypotheses by observation and experimental methodology. As a scientist, the psychologist is committed to a public, impersonal, objective pursuit of truth, using methods that can be repeated by others and faithfully interpreting results by predetermined standards. Although this traditional view of psychology's approach to truth is often challenged as naive and simplistic (Bevan, 1991; Toulmin, 1990) because it ignores the importance of the personal, political, and historical filters that are used just as much by scientists as by nonscientists, it still represents the values and methods in which most psychologists are trained. It also represents our belief as authors that the scientific method and the research skills of psychologists are the most essential and reliable tools we have available for examining the many important legal questions we address throughout the book.

Legal experts rely heavily on precedents in weakness of their proof of causation and noted his doubts that several rulings he had made in their favor would be upheld on appeal. In short, he played on the fears and doubts of both sides to produce a "risk-adverse" settlement.

On May 6, 1984, the day before trial, the parties settled for $180 million, a figure suggested by Judge Weinstein. How was the fund to be distributed? Judge Weinstein held that:

> Under the payment program, individual awards will be made only to exposed veterans who suffer from long-term disabilities and to the surviving spouses or children of exposed veterans who have died. . . . All deaths and total disabilities will be compensable, regardless of what disease was the cause, unless predominately caused by trauma, whether or not self-inflicted.

Judge Weinstein did not believe the plaintiffs could prove Agent Orange caused death and illness. In fact, he dismissed the case of 350 veterans who chose not to be part of the class action, because he felt they failed to prove causation through credible witnesses. He saw the class action as an opportunity, however, to fashion a just end to a national controversy, putting money (though not too much—the award for total disability was about $12,500 per claimant) in the hands of those suffering the most, while penalizing the chemical companies for producing an agent that could cause death and illness. Significantly, the money was to be distributed to anyone exposed without proof that death or illness was caused by Agent Orange. A veteran dying of a heart attack (never associated with Agent Orange) would be paid from the fund established by the chemical companies. The wives and children of the veterans, however, were not to be compensated for their miscarriages and birth defects. Why? Because Judge Weinstein knew that the fund was limited and wanted the money to go to those most directly affected: the veterans who were exposed.

The Agent Orange case is one in which the judge candidly sacrificed the quest for truth (did Agent Orange cause the plaintiffs' death and illness?) for a partial resolution of a national problem. The nation had betrayed its Vietnam veterans, and the settlement was a step toward making things right.

establishing new laws. When confronted with a case, judges and attorneys examine rulings in previous cases (as well as the Constitution and the statutes) for guidance. *Case law,* the law made by rulings in individual cases, is very influential; statutes and constitutional safeguards do not apply to every new situation, and so past cases often serve as precedents for deciding current ones. The principle of *stare decisis* ("let the decision stand") is important in this process. Judges typically are reluctant to make decisions that contradict earlier ones, as the history of the Supreme Court's school desegregation decision indicates. When the U.S. Supreme Court voted unanimously in May 1954, in *Brown* v. *Board of Education,* that public school segregation was contrary to the law, many reports claimed that it "supplanted" or even "overturned" a previous ruling, in the 1896 case of *Plessy* v. *Ferguson.* But when it comes to court decisions, things are not that simple or straightforward.

Judges usually are reluctant to hand down decisions that radically change the law or directly go against previous decisions. Even though the judges may believe that some previous law is now inappropriate or even immoral, they still try to find some precedents for their desired decision from past rulings. A brief history of rulings that led up to the *Brown* v. *Board of Education* (1954) decision illustrates this phenomenon.

During a train trip in Louisiana in the 1890s, Homer Plessy sat down in a railroad car labeled "Whites Only." Mr. Plessy's ancestry was mostly Caucasian, but he had one Negro great-grandparent. Therefore, according to the laws of Louisiana at that time, Mr. Plessy was considered a black (or "colored," in the prevalent term at that time). Mr. Plessy refused to move to a car designated for "colored" passengers, as a recently passed state law required. He took his claim to court, but a New Orleans judge ruled

that, contrary to Mr. Plessy's argument, the statute that segregated railroad cars by race did not violate the Fourteenth Amendment to the Constitution; that is, it did not fail to give Mr. Plessy "equal protection under the law."

Mr. Plessy persisted in his appeal, and eventually, in 1896, the Supreme Court acted on his claim. By a 7-to-1 vote, it affirmed the decision of the judge and the lower courts. Judge Henry Billings Brown, speaking for the majority, declared that laws that had established separate facilities for the races did not necessarily imply that one race was inferior to the other. Part of the judge's decision reflects the predominant view of those times, almost a century ago: "We consider the underlying fallacy of the plaintiff's [that is, Plessy's] argument to consist in the assumption that the enforced separation of the two races stamps the colored race with a badge of inferiority. If this be so, it is not by reason of anything found in the act, but solely because the colored race chooses to put that construction on it."

Although this opinion was a far cry from the 1954 decision, which highlighted the detrimental effects of segregation on the personality development of black children, intermediate decisions by the Court permitted this seemingly abrupt change to evolve more predictably. One of these was the case of *Sweatt* v. *Painter,* decided by the Supreme Court in 1950. Heman Sweatt was a black man who wanted to enroll in the University of Texas law school, in Austin. The university was at that time (the late 1940s) racially segregated, and so the board of regents' response was to build a separate law school (in Houston, not in Austin) for Mr. Sweatt and any other blacks who chose to apply. Mr. Sweatt took the decision to court.

The U.S. Supreme Court ruled in favor of Mr. Sweatt but *not* on the grounds that separate but equal facilities were unconstitutional. Rather, its decision was based on the conclusion that the separate facilities could not be equal to the law school at the University of Texas at Austin. The new school would not have the established law library or an experienced faculty or other qualities of the other school. It was not equal to the University of Texas, in the words of the Court, "in those qualities which are incapable of objective measurement but which make for greatness in a law school." Note that even though this decision preceded *Brown* v. *Board of Education* by only four years, the Court refused to conclude explicitly that all separate facilities are inherently unequal. It merely decided about a very limited type of public facility.

About the same time, the University of Oklahoma took a different strategy to deal with the first black person admitted to its graduate school of education. George McLaurin was allowed to enroll, but he was segregated from all his classmates. His desk was separated from all the others by a rail, to which the sign "Reserved for Colored" was attached. He was given a separate desk at the library, and he was required to eat by himself in the cafeteria. Everything else was "equal." In the case of *McLaurin* v. *Oklahoma State Regents*, also in 1950, the U.S. Supreme Court ruled unanimously that this procedure denied him his right to equal protection of the law; it concluded that such restrictions would "impair and inhibit his ability to study, to engage in discussion and exchange of views with other students." But, again, the Court did not strike down *Plessy* v. *Ferguson*.

It was not until Earl Warren was appointed chief justice in 1953 that enough momentum built to reverse *Plessy* v. *Ferguson*. Justice Warren was not a precise legal scholar; he was less concerned with the fine points of the law than with whether the law was just. He liked to ask "What is fair?" It was Warren who spearheaded the unanimous decision that finally overturned the idea that separate facilities can be "equal."

He wrote that to separate black children "from others of similar age and qualifications solely because of their race generates a feeling of inferiority as to their status in the community that may affect their hearts and minds in a way unlikely to ever be undone."

Law Functions by the Case Method, Psychology by the Experimental Method

For the attorney, each case is an entity in its own right. Although it may have similarities to previous cases so that precedents may be applied, each case has unique manifestations. In contrast, most experimental psychologists seek what is common to different examples and try to extract a common factor. It is this abstract, or theoretical, factor, rather than the incident or the case itself, that is the focus of empirical research methods.

Law Supports Contrasting Views of Reality; Psychology Seeks to Clarify One Muddled View of Reality

As indicated earlier, jurors must decide which of two conceptions of the truth is more acceptable in light of a mixed set of facts. Attorneys representing clients marshal all the facts that support their side. Although this procedure is similar to some scientific activities (a psychologist may do a study that pits predictions from two theories against each other), the psychologist is trained to be objective and open to all perspectives and types of data. The goal is to integrate or assimilate conflicting findings into one refined view of the truth, not to choose between alternative views. Once again, this portrayal of the psychologist's goals may be too idealistic when compared to a candid picture of his or her actual behavior. Social scientists also become personally invested in their favorite explanations for events and may show considerable selectivity and partisanship when defending these positions against critics, but they are still expected to behave "as if" they were objective and unbiased.

When representatives of one discipline invade the jurisdiction of the other, conflicts result. Mental health professionals are called by one side or the other when a criminal defendant pleads not guilty by reason of insanity. The court wants to know: "Is this person insane or isn't he?" Psychiatrists and psychologists are loath to answer such a question directly. Beyond the fact that *insanity* is a legal term, not a scientific one, their conclusions are often laced with ambiguity. They may want to say "I'm not sure" or "Sometimes he is; sometimes he isn't." They may try to answer the question in terms of more or less likelihood rather than "yes" or "no." Such a response reflects the imprecision felt necessary by a psychologist when dealing with a single case because psychologists are accustomed to thinking about the probability of events being true rather than about the certainty of their status. The legal system has difficulty with such inconclusive responses because it needs to arrive at a final answer for a dispute.

The foregoing distinctions only scratch the surface of the differences between law and psychology. We will encounter their implications many times in subsequent chapters. As with the previous choices, selecting one option here over the other one is not a satisfactory response. Use of both approaches moves us closer to the goal of an adequate understanding than does reliance on one. We must remain aware of the limits of our own perspective and realize that other viewpoints are essential for a full understanding.

However, the contrast in knowledge-generating procedures does raise serious procedural questions. For example, given the differences in approach, how should a psychologist respond to the challenge of studying the law?

What kind of role or roles should the psychologist play in understanding the legal system? The fact that science is empirical does not mean that scientists' choices are free of values. The scientist decides both what to study and how to study it; these matters are examined in Chapter 2.

SUMMARY

Laws are everywhere. They are human creations, which have as their major purpose the resolution of human conflict. As society changes, new conflicts surface, leading to expansion and revision of the legal system.

Many possible approaches exist for the study of the law. Anthropologists compare the legal procedures in differing societies and relate these differences to other characteristics of those societies. Sociologists examine the impact of social institutions (the family, the social class, the neighborhood) on adherence to the law or on social deviation. Philosophers examine how law reflects concepts of morality and justice. A psychological approach focuses on individuals as agents within a legal system, asking how their internal qualities (personality, values, abilities, experiences) and their environments affect their behavior.

Several basic choices must be made between pairs of options in the psychological study of the law. These options are often irreconcilable, because each is attractive but both usually cannot be attained at the same time. Society often devotes its efforts first to one, then to the other. The choices are (1) whether the goal of law is achieving personal freedom or ensuring the common good, (2) whether equality or discretion should be the standard for our legal policies, (3) whether the purpose of a legal inquiry is to discover the truth or to provide a means of conflict resolution, and (4) whether the methods of law or science are the best for making decisions.

CHAPTER 2

Psychologists and the Legal System

Chapter 1 described the psychologist's approach to the law as an empirical one. Does the value of a stolen item affect whether a victim will report a crime to the police? Do judges rely on a defendant's past record more than on the severity of the crime in setting the amount of bail? Does completing law school change a young person's values? In attempting to answer such questions, the psychologist collects data from the world of experience and offers answers only after such empirical activities are completed.

THE PLACE OF VALUES

Procedures for collecting and analyzing data are not always straightforward. The psychologist must first make two basic decisions: What questions are to be asked? And what should be done with the answers? In responding to these inescapable choices, psychologists reveal their values. Conflicts often exist between contrasting but equally desirable values, leading to dilemmas as thorny as those posed in Chapter 1.

For example, consider the case of *Plessy* v. *Ferguson* (1896), described in Chapter 1. One hundred years ago, when black people were required to ride in separate railroad cars in Louisiana, the Supreme Court concluded that forced separation of different races did not necessarily imply inferiority of status. Suppose a group of psychologists, *at that time*, had evaluated that claim empirically. Their conclusions would doubtless have been influenced by what questions they chose to ask. For example, if they compared the physical layout of the "white" and "colored" cars, the number of windows, the presence of restrooms, the padding of the seats, or even the passengers'

subjective feelings of comfort, they might conclude—*on the basis of empirical data*—that separation meant no inferiority. But suppose they had asked the black passengers other questions—for example, "Would you prefer to sit in the 'white' car?" "How does it feel to be seated in a car 'for colored only'?" "What does a separate car mean to you?" They might have reached different conclusions, again based on empirical data, that were more in keeping with Homer Plessy's preference for being seated in the "white" car. Sometimes science is called "value-free" because it tries to look objectively at the data collected. But it can never be value-free as long as the scientist has some choice in what questions are asked and what data are collected.

Psychologists must make other choices about the uses of their data. Many psychologists publish their findings in scientific journals that are read by their peers; others write articles for popular magazines or testify before legislative committees. Some psychologists generate research findings in order to assist underprivileged groups in our society. Decisions about where to publish or how to disseminate data and conclusions also reflect scholars' values, especially about the proper purposes of science. Psychologists do not agree about what their purposes should be (see, for example, an exchange between two psychologists about whether organizations of psychologists should have lobbied against the nomination of Robert Bork to the U.S. Supreme Court: Melton, 1990, 1991; Small, 1991). In this chapter we explore four possible roles for the psychologist in society, then we examine how these roles apply to psychologists who study the law and participate in the legal system, and we conclude by evaluating the possible ethical dilemmas resulting from each of these roles.

THE PSYCHOLOGIST'S RELATIONSHIP TO SOCIETY

What are appropriate activities for a psychologist in society? Most courses in psychology portray only two roles for psychologists: either that of the scientist who conducts basic research about the causes and development of behavior or that of the applied psychologist (usually the clinical psychologist) who tries to understand and assist individuals or groups confronting their problems. The possibilities are more elaborate, however. Four contrasting roles can be ordered on a continuum from isolation, on one end, to collaboration with persons from other disciplines and the public at large, on the other end.

The Psychologist as a Pure Scientist

A "pure" scientist pursues knowledge for its own sake. Basic researchers study a phenomenon simply for the joy of understanding it. They do not seek to apply their findings; many have no concern whether the knowledge they generate is ever put to any practical, problem-solving use. Some may even be hostile when, for example, a newspaper reporter takes their conclusions and applies them to a commonplace problem.

As an example of basic research, an investigator may study the relative importance of heredity and environment on intelligence. She may collect data on the similarity of IQ scores of identical twins compared with fraternal twins or with siblings born at different times. She may study identical twins who were put in separate foster homes at an early age, in order to tease out the effect of their differing environments. Her predominant motivation is to understand the phenomenon or to develop a theory about the genetic transmission of characteristics from one generation to the next.

The Psychologist as an Applied Scientist

Other psychologists are dedicated to applying knowledge in order to solve real-life problems. Most of the public's awareness of the psychologist's work reflects this role, whether this awareness comes from viewing the reruns of Bob Newhart's clinical psychologist sitcom or reading about psychologists who testify as expert witnesses in trials involving insanity pleas.

Clinical, counseling, and school psychologists apply scientific findings to the betterment of individuals who are having personal difficulties. Other psychologists seek to understand and alleviate social problems. Their underlying values reflect social service to a greater degree than do those of the "pure" researcher, whose basic goal is understanding. The Society for the Psychological Study of Social Issues (SPSSI), an organization of some 3000 psychologists and other professional people, concerns itself with matters that affect the well-being of substantial numbers of our compatriots, such as poverty, racism, pollution, and criminal behavior. Members of SPSSI believe that psychological facts ought to be brought to bear on policy dilemmas. For example, during the last decade, SPSSI worked successfully for congressional approval of a U.S. Institute for Peace, an impartial data-gathering and training institute whose purpose is to study nonviolent approaches to the management of international conflict.

The applied scientist often acts as a *consultant*. The director of a government organization or the principal of a school may approach the psychologist with a practical problem. Does exposure to pornography increase men's violence against women? What will improve the scholastic performance of schoolchildren? Psychologists may carry out new empirical studies to answer these questions, or they may study existing research to draw conclusions.

When the psychologist in the role of consultant provides a report, policy makers have the right to select what they consider the most relevant findings and base their policies or actions on these conclusions to the extent they desire. Thus, the policy makers retain the control and the power. But the psychologist has contributed, by presenting alternative positions and the empirical support for each, before the policy makers formulate a decision.

The Psychologist as a Methodologist and a Policy Evaluator

In addition to their knowledge of substantive problems, psychologists have methodological skills that they use in assessing how well an intervention has worked. Psychologists and other social scientists have been asked so frequently in the last three decades to conduct evaluation studies that a separate subfield, called *policy evaluation,* or *evaluation research,* has emerged. The policy evaluator provides data to answer questions like "I have instituted a change; how do I know whether it was effective?" Or, more ideally, "I want to make a change in our organization's procedures, but, before I do, I want to know how to design it so I will be able to determine later whether it worked."

The role of psychologist as policy evaluator blossomed in the late 1960s, partly as a manifestation of President Lyndon Johnson's goal of transforming American society. The eminent social psychologist Donald T. Campbell (1969) wrote at that time of a vision of an "experimenting society," in which psychologists would contribute their research expertise to help policy makers determine the effectiveness of Johnson's

"Great Society" attacks on the social problems of unemployment, poverty, racism, and sickness. The underlying value is that public policy will be more intelligently formed if decision makers have input from psychologists (Monahan, 1977).

The psychologist as evaluation researcher might be asked to determine how well programs such as Project Head Start achieved their goals. A cornerstone of President Johnson's War on Poverty, Head Start was a federally supported intervention program designed to improve disadvantaged children's readiness for school. Its efforts were many—from health examinations to school enrichment activities and parent training. This massive program begged for evaluation, and psychologists were called upon to evaluate it. Yet because of its immense and comprehensive nature, and because its planning did not permit systematic comparisons of children with and without training, the effectiveness of Head Start has remained unsettled and controversial (Saxe & Fine, 1981). It is an expensive reminder of the necessity of careful planning *before* changes are instituted, so that we will be able to know whether the changes did or did not make a difference.

The Psychologist as an Advocate

The final role for psychologists, the advocate, is often omitted from textbooks. It is the most controversial role because it is the most "activist." Its goal is to change society. One early advocacy effort by social scientists was to challenge the "separate but equal" doctrine that undergirded school segregation. A group of prominent social scientists in the early 1950s prepared a statement titled "The Effect of Segregation and the Consequences of Desegregation: A Social Science Statement," which became part of the legal brief submitted to the U.S. Supreme Court before its 1954 *Brown* v. *Board of Education* decision.

The statement began with a review of the detrimental effects of segregation, prejudice, and discrimination on black children. The statement asserted that these children learned from their environment that they belonged to what American society considered an inferior group. As Stuart W. Cook, one of the authors of the report, noted, "They react to this knowledge with a sense of humiliation and feelings of inferiority, and come to entertain the possibility that they are, in fact, worthy of second-class treatment" (Cook, 1984, p. 3). These feelings inevitably led to self-hatred and self-rejection for being black.

It is uncertain whether the Supreme Court, in its decision overturning school segregation, was influenced by the social science statement. (Several of the empirical findings and the social scientists' statement itself were cited in a footnote to the *Brown* v. *Board of Education* decision.) Seeking evidence of the social scientists' impact, some commentators have noted a resemblance between parts of the statement and one famous passage in the Supreme Court's *Brown* opinion:

> Segregation of white and colored children in public schools has a detrimental effect upon the colored children. The impact is greater when it has the sanction of the law; for the policy of separating the races is usually interpreted as denoting the inferiority of the Negro group. A sense of inferiority affects the motivation of a child to learn. Segregation with the sanction of law, therefore, has a tendency to retard the educational and mental development of Negro children and to deprive them of some of the benefits they would receive in a racially integrated school system. Whatever may have been the extent of psychological knowledge at the time of *Plessy* v. *Ferguson,* this finding is amply supported by modern authority.

The social protest and unrest of the late 1960s also contributed to the emergence of an advocacy role for psychologists. George Miller, a distinguished experimental psychologist previously known for his basic research on memory, gave a very uncharacteristic message as his presidential address to the American Psychological Association in 1969. He urged his colleagues to "give psychology away"—that is, to help others use psychological knowledge to solve the social problems encountered in everyday society. This may sound like the consultant's role, described previously, but Miller extended it. He noted that powerless groups in our society might better their conditions if they had the benefit of the skills and knowledge of psychologists. They could improve living conditions in the ghetto by effectively lobbying for better crime control, job-training programs, neighborhood schools, and community health and recreation services. Thus the goal for the advocate is to increase the *empowerment* of citizens (Rappaport, 1981, 1987); empowerment refers to the goal of helping disenfranchised groups gain increased control over their lives and increase their personal or collective power to influence social policy and community change.

Other psychologists began, about this time, to urge psychologists to take a partisan role in assisting underprivileged groups. Kenneth Ring (1971) called on his colleagues to take sides, to engage in research and other professional activities that challenged the entrenched establishment. In choosing sides, he stated, "one can, unthinkingly or through choice, ally oneself with the institutional forces which support professional psychology. Or, one may choose to side not with the powerful but with the weak" (p. 5). Some of us may not realize that psychologists take sides when they accept employment by a particular organization. An industrial/organizational psychologist who performs personnel assessment and selection for a large company is paid to help the company select the "best" job candidates; the psychologist is not paid to show concern for those who fail the selection test, nor does he or she ordinarily assist applicants to pass the selection test. Some psychologists may even deny they have any responsibilities to the job applicants.

By identifying with less powerful, less organized groups in society, the psychologist as advocate takes on two tasks: a traditional research task and a political task. The research task is to study how selected institutions affect the politically weak. An analog to the advocate's research task is the crusade over the last three decades of lawyer Ralph Nader and his "raiders" on behalf of consumer safety and protection (Blum, 1990). The political task is to ensure that the research is used to bring about recommended institutional changes. That might require publicity, lobbying, organizing of special-interest groups, and other forms of constructive social action (Haney, 1991).

Ring referred to the combination of advocacy research and partisan social action as "the psychology of the left," and he saw this as a plausible stance for psychologists, since—among the different academic disciplines—they are most likely to be political liberals or to the left of liberalism (Lipset & Ladd, 1970). An example of advocacy by a psychologist is the work of Hannah Levin.

While working as a consultant to a community mental health center, Levin observed that the people who lived in the surrounding area had little say about the operation of the center. The health authorities told the community residents that they could have an advisory board but that physicians would have to administer the actual health program. However, the people wanted the center to be administered by community residents. In the confrontation that resulted, Levin became an advocate for the people. She found that her arguments on behalf of the people motivated many of them to take action. She gave the people a new confidence that eventually empowered them to establish control over the health center's basic policies. One outcome of this community control was a shift in priorities from programs that emphasized suicidal and acutely disturbed patients to programs that emphasized youth. Levin's summary of her position in this health controversy is very explicit:

> Today a new tradition for professionals is being molded. We call ourselves radical professionals; that is, we use our skills to help make social change. Thus, as advocates for the powerless we assist these groups in gaining a redistribution of power rather than just a redistribution of services. We have given up our so-called professional neutrality for a partisan role. We believe that there is a conflict of interest between the groups we represent and other groups, and the recognition of this conflict is necessary in guiding our work. Our role has become that of aiding the poor in challenging today's standards rather than meeting them, and our relationship to the poor community and its organizations has been as employees rather than employers [1970, p. 122].

What tasks might an advocate pursue to improve the education of minority-group children? The research task might be to evaluate the quality of inner-city schools. In large cities, are the best teachers assigned to the schools in the affluent neighborhoods? Are well-qualified, well-trained teachers present in the same proportion in schools throughout the city? Do ghetto schools get short shrift in allocations of supplies? *If* adverse differences exist—if there is discrimination against inner-city schools, either by design or by accident—then the psychologist/advocate faces the political task of mobilizing support for change. Can new, more sympathetic, school board members be elected? Will the school administration be responsive to facts showing the neglect of the inner-city schools? Is it desirable to gain publicity through protest marches?

The four roles just presented vary in several respects. Each of them is fraught with dangers and ethical dilemmas. What is right? What is proper for a psychologist to do? Before considering such questions, we'll discuss how each role contributes to the study of the law.

THE PSYCHOLOGIST'S RELATIONSHIP TO THE LAW

The fact that the four roles differ on a dimension of "ivory tower" isolation versus involvement with the community is highlighted when we apply the four roles to psychologists' study of and work in the legal system.

The Psychologist as a Basic Researcher

Even though "pure scientists" choose topics without regard for their application, and even though they prefer to work alone or collaborate with a few like-minded souls in their laboratory, the basic knowledge they generate can promote a better understanding of the law.

For example, laboratory research on visual perception helps us understand just how accurate an eyewitness is to a crime or an accident; so does the research of psychologists who test different theories of memory. Basic research on the relationship of one's social attitudes to one's behavior can help us understand why people obey or disobey the law. Likewise, clinical psychologists' professional evaluations of criminal defendants have been found to be affected by their basic attitude about the causes of crime (Deitchman, Kennedy, & Beckham, 1991).

The study of conformity has been a popular basic research topic for social psychologists.

Conformity is an important consideration in jury decisions, and an analysis of the responses to conformity pressures by groups of subjects in the laboratory can provide clues for understanding the power of pressure from the majority to affect jury decisions.

In summary, opportunities to apply "pure" research findings to understanding the legal system are numerous.

The Psychologist as an Expert Witness

Psychologists who are interested in applying the findings of their profession to real-world questions can act as expert witnesses in legislative hearings (Box 2-1) or in a court of law.

During a trial, each side, as part of its presentation of the evidence, may ask the judge to allow expert witnesses to testify. Juries—and judges, too, for that matter—cannot be expected to be well versed in every topic from abscesses to Zinfandel wine. An expert witness is someone who possesses special knowledge about a subject, knowledge that the average juror does not have. Although people need not always have had formal training before they qualify as expert witnesses—an antique dealer or a gold prospector might be an expert on certain topics—most expert witnesses have had training. At any rate, the judge must be convinced that the testimony any expert will present is of a kind that requires special knowledge, skill, or experience and that the testimony will help resolve the dispute and lead jurors toward the truth. Experts are usually paid for the time they spend testifying in court, as much as $500 per hour for some specialties (Blum, 1989).

For example, if the trial is to determine the responsibility for injuries that a person suffered when a bridge collapsed, it is not likely that the jurors possess the technical knowledge to assess the adequacy of the bridge construction. (Were the steel girders thick enough? Was the right mix of concrete used?) Jurors in a murder trial probably have not had the medical training necessary to form accurate judgments about the causes of death. The topics calling for expertise are almost limitless. And psychologists, as expert witnesses, have been called on to testify in a variety of cases. Here are a few examples:

- The mental state of a defendant at the time of an alleged offense and the mental competence of the defendant to stand trial

- The degree of emotional or brain damage suffered by a victim in an accident
- The extent of mental retardation and the appropriateness of certain treatments for mental retardation
- Employee discrimination through selection and promotion procedures
- The effects of bilingualism in children
- Community standards regarding obscenity
- The battered woman syndrome
- The accuracy of identifications by eyewitnesses
- Trademark infringement and false advertising

| Box 2-1 | *Testifying in a Legislative Hearing— An Example of an Expert Witness/Consultant* |

Just like the problem of sentencing disparity (described in Chapter 1), the use of indeterminate sentences has been criticized as denying prisoners equal treatment before the law. Psychologist John Monahan (a law school professor at the University of Virginia) describes his actions on this issue and their impact:

The indeterminate sentence involves sentencing convicted offenders for vaguely specified periods of time (e.g., 1 to 20 years), with the actual release date determined by a parole board on the basis of psychological or psychiatric reports. As a psychologist, I was aware of the data on the failure of involuntary treatment (Geis & Monahan, 1976) and the inability of mental health

professionals to predict with any accuracy when an offender was violence-prone (Monahan, 1975b; Monahan & Cummings, 1975). But persuasive as the data were, they did not tell me how highly the community in question—prisoners, in this case—prioritized *this* policy issue as compared with others. It was only through reading the literature of prisoner advocates (American Friends Service Committee, 1972; Mitford, 1974), talking with officials of the Prisoners' Union, and seeing the thousands of letters written to legislators by prisoners themselves urging abolition of the indeterminate sentence that I became aware that this was not just one among many issues of community concern, but an extreme-

ly high-priority issue as well. Convinced that my choice of a target problem was consistent with the priorities of the community, and marshaling all the available empirical evidence, I advocated both in the popular media and before legislative committees (Monahan, 1975a) that the indeterminate sentence should be abolished. While the effect of any one person's testimony was doubtlessly marginal, the [California] legislature did take the evidence into account when it voted to abolish the indeterminate sentence effective July 1, 1977 [Monahan, 1977, p. 205].

This example also illustrates how a given psychologist may play two roles at the same time; in fact, being a consultant and being an advocate may be hard to separate.

- The impact on juries of sensationalistic pretrial publicity
- The effects of alternative child custody arrangements after divorce
- The cause of death in cases in which suicide is suspected
- The effects of warning signs or safety instructions on potentially dangerous equipment

Expert witnesses are usually proposed by one side in a trial, and the judge decides whether they will be allowed to testify. Many judges fear that an expert witness's testimony will be so powerful that it will usurp the jury as the fact finder in the case, and so judges may refuse to let experts testify, especially if their topic of expertise is one that most laypeople are familiar with. Thus, in matters of the accuracy of eyewitnesses, psychologists have often been denied the opportunity to testify. The late Robert Buckhout, who was a national expert on accuracy of eyewitnesses, reported that in New York "I have testified before juries in about 10 cases and been kept out of trials too many times to keep count" (1983, p. 67). A comprehensive review by Solomon M. Fulero (1988) indicates that by 1988 a total of 111 state and 29 federal judicial opinions had been published on the question of letting expert witnesses testify. Fulero concludes that psychologists have been allowed to testify about eyewitness accuracy for the defense in at least 450 cases in 25 states, but many states still prevent them from doing so.

Although a judge's decision not to permit a psychologist to testify is subject to reversal on appeal, the fact that some judges allow the testimony, whereas others refuse it, is an example of judicial discretion, one of the dilemmas identified in Chapter 1. A particular judge's decision (involving the senior author of this book) and the reasons for the judge's refusal are described in the following paragraphs.

First, we describe the case that led to the judge's decision.

Cathy Mills (not her true name) left her Topeka, Kansas, home for her job as a hospital nurse's aide on Friday, June 16, 1978, at approximately 10:20 P.M. Because her car was not working, she was on foot. Ms. Mills, a young white woman who was fearful of being raped, walked down the middle of the street because she had been told it was safer there. About three blocks from the hospital, she passed a parked car with its hood up. As she walked past the car, a man spoke to her and then, with a knife in his hand, he grabbed her. Ms. Mills described him as black, about 6 feet tall, weighing about 200 pounds, in his late twenties or early thirties, with watery eyes, a mustache, medium-length sideburns, and a medium-length Afro hairstyle. At knifepoint, the man forced her into his car, which she later described as a 1969 Ford LTD, black over white. At the trial five months later, she testified that the oil light on the dashboard stayed on the entire time he was driving the car. She further testified that the car had an automatic transmission and that there was a towel on the seat.

The man drove Ms. Mills through Topeka and finally stopped near a field. He got out of the car and told Ms. Mills to undress. Still holding the knife, the man told her to lie down and then had sexual intercourse with her. Afterward, Ms. Mills got dressed, and the man drove her toward the hospital, letting her out several blocks from it.

Ms. Mills then went to the hospital and informed her supervisor that she had been raped. This was approximately 11:00 P.M., about 40 minutes after she had started out for work. At the hospital, Ms. Mills was examined and treated, semen and loose pubic hairs were collected as possible evidence, and her clothes were kept for the police to examine. Later that night—a Friday night—she went to the police station to give a statement. On the next Monday night she returned to the police station and looked through a series of photographs contained in looseleaf books. She was unable to identify her assailant from examining any of those photographs.

On August 7, 1978—seven weeks later— she returned to the police station to look at some other photographs. From a group of five black-and-white photographs, she identified one of the subjects as the man who had raped her. Then, from a group of six color photographs, she also identified a photograph of the man who had raped her. The two photographs were of the same man, James Reed. Mr. Reed was the only person whose photograph appeared in both sets.

The police department's first contact with James Reed was on August 4, three days before Ms. Mills identified him from the photographs. He was stopped for a registration check on the car he was driving; it was registered in the name of his woman friend, Charlene Chambers. The same detective who was handling Ms. Mills's case stopped Mr. Reed. He reported that the car was a dark blue over white, four-door car in poor running condition. The detective noticed a small towel lying on the front seat.

The detective's next contact with Mr. Reed was on August 8, 1978, the day after Ms. Mills made her identification. Mr. Reed was placed in custody for investigation, and his clothes (similar to those the rapist was described as wearing) were taken from him, as was a knife.

Ms. Mills identified James Reed in person for the first time at the preliminary hearing, three months after the attack. She also identified him at the trial, about five months after the attack. With each subsequent identification, her confidence in the accuracy of her identification rose.

During the trial, she testified that she had been "scared to death" during the entire ordeal, fearing that the man would kill her.

Afraid to face him, she looked at him only now and then.

Because of the circumstances, plus the procedure used by the Topeka Police Department in identifying the assailant, the assistant public defender (who was Mr. Reed's attorney) asked the author to testify as an expert witness on the accuracy of eyewitnesses' identification. An additional reason for this request—and for the author's willingness to testify for the defense in a rape trial—was that a laboratory report from the Kansas Bureau of Investigation concluded that Negro pubic hairs taken from the pubic combings of Ms. Mills were microscopically dissimilar to the pubic hair sample taken from James Reed. Directly conflicting evidence on the identity of Cathy Mills's assailant was, therefore, expected at the trial.

Was the accuracy of eyewitness identification a proper subject for expert testimony in this case? The counsel for the defense argued that such expert testimony was well within the guidelines established by two Kansas cases. In one of these cases, the judges had been quite restrictive and had proposed that expert testimony could be admitted only when the topic was complicated and beyond the common knowledge of jurors. But the other case (*Massoni* v. *State Highway Commission*, 1974) qualified matters; in it, the judges had stated that, although expert witnesses may be permitted to give opinions bearing on the ultimate issues, they may do so only when the opinions will help the jury interpret technical facts or understand the material in evidence.

On November 9, 1978, Shawnee County District Judge Adrian J. Allen denied the defense counsel's motion to allow an expert to testify, stating:

The Court is of the opinion such testimony is not admissible because laymen jurors are perfectly capable to draw proper conclusions from eyewitness identification testimony, particularly since the testimony is, of course, subject to cross-examination. In the opinion of the Court, expert testimony in the field of eyewitness identification does not involve a subject sufficiently beyond the common knowledge of ordinary persons and, therefore, is not a subject upon which the jurors would find the testimony of an expert particularly helpful.

Most psychologists would, of course, disagree with the judge that they have nothing to contribute "sufficiently beyond common knowledge" (their claims will be examined in Chapter 7). Whether the testimony of an expert witness would alter the verdict in a specific trial is, of course, impossible to know; in this trial, the jury found James Reed guilty.

The Psychologist as a Policy Evaluator

The legal system is no different from other elements of our society in its frequent implementation of changes that have not been properly evaluated. As noted in Chapter 1, new laws are constantly being created and old ones revised and reinterpreted as a result of changes in society. These legal modifications cry out for evaluation. What are the effects of changing the legal drinking age from 18 to 21? Does a police crackdown on speeders reduce traffic accidents? Is the death penalty a deterrent? Such questions encourage evaluation research on legal issues.

Likewise, the law enforcement and criminal justice systems frequently alter their operating procedures. For example, police departments may change from automobile patrols to foot patrols in order to increase surveillance and to improve police/community relations. New programs are established to discourage or prevent the sexual abuse of children (Bales, 1988a). Often these innovations are introduced with-

out adequate planning about how they can be evaluated; hence their outcomes, whether good or bad, cannot be determined (Reppucci & Haugaard, 1989). The methodological skills of the psychologist as evaluation researcher are essential in designing an innovation so that its effects can be tested, in order to eliminate other possible explanations for any changes. For example, a judge in New Philadelphia, Ohio, in an effort to reduce drunk driving, routinely ordered first offenders to spend 15 days in jail plus pay a $750 fine. His practice was well known in the county, and you might expect that it would deter drunk driving. But researchers did anonymous spot checks of drivers, including breathalyzer tests, in New Philadelphia and also in Cambridge, Ohio, a neighboring county where sentences were less severe. Similar numbers of drunk drivers were found in both localities, implying that the extreme punishments weren't effective deterrents.

Claims of employment discrimination provide an opportunity for using statistical analyses conducted by an evaluation researcher. Tomkins (1988b) identifies several recent Supreme Court cases in which plaintiffs used statistical data and social science evidence to bolster their contentions of having been unfavorably treated by employers because of their race or gender. In one of these, the plaintiff, Ann Hopkins, claimed that she had been rejected for an appointment as a partner in Price, Waterhouse, a "big eight" accounting firm, because her behaviors had been evaluated as too "unladylike" and aggressive by the current partners. (Ms. Hopkins's record and productivity at the firm surpassed those of the men who had been promoted to partner.) In the spring of 1989, the Supreme Court ruled in Ms. Hopkins's favor. In reaching its decision, the Court cited the expert testimony that social psychologist Susan Fiske had given in the case about the indications and effects of gender-based stereotyping and how such stereotyping was revealed in Ann Hopkins' employment experiences (Fiske, Bersoff, Borgida, Deaux, & Heilman, 1991).

The Psychologist as an Advocate

One major difference between the consultant and the advocate is the fact that the latter identifies with one side. Even if a consultant is paid by one side in a trial, as an expert witness he or she is under oath to tell "the truth, the whole truth, and nothing but the truth." Advocates, although using psychological methods and trying to render an objective analysis of data, commit their skills to one side; they become partisans. The contrast with the expert witness role can be best illustrated by the actions of a group of social scientists who aided the defense team in the trial of the "Harrisburg Seven." This trial, by the way, was the first highly publicized application of so-called *scientific jury selection procedures*, further described in Chapter 13. Box 2-2 describes the case and the procedures that the social scientists used.

Much has been written about these procedures since they were first publicized in 1973 (Schulman, Shaver, Colman, Emrich, & Christie, 1973). More recently, the national media devoted extensive coverage to the use of jury consultants by William Kennedy Smith in his highly publicized 1991 trial on rape charges. Critics have labeled these techniques "jury rigging" and jury manipulation (Etzioni, 1974a, 1974b) or argued that there are few, if any, convincing demonstrations that scientific jury selection is more effective than routine jury selection (e.g., Fulero & Penrod, 1990; Hans & Vidmar, 1986; Saks, 1976).

For their part, jury consultants usually offer two justifications for these methods. Richard Christie, a pioneer of jury consultation, did not see the techniques as a "radical departure from more traditional legal practice" (1976, p. 265); rather, they differ from lawyers' traditional jury selection procedures more in degree than in kind. But Christie's own comparison of the two approaches reflects qualitative differences. For example, in assessing characteristics of possible jurors, lawyers traditionally use their personal knowledge of specific individuals plus their experience with previous jury pools, whereas social scientists carry out new surveys and analyze demographic studies. In making observations of prospective jurors, lawyers typically rely on intuition, seasoned by their past experience, whereas social scientists make systematic ratings, guided by psychological theory. In trying to compose the actual jury—to the degree that they have control over the outcome—lawyers usually focus on the selection of key jurors, whereas social scientists more systematically apply findings from small-group research.

The second defense of jury selection is based on a perception that the "dice are often loaded" in favor of the prosecution. The social scientists in the Harrisburg Seven case applied their procedures because they believed that the defendants' rights to presumption of innocence were seriously threatened. They noted:

> The Government chose a conservative location for the trial. J. Edgar Hoover proclaimed the defendants' guilt long before the trial began. William Lynch [the chief prosecuting attorney] made public some of the controversial Berrigan-McAlister letters. As in most criminal and political trials, the investigatory and financial resources of the government far outweighed those of the defendants. . . . For these reasons we believed, and still believe, that our partisanship was proper [Schulman et al., 1973, p. 84].

In recent years, psychologists' involvement in trial consultation has increased. Nationally, the number of companies or individuals who work full-time in jury consultation has grown rapidly. Litigation Sciences, a firm established by Donald E. Vinson in 1979, employs more than 20 Ph.D.-level social scientists and market

researchers; within its first ten years, the firm assisted attorneys in more than 900 cases and interviewed 20,000 jurors (Cox, 1989). In con-

---

| Box **2-2** | *"Scientific Jury Selection" in the "Harrisburg Seven" Trial* |

In 1971 Philip Berrigan and seven other defendants were arrested and charged with conspiracy to plan a number of antiwar activities, such as raiding draft boards, blowing up heating tunnels in Washington, DC, and kidnapping Henry Kissinger, then secretary of state. The federal government chose to hold the trial in Harrisburg, Pennsylvania, considered to be the most conservative, progovernment locality in the district. For the first time, a team of social scientists joined the defense attorneys in an effort to select a favorable jury from a largely unfavorable community. A "recipe for a jury" was formulated (Schulman, Shaver, Colman, Emrich, & Christie, 1973). As their first step, the team of social scientists sought to determine whether the pool of prospective jurors was representative of the local population. They compared the demographic characteristics of those drawn in the pool to a random sample of registered voters in the community and found that the average member of the venire was somewhat older. Partly because of these findings, the presiding judge ordered the drawing of a second, more representative, jury pool. Score a minor triumph for the social scientists!

The defense team next sought

to discover what background characteristics were related to potential jurors' biases toward conviction or acquittal. They interviewed 252 people from the Harrisburg area, in order to find out whether such qualities as age, religion, gender, and level of education were related to attitudes such as trust in the government and tolerance for protest by dissidents. As it turned out, community members who were Episcopalians, Presbyterians, Methodists, or members of fundamentalist churches tended to side with the prosecution, whereas those who were Roman Catholics, Lutherans, or members of the Church of the Brethren were more sympathetic to the defense. Counter to their expectations, the social scientists found that people with more education and exposure to metropolitan news media were more conservative politically and more sympathetic to the prosecution. But, as expected, members of the Democratic party tended to side with the defense. In summary, the social scientists concluded that their ideal juror would be a female Democrat with no religious preferences who held a white-collar job or a skilled-laborer position. Guided by these survey results, the defense sought such jurors.

The task was not easy. There were few such people in the panel. But, in a sense, the defense team was successful. The trial ended with a hung jury, split 10–2 with the majority favoring a verdict of "not guilty." The U.S. government decided not to hold a second trial. All the charges were dropped. And yet, at another level, the social scientists were completely off base in their selection of two of the jurors—the two who became holdouts for guilt. One of these jurors, a Lutheran man in his fifties who owned two grocery stores, had expressed vaguely antiwar attitudes during jury selection. But, as soon as the deliberations began, it became clear that his true feelings were far from peace loving. The other, a 68-year-old woman, belonged to a pacifist church; four of her sons were conscientious objectors to wars on religious grounds. The defense team accepted her immediately on hearing that. But in the deliberations she showed that she did not share her sons' feelings. In their ratings of prospective jurors, the defense had given rather positive evaluations to both of these people—more positive than for some of the other jurors they had to take.

trast to the Harrisburg Seven defendants, most clients of Litigation Sciences are large corporations involved in huge civil trials dealing with claims of antitrust, product-liability, or toxic-waste violations.

ETHICAL CONSIDERATIONS IN EACH ROLE

Whatever role a psychologist chooses, it carries standards about what is acceptable and unac-ceptable behavior. Indeed, every day we all face choices about what is right and wrong. (Chapter 3 reviews some of the factors we consider in these decisions.) Professions often develop explicit statements of ethical standards of behavior for that profession. For psychologists in general, the American Psychological Association (APA, 1992) has specified a Code of Ethical Principles of Psychologists. Members who violate any of these ethical principles may be expelled from the organization.

But making the right choice is complicated by the fact that the principles specified by the ethics code may conflict with the psychologist's legal responsibilities. The most explicit illustra-

---

Box 2-3 | **The Tarasoff Case and the Duty to Protect**

It's hard to get a handle on the true personality of Titania ("Tanya") Tarasoff, even though a docudrama-type book has been written about her life and death (*Bad Karma*, Blum, 1986). Was she a manipulative, scheming seductress, or was she a sincere naif interested in foreign students because, despite her living in Berkeley, California, her parents were from Russia, she had been born in Shanghai, and she had spent her early childhood in Brazil? What is clear is that she confused and frustrated Prosenjit Poddar, a student from India who met her shortly after he came to the University of California as a graduate student in naval engineering. Not only was Poddar inexperienced in American customs—he didn't know what to make of Tanya's phone calls or visits to his dorm room—but he had led a sheltered life in India and never had had a close relationship with a young woman. At first Poddar felt that he was falling in love with Tanya Tarasoff, but her inconsistencies—she would be very friendly toward him one day but avoid him at the International House folk dance the next night; she would accept a date with him but during it talk about other men who interested her—came to mystify Poddar, as they would most of us. Poddar became angry and even fantasized hurting or killing Tanya; he never threatened her, but his comments to his friends led one of them to accompany Poddar to the campus mental health clinic. After several visits, Poddar's psychotherapist warned the police that Poddar had made death threats (he never mentioned Tanya's name); the police detained him only briefly. Two months later, Poddar went to the Tarasoff home, encountered Tanya, and stabbed her to death.

The parents of the young woman brought suit against the staff members and the university, claiming they were negligent by failing to show reasonable care; they should have confined Poddar and taken steps to warn or protect Tanya. Basically, the supreme court of the state of California agreed; it established a standard for psychotherapists whereby they have a duty to use "reasonable care" to protect potential victims from clients in psychotherapy who threaten violence. After that decision, made in 1976, courts in several other states rendered similar decisions. Some cases extended the duty to the protection of property, and other decisions applied the duty to protect all foreseeable victims, not just identifiable ones.

tion of this dilemma is the ethical obligation of confidentiality versus the legal duty to warn potential victims of clients' threats. This conflict was most apparent in the *Tarasoff* decision by the supreme court of the state of California (see Box 2-3).

Furthermore, each of the psychological roles that serve as the framework for this chapter carries somewhat different ethical obligations, as described in the following sections. In keeping with this diversification, Division 41 (American Psychology-Law Society) of APA has developed a set of guidelines for forensic psychologists, under the direction of Stephen L. Golding, Thomas Grisso, and David Shapiro. These Specialty Guidelines for Forensic Psychologists, published and approved by the division's membership in 1991, provide "specific guidance to forensic psychologists in monitoring their professional conduct when acting in assistance to courts, parties to legal proceedings, correctional and forensic mental health facilities, and legislative agencies" (Committee on Ethical Guidelines for Forensic Psychologists, 1991). The guidelines amplify the Ethical Principles of Psychologists in several areas of forensic practice such as confidentiality, methods of evaluations and reports, and relationships between the psychologist and the contending parties in litigation.

So far, so good, you might say. Isn't it society's responsibility, through laws and court decisions, to provide each of us with safety? But the *Tarasoff* decision reflects the first dilemma described in Chapter 1: the rights of individuals versus the common good. To require psychotherapists to reveal what has been told to them in confidence conflicts with their professional standards. Beyond that, many clients are not likely to reveal their innermost fantasies and frustrations—violent or not—unless they are assured that their revelations will be held in confidence. Does the *Tarasoff* decision mean that a psychotherapist has to confront incoming clients with something akin to a *Miranda* warning? If so, how can trust result?

Tanya Tarasoff has been dead for 20 years, but the principle that indirectly was illuminated by her death still is not consistently implemented. For example, several state legislatures, beginning with California, reacted to *Tarasoff* by passing laws that limit the liability of psychotherapists in such "duty-to-protect" situations. Typically, this new legislation exempts psychotherapists from being sued for failing to warn or protect victims, unless their client has told them of a "serious threat against specific or identifiable persons" (Bales, 1988b, p. 18). If that has happened, the psychotherapist is usually required "to make reasonable efforts to communicate the threat to the potential victim, a law enforcement agency, or both" (Bales, 1988b, p. 18).

In a related fashion, a jury in Georgia ruled that a psychologist was not obligated to violate the confidentiality of his patient's revelations by notifying the police of the patient's violent thoughts and feelings (Buie, 1989). This was the verdict despite the fact that the patient, a parolee from the state penitentiary, had murdered a young woman. Her parents, who brought suit against the therapist, argued that he knew or should have known that his client was dangerous and that he should have told the police that the parolee had expressed homicidal wishes during therapy. In his defense the psychotherapist reported that the murderer's vague expression of violence never targeted any specific victim. Furthermore, the therapist had facilitated the commitment of the client to a locked ward of a hospital for treatment. It was only after the parolee's release from the hospital that he committed the murder.

The Ethics of the Basic Researcher

The APA Code of Professional Ethics provides only an overview of the responsibilities of the basic researcher. Procedures for experimentation with human subjects dictate that the subjects be informed of the risks in participating and that their consent be obtained. When using animals as subjects, experimenters are to avoid inducing pain or injury unless there is no other way for the research question to be studied. Recently, supporters of animal rights have criticized the use of animals by experimental and neuropsychologists (Cowley, 1988).

Basic researchers also must follow standards of objectivity in collecting and analyzing data and in writing up their results for publication. Their procedures need to be described thoroughly in their publications so that other scholars can repeat their procedures and check the findings. Any material they publish should be their own work, of course. However, despite these rules, examples of plagiarism and falsification of data still periodically appear in psychology, as well as in other sciences (Hostetler, 1988).

The Ethics of the Expert Witness

The psychologist as expert witness represents a profession that stands for objectivity and accuracy in its procedures. Even though expert witnesses are usually hired (and paid) by one side, they are responsible for reporting all their conclusions, whether these favor the side paying them or not. Furthermore, it violates the ethical standards of both psychologists and lawyers for expert witnesses to accept payment that is contingent on the outcome of the case.

But achieving objectivity is by no means easy. Horgan (1988) argues that, from the jury's perspective, the psychologist is perceived as an advocate rather than as an unbiased scientist. Regardless of this perception, a psychol-

ogist, when asked to testify, has an ethical requirement to be explicit with the attorney about his or her orientation. Still, psychologists may be tempted to sympathize with the side that has employed them. This sympathy may not even be conscious; instead, the psychologist may simply filter the facts of the case through perceptions motivated by a spirit of helpfulness to his or her client.

Some experts provide testimony that is ethically questionable because of the methods they use in arriving at their conclusions. One example stems from the case of Thomas Andy Barefoot, a convicted murderer of a police officer, who was ultimately executed by a lethal injection in a Texas prison. The jury that convicted Barefoot and imposed the death penalty had heard testimony from a Dallas psychiatrist, Dr. James Grigson, that the defendant had a "100 percent and absolute" chance of committing future violent acts and that he would be a continuing threat to society (Work, 1985, p. 65). The psychiatrist *had never examined* Barefoot.

Dr. Grigson has testified in more than 120 capital murder cases in Texas (Rosenbaum, 1990). In this state—unlike most others that permit the death penalty—the jury may recommend capital punishment only if it concludes that it is probable that the defendant will commit further acts of violence and will be a continuing threat to society. Dr. Grigson characteristically testifies that the offender is dangerous, regardless of whether he actually has examined the person; in all but nine of the trials in which he has testified the defendant was sentenced to death (Belkin, 1988).

When the decision to sentence Barefoot to death was appealed, the American Psychiatric Association strenuously objected to the admissibility of testimony by a psychiatrist who had not personally examined the defendant, especially to the prediction about his future dangerousness. But the U.S. Supreme Court upheld both the decision and the admissibility of the psychiatrist's testimony—though not without dissent from Justice Harry Blackmun, who wrote: "The specious testimony of a psychiatrist, colored in the eyes of an impressionable jury by the inevitable untouchability of a medical specialist's words, equates with death itself" (quoted in Work, 1985, p. 65).

However, in another case appealed to the Supreme Court, Grigson did examine the convicted murder defendant, John T. Satterwhite. As usual, Dr. Grigson told the jury that Satterwhite was dangerous and beyond the reach of psychiatric rehabilitation. But because the examination took place without the presence or the knowledge of the defendant's attorney, the Supreme Court (in May 1988) unanimously reversed the death sentence and ordered a new sentencing hearing (Brigham, 1988).

A further problem occurs whenever the adversary system forces an expert to make absolute, "either/or" judgments. Which parent would be better for the child in a custody case stemming from a divorce? Does the evaluation of a defendant indicate he is insane? Shana Alexander (1979), in her report of the trial of Patricia Hearst, contrasts the black-or-white opinions that are required in trials against the various shades of gray that usually characterize the testimony of psychiatrists and psychologists.

When psychologists are allowed to testify about the accuracy of eyewitnesses, another ethical question arises. Do they really have anything to say that is accurate, precise, and relevant to that particular witness? Is their testimony really beyond the common understanding and experience of the average juror? Psychologists differ in their responses to such questions. Most (for example, Brigham & Bothwell, 1983; Loftus, 1984; Wells, 1984) conclude that the chances are slim of finding 12 jurors who are well informed about the accuracy of eyewitnesses. Furthermore, the vast majority of research

psychologists who possess expertise about the relative accuracy of eyewitnesses consider the phenomenon a legitimate one for their testimony (Kassin, Ellsworth, & Smith, 1989). But a few psychologists, especially Michael McCloskey and Howard Egeth (1983), have argued that psychologists' knowledge of eyewitnesses is not beyond the common understanding and experience of the average juror.

The Ethics of the Evaluation Researcher

The psychologist who evaluates court reforms and other changes in the law enforcement system faces ethical responsibilities similar to those of the expert witness. The standard canons of scientific procedure apply, but, again, because of the source of payment, there are pressures to interpret results in a certain way.

Consider, for example, a large state prison that wants to improve its parole system. Prison officials have identified a problem with convicts eligible for parole who are heavy drug users. If released into society, they are likely to commit further crimes to maintain their drug habit. Hence, they will soon return to prison. So the prison seeks to introduce and evaluate an innovative halfway-house program for those parolees with a history of narcotics addiction. It hires an evaluation researcher to design a study and evaluate the effects of this innovation. The prison provides money to carry out the study, and prison officials are sincerely committed to its goals. Assume the psychologist concludes that the halfway house does *not* significantly reduce drug use by parolees. The authorities are disappointed; they may even attack the integrity of the evaluation researcher. Yet, as scientists, program evaluators must "call 'em like they see 'em," regardless of the desirability of the outcome.

Even if the program is successful, the evaluation researcher faces other ethical dilemmas. To assess such an innovative program, the researcher might have to deny some parolees access to the program and place them in a "status quo" control group. The ethical dilemma becomes more critical when some potentially lifesaving innovation is being evaluated. But often it is only through such research methods that a potentially helpful new program can be convincingly proven to be effective.

Evaluation researchers who study the criminal justice system also need to be aware of the potential narrowness of their viewpoint and its effect on their conclusions. Faced with the fact that almost two-thirds of ex-prisoners are rearrested within three years of their prison release (Lacayo, 1989), the psychologist is tempted to blame the individual ex-convict as the cause of the problem, even though variables more appropriate to sociological or economic perspectives—community orientation, unemployment rates, "secondary deviance" (see Chapter 5)—are equally applicable.

The Ethics of the Advocate

As we noted earlier, when the psychologist becomes an advocate for one side in the selection of jurors, ethical problems emerge. Just how far should the selection go? Christie has concluded that in political cases most potential jurors are biased toward the prosecution. He seems to be implying that in an adversary system it is all right to select people "initially favorable to the defense" (1976, p. 269). But in the same paragraph he writes that "the central problem in jury selection is the careful evaluation of those who are not so biased that they cannot be *fair and impartial jurors*" (pp. 269–270; italics added). Incidentally, the latter goal—that of a fair jury—is endorsed by the Sixth Amendment to the U.S. Constitution, which guarantees the individual a right to trial by an impartial jury.

Not only may systematic jury selection upset the balance of a jury, but it also may influence the power structure and the sociometric network within the group. In his case history of the selection of the Gainesville Eight jury, Christie (1976) describes how his team was able to arrange the composition of the jury so that the team's choice would be elected foreperson. Their choice was an art teacher whose husband was an administrator at the University of Florida. Her reputation in the community was that she was politically conservative but fair. The defense team rated her as a natural leader. Christie writes: "Basing their strategy on this assumption the defense team then decided to strike high-status males who looked like potential leadership rivals, especially since none of them came across as favorably as she did" (1976, p. 273). The expectations were upheld; this juror was selected by her colleagues as foreperson, and eventually the jury voted unanimously to acquit the Gainesville Eight.

What, then, is "fair"? Can there be fairness and impartiality in an adversary system? Systematic jury selection may illustrate a situation in which social scientists and lawyers, in concert, are in conflict with the way most people interpret the intent of the law.

When psychologists become advocates in jury selection, they subscribe to the ethical code of the attorneys, who, after all, are in charge of the trial preparation. The Ethics Code of the American Bar Association admonishes its members to defend their clients to the best of their abilities, short of lying or encouraging lying. Every defendant, regardless of the heinousness of the crime or the mass of evidence against him or her, is entitled to the best defense possible, including the use of psychological techniques to assess the relative favorability of prospective jurors. (The prosecution is entitled to the same opportunities to employ psychological knowledge, but prosecutors rarely use psychologists to assist them in selecting juries.)

Although psychologists rely on lawyers' ethics when acting as part of a defense team, they do not thereby abandon the ethics of their own profession. They must not misrepresent research results, fake data, or plagiarize. They do not disguise "personal values as scientific conclusions and then foist them on an unsuspecting public" (Monahan, 1977, p. 206). Rather, they apply their knowledge and skills for a particular desired outcome, and they are candid about doing so. Are psychologists who work for an advertising agency unethical when they use professional knowledge to encourage consumers to buy one brand of dogfood rather than another? Many of us would say no; the free enterprise system permits any such procedures that do not falsify claims. Is this example analogous to jury selection? Probably, especially given that rival attorneys always try to select jurors who will sympathize with their version of the facts. The adversary system rests on the expectation that each side will eliminate those jurors most favorable to the other side, thus resulting in an unbiased jury. As long as the adversary system permits attorneys from each side to eliminate some prospective jurors without giving reasons, it does not seem unethical for psychologists to assist them—as long as the psychologists maintain their responsibilities as data-based decision makers. However, psychologists who make exaggerated claims about the effectiveness of their jury selection techniques are misrepresenting their services, which is a clear violation of APA ethical standards (Cutler, 1990).

SUMMARY

Although empirical in their orientation, psychologists face choices when deciding what role they will play in studying the law or working in the legal system. Four possible roles are identified in this chapter: the psychologist (1) as basic researcher, (2) as consultant, (3) as methodologist or policy evaluator, and (4) as advocate. Basic researchers are interested in knowledge for its own sake; they do not seek to apply their findings to the solution of practical problems. Yet many basic research findings are relevant to practical problems—for example, findings on how memory works, on why eyewitnesses to crimes may be inaccurate, or on how attitudes relate to behavior. In the consultant role, the psychologist may apply basic research knowledge to a particular problem, in response to requests from personnel working in the legal system. Psychologists who serve as expert witnesses—in, for example, child custody disputes or trials involving the insanity plea—exemplify the consultant role. They supply needed information and opinions; their contact with the legal system is initiated by others—judges, law enforcement officials, prison wardens, defense attorneys. As a policy evaluator or an evaluation researcher, the psychologist capitalizes on methodological skills. Policy evaluators design and conduct surveys and experiments so that innovators can learn what effects their innovations have had. The fourth role, the advocate, is the most controversial. The advocate supports and represents segments of the community who seek greater power and influence. This role contains both a research function and a political function. Within the field of law, a psychologist who helps a team of defense attorneys select a jury sympathetic to the defendant is acting as an advocate. Similar problems of ethics are associated with each role, but to some extent the ethical dilemmas for each are different.

CHAPTER 3

Legality, Morality, and Justice

W hat would you have done if you had been a juror deciding the fate of Lester Zygmanik? Here's the dilemma: He was charged with murdering his own brother, George. A motorcycle accident a few days earlier had left George—at the age of 26—paralyzed from the neck down. He saw his future as promising him only pain, suffering, and invalidism; as he lay in agony, he insisted that his younger brother Lester, age 23, swear he would not let him continue in such a desperate state. "I want you to promise to kill me; I want you to swear to God," George said. (Other family members later verified that this had, in truth, been George's wish.) So, on the night of June 20, 1973, Lester slipped into his brother's hospital room and shot him in the head with a 20-gauge shotgun. Dropping the gun by the bed, he turned himself in moments later. There was no question about the cause of death; later, on the witness stand during his murder trial, Lester told the jury that he had done it as an act of love for his brother. (The book recounting this case, by Paige Mitchell, 1976, is also titled *Act of Love*.) Because New Jersey had no laws regarding mercy killing, the state felt it could make a case for charging Lester with first-degree murder. And in New Jersey, at that time, such a conviction would require the judge to sentence Lester to life in prison.

The state believed it had a good case against Lester. His actions conformed with every one of the elements that the law required for his guilt to be proved. There was, first of all, premeditation, or formation of a plan to kill; there was deliberation (as defined in the New Jersey criminal code, "the weighing of the 'pros' and 'cons' of that plan, which weighing only need take a few seconds"); and there was willfulness ("the intentional carrying out of that plan"). Lester had even sawed off the shotgun before hiding it under his coat, and he had packed the bullets with candle wax, which compacted the explosion and made it more deadly. Lester forthrightly told his lawyer:

> I gave it a lot of thought. You don't know how much thinking I did on it. I had to do something I knew that would definitely put him away. And the only thing I knew that would definitely do that would be a gun. . . . I wanted to make sure this was done fast and quick. I knew, I felt . . . I'd have one chance to do this. I gave it a lot of thought. You understand? I wanted to make sure he would definitely die [Mitchell, 1976, p. vii].

At his trial, Lester took the stand and described his motivations. He did not fall back on the insanity plea; he simply explained that his actions followed his brother's wishes.

If you had been a juror in this trial, how would you have voted? College students usually split just about evenly between verdicts of "guilty of first-degree murder" and "not guilty." Those who vote guilty, though often hoping that the sentence will be a humanitarian one, believe it is their duty to follow the prevailing evidence and the law. Certainly this was an act of murder, they say, regardless of its well-meaning intentions. But those who vote "not guilty" often feel that it is appropriate, on occasion, to disregard the law when mitigating circumstances are present or when community standards argue for forgiveness. Such a diversity of reasonable reactions is one manifestation of the dilemma between treating similar defendants equally and showing discretion if circumstances warrant. Jurors in such cases are also faced with another of the conflicts we posed in Chapter 1—that is, responding to society's needs for protection against offenders while preserving the rights of individuals. Did Lester's brother have the right to coerce Lester into taking his life?

As the trial began, the prosecutor was confident that Zygmanik would be found guilty. The jury, composed of seven men and five women, was tough, conservative, blue-collar; all jurors were over age 30. And the judge had even ruled that the term *mercy killing* could not be used in the trial.

But after deliberating for less than three hours, the jury found Lester Zygmanik not guilty. The jurors focused, apparently, on the relationship between Lester and his brother, and they concluded that Lester had been overcome by grief, love, and selflessness. In rendering their decision, they implicitly acknowledged that moral considerations—that is, commitments to care for others—were more important in their decision than following the strict guidelines of the law. Perhaps, too, they felt that a prerequisite of a crime, not mentioned in the law, is the absence of consent of the victim. During the trial Lester testified that on the night of the killing "I asked him if he was in pain. At this time he couldn't speak at all. He just nodded that he was. He nodded yes. So, I says, 'I am here to end your pain—is that all right with you?' And he nodded yes. And the next thing I knew, I shot him" (Mitchell, 1976, p. 195).

The criminal justice system of the United States contains no provision for such mitigating circumstances. In contrast, Belgium, France, Germany, and the Netherlands have laws that recognize a "compassionate" or an "altruistic" motive for killing. As Mitchell (1976, p. 245) notes, in Czechoslovakia, Switzerland, Peru, and Uruguay, the request by a victim constitutes an extenuating circumstance, and often no penalty is provided. Since the case was in the United States, however, Lester technically broke the law.

The Lester Zygmanik trial is not the only one in which the defendant claimed his act was a "mercy killing." In other such cases, juries have not always responded as his did. Certainly there can be no more dramatic demonstration of discretion in jury verdicts than in comparing the outcomes of the trial of Lester Zygmanik to that of Roswell Gilbert.

"My wife begged to die," screamed newspaper headlines about Roswell Gilbert's trial. Emily Gilbert, age 73, suffered from Alzheimer's disease and osteoporosis, both of which were incurable. She pleaded for someone to end her constant suffering. Roswell Gilbert, age 75 at the time and a retired electrical engineer, shot his wife twice in the back of her head as she sat on a sofa, looking out a window in their tenth-floor condominium. He was indicted for first-degree murder but claimed it was a mercy killing, done out of compassion for her suffering. At his trial, witnesses testified that Mrs. Gilbert had longed for and begged for death. The Fort Lauderdale, Florida, jury that heard his trial could have convicted him on a lesser charge (like second-degree murder or manslaughter), or, of course, it could have found him not guilty of any crime. But the ten-woman, two-man jury went along with the prosecution's request for a first-degree murder conviction. One of the jurors later said "We had no choice. The law does not allow for sympathy."

Roswell Gilbert was sentenced to life in prison, with a 25-year minimum mandatory term. Because the state waived the death penalty in his case, under Florida law there is no other punishment for first-degree murder. However, after serving five years in prison, he was granted clemency and released from prison in August 1990.

One reason why the jury verdict in the Gilbert trial differed from the verdict in the Zygmanik trial may be that the defendant refused to disclose much about his wife's agony when he testified, despite the fact that he had witnessed it repeatedly. Roswell Gilbert's attorney reported that "much of the time Emily was incontinent; he had to clean her, bathe her, change her underwear, put on her makeup, floss her teeth . . . do everything for her." Several days before the shooting, Mr. Gilbert had taken his wife to the hospital after she had fallen and was in agony. She was also angry and confused; she balked at disrobing at the hospital, wouldn't be X-rayed, refused a bone scan, pulled a needle out of her arm, and ran through the hospital hallways trying to escape. Finally, the hospital authorities asked the Gilberts to leave, saying they couldn't help her. Mr. Gilbert later told his attorney: "Hospitals wouldn't take her, [private] nursing homes wouldn't take her. . . . In a state hospital they'd have to strap her down. She'd be dehumanized." But, as the attorney later said, "We couldn't get any of this out of him on the stand. He wouldn't talk about it. He thought it would soil her memory. . . . He didn't even tell their daughter."

Nevertheless, the outcome once more emphasizes the power of discretion in the legal system. Two years before, a grand jury in the same Fort Lauderdale courthouse failed to indict a man facing similar mercy-killing charges. The man had shot his wife—who also suffered from Alzheimer's disease—in the brain.

LEGALITY VERSUS MORALITY

Cases like these cause us to examine whether legality and morality are always the same phenomenon. On first thought, we might assume that what is law abiding and what is morally right would be consistent with each other. But, in the Zygmanik example, the jury concluded that a morally right action and the law were inconsistent. Legislatures and scholars have argued for centuries whether the law should be consistent with morality. For example, prostitution is universally condemned as immoral; yet it is legal in parts of Nevada and in some European countries. Acts of civil disobedience, whether in racially segregated buses in Montgomery, Alabama, three decades ago or on college campuses today, are applauded by those who consider annoying laws to be ethically indefensible. Further examples, in the following paragraphs, illustrate how the legal system struggles over this issue.

The Case of the Drowning Fisherman

You are sitting on the edge of a pier, eating a hero sandwich and watching the sunset, when the fisherman next to you leans forward and tumbles into the ocean. As he thrashes around, he shouts to you "Help me—I can't swim! Throw me a life preserver!" You see a life preserver only 5 feet from you, but you make no effort to throw it to him, even though you could with absolutely no danger to yourself and only the most minimal effort. Instead, you sit placidly watching the sun go down, while you munch on your sandwich.

Have you committed any crime by failing to respond? No, the late John Kaplan, a law professor at Stanford University, once wrote: "Under the law of essentially every Anglo-American jurisdiction you are guilty of no tort [that is, wrong] making you civilly liable to the family of the fisherman you permitted to drown, nor would you be criminally liable in any way for his death" (1972, p. 219). Despite "Good Samaritan" laws passed by many states, this fundamental principle still applies.

Neither civil nor criminal law is very concerned about those good acts that we *fail* to do. Why? Kaplan offers several answers.

The first is the principle of individualism, or the right to be left alone. The law, at least in the United States, does not require you to be "your brother's keeper." As noted in Chapter 1 in describing the conflict between personal rights and society's needs, one predominant value in our society is individualism, or the right to "do your own thing." Kaplan concludes that the law "regards the fisherman's falling into the water as an imposition upon the freedom of those around him and asks why should the law permit the fisherman, merely by being careless, to impose legal duties on others and to interfere with their freedom to behave as they wish as long as they do not harm anyone?" (1972, p. 220).

The second issue is the principle of "why me?" Imagine that, instead of you alone, there were 200 people on the pier and no one helped. If there were a legal duty to aid, all would be liable. Who, then, would be prosecuted? The district attorney could not prosecute all 200, so he or she would pick a few. "Why me?" those few might ask. Although the government occasionally picks a few violators to prosecute in order to bring public attention to a matter, no standard exists in this situation to tell the district attorney just which bystanders to pick.

What if the fisherman had been your son, who is a minor in the eyes of the law? Or if the fisherman were on a boat and you were the captain? Now we have a different case. In both these examples, you would have been legally liable because of your special relationship to the victim.

And what if you had tried to save the fisherman but had thrown the life preserver so clumsily that it landed far away from him and he drowned before he reached it? Kaplan warns us that the courts "are unanimous in imposing some liability where some argument can be made that your bungled attempt to help the fisherman placed him in an even worse position than he was in before you made the attempt" (1972, pp. 221–222). This is especially true if your act prevented others from providing competent help—if, for example, you squandered the only life preserver available. Hence another legal justification emerges for the ethically questionable position of doing nothing.

The Hiker in Danger

Consider another example: You are sitting beside the road, and you see a car bearing down on a hiker. It is too noisy for a shout to be heard, so all you can do is push the hiker out of the path of the car. But, in doing so, you are struck by the car and injured.

Is the driver liable? Can you sue successfully? In earlier times the legal system said no, you can't sue, inasmuch as you risked your life without any requirement to do so. The rescue attempt was solely your responsibility, and you therefore could not collect for your injury from the driver, even if the hiker could have done so. Does this interpretation of the law encourage moral behavior? Of course not.

And hence modern law has changed, to reflect and promote the helper's rights. In fact, such a shift appears to be one of those rare ones that, in terms of the conflict posed in Chapter 1, aid society's needs for protection while also substantiating individual rights. What has emerged is a principle that "danger invites rescue" and hence "the driver's act of endangering the hiker was also a threat to those around him who might attempt to rescue the hiker" (Kaplan, 1972, p. 225).

The Concept of Intention in Law and Psychology

A fundamental question of criminal law is: When are people responsible for the consequences of their own actions? Is a person who gets drunk in his own apartment, passes out with a lighted cigarette in his hand, and sets the building on fire responsible for killing residents in another apartment who perish in the resulting conflagration? For a fact finder (a jury or a judge) to conclude that a defendant is guilty of certain crimes, the element of intention has to be proved. Yet the law and psychology differ somewhat in their definitions of *intention*; here we see a manifestation of the fourth dilemma posed in Chapter 1: science versus the law as a source of decisions.

The law sees intention as committing an act deliberately, willfully, knowingly, as distinguished from committing an act by mistake, by accident, by negligence, or by carelessness. Intention must be voluntary; any act committed under external compulsion is not considered an intentional act. (Note the black-or-white distinctions in the description of the fourth dilemma in Chapter 1.)

However, certain qualifications accompanying this definition result in a broader interpretation of "intention." For example, if an armed robber intends only to rob a liquor store but his gun goes off accidentally and he kills the clerk, he can be charged with felony murder, even if he did not intend to kill or even wound the victim. And the law does not relieve law violators of responsibility if their behavior is psychologically compulsive or is the result of a self-induced state, such as intoxication. Jurors have difficulty, at times, applying these concepts to specific cases. Joel B. Steinberg was tried in New York City for the second-degree murder of his adopted daughter, Lisa. But, instead, the jury found him guilty only of first-degree manslaughter. Even though he had beaten her repeatedly, several jurors—aware that he had used cocaine for days—were not convinced that his drug-dulled mind could reflect the "depraved indifference" for another person's life that is one of the elements of second-degree murder (Glaberson, 1989). Was he so intoxicated that he could not form the intent to kill his daughter? The jury apparently so concluded.

The relative importance of a person's intention versus the ultimate outcome of his/her behavior creates problems for the law. Alan Dershowitz, a law professor at Harvard University, poses the following challenging question: "Can a defendant be convicted of attempted murder if he shoots at an object that he believes to be a living human being, but turns out to be a corpse or dummy?" (1982, p. 85).

An early relevant case, called the *Damms* case, dealt with a man who took his wife for a car ride, stopped the car, and brandished a gun. His wife started to run away, but Mr. Damms caught her. He raised the pistol to her head. Slowly, deliberately, he pulled the trigger. The gun did not fire. He had forgotten to load it! Two police officers witnessed the event and heard Mr. Damms exclaim, after he pulled the trigger of the unloaded gun, "It won't fire. It won't fire." (There was no evidence of whether the exclamation was made in a tone of assurance, disappointment, surprise, or desperation.) Mr. Damms was found guilty of attempted murder, but he sought the reversal of his conviction on the ground that it had been impossible to kill his wife with an unloaded gun. The court upheld his conviction, concluding that "the fact that the gun was unloaded when Damms pulled the trigger did not absolve him of (attempted murder) if he *actually thought* at the time that it was loaded" (quoted in Dershowitz, 1982, p. 87).

Intention is central here; at least for the charge of attempted murder, it is more important than the consequences of the act. The judges concluded that Mr. Damms assumed he had put bullets in the gun. And, if he had, his wife would have been dead. But note also that Mr. Damms was charged with *attempted* murder, not "intention to commit murder"; even the law sometimes recognizes the slippery nature of the term *intention*.

Is there any difference in the morality of the perpetrator's act in the two situations of the gun failing to fire versus the gun firing and killing his wife? Dershowitz argues that there is no real moral difference because intention determines the morality of an act. Why, he asks, should matters of chance "determine the extent of a defendant's punishment" (1982, p. 88)?

What if someone shoots another person, thinking he is already dead, but it is possible that he was still alive at the time? The law has had even greater trouble clarifying its position on such perplexing matters.

One night a number of years ago, Melvin Dlugash went drinking with two friends, Mike Geller and Joe Bush. Mike had a basement apartment, and Joe had been staying with him for several months. Joe was supposed to share the rent, but he hadn't been doing so. Mike asked Joe about this several times during the evening, and Joe responded angrily that he didn't owe anything and that, if Mike persisted, he was "going to get hurt."

About midnight the three returned to Mike's apartment and continued to drink. After two or three hours the argument grew more intense. Mike demanded the rent money ($100), and Joe threatened to hurt him if he didn't lay off. But Mike repeated the demand.

Suddenly Joe pulled a .38 revolver from his pocket and fired it point-blank at Mike's heart, three times. Joe then turned to Mel Dlugash, pointed his gun at him, and said "If you don't shoot him, I'll shoot you." Joe wanted it to appear that they were in it together, so that Mel would not be able to point an accusing finger at Joe. After some understandable hesitation, Mel walked over to Mike's prone and motionless body and fired five bullets from his .22 pistol into Mike's head.

Mel was arrested by the police. (Joe had run away.) Mel told the police what had happened; he reported that there had been three to five minutes between Joe's shooting and his. Why did he do it? Mel said he feared for his life, and, besides, Mike was already dead when he fired at the body. But Mel was arrested and charged with murder.

Joe Bush was caught and charged with murder, too. But he plea-bargained (see Chapter 10), and his murder charge was dropped in exchange for his plea of guilty to a charge of manslaughter. He was sentenced to five to ten years in prison.

Mel, in contrast, refused to plead guilty to manslaughter because Mike was dead when he shot him. So Mel went to trial, and the judge instructed the jurors that they could convict him of murder only if they were convinced that Mike was alive when Mel shot him *and* that Mel assumed him to be alive and intended to kill him. But they could instead convict him of attempted murder. The jury deliberated for several days and returned a unanimous verdict: Mel was found guilty of murder. So Mel was sentenced to a mandatory term of 15 years to life imprisonment for murder, a much longer term than Joe received.

Alan Dershowitz (the source of the information reported here) assisted in Melvin Dlugash's appeal of his conviction. Much of his legal brief dealt with the issue of "impossible attempts." In a hypothetical English case, Lady Eldon travels to France and purchases some fine lace, which is subject to a steep import duty. As she tries to smuggle it past the English customs inspector, she is caught. He looks at it carefully and tells her "This is not fine Belgian lace; it is a cheap English imitation, and you don't need to pay any duty on it." Most legal authorities concluded that Lady Eldon could not be found guilty of smuggling. But some disagreed; after all, she had intended to break the law and had acted on this intention.

Dershowitz's brief was effective; the appeals court overturned Dlugash's conviction. It concluded that the prosecution had "failed to prove beyond a reasonable doubt that Geller had been alive at the time he was shot by the defendant." But the state appealed this decision, and a higher-level appeals court ruled that Mel was guilty of attempted murder, since there was—in the judges' minds—sufficient evidence that he *believed* Mike was alive when he shot him.

Several states, including New York, have passed new laws covering this "impossible attempt" issue. In New York, actual impossibility does not constitute a defense as long as the crime that was attempted "could have been committed had the attendant circumstances been as [the defendant] believed them to be." The purpose of the New York law apparently is to punish people for acting out their bad intentions.

In light of these developments, Dershowitz requested a new trial for Melvin Dlugash. The request was granted, but Mel was willing to plea-bargain if a guilty plea to a lesser crime would permit him to be free. (He had already served some prison time by then.) The district attorney wanted Mel to plead guilty to manslaughter, but he refused; that would still constitute an acknowledgment that he had killed Mike. Dershowitz countered with an offer that Mel plead guilty to unlawful possession of a gun. Not surprisingly, the prosecutor said no. So they decided to create a new crime category. Mel pleaded guilty to "attempted manslaughter," the judge accepted the plea, and Mel was sentenced to five years' probation. Finally, he was free.

Psychology's approach to intentions reflects its greater range of differentiations and less clear-cut distinctions than those of the legal system, as described in the fourth dilemma in Chapter 1. Psychology observes a continuum of behavior from unconscious to conscious. Marshall (1968, p. 72) posits eight categories of intention along this continuum:

1. Pure accident
2. Reflex action
3. Action out of unconscious
4. Action under stress
5. Action under hypnotic suggestion
6. Action interrelated with social transactions (social suggestion)
7. Action where the consequence is foreseeable
8. Conscious action with conscious intent

Even this continuum may oversimplify variations in intention because it minimizes the importance of the environmental situations and cultural expectations that different persons face. The overall social context in which behavior occurs can exert a strong influence on a person's intention to behave in different ways. Different contexts may make it all but impossible for an individual to conceive of certain behavioral options; therefore, that person's ability to intend a given behavior might be much more limited than that of another person who operates in a context where many more behavioral alternatives are possible.

Psychology has also studied how people assign causes, including intentions, to the behavior of others and themselves. The rapidly developing field of attribution theory has led to a number of conclusions, including these:

1. When making inferences about the cause of *another person's* behavior—especially behavior that has negative consequences—we tend to attribute the cause to something within the person; that is, we are inclined to believe that others are disposed to act the way they do.
2. But when our *own* actions lead to negative outcomes, we are more likely to blame the situation or the environment for the outcome.

Later chapters apply attribution theory in greater detail to illustrate how psychology interprets the concept of intention. Throughout this book, we confront the conflict between how psychology views the causes of behavior and how the law sees matters.

THE DEVELOPMENT OF CONCEPTIONS OF MORALITY

The foregoing examples make clear that what is right, for most of us, is not always what the law prescribes. But individuals differ in the standards that determine what is right and wrong. Some of us rely on the law almost entirely; others of us use internalized principles of morality as beacons for action, whether they agree with the law or not. A better understanding of these differences—as well as of the conflict between the law and the social sciences—can be gained by examining psychological theories of how our beliefs about right and wrong develop.

Lawrence Kohlberg's Theory of Moral Development

Why do we obey traffic signals? Why do some of us return a missing wallet to its rightful owner, even if it contains hundreds of dollars? Most of the psychological explanations of morality (for example, those by Sigmund Freud and by Jean Piaget) take a developmental perspective, positing that people's thoughts about moral behavior become more sophisticated as they mature. That is, infants are seen as self-centered, selfish, amoral creatures; as children grow older, they develop new cognitive capabilities and acquire new and higher conceptions of morality. Whereas the infant knows no other way than to "look out for Number One," older children and adolescents move through different stages that reflect an awareness of more socially acceptable degrees of morality.

The most extended explication of the developmental perspective is the theory of moral judgment advanced by the late Harvard psychologist Lawrence Kohlberg (1958, 1963, 1981; Colby, Kohlberg, & collaborators, 1987), who proposed

that humans experience six stages of moral development as they move from infancy to childhood to adolescence and adulthood. Although the sequence of stages is the same, said Kohlberg, not all persons will attain all stages. Some remain stuck at one stage and continue to use that as a filter through which they resolve moral dilemmas for the rest of their lives. "Moral dilemmas" are central in Kohlberg's approach; they are choices that all of us face, and our choices reflect how we think about what is right and wrong. The determination of what is correct is qualitatively different at each stage. (An example of a dilemma used by Kohlberg is presented in Box 3-1.) As people progress through the six stages, they move from one level of moral maturity (or, actually, immaturity) to the next, changing and refining the ability to make choices in their behavior.

Kohlberg's three levels and the two stages within each level are as follows:

1. *Preconventional level.* Young children respond to rules and labels of behavior such as "good" and "bad" or "right" and "wrong." But children interpret these labels in light of the *physical consequences* of their actions (that is, whether the action leads to being punished or rewarded). Further, young children at this level of "subnormal moral development" interpret "good" or "bad" in light of the physical power of those who make the rules and apply the labels. At this level, "might makes right."

The first stage reflects a *punishment and obedience orientation*. To the child at this stage, the consequences of his/her action determine the goodness or badness of the action. If the child does something and gets caught and punished for it, such as taking cookies from the cookie jar, the child concludes that the act must have been wrong.

The second stage is, in Kohlberg's language, the *instrumental relativist orientation*, or *hedonis-*

tic orientation. At this stage, the child considers "right actions" to be those that satisfy his or her own immediate needs and personal interests and occasionally the needs and interests of others. Children at this stage are still "preconventional" because their actions are still motivated by selfishness. Although acts might appear to be unselfish—a child helps her grandmother across a busy street—they are done to benefit the child herself in the long run. Human relations are viewed in the language of the marketplace: "You scratch my back and I'll scratch yours." Something that is a "good deal" for both parties is considered morally right at this stage.

Although this orientation comes rather early in Kohlberg's scheme of development, it is often reflected in many behaviors by adults in our society. In fact, parents sometimes encourage "mor-

al" behavior in their children by appealing to the children's selfish interests: "You should help your grandmother across the street because then she'll remember you in her will."

2. *Conventional level.* According to Kohlberg, morality, for most Americans, means either obeying the laws and rules or behaving the way people expect you to. In moving to this conventional level, a person shifts from the self-centered orientation of the preconventional stages to one that reflects awareness of the rights, feelings, and concerns of others. Fulfilling the expectations of one's family, religious group, or country becomes valuable in its own right, regardless of the immediate consequences to the person. The attitude reflects not only conformity to the social order but also loyalty to it. Emphasis is on actively maintaining,

---

Box **3-1** | *Kohlberg's Moral Dilemmas*

To determine a person's stage of moral development, Kohlberg used a set of moral dilemmas and interviewed the person with regard to his or her responses to each of these dilemmas. In assigning a stage to the answers, Kohlberg proposed that the reasons the person gave for his or her decision in a semistructured interview were just as important as the decision itself.

A typical Kohlberg dilemma is the case of Heinz. In Europe, a woman was near death from a special kind of cancer. There was one drug that the doctors thought might save her. It was a form of radium that a druggist in the same town had recently

discovered. The drug was expensive to make, but the druggist was charging ten times what the drug cost him to make. He paid $200 for the radium and charged $2000 for a small dose of the drug. The sick woman's husband, Heinz, went to everyone he knew to borrow the money, but he could only get together about $1000, which was half of what it cost. He told the druggist that his wife was dying and asked him to sell it cheaper or let him pay later. But the druggist said "No, I discovered the drug and I'm going to make money from it." So Heinz got desperate and broke into

the man's store to steal the drug for his wife. Should the husband have done that? Why?

In Kohlberg's system, a *preconventional* answer would be that Heinz should not steal the drug because, if he did, he would probably be caught and put in jail. One *conventional* answer might be that Heinz should steal the drug because he loves his wife and should care for her; another would be that he should not steal the drug because it is wrong to steal. Several *postconventional* answers to this dilemma are possible; can you think of what some of them might be?

supporting, and justifying the social order and identifying with persons and groups in it.

The *interpersonal concordance* or *good-boy/ nice-girl orientation* is the third stage in Kohlberg's theory. Moral behavior, as defined by the person operating at stage three, is that which pleases, helps, or is expected by others. Intentions are important in defining morality here; the notion that someone "means well" becomes salient for the first time, and one earns approval for being "nice."

For example, a teenager faced the dilemma of going out with his friends after a dance when he knew his mother wanted him at home. He decided to go home, not because of a desire to avoid punishment (which would have been a stage-one morality) but because "my mother would have worried about me all night if I stayed out" (Gilligan, 1988, p. xxxiv).

The next stage at this conventional level is the *law-and-order orientation*. Here the focus is on fulfilling the duties to which you have agreed and on obeying laws and rules and maintaining the social order. Moral behavior at this fourth stage consists of doing one's duty, showing that one respects authority, and perpetuating the given social order *because* it is the given social order (Kohlberg, 1958).

3. *Postconventional,* or *principled, level.* At the third and, in Kohlberg's conception, highest level of morality, the person further internalizes individual standards of morality. The person makes an effort to define moral values and codes of conduct apart from the authoritativeness of the groups or persons who advocate these principles and apart from his or her own degree of identification with these groups. The person's code of conduct reflects emerging principles that may or may not agree with the rules and laws directing the groups of which the person is a member.

The *social contract* or *legalistic orientation* falls in this level of moral development and is the fifth stage, according to Kohlberg. At this stage the person operates from internalized principles but realizes that these principles may be at odds with the norms, rules, or laws of society or with the viewpoint of the majority. Such a principle might be a belief that no one has the right to take another person's life. Thus the person at stage five, although objecting to the death penalty on the ground that it violates the principle of maintaining human life, still recognizes that the death penalty for certain crimes remains the law of the land (or at least of that state). The essence of the stage-five orientation is the attempt by the person to change the laws or rules through democratic means. The stage-five orientation leads the person to say, in effect, "I believe the death penalty is wrong in principle, but I accept that it is the law, and the law is a representation of consensus views. Therefore, I may lobby to change the law; I may write letters to newspapers; I may circulate petitions; I may campaign for political candidates who promise to abolish the death penalty." The person at stage five may disagree with society's consensus on some issues but realizes that he or she must exist in society and work within it to change it. This fifth stage represents the "official" morality of democratic governments and the U.S. Constitution.

The *orientation of universal ethical principles* is the sixth stage in Kohlberg's scheme. At this highest stage, what is morally right is defined not by the laws and rules of the social order but by one's own conscience, in accordance with self-determined ethical principles. Rather than being concrete moral rules, these principles are abstract; they include universal principles of justice, principles of reciprocity and equality of human rights, and respect for the dignity of human beings as individuals. For example, opposite positions regarding the acceptability of abortion on demand may reflect a commitment to principles about the sanctity of human life or to principles about the rights of individuals to control their own bodies—but both of these positions may be derived from stage-six principles. Likewise, one's attitudes about the morality of assisting a terminally ill person commit suicide might reflect a principle that human beings should be able to control their ultimate destinies, or it might embody a belief that all human life is sacred and cannot be sacrificed for personal preference. This particular debate has been sharpened by the highly publicized case of Jack Kevorkian, a Michigan physician who, having built "suicide machines" with which he admits he has aided chronically ill persons commit suicide, was charged with the murder of two women who used his machines.

Kohlberg has found that postconventional morality (both stage five and stage six) "is probably attainable only in adulthood and requires some experience in moral responsibility and independent choice" (1973, p. 500). Clearly, stage six is the most controversial of Kohlberg's stages, and thus it receives extended review in Box 3-2.

A central assumption of Kohlberg's theory is that a person advances from a lower to a higher stage of morality only as a result of being confronted by an expression of this higher level of moral reasoning by another person or by a group. If there is no confrontation with examples of principled morality, movement toward the higher stages cannot occur. Perhaps each of

---

Box 3-2 | How Do You Know a Stage-Six Person When You See One?

Kohlberg considered a person operating out of universal ethical principles to manifest the highest level of moral development. But certain actions can be attributed to different levels of moral development. During the late 1960s and early 1970s, did antiwar activists protest out of principles of nonviolence or out of fear that they could go into the Army and lose their life? Kohlberg's examples of stage-six behavior—Jesus Christ, Gandhi, Martin Luther King—were willing to *sacrifice* for their actions and, in fact, did so. Acceptance of the potentiality of punishment for one's principles separates the stage-six act from a similarly appearing protest that is done for selfish reasons.

Contemporary manifestations of stage-six behavior include the following:

Dorothy Eber is an antiwar, antinuclear activist and protester. She and several companions broke through a fence at a nuclear missile site in Missouri. They planted some flowers, then plopped down on the concrete lid and prayed. Mrs. Eber, a 64-year-old widowed grandmother, was arrested for trespassing on government property and was sentenced to a two-year term in a federal penitentiary (Royko, 1989).

John Ryan was an FBI agent who was fired in 1987, after more than 20 years of service. He was scheduled to retire at full pension in 10 months, at the age of 50. The rea-

son for the firing: he refused to investigate peace groups because of his "personal, religious, and human beliefs." Ryan, a devout Roman Catholic and committed pacifist, had been instructed to investigate two peace-oriented organizations suspected of vandalizing military recruiting activities in Chicago.

Not everyone would agree that these actions reflect the highest stages of morality. And some would argue that, if everyone operated out of universal ethical principles, the result could be anarchy. Regardless, Kohlberg's theory is of enormous heuristic value in thinking about the basis of moral actions.

you has experienced an incident in which someone else's conduct has led you to reexamine the values upon which you have based your own behavior.

The notion that an individual must pass through a series of stages to achieve moral maturity is quite an assumption. But a comparison of different theories, including those based on the contrasting perspectives of Freud and of Piaget, reveals that their differing conceptions arrive at the same end positions—a stage in which one relies on principles rather than rules and in which actions are autonomous.

A developmental conception can also be applied to a person's conception of the law. In fact, June Tapp and Felice Levine (1970, 1974; Levine & Tapp, 1977) have applied a similar structure to the socialization of legal development, as defined by people's problem-solving strategies toward the law. The preconventional level emphasizes obedience or deference to the law. At this level, people obey the law out of fear of punishment or deference to authority. The conventional level focuses on law maintenance; that is, people follow laws in order to maintain the social order of the community. Group norms are thus more important than individual rights. At the postconventional level, people are concerned with law creation. Thus people follow the laws only if they coincide with independently derived ethical categories. A subsequent analysis (Cohn & White, 1990) assumes that these cognitive factors—these beliefs and mental perspectives—interact with responses we learn from our social environment. For example, we learn what the norms are for enforcing rules and laws (Cohn, Carlson, & White, 1984).

Empirical studies of moral development and legal socialization among children, adolescents, and adults provide some general support for the conceptions of Kohlberg and of Tapp and Levine, as do the infrequent studies that assess children's moral judgment levels and then retest the subjects 5, 10, or 20 years later (Colby, Kohlberg, & collaborators, 1987; Kohlberg, 1958, 1963, 1981; Snarey, 1985; Walker, 1989).

Proposing a Different View of Morality: A Feminine View

Kohlberg based his theory on the responses of boys and men; in doing so, he did little to discourage others from assuming that this conception also characterized girls' and women's development. Kohlberg believed that fewer women than men achieve the higher stages of moral development, because their allegiance to their children (stage three) precludes their developing the abstract moral principles requisite for stage six. A more-than-implicit developmental inferiority is attributed to women in Kohlberg's theory (Walker, 1984). Carol Gilligan (1977, 1982), a former student of Kohlberg's and later a colleague of his at the Graduate School of Education at Harvard University, has objected to the male-oriented nature of his theory and its failure to apply to the socialization and experience of women. She has forced scholars to rethink the existing theories of the development of moral thought.

Gilligan developed a systematic conception of women's moral development that differs radically from Kohlberg's in content, even though it resembles Kohlberg's in structure. It is similar because it proposes that young children of both genders share an inability to distinguish the perspective of others from their own perspective. Gilligan also proposes that women pass through three levels and that, like the men in Kohlberg's theory, they move from self-centeredness to an other-oriented and then to an autonomous conception.

But although Kohlberg's approach—for men—has a rules orientation, with emphasis on abstract concepts and especially the concept of justice, women, Gilligan finds, possess a responsibility orientation, with emphasis on sensitivity to others and the concepts of compassion and care. Women's development is best understood within a context of complex relationships, in connection to other people. In contrast to boys and men, whose identity is defined through their separation from others—especially their mothers—for girls and women identity is defined through attachment and an "ethic of care" (Gilligan, 1982, p. 8). Perhaps the connectedness orientation of women stems from the fact that females develop their gender identity while remaining psychologically identified with their mothers (Chodorow, 1978). For women, moral dilemmas result not from competing rights, as they do for men, but from competing responsibilities. In Gilligan's words, for women the moral dilemma "requires for resolution a mode of thinking that is contextual and narrative rather than formal and abstract" (Gilligan, 1982, p. 19). Acts of caring are designed to sustain "the web of connection so no one is left alone" (1982, p. 62). In fact, abstract thinking would bring unwanted impersonality to a woman's exercise of her responsibility for the care of others as individuals.

Like Kohlberg, Gilligan bases her theory on responses to moral dilemmas. But Kohlberg has been criticized for the unfamiliarity and possible irrelevance of his dilemmas involving fictitious persons. Hence, Gilligan interviewed 29 women who were facing a personal decision about whether or not to abort a pregnancy. Gilligan's use of personal decisions about everyday problems reflects her belief that the feminine conception of morality is embedded in relationship with actual people. Some of Gilligan's subjects were unmarried and still in public school; others were married but for one reason or another were unsure that they wanted to have the baby.

On the basis of these detailed interviews and follow-up interviews a year later, Gilligan concludes that women move through three levels of moral development. In all, the conflict is between the obligations and responsibilities to one's self and those to others. The first level, like Kohlberg's preconventional morality, is selfish. The self is the sole object of concern in what Gilligan calls the *orientation to individual survival*. When asked what one "should" do, the only thought is what one "would" do for oneself. If there is any sense of obligation—seen by Gilligan as central to women's development—it is only obligation to one's own survival. No awareness of conflict exists at this level.

But some women move from selfishness to a sense of responsibility and a different interpretation of *obligation*. The young woman may feel conflict within herself. For example, she values her independence and yet she wants to establish connection with another person; marriage and motherhood have attractions but also limitations. Similarly, the criterion for judgment changes, and "should" and "would" begin to conflict. What one wants isn't always right.

This awareness of conflict leads to level two, the conventional level of morality, which Gilligan calls *goodness as self-sacrifice*. Morality here is defined as meeting the expectations of others and submitting to the norms of society. Primarily, there is a concern over meeting others' needs and not hurting others (Gilligan, Ward, & Taylor, 1988).

In considering whether to abort a fetus, a woman must "confront the seemingly impossible task of choosing the victim" (Gilligan, 1982, p. 80). If she is an unmarried high school student who decides to have the baby, the victim may be herself—expelled from school, subjected to ridicule by her peers, abandoned by her boyfriend, and ostracized by her parents. Or, if she is a working woman with little income, having the baby may make the infant a victim of limited funds, little maternal support, and an impoverished future. For the woman at level two, the concerns of others are salient. Will the child suffer? What will my parents think? Will another child place a financial burden on our family resources? The "right" way to resolve the dilemma at level two is to decide in a way that hurts others the least. But the stakes are high for the woman herself; her own needs are sacrificed in the decision, and she may soon struggle to free herself from the powerlessness of her own dependence.

As some women move beyond level two, they scrutinize the logic of self-sacrifice; the word *selfish* comes back in, but at a higher level of analysis. The woman begins to ask whether it is "selfish or responsible—moral or immoral—to include her own needs within the compass of her care and concern" (Gilligan, 1977, p. 498). She becomes aware of her own inner judgment as well as what other people think. The woman includes herself in the injunction to protect and care for people (L. V. Davis, 1985). The new goal is to be honest with oneself. Gilligan calls this third level the *morality of nonviolence*. The basic injunction is one against hurting, and it becomes a principle governing all moral judgment and action in its condemnation of exploitation and hurt.

At level three, the determinants of the decision whether to have an abortion center on the woman's responsibilities to herself—to her own moral code, to her own development and maturity—as well as to others.

In summary, for Kohlberg and for men, the moral imperative is to use rules in order "to respect the rights of others and thus to protect from interference their rights to life and self-fulfillment" (Gilligan, 1982, p. 100). The choice, hence, is between competing *rights*, with a perspective colored by *rules*. In Gilligan's view, for women the moral imperative is to alleviate the troubles of the world. The choice is

between competing *responsibilities*, and the operating principle is *care*. For women, the right to property—or even the right to life—is not weighed in the abstract, in terms of some logical priority, as the law sees it, but "in terms of the actual consequences that the violation of these rights will have in the lives of the people involved" (Gilligan, 1982, p. 95).

At this point a clarification is in order: throughout this discussion, the morality of "men" and "women" has been contrasted. But the difference is not an inborn gender difference so much as it is a difference in the socialization and childhood experiences of males and females in our society. In addition, not all men and women respond on moral-dilemma tests with the values "typical" of their gender. For these reasons, it is more appropriate to refer to two differing conceptions of morality, *masculine* and *feminine*, than to speak simply of male/female differences. In fact, recent evidence (see Berk, 1991; p. 499 for a review) suggests the absence of sex differences on the supposedly more masculine justice-oriented measures of moral reasoning. Even if conceptions of morality are not strongly linked to gender, Gilligan's work has helped expand our notions of how very moral persons (of either gender) might think and behave. In addition to being committed to abstract principles of fairness, the highly moral person remains concerned about caring for the welfare of individuals.

Consider a couple of biblical examples that illustrate these different emphases. The patriarch Abraham prepared to sacrifice the life of his son to demonstrate the integrity and supremacy of his faith. And in Judges, Chapter 11, we are told of Jephthah, who led the forces of Gilead in battle against the Ammonites. Jephthah made a rash promise to the Lord: if he was granted victory over the enemy, he would offer as a burnt offering to the Lord "whatsoever cometh forth from the doors of my house to meet me" (Judges 11:31, King James Version). Jephthah doubtless assumed that this would be a sheep or a goat, but when he returned as victor, his daughter rushed out of the house to greet him, dancing and playing a tambourine. Jephthah was in anguish; he had made a solemn vow to the Lord, and thus he offered his only child as a sacrifice.

In the traditionally masculine conception, the relationship of concern is that between Jephthah and the Lord, because the orientation is to abstract principles, including "keeping your promises." If the daughter is considered, it is done within a question of whose *rights* should prevail. As L. V. Davis (1985, p. 108) observes, the rules developed in the masculine orientation provide idealized guidelines by which conflicts are rationally and fairly resolved. This orientation abstracts these conflicts from the individuals who experience them. In Kohlberg's conception, even persons operating at stage six, who might advise Jephthah to disregard his vow, would emphasize the *right* of human life, including the life of his daughter. But Gilligan would propose that a woman would focus on Jephthah's *responsibility to his daughter*. For women, moral development reflects concern with attachments and relationships, rather than autonomy and achievement. Gilligan's biblical exemplar is the woman who comes before Solomon and "verifies her motherhood by relinquishing truth in order to save the life of her child" (1982, pp. 104–105). In her view, a woman's morality depends on the extent to which her actions live up to her ideal of care.

WHAT IS JUSTICE?

The foregoing comparison of Kohlberg's and Gilligan's conceptions suggests that justice can be seen from two different vantage points. It can be based on abstract ideals, or it can be derived from the nature of the relationship between interested parties. We can apply these contrasting perspectives to real-world dilemmas. For example, should the parents of a teenager charged with murder comply with the court's order to testify against him?

A Houston, Texas, couple spent several months in jail after refusing to testify before a grand jury. Their son was a suspect in the abduction and shooting death of a mail carrier. Mrs. Odette Port, stepmother of the suspect, said: "I was faced with a choice, a choice between the law of the land and the law of my conscience." She refused to provide information about the crime scene, the murder weapon, and other facts that might implicate her stepson. As a consequence, she served four and a half months in a Houston jail. Her husband and the father of the suspect, Bernard Port, spent two months in jail before he testified and was released. Before being sent to jail, he had argued that a right of privileged communication exists between parents and children, just as it does between attorneys and clients or between spouses. But the courts rejected the claim. His son, David Port, 17, was later found guilty of murder and sentenced to 75 years in prison.

In general, justice means *fairness*. Justice is an outcome of the process in which people receive what they deserve or are due. There are several guidelines to help us identify whether justice has been done. One of these, used extensively by psychologists, is equity theory (discussed in the next section of this chapter).

Not only do we want standards for determining whether justice has been done, but additionally we want to believe that outcomes in the world are usually the appropriate or just ones; it is threatening to us to believe that unfairness can prevail. The final section of the chapter examines this need to believe in a "just world."

EQUITY THEORY— AN ATTEMPT TO UNDERSTAND JUSTICE

Determinants of justice may be understood through an analysis of the concept of *equity*. Usually equity refers to the distribution of rewards in society according to some criterion of merit. This is a demonstrable value throughout the world. Fromm (1956) finds a "fairness principle" in almost every society; for instance, most societies have some implicit desire to "equitably" apportion rewards and costs among participants.

Definitions of Equitable Relationships

Equity theory tries to determine what *is* "equitable." Psychologists define equitable relationships as those in which all participants in a group receive outcomes that reflect their relative contributions to the group's activity (Lerner, 1974, 1977; Leventhal, 1976; Walster, Walster, & Berscheid, 1978); that is, the outcomes (or payoffs) for person A divided by the inputs of person A equal the outcomes for person B divided by the inputs of person B. (Inputs are the participants' contributions to the activity.)

Say, for example, that persons A and B cut person C's lawn. A works two hours and B works one hour. C has told them he will pay them a total of $15 for the job. How do they divide the $15? Your first reaction probably is that A should get $10 and B $5, since A worked twice as long as B. And that is eminently reasonable; when we are determining how to measure inputs, length of work time is a very plausible choice.

But it is not the only one. Suppose it is true that person A works two hours and person B only one hour, but it happens that A is in excellent physical condition whereas B has a broken leg. Furthermore, his cast is heavy and awkward, so an hour's yard work has caused him great pain and fatigue. Given those facts, what is equity in assigning payoffs? Should B receive a greater reward than one-third because his effort entailed more pain and suffering? His work certainly required more effort and energy per hour than A's work did. Maybe his inputs are even greater than A's, even though he worked half as long.

So the standards for determining relative inputs reflect value judgments, and there are no easy answers (Sampson, 1975). Remember the conflict in Chapter 1 between equality and discretion; it can be argued that each is, in a different sense, fair and just. But, of necessity, laws must develop agreed-on definitions or measures of inputs. Recently, in response to Title VII of the U.S. Civil Rights Act of 1964, which made it illegal to pay one person less than another because of the person's gender, some states and cities tried to achieve the principle of "equal pay for work of comparable worth" by passing new laws and regulations that defined comparable worth. For example, is the work of a teacher of comparable worth to that of a newspaper reporter? A practical nurse's work to that of a gardener? During the 1980s, several states instituted salary readjustments for state employees based on such a principle (Lowe & Wittig, 1989). Despite criticism that different jobs were not objectively comparable, the state of Washington, as one example, made comparisons based on four criteria: (1) knowledge and skills, (2) mental demands, (3) accountability, and (4) working conditions. This comparable-worth study found that the jobs of warehouse worker and clerk/typist were both rated at a 94-point level, but warehouse workers, typically men, were paid 25% more than were clerk/typists, who were typically women. Shortly after Washington State initiated plans to eliminate such pay discrepancies, the Ninth U.S. Circuit Court of Appeals refused to authorize the procedure, and the state was forced to accept prevailing marketplace rates as the determinants of state employees' salaries. Marketplace rates reflect different criteria from those used by the state of Washington; they are more in keeping with the beliefs found by Dornstein (1988) in a cross-sectional public opinion sample of employees, which indicated that the prestige of the occupation and the physical demands of the job should be the major determinants of its pay.

Reactions to Inequity

Despite the difficulty in obtaining agreed-on measures of equity, each of us has subjective feelings of what is fair. According to equity theory, people become distressed and resentful when they participate in inequitable relationships. Those who receive less than they deserve usually feel anger, whether the payoff is pay for work, tangible goods, or even appreciation and recognition.

Those who receive more than they deserve may feel guilt. Although they want to maximize their outcomes, they also feel embarrassed and guilt ridden. The greater the inequity, the greater the distress and the stronger the efforts (by some, at least) to restore equity.

How Is Equity Restored?

How do you react when you have been overcompensated for some action? You may have received a higher grade than you deserved or been paid more than you consider fair. Or you may have inadvertently caused someone else to suffer an unfair outcome; how do you, as a harmdoer, restore equity?

First, if feasible, we may seek to compensate those who have been undercompensated. We may say "Here, take part of my pay; you deserve it." Or we may, on future occasions, overreward the other person.

But we may also engage in self-deprivation. We may reduce our own outcomes to the other person's level.

Others, however, may ridicule the people who received undercompensation, either to their faces or, more likely, behind their backs. Your being *over*compensated may be so threatening that you cannot acknowledge it. Instead, your reaction may be to make jokes about those who have suffered for your benefit.

Equity versus Equality— Which Is Justice?

Equity is reflected in the allocation of rewards based on relative contributions. But some have questioned whether this is the most fitting definition of justice (see, for example, Sampson, 1975). Other rules for allocating rewards include the norms of equality, or reciprocity, or individual need (Deutsch, 1975; Elliott & Meeker, 1986; Rusbult, Lowery, Hubbard, Maravankin, & Neises, 1988). For example, some people believe justice is reflected by giving the same reward to all, regardless of their contributions. This controversy spans a number of settings; for example, in determining salary raises for professors, some colleges prefer "across the board" raises (that is, equality), whereas others base each raise on each professor's "merit" (that is, equity).

Psychologists have conducted experiments to identify the conditions under which equity or equality operates (Walster et al., 1978). A typical procedure is to have subjects act as a set of workers who simultaneously complete similar tasks but whose collective outcomes will depend on their combined performances. After working on their task, subjects receive feedback about their relative task performance. Subjects might be told, for example, "You earned 75 points and the other person earned 50 points." Then they are asked to suggest a division of the rewards.

Does equity obtain in such situations? Sometimes it does. Yet some studies have found a tendency for subjects to accept higher outcomes for themselves, but not lower outcomes, when there had been a difference in performance that ordinarily would prescribe an unequal division of rewards (Benton, 1971; Lane & Messe, 1971).

Gender Differences in the Allocation of Rewards

Do men and women use the same standards in assigning credit or payoffs? Some early studies found that females opted for equality rather than equity, regardless of relative inputs. In one such study (Leventhal & Lane, 1970), pairs of males and pairs of females worked individually on multiplication problems and then were told that one member of the pair had performed much better than the other. Then they were informed that one of them would be chosen at random to allocate the payoffs that had accrued from their team performance. Members of the pair were isolated from each other, and each was told that he or she was the member designated to divide the money.

Men, on the average, took about 60% of the outcome when their performance was higher than their co-worker's; they typically took 40% for themselves when their performance was the lower. But women took only 50% when theirs was the higher performance level and 34% when theirs was lower. So apparently women tend to downgrade their own achievement, but the women do not report relying so much on performance differences in making their allocations (Harvey & Smith, 1977). Further evidence that

women underestimate the worth of their own work is found in the findings of researchers Brenda Major, Dean McFarlin, and Diana Gagnon (1984). They found that, when women were asked to do as much work as they thought fair for a fixed amount of money, they worked 25% longer than men did under conditions of no supervision. When told that someone was monitoring them, women worked 52% longer than men did. The women did more work and produced more correct work than the men.

We need to make several qualifications to this apparent conclusion that there are gender differences in the use of equity versus equality (Kahn, Nelson, & Gaeddert, 1980). First, in the early studies subjects were led to believe that there would be no future contact between the two participants. But when the two persons anticipate future contact with each other, their use of equality as a standard for allocating rewards increases. Perhaps some of us who think we have performed better do not want the discomfort of appearing "grabby" to someone we are going to spend additional time with. For example, roommates tend to distribute rewards equally rather than on the basis of relative merit (Austin, 1980). And in general, within groups of people who must work closely together, the norm of equity can produce tension, antagonism, and competition, and so a shift toward equality may occur.

Second, in a different set of studies in which a man decided the allocations of payoffs and a woman was his partner—and the man had done better—he typically assigned himself a smaller amount than if his partner had been a man (Kahn et al., 1980).

Certain contextual qualities may also affect this interpretation. The use of money as a reward in these experiments is very male oriented. Most of the studies employ an industrial simulation or similar work setting. Men are more experienced and comfortable in this business-oriented social exchange. Perhaps most important is the fact that the tasks used in these early studies (such as solving mathematical problems) are ones at which men are expected to excel.

More recent studies have addressed these limitations. Reis and Jackson (1981) had male and female subjects work on one of two tasks. One task was male oriented and the other female oriented. In both tasks objects were flashed on a screen and subjects were asked to describe their functions, but in the first task the objects were ones men are more familiar with and in the second the objects were more typical of women's experience. Men used equity to divide rewards on both tasks. When the task was male oriented, the females did not divide the reward equitably, but they *did* use the norm of equity when they worked on a female-oriented task.

Regardless of the qualifications just stated, the search has continued for a gender difference in the standards for assigning rewards. If women prefer equality as the determinant, their preference may reflect a different type of concern. David Bakan (1966) makes a distinction between the states of *agency* and *communion*. Agency refers to a striving for achievement, prominence, and success, whereas communion reflects a concern with intimacy, interpersonal relationships, and attachment. There are indications that females base their allocations more on communion than on agency; they are more accommodating than males and more concerned with interpersonal harmony and intimacy (Vinacke, 1959; Watts, Messe, & Vallacher, 1982).

Furthermore, according to Crano and Messe (1982, p. 340), "females might place a higher value on the actions of others that provide them with social approval, whereas males might find greater values in an indication by others that their past successes have been recognized." Again, the gender distinction between agency and communion emerges.

BELIEF IN A "JUST WORLD"

People have a need to believe that justice exists in the world, and most of us assume that people get what they deserve in life (Lerner, 1980). This need reflects more than just believing in a predictable world. The need to believe in a "just world" occurs so that people can go about their daily lives with a sense of trust, hope, and confidence in the future.

Furthermore, people structure the world to fit their beliefs. If something bad happens to someone we know, we may sympathize, but we also may be tempted to believe that the person must have deserved it—or even provoked it. Otherwise, it would not have happened.

If an apparently innocent person suffers, this inconsistency threatens our own belief in a just world. So we may come to *derogate the victim*. In a recent year, 1500 women in the United States were murdered by their husbands or boyfriends (Goodman, 1989). These men served prison terms, on the average, of only two to six years. The massive number of lenient sentences may reflect an implicit belief that the victim deserved her fate; otherwise, it would be too threatening to conclude that innocent people could become victims of such heinous acts. In other types of trials, it might be particularly important to try to counter just-world sentiments; for example, expert testimony about reactions of battered women (Schuller & Vidmar, 1992) or rape victims (Frazier & Borgida, 1992) is often used by attorneys to dispel some just-world assumptions jurors might hold about the behavior of a woman in violent encounters.

This blaming of an innocent victim happens whenever observers are unable to intervene on behalf of the victim. In such circumstances, people seem to work backward in their reactions to victims. They assess what is happening and then calculate what it would take for someone to deserve that fate. Reactions to injustice include an initial state of upset and then an effort to restore justice. But, if justice cannot be restored, observers will be motivated to find evidence that the victim actually deserved his or her fate (Lerner, 1980).

Martyred victims (those who choose to suffer so that others will not) receive even more derogation than innocent victims. The less deserved a person's suffering has been, or the less compensation the person has received for having suffered, the greater the likelihood that the person will be devalued (Lerner & Simmons, 1966).

Although the foregoing statements imply that the need to believe in a just world is a prevalent orientation among us, there are individual differences in the strength of this response. Some people are so threatened by the possibility that negative outcomes can occur without reason that they always grasp at opportunities to blame the victim. Others are more able to tolerate the irrationality of everyday unpleasant occurrences. Rubin and Peplau (1975) have developed an attitude scale, called the Beliefs in the Just World Scale, to measure these individual differences. People who have strong beliefs in a just world tend to be conventional people who subscribe to traditional religious beliefs. They justify the status quo, are more likely to give harsh sentences to defendants, and yet are generally optimistic people.

SUMMARY

What is considered moral is not always what is ruled legal, and vice versa. And sometimes what most of us would consider an immoral failure to act in an emergency is not against the law.

People also differ in their standards for determining right and wrong. Some of us rely on the law almost entirely; others have internalized principles of morality that may be inconsistent with the laws. Various theories seek to explain the development of moral judgment. Lawrence Kohlberg proposes six stages of moral development that may be experienced by persons in all cultures; the way a person decides what is correct behavior is qualitatively different at each stage. Although extensive empirical evidence supports Kohlberg's theory, Carol Gilligan has criticized it, proposing that women's development may be described better by a different kind of morality. Whereas Kohlberg's theory has an orientation toward rules, with an emphasis on abstract concepts and especially the concept of justice, Gilligan argues that women possess a responsibility orientation, with emphasis on sensitivity to others and the concept of care.

Regardless of the differing conceptions, justice can be defined as fairness. Psychologists use equity theory to identify standards for determining whether justice has been done. Equity is defined as a state in which each person's rewards are in keeping with his or her relative contributions. As a standard for allocation of resources, equity can be contrasted with equality, in which the same levels of resources are assigned to every participant, regardless of how much he or she contributed. There is some tendency for gender differences to exist in the allocation of rewards: men characteristically use equity as a norm; women sometimes use equity, sometimes equality.

The need to believe in justice can be so strong that people will adopt the "just world" explanation for events that really are only chance happenings. For example, if a friend is a victim of a rape or a serious accident, some people will blame the victim for the tragedy. This reaction is a response to the threat that such terrible occurrences could happen, without reason, to innocent people.

4

Lawyers: Socialization, Training, and Ethics

Throughout this book we emphasize the dilemmas resulting from efforts to make the legal system work effectively. The conflicting values of equality and discretion, the alternative pathways to knowledge from science and the law, and the sometimes incompatible goals of truth and stability all place burdens on those who administer the legal system. Lawyers are, of course, primarily responsible for the system's effectiveness—not just practicing attorneys but also the judges, legislators, mayors, governors, and even presidents, trained as lawyers, who determine whether there will be reform in the legal system. It is therefore important at this point to examine the backgrounds, training, and values of the legal profession.

What kinds of people become attorneys? Do their values change as they traverse through law school? Does legal education prepare lawyers for the choices they face on the job? What kinds of guidance are given to resolve ethical dilemmas? These are examples of the issues considered in this chapter.

WHO DECIDES TO BE A LAWYER?

In the United States, there are close to 800,000 attorneys, or one for every 300 people in the country. This number is more than twice the figure in 1970 and four times the figure in 1950. Washington, DC, has one lawyer in private practice for every 64 residents; in contrast, in West Virginia there is one attorney for every 1100 persons. Two-thirds of all the lawyers on earth live in the United States, although this country accounts for only about 6% of the world's population. The United States has three times as many lawyers, per capita, as Great Britain and 25 times as many, per capita, as Japan. Los Angeles

County has more lawyers than all of France, a country seven times larger in population. Sometime before the turn of the next century, this country probably will have more than a million persons with law degrees (Goldstein, 1988a). While vice president, Dan Quayle (who has a law degree) ended a well-publicized speech to the American Bar Association in August 1991 with the following rhetorical questions: "Does America really need 70% of the world's lawyers? Is it healthy for our economy to have 18 million new lawsuits coursing through the economy annually? Is it right that people with disputes come up against staggering expense and delay?" (Johnson & Kamlani, 1991).

Law School Enrollments and the Proliferation of Lawyers

What are the psychological and sociological implications of the huge numbers of lawyers currently in the United States? Are there too many lawyers? Do their numbers lead to frivolous lawsuits and unnecessary legislation? These matters are considered further at the end of this chapter, in a section on society's evaluation of the legal profession.

The proliferation of lawyers is partly a result of the boom in the market for legal employment, which has contributed to the rapid increase in law school enrollments over the last two decades. In 1965 about 24,000 first-year law students were enrolled in U.S. law schools. The number increased steadily during the 1970s and peaked at 42,000 in 1980. Since then, first-year enrollments have remained fairly stable, even though applications increased by 5% to 15% a year during the late 1980s (Herzfeld, 1988). By the beginning of the 1990s, approximately 83,000 applicants were seeking admission each year to our country's law schools.

What do all these attorneys do? Two-thirds

of law school graduates are in the private practice of law, in anything from one-person storefront law offices to large firms employing 200 or more attorneys. One U.S. firm includes 1330 attorneys. About 10% of law school graduates work for government agencies (including over 10,000 judges in federal and state courts). Another 10% are in private business as salaried lawyers or in management. The rest (about 15%) have a variety of jobs; some are directly law related (including professorships in law schools), and some are positions in which their legal training is of great assistance (insurance, banking, politics). Of 9500 FBI agents, 1500 have law degrees (Sessions, 1989). Some are far removed from their legal training. Fidel Castro, Francis Scott Key, Oakland A's manager Tony LaRussa, and Peter Ilyich Tchaikovsky share one characteristic—they all were once lawyers (Margolick, 1989a).

Women and Minorities in Law School and in the Profession

Not only have the numbers of law students and lawyers been multiplying, but their demographic qualities have been changing. From 1950 to 1970 the proportion of lawyers who were women remained relatively steady, at between 2.5% and 3%. But by 1980 more than 7% of lawyers were women (M. J. Davis, 1985). A very small percentage of older attorneys are women, but more than a third of younger attorneys are. In recent years, about 40% of law students have been female, and demographers predict that by the year 2000 women will constitute almost that percentage of the law profession (Goldstein, 1988b).

What might be the effects of this increased number of females on the practice of law? Do female attorneys hold the feminine conceptions of justice portrayed in Chapter 3? Do they approach this "masculine" profession in a differ-

ent way? Will they "humanize" the profession? Or do women who select the law as a career already have an orientation to the law that is different from the orientation of most women? These are questions for which research answers are only beginning to emerge (see Box 4-1). However, there is some indication that women and minority-group members plan, to a greater degree than white male lawyers do, to work as public defenders, poverty lawyers, or public-interest attorneys (Kirby, 1976).

Because women have entered the law profession in large numbers only relatively recently, few women have achieved partnerships in law firms; only about one out of every 13 partners is a woman (Goldstein, 1988b). Typically, attorneys are initially hired as "associates"—that is, salaried employees. Some will "make partner" after five to ten years in associate status; others will be retained as permanent associates or dismissed.

Another reason for the low percentage of female partners may be a traditional orientation in some firms that rejects women for promotion even if they are as capable as the men who are promoted. Of the graduates of the Harvard Law School class of 1974 who entered private practice, the proportion of men who were partners six years later was more than twice that of women (Abel, 1989). Elizabeth Anderson Hishon, who was denied partner status in a large law firm, brought suit against her employer. She had worked for a prestigious Atlanta law firm for seven years when she was denied partnership status in 1979. She sued the firm, invoking Title VII of the Civil Rights Act of 1964, claiming that sexual discrimination was the reason for the partners' decision to exclude her. (At the time, the firm had no females or blacks among its 50 partners.) The law firm responded that Title VII did not apply to decisions about admission to partnership because such decisions involved a change in status from employ-

ee to employer. The firm also pleaded that lawyers made such a "distinctive contribution" to
society that they deserve special constitutional
protection for their "freedom of association."
Surprisingly, two lower courts sided with the
firm, but Hishon carried her appeal to the nation's highest court, and in May 1984 the Supreme Court ruled unanimously that federal

antidiscrimination laws apply to law partnerships. The decision did not award her a partnership, but it permitted her to bring suit against
the firm and to gain access to records containing the law firm's reasons for rejecting her as a
partner. She is now a partner in another Atlanta law firm.

In 1988, the American Bar Association

Box **4-1** | *Being a Woman and a Lawyer*

The legal profession is one of the
most masculine of occupations, in
the sense that "masculine" refers
to an orientation toward rules and
abstract principles and an emphasis on a separate identity and competitive advantage. How do women
who enter the legal profession accommodate a personal moral orientation that might be in tension
with the presuppositions of the system? Jack and Jack (1988) interviewed all 18 of the women who
were practicing law in a county in
the Northwest. On the basis of
these interviews, they identified
three patterns of adjustment.

At age 36, "Jane" emulated the
masculine model; she denied the
feminine, or relationship, side of
her self and became an ardent advocate. Defending a guilty client
was not "a problem for me. . . . It's
your job to present the case and
make sure that the person—if they
have a defense—has an opportunity to present it. . . . There's no reason for you to feel badly about it"
(quoted by Jack & Jack, 1988,
p. 270).

The suppression of her more
feminine values began in law
school: "I know people thought I
was crazy, but I can remember first-
year law school—I have the feeling
when I was being forced to change
my sex and I can feel it. . . . I don't
think you ever look at the situation
the same after you go through
three years of legal training"
(p. 271). Relevant to Jane's strategy is the study by the Boston Bar
Association of 2000 local lawyers;
it found that its women members
were significantly more likely than
its men members to be single, divorced, or without children (Goldstein, 1988b).

A second strategy, used by the
majority of women lawyers, was to
divide the self into two parts: the
lawyer self and the caring self. "At
work, the lawyer self dominates the
foreground and the caring self remains subdued. Outside of the office, the positions are reversed. This
allows the appropriate self to respond to each setting in a manner
consistent with its training and values" (Jack & Jack, 1988, p. 277).

But the separation wasn't always achieved easily. The caring
self often did not remain neatly
"boxed up" at the office. Moreover, the compartmentalizing of
selves frequently led to tension
rather than mental health.

Two of the 18 lawyers employed
a third strategy: they shaped their
role as lawyers on the basis of their
personal morality. They integrated
care into their job definition as an
attorney; they kept clients informed, responded to clients in
need, and avoided hierarchical office relationships. The major problem here is dealing with the stress
of caring within the context of a
profession. The involvement with
clients can lead to burn-out. Yet
such women can stimulate the profession to change. As Gilligan has
observed, in the legal system the
question "is no longer either simply about justice or simply about
caring; it is about bringing them together to transform the domain"
(quoted by Jack & Jack, 1988,
p. 287).

adopted a resolution to "refuse to participate in, acquiesce in, or condone barriers to the full integration and equal participation of women in the legal profession." Some jurisdictions even have passed *ethical* rules against gender discrimination in employment; for example, in the District of Columbia, it is unethical to discriminate on the basis of gender, sexual orientation, or responsibility for child care.

Despite these forward steps, women have not achieved full equality within the profession. Although women perform as well as men in law school, they are disadvantaged in every career path: in disproportionate numbers, female teachers are off the tenure track or are employed at nonelite schools, female judges serve in lower courts, and female private practitioners are associates rather than partners. In part the disparity in treatment is explainable by the fact that child-bearing is, or is assumed to be, the responsibility of women; consequently, women of child-bearing age face subtle discrimination from employers who assume motherhood is incompatible with the practice of law (Abel, 1989). The emergence of "mommy tracks" within large firms is intended to accommodate women who wish to work part-time while their children are small. Women who opt for the mommy track, however, are likely to be left behind when decisions are made about choice assignments or partnerships (Kingson, 1988).

As in other aspects of American life, discrimination against blacks has been the norm in the legal community. When the American Bar Association inadvertently admitted three blacks in 1914, it "persuaded" them to resign, after which it formally excluded blacks until 1943 (Abel, 1989, p. 100). Although blacks are well represented in government work and small group practice, until recently they have been virtually shut out of large firm practice. As recently as 1983, two-thirds of the largest U.S. firms had no black partners and a sixth had no black lawyers at all. More than three-quarters had no Hispanic partners and half had no Hispanic lawyers at all (Abel, 1989, p. 108) A 1989 survey of minorities in the nation's 250 largest law firms revealed that about 2% of the 23,000 partners and their associates are minorities (Bates & Whitehead, 1990). The percentage of minorities in law schools is holding constant at about 5%. Although high-profile lawyers like U.S. Supreme Court Justice Clarence Thomas demonstrate that race is no inherent impediment to success, we expect that minorities will continue to be underrepresented in the legal profession, particularly in positions of leadership.

Even though the pattern is changing, especially with regard to women, the profile of those aspiring to the legal profession remains characteristically white, male, and affluent (Astin, 1984; one exception is California, where only 49% of the lawyers with five years or less of experience are white males). This profile reflects the image of law as a *traditional* occupation; the ages at which students decide to go to law school and the reasons for these decisions reflect this conception and the value that the profession places on stability and on maintenance of ongoing traditions. These orientations contribute to the conflict in legal processes as straightforward searches for truth versus negotiated mechanisms for resolving disputes.

The Decision to Study Law

Thielens (1980) asked the entering law school class at Columbia University when they had first considered the study of law. A quarter of the students reported that it occurred when they were 15 or younger; a third considered it during the first year of college. Early consideration of the law as a career was facilitated by having a parent who was an attorney.

But why go to law school? The vast majority of law students (88%) responded, predictably, that they planned to practice law. Slightly more than a tenth of first-year law students at Columbia University even reported that they already had a definite law job lined up. However, they expressed other attractions to law school, too; 20% felt that law training was good discipline even if they never practiced law. More than a fifth reported that they were indecisive about a career and had decided to try law school.

In keeping with the portrayal of a tradition-oriented profession, 38 of the 246 Columbia first-year students had a parent who was an attorney. Although other studies have confirmed this figure of 15% of law students aspiring to become second-generation lawyers, the percentage has dropped recently, partly because of the increased number of students entering law school.

Even as the "my parent is a lawyer" tradition erodes, law students remain a rather exclusive group (Stevens, 1973). They tend to come from families that are well off financially, and they are more likely than other college graduates to have gone to private colleges that charge high tuition. Half of the entering law students in 1980–1981 had been in the top 25% of their undergraduate class (Astin, 1984). Not only are students with solid academic performance more likely to be admitted to law school than those with lower grades, but they are more likely to *apply*.

The decision to become a lawyer is not made capriciously. Students often consider how well the requirements of law school mesh with their personalities, as well as their scholastic abilities. We would expect that students who enroll in law school, especially those who persist, have personality characteristics and motivations that distinguish them from other students. Miller (1967) compared the dropout rate for students of different personality types at four law schools. Students who had finished their first year in good standing but did not enter their

second year the following fall were considered dropouts. Of those studied, 13.8% dropped out at this point. The decision to quit was related to the students' personality types. On the basis of their responses to the Myers-Briggs Type Indicator (a Jungian measure of personal styles), those students classified as "thinking types" had a dropout rate of 11%, whereas "feeling types" had a dropout rate of 20%. The dropout rate (28.1%) was even higher for those feeling types who were especially idealistic and people oriented. This type of student was underrepresented in law school, compared with the undergraduate population, implying that the high dropout rate may reflect a response to a problematic mix of personality style and occupational demands. In the thinking-versus-feeling classification used in the Myers-Briggs inventory, 75% of male lawyers and 60% of female lawyers are "thinkers" rather than "feelers," compared to 60% and 40%, respectively, of the population at large. Furthermore, feelers, who tend to make decisions based on personalized subjective values, tend to be the unhappiest lawyers (Moss, 1991).

Social scientists have sought to identify other relevant qualities of beginning law students. One survey (Stevens, 1973) found that 55% of the entering Columbia University law school class considered "independence" to be "of great importance" in their decisions; 51% valued the professional training, and 47% reported a strong interest in the subject matter of law school.

Clearly, many factors are important, as Willging and Dunn (1982, p. 331) note:

1. "Law students are not primarily concerned with implementing individual judgments about the restructuring of society to improve social justice"; that is, becoming an activist or advocate for underprivileged groups is not a strong motivation.
2. "Individual and independent control over the

work presented by clients is a widespread expectation of aspiring lawyers," implying that law students need to have control over their lives and work.

3. "Concerns about prestige and financial reward are not reported to be of greatest importance."

Generalizations (particularly the preceding ones) are suspect because men and women study law for many reasons. Whereas some are attracted to the law as an intellectual exercise, others see themselves as social reformers. Some choose law for family reasons, some as a natural step up from a related career (for example, paralegal work), some as an opportunity for prestige and money (perhaps influenced by viewing *L.A. Law*). Some students profess to have "always wanted to be a lawyer," and others turn to law school because there seems to be nothing else to do with a liberal arts degree.

John Hunter, a general practitioner in Raleigh, North Carolina, describes his decision to attend law school as follows:

In my own case, I became interested in the law as a profession largely as a result of two factors which touched me entirely by chance. First, I was born and grew up in a neighborhood in which my family lived across the street from a very good lawyer who often talked with me about his profession, and secondly, I happened to take a course in public speaking during my first year in high school which led to a great interest in it and developed in me a skill in speaking in public which could be nicely worked in with the practice of law. In addition, I discovered in connection with the work I did in some of my English courses that I liked to work with words and particularly to express ideas in written or spoken language. The result was that by the time I entered college, I knew definitely that I wanted to be a lawyer, even though I had virtually no experience that touched upon the law itself or the type of work a lawyer does [Love & Childers, 1963].

Hunter is representative of those who went

to law school because of a perceived aptitude for the study and practice of law. Alan Dershowitz, the youngest professor to attain tenure at Harvard Law School and a defender of unpopular clients, reflects the motivation to "argue and debate," a motive described as of great importance by 26% of the respondents in Stevens's survey. Dershowitz started talking about the law while growing up in a devout Jewish household in Brooklyn; he remembers his father and uncles spending hours discussing the Talmud, the basic treatise of Jewish law (Bayles, 1984). "The Jewish religion is a very argumentative religion," Dershowitz says. "You argue with everyone. You essentially put God on trial." The experience left him with "a problem with authority." He is quoted as saying "Teachers were always telling me 'You're stupid, but you have a big mouth so you ought to be a lawyer'" (Bayles, 1984).

"Restructuring society" is another motivation for Dershowitz; he sees himself as a spokesperson for civil liberties and the rights of citizens, and he thinks "it's perfectly acceptable to have an influence on the American legal system."

Another exceptional lawyer, with regard to his willingness to disclose his innermost motivations and fears, is Gerry Spence, a Wyoming attorney who has ranged across the country successfully representing victims in personal injury cases. He represented Miss Wyoming in a libel suit against *Penthouse* magazine (to be described in Chapter 19) and Karen Silkwood in her plutonium contamination trial against the Kerr-McGee Corporation. A segment on *60 Minutes* described him as possibly the best trial lawyer in the United States today.

Spence sees himself as a gunfighter in the courtroom. "Why are we such fighters?" he asks. "I had some ideas about it."

The ideas had to do with fear, of my own fear of walking into a courtroom and laying it all down for a judge and a jury, all of me. It *is* I always, not the client, on trial. I have seen many clients asleep while the jury is out and I pace the floor in misery.

And all the young gunfighters want to take me on because it's a no-lose proposition for them. To be beaten by Gerry Spence is expected. It is an honor in a way. "He got me for half a million dollars last week," some trial man boasts of a case he could have settled with me for sixty thousand dollars. He was happy he had lost. It was a notch on my gun, but on his, too, because he had been in a fight with the big gunfighter, and others had not [Spence & Polk, 1982, pp. 15–16].

Undoubtedly, as Stevens's (1973) survey suggests, many lawyers and law students believe in service to the underprivileged. Thousands of volunteer lawyers provide legal services to the indigent through various state and local pro bono programs; the American Bar Association has successfully resisted the efforts of the Reagan and Bush administrations to eliminate the Legal Services Corporation, the federally funded program of legal services for the poor. Although societal views have hardened in the last 20 years, a 1971 study of first-year law students was encouraging. Steele (1971) found that 91% agreed and 58% expressed complete agreement with the statement "In spite of people who have done wrong, I still have faith in the basic decency of human beings." Exposure to lying and amoral clients, however, taxes even those with the most sanguine view of human nature. Consider the following reflection of criminal defense lawyer Seymour Wishman:

The most disturbing question people often put to me—a question asked accusingly, over and over, but without touching me until now—was: "Don't you take responsibility for what a criminal you get off may do next?"

"Very little. About as much as a doctor who repairs the broken finger of a killer," I used to answer flippantly.

I could no longer give that answer.

. . . My initial response had been to overlook the fact that defendants lie, or, if I could not overlook it, to forgive them for it somehow. In a perverse way, I didn't feel it was as outrageous for them to lie as for other people. Defendants were desperately trying to stay out of prison, and I could sympathize with that desire after having spent so much time in prisons myself, as a visitor.

But it was more than that. I saw the defendants as victims, helpless and at the mercy of others. Somehow I did not hold them accountable for their behavior in the same way I would others. "If you understand their backgrounds, that they'd been through. . . ." Or, I have heard myself say, "They have a different morality. They lead desperate lives, and in order to survive, they see nothing wrong in robbing, raping, mugging, murdering, or are compelled to (fill in the crime)" [1981b, pp. 36–37].

Anxiety Level of Law Students

Law students appear to be anxious students. A comparison of first-year law, medical, and nursing students at Yale University (Eron & Redmount, 1957) showed significantly higher anxiety levels in the law students. Possible reasons include the fact that law students face a new type of teaching, with only a final exam to determine their entire grade in a course. Their rank in their class is very important, determining future jobs and salary level. According to Horowitz and Willging (1984), many law professors view increased anxiety as "a necessary component of preparation for a profession in which coping with anxiety is a vital attribute" (p. 54). However, extremely high anxiety levels interfere with effective scholastic performance. A survey of first-year law students at the University of Wisconsin found that those who exhibited either very high or very low levels of anxiety did worse on their exams than their Law School Aptitude Test (LSAT) scores would have predicted (Comment, 1968).

High anxiety also impedes the students' ability to perform effectively in law school. Patton (1968) divided law students into two groups: those who had performed better in their first year than would have been expected from their undergraduate grades and scores on the LSAT and those who had performed worse. Those who had done less well were more anxious about the Socratic teaching method (described later in this chapter) and test taking and also more doubtful about their ability to interact with other students and faculty members in task-related situations.

Students' anxiety levels do not seem to drop during the three years of law school. Eron and Redmount (1957) conclude that the anxiety generated by the initial adjustment to law school is replaced by other types of anxiety as students go through law school. Putting their conclusion together with Lempert's (1972) finding that law students respond negatively to a pass/fail system, one begins to speculate that there is almost a need for the torment—that the pressure and the resulting anxiety become a necessary external motivating device if best levels of performance are to be achieved. On the other hand, whether law students "need" to be anxious or not, law school education is structured in such a way that increased anxiety is a predictable consequence for many students facing the pressures of law school.

Full-Time Commitment

Training for the legal profession has always required intensity and commitment. Back 250 years ago, when William Livingston began his legal education, he had to contract with his teacher that "for the term of his apprenticeship he would not go to the theater or tavern, play cards or dice, commit fornication or get married, or at anytime leave the mas-

ter's premises without permission" (Pipkin, 1982, pp. 1109–1110). Matters have changed in many respects, but law school remains an intensive and competitive environment. Class preparation and review are time consuming; immense amounts of material must be mastered. Therefore, law schools maintain policies to ensure that students will not be diverted from full-time study. In Coser's (1974) terms, law school is a "greedy institution," demanding the entire time, energy, and loyalty of its participants (Pipkin, 1982). The American Bar Association (ABA) states that "full-time student means a student who devotes substantially all working hours to the study of law" (American Bar Association, 1979, p. 10). Consistent with the ABA definition, many schools advise law students to avoid part-time work completely. As Pipkin notes, although contemporary law students do not have to sign a contract like William Livingston's in 1742, they may at times have to adhere to it! (See also Box 4-2 for an insider's view.)

THE LAW SCHOOL EXPERIENCE

Why does law school demand so much time and energy? What are the goals of a legal education, and what happens in law school? Law professors describe the primary purpose of law schools as teaching students to "think like lawyers." What does this mean?

"Thinking Like a Lawyer"

Students and law school alumni agree with the faculty about the importance of this goal. Gee and Jackson (1977) asked students at eight law schools across the country to rate themselves on 13 skills that were part of a legal education. "Ability to think like a lawyer" was the skill on which they rated themselves highest. Being able to reason logically, or analytically, is one way to define this skill; it includes the ability to see various sides of a problem and then to express one's ideas articulately, whether through oral or written expression. "Thinking like a lawyer" means thinking unemotionally in the sense that the human element in complex issues can be put aside (Willging & Dunn, 1982, p. 321). Such descriptions support the conclusion in Box 4-1 that law school promotes a traditionally "masculine" conception of justice (as presented in Chapter 3).

The Case Method and the Socratic Teaching Procedure

The case method of teaching, developed by Dean Christopher Columbus Langdell at Harvard University over 100 years ago, is now used by many law professors. The raw material for class discussions emerges from actual cases that have been reviewed by appellate courts. The focus is on identifying underlying principles so that students can learn to isolate the critical factors in each case.

The case method is usually used in conjunction with what is called the Socratic teaching style (the name originating with the procedures

---

Box 4-2 | Law School as a "Jealous Mistress"

Scott Turow (1977), while a first-year law student at Harvard, kept a diary of his year. His account reflects how the pressure toward total participation weakens ties with other institutions and persons who dare to make competing claims. He writes:

At home, things are in a trough. Annette's patience with the law school wife bit appears to have worn thin and we are bickering often. For A., I guess it is hard not to feel cheated. She's been dragged across the country and stuck in an exhausting job, while I am treated to the glories of Harvard Law. It does not help that in the little time we get together, I am frequently too preoccupied to be fully at-

tentive. And since we are in a new place there is not an established circle of friends who might bolster her spirits. The law school has not provided a community with which we're eager to get involved. It's not a social place. On the weekends we're all just as happy not to see each other. And with good reason. On the few evenings we've had law school friends here, as we did last night, the conversation has centered obsessively on HLS.

For Annette, there is no easy solution, and she's often left frustrated and alone. During the daytime on weekends, she has taken to heading off for outings in the city by herself—to

museums, to exhibits, on shopping expeditions. But there are instants when it is plain that she is bitter at how unavailable I am. Last week she told me that I am more intimate with the law than with her, a not-so-subtle reference to the fact that we have been getting together in the bedroom infrequently. (From the drift of conversations around school, I take it that that problem is not unique to us.) All of it leaves me feeling toweringly guilty at moments, and also helpless, since I cannot make the law school and its demands dissolve [Turow, 1977, p. 141].

Socrates used with his pupils). In the Socratic method, the professor asks individual students questions designed to explore the case and determine the legal principles that the courts applied in reaching their decision. The professor encourages the student to relate the case to others like it or to distinguish it from similar but inapplicable precedents. As the professor goads and stimulates, the Socratic style can be exhilarating; it can also be an instrument of degradation. A law professor (Josephson, n.d.), in a booklet of advice to first-year students, offers Rule 1 about the Socratic method: the game is rigged, and the lions are supposed to win. After all, the professors are more experienced, and they have refined their questions to tease out subtle distinctions between cases or between hypothetical situations. Students who get "shown up" should not take it personally or feel humiliated, Josephson claims.

Scott Turow (1977), in his diary of life as a first-year law student at Harvard, provides an example of the Socratic method. (It should be noted that the contracts course with Professor "Perini" is an extreme example.)

> As he went on describing the subjects with which we would soon be dealing—offer, acceptance, interpretation; the list was extensive—I began to think that, like Mann, he would let the hour slip away. No one would be called and we'd all be safe for one more day. But at six or seven minutes to twelve he returned to the lectern and looked down at the seating chart.
>
> "Let's see if we can cover a *little* ground today." Perini took a pencil from his pocket and pointed it at the chart. It might as well have been a pistol. Please, no, I thought.
>
> "Mr. Karlin!" Perini cried sharply.
>
> Nearby, I heard a tremendous thud. Five or six seats from me a man was scrambling to grab hold of the books that had been piled before him, two or three of which had now hit the floor. That, I was sure, was Karlin who had jolted when he heard his name called. He was a heavyset man,

pale, with black eyeglasses. He was wearing a yarmulke. His eyes, as he struggled with his books, were quick with fright, and at once I felt terribly sorry for him and guilty at my own relief.

> "Mr. Karlin," Perini said, ambling toward my side of the room, "why don't you tell us about the case of *Hurley* v. *Eddingfield?*"
>
> Karlin already had his notebook open. His voice was quavering.
>
> "Plaintiff's intestate," he began. He got no further.
>
> "What does *that* mean?" Perini cried from across the room. He began marching fiercely up the aisle toward Karlin. "In-*tes*-tate. What is that? Something to do with the *stomach*? Is this an anatomy class, Mr. Karlin?" Perini's voice had become shrill with a note of open mockery and at the last word people burst out laughing, louder than at anything Perini had said before.
>
> He was only five or six feet from Karlin now. Karlin stared up at him and blinked and finally said, "No."
>
> "No, I didn't think so," Perini said. "What if the word was 'testate'? What would that be? Would we have moved from the stomach"—Perini waved a hand and there was more loud laughter when he leeringly asked his question—"*elsewhere?*"
>
> "I think," Karlin said weakly, "that if the word was 'testate' it would mean he had had a will."
>
> "And 'intestate' that he didn't have a will. I see." Perini wagged his head. "And who is this 'he,' Mr. Karlin?"
>
> Karlin was silent. He shifted in his seat as Perini stared at him. Hands had shot up across the room. Perini called rapidly on two or three people who gave various names—Hurley, Eddingfield, the plaintiff. Finally someone said that the case didn't say.
>
> "The case doesn't *say!*" Perini cried, marching down the aisle. "The case does *not* say. Read the case. *Read* the case! *Care*fully!" He bent with each word, pointing a finger at the class. He stared fiercely into the crowd of students in the center of the room, then looked back at Karlin. "Do we really care who 'he' is, Mr. Karlin?"
>
> "Care?"

"Does it make any *difference* to the outcome of the case?"

"I don't think so."

"Why not?"

"Because he's dead."

"He's *dead!*" Perini shouted. "Well, that's a load off of our minds. But there's one problem then, Mr. Karlin. If he's dead, how did he file a *law*suit?"

Karlin's face was still tight with fear, but he seemed to be gathering himself.

"I thought it was the administrator who brought the suit."

"Ah!" said Perini. "The ad*min*istrator. And what's an administrator? One of those types over in the Faculty Building?"

It went on that way for a few more minutes, Perini striding through the room, shouting and pointing as he battered Karlin with questions, Karlin doing his best to provide answers. A little after noon Perini suddenly announced that we would continue tomorrow. Then he strode from the classroom with the seating chart beneath his arm. In his wake the class exploded into chatter [Turow, 1977, pp. 51–53].

What Is Taught and What Is Not Taught

In the traditional law school curriculum, all the first-year courses are required ones; they cover the staples of legal practice, such as contracts, civil procedure, criminal law, and torts. (Torts are private wrongs resulting from a breach of a legal duty even if a contract does not exist.) Electives are available in the second and third years, although there are still required courses, including, at most schools, a course on legal ethics. Opportunity for specialization within law school is a relatively recent phenomenon; among major types of specialization are corporate law, taxation, antitrust law, family law, and patent law. Specialization may serve as an effective antidote to third-year boredom, according to Dean Ronald Cass of Boston University:

"There is much more coordination in other academic areas, moving people along a track. It struck me that it shouldn't be that difficult to bring more coherence to teaching."

The legal curriculum emphasizes principles of the law. Law faculty generally discourage teaching the practical aspects of "lawyering," such as setting up a law office, preparing deeds, or learning the courtesies of appearing before a judge. J. R. Nielsen, a professor at Hastings College of Law in San Francisco, writes:

> It is a fact that a student can graduate from this, the fourth largest law school in the United States, without ever having written a pleading, a contract, a will, a promissory note, or a deed. It's worse than that. It is a fact that most students graduate from this law school without ever having *seen* a real honest-to-God pleading, or contract, will, promissory note, or deed. A student can graduate without ever having set foot in a courtroom and without ever having spoken to, or on behalf of, a person in need of advice or counsel. A student can graduate without once being exposed to the operation of the rules of the court [1984, p. 15].

But recently the trend has been toward incorporating more training in the "nuts and bolts" of law practice into the curriculum. Law students are asking for such opportunities, and many legal educators believe that leaving such training to law firms, after students have graduated, is an abdication of responsibility. In response, most law schools are now providing "skills training," through simulation courses and clinics. In simulation courses students perform in "make-believe" cases with other students acting as clients and witnesses. Clinics, on the other hand, give students an opportunity to deal with real clients under the supervision of an instructor or practicing lawyer. Despite this trend, relatively few credit hours in the three-year curriculum are available for such courses, and full-time faculty members with the skill and desire to teach them may be few, so that such courses cannot always accommodate all interested students.

CHANGES IN VALUES AS A RESULT OF LAW SCHOOL

Given the commitment that students must make to the demands of law school and its impact on them, we would expect changes in values to occur. For example, critiques of legal education during the period of activism in the early 1970s claimed that law school retarded students' moral development. However, Willging and Dunn (1982, p. 321) report that the few empirical studies of value changes during law school do not support these claims.

Likewise, there is little indication of any shift in idealistic concerns. Thielens (1980) compared service and income as goals at each year of law school. His results show no dramatic changes, except that idealism tends to increase over the law school experience.

Thielens also reported that, among his sample of Columbia law students, the valuing of competition decreases, especially as a result of the first-year experience. Yet both professors and law students agree, almost unanimously (93% and 90%), that law students are very competitive (Auerbach, 1984). Some students and observers report that, over the law school experience, imagination and creativity seem to be demoted in favor of attaining legal tools, vocabulary, and the skills of analysis (Turow, 1977). Certainly the latter qualities are part of "thinking like a lawyer."

Other observers sense an increasing cynicism and "hardness," the development of a professional callousness manifested in views like "You win some; you lose some." Not all attorneys show such reactions; nor, in fact, do the data on changes in moral development scores during the first year of law school. Willging and Dunn (1982) found that law students' stage of moral development, as measured by their responses to Kohlberg-type ethical dilemmas, did not change—either forward or backward—during the first year of law school. Law students maintained a conventional orientation to morality (Kohlberg's stages three and four; see Chapter 3). Many attorneys remain ego-involved with their clients and their cases, some even to a detrimental degree. Lawyers are not encouraged to become emotionally involved with clients. The paradigm is the lawyer zealously representing the client—but at arm's length, a principle illustrated by the story of the defense lawyer who pulled out all the stops (ethically, of course) in a murder case only to see the jury return a verdict of guilty. As the judge pronounced sentence, the client whispered to the lawyer "What are we going to do now?" To which the lawyer responded "I don't know about you, but I think I'll go to lunch." The point, of course, is that the lawyer didn't make the facts and wasn't on trial.

Many effective trial lawyers, however, have great ego involvement, but usually with the case, not the client. Gerry Spence, the highly successful Wyoming attorney, reflects ego involvement by seeing himself on trial in every court case. He writes:

> The jury accepts or rejects *me*, not my case, I make the case. I am the director, the producer, its principal actor—it is my courtroom, my judge, my jury—it is I, and when the jury says no, it is the ultimate rejection because they are not saying no to just an idea, but they are saying no to all of me since I have put all of me in the pit [Spence & Polk, 1982, p. 15].

Of course, we do not know how much of the competitiveness of attorneys stems from their law school experiences and how much of it is present in students before they enter law school. Students, after all, are not randomly assigned to law school or some other profession. Those who choose law school made that selection partly because they assumed that their temperament and motives were congenial with the responsibilities they expected in the profession of law.

LAWYERS AND ETHICS

Lawyers are human, and it is inevitable that some will behave unethically or even criminally. Every state attempts to protect the public against unethical lawyers through a code of ethics (usually patterned after the ABA's Model Rules of Professional Responsibility; see Box

4-3), enforced by a disciplinary body whose decisions are reviewed by the highest court of the state. The disciplinary body can censure, suspend, or even disbar unethical lawyers. In addition, most states have created "client security funds" to reimburse clients whose money has been embezzled by lawyers.

Public criticism of the disciplinary process generally takes two forms: (1) an assumption that lawyers "get away with anything," based on the fact that disciplinary proceedings are often closed and the disciplinary tribunal is composed primarily of lawyers; and (2) a perception that the ethical rules—the lawyers' code—does not provide relief for those who are overcharged or poorly represented. Both criticisms are just. The public can never be expected to accept a disciplinary process that takes place behind closed doors, and the failure of bar associations and disciplinary tribunals to come to grips with

---

Box 4-3 | *History of the Lawyer Codes*

The American Bar Association is a private organization with no power to impose its rules on anyone. The ABA has served, however, as a source of rules, adopted by the several states in whole or in part.

The ABA's first codification came in 1908 as 29 "Canons (or Laws) of Ethics," which were widely adopted by the states and which served as general rules of conduct until 1970. In that year the ABA (and soon thereafter all the states in some form) adopted the Code of Professional Responsibility, which consists of nine general statements

(called "canons" in the Code), each followed by a set of rules and a set of "ethical considerations," the latter intended to guide well-meaning lawyers. Under the Code, violation of a rule could result in discipline for the erring lawyer, but violation of an ethical consideration could not.

Dissatisfaction with the format and coverage of the 1970 Code (too much emphasis on litigation) led to the 1983 Model Rules of Professional Responsibility. Now adopted by about two-thirds of the states, the Rules are in a format

familiar to most lawyers: a set of rules, each followed by comments to be used in interpreting the rules (Gillers & Dorsen, 1989).

In addition, the ABA Committee of Ethics and Professional Responsibility, along with its state counterparts, issues advisory opinions on matters that are not definitively answered by the Rules. Lawyers are encouraged to seek the advice of their respective states' ethics committees when in doubt as to the proper course of conduct.

price gouging and/or inept lawyers explains in part why the public perception of lawyers is as low as it is.

The Model Rules of Professional Responsibility do, however, provide answers for many of the difficult problems with which lawyers must deal. Suppose, for example, that a client tells the lawyer in confidence that he intends to burn down his business in order to collect the insurance proceeds. One might expect that the lawyer should inform the police of the impending arson. Because of the importance assigned to client confidences, however, the Model Rules require the lawyer to keep silent unless the lawyer reasonably believes that the fire might endanger someone within the building. The lawyer may, of course, try to talk the client out of the planned crime, but ultimately the lawyer is required to keep the information confidential.

Take another example: Suppose a couple planning on an amicable divorce decide to hire a lawyer who has helped the husband with his business over the years. The couple ask the lawyer to "help them with the divorce." Can the lawyer represent both? The Model Rules allow the lawyer to represent both only if the lawyer reasonably believes that the husband and wife are in total agreement and that there is little likelihood that they will fall into conflict during the course of the divorce proceedings. Even then the lawyer must be careful, because the wife will need to know her husband's business transactions in order to enter into a fair property settlement. The lawyer cannot fairly represent the wife's interest unless the husband is willing to authorize the lawyer to tell the wife about matters earlier communicated to the lawyer in confidence.

One more example: Suppose a lawyer represents a client engaged in secret negotiations to buy a farm for development as a shopping center. Can the lawyer ethically buy the adjoining farm—which the client is not interested in—in anticipation of profiting when the shopping center is developed? The answer is: only with the client's consent. As the client's agent, the lawyer cannot use confidential information to make a side profit unless the client consents.

There are, of course, ethical conundrums in the law, which have been debated in Legal Ethics courses, law journal articles, and TV talk shows. Some of these problems have no satisfactory answers because the Rules do not resolve all questions and sound arguments can be advanced for contrary positions. You might try to develop arguments for different solutions to some of the best of these legal puzzles, such as the following:

- On examining his client's back tax returns, the lawyer tells the client that he probably will be charged with tax fraud. The client asks the lawyer for a list of countries that do not have extradition treaties with the United States. May the lawyer provide this information, knowing that the client may flee to escape prosecution?
- On being interviewed by his lawyer, the client tells a patently unbelievable story about the alleged crime. To what extent can the lawyer closely question the client when the result may be an equally false, but more believable, story?
- In a criminal case, the defense lawyer knows that his client robbed the victim. In cross-examining the victim, may the lawyer ethically suggest that she is mistaken in her identification of the defendant as the assailant? May the lawyer ethically suggest that the victim is lying?

CRITICISMS OF LAWYERS

The legal profession has been criticized for reasons other than its self-serving definition of ethics. Lawyers, it is claimed, fail to adequately serve the "middle 70%" of the population. Rich criminal defendants can afford expensive law firms to represent them; corporations have the resources to pay for extensive legal research and preparation. At the other end of the economic scale, poor people are provided lawyers without cost if they are defendants in criminal trials, and they may rely on legal aid clinics, including volunteer private attorneys, if they are involved in civil suits. It is middle-income families who have difficulty obtaining legal assistance because attorneys' fees of $75 to $200 an hour quickly become prohibitive. Lawyers would respond that such cases demonstrate the merits of the contingency-fee procedure. If you believe that, for example, your physician's negligence has caused you a serious illness or injury, you can ask an attorney to represent you in a civil suit against the physician. If the case is settled in your favor, your attorney receives a percentage (usually 33% to 40%) of whatever is awarded to you. But, if you lose, you do not have to pay your attorney any fee.

Lawyers are also charged with complicating the law unnecessarily so that consumers must hire an attorney to interpret the law for them. Lawyers' organizations will charge others with the unauthorized practice of law ("U.P.L.") if the latter carry out legal matters without being licensed to do so. Rosemary Furman, a Jacksonville, Florida, legal secretary, began dispensing do-it-yourself legal kits, mostly for couples seeking a divorce. She was prosecuted and sentenced to 30 days in jail for dispensing legal advice without a license. Shortly after this, and perhaps not independently of it, the Florida Bar Association developed a new procedure so that in Florida childless couples who agree to divide their assets and debts can receive a divorce at a cost of less than $100 in filing fees without the assistance of an attorney. Along the same lines, an ABA study disclosed that nearly half (47%) of 1985 divorces in Phoenix were accomplished

without a lawyer. An ABA spokesperson responded to the finding by saying that the organized bar should assist, not hinder, those who wish to represent themselves (Moss, 1988).

Criticisms of fee setting include the practice of charging by the hour, which can encourage delays and extend debate. In large law firms, the associates must generate a certain number of "billable" hours a year; the average number of annual billable hours at some large New York City law firms increased from around 1700 in the late 1970s (Brill, 1978) to between 2300 and 2500 ten years later (Kingson, 1988). If we divide 2400 hours by 50 weeks (giving each associate a two-week paid vacation each year), we get the requirement of about 48 billable hours per week, every week—that is, 48 hours in which the young attorney meets with clients, conducts legal research on the clients' behalf, meets with opposing attorneys, takes depositions, litigates cases in court, talks on the telephone with or for clients, dictates correspondence, or prepares requested materials such as wills or contracts. This is a challenging standard. Young attorneys in large firms feel pressured to bill as many hours as are legitimate and possible.

Sometimes these efforts lead to excessive outcomes. One West Virginia lawyer billed the state for 75 hours of work for one day's work representing indigent criminal clients. How is that possible? He charged the state travel and court time separately for each client—a total of 22 hours travel and 53 hours court time—though he traveled less than an hour and was in court only four hours. In censuring the lawyer, the West Virginia Supreme Court commented "When an attorney spends one hour traveling to represent six clients at a hearing he does not actually travel six hours—he travels for one hour. When an attorney spends two hours representing six clients at a hearing, he does not actually work for 12 hours—he works for two hours" ("No Author," 1987). The late Edward Bennett Williams, one of the preeminent lawyers of the 20th century, bragged to reporters that he had billed 3200 hours in 1984—more than 60 hours per week, in spite of having undergone surgery twice in the year. According to his official biographer, the fact that he billed 3200 hours did not mean that he worked 3200 hours. The way Williams calculated the number of hours to bill on a given case was to figure out what he was worth—an arbitrary figure—and divide by his hourly rate, which at the time of his death was $1000 an hour (Thomas, 1991).

Such abuses lead to the cynic's response to the question "What do you call a lawyer who bills 2800 hours a year?" Answer: "A liar." A litany of abuses has been catalogued in the legal and popular press: double billing (the example above), minimum billing (where every phone call, no matter how brief, is billed at some minimum multiple of an hour), value billing (where research done for client A that benefits client B is billed to both), separate charges for overhead, and use of two (or three) lawyers when one will do.

Because of such abuses, clients are increasingly shopping around before hiring a lawyer and demanding detailed invoices, cost estimates, and cost controls. Lawyers or law firms that are inefficient and/or larcenous can be expected to fall by the wayside.

It is from the income of associates that the partners make their profits. Brill (1978) notes that a good rule of thumb is that an hourly rate for associates be equal to about twice their annual salary divided by 1000. For example, the work of a $50,000 associate gets billed at $100 an hour. Thus, if the associate logs just 500 hours a year, the firm gets back the salary (500 x $100 = $50,000). Add another $50,000, or 500 hours, for secretarial services and other overhead, and you get a total of $100,000 or 1000 hours for the cost of keeping him or her working. The rest (say,

1400 hours or $140,000) is profit for the partnership. One giant New York City firm reported profits per partner in 1987 at $885,000 (Torry & Lawrence, 1989).

But young law graduates, awed by starting salaries upward of $70,000 at Wall Street's most prestigious firms, need to realize that their toil for five to ten years of 70-hour weeks does not guarantee a partnership. In fact, it is not uncommon for firms to offer partnerships to only one out of every seven or eight associates who have logged the requisite years (Lacayo, 1986).

Partners generate income for the law firm through their own billable hours too, of course, though with fewer hours than associates. In the New York survey, the average number of hours billed per year for partners was 1468, much less than for associates. Then, too, partners bill at a higher rate; senior partners of top firms charge $200–$300 an hour.

The need to bill hours contributes to criticisms that some attorneys file too many frivolous lawsuits and motions. In 1962 slightly more than 85,000 lawsuits were filed in *federal* courts across the nation. Twenty years later, the figures had swelled by 180%, to almost 240,000 lawsuits. By the start of the 1990s, it was estimated that about one million federal lawsuits were being filed every year. Civil litigation has grown to be an enormous industry; some estimates place its total costs and income at 80 billion dollars per year. State and local courts now have about 8 million lawsuits pending, one for every 29 people in the country. Horror stories abound: pro football fans suing the referee over a bad call, umpires suing baseball managers over name calling, an adult man suing his parents for lack of love and affection, a man suing a woman over a broken date, one prisoner suing his guards for "allowing" him to escape, another inmate suing prison officials for denying him the chance to contribute to a sperm bank.

The former U.S. Supreme Court Chief

Justice Warren Burger (1982) criticized his fellow attorneys for deluging the dockets with "absurd" lawsuits; in a speech before the ABA convention in 1984, he even called them "hired guns" and "procurers" who advertised their services as if they were selling "mustard, cosmetics, and laxatives." (Lawyers were first given the right to advertise in 1977, in a Supreme Court decision concluding that an Arizona ban on advertising violated an attorney's right to free speech. Burger dissented from the majority in that decision.) The chief justice also criticized his colleagues for contributing to court congestion by their failure to encourage out-of-court settlements of disputes.

Burger's rebuke fits the public image of greedy lawyers ready to sue at the slightest provocation. But an analysis of ways for resolving legal disputes questions the accuracy of that image. David Trubek, a law professor at the University of Wisconsin, and his colleagues (Trubek, Sarat, Felstiner, Kritzer, & Grossman, 1983) surveyed how potential legal disputes were settled in 5000 households in five parts of the country. For every 1000 grievances, only about 100 resulted in hiring a lawyer and only 50 in filing a lawsuit. The Wisconsin researchers also followed 1650 civil lawsuits through state and federal courts and interviewed 1300 lawyers who were involved in many of them. On the average, the attorneys spent about 30 hours on a typical case; this earned them less than

---

Box 4-4 | Alternative Dispute Resolution

Psychologists, especially social and clinical psychologists, have had an extended interest in conflict and its resolution. Around 1970, interest began to focus on third-party intervention in disputes (Smith, 1987); among these disinterested third parties are labor mediators, marriage counselors, divorce mediators—and, increasingly, attorneys.

Despite the fact that more than one million divorces are granted in the United States yearly, attorneys a decade or so ago considered divorce mediation as heresy. But now law school courses and continuing legal education (CLE) workshops on the topic are increasingly popular. The ABA has formed a Special Committee on Dispute Resolution, and the book *Getting to Yes*, by law professors Roger Fisher and William Ury, was a critical success.

The Harvard Law School now offers a trend-setting Program on Negotiation. Moreover, the theme of the 1989 ABA convention, held in Honolulu, was "Resolving Disputes in Pacific Ways" (the double entendre was doubtless intended!).

About a thousand of the 4000 trained divorce mediators in the United States are attorneys. Approximately one-half of the states require mediation in certain types of divorce cases, especially if children are involved.

As noted by Emery and Wyer (1987), divorce mediation differs from the two traditional procedures (litigation and out-of-court negotiations between two opposing attorneys) in three important ways: "(a) In mediation communication takes place with a single professional, (b) mediation is based on an assumption of cooperation rath-

er than competition, and (c) parties make their own decisions in mediation" (Emery & Wyer, 1987, p. 472).

The goal of mediation is not to reconcile combative spouses; rather, it is to help couples reach mutually satisfactory agreements on such emotionally charged issues as who raises the children, who keeps the house, and who pays whom how much. The mediator may save the couple further aggravation as well as attorney's fees (high-profile divorce lawyers like Raoul Felder and Marvin Mitchelson charge $350–$450 per hour). Once the mediator has helped the couple form a memorandum of understanding, each spouse has it reviewed by his or her own attorney to make sure its terms are legal and fair.

Psychologists can play the role of evaluation researchers (see

$2500. In many of these cases, pretrial discovery (the early phase in which each attorney seeks to learn what evidence the other side has) was quite limited, despite Chief Justice Burger's claim that it caused interminable delays and impeded litigation. In addition, separate studies conducted by the National Center for State Courts, the American Bar Foundation, and the RAND Corporation's Institute for Civil Justice all dispute claims that a litigation explosion has occurred in recent years. Only modest increases in lawsuits between private citizens were observed, in contrast to very large increases in bankruptcy cases, contract disputes, and suits between corporations.

Justice Burger also advocated that the legal profession—which he sees as currently mesmerized by the thrill of courtroom battles—move away from total reliance on adversarial contests for resolving all disputes. "Our system is too costly, too painful, too destructive, too inefficient for a truly civilized people," he said. The legal profession is exploring negotiation and other means of dispute settlement (see, for example, Sacks, 1984; Sander, 1984; Williams, 1984). As just one example, many states are encouraging and increasingly using divorce mediation, in which a divorcing couple work with a lawyer/mediator to develop a dissolution agreement that is both fair and workable rather than resolving their disputes in an adversarily contested trial (see also Box 4-4). Alternative

Chapter 2) in assessing alternative dispute resolution techniques (Tomkins, 1988a). Several studies have found that divorce mediation is associated with numerous positive outcomes, including greater satisfaction with the process among divorcing couples. However, mediation may not be equally beneficial for men and women. Mediated settlements appear to be especially popular with men, who may, because of greater power or more resources, fare better in the negotiation process than women (Grych & Fincham, 1992).

Mediation has also become a popular approach to other legal matters. For example, judges—in order to alleviate crowded court dockets—have begun to use the *summary jury trial* as an alternative dispute resolution procedure. In a summary jury trial, a six-person jury listens as attorneys for each side in a civil suit summarize the evidence. No witnesses are presented. The jury then renders a nonbinding verdict. Everything is done in one day. It is hoped that the result will facilitate a settlement and avoid a long, costly trial. The U.S. Congress is considering legislation to give judges the right to mandate summary jury trials in certain circumstances. As Tomkins (1988a) notes, psychological research on effectiveness is warranted.

Mediation has extended beyond the preceding examples to other types of conflicts, such as those between neighboring families, landlords and tenants, or customers and storekeepers. The ABA estimates that the more than 300 dispute resolution centers in the United States process over 230,000 cases a year (Pruitt, 1987), thus easing pressure on court calendars.

Psychologists' evaluations of the effects of dispute resolution centers show, in Pruitt's words, "remarkable consistency." To quote him:

Agreements reached in mediation are usually satisfactory to the disputants and hold well over time. Relationships between the disputants often improve after the hearing. In addition, both sides tend to be pleased with the treatment they have received in the hearing and see the outcome as fair. A large majority of them say that they would return to the center if they had another problem and would recommend the service to a friend. Mediation generally receives higher ratings in all of these areas than do court hearings [Pruitt, 1987, p. 60].

dispute resolution methods are discussed further in Chapter 12.

TOO MANY LAWYERS?

This chapter began with the observation that the United States has many more lawyers per capita than any other country—one for every 300–320 residents (by contrast, Japan has one lawyer for about every 9000 residents and England has one for every 1200 persons). Does it have too many? Some lawyers think so. William K. Coblentz, a San Francisco attorney, writes:

> The trouble is, lawyers don't do much. Sure, they are busy. Sometimes they help people. My law professors used to assure us as we prepared to graduate that lawyers are the grease that lubricates the wheels of society. Nonsense! A few are needed to give advice, draft contracts and protect people from bureaucratic excesses. But mainly lawyers deal in process. They don't have to produce anything useful, rehashing past events in such a way as to distribute wealth from one person to another. They think up new situations and theories for redistribution. When wealth is simply redistributed, society has no net gain. And we all incur a cost equal to the value of the resources used in the redistribution, as well as the useful production the redistributors could have been contributing [1983, p. 17].

This claim that our country's talents are being wasted by the profusion of competent people marching into the legal profession is reaffirmed by Derek Bok, president of Harvard University and former dean of its law school. In his 1983 report to the Harvard Board of Overseers (quoted in Benenson, 1984), he wrote that "far too many" of the nation's brightest young people "are becoming lawyers at a time when the country cries out for more

talented business executives, more enlightened public servants, more inventive engineers, more able high school principals and teachers."

But a contrasting viewpoint is equally legitimate. We have more lawyers now than we had 20 years ago because our society has grown more diverse and complex, because we have more laws and rules, and because our society has become more bureaucratized. Michael Davis (1985), a former law school dean, has identified four developments over the last 30 years that have increased the need for lawyers:

1. *Prosperity.* A better standard of living leads people to go more places, form more corporations, buy more property, seek more tax shelters, and engage in many other activities that increase the demand for legal advice.
2. *Regulation.* Over the last three decades, increased civil rights, pension reform, improved standards for safety in the workplace, greater environmental protections, and similar developments have created a need for lawyers to operate and enforce the new regulations.
3. *Expanded rights.* There has been a substantial increase in constitutional protections for individuals, including indigent defendants and juvenile offenders.
4. *Litigiousness.* With the depersonalization of urban living, the secularization of society, and the weakening bonds of family structure, people seek other means—the courts—to assist them redress their misfortunes. Former President George Bush described this phenomenon as "America's love affair with the lawsuit."

We need lawyers in order to maintain a free society. Disputes will always be with us, and a necessary cost of a complex society is the maintenance of a profession whose job it is to help us resolve disputes.

If a society finds itself with too many lawyers,

then another kind of law, the law of supply and demand, will take over as at least a partial corrective, for legal services are, after all, like any other commodity in a free marketplace.

SUMMARY

The United States has more lawyers per unit of population than any other country in the world—nearly 800,000 at last count. Despite rapid increases in recent law school enrollments, the profession remains predominantly white, male, and traditional in its orientation.

Law school attracts a particular type of student. Law students are more likely to come from families of higher economic status and to have attended private colleges, and they possess above-average scholastic aptitude. Among prime motivations for a legal career are control over one's work environment, intellectual stimulation, and varied work activities.

Anxiety levels are high among entering law students and remain so throughout the law school years. One possible reason is the Socratic method, with its goal of training students to "think like a lawyer." As a body of material to be taught, the law remains a traditional subject, with emphasis on basic principles. But recently the trend is toward more training in practical aspects of the law.

Despite speculations to the contrary, there is little empirical evidence that personal values change during law school, whether the topic is idealism, cynicism, or level of moral development.

Every state requires lawyers to adhere to a Code of Conduct (usually patterned after the ABA Model Rules of Professional Responsibility) or risk censure, suspension, or disbarment. In addition, state ethics committees offer guidance to lawyers about proper ethical behaviors.

Criticisms of the law include the failures of self-regulation of the profession, the efforts to keep nonlawyers from offering consumers the same services at lower prices, the expense of legal assistance, and the proliferation of attorneys, which allegedly leads to unnecessary lawsuits.

Theories of Crime

In 1991, the most recent year for which complete police statistics were available to us, more than 23,000 homicides were committed in the United States, more than 3 million burglaries totaling over 3.4 billion dollars in losses occurred, and about 1.6 million Americans were raped, robbed, or seriously assaulted. In the words of Aric Press (1988, p. 67)" . . . In some American cities, particularly in the poorest neighborhoods, crime has become a 'deadly plague.'" By some estimates, violent crime in the United States is 10 to 20 times higher than in the countries of Western Europe (Katz, 1988).

What can be done to control crime? Should we hire more police, develop more courts, build more prisons? Controlling crime is a major social and political issue in the United States. An extremely successful element in George Bush's 1988 presidential campaign was his attack on his opponent, Michael Dukakis, for having permitted the furlough of Willie Horton, a Massachusetts convict who subsequently raped a Maryland woman on his furlough. Congress has passed several anticrime bills that expand the use of capital punishment to a wider spectrum of crimes and place new controls on the purchase of certain firearms. The Supreme Court has issued a series of rulings that strengthen the powers of law enforcement officials in the areas of search and seizure, interrogation of criminal suspects, and the pretrial detention of persons who have been arrested. All these steps have been justified, in part, as remedies for the relentless increase in crime in the United States.

But, in order to ease the crime problem, psychologists would argue that we must first understand its causes. Why does crime happen? What motivates people to commit illegal acts? Bad genes? Inadequate parents? Failed schooling? Twisted impulses? Harsh environments? Delinquent friends? Social disadvantage? Drug addiction? Some combination of these? Can crime

be predicted from a knowledge of a person's early life? Or are many people capable of crime, given an unlucky mix of intoxication, anger, and unprotected victims? Are some crimes so extreme that they defy any scientific explanation (see Box 5-1)? These questions, applied to many different forms of crime, are the concern of *criminology*, which is the study of crime and criminal behavior. In this chapter, we summarize the major theories of crime, beginning with a very brief review of the historical predecessors of 20th-century criminology.

THEORIES OF CRIME AS EXPLANATIONS OF CRIMINAL BEHAVIOR

Theories of crime are probably as old as crime itself. Aristotle claimed that "poverty is the parent of revolution and crime," but most early explanations of crime took a religious tone: crime was either equivalent or due to sin—a view that was also very popular throughout the Middle Ages.

In the 17th century, Sir Francis Bacon argued that "opportunity makes a thief." During the 1700s, philosophers and social critics such as Voltaire and Rousseau emphasized legal and social concepts such as free will, hedonistic decision making, and the social contract whereby individuals surrender some personal autonomy to the state in exchange for greater collective liberties. These principles ultimately grew into the *classical school* of criminology.

The two leading proponents of classical criminology were the Italian intellectual Cesare Beccaria and the British philosopher Jeremy Bentham, who believed that lawbreaking was the result of people, faced with a choice between right and wrong conduct, choosing to behave wrongly. People made pro-crime decisions when they believed that the gains of crime would outweigh its losses. Classical theorists interested in reforming the harsh administration of justice in post-Renaissance Europe insisted that punishment of criminals be administered in a reasonable and fair manner. This principle required the state to use punishments that were proportionate to the crimes committed: the punishment should fit the crime. Classical theory has influenced several fundamental principles of justice in Western societies (e.g., the Eighth Amendment ban against "cruel and unusual punishment"), and, as we shall see in Chapter 18, it still exerts an important influence on modern correctional philosophy.

Most 20th-century theories of crime developed from the *positivist school* of criminology. Positivists emphasized factors *deterministic* of criminal behavior rather than the free will of people to behave as they chose. Positivists sought to understand crime through the scientific method and empirical data, but their determinism took many different forms. Some stressed sociological factors, whereas others preferred biological, psychological, or environmental variables. Additionally, there is nothing inconsistent about a positivistic explanation of choice, whereby classical and positivistic theories share common ground. In practice, however, such combinations have been rare.

Cesare Lombroso, Enrico Ferri, and Raffaelo

| Box **5-1** | *Are All Crimes Explainable?* |

When police entered Apartment 213 at the Oxford Plaza Apartments in Milwaukee, Wisconsin, on July 22, 1991, they encountered one of the most horrifying crime scenes in this country's history. Severed human heads were discovered in the refrigerator, photographs of dismembered bodies were tacked to the walls, and human body parts were discovered immersed in a vat of acid. Ultimately, police discovered the remains of 11 male victims in and around the grimy, stench-filled one-bedroom apartment. Shortly after discovering these monstrosities, police arrested Jeffrey L. Dahmer, a 31-year-old chocolate-factory worker who soon confessed to a total of 17 killings. Dahmer provided authorities with the details of his slayings, which typically involved luring men to his apart-

Jeffrey Dahmer

ment, having sex with them, killing them, dismembering their bodies, and hoarding the remains. He admitted to performing sex acts on the corpses and also said that he cut one man's heart out and stored it in his freezer, intending to eat it later. He apparently ate body parts of the victims "he liked the most."

Can any theory of crime offer a

reasonable explanation of this gruesome carnage? Does Jeffrey Dahmer's history, even viewed now with the full knowledge of his terrifying crimes, offer any satisfying account of how a human being could engage repeatedly in such conduct? Or is Dahmer's behavior so extreme that it embarrasses social science explanations as shallow, pale excuses that fail to confront the fundamental evil that seems to lurk in a man like Dahmer?

A review of Dahmer's life has failed so far to uncover the trauma or prolonged mistreatment or environmental deprivations that would sufficiently explain his serial murders; neither is there convincing evidence that Dahmer suffered from a mental illness serious enough to compel this conduct. Dahmer was raised in a middle-

Garofalo were three important early positivists. They were preceded by A. M. Guerry in France and Adolphé Quetelet, a Belgian statistician, who, nearly 50 years before Lombroso, studied crime data and concluded that crime occurred more frequently in certain geographical areas and in the presence of specific social conditions. For various reasons, however, these early *ecological theories* were not as influential as those of the Italian positivists.

Lombroso (1876) and Garofalo (1914) emphasized the physical characteristics of criminals that implied a heavy biological predisposition to crime. Ferri (1917) also acknowledged physical factors but stressed social and environmental factors. The early positivists thought of themselves as scientists, but their science was crude by current standards and led to conclusions that are not taken seriously today despite evidence that biological factors play some role in criminality. Positivists believed that punishment should fit the criminal rather than the crime, a position that foreshadowed rehabilitation as a correctional priority and the indeterminate sentence as a means for achieving it.

Most modern theories of criminal behavior are a legacy of the positivist tradition. Almost every scholarly field, including biology, genetics, psychology, sociology, economics, anthropology, and religion, has spawned at least one theory of crime. The empirical status of these theories varies greatly. None of them explains

class family in a prosperous suburb. Neighbors recalled him and his younger brother as "very polite children." In high school, Dahmer showed erratic behavior, became gradually isolated from friends, and earned a reputation as an outcast for his weird humor (one classmate recalls that he liked to trace the outlines of nonexistent bodies on the ground). In 1978, Dahmer's parents went through a bitter divorce that apparently led to a marked worsening of Dahmer's drinking problems, which had been present since junior high school. Dahmer had attended Ohio State University briefly in 1978, but he did poorly and dropped out to join the Army in 1979. He was released early from the Army in 1981 because of his drinking problems. He then went to live with his grandmother in West Allis, Wisconsin. In 1985, he began the laborer's job at the Ambrosia Chocolate Factory that he held until shortly before his arrest. In 1988, after moving out of his grandmother's house, Dahmer was arrested for molesting a 13-year-old boy and was sentenced to five years' probation. Sometime later, he began his Milwaukee killing spree.

Clearly, Jeffrey's Dahmer's life began to unravel seriously in the late 1980s. But, as his troubles unfolded during this time, they did not appear so different from those of many lonely, alcoholic men—men who, despite the tragedies of their lives, did not lure multiple victims into traps of violent death. Although social scientists may attempt to link the crimes of Jeffrey Dahmer to any of several factors in his life, including the diagnosis that he had a serious personality or sexual disorder or that he was sexually abused as a child, we doubt that any current scientific theory can come to terms adequately with the enormity of these murders.

Attributing Dahmer's crimes to "evil" or fundamental moral failure is no more satisfying an alternative, because one must still answer why moral failure would be manifest in this excessive way.

Jeffrey Dahmer is so frightening to us all not only because of what he did but also because of our inability to comprehend why he did it. Although Dahmer's acts seem beyond comprehension, a jury found that he was not insane during his crimes, and he was sentenced to life in prison.

all forms of criminality equally well; some explain very little criminality. Empirical data, rational analyses, moral values, and political ideologies all play a role in shaping preferences for the leading theories in criminology.

Theories of crime can be grouped into one of four categories: (1) *sociological*, (2) *biological*, (3) *psychological*, and (4) *sociopsychological*. What are the important distinctions among these four approaches?

Sociological theories explain crime as the result of social or cultural forces that are *external* to any specific individual, that exist *prior* to any criminal act, and that *emerge* from social-class, political, ecological, or physical structures affecting large groups of people (Nettler, 1974). Individual differences are deemphasized in favor of factors that put groups of people at risk for crime.

Sociological theories can be subdivided further into *subcultural* and *structural* explanations. (We describe a third type of sociological approach, *control theory*, under *sociopsychological theories*.) Structural theories emphasize that most people have similar interests but differ dramatically in opportunities to employ their talents in socially legitimate ways. Discrepancies between aspirations and means of attainment create strains on people that lead them to crime. Structuralists search for the disorganized social arrangements that thwart legitimate attainments and result in illegal conduct.

Subcultural theories hold that crime originates when various groups of people adhere to cultural values that are inconsistent with the dominant, general rules of society. In this view, crime is the product of subcultural deviation from the agreed-upon norms that underlie the criminal law.

Biological theories usually stress one of the following factors: genetic influence, chromosomal abnormalities, biochemical irregularities, or constitutional (body type) determinants. Biological theorists believe that biophysical factors predispose certain people to crime, but they usually retain a healthy respect for environmental and social influences.

Psychological theories emphasize the idea that crime results from personality attributes uniquely possessed, or possessed to a special degree, by the potential criminal. For example, there are several variations on the psychoanalytic theme that crime is the result of an immature ego and superego, which are too weak to control the sexual and aggressive instincts of the id. Other psychologists have tried to paint a psychological portrait of the "criminal type." Although personality researchers have found a number of traits that distinguish delinquent persons from nonoffenders, their methods do not allow us to conclude that the traits in question caused the crimes observed.

Sociopsychological theories (or *social process theories*; Nettler, 1974; Reid, 1976) bridge the gap between the broad environmentalism of sociology and the narrow individualism of psychological or biological theories. All sociopsychological theories are learning theories. They differ in their view of "what" is learned and "how" it is learned. *Control theory* assumes that people will behave antisocially unless they learn not to offend through a combination of inner controls and external constraints on their behavior. *Learning theory* stresses the ways individuals acquire specific criminal behaviors through different forms of learning.

SOCIOLOGICAL THEORIES OF CRIME

Structural Explanations

One key concept of structural approaches is the fundamental inequality we experience in opportunities to achieve the goals valued by society. Living in the United States instills in most of us aspirations for wealth, success, and education, as well as hopes to possess many material possessions. Not all of us can obtain these goals—at least through legally acceptable means. Some of us, because of our education, the affluence of our family, our abilities, or our good looks, have greater opportunities to achieve the goals that society prescribes. Those who are thwarted from reaching these goals through legitimate means may ultimately turn to illegal means to do so.

Differential opportunity is the basis of the structural theory of crime proposed by Cloward and Ohlin (1960) in their book *Delinquency and Opportunity*. This theory can be traced to Emile Durkheim's ideas about the functional necessity for moral bonds between individuals in society. Durkheim thought that life without moral obligations or social requirements would become intolerable and result in *anomie*, a feeling of normlessness that may precede destructive behaviors like suicide or crime. One implication of anomie theory was that unlimited aspirations produce a pressure for deviation from social norms.

Modern sociologists have given a more limited meaning to Durkheim's anomie, emphasizing the fact that society presents conflicting demands between its endorsed goals of conduct and the available means of achieving these goals. Merton (1968) applied *anomie* to situations in which the social structure stimulates common aspirations (e.g., wealth, property ownership) at the same time that it limits the means of acceptable attainment.

Cloward and Ohlin hypothesize that people in the working-class subculture usually want to succeed through legal means, but society denies them legitimate opportunities to succeed. Barriers include cultural and language differences, financial hardships, and limited access to the resources that are crucial for upward mobility. Poor people cannot, for example, afford advanced education. Also, the crowding in large cities makes class distinctions more apparent.

When legal means of goal achievement are blocked, intense frustration results, people cultivate illegal methods, and crime surfaces. Youthful crime, especially in gangs, is one example of this sequence.

The theory of differential opportunity assumes that persons who grow up in crowded ghettos with a different cultural background still possess the conventional goals of the middle class. Thus the crime that results from this discrepancy is a response to a structural strain; it is distinctive in its illegal means more than in its ends.

Gottfredson (1986) and Gordon (1986), a sociologist team, attempted to explain the higher crime rate of lower-class black youths by their less-than-satisfactory scholastic performance. Denied job opportunities because of their aptitude scores or grades, these youths discover that they can make $500 or $600 a week dealing crack cocaine. (In fact, with the advent of crack cocaine, arrests of juveniles in New York City, Detroit, Washington, DC, and other cities tripled between 1983 and 1987.)

The theory of differential opportunity has several limitations (Lilly, Cullen, & Ball, 1989, pp. 76–78). First, research indicates that seriously delinquent youths display many differences from their law-abiding counterparts in addition to differing educational opportunities. Second, there is no evidence that lower-class youth find their limited success in school more frustrating than middle-class youngsters. On the contrary, one might expect the exact opposite to be true (Nietzel, 1979). The assumption that lower-class juveniles characteristically aspire to middle-class membership is also unproved.

Furthermore, the major terms in the theory, such as *aspiration*, *frustration*, and *opportunity*, are defined too vaguely; the theory is not explicit about what determines the choice of adaptation to blocked opportunities by those who are deprived (Sheley, 1985).

Last, and most apparent, crimes are often committed by people who have never been denied opportunities. Think of Leona Helmsley's conviction for income tax fraud or Michael Milken, the highly successful Wall Street stockbroker convicted of fraudulent business practices. Another example is the fascinating case of "the Falcon and the Snowman"—two young men from the wealthy Los Angeles suburb of Palos Verdes, Christopher Boyce and Daulton Lee, who collaborated for two years in order to steal secrets about U.S. spy satellites and sell this information to the Soviet Union (Lindsey, 1979, 1983).

Albert Cohen's (1955) *Delinquent Boys: The Culture of the Gang* proposes a structural hypothesis that relates crime to social-class differences and social status. Cohen emphasizes the *reaction* of lower-class youths to the goals of the middle class; these goals, being unattainable, are ultimately repudiated through destructive, vandalistic crime. According to Cohen, lower-class youths are evaluated by the "middle class measuring rod" in institutions where the lower class must function (e.g., the schools). The schools, however, are operated by middle-class individuals who require lower-class youths to accept their standards.

The lower-class juvenile lacks the prior socialization necessary for successful middle-class achievement. Instead, he has been reared in an environment that values immediate gratification and physical aggression. Although he has been trained to endorse middle-class values, he is ill equipped to translate these aspirations into effective actions.

The frustration and lower self-esteem caused by these failures lead to a delinquent subculture in which the middle-class measuring rod is vigorously repudiated. Cohen explained delinquent subcultures using the psychoanalytic concept of *reaction formation*: the norms of the previously accepted middle-class orientation are defied by replacing them with their most offensive opposites. However, reaction formation involves only an apparent rejection; the delinquent youth still secretly desires what he openly repudiates.

Delinquent subcultures develop so that gang members can express their resentment and anger toward middle-class respectability. Their typical crimes are *negativistic* ("the delinquent's conduct is right, by the standards of his subculture, precisely because it is wrong by the norms of the larger culture"—Cohen, 1955; p. 28) and *malicious* ("enjoyment in the discomfiture of others, a delight in the defiance of taboos itself "—p. 27).

Cohen's theory agrees with differential opportunity theory that social stratification, and the accompanying loss of status for lower-class persons, causes crime. However, the two theories diverge on the type of crime that such conflict produces. Cohen describes crime that is nonutilitarian, gratuitous, and expressive rather than the "rational," utilitarian crime described by the differential opportunity theorist.

As with differential opportunity theory, empirical support for Cohen's theory is limited. The biggest weakness is the assumption that members of the lower class adhere to middle-class values. If social class is as powerful as sociologists urge, would it not be more reasonable to suppose that the socialization practices of the lower class would insulate its members against indoctrination into middle-class preferences? Also, Cohen's descriptions of typical gang-affiliated crime are not accurate (Kitsuse & Dietrick, 1959). Most lower-class delinquency has a functional quality to it. By contrast, middle-class crime often involves random destruction and vandalism. As with Cloward and Ohlin's theory, Cohen's description may be partially right about the wrong people.

One last, special form of structural theory involves what Nettler (1974) termed *rational crime*. Rational crime involves illegal behavior that "makes sense" because the person is rewarded for doing it, and it can be committed with a relatively low risk of detection. It is crime encouraged by some nearly irresistible "golden opportunity."

Nettler discusses four contexts in which rational crime occurs. First, there are situations where money or objects are easy targets for theft. Shoplifting, thefts by employees, and embezzlement are examples. Second, there are circumstances associated with otherwise legitimate work that "demand" certain crimes. Price fixing, fraud, and business crime are examples. Third, there is crime as a preferred livelihood. Included here are theft rings and "organized crime." The final example of rational crime is crime organized as a business. These activities involve the major products of organized crime: the illegal provision of liquor, drugs, prostitution, and gambling.

Rational crime shares similarities with other structural theories. It applies only to limited, albeit different, categories of offense. It also describes most crime as functional or useful. The major distinction is that, whereas most structuralists see crime as an understandable reaction to social disadvantage, the "rationalist" views crime as an understandable reaction to the advantages of particular social arrangements. We see two major limitations to "rational crime" theory. First, it does not explain repeated, violent crimes; second, it does not explain why, given the same "golden opportunities," some people offend while the majority do not.

Subcultural Explanations

The second type of sociological approach focuses on subcultural explanations and emphasizes the discrepancy in norms for different groups. The subcultural perspective holds that conflicts in norms cause criminal behavior when various ethnic or class groupings of people endorse subcultural norms that pressure people to deviate from the norms underlying the criminal law (Nietzel, 1979). Gangs, for example, enforce norms about how to behave. For some youths, the gang supplants their parents as the source of norms, even when the parents attempt to instill their own values.

This theme of cultural conflict is illustrated by Walter Miller's theory of "focal concerns." Miller attributes the criminal activities of lower-class adolescent gangs to their attempt to achieve the ends that are valued in their culture through the behaviors that they perceive as the most feasible means of obtaining those ends. Thus, adherence to the traditions of the lower class is essential. What are these characteristics? Miller (1958) labels them as trouble, toughness, smartness, excitement, fate, and autonomy. For example, lower-class boys pick fights to show their toughness, and they steal to demonstrate their shrewdness and daring (Sheley, 1985). Hundreds of gang-related murders occur in Los Angeles each year; many are committed to demonstrate adherence to gang values. Table 5-1 summarizes the six focal qualities that are important to gang members and then distinguishes between what the gangs consider to be desirable and undesirable alternatives.

The theory of focal concerns does not explain crime by individuals who are not socially disadvantaged, such as the rich hotel owner or the television evangelist. Here again, key concepts are vague. How do cultural standards originate? How are they transmitted from generation to generation? And how do they control the behavior of any one individual? The most troublesome concept is the central one, subculture. Some critics reject the assumption of major value differences among groups.

Other social scientists (Elliott, 1988) question whether social class and urban living are strongly related to crime by youths. Based on self-reports by youths over a ten-year period, Elliott's study found very small differences in the delinquency rates with respect to race and social class. Elliott also found little difference

Table 5-1 Miller's "Focal Concerns" of Lower-Class Culture

Area	Perceived alternatives	
1. Trouble	Law-abiding behavior	Law-violating behavior
2. Toughness	Physical prowess; skill; "masculinity"; fearlessness; bravery; daring	Weakness; ineptitude; effeminacy; timidity; cowardice; caution
3. Smartness	Ability to outsmart, dupe, "con"; gain (of money) through "wits"; shrewdness; adroitness in repartee	Gullibility, "conability"; gain (of money) through hard work; slowness, dull-wittedness; verbal maladroitness
4. Excitement	Thrill; risk; danger; change; activity	Boredom; "deadness"; safeness; sameness; passivitiy
5. Fate	Perception as favored by fortune or as being "lucky"	Perception as ill-omened or as being "unlucky"
6. Autonomy	Freedom from external constraint; freedom from superordinate authority; independence	Presence of external constraint; presence of strong authority; dependency; state of being "cared for"

Adapted from Miller (1958).

between rural and urban young men with respect to self-reported criminal behavior. Although crimes in rural areas are less likely to be reported to the police, rural youths claim to have committed almost as many crimes as urban young men (Rensberger, 1988).

BIOLOGICAL THEORIES OF CRIME

Biological theories of crime search for genetic deficiencies, physiological excess, or constitutional deficits that predispose people to criminal behavior. This disposition is then translated into specific criminal behavior through environments and social interactions spanning a long period of time.

Historical Background

The early positivists advocated biological theories, particularly Lombroso with his concept of *atavism*, which held that the criminal was a congenital throwback to a primitive, savage type of man. Another neo-Lombrosian view of crime was developed by the Harvard anthropologist Ernest A. Hooton in his controversial volume *Crime and the Man* (1939). Hooton sought to discover anatomical distinctions among different types of criminals and between criminals and "civilians" (his noncriminal controls). Physical measures were taken on more than 17,000 persons, approximately 14,000 criminals and more than 3000 civilians.

It should come as no surprise that Hooton discovered a multitude of physical differences between these groups. Burglars were found to possess short heads, golden hair, and undershot jaws. Robbers were conspicuous by their long wavy hair, high heads, short ears, and broad faces. Sex offenders "include among the rapists no few of full-bodied and probably over-sexed ruffians, but also, and especially in the other sex category, a majority of shrivelled runts, perverted in body as in mind, and manifesting the drooling lasciviousness of senile decay" (Hooton, 1939, p. 374).

Hooton's theory has not weathered well the criticisms of modern behavioral scientists. The major objections have centered on the inadequacies and biases of his sampling procedures.

Constitutional Theories

William A. Sheldon, both a psychologist and a physician, posited a somatic typology composed of three dimensions of physique and their corresponding temperaments (Sheldon, 1942, 1949). Sheldon described three somatotypes, or body builds: the *endomorph,* who tended to be obese, soft, and rounded, the *mesomorph,* who was muscular, athletic, and strong; and the *ectomorph,* who was tall and thin but had a well-developed brain. According to Sheldon, endomorphs were fun loving, sociable, and jolly. Ectomorphs were introverted, sensitive, and nervous. Mesomorphs were assertive, vigorous, and bold.

Based on his comparative analysis of 200 delinquent men and 200 nondelinquent men, Sheldon proposed that the mesomorph was best suited for criminal behavior. He thought the mesomorph's aggressiveness, along with a lack of inhibitory controls, produced a prime candidate for criminality. Sheldon did not believe that all mesomorphs became criminals; neither did he believe that environment was unimportant. However, he was convinced that physical variables were being neglected in most attempts to explain crime.

Today, Sheldon's ideas are largely ignored or ridiculed. His sampling methods were faulty, and his definition of delinquency was too vague. The most common objection is that Sheldon's somatotypes were little more than stereotypes, not deserving of serious scientific attention.

However, the search for constitutional predispositions to delinquency has persisted. In their classic study *Unravelling Juvenile Delinquency* (1950), Eleanor and Sheldon Glueck compared 500 chronic delinquents with 500 nondelinquents. The two samples were matched on a host of demographic variables (Glueck & Glueck, 1950, 1956). Using Sheldon's classification scheme, plus a fourth typol-

ogy they called *balanced,* the Gluecks claimed that significantly more delinquent than nondelinquent youths were mesomorphic. However, a substantial percentage of delinquents were not mesomorphic. In interpreting these data, the Gluecks suggested: "It is quite apparent that physique alone does not adequately explain delinquent behavior; it is nonetheless clear that, in conjunction with other forces, it does bear a relationship to delinquency" (Glueck & Glueck, 1956, p. 246).

Another attempt to include constitutional factors with sociocultural variables was Juan Cortes's *Delinquency and Crime* (1972). Using his own method of somatotyping a sample that included 100 delinquents, 100 nondelinquents, and 20 convicted felons, Cortes discovered significant relationships among delinquency, predominant mesomorphy, and self-evaluated traits of personality, such as need for achievement, risk taking, and extraversion. Cortes was not convinced that a mesomorphic condition was a necessary or sufficient cause of crime, but he believed that constitutional influences should not be overlooked in explaining criminal behavior.

In summary, typologies have several limitations. When we use a few all-or-none categories, we force on nature an oversimplified scheme. Even if an individual can be accurately described as an introvert or an aggressive type, such a description is inadequate. First, it ignores hundreds of other attributes of the individual that could be used in categorizing that person. Second, it assumes that two individuals tossed into the same psychological pot have the same attributes. Almost always, we find that explanations are not a matter of black or white; they are a question of shadings.

When physique is proposed as the direct cause of criminal behavior, further problems emerge. Even if there is a correlation between the two, it does not necessarily mean that one causes the other. It is quite likely that, as children, males with a mesomorphic physique were more likely to find that aggressive ways of demanding what they wanted were the ways that "worked." Having been rewarded for this bullying, they persist as adults in terrorizing their peers (see Box 5-2). Thus, it may be that a social-learning-theory explanation (to be described later in this chapter), rather than a constitutional one, is most appropriate for the findings of the Gluecks and William Sheldon.

Genetic Theories

All sorts of conditions, good and bad, have been attributed to a person's biological inheritance. So it is with criminals who are thought to suffer a hereditary taint that either singly, or in collaboration with a pernicious environment, produces antisocial behavior.

The earliest methodology for studying genetic contributions to criminality was the *genealogy*, or study of family lines. This method requires completing a record that traces the ancestry of an individual or charts the descent of various offspring from one common ancestor (see Box 5-3). Two famous genealogies in criminology are Henry Goddard's study (1916) of the fictitiously named Kallilak family and Richard Dugdale's (1877) examination of the Jukes. Both families were cursed by a large progeny of scoundrels, leading the investigators to suspect the influence of heredity. This suspicion was particularly strong for Goddard, who believed that "feeblemindedness" could be inherited and was associated 50% of the time with eventual criminality. The genealogical method suffers from several limitations, the major one being that the method does not permit an unambiguous conclusion about what the

---

Box 5-2 | Once a Bully, Always a Bully?

A longitudinal study (Huesmann, Eron, & Yarmel, 1987) carried out over a 22-year period followed 870 children from Columbia County, New York, from the ages of 8 to 30. At age 8, the incipient male bully was seen by other children as starting fights over nothing, being quick to anger, and taking things without asking (Goleman, 1987). He was often a social outcast and disliked school, expressing his defiance through tardiness and truancy. By age 19, he was likely to have dropped out of school. At that point, he was

three times more likely than others to have been in trouble with the law (Goleman, 1987). At age 30, his wife saw him as aggressive, even abusive. His run-ins with the law ranged from drunken driving to crimes of violence. As a parent, he was uncaring and punitive; his children tended to follow his own earlier pattern of being a bully (Goleman, 1987). Likewise, females who were aggressors as children were more likely to severely punish their own children.

In fact, the bully's characteristics can be traced over three gener-

ations (Huesmann et al., 1987). The parents of incipient bullies discipline them severely; when the younger generation become parents, their children, too, tend to be troublemakers, even in elementary school.

Eron and his associates found that bullies did not have lower IQ scores than other children, but as teenagers and adults they performed below their expected level on achievement tests and often held jobs below their level of abilities.

family transmits—genetic predisposition, psychosocial characteristics, or both.

In the *twin study* the researcher compares the *concordance rate* (the percentage of twin pairs sharing the behavior of interest) for *monozygotic twins* (genetically identical twins) and *dizygotic twins* (commonly called fraternal twins, who share 50% of the same genetic material). If the monozygotic concordance rate is significantly higher, the investigator concludes that the behavior in question is genetically influenced, because monozygotic twins are genetically identical but dizygotic pairs are not. This method assumes that environmental differences for any pair of twins are equivalent for the two types of twins, an assumption that may not always be accurate. Finally, the discovery of any *discordant monozygotic twins* indicates that some nongenetic factor influences the behavior being studied.

The first twin study of crime was conducted in Germany by Johannes Lange (1929). Lange obtained data on 13 monozygotic and 17 dizygotic pairs. In each twin pair, one member, the twin first studied, had been imprisoned. The criminality concordance rate for the monozygotic twins was 77%, compared to the dizygotic rate of 12%, leading Lange to conclude that inherited tendencies play a "preponderant part" in causing crime.

Kranz (1936) obtained 32 monozygotic, 43 same-sex dizygotic, and 50 opposite-sex dizygotic twins. The concordance rate for a criminal record was 66% for monozygotics, 54% for dizygotics of the same sex, and 14% for opposite-sex dizygotics. The difference between the identical and same-sex fraternal twins was not statistically significant. Rosenthal (1970) interprets the substantial difference between same-sex and opposite-sex dizygotic twins as evidence "that environmental factors are of overriding importance with respect to the legal criterion of

---

Box 5-3 | *All in the Family*

Effie Ramsey has ten sons, but she doesn't see any of them very often. Nine are in prison or in jail; the tenth is in a halfway house for law violators. At the time of this writing, the sons range in age from the mid-twenties to the early forties; all have done time in prison. Most of their crimes were of moderate severity, like robbery and burglary, but recently two of them were charged with the first-degree murder of a Kansas City couple. The sons average four criminal convictions each.

Authorities don't know exactly where the family went wrong. They were poor but always had food. Unlike many inner-city children, the ten brothers were raised by both parents living together. In fact, one or the other of the parents participated at almost all of their sons' hearings in juvenile court; they made sure that the boys attended juvenile court counseling sessions. Their mother was cooperative with the police and often helped locate her sons when they were wanted by law officers. But

authorities said that the parents did not supervise their children and that the sons lacked role models. Once the older brothers turned to crime, the others followed. Despite the statistical improbability that ten out of ten siblings would be lawbreakers, the simplistic explanation—that they had each inherited criminal tendencies from their parents—is less likely than an explanation using social-learning theory.

Adapted from Kraske and Kaut (1989).

Table 5-2 Relationship of Criminality between Biological and Adoptive Parents and Their Sons

	Are biological parents criminal?	
	Yes	No
Are adoptive parents criminal?		
Yes	24.5% (of 143)	14.7% (of 204)
No	20.0% (of 1226)	13.5% (of 2492)

From Mednick, Gabrielli, and Hutchings (1984). The number in parentheses is the total number of adopted males for each cell.

whether or not one obtains a criminal record" (p. 134).

Christiansen (1977a) obtained data on a national sample of twins born during a specific time period. Based on a sample of 3586 pairs of twins born in Denmark, Christiansen first identified persons with criminal convictions. He found that 50% of the monozygotic twins were concordant for criminal behavior compared to 21% of same-sex dizygotic twins.

After reviewing twin studies conducted over four decades in Germany, Holland, the United States, Japan, Finland, and Norway, Christiansen (1977b) concluded that the concordance rates for crime between monozygotic twins hovered around 69%, whereas for dizygotic twins the concordance rate averaged 33% (see also Wilson & Herrnstein, 1985).

Another effective strategy for separating genetic from sociocultural influences, both of which are transmitted within families, is the *adoption study*, in which the adopted offspring of parents with a disorder are compared to their biological and adoptive parents or to the adopted offspring of parents without the disorder. For example, Schulsinger (1972) compared the records of biological relatives of adoptees diagnosed as psychopathic with the diagnoses of the adoptive relatives and members of the adoptive families. A greater proportion of biological relatives than of either of the two adop-

tive-relative groups were diagnosed with psychopathic characteristics.

The largest adoption study of criminality was conducted in Denmark on 14,427 adoptees and their biological and adoptive parents (Mednick, Gabrielli, & Hutchings, 1984). Table 5-2 summarizes data for adopted boys having different combinations of criminal and noncriminal biological and adoptive parents. As shown, when neither set of parents had a conviction, 13.5% of their sons had been convicted of a crime. When the adoptive parents had a conviction but the biological parents did not, 14.7% of the sons were criminal. Twenty percent of the boys had been convicted if their biological parents had been convicted but their adoptive parents had not. If both sets of parents had a conviction, the criminality in the sons increased to 24.5%. In addition, biological parents who were chronic offenders (three or more convictions) were three times more likely to have sons who were also criminal than were biological parents with no convictions.

The bulk of the evidence suggests that genetic factors exert some influence on criminal behavior (DiLalla & Gottesman, 1991). How large an influence is not yet clear, but it is enough to require our attention. Any decision that crime is even partially determined by genetic factors still begs the obvious question: what, exactly, is inherited? There is a lengthy list of likely candidates (Moffitt & Mednick, 1988), but five possibilities are usually emphasized.

1. *Constitutional predisposition.* The data are inconclusive about this factor and do not carry us much beyond the obvious intuition that strong, athletic, muscular youths are bigger bullies than their portly or puny peers.

2. *Cortical abnormalities.* High rates of abnormal electroencephalogram (EEG) patterns have been reported in prison populations and in violent juvenile delinquents and may be related to crime through the association of EEG irregularities with poor impulse control and impaired judgment. Unfortunately, in the general population, a high percentage of persons have EEG abnormalities, thus limiting the diagnostic utility of the EEG. Further, some studies have not found a significant relationship between EEG pathology and delinquent behavior (Loomis, 1965).

3. *Intellectual deficit.* Offenders' IQs are about 8–10 points lower than those of non-offenders. This difference is mainly in verbal (as opposed to performance) IQ scores, which implies that offenders are less able to (1) postpone impulsive actions and replace them with better-planned alternatives and/or (2) achieve academic success as a route to socially approved attainments (Binder, 1988). A frequent criticism of these findings is that the IQ of incarcerated delinquents is not representative of delinquents at large. However, recent data indicate that, regardless of whether they are incarcerated or not, delinquent youths perform more poorly on IQ measures than their nondelinquent peers but do not differ among themselves (Moffitt & Silva, 1988).

4. *Autonomic nervous system differences.* The autonomic nervous system (ANS) carries information between the brain and all organs of the body. Because of these connections, emotions are associated with changes in the ANS. If fact, we can "see" the effects of emotional arousal on such ANS responses as heart rate, skin conductance, respiration, and blood pressure.

Criminals appear to differ from noncriminals in their physiological responsiveness to stimulation (Mednick & Christiansen, 1977). These differences, which might also involve hormonal irregularities (Olweus, 1987), could cause some criminals to have difficulties in learning how to inhibit behavior that is likely to lead to punishment. These difficulties in conditioning are considered an important predisposing factor by some sociopsychological theorists (discussed at the end of the chapter).

5. *Physiological differences.* A number of physiological factors might lead to increased aggressiveness and delinquency. Among the variables receiving current attention are (1) high levels of testosterone, (2) increased secretion of insulin, and (3) lower levels of certain metabolites of serotonin (DiLalla & Gottesman, 1991).

PSYCHOLOGICAL THEORIES OF CRIME

Psychological explanations of crime emphasize individual differences in the way people think or feel about their behavior. These differences can be subtle influences that make some people more prone to criminal conduct. Or they can be more extreme disturbances that involve major psychological dysfunction and/or personality disorders.

Psychoanalytic Explanations

Psychoanalysts assume that crime results from personality disturbance in which the ego and superego cannot restrain the antisocial instincts of the id. Although the unique history of the individual should reveal the specific factors that produced a defective superego, the most common factor is faulty identification by a child with his or her parents.

Freud believed that the criminal suffers from a compulsive need for punishment to alleviate guilt feelings stemming from the unconscious, incestuous feelings of the Oedipal period. "In many criminals, especially youthful ones, it is possible to detect a very powerful sense of guilt which existed before the crime, and is therefore not its result but its motive. It is as if it was a relief to be able to fasten this unconscious sense of guilt onto something real and immediate" (Freud, 1961, p. 52).

Franz Alexander (e.g., Alexander & Healy, 1935) believed that the criminal cannot postpone immediate gratification in order to obtain greater rewards in the future. The criminal does not orient his behavior with the *reality principle*, which is a basic lesson to be learned during the anal stage of development. Alexander regarded the antisocial activities of the adult as exaggerated anal characteristics acquired in childhood. In addition to these tendencies, Alexander thought family and general social forces also contributed to criminality. In *Roots of Crime*, written with William Healy in 1935, Alexander argued that "criminal acts are not always committed by certain individuals who can be defined and characterized psychologically or in terms of personality as specifically inclined to crime, but neither are criminal acts restricted to certain social groups which can be characterized and defined sociologically . . . both personality and sociological factors are active at the same time; either of them may be predominant in one case, negligible in another . . . " (p. 273).

Other psychoanalysts have suggested that criminal behavior is a means of obtaining substitute gratification of basic needs such as love, nurturance, and attention, which should have been satisfied normally within the family. The late John Bowlby's work (1949, 1953; Bowlby & Salter-Ainsworth, 1965) holds that "maternal separateness and parental rejection are believed together to account for a majority of the more intractable cases (of delinquency) including the 'constitutional psychopath' and the 'moral defectives' " (Bowlby, 1949, p. 37).

Psychoanalytic theories often trap their adherents in tautological circles. Antisocial instincts may simply be alternative names for the behaviors they are intended to explain. Psychoanalytic interpretations of crime also differ vastly from patterns of real criminal conduct. Freud's idea that the criminal commits crimes in order to be caught and punished ignores the obvious extremes to which most offenders go to avoid detection of their wrongdoings. Most offenders do not appear frustrated or guilt ridden by the fact that their "crimes pay" at least some of the time. In fact, the success of their crimes seems to be a major gratification in their lives. Finally, psychoanalytic descriptions are at odds with the observation that many forms of crime are more calculated than compulsed, more orchestrated than overdetermined, and more devised than driven.

Criminal Thinking Patterns

In a controversial theory spawned from their frustration with traditional explanations of criminality, Samuel Yochelson and Stanton E. Samenow (1976; Samenow, 1984) propose that criminals possess a different way of thinking; that is, the thinking of criminals, though internally logical and consistent, is erroneous and irresponsible. Consistent lawbreakers see themselves and the world differently than the rest of us do.

Yochelson and Samenow reject sociological and environmental explanations of criminality, such as a broken home or unemployment. Rather, they propose, criminals become criminals as a result of choices they start making at an early age. These patterns, coupled with a pervasive sense of irresponsibility, mold lives of crimes that are extremely difficult to change.

Yochelson and Samenow described the criminals they studied as very much in control of their own actions, rather than as victims of the environment or as "sick." These criminals were portrayed as master manipulators who assign the blame for their own behavior to others. They are such inveterate liars that they can no longer separate fact from fiction. They use words to control and manipulate, not to represent reality.

These psychiatrists based their conclusions on intensive interviews with a small number of offenders, most of whom were incarcerated "hardcore" criminals or men who were hospitalized after having been acquitted of major crimes by reason of insanity. No control groups of any sort were studied. Yochelson and Samenow have portrayed one type of criminal, but their analysis does not accurately represent the majority of lawbreakers in our society. Furthermore, the "criminal thinking pattern" theory does not explain how these choices are made in the beginning (Pfohl, 1985), although Samenow's more recent book, published in 1984, hints at genetic predispositions to crime. In fact, in some ways this theory is similar to the notion of the psychopathic personality, which we turn to next.

Personality Defect as an Explanation of Criminality

Many laypersons attribute the cause of crime to a personality defect in the offender. This explanation forms the basis for theories that posit a basic antisocial or psychopathic nature to the criminal. The concept of *psychopathy* has a long history; generally it refers to persons who have frequent and repetitive criminal activity. More recently, the focus has been on the underlying unsocialized character, the lack of conscience,

that brings such persons into repeated conflict with society, often from very early ages. They are superficial, arrogant, and unable to learn from experience or to feel guilt; they lack empathy and loyalty to individuals, groups, or society's values (Hare, Hart, & Harpur, 1991). They are grossly selfish, callous, and irresponsible; they tend to blame others or to offer plausible rationalizations for their behavior.

The official diagnostic designation for the psychopath is *Antisocial Personality Disorder*. About 80% of psychopaths are men (Goleman, 1987). The person described as a psychopathic personality is easy to identify but difficult to rehabilitate. Fortunately, psychopaths account for a small percentage of lawbreakers. However, they commit a disproportionately large percentage of violent crimes (McCord, 1982), and their acts often garner massive publicity (see Box 5-4).

There are a multitude of theories about the causes of psychopathic behavior. One view is that psychopathic persons suffer a cortical immaturity that makes it difficult for them to inhibit behavior. Robert Hare (Hare & McPherson, 1984) has proposed that psychopaths may have a deficiency in the left hemisphere of their brains that impairs their ability to plan and regulate behavior carefully.

Psychopathic persons are also thought to have a reduced anxiety level and to be relatively underaroused in the resting state as well. This combination of low cortical and autonomic arousal results in a high need for stimulation. Consequently, the psychopath prefers novel situations and tends to "shorten" stimuli, thereby being less controlled by them. Quay (1965) has advanced a *stimulation-seeking* theory positing that the thrill-seeking and disruptive behavior of the psychopath serves to increase sensory input and arousal to a more tolerable level.

One result of this thrill seeking is that the psychopathic person may be "immune" to many social cues that govern behavior. Eysenck

(1964) proposed a theory that emphasizes the slower rate of classical conditioning for persons classified as psychopaths: because socialization and conscience development depend on acquiring classically conditioned fear and avoidance responses, psychopathic individuals' conditioning deficiencies may account for their difficulties in normal socialization.

Another popular explanation for psychopathy involves familial disturbance, especially parental rejection and parental absence brought about by divorce or separation. Buss (1966) identified two parental patterns that might foster psychopathy. First, there are parents who are cold and distant. The child who imitates these parents develops a cold, detached interpersonal style that gives the superficial appearance of social involvement but lacks the empathy required for stable, satisfying relationships. Second, there are parents who are inconsistent in their use of rewards and punishments, making it difficult for the child to imitate a stable role model and to develop a consistent self-identity. Buss felt that a child in this situation learns how to avoid blame and punishment, rather than how to distinguish right and wrong behavior.

The major drawback of psychopathy as an explanation of crime is that it describes only a small percentage of offenders. It might be tempting to classify most offenders as psycho-

---

Box 5-4 | Ted Bundy—Why?

Born in 1946, Theodore Robert Bundy seemed destined for a charmed life; he was intelligent, attractive, and articulate (Holmes & DeBurger, 1988). A Boy Scout as a youth and then an honor student and a psychology major at the University of Washington, he was at one time a work-study student at the Seattle Crisis Clinic. Later he became assistant to the chairman of the Washington State Republican Party. It was probably about this time that he claimed his first victim: a college-age woman who was viciously attacked while sleeping and left alive but brain damaged. During the years from 1974 through 1978, Bundy stalked, attacked, killed, and then sexually assaulted as many as 36 victims in Washington, Oregon, Utah, Colorado, and Florida. Apparently

Ted Bundy

some of the women were distracted when the good-looking, casual Bundy approached, seeming helpless because of being on crutches or with an apparent broken arm. He usually choked his victims to death and then sexually abused and mutilated them before disposing of their bodies in remote areas (Nordheimer, 1989).

It is characteristic of the psychopathic personality or sociopath to maintain a facade of charm, so that acquaintances will describe him (as they did Bundy) as "fascinating," "charismatic," and "compassionate." At his trial for the murder of two Chi Omega sorority sisters in their bedrooms at Florida State University, he served as his own attorney (Bundy had attended two law schools). But he was convicted; he was also found guilty of the kidnapping, murder, and mutilation of a Lake City, Florida, girl who was 12 years old.

Bundy was sentenced to death. Shortly before he was executed on January 24, 1989, Bundy gave a television interview to California evangelist James Dobson in which he attributed the cause of his problems to pornography. He said:

paths and feel content that their crimes had now been explained. But, in fact, most offenders are not psychopathic. We must look to other factors to account for their illegal behavior.

SOCIAL-PSYCHOLOGICAL THEORIES OF CRIME

Social-psychological explanations view criminality as being learned through social interaction. (Sometimes these formulations are called "social process" theories, in order to draw attention to the processes by which an individual becomes a criminal.) Social-psychological theories are of two categories: control theories and direct learning theories.

Control Theories

Control theories assume that people will behave antisocially unless they are trained not to (Conger, 1980). Some people never form bonds with significant others, so necessary controls over antisocial behavior are never internalized. For example, Hirschi's (1969, 1978) model stresses four control variables, each of which represents a major social bond: (1) attachment,

"Those of us who are . . . so much influenced by violence in the media, in particular pornographic violence, are not some kind of inherent monsters. We are your husbands, and we grew up in regular families" (quoted by Lamar, 1989, p. 34). Bundy claimed that he spent his formative years with a grandfather who had an insatiable craving for pornography.

He told Dr. Dobson: "People will accuse me of being self-serving but I am just telling you how I feel. Through God's help, I have been able to come to the point where I, much too late, but better late than never, feel the hurt and the pain that I am responsible for" (quoted by Kleinberg, 1989, p. 5A).

The tape of Bundy's last interview, produced by Dobson and titled "Fatal Addiction," has been widely disseminated, especially by those who seek to eliminate all pornography. (Dr. Dobson served on a federal pornography commission during the Reagan administration.) But Bundy's claim that pornography was the "fuel for his fantasies" has been received skeptically by others, who saw it as one last manipulative ploy to gain further time. Even his mother stated that no evidence existed in her son's first 28 years (before he became a murder suspect for the first time) that hinted at any aberrant behavior (Nordheimer, 1989). In none of his previous interviews, including extensive conversations in 1986 with Dorothy Lewis, a psychiatrist he had come to trust, did he ever cite "a pornographic preamble to his grotesqueries" (Nobile, 1989, p. 41). Bundy had decided at that time that he needed psychiatric testimony in order to escape the electric chair—that is, he wanted to be diagnosed as not competent to stand trial because he was too confused and irrational to assist in his own murder defense. Despite Dr. Lewis's testimony in 1986, the judge would not declare Bundy incompetent. Thus, perhaps at that time he decided to portray himself as a normal youth who had been corrupted by pornography (Nobile, 1989).

According to psychiatrist Park Dietz, most serial sex killers have two distinct qualities: sexual sadism and psychopathy, or the lack of normal inhibitions about acting on their desires (quoted by Nobile, 1989). This classification seems a succinct summary of Ted Bundy.

(2) commitment, (3) involvement, and (4) belief. Young people are bonded to society at several levels; they differ in (1) the degree to which they are affected by the opinions and expectations of others, (2) the payoffs they receive for conventional behavior, and (3) the extent to which they subscribe to the prevailing norms.

Another example is Walter Reckless's (1961, 1967) containment theory. Reckless proposes that it is largely external containment—that is, social pressure—that controls crime. If a society is well integrated, with well-defined social roles and limits on behavior, effective family discipline and supervision, and reinforcement for positive accomplishments, crime will be contained. But if these external controls weaken or disappear, control of crime will depend on internal restraints, or the individual's superego. Thus a positive self-concept becomes an insulator against delinquency. Strong inner containment is inferred from the abilities to tolerate frustration, to be goal directed, to resist distractions, and to find substitute satisfactions (Reckless, 1967).

Containment theory is a good "in-between" view, neither rigidly environmental nor entirely intrapersonal. Containment can account both for the law-abiding individual in a high-crime environment and for the law violator from a low-crime background. But containment theory explains only a part of criminal behavior, as even its own advocates (such as Hirschi, 1969) admit. It does not apply to crimes within groups organized around a commitment to deviant behavior.

The British psychologist Hans Eysenck believes "heredity plays an important, and possibly a vital part, in predisposing a given individual to crime" (Eysenck, 1964, p. 55). Socialization practices then translate these innate tendencies into criminal acts.

Socialization depends on two kinds of learning: operant learning and classical conditioning. In *operant learning*, behavior is acquired and maintained by its consequences: responses followed by rewards are strengthened, whereas responses followed by aversive events are weakened. An important principle of operant conditioning is that immediate consequences are more influential than delayed consequences. However, according to Eysenck (1964, p. 101), in the real world the negative effects of punishment are usually "long delayed and uncertain (while) the acquisition of the desired object is immediate; therefore, although the acquisition and the pleasure derived from it may, on the whole, be less than the pain derived from the incarceration which ultimately follows, the time element very much favors the acquisition as compared with the deterrent effects of the incarceration."

Because of punishment's ineffectiveness, restraint of antisocial behavior depends on a second element, the conscience, whose development comes from *classical conditioning*. Eysenck believed that conscience is conditioned through close pairings of a child's undesirable behaviors with the prompt punishment of these behaviors. The taboo act is the *conditioned stimulus*, which, when associated frequently enough with the *unconditioned stimulus* of punishment, will produce an unpleasant physiological and emotional response. Conscience becomes an inner control that deters wrongdoing through the emotions of anxiety and guilt.

Whether conditioning builds a strong conscience depends on the strength of the autonomic nervous system. Eysenck believes there are large individual differences in this area. In some people, conditioned responses develop slowly and extinguish quickly. In others, conditioning progresses rapidly and produces strong resistance to extinction.

Underlying these differences are three major dimensions of Eysenck's personality theory: *extraversion, neuroticism,* and *psychoticism* (Eysenck & Gudjonsson, 1989). Extraverted people are outgoing, active, aggressive, and impulsive. Persons high in neuroticism are restless, emotionally volatile, and hypersensitive. Persons high in psychoticism are troublesome, lacking in empathy, and insensitive to the point of cruelty.

Extraversion, neuroticism, and psychoticism are also associated with important physiological differences, some of which we discussed in the section on psychopathy. High extraverts have low levels of cortical arousal, slowing their ability to be conditioned and also causing those responses that are conditioned to be extinguished easily. Conditioning is also impaired because physiological arousal dissipates more slowly in extraverted people and in persons classified as psychopaths. As a result, avoiding a previously punished act may be less reinforcing for such people because they experience less reduction in fear following their avoidance of the taboo behavior.

Persons high in neuroticism have a reactive autonomic nervous system and react excessively to stimuli. Therefore, high neuroticism interferes with efficient learning because of the irrelevant arousal that is evoked. In addition, high neuroticism leads to greater drive to carry out behavior of all sorts, including crimes.

Eysenck believed that high scores on extraversion and neuroticism would result in poor conditioning and, consequently, inadequate socialization. Poor conditioning leads to a faulty conscience, which in turn produces a higher risk for criminality. Additionally, if the person is high on psychoticism, he or she would tend to be more of a primary "tough-minded" psychopath.

The data on the relationships of extraversion, neuroticism, and psychoticism to criminality support a positive association between elevated extraversion and increased lawbreaking. However, the association between neuroticism and psychopathy is less clear; in fact, neuroticism may actually be lower in most psychopaths than in normal controls (Doren, 1987).

Another problem is that Eysenck has not clearly separated a different predisposition to be conditioned from the different conditioning opportunities that children experience. Genetic differences will be accompanied by different conditioning histories. A family of extraverts may transmit a potential for crime not only through inherited personality qualities but also through laissez-faire discipline whereby conditioning is too infrequent or inconsistent to be effective.

Learning Theories

Learning theory focuses on the ways in which criminal behavior is learned. One example is Edwin H. Sutherland's (1947) differential association approach. According to this theory, criminal behavior requires socialization into a system of values conducive to violating the law; thus the potential criminal learns "definitions" that are favorable to deviant behavior. If these definitions of criminal acts as acceptable are stronger and more frequent than the definitions unfavorable to deviant behavior, then the person is likely to commit a criminal act. Sutherland suggested that the difference between those who break the law and those who don't "lies not in their personal fiber but in the content of what they have learned" (Lilly et al., 1989, p. 58). For example, all of us value money; but some of us acquire it legally, others illegally. What is relevant is the values we place on specific behaviors by which to obtain money (Sheley, 1985). But these definitions need group support; crime will not persist in the absence of a "subculture of violence."

It is not necessary to associate with criminals directly. Children might learn procriminal definitions from middle-class parents, by watching their father pocket too much change or hearing their mother brag about exceeding the speed limit. Box 5-5 lists nine postulates of the differential association approach.

Differential association has survived because

of its broad scope and its ability to organize many research findings (Cressey, 1979). Furthermore, the theory is useful because it attempts to explain crime in places where it would not, on first blush, be expected—for example, among lawbreakers who grew up in affluent environments and who were granted their material wants. But it has difficulty explaining crimes of passion or impulsive violence. One reason is that "excess of definitions" is difficult to operationalize. Second, the theory does not explain why certain individuals, even within the same family, have the different associations they do—why are some people more likely than others to form criminal associations?

Social-Learning Theory

Although social-learning theory acknowledges the importance of differential reinforcement for developing new behaviors, it stresses cognitive factors and observational or *vicarious learning*. Albert Bandura (1986) claims that "most human behavior is learned by observation through modeling" (p. 47). Learning through modeling is more efficient than learning through differential reinforcement. Observation of competent models eliminates the hazards of unguided trial-and-error behavior. Sophisticated behaviors such as speech and complex chains of behavior such as driving a car require models. In all likelihood, so does crime.

Observational learning depends on: (1) *attention* to the important features of modeled behavior, (2) *retention* of these features in memory so that they guide later performance, (3) *reproduction* of the observed behaviors, and (4) *reinforcement* of attempted behaviors, which determines to a great extent whether they will be performed again.

The most prominent attempt to apply social-learning theory to criminal behavior is

---

Box **5-5** | *Postulates of the Differential Association Theory*

1. Criminal behavior is learned.
2. Criminal behavior is learned in interaction with other persons in a process of communication.
3. The influential aspect of the learning of criminal behavior occurs within intimate social groups.
4. When criminal behavior is learned, the learning includes (a) techniques of committing the crime, which are sometimes very complicated, sometimes very simple, and (b) the specific direction of motives, drives, rationalizations, and attitudes.
5. The specific direction of motives and drives is learned from definitions of the legal code as favorable or unfavorable.
6. A person becomes delinquent because of an excess of definitions favorable to violation of law over definitions unfavorable to violation of law.
7. Differential associations may vary in frequency, duration, intensity, and priority.
8. The process of learning criminal behavior by association with criminal and anticriminal patterns involves all the mechanisms that are involved in any other learning.
9. Although criminal behavior is an expression of general needs and values, it is not explained by those general needs and values, since noncriminal behavior is an expression of the same needs and values.

Adapted from Sutherland and Cressey (1974).

Bandura's (1973) book *Aggression: A Social Learning Analysis*. An abbreviated version of this theory is provided in Ribes-Inesta and Bandura (1976; see also Platt & Prout, 1987). The theory emphasizes modeling of aggression in three social contexts.

1. *Familial influences*. Familial aggression can assume many forms, from child abuse at one extreme to aggressive parental attitudes and language at the other. It is in the arena of discipline, however, where children are most exposed to frequent, vivid examples of coercion and aggression as a preferred style for resolving conflicts and asserting desires.

2. *Subcultural influences*. Some subcultures provide a rich schedule of aggression as well as rewards for their most combative members. "The highest rates of aggressive behavior are found in environments where aggressive models abound and where aggressiveness is regarded as a highly valued attribute" (Bandura, 1976, p. 207).

3. *Symbolic models*. The major influence of symbolic models on aggression has been attributed to the mass media, particularly television. A large number of studies have investigated the effects of televised violence on viewers, especially children. Interpretations of this literature vary as to whether viewing televised violence causes later aggression in viewers. The consensus is that TV violence does increase aggression for children and adolescents, that this influence is of small, but meaningful, magnitude, that short-term effects have been demonstrated more clearly than long-term effects, and that TV violence may have a greater impact on children who are initially more aggressive (Friedrich-Cofer & Huston, 1986; Pearl, Bouthilet, & Lazar, 1982; Surgeon General's Scientific Advisory Committee on Television and Social Behavior, 1972; for the dissenting view that TV violence has not been shown to increase aggression, see Freedman, 1984, 1986).

Social-learning theory stresses the importance of environmental cues that increase antisocial behavior. These "instigators" (Bandura, 1976) signal when it might be rewarding to behave antisocially versus when it might be risky to do so. Six instigators deserve special mention and are summarized in Table 5-3.

According to social-learning theorists, people also regulate their behavior through self-reinforcement. Individuals who derive pleasure, pride, revenge, or self-worth from their ability to harm or "rip off" others will persist in these activities—at times enjoying an almost sensual pleasure in criminal behavior (Katz, 1988). Conversely, people will discontinue conduct that results in self-criticism and self-contempt. Bandura emphasizes the ability of people to exempt themselves from their own conscience after behaving antisocially. These tactics of "self-exoneration" can assume many forms: minimizing the seriousness of one's acts by pointing to more serious offenses by others, justifying aggression by appealing to higher values, displacing the responsibility for misbehavior onto a higher authority, blaming victims for their misfortune, diffusing or sharing responsibility for wrongdoing, dehumanizing victims so they are stripped of sympathetic qualities, and underestimating the damage of one's actions.

The major asset of the social-learning approach is its account of how specific patterns of criminality can be developed in individual offenders. A second strength is that it can be applied to a wide range of crime.

The major limitation of social-learning theory is that there is little empirical evidence that "real life" criminal behaviors are learned according to the principles of behaviorism. Most of the data come from laboratory research in which the experimental setting nullifies all the legal and social sanctions that actual offenders must risk.

A second problem is that the theory does

Table 5-3 Instigators to Criminal Behavior

Models	Modeled aggression is effective in prompting others to behave aggressively, particularly when observers have been previously frustrated or when the modeled aggression is seen as justified.
Prior aversive treatment	Assaults, threats, reductions in available reinforcers, blocking of goal-directed behaviors, and perceptions of inequitable treatment can lead to increased aggression and can enhance the perceived rewards of aggression.
Incentive inducements	Antisocial behavior can be prompted by the anticipated rewards of misbehavior. Bandura (1976) suggests that aggression is sometimes stimulated and temporarily sustained by erroneously anticipated consequences. Habitual offenders often overestimate their chances of succeeding in criminal acts and ignore the consequences of failing.
Instructions	Milgram's (1963) famous experiment demonstrating widespread willingness to follow orders to inflict "pain" on another person suggests that antisocial behavior can be instigated by commands from authorities. The strength of instructional control is limited to certain conditions and is an infrequent source of instigation in most crimes.
Delusions	Individuals occasionally respond aggressively to hallucinated commands or paranoid jealousies and suspicions. People who suffer delusional symptoms also tend to be socially isolated, a factor that sometimes minimizes the corrective influences that a reality-based environment could have on them.
Alcohol and drug use	Alcohol and drugs must be reckoned with as potent instigators of antisocial conduct. A strong positive association between crime and alcohol use is undeniable, especially in violent crime. By depressing a person's responsiveness to other cues that could inhibit impulsive or aggressive behavior, alcohol and drugs often lead to an increase in antisocial behavior even though they are not stimulants. Narcotics use, by virtue of its cost and its deviant status, acts as a catalyst or amplifier of criminality, especially property crime.

not explain why some people fall prey to "bad" learning experiences while others resist them. Learning might be a necessary ingredient in developing criminality, but it is probably not a sufficient one. Individual differences in the way people respond to reinforcement need to be considered, as they are in the theory that we review next.

Wilson and Herrnstein's Constitutional-Learning Theory

Some theorists have integrated multiple learning processes into a comprehensive, learning-based formulation of criminality (e.g., Feldman, 1977). The most influential and controversial multiple-component learning theory is found in Wilson and Herrnstein's (1985) *Crime and Human Nature*. Wilson and Herrnstein observe that both criminal and noncriminal behavior

have gains and losses. Gains from committing crime include revenge and peer approval. Gains associated with not committing crime include avoiding punishment and having a clear conscience. Whether a crime is committed depends, in part, on the net ratio of these gains and losses for criminal and noncriminal behavior. If the ratio for committing a crime exceeds that for not committing it, the likelihood of the crime being committed increases (this idea is similar to what Cornish & Clarke, 1986, call *rational choice* theory).

Wilson and Herrnstein argue that individual differences influence these ratios and determine whether an individual is likely to commit a crime. For example, like Eysenck, the authors propose that individuals differ in the ease with which they learn to associate, through classical conditioning, negative emotions with misbehaviors and positive emotions with proper behaviors. These conditioned responses are the foundation of a strong conscience, which increases the gains associated with noncrime and increases the losses associated with crime.

Another important personality factor is impulsivity, or what Wilson and Herrnstein call "time discounting." All reinforcers lose strength the more remote they are from a behavior, but persons differ in their ability to delay gratification and obtain reinforcement from potential long-term gains. More impulsive persons have greater difficulty deriving benefits from distant, albeit powerful, reinforcers. Time discounting is important in understanding crime because the gains associated with crime (revenge, money) occur immediately, whereas the losses from such behavior (punishment) occur much later in time, if at all. Thus, for impulsive persons, the ratio of gains to losses shifts in the direction of criminal behavior.

Equity, a term we discussed in Chapter 3, is another important influence on criminality. Equity theory states that people make comparisons between what they feel they deserve and what they observe other people receiving. Inequitable transactions are perceived when one's own ratio of gains to losses is less than that of others. Judgments of inequity change the reinforcing value of crime. If we perceive ourselves as being unfairly treated by society, this sense of inequity can increase the gains associated with a crime like stealing because such behavior will help to restore our sense of equity.

Another major component in their theory is what Wilson and Herrnstein call "constitutional factors," which are present at birth or soon after. These factors include gender, intelligence, variations in physiological arousal, and the aforementioned impulsivity—all of which conspire to make some persons more attracted to wrongdoing and less deterred by the potential aversive consequences of crime.

Of several social factors linked to criminal behavior, Wilson and Herrnstein believe that family influences and early school experiences are the most important. Families that foster (1) *attachment* of children to their parents, (2) *longer time horizons* whereby children consider the distant consequences of their behavior, and (3) a strong *conscience* about misbehavior will go far in counteracting criminal predispositions. The work of Gerald Patterson and his colleagues is pertinent to this aspect of Wilson and Herrnstein's theory. Based on extensive observation of families with and without aggressive and conduct-disordered children, Patterson (1982, 1986) identified four family interaction patterns associated with later delinquency: (1) poor disciplinary techniques involving either overinvolved nagging or indifferent laxness, (2) lack of positive parenting and affection toward children, (3) ineffective parental monitoring of a child's behavior, and (4) failure to employ adequate problem-solving strategies to reduce stress and irritability within the family.

Remedies to these harmful patterns involve warmth and supportiveness combined with consistent enforcement of clear rules for proper behavior. Unfortunately, these methods are not likely to be practiced by parents whose own traits reflect the predispositions they have passed on to their children. Therefore, such children face the double whammy of problematic predispositions coupled with inadequate parental control.

Of additional importance is an interaction between biological factors and early school experiences. Not only are impulsive, poorly socialized children of lower intelligence more directly at risk for criminality, but their interaction with cold, indifferent schools that do not foster educational achievements is an additional liability that discourages traditional social conformity.

Because they took hereditary and biological factors seriously, Wilson and Herrnstein have come under heavy fire from critics who have portrayed their theory as a purely genetic one. It is not. What they have done is restored psychological factors (some inheritable, some not) and family interaction variables to a place of importance in criminology, which for decades has been dominated by sociological concepts.

The Social-Labeling Perspective

The most extreme version of the social-psychological approaches is the *social-labeling perspective*. Its emergence as an explanation of criminality reflects (1) frustration about the inability of previous approaches to provide comprehensive explanations and (2) a shift in emphasis from "Why do people commit crimes?" to "Why do some people come to be called 'criminals'?" (Sheley, 1985).

Some examples will illustrate this shift. In one study (Heussanstamm, 1975), a group of college students in Los Angeles—each of whom had a perfect driving record in the previous year—had "Black Panther" bumper stickers put on their cars. Within hours, they began to get tickets for traffic violations, such as improper lane changes. These results imply that the Los Angeles police were labeling behavior differently, based on the presence of the bumper sticker.

A second researcher (Chambliss, 1984) studied one town's reactions to two groups of high school boys: a middle-class group he called "the Saints" and a working-class group known as "the Roughnecks." The two groups had a delinquency rate that was about equal, but "the community, the school, and the police react[ed] to the Saints as though they were good, upstanding, nondelinquent youths with bright futures but to the Roughnecks as though they were tough young criminals who

were headed for trouble" (Chambliss, 1984, p. 131).

The basic assumption of labeling theory is that deviance is created by the labels that society assigns to certain acts. Deviance is not based simply on the quality of the act; rather, it stems also from the consequences, the reactions to the act. Social-labeling theory makes a distinction between primary deviance, or the criminal's actual behavior, and secondary deviance, or society's reaction to the offensive conduct (Lemert, 1951, 1972). With regard to the primary deviance, offenders often rationalize their own behavior as a temporary mistake, or they see it as part of a socially acceptable role (Lilly et al., 1989).

Box 5-6 lists five basic assumptions of this perspective. The stigma of being labeled a deviant can create a self-fulfilling prophecy (Merton, 1968). Many ex-convicts who seek an honest and law-abiding life are spurned by prospective employers and by their families and are labeled "ex-cons." Frustrated in their efforts to make good, they may adopt this label and engage in further lawbreaking (Irwin, 1970). According to this perspective, the criminal justice system produces much of the deviance it is intended to correct.

The social-labeling approach is helpful because it raises our consciousness about the difficulties faced by offenders in returning to society. Moreover, it reminds us that some lawbreakers—for example, those who live in crime-prone neighborhoods frequently patrolled by police—are more likely to be caught and "criminalized" than are others. But the social-labeling approach does not explain all criminal behavior. Primary deviance—that is, a law violation in the first place—has to occur before secondary deviance takes its toll. Many lawbreakers develop a life of crime before ever being apprehended (Mankoff, 1971), and differences among people exist and persist despite the names we call them.

SUMMARY AND INTEGRATION OF THEORIES OF CRIME

Where do all these theories leave us? Do any of them offer a convincing explanation of crime? Are there implications for how we can best intervene to prevent or reduce crime in our society? Although many commentators routinely decry the lack of a convincing theory of crime, we believe there is an increasing fund of knowledge about the causes of serious crime that offers valid explanations for how criminality develops and also suggests reasonable strategies for controlling it.

Serious criminality is extraordinarily versatile, involving careers that include violent crime, property crime, vandalism, and substance abuse. One implication of this diversity is that persons travel several causal pathways on the way to their brand of criminality. No single variable causes all crime, just as no one agent causes all fevers or upset stomachs. However, several etiological factors have been reliably associated with criminality. Any one of these factors is sometimes a sufficient explanation for criminal behavior; more often, however, they act in concert to produce criminality. The factors of greatest importance are the following:

1. Certain *environments* are rich in opportunities and temptations for crime. They achieve this quality because of social impoverishment and disorganization, fundamental economic inequalities, a tradition of tolerating if not encouraging crime, social dissension and strife, and an abundance of inviting targets and easy victims of crime.

2. Likewise, certain *persons* are particularly vulnerable to behaving criminally, and this predisposition becomes stronger when such persons find themselves in risky environments. Predispositions to criminality tend to be correlated with poor social skills, lower verbal intelligence, and disturbed physiological arousal that interferes with classical conditioning and inner restraints. Consequently, some people appear

---

Box 5-6 | Assumptions of the Social-Labeling Perspective

1. Before persons can be labeled as criminals, their behavior must be noticed, or at least assumed to be noticed, by society.
2. Observation must be followed by reaction. Individuals cannot be labeled as criminals unless society reacts to their alleged offenses; that is, an act is devoid of social meaning until society attempts to give it meaning.
3. Society's attempt to label people as criminals may succeed or may fail. The attempt to label does not guarantee the successful imposition of a label.
4. The outcome of the negotiation of a label between society and individuals involves more than just the qualities of alleged criminal acts. Characteristics of the alleged violator, such as race, gender, or socioeconomic status, and the social or political climate in which the negotiation occurs, will also influence the outcome.
5. Whether the effects of the labeling are long-lasting is also negotiable and depends on individuals' reactions to their labels, society's perceptions of those reactions, and society's willingness to negotiate.

Adapted from Sheley (1985, pp. 233–234).

well stocked in attitudes, thinking, and motivations that encourage antisocial behavior and that also render them relatively immune to negative consequences for misconduct.

3. Delinquency and serious criminality are correlated with childhood histories of poor behavioral control and conduct problems. This association is consistent with the role of predispositions, and it points to the crucial influence of parents on later delinquency. The failure of parents to control their children's initial episodes of impulsive and acting-out behavior is an early precursor of delinquency.

4. Modeling and peer pressure promote criminality. Crime increases when peers support it, as is sometimes the case in the criminal justice system itself when, by virtue of its official processing of offenders, "beginning" criminals associate frequently with more serious offenders.

5. Contingencies for crime are often favorable because the short-run positive payoffs for offending are stronger and more probable than the long-run risks of apprehension and punishment. Crime often does pay, and therefore any factor—social, psychological, or biological— that weakens a person's internal resistance to wrongdoing (even temporarily, as with alcohol or drug use) increases the probability of criminality.

6

The Police and the Criminal Justice System

In any survey list of public concerns, "crime" is always near the top. This ranking stems from the pervasiveness of crime in our country as well as the fear that crime causes in each of us. In any recent year, approximately one of every four households in the United States experienced a serious crime, according to statistics compiled by the National Crime Victimization Survey. These figures also indicate that at least two to three times as many crimes occur as are officially reported to the police. Only crimes that are detected and reported to the police find their way into the criminal justice system. But the physical, financial, and psychological effects of being a victim of crime persist even when the victimization is never made known to the police.

The process from report of a crime to punishment of a convicted offender can be long and tortuous. The flowchart in Box 6-1 illustrates the movement of a case through the

---

Box **6-1** | *The Sequence of Events in the Criminal Justice System*

Entry into the System

Prosecution and Pretrial Services

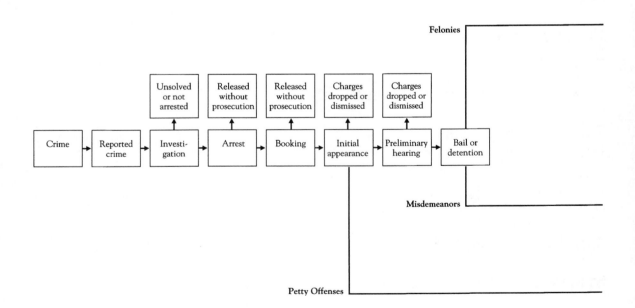

criminal justice system. Procedures in individual jurisdictions may vary from the pattern shown here, and some jurisdictions use differing terminology for the same action. But the pattern shown is generally representative.

The major purpose of this chapter is to describe the selection, training, and behavior of police officers. This chapter also serves as an introduction to the next two chapters, on crime detection.

Police occupy the front line of the criminal justice system. They are the face-to-face confronters of criminal activities, and we expect them to keep our streets safe and our homes secure. They are our "thin blue line" against public disorder. The visibility of the police is heightened by the uniforms they wear, the weapons they display, and the special powers they are given. This visibility makes the police convenient targets for the public's frustrations with the crim-

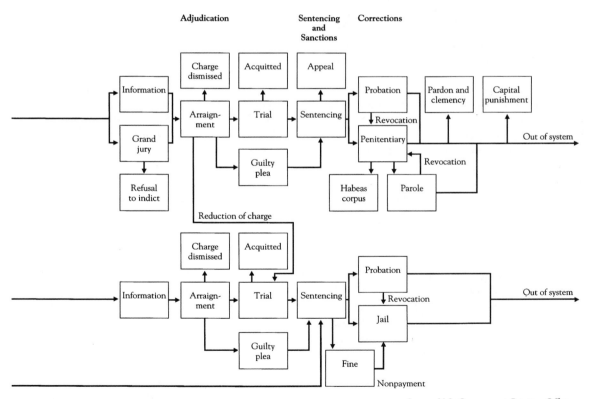

Source: U.S. Government Printing Office

inal justice system. On the other hand, the police are usually the first people citizens call in an emergency. Consequently, the public holds conflicting attitudes about the police. They demand protection by them at the same time that they resist interference from them.

Police perform a complex set of tasks in the criminal justice system. Street officers must combine physical prowess, perceptual acuity, interpersonal sensitivity, and intelligent discretion to succeed at their jobs. They need to make quick judgments about all sorts of human behavior under frequently stressful conditions. They should be versed in the law and at least intuitively knowledgeable about the social sciences. In exchange for these demands, police are usually overworked and unappreciated. These factors, along with the job pressures they face, the criminal elements they encounter, and the isolation in which they often work, render the police subject to the lures of bribery, corruption, and abuse of power.

When we consider the police from a psychological perspective, we encounter each of the dilemmas introduced in Chapter 1. Many individuals see the police as intruding on their rights to privacy and freedom; yet society recognizes that an institution like the police is necessary to protect society and to do its dirty work. Police officers investigate crimes—their job is to find out what happened—but they also feel compelled to make arrests. In their quest for convictions, or for the truth as they see it, police officers may go beyond the accepted legal procedures. Chevigny (1969) notes that, in a dynamic society in which occasional injustices are inevitable, it is difficult to obtain efficiency, quick work, and order from the police and at the same time attain due process and equal justice. Another conflict often arises when social science findings question the validity of techniques advocated by the police, such as hypnosis and lie detector tests. And last, but of great importance to the police, is the dilemma of equality versus discretion. When

should an arrest be made and when should only a warning be issued? How much force can legitimately be used in an arrest? Should all suspects be treated the same way?

SELECTION OF POLICE OFFICERS

One purpose of this chapter is to examine the police officer from a psychological perspective. How are police officers selected? Do the selection criteria work? Is there a set of personality characteristics that officers share? How are they trained, and does their training reflect their actual duties on the job? Can the police officer's image in the community be improved?

Psychological evaluation of police personnel began inauspiciously in 1916, when Lewis Terman, the Stanford University psychologist who revised Alfred Binet's intelligence scales to produce the Stanford-Binet intelligence test, tested the intelligence of 30 police and firefighter applicants in San Jose, California. Terman (1917) found that the average IQ score among these applicants was 84 and recommended that no one be accepted for these positions whose IQ fell below 80. A few years later, L. L. Thurstone tested the intelligence of 358 Detroit policemen, using the Army Alpha Intelligence Examination. Like Terman, he reported below-average IQ scores, but he also found that police of higher ranks scored lower than entry-level patrolmen.

Throughout the years, psychologists have continued to assess police candidates, although this work was often unsystematic and poorly evaluated. As late as 1955, only 14 U.S. cities with populations greater than 100,000 used a formal program of testing police candidates; by 1965, 27% of local police agencies reported some psychological evaluation of applicants (Ostrov, 1986). In the 1960s and 1970s, the period when police psychology became an established specialty, several national commissions, including the 1967 President's Commission on Law Enforcement and the Administration of Justice and the 1973 National Advisory Committee on Criminal Justice Standards, called for formal psychological assessment of police personnel in all departments. By the mid-1980s, at least 11 states required psychological screening of police candidates, and more than 50% of the country's departments psychologically screened beginning police officers (Benner, 1986).

Psychological evaluation of police applicants can focus on selecting those candidates who seem most desirable or psychologically fit or on eliminating individuals who seem least suited for police work. Most selection concentrates on screening out disturbed candidates because consensus on what constitutes the "ideal" police profile (see Box 6-2) is hard to achieve. Despite serious concerns about the validity of psychological evaluations in police selection (Kent & Eisenberg, 1972; Levy, 1967), many commentators (Bartol, 1983; Ostrov, 1986; Reiser & Klyver, 1987; Spielberger, 1979) believe that psychological screening is useful in the selection process and should be included. In addition, several court decisions (e.g., *Bonsignore* v. *The City of New York*, 1981) holding cities liable for the dangerous acts of their employees have required municipalities to demonstrate that they have taken reasonable precautions not to hire and/or retain people who are psychologically unfit for certain duties. Comprehensive psychological evaluations are one obvious way to demonstrate such precautions. In general, the courts have upheld psychological screening of police candidates as long as the evaluation and testing involved do not violate the provisions of various civil rights acts and are in compliance with federal guidelines.

Psychologists who evaluate police candidates rely on three tools: (1) personal interviews, (2) observations of candidates performing in structured situations contrived to capture real-world characteristics of police work, and (3) psychological tests. How much emphasis different psychologists place on these tools depends on several factors, including their professional background and training, the resources available for the evaluation, and the focus of the assessment questions (e.g., different strategies will be used for assessing mental disorders than for predicting what type of person will do best in which kind of position).

The Interview

Personal interviews are the most widely employed assessment tool despite evidence that interviews are subject to distortion, low reliability, and questionable validity. The extent to which an interview yields the same information on different occasions or with different interviewers (*reliability*) and the degree to which that information is accurately related to important criteria (*validity*) have not been clearly established (although there is good evidence that reliability, at least, increases as interviews become more structured).

Interviews are valuable as a rapport-building introduction to the evaluation process. They increase applicants' cooperation at the same time that they soothe anxiety and apprehension. Another reason interviews are popular is that they are flexible and economical. However, because they are subject to deliberate distortions and impression management by candidates, interviews are more useful for orienting candidates to the evaluation than for predicting candidates' subsequent performance.

Situational Tests

Situational tests have been used from time to time in police selection. For example, Mills, McDevitt, and Tonkin (1966) administered three tests intended to simulate police abilities to a group of Cincinnati police candidates. The

"Foot Patrol Observation Test" required candidates to walk a six-block downtown route and then answer questions about what they remembered having just observed. In the "Clues Test," candidates were given ten minutes to investigate a set of planted clues about the disappearance of a hypothetical city worker from his office. They were observed as they performed this task and were graded on the information they assembled. The "Bull Session" was a two-hour group discussion of several topics of importance in police

work. Performance on the Clues Test correlated significantly with class ranking in the police academy, but scores from the Foot Patrol Observation Test did not. Although independent "grades" for the Bull Session were not derived, it was viewed as an important measure of emotional and motivational qualities. In addition, Mills et al. (1966) discovered that the Clues Test was not correlated with intelligence—indicating the advantage of including a measure of nonintellectual abilities in the selection battery.

Box 6-2 | Selection of "Ideal" Police Officer

If it were your task to select police officers from a pool of applicants, what psychological qualities would you look for? Your answers probably reflect your values, as well as your image of what police officers do. Among the psychological characteristics usually generated in such a list are the following:

1. *Incorruptible.* A police officer should be of high moral character. Reports of officers taking bribes are especially disturbing because the police officer must treat all citizens fairly within the rules of law.

2. *Well adjusted.* A police officer should be able to carry out the hazardous and enervating duties of the job without "cracking up." Officers are always in the public view. They need to be thick skinned enough to operate without defensiveness; yet they need to be sensitive to the needs of others. Likewise, they need to cope with the ever-present danger and stress of their jobs, in-

cluding the constant realization that death may lurk around the corner. Throughout the 1980s, about 100–150 police officers were killed annually in the line of duty.

3. *People oriented.* A police officer's major duty is service to others. An officer needs to have a genuine interest in people and a compassionate sense of their innate dignity. At the commencement program of the New York City Police Academy, new officers were told: "There is one thing we cannot teach you and that is about people. The bottom line is to treat people as people and you'll get by" (quoted by Nix, 1987, p. 15).

4. *Free of emotional reactions.* Although a degree of chronic suspiciousness may be desirable for the job, the police officer should be free of impulsive, emotional, overly aggressive reactions. Restraint is essential because officers are trained to take an active position in crime detection and are even encouraged by

their superiors to be wary of what is happening around them (Greenberg & Ruback, 1984). For example, a Chicago Police Department training bulletin states:

> Actions, dress, or location of a person often classify him as suspicious in the mind of a police officer. Men loitering near schools, public toilets, playgrounds, and swimming pools may be sex perverts. Men loitering near bars at closing time, or any other business at closing time, may be robbery suspects. Men or youths walking along looking into cars may be car thieves or looking for something to steal. Persons showing evidence of recent injury, or whose clothing is disheveled, may be victims or participants in an assault or strong arm robbery [quoted in Greenberg & Ruback, 1984, p. 72].

A new police officer, reflecting on

Despite the fact that situational tests have an intuitive appeal as selection devices, they have not proven to be superior predictors of performance compared to paper-and-pencil tests in most studies. Because they are time consuming and expensive, they are used mainly to supplement psychological tests.

Psychological Tests

Psychological tests typically have adequate reliability and can be standardized, objectively scored, and administered to large groups of subjects at the same time; as a result, they are the backbone of police screening methods. Two types of tests are included in selection batteries: tests of cognitive or intellectual ability and tests of personality traits or emotional stability.

Most recent studies of police officers confirm that they have average to above-average intelligence as a group (Poland, 1978). Intelligence tends to correlate fairly strongly with the perfor-

---

the effect of his training, said "I've always been suspicious. [But now] I find myself looking up at the roofs of buildings to see if people are going to throw anything off" (quoted by Nix, 1987, p. 15).

5. *Logical.* Police officers should be able to examine a crime scene and extract hypotheses about what happened and what characteristics might describe the lawbreaker. An example of this deductive ability comes from the actions of Al Seedman, former chief of detectives of the New York City Police Department, who explained to an interviewer that he had been helping some detectives from a small Connecticut town investigate a case:

In the woods just outside town they found the skeleton of a man who'd been dead for three months or so. They figured they'd find out who he was as soon as his family reported him

missing, but it's been three months since he was found—which makes six months since he died—and nobody has claimed him. They don't know what to do. . . .

Once I got the answer to one question I was able to give them a method. I asked whether this skeleton showed signs of any dental work, which usually can be identified by a dentist. But according to the local cops, they said no, although the skeleton had crummy teeth. No dental work at all. Now, if he'd been wealthy, he could have afforded to have his teeth fixed. If he'd been poor, welfare would have paid. If he was a union member, their medical plan would have covered it. So this fellow was probably working at a low-paying non-unionized job, but making enough to keep off public assistance. Also, since he didn't match up to any family's miss-

ing-person report, he was probably single, living alone in an apartment or hotel. His landlord had never reported him missing, either, so most likely he was also behind on his rent and the landlord probably figured he had just skipped. But even if he had escaped his landlord, he would never have escaped the tax man.

The rest was simple. I told these cops to wait until the year is up. They can go to the IRS and get a printout of all single males making less than $10,000 a year but more than the welfare ceiling who paid withholding tax in the first three quarters but not the fourth. Chances are the name of their skeleton would be on that printout [quoted in Seedman & Hellman, 1974, pp. 4-5].

mance of police recruits in their training programs; however, intelligence scores are only weakly related to actual police performance in the field (Bartol, 1983). These results point to the problem of predictive validity, which is a pervasive difficulty that we discuss in the next section.

The Minnesota Multiphasic Personality Inventory (MMPI) is by far the most often used test of personality in police screening, followed by the California Psychological Inventory (CPI) and the Sixteen Personality Factor Questionnaire (16PF). Evidence for the validity of these tests in screening out unsuitable candidates for police work is mixed. Several investigations support the validity of the MMPI (Bartol, 1991; Beutler, Storm, Kirkish, Scogin, & Gaines, 1985; Hiatt & Hargrave, 1988) and the CPI (Hogan, 1971; Spielberger, Spaulding, & Ward, 1978), but others (Lester, Babcock, Cassissi, & Brunetta, 1980; Mills & Stratton, 1982) have questioned the value of psychological testing of police recruits in general.

One personality test designed specifically to identify psychologically unsuitable law enforcement candidates is the Inwald Personality Inventory (Inwald, Knadz, & Shusman, 1983). It consists of 26 scales that tap past and present behaviors presumed to have special relevance for law enforcement applicants; examples include Lack of Assertiveness, Trouble with Law and Society, Undue Suspiciousness, and Driving Violations. Preliminary research with this instrument has revealed good reliability and validity, although its predictive validity does not appear to be significantly better than that of the MMPI (Bolton, 1985; Swartz, 1985).

An excellent study of psychological test validity is provided by Beutler et al. (1985), who examined the relationship between several tests (including the MMPI and five other standardized tests) and various measures of performance for 65 subjects who had been recently accepted for police work. Twenty-two of these officers were employed in an urban police department, 27 worked in a department associated with a major state university, and 16 were from a community college department. The investigators gathered an extensive list of criteria on how well each officer performed on the job. Ratings of *interpersonal ability* and *technical proficiency* were obtained from supervisors, and seven criteria of performance were collected from each officer's personnel record: reprimands involving use of vehicles, reprimands involving use of force, grievances, suspensions, referrals for counseling, attendance at continuing-education activities, and commendations.

The results suggest that performance on the different criteria was predictable by psychological tests, and these predictions even generalized across different types of police departments. The MMPI profile was particularly effective in predicting reprimands, grievances, and suspensions. However, another discovery points to the difficulty in measuring police performance: supervisors' ratings were not strongly related to criteria obtained from the personnel records (such as suspensions and reprimands.) Beutler et al. (1985) suggest that supervisor bias might account for this result, and they caution against relying too heavily on supervisor ratings as measures of police job performance.

THE VALIDITY OF POLICE SCREENING

Although experts disagree on the usefulness of psychological screening of police, they all agree that good empirical research on this topic is difficult to conduct (Inwald, 1986). Studies of predictive validity using actual police performance in the field as the criterion are so time consuming and expensive that most departments cannot afford them. Instead, they settle for research that examines the relationship between screening tests and performance by police recruits in their training schools. This relationship is usually positive, but success or failure in training is not the criterion of real interest.

Another problem with studies of validity is that the police candidates who do poorly on the screening evaluations are eliminated from the pool of trainees and potential employees. Although this decision is reasonable, it makes it impossible to study whether the prediction of poor performance would have been valid.

Finally, selecting adequate criteria to measure effective police performance is notoriously difficult. Supervisor ratings are often inflated or biased by interpersonal factors that are irrelevant to actual achievements or problems. In some departments, especially smaller ones, the individual police officer will be expected to perform so many diverse functions that it becomes unreasonable to expect specific cognitive abilities or psychological traits to be related in the same way to the multiple facets of performance. Also, if we are interested in predicting which officers are likely to act in risky, dangerous, or inappropriate ways, our predictions will be complicated by the fact that such behaviors occur only rarely in any group of people. As a consequence, these assessments will be plagued by numerous situations in which the predicted event does not take place.

can order an officer to undergo an evaluation of fitness to continue duty.

These evaluations pose difficulties for everyone involved. Administrators must balance the need to protect the public from a potentially dangerous officer against the legal right of the officer to fair employment. Clinicians have to navigate a narrow path between a department's need to know the results of such an evaluation and the officer's expectation that the results will be kept confidential. Finally, the officers themselves face a dilemma: they can be honest and reveal problems that could disqualify them from service, or they can distort their responses in order to protect their jobs but consequently miss the opportunity for potentially beneficial treatment.

Two different models of fitness-for-duty evaluations are used. In the first, departments use the same psychologist to perform the fitness-for-duty evaluation and to provide whatever treatment is necessary for the officer. In other departments, the psychologist who evaluates the officer does not provide any treatment, thereby preventing a conflict of interest between keeping the therapy confidential and disclosing an officer's psychological functioning. In most circumstances, the second model is the preferred one. In-depth discussions of ethical dilemmas facing police psychologists are provided by Dietz and Reese (1986), D'Agostino (1986), and Weiner (1986).

FITNESS-FOR-DUTY EVALUATIONS

Another type of psychological assessment of police officers is the fitness-for-duty evaluation. As a result of a critical incident, a series of problems, or other indicators that an officer is psychologically impaired, police administrators

TRAINING OF POLICE OFFICERS

Once candidates for police training have been selected, they participate in a course of training that usually lasts several months. For example, the New York City police academy requires a 24-week training program, with 40 hours of training per week. Other jurisdictions have training programs averaging 14 to 16 weeks.

Two types of criticism of these programs have emerged. One is that, after rigorous selection procedures, few trainees fail the training program. For example, of 1091 recruits who began the training program in New York City in 1987, only 65 dropped out or were dismissed for a variety of reasons, including physical or academic inadequacies (Nix, 1987). Advocates count this rate of success as an indication of the validity of the selection procedures, but critics complain that graduation is too easy or predictable, especially given the burn-out rate of on-the-job police officers.

A second criticism is that there is insufficient training in the field, as well as a lack of close supervision of trainees during the time they spend on patrol. The limited time trainees spend with veteran training officers on patrol may give them a false sense of security (Beck, 1987) and may deprive them of learning different ways of responding to citizens from various cultural backgrounds.

TRAINING IN CRISIS INTERVENTION

The police are often asked to maintain public order and defuse volatile situations involving persons who are mentally ill, intoxicated, angry, or motivated by politically extreme views. Because of the instability of the participants in such disputes, they pose great risks to the police as well as to bystanders. In this section, we examine three types of crisis situations to which police are often called—incidents involving the mentally ill, family disturbances, and hostage taking. Psychologists have made important contributions to each of these areas by con-

ducting research, designing interventions, and training the police in crisis intervention skills.

Interactions with the Mentally Ill

For the past two decades several factors have forced mentally ill persons from the mental institutions in which they were formerly maintained to settings such as halfway houses, community mental health centers, general hospitals, "flophouses," the streets, and local jails. This deinstitutionalization movement has resulted from (1) advances in antipsychotic medications that allow persons to function outside of hospitals, (2) increased restrictions on the involuntary commitment of the mentally ill to hospitals, (3) changes in the patterns of psychiatric hospitalization, and (4) decreased public funding for mental health programs (Kiesler, 1982; Teplin, 1984b). The rise of the homeless or "street people" population, among whom problems of substance abuse and mental illness are frequent and severe (Fischer & Breakey, 1991), is also linked to declining availability of publicly supported mental health treatment. Another result of deinstitutionalization (which in itself is an admirable goal *when sufficient funding for alternative, noninstitutional care is ensured*) is that supervision of the mentally ill has become more of a responsibility for the police than it was previously.

Research on how the police handle mentally ill persons has concentrated on the discretion officers use in crisis incidents. Will they arrest the citizen, or will they try to have the person hospitalized? Will they attempt on-the-spot counseling themselves, a referral to a mental health agency, or a return of the person to a safe place, to relatives, or to friends? Early research on these questions suggested that the police were reluctant to use their power to arrest or to arrange emergency hospitalization of the mentally ill unless these people's behavior presented an obvious danger to themselves or others (Bittner, 1967). These findings are consistent with research on police discretion in general, which suggests a tendency to avoid arrest in nonserious incidents unless the suspect is disrespectful to the officer, the complainant prefers that an arrest be made, or the officer perceives the benefits of arresting the subject to outweigh the perceived costs. Other studies, however, have shown that the police might prefer arrest over hospitalization when dealing with mentally ill persons (Matthews, 1970), especially if there is less "red tape" involved in completing an arrest versus finalizing a hospitalization.

The best research on the question of how frequently the mentally ill are arrested by the police has been conducted by Linda Teplin, a sociologist at Northwestern University. Teplin (1984b) assembled a team of psychology graduate students and trained them to observe and code the interactions of police officers with citizens over a 14-month period in two different precincts in a large American city. Observers used a symptom checklist and a global rating of mental disorder to assess mental illness in the citizens observed.

Teplin studied 884 nontraffic encounters involving a total of 1798 citizens, of whom 506 were considered suspects for arrest by the police. Arrest was relatively infrequent in these incidents, occurring in only 12.4% of the encounters; in terms of individuals (some incidents involved several suspects), 29.2% were arrested. The observers classified only 30 (5.9%) of the 506 suspects as mentally ill. The arrest rate for these 30 persons was 46.7% compared to an arrest rate of 27.9% for suspects who were not rated as having mental disorders. This greater probability of arrest for the mentally ill suspect was found regardless of the type or seriousness of the incident involved. Teplin concluded that the mentally ill were being

"criminalized" and that this outcome was the result not only of the provocative nature of their psychological symptoms but also of the inadequacies of the mental health system in treating such persons. As a result, the criminal justice system has become a "default option" for patients whom hospitals refuse to accept for treatment because they are too dangerous, are not dangerous enough, or suffer a disorder that the hospital does not treat. And, not surprisingly, the rate of severe mental disorders in jail populations, often combined with diagnoses of substance abuse and personality disorder in the same individuals, is alarmingly high (Abram & Teplin, 1991).

The jailing of the mentally ill does not reflect improper behavior by the police as much as a failure of public policy regarding the treatment and protection of the chronically mentally ill. More and better training of police officers in the recognition and short-term management of the mentally ill is necessary (Drucker & Goldstein, 1983, and Godschalx, 1984, discuss such programs), but an adequate resolution of this problem will require large-scale changes in the way services for the seriously mentally ill are organized, delivered, and funded (Abram & Teplin, 1991; Teplin, 1984b).

Domestic Disturbances

When violence erupts in a family or between a couple, the police are often the first people called to the scene. What they might encounter when they arrive is unknown. Will the participants be armed? Are they intoxicated or psychologically disturbed? How much violence has already taken place? What is certain is that responding to such family disturbances is one of the most dangerous activities that the police perform. The amount of time police spend dealing with domestic disturbances exceeds the time they spend investigating murder, rape, and all forms of aggravated assault

(Wilt, Bannon, Breedlove, Sandker, & Michaelson, 1977). Approximately 25% of police deaths and assaults on officers occur during police intervention in family disturbances (Ketterman & Kravitz, 1978).

Because of their danger and frequency, family disturbances pose a difficult challenge for the police. Can they be handled in a manner that protects potential victims, reduces chances of recurrence, and limits the risks of injury to responding officers? The first project on crisis intervention with domestic disputes was developed by Morton Bard, a psychologist in New York City. Bard (1969; Bard & Berkowitz, 1967) trained a special group of New York City police

officers (nine black and nine white volunteers) in family disturbance intervention skills for a project located in West Harlem. The month-long training program focused on development of interpersonal strategies that would allow officers to intervene in family disputes without making an arrest. The training emphasized the psychology of family conflict and issues of cross-racial differences. Role playing was used to acquaint officers with techniques for calming antagonists, lowering tensions, reducing hostilities, and preventing physical violence.

For two years after the training, all family crisis calls in the experimental precinct were answered by the specially trained officers. They

---

Box 6-3 | *Family Violence—Now Finally Recognized*

"People are more likely to be killed, physically assaulted, hit, beat up, slapped, or spanked in their own homes by other family members than anywhere else, or by anyone else, in our society" (Gelles & Cornell, 1985, p. 12). As the text indicates, police intervention into family violence is dangerous work. Because of the many risks and the few rewards for doing so, police officers are seldom motivated to get involved.

Not only is the dangerousness of the intervention a problem, but also many police officers—like many others among us—accept certain myths about the nature of family violence. Gelles and Cornell (1985) list these false assumptions as the following:

Myth 1: Family violence is rare. It is difficult to get accu-

rate statistics on child abuse and other forms of family violence because no agency systematically gathers such data. But it is not a rare phenomenon; it is estimated that 14% of children in the United States are abused within their families each year and that the lifetime incidence of spousal abuse may be as high as 50% of married couples.

Myth 2: Family violence is confined to mentally disturbed or sick people. When we hear or read that a woman has plunged her 2-year-old son into a tub of boiling water or that a man has had sexual intercourse with his 6-year-old daughter, our first reaction might be "That person is terribly sick!" The way family violence is portrayed in the mass

media (Steinmetz & Straus, 1974) leads to a conclusion that normal people do not beat their relatives. But sociologist Murray Straus (1980) estimates that fewer than 10% of all instances of family violence are caused by mental illness or psychiatric disorders.

Myth 3: Family violence is confined to people in poor economic circumstances. Although there is more reported violence and abuse among families with fewer economic advantages, these responses are by no means limited to such families. Among middle-class couples seeking a divorce, 23% mentioned violence as one of the reasons for wanting to end the marriage (Levinger, 1966). One of President Reagan's prime executive-branch appointees, John Fed-performed 1375 interventions with 962 families. Evaluation of the project focused on six outcomes: (1) a decrease in family disturbance calls, (2) a decrease in repeat calls from the same families, (3) a reduction of homicides in the precinct, (4) a reduction of homicides among family members, (5) a reduction of assaults in the precinct, and (6) a reduction of injuries to police officers. However, the results supported only two of these expectations. There were fewer assaults in the precinct, and none of the trained officers was injured (compared with three police officers who were not part of the program but were injured while responding to family disturbances).

In addition to these outcomes, Bard discov-
ered that some stereotypes about domestic violence were often incorrect (see Box 6-3 for elaboration). For example, in only 10% of the calls did the complaining party allege that the other person was drunk. Also, although husbands and wives were about equally likely to use violence to resolve a disagreement, husbands inflicted much more physical injury than wives.

Evaluations of similar domestic crisis units in other cities have yielded mixed results (Pearce & Snortum, 1983). Specially trained officers typically rate their resolutions of disturbance calls more favorably than do officers without special training. However, the long-term effects of the special interventions

ders, was forced to resign his position when it was revealed, as part of a divorce hearing, that he had frequently abused his wife.

Myth 4: Battered wives like being hit—otherwise they would leave. Faced with the fact of wife battering, most persons seek rational explanations. These often take the form of (1) the woman must have provoked the violence, and/or (2) she must like it because she didn't leave after the first beating. Many people blame the victim (see Chapter 3). However, the concept of "learned helplessness" better explains why so many women endure such extreme violence for so long (Walker, 1979). Psychologist Lenore Walker observes that women who suffer continued physical violence at the hands of their husbands have much more negative self-concepts than women whose marriages are free from violence. She proposes that the repeated beatings leave these women feeling that they won't be able to protect themselves from further assaults and that they are incapable of controlling the events that go on around them (Gelles & Cornell, 1985).

Myth 5: Alcohol and drug abuse are the real causes of violence in the home. "He beat up his children because he was drunk" is another popular explanation of domestic violence. We need to be precise here. Yes, most studies find a considerable relationship between drinking and violence (Gillen, 1946;
Wolfgang, 1958). Perhaps as many as half the instances of violence and abuse involve alcohol or drugs (Gelles & Cornell, 1985); in the case of violence directed toward a spouse, both the offender and the victim may have been drinking extensively before the violence. But does the drug taking *cause* the violence? Some people assume that alcohol is a *disinhibitor*—that it unleashes violent behavior. But in other societies people drink and then become passive (Mac-Andrew & Edgerton, 1969). Reactions to drinking are largely a function of our expectations, which often provide an excuse to the violent offender: "I was drunk and didn't know what I was doing."

are less clear; sometimes they lead to an increase in "repeat" callers, but in other cases this effect is not observed.

In recent years, crisis intervention and other nonarrest methods for resolving family disturbances have come in for increased criticism, especially from women's rights groups that have filed lawsuits against law enforcement agencies that have not arrested seriously assaultive domestic batterers. These critics maintain that, when actual assaults have taken place in a family, arrest is the most appropriate response to protect victims and reduce future violence (Dutton, 1987).

In response to these concerns, some police departments have developed guidelines for when arrests should be made in domestic disputes. Chicago, for example, adopted the following seven indicators that an arrest of a domestic attacker is necessary (Loving & Quirk, 1982): (1) conflict that is emotionally intense, (2) threatened or actual use of weapons in the conflict, (3) previous injuries from assaults by this attacker, (4) previous court appearances by this attacker, (5) previous attempts by the parties to separate from each other, (6) a second call for help to the police, and (7) involvement of children or of intoxicated or mentally disturbed participants.

Domestic disputes illustrate an interesting phenomenon often encountered when attempting social reforms. Social problems and well-intentioned efforts to modify them tend to revolve in a cyclical fashion rather than moving in a straight line toward progress and increased sophistication. Today's reform, aimed at correcting some social evil, often develops its own difficulties or inequalities and ultimately becomes itself a target in need of reformation. Crisis intervention, originally preferred over arrest as a more psychologically sophisticated police response to family disturbances, has now come full circle to the point that it is seen as an inadequate control for problems of serious domestic violence; in these cases, official arrest is once again identified as the most effective intervention.

Hostage Negotiation

Most experts agree that the massacre of 11 Israeli athletes taken hostage at the 1972 Munich Olympic Games by Palestinian terrorists spurred the creation of new law enforcement techniques for resolving hostage incidents. These techniques of hostage negotiation, although still being revised, were developed through extensive collaboration among military, law enforcement, and behavioral science experts.

Soskis and Van Zandt (1986) identified four types of hostage incidents that differ in their psychological dynamics and appropriate techniques for resolution (see also Gist & Perry, 1985). A large percentage of hostage incidents involve persons suffering a *mental disorder* or experiencing serious personal or family problems. In these situations, hostage takers may have a history of depressive or schizophrenic illness, or they may be persons whose feelings of chronic powerlessness, anger, or despondency compel a desperate act that demands attention to their needs. Disturbed hostage takers pose a high risk of suicide, which they sometimes accomplish by forcing the police to kill them, an act that is termed *victim precipitated death*.

A second, common type of hostage situation involves the *trapped criminal*. Here a person who is trapped by the police during the commission of a crime takes anyone who is available as a hostage in order to bargain with the police for freedom. Because these incidents are unplanned and driven by panic, they tend to be, especially at their early stages, very dangerous to the victims and the police.

The third type of hostage situation, also involving criminals, is the *takeover of prisons* by inmates who capture prison guards or other inmates as hostages. In these incidents the passage of time tends to work against nonviolent resolutions because the hostage takers are violent people, working as a group with volatile leadership.

The fourth type of hostage taking, and the one that is most highly publicized and discussed, is *terrorism*, defined as "the use or threat of violence to achieve a social, political, or religious aim in a way that does not obey the traditional rules of war" (Soskis & Van Zandt, 1986). Terrorists usually plan their kidnapping of hostages, and they are typically motivated by organizational goals. These goals may require their own deaths as a necessary, but honorable, sacrifice for a higher cause. For this reason, terrorists are seldom responsive to typical hostage negotiation techniques that appeal to rational themes of self-preservation.

Successful hostage negotiation requires an understanding of the dynamics of hostage incidents so that these dynamics can be manipulated by the negotiator to contain and ultimately end the incident with a minimum of violence (Schlossberg & Freeman, 1974). For example, in many hostage situations a strong sense of psychological togetherness and mutual dependency develops between the hostages and their kidnappers. These feelings emerge from (1) the close, constant contact between the participants, (2) their shared feelings of fear and danger, and (3) the strong feelings of dependency that prolonged captivity produces. This relationship, dubbed the "Stockholm syndrome," involves positive feelings on the part of the hostages toward their kidnappers as well as reciprocated positive feelings by the kidnappers toward their hostages (see Box 6-4). Hostage negotiators try to take advantage of this dynamic by becoming a part of it themselves. They attempt to become a psychological member of the hostage group who has important ties to the outside world that can be used to bring the crisis to a peaceful end.

The successful negotiator makes contact with hostage takers in as nonthreatening a manner as possible and then maintains communication with them for as long as necessary. Generally, the negotiator will attempt to isolate the hostage takers from other outside communication in order to foster dependency on the negotiator as the crucial link with other people. Once communication is established, the negotiator will try to reduce the fear typically felt by the hostage takers so that they will be more willing to agree to a reasonable solution. The negotiator will try to structure the situation in ways that maximize predictability and calmness. The negotiator may also offer to help with any medical needs that the hostage group has, thereby gradually fostering positive components of the Stockholm syndrome. Finally, through gradual prompting and reinforcement, the negotiator tries to promote behaviors that are indicative of positive negotiation progress. Examples of such behaviors are increased conversation between the negotiator and the hostage taker, the passage of deadlines without threatened violence taking place, and less violent content and fewer threats in the speech of hostage takers.

THE POLICE OFFICER'S JOB

In the eyes of most citizens, the job of the police officer is to catch criminals and enforce the law, just as *Cagney and Lacey* or the police on *Miami Vice* used to do weekly on TV. But there are broader functions than these. The major duties of the police are divided into three general areas:

1. *Enforcing the law*, which includes investigation of complaints, arrest and prosecution of suspects, and efforts at crime prevention. Although law enforcement is perceived by most citizens as the most important function of the police, it accounts for only about 10% of police activity.
2. *Maintaining order*, including intervening in and arbitrating family and neighborhood disputes and keeping traffic moving, noise levels down, rowdy persons off the streets, and disturbances of the peace at a minimum. It is estimated that three out of every ten requests for police officers deal with this type of activity.
3. *Providing services*, such as giving assistance in medical and psychological emergencies, finding missing persons, helping stranded motorists, escorting funerals, and even rescuing cats from trees. An analysis of all the calls made to police cars in Syracuse, New York, in one week classified 37% of them in this category (Wilson, 1978).

Should the police spend so much of their time on community services? The major objections to community services are that they waste police resources and distract the police from the crucial roles of law enforcement and public protection for which they are specially trained. However, there are two advantages to the police continuing to provide such services. First, short of spending massive amounts of money to train and employ a new cadre of community service workers, there is no feasible alternative to the police in this capacity. Second, by providing these services, the police create a positive identity in the community that carries good will, respect, and cooperation over to their crime-fighting tasks. These side effects also serve as a "normalizing

---

Box 6-4 | The "Stockholm Syndrome"

The "Stockholm syndrome" resurfaced during the period in 1985 when 39 passengers from TWA Flight 847 were kept as hostages for 17 days by Beirut hijackers. The term comes from a 1973 incident in which hostages held in a Swedish bank developed a close emotional attachment to their captors (Eckholm, 1985). Hostages may come to sympathize with the lawbreakers and even adopt, at least temporarily, their captors' ideological views. The behavior of Patricia Hearst, who was kidnapped in 1974 and later helped her captors rob a bank, has been explained through this syndrome. Allyn Conwell, the spokesperson for the hostages in the 1985 TWA hijacking, was criticized for his statements expressing "profound sympathy" for his captors' Shi'ite position, but he explicitly denied that he was influenced by the Stockholm syndrome (Eckholm, 1985).

According to Martin Symonds, a New York psychiatrist and expert on terrorism, the syndrome is more likely to emerge when the hostages are purely "instrumental" victims, of no genuine concern to the terrorists except as levers over a third party. In such situations, the captors say "We'll let you go if our demands are met," and the captive begins "to misperceive the terrorist as the person who is trying to keep you alive" (Symonds, quoted in Eckholm, 1985, p. 6). For this reason, it is especially important for the police to determine the motivations of any hostage takers, as well as their specific goals.

buffer'' for the police by giving them opportunities to interact with people who are not behaving criminally, thereby decreasing the tendency of police to develop a cynical, suspicious attitude toward others.

Not only is the police officer's job composed of multiple duties, but the requirements of those duties may lead to personal conflict and eventually to psychological problems.

STRESS AND THE POLICE

Scores of books, technical reports, and journal articles have been written on the causes and treatment of police stress (e.g., Alkus & Padesky, 1983; Duncan & Kravitz, 1979; White, Scott, Biggerstaff, & Grubb, 1985). A journal is devoted to this specific topic (*Police Stress*), and a special organization, the International Law Enforcement Stress Association, has been formed.

One problem that emerges from the job of police officer is the "life in a fishbowl" phenomenon. Officers are visible to the public, and they are aware that their every act is being evaluated. Often they perform their job differently than the public wants them to (Lefkowitz, 1975). They are sensitive to public criticism, and this criticism also leads their spouses and children to feel isolated and segregated.

The police officer's role is among the most stressful of any. The National Institute on Workers' Compensation lists it among the "ten toughest jobs" (A. Miller, 1988, p. 43). Several investigators have divided the stress of police work into different categories according to the sources of the stress or the type of problem involved (Ostrov, 1986; Spielberger, Westberry, Grier, & Greenfield, 1980). The leading example of an instrument designed to measure police stress is the Police Stress Survey (PSS)

(Spielberger et al., 1980), which in its original form consisted of 60 items.

A revision of the PSS resulted in an additional 25 items derived from open-ended interviews with police officers (White, Lawrence, Biggerstaff, & Grubb, 1985). The following three categories of stress are the ones most commonly experienced by the police:

1. *Physical and psychological threats.* Included here are events related to the unique demands of police work. Items referring to using force, being physically attacked, confronting aggressive people or grisly crime scenes, and engaging in high speed chases load heavily on this factor (see Box 6-5 for further discussion). Danger can emerge from the most innocuous circumstances. Three police officers in Inkster, Michigan, made a routine call at a motel to serve a warrant for writing a bad check. They were met with a fusillade of gunfire; all three were killed. Patrolman Gary Lorenzen was one of the first officers to discover the bodies; "I haven't had anyone here I could talk to—I'm hurting like a son of a bitch inside but I have to be strong for the other officers," he said (Clancy, 1987, p. 1A).

2. *Evaluation systems.* These stressors include the ineffectiveness of the judicial system, court leniency with criminals, negative press accounts of the police, and putdowns and mistreatment of police officers in the courts.

3. *Lack of support.* Examples of these stressors include inadequate support by administrators within the department, weak support from supervisors, and poor job performance by fellow officers.

Stress is inevitable, given the demands placed on the police. Yet, police officers often have difficulty admitting that the stressful nature of their job is affecting them. A stigma exists about admitting a need for professional help. There may even be what Zimbardo

(1970) calls "dehumanization in self-defense"—that is, a process of protecting oneself from overwhelming emotions by treating others as objects rather than as persons. Better this, the officer thinks, than being "unprofessional." Officers with "problems" are relieved

of their weapons and badges, the symbols of their unique position and authority, and often they are placed in a limited-duty assignment (sometimes called the "bow and arrow" squad).

Stressful working conditions also lead to burnout. Only in the last decade has burn-out become

---

Box 6-5 *Reactions of Police Officers Involved in Shooting Incidents*

Solomon and Horn (1986) studied 86 police officers who had been involved in line-of-duty shooting incidents. These officers, 53% of whom had been involved in a shooting in which a person was

killed, were attending a three-day workshop on postincident trauma at the time.

Below are the percentages of officers who experienced at least a moderate amount of each of 18

postincident reactions, followed by the percentages of officers who suffered certain perceptual distortions during or after the incident.

Reaction	Percentage
1. Heightened sense of danger	58
2. Anger	49
3. Nightmares	34
4. Isolation/withdrawal	45
5. Fear and anxiety about future situations	40
6. Sleep difficulties	46
7. Flashbacks/intruding thoughts	44
8. Emotional numbing	43
9. Depression	42
10. Alienation	40
11. Guilt/sorrow/remorse	37
12. Mark of Cain	28
13. Problems with authority figures, rules, regulations	28
14. Family problems	27
15. Feelings of insanity/loss of control	23
16. Sexual difficulties	18
17. Alcohol/drug abuse	14
18. Suicidal thoughts	11

Perceptual Distortions	
1. Slow motion (perceiving the event to occur in slow motion)	67
2. Fast motion (perceiving the event to occur in rapid motion)	15
3. Diminished sound during the event	51
4. Intensified sound during the event	18
5. Tunnel vision during the event	37
6. Heightened detail during the event	18

recognized as a predominant problem for persons who deliver services to the public. It has been defined as "a syndrome of emotional exhaustion, depersonalization, and reduced personal accomplishment that can occur among individuals who work with people in some capacity" (Maslach & Jackson, 1984, p. 134). Emotional exhaustion reflects feelings of being emotionally overextended and "drained" by one's contact with other people. Depersonalization may take the form of a callous or insensitive response to other people, particularly crime victims and others requesting police assistance. Reduced personal accomplishment is manifested in a decrease in one's feeling of competence at the end of a day's work with other people (Maslach & Jackson, 1984).

Burn-out also affects behavior off the job. In their study of police officers and their families, Jackson and Maslach (1982) found that emotional exhaustion was, in fact, more likely than any other factor to affect behavior at home. Police officers were described by their wives as coming home upset, angry, tense, and anxious.

Burn-out may also result from an extended number of years at the same job. Patrol officers sometimes speak of the seven-year syndrome. Initially, officers are eager and anxious about their job performance. The tasks are initially interesting and challenging. But after several years some officers lose interest; the job feels stale and no longer encourages self-actualization and self-development. Enthusiasm is lost.

What can be done to reduce stress and burn-out in police officers? From their analysis of the research on organizational behavior, Jackson and Schuler (1983) hypothesized four qualities of the organization that increase burn-out in employees: (1) lack of rewards (especially positive feedback), (2) lack of control, (3) lack of clarity, and (4) lack of support. Although each of these is especially problematic for police officers, certain interventions can reduce the likelihood of burn-out (see Box 6-6 for other interventions).

For example, the police officer seldom hears when things go well for a client but often hears of the complaints of enraged citizens. Police officials could create opportunities for citizens to express their appreciation of what police officers are doing daily.

Officers often feel a lack of control in their jobs. They must react to calls; they cannot change the flow of demands. Furthermore, citizens expect them to respond immediately. Although the level of demands cannot be changed, officers can be given greater flexibility in how they respond to these demands. Their daily duties can be restructured so as to increase a sense of choice of activities. The place of discretion can be emphasized to the officers, because they do have a great deal of it when dealing with suspected offenders (Powell, 1981; Siegal, Sullivan, & Greene, 1974). As Greenberg and Ruback (1984) note, officers do not always make an arrest even when they catch a suspect breaking the law. In one study, police officers did not make an arrest in 52% of the misdemeanors and 43% of the felonies they investigated, even when they had probable cause to believe that the suspect had committed a crime (Reiss, 1971). LaFave (1965) provides one illustration:

> A traffic officer stopped a car that had been going 15 m.p.h. over the speed limit. The driver was a youth, but he had a valid driver's license. Although the 15 m.p.h. excess was beyond the ordinary toleration limit for speeding violations, the officer only gave the youth a severe warning. The officer knew that the law required suspension of the license of a juvenile driver for any moving violation [p. 138].

One strategy for decreasing burn-out among police is the use of *team policing*. Team policing involves a partial shift of decision making from a centralized authority to front-line officers and their immediate supervisors, who share the responsibility of making policy and management decisions. Teams are often organized around neighborhoods, and within a neighborhood team, members perform several different functions so that they come to realize how important each team member is to the overall success of the group.

IS THERE A POLICE PERSONALITY?

Given that the job description of a police officer requires a number of challenging tasks and that the job is highly public and visible, the public has a tendency to label police officers as having a certain set of qualities. Is there a distinct "police personality"? Do police officers share a cluster of personality characteristics that differentiates them from other people?

If there is a "police personality," how does it come about? Are police officers, by nature, a homogeneous group? Do they differ from other occupational groups and from the general population, and do individual officers cluster narrowly together with respect to their positions on many personality traits? Or is the personality of police officers shaped gradually over their careers as a result of common occupational demands and experiences? There are different opinions about the correct answers to these questions, but the consensus is that career socialization is a stronger influence than preexisting differences that lead certain individuals to become police officers.

Box 6-6 | Stress Reduction with the Police

The negative consequences of stress can be especially troublesome for police officers, because they are exposed to dangerous situations, they are armed with deadly weapons, and they are given special powers to use force. All these facts add to the risks of serious consequences for police who experience high levels of stress and make it important that police receive effective treatment for stress-related disturbances.

In recognition of these concerns, many police agencies have developed their own stress management programs or referred their officers to other agencies for counseling. These programs emphasize the prevention of stress through such techniques as relaxation training, stress inoculation, detection of early signs of stress, and effective problem solving (Reiser & Geiger, 1984).

Another approach to stress-related problems is to change those aspects of police work that officers find the most frustrating. These system-level changes are usually aimed at organizational difficulties that complicate police work. One example of this type of change is *team policing*, which we described in the text.

Despite attempts to prevent stress and to change organizations in positive ways, some officers will experience stress-related problems that require counseling. Psychological treatment of police officers is complicated because, as a group, the police are resistant to personal counseling. First, they tend to believe that really capable officers should be able to withstand any hardships and that failure to do so signals a lack of professionalism, machismo, or emotional control (Reiser & Geiger, 1984). Second, police fear that counseling attaches a stigma of mental disorder to them that will undercut respect from their peers. Finally, officers are justifiably concerned that the department's need to know their psychological status with respect to their fitness for continuing duty will override their rights of confidentiality and lead to embarrassing disclosures of personal information.

Police departments have developed several alternatives for providing psychological counseling to their officers. Although none of these options solves all the problems mentioned above, each tries to overcome the more common obstacles facing police counseling programs. One popular approach is peer counseling,

Among the most influential conceptions of a police personality is Joel Lefkowitz's description of the psychology of the police. After studying a host of variables, Lefkowitz concluded that the police do not differ from other groups in terms of psychological disorders or intelligence, but he suggested that there were other important differences. Lefkowitz (1975, p. 6) writes:

> . . . there exists a constellation of traits and attitudes or a general perspective on the world which particularly characterizes the policeman. This constellation . . . presumably [comprises] such interrelated traits as authoritarianism, suspiciousness, physical courage, cynicism, conservatism, loyalty, secretiveness, and self-assertiveness.

Lefkowitz and subsequent others (Charles, 1986; Muir, 1977) identified two clusters of personality traits that have been viewed as distinctive of police officers, but not in any pathological way.

Cluster One includes the traits of isolation and secrecy, defensiveness and suspiciousness, and cynicism. The image in this portrait is one of a close-knit group of people whose occupational isolation and accompanying secrecy lead to strong feelings of being misunderstood by outsiders, who are in turn viewed with suspiciousness and cynicism by the police. Feelings of insecurity also develop and underlie the officers' desire for a uniform and badge as symbols to bolster their limited sense of personal adequacy to meet the extraordinary challenges of

whereby police officers with or without special training in peer-counseling methods share their personal problems and discuss different ways of coping with the stress of their work. Describing their experiences with peer counseling in the Los Angeles Police Department, Reiser and Klyver (1987) report that 200 trained peer counselors conducted about 5000 hours of counseling with their fellow officers in one year alone. Most of this counseling was aimed at relationship problems and job dissatisfactions.

A second method is to provide counseling for specific problems that police officers suffer. The most noteworthy example of these focused interventions is counseling for officers who have been involved in the use of deadly force (see Blau, 1986; also refer to Box 6-5). The

emotional aftermath of shooting incidents is among the most traumatic experiences the police encounter and can often lead to symptoms of posttraumatic stress disorder (Reiser & Geiger, 1984; Solomon & Horn, 1986). Providing post-incident counseling is a common service of police psychologists; in some departments, counseling officers involved in shooting incidents is mandatory (McManis, 1986). The goals of this counseling, which also often relies on peer support (Klyver, 1986), are to reassure officers that their emotional reactions to incidents are normal, to give them a supportive place to express these emotions, to help officers understand the natural process of traumatic reactions and grieving, to help them reduce stress, and to promote a well-paced return to duty.

Although many ethical dilemmas are involved in psychological counseling for police officers (D'Agostino, 1986), the most difficult ones revolve around questions of confidentiality. Police counseling services are usually offered in one of two ways: by an "in-house" psychologist who is a full-time employee of the police department or by an "outside" psychologist who consults with the department on a part-time basis. In-house professionals are more available and knowledgeable about police issues. Outside consultants, because they are independent from the department, are better able to protect the confidentiality of their clients' disclosures.

their jobs. In fact, feelings of being misunderstood by the public are one of the three most frequent problems reported by police officers. The segregation that results from the uniform and from their role in the community leads to what Lefkowitz (1975) calls socio-occupational isolation, which only intensifies the solidarity with other police officers.

Lefkowitz's second cluster, "Trait Syndrome II: Authoritarianism, status concerns, and violence," is much more controversial and includes a penchant for violence, as well as several dimensions of authoritarianism. Authoritarianism, as conceived by Adorno and his colleagues (Adorno, Frenkel-Brunswik, Levinson, & Sanford, 1950), is a cluster of beliefs that reflect identification with and submissiveness to authorities, an endorsement of power and toughness, intolerance of outgroups and minorities, pressure for conformity to group norms, and rejection of anything unconventional as "deviant" or "sick."

Although the police appear submissive to authority and tend to be politically conservative, they do not, as a group, score as particularly authoritarian on the California F Scale of Authoritarianism or particularly rigid on Rokeach's Dogmatism Scale (Carlson, Thayer, & Germann, 1971; Fenster & Locke, 1973). In some studies, they score lower than college students and teachers. If they are authoritarian, it is primarily in the sense of enacting middle-class conventionality. Police may also become more aggressive when they perceive their personal authority to be questioned, and they work at a job that justifies (and sometimes overjustifies) the use of force. Police also appear more responsive to politically powerful figures than to powerless ones. In a provocative investigation, Wilson (1978) asked police officers how they would respond if they saw a car with a very low license number—for example, license "NY 2"—speeding. Such low-number plates are offered to politicians in many states. Police officers in two New York communities, Amsterdam and Newburgh, responded without hesitation that they would "mind our own business." Police officers do not express similar concerns toward groups and individuals who lack political clout. Greenberg and Ruback (1984) summarize the relevant body of literature by stating:

> Several studies provide evidence of police discrimination against persons of lower socioeconomic status and members of minority groups (Cochran, 1971; Skolnick, 1975; Westley, 1970; Wilson, 1978). Chambliss and Seidman (1971), among others, contend that suspects of lower socioeconomic status are discriminated against by the police because they wield less political power than middle-class suspects. Chambliss and Seidman further contend that because the police associate minority-group membership with lower socioeconomic status, minority-group members have become the objects of police discrimination [p. 82].

The labels "authoritarian" and "violent" may be justified for police officers, but only in a much narrower sense than usually applied. Surveys and informed opinion agree that police officers tend to be a politically conservative, conventional group, very loyal to one another and concerned with assertively maintaining the status quo. They are authoritarian in the sense of respecting the higher authority of the law, the nation, and the government they serve. Pepinsky (1975) observes:

> If a citizen behaves disrespectfully toward the [police] officer, the citizen is not seen by the officer as merely showing disregard to the officer as an individual. The citizen is seen as disregarding the larger authority the officer believes he represents. This disrespect to the officer represents the best evidence the officer is apt to have of disrespect for the law itself—hence, of a citizen's determination not to adhere to the dictates of the law in the future [p. 37].

The predominant psychological motivation to become a police officer appears to be the need for security, probably a manifestation of the working-class backgrounds from which most police officers come (Gorer, 1955; Niederhoffer, 1967). The second-commonest motive is a desire to be of social service, with emphasis on the "social," or working with others. Successful police officers are *less* motivated than most people by a desire for autonomous work or a chance to make one's own decisions.

Research indicates that police officers *do not* possess pathological extremes of personality. Most studies indicate that, as a group, they are "normal" or "healthy" in their adjustment. The group's average IQ is consistently within the high-average range.

POLICE/COMMUNITY RELATIONS

Police officers are justified in feeling that they live in a "fishbowl," for their performance is constantly being reviewed by the courts and evaluated by the public. Several amendments to the U.S. Constitution impose limits on law enforcement officers; such limits are part of the first ten amendments, known as the Bill of Rights. The Fourth Amendment protects against unreasonable search and seizure of persons or property. The Fifth Amendment provides guarantees for persons accused of a crime; for example, no such person "shall be compelled in any criminal case to be a witness against himself, nor be deprived of life, liberty, or property, without due process of law." As will be shown in Chapter 9, limits on police activities are frequently reevaluated on the basis of current court interpretations of these amendments and recent cases. The Sixth Amendment

guarantees the accused "the right to a speedy and public trial" and "the assistance of counsel for his defense"; the way these provisions are interpreted has implications for police procedures. Protection against "cruel and unusual punishment" is promised by the Eighth Amendment, and the Fourteenth Amendment guarantees all citizens "due process." These amendments also direct and constrain police behavior.

During the last two decades, citizens' groups have been increasingly critical of the police. Two types of concerns can be identified. The first deals with interrogation practices used by the police to elicit confessions from suspects. Although the coercion of confessions is covered extensively in Chapter 8, one example here illustrates the concern. Wald, Ayres, Hess, Schantz, and Whitebread (1967) observed 127 interrogations carried out during 11 weeks by the New Haven, Connecticut, Police Department. Manipulative tactics to induce confessions were used 65% of the time. The most common approach was "to overwhelm the suspect with damaging evidence, to assert a firm belief in his or her guilt, and then to suggest that it would be easier for all concerned if the suspect admitted to his or her role in the crime" (Kassin & Wrightsman, 1985, p. 75). Along with this plea, police often expressed concern for the suspect's welfare. The researchers did not observe undue force used by the police detectives, but they did report the frequent use of promises of lowered bail, reduced charges, or leniency by the judge and vague threats about harsher treatment. In three of the 127 cases, detectives implied that they would make trouble for the suspects' friends or families if they refused to cooperate.

A second concern of community groups is excessive force or brutality by the police (Fyfe, 1988). During the protests of the 1960s that took place in Watts (a section of Los Angeles), in Detroit, and throughout the South, blacks demonstrated against police harassment of innocent people. The police officer is often viewed in the ghetto as a representative of an all-male, lily-white, overbearing colonial power that exerts economic, political, and social control over its inhabitants (Blauner, 1972). Law enforcement officers are trained to act within legally prescribed boundaries, but charges of police brutality frequently appear in local newspapers. During the late 1980s, it was estimated that approximately 2500 cases of police brutality were reported and investigated annually.

The beating or killing of suspects by the police draws extensive attention in the media. A recent example of this phenomenon occurred in Los Angeles in March 1991, when police chased a black motorist who they alleged was speeding through an L.A. suburb in his 1988 Hyundai. As the unarmed man emerged from his car, a police officer felled him with a blast from a 50,000-volt stun gun, and three patrolmen proceeded to beat and kick him while a police helicopter hovered overhead. As a result of this attack, which was witnessed by at least 11 other police onlookers, Rodney King, a 25-year-old man who it was later learned was on parole, lay seriously injured with multiple wounds, a broken ankle, a cracked cheekbone, and several internal injuries. One special feature of this attack was that a nearby citizen captured part of the episode on his videocamera; within hours the tape of this terrifying beating was played across the country on network news programs. Soon thereafter, local, state, and federal agencies launched investigations into the beating and the entire L.A. Police Department. In their first trial, three of the four officers who were charged with beating King were acquitted of all criminal charges against them, an outcome that shocked millions of Americans.

Even the U.S. Supreme Court has recently restricted the use of deadly force by police. It struck down a Tennessee law that allowed police to shoot to kill, even when an unarmed suspect fleeing a crime scene showed no apparent threat (Duning & Hanchette, 1985; Fyfe, 1982). The incident that sparked the decision involved a Memphis police officer who responded to a call about a late-night prowler breaking into a house. Spotting an intruder darting across the backyard, the officer commanded him to halt. The figure instead began to climb a fence and escape; fearing that he could not do likewise, the policeman fired. The 15-year-old unarmed robber was fatally shot in the head. He had stolen a purse and ten dollars. (Three justices, Sandra Day O'Connor, Warren Burger, and William Rehnquist, dissented from the majority opinion and stated that it would give suspects a constitutional right "to flee unimpeded" from the police.)

What causes the police to act brutally? How can we explain incidents in which officers clearly have used excessive force? One popular explanation is that police excesses stem from the personality problems of "a few bad apples" among the police. In this view, brutality reflects the sadistic extreme of the aggressive, tough pole of the authoritarian personality that we have already discussed. An opposing explanation is that brutality is the unfortunate price occasionally extracted from situations in which rising numbers of violent, even deadly, criminals demand forceful responses from the police. Which view is correct?

Police brutality is another example of a problem for which psychology seeks explanations neither in individual personalities nor in environmental situations but in the *interactions between persons and the situations in which they function.* From this perspective, we begin with police officers who, on average, are strongly committed to maintaining the conventional order and to protecting society. We repeatedly put them into potentially dangerous situations, we arm them well, and we authorize them to use appropriate force. The result from the mix of this type of person with these types of situations is predictable: in some unknown number of encounters, the police will use excessive force against citizens who are incorrectly suspected of wrongdoing that threatens public safety.

During the last two decades, but particularly since the Rodney King episode, a number of attempts have been made to improve police relations with people in the community. Beyond concern with community relations, our society has increasingly realized that traditional policing methods don't work. Skolnick and

Bayley (1986) summarize the research findings in Box 6-7.

We have already described team policing as one effort to make the police officer's job less stressful and to respond to some community concerns about the way police perform their jobs. Evaluations of this type of innovation are inconsistent. In some cities only minor changes were made, such as stenciling "Neighborhood Police Team" on several radio cars; it was unlikely that such trivial actions would improve police/community relations. In other cities, proposed changes were thwarted by higher levels of police administration. But after team policing was introduced in Newark, New Jersey,

---

Box 6-7 | Police Methods: Myths and Facts

The effectiveness of traditional police strategies has been questioned by recent research findings. For example:

1. Increasing the size of the police force does not necessarily reduce the rate of crime or increase the proportion of crimes that lead to convictions. Crime rates and conviction rates are best predicted by conditions in the locality and society in general, such as income level, unemployment rate, population, and income distribution (Clark & Heal, 1979; Morris & Heal, 1981).

2. Use of police cars patrolling through neighborhoods does not reduce crime or increase the chance of catching suspects.

Furthermore, it doesn't reassure citizens appreciably, nor does it increase trust in the police (Kelling et al., 1974). But regular patrols by police officers on foot do reduce citizens' fear of crime, although there is little evidence that they reduce the crime rate (Police Foundation, 1981).

3. Two-person patrol cars are no more effective than one-officer cars in reducing the crime rate or catching lawbreakers. Also, injuries to police officers are no more likely in one-person patrol cars (Pate & Kelling, 1980).

4. Highly saturated patrolling reduces the crime rate, but only temporarily. One major effect is to displace this crime to other areas.

5. Major crimes—robbery, muggings, rape, murder—are rarely encountered by police while they are on patrol (Reiss, 1971). As Skolnick and Bayley (1986, p. 4) observe, only "Dirty Harry" has his lunch interrupted by a bank robbery in progress.

6. Crimes are most often "solved" because the offenders are caught almost immediately or because someone provides a *specific* identification—name, address, or license plate number. If neither occurs, the chances that the crime will be solved are less than 10% (Greenwood & Petersilia, 1976).

Adapted from Skolnick and Bayley (1986).

crime rates decreased dramatically and officer morale was reported to be high.

As Skolnick and Bayley (1986) observe, structural changes like team policing must be accompanied by changes in operating philosophy too. One of the most promising reforms found in a survey of six innovative police departments (Houston, Detroit, Denver, Oakland, Newark, and Santa Ana, California) was what Skolnick and Bayley call *civilianization,* or the increased employment of civilians in the police department. In Santa Ana, these police employees wear uniforms but not guns or billy clubs. They carry out service-related activities and relieve the regular police officers of duties that take time away from patrol and crime investigation.

A change in the function of the police is reflected in the philosophy of some police departments. Traditionally, police have been only reactive; they have responded to crimes. But now police officials are asking if they can reduce crime by managing the problem rather than just responding to manifestations of it (Wilson & Kelling, 1989).

"Managing the problem" includes, for example, preventive maintenance. The philosophy behind this approach is as follows: "If the first broken window in a building is not repaired, soon all the windows will be broken; likewise, when disorderly behavior is left unchallenged or neighborhood decay is left unattended, the disorder escalates and the decay spreads" (Wilson & Kelling, 1989, p. 23). So Los Angeles police have organized citizens' groups to paint out graffiti and have prompted city agencies to tow away abandoned cars. The goal is to "harden the target" so that criminals have reduced opportunities to commit their crimes. Houston has opened up store-front police stations, as another example of the community problem-solving orientation. In this conception, known as *community-based*

policing, the officer thus becomes a sort of Peace Corps community organizer; rather than nightly busting drunks who congregate in an empty lot, the police help convert the lot into a vest-pocket park (Anderson, 1988; Press, 1988). The police can deal more directly with citizens' requests and needs than would be possible through official dispatches received from a centralized police communications center. Community-based policing seeks to humanize police and citizens to each other.

Community police administrations are beginning to acknowledge the need for changes in attitudes in individual officers. Recognizing the absence of dialogue between the police and the black community in many cities, Teahan (1975a) used role playing and interpersonal feedback during police academy training to improve communication and relationships between black and white police officers. An example of the role-playing situations that Teahan used to improve black/white relations is the following:

> Two officers representing scout car partners were chosen (or volunteered) from the group. A third officer was then assigned the role of citizen. The scout car men were given a card stating: "You are cruising in your scout car at 12 P.M. in the 13th precinct when you receive information over the car radio that an armed robbery has just been committed a few blocks away. The suspect is described as a young adult male in his early twenties, dressed in a dark overcoat. Suddenly, you notice a young man fitting that description ahead of you. You pull up beside him and. . . . "
>
> The officer designated as the citizen received a similar card reading: "You are a black university student who has just finished seeing a movie a few blocks away. It is 12 P.M. and you are hurrying home to your apartment when a police squad car pulls up beside you" [Teahan, 1975a, p. 38].

The results were mixed. The black officers felt the workshops were beneficial; they showed greater concern over racial issues and felt that relationships between black and white officers were even better than they had been at the beginning of training.

But white officers became *more* prejudiced toward blacks. (White officers in control groups who did not participate in the workshops became less prejudiced.) Furthermore, they reported less contact with blacks at the end of the project.

Results were even more disappointing to Teahan when, in a second study, he followed up police officers 18 months after participation in these police academy workshops (Teahan, 1975b). He found radical increases in racial animosity between black and white officers over the 18 months. All officers seemed to become more impersonal and detached; they more easily developed feelings of hostility toward authority figures. As black officers progressed through the academy and on to regular police work, they became increasingly negative toward whites and disillusioned with the department; they began to shift in the direction of a greater sense of black unity and polarity against whites. Whereas blacks saw greater preference being given to whites, white officers perceived things to be the opposite. The result was that both groups became more ethnocentric and polarized.

One solution to the problem of race relations would be more representation of minorities on police forces. And some cities are actively recruiting minorities. But in other cities the use of a written Civil Service examination as the major basis for promotion has kept minority-group members from advancing because of racial biases associated with the tests that may compromise their validity. For example, of the 377 police officers in New York City promoted after 1989 testing, only 3 were black, 16 Hispanic, and 1 Asian-American (Pitt, 1989).

SUMMARY

Policing is necessary in any society concerned with maintaining public order, even though some people in our society see police activity as restricting the freedom of individuals. Police officers daily face the dilemma of equality versus discretion: whether to treat all suspects or lawbreakers equally or whether to temper justice with mercy.

Selection of police officers usually includes the completion of a set of psychological inventories and a clinical interview as well as situational tests, in which the candidate role-plays responses to real-life challenges that would face a police officer, such as intervening in a dispute between a wife and her husband or aiding an injured man in a public place. Although responses to these situational tasks are valuable additions to psychological testing and interviewing, many police departments are reluctant to adopt them because they are costly and time consuming.

Training of police officers usually covers a variety of topics, including criminal law, human relations training, self-defense, and use of firearms. Many training programs last about 15 weeks. Recently police recruits have been trained in crisis intervention, including handling the mentally ill, resolving family disputes, and responding to hostage taking.

The police officer's job is multifaceted. Law enforcement (including investigation of complaints, arrest and prosecution of suspects, and efforts at crime prevention) accounts for only about 10% of police activity. Maintaining order (intervening in family and neighborhood disputes, keeping traffic moving, responding to disturbances of the peace, and so on) accounts for about 30% of police activity. Providing services is even more time consuming.

As the Gilbert and Sullivan operetta tells us, "A policeman's lot is not a happy one." Three problems are especially significant: the "life in a fishbowl" phenomenon, job-related stress, and burn-out. Job duties and perceptions of the officer's role can be modified to reduce burn-out. Special psychological interventions are also available to counteract stressful reactions suffered by the police.

Whether a specific "police personality" exists is controversial, but research suggests that two clusters of traits exist: (1) isolation and secrecy, defensiveness and suspiciousness, and cynicism; and (2) authoritarianism, status concerns, and violence. The evidence for the existence or strength of the second cluster is less convincing than for the first, and there is no indication that police officers as a group possess pathological personalities.

In recent years, community groups have been very critical of police behavior. Manipulative tactics used to coerce confessions from criminal suspects have been documented. Brutal treatment of innocent citizens, especially those of racial minorities, has been highly publicized. Efforts to improve police/community relations include team policing, reorganizations within the police department that restructure the traditional chain of command, community-based policing, and interracial human relations workshops. These interventions have had only a limited degree of success.

7

Crime Investigation: Eyewitnesses

As we saw in Chapter 6, the tasks facing the police include investigating crimes and accumulating evidence so that suspects can be identified and arrested. Particularly at the early stages of an investigation, eyewitnesses are important to these tasks. Sometimes they provide the only solid leads for the police. But in their attempts to solve crimes—and especially in their use of observers—the police face the kinds of dilemmas described in Chapter 1.

Witnesses often make mistakes in their identification. The police may pressure them to point the finger at a suspect; often the desire to get a case "nailed down" (the goal of conflict resolution and stability described in Chapter 1) dominates over the goal of discovering the truth. Hence the reports of eyewitnesses can lead the police down blind alleys or cause them to arrest the wrong suspect; the testimony of mistaken observers can even lead to wrong verdicts by judges and juries. In fact, a leading researcher, Elizabeth Loftus, has stated that "Faulty eyewitness testimony, in my opinion, is the major cause of wrongful conviction in this country" (quoted in Leary, 1988, p. 23). (And, as noted by Wells and Loftus, 1984, concern about eyewitnesses' accuracy is not restricted to criminal cases. The results of civil lawsuits and safety inquiries are often affected by the reports of eyewitnesses.)

Many crimes have only one eyewitness. A rape, for example, is usually witnessed only by the victim; the same is true for the sexual abuse of children. Eyewitness testimony, even from one person, can be very convincing. In England, of cases in which the only evidence was eyewitness testimony, 74% resulted in conviction. Half of these (169 out of 347) had only one eyewitness (Loftus, 1979). Society clamors for the prosecution of crimes and the punishment of lawbreakers, but innocent individuals deserve to be treated fairly by the criminal justice system. As you will discover in the next section, the latter goal is sometimes sacrificed through a combination of witness mistakes and faulty investigatory procedures.

EXAMPLES OF MISTAKEN IDENTIFICATION

In a book aptly titled *Wrongful Imprisonment*, Brandon and Davies (1973) cite 70 cases in which eyewitness testimony was the main factor in an innocent person's conviction. How does this happen?

The ordeal of Bernard T. Pagano is illustrative. A number of crimes near Wilmington, Delaware, came to be called the "Gentleman Bandit" robberies because of the nice manners of the criminal, who frequently apologized to his victims. The police published composite drawings based on different victims' descriptions of the robber's appearance, and these encouraged an anonymous report that the drawing resembled Father Bernard T. Pagano, the assistant pastor of a Catholic church in Bethesda, Maryland. Fr. Pagano was charged with the robberies, all the while proclaiming his innocence. At his trial, seven victims identified the priest as the robber. Although there was no other major evidence against him, a conviction looked likely. But, during the trial, a man already in jail came forward and confessed to these crimes. Though 15 years younger, he bore a striking resemblance to Fr. Pagano. The true criminal had a police record and even had committed similar robberies in the past. He also knew unpublished information about the crimes charged to the cleric. Fr. Pagano was released; but, had the perpetrator not come forward, it is very likely that the priest would have become a prisoner.

One reason why such mistakes proliferate is that, when eyewitnesses make a tentative identification, police stop investigating other leads. The goal of finding the truth is submerged—often unintentionally—in the rush to resolve the conflict over the cause of a crime.

Although the Pagano case illustrates one type of eyewitness error—associating a composite drawing with the face of an innocent person—other sources of error are possible. Richard M. Nance (notice the middle initial M) was arrested in Los Angeles. His was not a very serious charge, but he was found guilty and given a brief jail term. In the midst of his ten-day sentence, a nationwide computerized crime network spat out the information that a Richard *Lee* Nance was sought in Sonoma County, in northern California, on a burglary charge.

The Sonoma County Sheriff's Department's warrant for Richard Lee Nance said he was born on July 3, 1946, was 5 feet, 10 inches tall, and had brown hair and brown eyes. The L.A. prisoner's middle name was Marion, not Lee; he was born on July 6, 1946, not July 3; and his eyes were blue, not brown. Yet he was flown to Sonoma County and put in jail with bail set at $5000. During the pretrial hearing, the burglary victim even pointed to Richard M. Nance and identified him as the man who had stolen a valuable ring and $100 from his farmhouse. Because Richard M. Nance was there at the hearing, labeled as the defendant, the victim was quick to assume that Nance was the robber, even though his fingerprints differed from those left at the scene of the crime. As Nance said later, "I can laugh about it now but can you believe me sitting there in the bright orange [jail] jump suit. Who else is the guy going to point to? The judge?" Despite the inconsistencies in name, appearance, and fingerprints, it took an investigator from the public defender's office almost a month to unravel the case and get Nance released from jail.

Nance asked rhetorically "Who else is the witness going to point to?" but witnesses have sometimes pointed to the wrong person. In a trial in Washington, DC, two different U.S. Park Police officers, on the stand, pointed to the defense attorney rather than the defendant when asked to identify the protester charged with assaulting a police officer. After the first witness erred, the defense attorney moved his note pad and papers in front of his client, who began to scribble furiously, thus contributing to the impression that the defendant was the attorney, and vice versa. After the second misidentification, the government dropped the charges (Strasser, 1989).

During the last few years, the public has become more aware that mistaken identifications can be made. The case of Lenell Geter (see Box 7-1) was portrayed on *60 Minutes*; this publicity, plus newspaper articles and intervention by government authorities, led the Dallas, Texas, district attorney eventually to release Geter.

POINTS AT WHICH A MISTAKEN IDENTIFICATION CAN OCCUR

Jurors in a criminal trial see a victim take the witness stand and confidently identify the defendant as his or her attacker. Not only may the jurors assume that this identification is accurate, but they are likely to believe that the victim was just as confident about the initial description or identification. These assumptions fail to recognize the many problems that can plague the accuracy of a criminal identification (Wells, in press).

Mistakes in the process can occur the moment the crime is committed. It may be too dark, events may move too swiftly, or the encounter may be too brief for the victim to form an accurate perception of the incident. Yet victims are forced to form impressions—about the criminal's height, hair color, voice, and other identifying features. We have all had the experience of spotting someone we think we instantly recognize and realizing that he or she is a stranger only when we start to say hello. Similar mistakes can be made at the time of a crime. "The robber looked familiar," a clerk may think.

During the investigation of a crime, the police will ask the victim to examine a book of photos or a lineup of suspects. They may coax reactions from eyewitnesses. At this point the victim wants to help the police solve the crime; victims feel implicit pressure to identify *someone,* even if the police do not deliberately encourage it.

Police detectives have been given several suggestions for conducting a lineup properly. For example, it is preferable to ask witnesses "Is he there? Do you see him?" rather than "Which one of these is he?" The second question suggests to the witness that the suspect is actually present in the lineup, whereas the first one does not. But, even if the preferred questioning is used, about 60% of the time the viewer picks someone from the lineup as the criminal. Is this a desirable outcome? We cannot say, because we do not know what percentage of lineups include the true criminal. Most lineups are composed of five or six persons, one of whom is the suspect; the others—called "foils"—are people known to be innocent of the crime (often the foils are police officers or offenders in jail for other crimes). However, even if the police avoid improper suggestions in their procedures and use appropriate foils, many witnesses will assume that the police would not have scheduled a lineup if they did not have a good suspect as part of it (Malpass & Devine, 1984).

A better procedure would be to show suspects and foils one at a time. Cutler and Penrod (1988), using a 1½-minute videotape of a staged liquor-store robbery, found that, when persons

---

Box 7-1 | *Lenell Geter: What If His Case Hadn't Been Publicized?*

Lenell Geter, a 26-year-old engineer, was convicted of armed robbery of $615 from a Kentucky Fried Chicken store in a small Texas town. He was sentenced to life in prison, even though he had a strong alibi: nine of his co-workers insisted that he was at work at the time of the robbery, in the middle of the afternoon on August 23, 1982. His place of employment, E-Systems, in Greenville, Texas, was 50 miles from the robbery site. Geter, a black man with a college degree, had no criminal record. The prosecution presented no physical evidence linking him with the holdup. In fact, initial reports by the restaurant workers described the criminal as about 5 feet, 6 inches. Geter is 6 feet tall.

But Geter was convicted by an all-white jury, on the basis of the testimony of five employees of the store, all white, who mistakenly identified him as the gunman by picking his picture out of a police photo array. Despite the apparent injustice and the widespread media coverage it generated, the Dallas County prosecutors did not let Geter go free *until another suspect was identified as the criminal* by four of the original five eyewitnesses. That happened in March 1984, almost two years after the crime and after Geter had served most of the intervening time in prison. Since his release, Geter married, had a child, and returned to his native state of South Carolina, where he is now a social worker.

were shown individually, the witnesses picked the wrong individual only 19% of the time, whereas in a traditional lineup of six persons they falsely accused an innocent person 39% of the time.

Police departments differ in the care they give to creating a lineup of persons who resemble the suspect. They may place the suspect in a lineup of people who differ markedly from the suspect in height, weight, physique, hairstyle, and other significant features mentioned in the witness's description of the offender. Here are some examples: "In one case . . . the defendant had been picked out of a line-up of six men, of which he was the only Oriental. In other cases, a black-haired suspect was placed among a group of light-haired persons, tall suspects have been made to stand with short suspects, and, in a case where the perpetrator of the crime was known to be a youth, a suspect under twenty was placed in a line-up with five other persons, all of whom were forty or over" (*United States* v. *Wade,* 1967). In assembling lineups, police should use foils who match the witness's description of the culprit as much as possible (Luus & Wells, 1991), just as a challenging multiple-choice question should have alternative answer choices that are plausible though wrong. Psychologists have developed procedures to measure how many of the foils in a lineup truly act as legitimate alternatives (Brigham, 1989).

Lineups are time consuming to create, and adequate types or numbers of foils may not be available. Thus police departments often use a book of photographs, or "mug book," to identify suspects. The problem here is of another kind; victims may be asked to look at a large number of photographs in a short period of time (as many as 500 in an hour). Before the trial, there will be a preliminary hearing, at which the suspect is present. The victims or other eyewitnesses will be asked whether the suspect is the person who committed the crime. It is hard for witnesses to change their public statement at this point. If

they have picked the suspect out of a lineup or a photo array, most would be very reluctant now—in front of a judge and the attorneys—to say "I'm not so sure" or "I've changed my mind about him." Also, their current identification of the suspect may now be determined more by their recognition of the mug-book picture than by their recall of the original crime.

In response to being challenged by an opposing attorney, many eyewitnesses become even more confident in their identifications. Additionally, they may try to become more convincing by providing more details and embellishments during subsequent steps in the investigation and trial process. For example, the defense attorney may propose a *suppression hearing,* in which the judge is asked to rule that the eyewitness cannot testify at the actual trial because of the inaccuracy in his or her report. (Judges rarely accede to such requests, but defense attorneys try anyway.) At the suppression hearing, the eyewitness may again be called on to make an identification of the accused; and so again, of course, at the actual trial.

We have just seen some of the ways that the processes of crime detection and investigation can contribute to errors in identification. But all of us, as observers, have the capacity within our own perceptual and memory processes to make errors too. To illustrate these sources of error, we now consider the steps in the process of acquiring information from the outside world and recalling it.

BASIC INFORMATION PROCESSING: PERCEPTION AND MEMORY

To process information, we must first perceive a stimulus and at least momentarily retain it.

Failures and errors can emerge at any step along the way.

Perception

Although our perceptual abilities are impressive (Penrod, Loftus, & Winkler, 1982), we do make errors. We tend to overestimate the height of criminals, and we overestimate the duration of a brief witnessed event while underestimating the duration of prolonged incidents. When watching a short film, we notice more about the actions than about the persons doing the acting. If a weapon is present when a crime is committed, we devote our attention to it more than to the facial features or other physical aspects of the person who has the weapon. This "weapon focus effect" has been demonstrated even when people watch a film of a crime (Loftus, Loftus, & Messo, 1987; Tooley, Brigham, Maass, & Bothwell, 1987). It appears to be caused not so much by emotional arousal as by the fact that witnesses narrow their attention to the weapon, thereby limiting the amount of attention they pay to other aspects of the situation, such as physical features of the perpetrator (Kramer, Buckhout, & Eugenio, 1990; Maass & Köhnken, 1989).

Memory

Experimental psychologists subdivide the building of a memory into three processes: (1) encoding, (2) storage, and (3) retrieval. We will consider each in turn.

Encoding. *Encoding* refers to the acquisition of information. Many aspects of a stimulus can affect how it is encoded; stimuli that are only briefly seen or heard are not encoded fully, of course. How complex a stimulus is affects its acquisition, but the relationship is not a straightforward one. As the complexity of an event increases—consider, for example, an earthquake or an explosion—some portions of the event probably will be misremembered, whereas other aspects of the event will be accurately recalled.

Contrary to what many people believe, a stressful situation does not enhance the encoding of events. A mild level of stress or arousal may produce alertness and interest in the task at hand, but extreme stress usually causes the person to encode the information incompletely or inaccurately. This principle reflects an application of the Yerkes-Dodson law, which describes the effects of arousal on learning. Under extremely low levels of external stress, the person is in such a relaxed state that little learning takes place. On the other hand, if the environment contains excessive stressful components, perception is narrowed, information is funneled, and less learning occurs than under mild levels of stress. Performance on many tasks is best when the level of arousal is moderate—enough to ensure a person's attention but not so high as to disrupt accuracy.

Characteristics of the witness also affect encoding. We all differ in visual acuity and hearing ability. We also have a tendency to see what we expect to see; preexposure instructions about what to notice have their desired effects.

Storage. The second step in building a memory is the *storage* of stimulus information. How well do we retain what we encode? Many years ago the experimental psychologist Hermann Ebbinghaus showed that early memory loss is rapid. Lipton (1977) illustrated this phenomenon in a setting relevant to the concerns of this chapter. Subjects were shown a film of an armed robbery and shooting without any prior knowledge that they would be serving as eyewitnesses. Those who were questioned after one week generated 18% less memory information than those who were questioned immediately after viewing the film.

But a second phenomenon also occurs during the storage phase—a surprising and potentially disturbing one. Activities that eyewitnesses carry out or information they learn *after* they observe an event can alter their memory of the event. For example, viewing mug shots of suspects can alter an eyewitness's capacity to recognize faces that he or she viewed before the mug shots (Brown, Deffenbacher, & Sturgill, 1977; Gorenstein & Ellsworth, 1980); that is, the new activity can interfere with memory of the old.

A similar conclusion derives from the ingenious studies of Elizabeth Loftus (1975, 1979). In one of her projects, subjects viewed a one-minute film of an automobile accident and were later asked a series of questions about it. The first question asked either how fast the car was going "when it ran the stop sign" *or* how fast it was going "when it turned right." Then, on the last question, all subjects were asked whether they had seen a stop sign in the film. In the first group, which had earlier been asked about the speed of the car "when it ran the stop sign," 53% said yes, whereas only 35% said yes in the second group. The effect of the initial question was to "prompt," or refresh, the memory for this part of the film. In a second study, Loftus included a misleading follow-up question that mentioned a nonexistent barn. When questioned one week later, 17% of the subjects reported seeing the barn in the original film! In essence, the new information was added to the same memory store as the original stimulus.

Retrieval.   The third and last step in establishing memory is the retrieval of information. This is not as straightforward a process as you might at first think. We all have experienced the "tip of the tongue" phenomenon: we know an answer or a movie title or a person's name but can't dredge it out of our memory store.

Again, at this phase, wording of questions can influence output. For example, in one experiment, subjects first watched a brief film and then were asked questions about it. Subjects who were asked "Did you see the broken headlight?" were two to three times more likely to answer "yes" than subjects who were asked "Did you see a broken headlight?" (Loftus & Zanni, 1975). (There was no broken headlight in the film.) Similarly, the verb that described the action in a retrieval question influenced estimates of the action in the film. Loftus and Palmer (1974) asked "How fast were the cars going when they smashed?" " . . . when they collided?" " . . . when they bumped?" " . . . when they hit?" or " . . . when they contacted?" The average response was 40.8 miles per hour for "smashed," 39.3 mph for "collided," 38.1 mph for "bumped," 34.0 mph for "hit," and 31.8 mph for "contacted."

In recalling information from our memory store, we often generate memories that are, in a sense, accurate but are not relevant to the task at hand. For instance, victims will sometimes pick from a lineup or a photo array the face of a person whom they have seen before but who is not the actual criminal. For example, a clerk at a convenience store who is the victim of a late-night robbery may mistakenly identify an innocent shopper who frequents the store. In an actual case, a Los Angeles judge who was kidnapped and attacked while she was jogging picked a suspect's picture from the police mug book after the attack, and on that basis he was charged with the crimes. She later stated that she had not remembered at first that he had appeared before her in court four years earlier, for similar offenses, and that she had sentenced him to unsupervised probation (Associated Press, 1988). This phenomenon, called *unconscious transference,* was demonstrated by Robert Buckhout (1974), who staged a mock assault before an unsuspecting class of 141 students. Seven weeks later, when the students were asked to pick the assailant from a group of six photographs, 40% were able to select the assailant. But, of the 60% who failed to make the correct identification, two-thirds selected a person who had been at the "crime scene" as an innocent bystander. This is one means by which innocent persons are thrust into a process that eventually convicts them of crime.

In summary, as Hall, Loftus, and Tousignant (1984) conclude, testing one's memory for an original event can alter the memory for that event; indeed, "the witness reacts as if original memory and postevent information had been inextricably integrated" (p. 127).

PSYCHOLOGICAL TESTS OF EYEWITNESSES' ACCURACY

Throughout this chapter we have implied that the testimony of eyewitnesses to crime is sometimes in error and that law enforcement officials, in their zeal to prosecute offenders, contribute to this error by their emphasis on closing out a case. But how often does this occur? How much error is there? The legal system does not give priority to these questions because it has other questions that it considers more urgent. One contribution a psychologist can make to the law is to provide empirical data that are relevant to the specific question "In a controlled situation, where we know the correct answer, just how many errors do eyewitnesses make?"

As we saw in the description of unconscious transference, psychologists can stage mock crimes in front of captive audiences such as college classes. When Buckhout (1974) did this, the accuracy rate of only 40% (when the students were questioned seven weeks later) was higher than the outcome from sheer guessing (1 out of 6, or 16.7%) but was hardly strong enough to convict anyone of a crime.

You might think that the seven-week delay reduced accuracy at least somewhat. Perhaps, but even testing done more promptly after the crime does not produce 100% accuracy. In one study, after a 35-day delay the accuracy rate was 56%, and after only a 2-day delay it was 75% (Ellison & Buckhout, 1981). These modest rates of accuracy, especially after some time interval, are related to higher "false alarm" rates, which result when a witness falsely identifies a suspect *as the culprit*, even when the true criminal is not in the lineup. As many as 80% of the eyewitnesses in some studies choose someone, even when none of the lineup members is the true criminal.

And there are further worries. Laboratory studies, usually conducted with college-aged subjects, may actually overestimate the degree of accuracy in real-world crime detection. In the real world, criminals disguise themselves, prevent victims from looking at them, and instill fear in their victims, many of whom may be older than the typical experimental subject. Usually the viewing time is brief, the illumination is poor, and the criminal moves rapidly. Buckhout (1975) staged a simulated crime on a television news broadcast and asked members of the viewing audience to phone in their choice of suspects shown shortly after the crime. Out of 2145 viewer-witnesses who called in, only 14.7% were correct, an accuracy rate that was no different from the one achieved by simply guessing. Eyewitness accuracy also declines a bit with age, particularly after age 50; but the effects of other variables, such as weapon focus or biased instructions, appear to operate very similarly regardless of the age of subjects (O'Rourke, Penrod, Cutler, & Stuve, 1989).

Another difficulty stems from the use of *observers* as the subjects in most simulated crimes.

You might think that *victims* would be more accurate eyewitnesses than observers, who often may not be paying much attention. But research by Kassin (1984) finds the opposite result: in a simulated theft, bystanders later reported more correct information about the perpetrator than did the person who witnessed his own possession being stolen. The emotion generated by being a crime victim may get in the way of attending to details of the criminal.

THE EYEWITNESS IN THE COURTROOM

Despite the limitations in the accuracy or reliability of their identifications, eyewitnesses are among the most influential resources the prosecuting attorney uses to convict a defendant in a criminal trial. Eyewitnesses are believed by jurors most of the time. Loftus (1974) gave subjects a description of an armed robbery that had resulted in two deaths. Of mock jurors who heard a version of the case that contained only circumstantial evidence against the defendant, 18% convicted him. But when an eyewitness's identification of the defendant was presented as well, 72% of the mock jurors convicted him. A third group of mock jurors was told that the eyewitness had very poor vision (20/400) and was not wearing eyeglasses on the day of the crime; still, 68% of the mock jurors found the defendant guilty! It is hard to overestimate the power of innocent eyewitnesses to convince a jury of the correctness of their testimony.

Psychological research shows that jurors overestimate just how accurate eyewitnesses are. In one study, Gary Wells and his associates (Wells, Lindsay, & Ferguson, 1979) staged a "theft" under viewing conditions that were either good, moderate, or poor for witnesses. As you might expect, eyewitnesses did a better job when the viewing conditions were good; 74% of them were accurate, compared with 50% in the moderate viewing conditions and 33% in the poor viewing conditions. Then, in Wells's study, some mock jurors watched an eyewitness being cross-examined, after which the jurors indicated whether they believed the eyewitness. Belief rates for the good, the moderate, and the poor witnessing conditions were, respectively, 69%, 57%, and 58%. Thus, when the viewing conditions are only so-so or poor, jurors tend to overestimate how accurate the witnesses are. In another study whose results were consistent with these, Brigham and Bothwell (1983) found that as many as 83% of their mock jurors exaggerated the accuracy of eyewitness identifications.

Jurors overestimate the validity of eyewitnesses' testimony because they appear to be unaware of several of the factors that compromise eyewitness accuracy. For example:

1. Jurors are insensitive to biases that may be introduced by police investigation procedures. For instance, someone may falsely testify about an identification in order to avoid prosecution himself (Hastie, 1980).
2. Jurors have little awareness of the factors that interfere with accurate retention, such as weapon focus, amount of violence in a criminal event, effects of prior exposures, and so on (Cutler, Penrod, & Dexter, 1990).
3. Jurors show a lack of sophistication about police procedures for testing recognition (Cutler et al., 1990; Loftus & Wagenaar, 1990).
4. Jurors put too much emphasis on witnesses' statements about the confidence of their identifications. In fact, Cutler, Penrod, and Stuve (1988) found that, for laypersons, the witness's level of confidence was the most

important criterion for judging the witness's truthfulness. As we discuss in detail later, an eyewitness's confidence is *not* a strong indication of accuracy.

Furthermore, jurors are usually not told about those eyewitnesses who could *not* identify a suspect; even the defendant's attorney may not be aware of these misses (Wells & Lindsay, 1980). There are a number of guidelines that jurors could use to gauge the reliability of an eyewitness. Some of these are listed in Box 7-2.

EXPERT TESTIMONY BY PSYCHOLOGISTS

Given the problems of eyewitnesses' testimony, it would seem that truth would be better served if there were a means by which jurors could be alerted and educated about these problems. There are two ways that this might be done.

First, psychologists who are knowledgeable about the relevant research on perception and memory could testify to juries about their findings. Second, the judge might instruct the jury about how to interpret this testimony. We describe each of these alternatives in this section.

Evaluating the Testimony of Psychologists

Psychologists could have much to say to jurors about experimental research on eyewitness testimony: that eyewitnesses are often inaccurate, that extreme stress usually inhibits accurate and complete encoding, that the presence of a weapon deflects attention from the offender's appearance, that white victims make more errors when the offender is of a different race, that extremely confident eyewitnesses are not especially accurate, that differences in the way lineups are formed and introduced to witnesses affect eyewitness accuracy, and that jurors' ability to discriminate

---

Box **7-2** | *Which Eyewitnesses Are Suspect?*

What factors should especially alert us to question the accuracy of an eyewitness's testimony? Here is a list of conditions that point to potential problems:

- If the witness originally stated that he or she would be unable to identify anyone (Wall, 1965).
- If the identifying witness knew the defendant before the crime but made no accusation against him or her when questioned by the police (Wall, 1965).

- If a serious discrepancy exists between the identifying witness's original description of the perpetrator of the crime and the actual description of the defendant (Luus & Wells, 1991).
- If, before identifying the defendant at the trial, the witness identified another person (*United States* v. *Wade*, 1967).
- If the witness and the person identified are of different racial groups (Bothwell, Brigham, &

Malpass, 1989; Platz & Hosch, 1988).
- If a considerable period of time elapsed between the witness's view of the criminal and his or her identification of the defendant (Goodman & Hahn, 1987).
- If suggestive or improperly formed lineups have been used (Loftus & Wagenaar, 1990).

between accurate and inaccurate identification is poor.

But, as noted in Chapter 2, often psychologists are not allowed to testify about these matters (Loftus & Schneider, 1987), and appellate courts have generally upheld such decisions. The decision is up to the presiding judge—another example of the breadth of discretion present in the legal system. This discretion challenges the goal of equality, because sometimes psychologists are denied the right to testify in cases that are almost identical to others in which expert testimony is admitted.

Judges are reluctant to let psychological experts testify for several reasons. First, some judges believe that scientific research on eyewitness identification is not well enough established to provide valid research findings. (As noted in Chapter 2, a few psychologists would even agree with this opinion—for example, Egeth & McCloskey, 1984; Konecni & Ebbesen, 1986; McCloskey & Egeth, 1983; McCloskey, Egeth, & McKenna, 1986.) Second, judges may believe that such expert testimony would not provide facts that are beyond the common knowledge of most jury members but instead would invade the province of the jury as finders and triers of fact. (In Chapter 2 we saw an example of such a judge's decision, reflecting the reluctance of the legal profession to yield part of the fact-finding process to other disciplines.) Third, judges fear that admitting such expert testimony would open the gates to conflicting expert testimony, leading to a confusing and uninformative "battle of the experts." (Such battles have occurred in some highly publicized trials involving a criminal defendant's claim of insanity; see Chapter 16.) Finally, judges also worry that this type of testimony might lead jurors to give too little weight to eyewitness evidence (Woocher, 1986).

When psychologists have been allowed to testify, the outcomes have been beneficial to the goal of achieving the truth, at least in mock jury studies. Loftus (1980) presented student jurors with one of two trial summaries, one about a mild assault and the other about a murder. In both cases, eyewitness testimony was an important part of the evidence. Some subjects read standard versions of the trials; others read versions in which an expert witness testified for the defense about factors known to diminish the accuracy of eyewitnesses. The expert testimony reduced the conviction rates of individual jurors from 68% to 43% in the murder case and from 47% to 35% in the mild assault. The testimony also had the effect of increasing the amount of time the jury spent in deliberations, discussing and evaluating the eyewitnesses' testimony.

In perhaps the most comprehensive study of the effect of expert testimony on jurors' judgments, Cutler, Penrod, and Dexter (1989) showed undergraduate subjects a realistic videotaped trial that focused on the accuracy of an eyewitness's identification of an armed-robbery defendant. Some subjects also heard an expert testify about the effects of eyewitness and identification conditions on accuracy, whereas other jurors heard no expert testimony on these matters. The results indicated that students who were exposed to the expert testimony gave more weight to various witnessing and identification factors (e.g., weapon focus, lineup procedures) when judging the credibility of eyewitnesses than did students who did not hear such testimony. Students who heard an expert also gave less weight to the expressed confidence of eyewitnesses in their own accuracy than did students who did not hear an expert (of course, this is a desirable finding in light of evidence that witness confidence and witness accuracy are only weakly related). Finally, there was no evidence that students who heard an expert testify about eyewitness accuracy actually increased their skepticism about the witness's credibility.

Is it possible that any special advantages of expert testimony on eyewitness accuracy occur only in the context of mock jury research, where actors play the roles of the prosecuting and defense attorneys? Perhaps "real" lawyers could question witnesses more incisively and critically, so that jurors would be better able to separate accurate from inaccurate witnesses without the assistance of expert testimony. A recent experiment (Lindsay, Wells, & O'Connor, 1989) in which experienced trial attorneys were used to question witnesses to a staged crime showed that, even with the use of highly experienced attorneys, jurors were still unable to distinguish the accurate from the inaccurate witnesses; subjects believed the testimony of 68% of the accurate witnesses, but they also believed 70% of the witnesses who falsely identified an innocent party.

Most studies, including those using members of the community as jurors, lead to similar conclusions (Fox & Walters, 1986; Hosch, Beck, & McIntyre, 1980). But not all do. Occasionally the expert has no measurable effect on verdicts, perhaps because the jurors have already made up their minds (especially if the case is one-sided) or perhaps because the psychologist is not convincing. A study by Maass, Brigham, and West (1985) found that, if the expert presented testimony about the particular eyewitness under consideration, the expert had to give reasons for his or her conclusion that the person's accuracy should be questioned; otherwise, jurors were influenced very little by the psychologist's opinions.

A report of one actual crime also lends anecdotal support to the conclusion that the testimony of an expert witness has impact. Loftus (1984) describes the trial of two Arizona brothers charged with the torture of three Mexicans. Two juries were in the courtroom at the same time, one deciding the verdict for Patrick Hanigan, the other deciding the fate of his brother,

Thomas. Most of the evidence was from eyewitnesses, and it was virtually identical for the two defendants. However, expert testimony about the inaccuracy of eyewitnesses was introduced in Thomas's trial only. (The jury hearing Patrick Hanigan's case waited in the jury room while this evidence was presented.) Patrick Hanigan was convicted by one jury; his brother was acquitted by the other. This is as close to a "natural experiment" as the legal system has come for assessing the influence of a psychologist in the courtroom.

The Effect of Instructions from the Judge

A second way to alert jurors to the limitations of eyewitnesses is through a judge's instruction to them. Within the last two decades, both the federal courts and many state courts have encouraged trial judges to alert jurors to possible misinterpretations. In *Neil* v. *Biggers* (1972), the U.S. Supreme Court specified five conditions that should be considered in evaluating identification evidence:

1. The opportunity for witnesses to view the criminal at the time of the crime.
2. The length of time between the crime and the later identification.
3. The level of certainty shown by the witnesses at the identification.
4. The witnesses' degree of attention during the crime.
5. The accuracy of the witnesses' prior description of the criminal.

These conditions were restated and reaffirmed five years later in *Manson* v. *Braithwaite* (1977).

Although psychologists were pleased to see the Supreme Court take this action, they did not agree with all its strictures (Wells & Murray, 1983). Research supports consideration of the first two guidelines. The fourth and fifth conditions are plausible; however, little research has been done to substantiate the importance of these conditions as contributors to accuracy. It is recommendation number 3—to take into account the witnesses' level of certainty—that is most in question as a factor in evaluating identification evidence. At least 35 studies have been done on this point, with mixed results (Bothwell, Deffenbacher, & Brigham, 1987). Some have found no relationship between accuracy and certainty, whereas others report confident witnesses to be more accurate than hesitant ones. The average correlation across these studies is +.25 (Bothwell et al., 1987). However, the correlation between accuracy and confidence is affected by the length of time a witness has to look at a target; the longer

the exposure of the target to the witness, the stronger the correlation between the witness's confidence and the accuracy of identification.

Many states have followed the Supreme Court's lead in using a cautionary instruction similar to that from *Neil* v. *Biggers.* One of the more succinct of these is reprinted in Box 7-3. Note that it contains "degree of certainty" as a criterion, despite the equivocal evidence about the importance of witness certainty. Here we have another example of the conflict (discussed in Chapter 1) between the law and social science as ways of establishing truth.

Cautionary instructions have not been universally accepted in the courts, however. Some individual judges have been reluctant to apply the instruction. One side (usually the defense)

Box **7-3** | *An Example of a Cautionary Instruction*

Kansas judges are instructed by the state supreme court to give the following instruction (from *State* v. *Warren,* 1981) whenever the judge believes there is any serious question about the accuracy of testimony by an eyewitness.

Eyewitness identification:
The law places the burden upon the state to identify the defendant. The law does not require the defendant to prove he had been wrongly identified. In weighing the reliability of eyewitness identification testimony you first should determine whether any of the following factors existed and if so the extent to which they would affect

accuracy of identification by an eyewitness. Factors you may consider are:

1. The opportunity the witness had to observe. This includes any physical condition which could affect the ability of the witness to observe, the length of the time of observation, and any limitations on observation like an obstruction or poor lighting.

2. The emotional state of the witness at the time including that which might be caused by the use of a weapon or a threat of violence.

3. Whether the witness had ob-

served the defendant(s) on earlier occasions.

4. Whether a significant amount of time elapsed between the crime charged and any later identification.

5. Whether the witness ever failed to identify the defendant(s) or made any inconsistent identification.

6. The degree of certainty demonstrated by the witness at the time of any identification of the accused.

7. Whether there are any other circumstances that may have affected the accuracy of the eyewitness identification.

may request that the instruction be given, but judges sometimes refuse. *State* v. *Brown* (1982), a Kansas case, is relevant. Thomas E. Brown, Jr., had been convicted of armed robbery of a tavern. No cautionary instruction was given regarding the eyewitnesses' testimony, despite the defense attorney's request. In a previous Kansas case (*State* v. *Warren*, 1981), the state supreme court had held that, in any criminal trial in which identification by eyewitnesses is a critical part of the prosecution's case and there is serious question about the accuracy of the identification, a cautionary instruction should be given to the jury about the factors to be considered in weighing the credibility of that testimony.

In responding to Thomas Brown's appeal, the Kansas supreme court concluded that the trial judge did not commit an error when he failed to give the requested instruction. They wrote:

> Although it is undisputed that eyewitness identification was a critical part of the prosecutor's case, we fail to find that there was a serious question about the reliability of identification. In reaching this conclusion, we have considered the following evidentiary factors: The three young black males came to the tavern at about 9:00 P.M. The robbery occurred about one hour later at 10 P.M., after the robbers had been in the tavern where they could be observed by the witnesses. The robbery itself took 10 to 15 minutes. All of the witnesses' descriptions of the robber were consistent with each other and with the defendant's actual description. Witness Babcock, owner of the Whiz, had met two of the robbers in the tavern the week before the robbery, including the defendant, Brown. She knew his name was "Thomas." Her testimony was that she talked to the defendant for about an hour at that time. Another witness, the bartender, also testified that she had seen the defendant when he was at the tavern one week before the robbery. One of the witnesses testified that the defendant was close enough to put a gun near her arm and shoot it off.

There was a blank in the gun, however, so she was not hurt. She testified that she was able to identify the defendant as the robber as she remembered his face. The witnesses also identified the defendant at a photographic display two weeks after the robbery [*State* v. *Brown*, 1982, pp. 500–501].

The justices noted that the facts in Brown's case were substantially different from those in *State* v. *Warren* (1981). In the latter, the robbery of the Chateau Briand restaurant in Wichita had lasted less than a minute and a half. The identification of the defendant by the victim was made almost five months after the crime, "under highly questionable circumstances." Furthermore, the victim's report contained many contradictions and inconsistencies. So the fact that a cautionary instruction is available does not guarantee that a trial judge will use it or will even be required to by an appellate court.

A second reason for judges' failure to use cautionary instructions is the concern that such instructions reflect a bias in favor of the defense. One of the most frequent cautionary instructions is called the *Telfaire* instruction (from *United States* v. *Telfaire*, 1972). All but one of the federal circuit courts have approved the use of a cautionary instruction like it (Greene, 1988). But, when asked whether they would use the *Telfaire* instruction in their courts, 78% of the judges polled by Edith Greene (1988) said that it was improper to give to the jury. (Only 12% approved; 10% did not respond.) Disapproving judges felt that the instruction seemed to comment on the evidence and take the decision out of the jury's hands.

One study has compared how jurors react to a psychologist's expert testimony with how they react to a judge's cautionary instruction. Warner (1987) showed mock jurors different versions of a videotape of a trial for armed robbery of a liquor store. Of jurors who did not hear either the judge's instructions or a psychologist's testimony, 78% concluded that the defendant was guilty. Testimony of an expert witness, a prominent psychologist, reduced the guilty verdicts only slightly, to 70%. Some jurors heard the judge read one of two types of instructions. A long set of instructions (about five pages, double-spaced) that said much of what the psychologist said, but in the judge's words, was about as effective as the psychologist; 69% of the jurors still found the defendant guilty. The *most* influential procedure was a brief (one and a half pages) instruction based on the *Telfaire* instructions but modified by Edith Greene (1988) to make them more readable and organized. When this was included as part of the trial, 64% of jurors voted to convict, compared with the 78% conviction rate without it. Although Warner's study suggests that educating jurors about the difficulties faced by eyewitnesses can be achieved as effectively by a brief instruction by a judge as by a psychologist, the bulk of the research on the effectiveness of judges' instructions indicates that such instructions, in general, are usually not effective.

USE OF HYPNOSIS WITH EYEWITNESSES

Most eyewitnesses cannot remember everything that happened during the crime; their memories are often fragmented, uncertain, and vague. One reason they are inaccurate is that witnesses fill in the gaps in what they can remember, often with erroneous information. Are there ways to enhance the memories of eyewitnesses, to help them accurately remember facts and details?

Law enforcement officials are eager to use techniques that will increase the detail, the accuracy, and the usefulness of recollections by victims and other witnesses. Hypnosis has been investigated as an aid to memory and has been credited with helping solve some of this country's most notorious crimes. Hypnosis was used in the Sam Sheppard murder case, the trial of the Boston Strangler, and the investigation of the assassination of Robert Kennedy. Probably the most notorious example of its use involved the 1976 Chowchilla, California, kidnapping case, in which a busload of 26 schoolchildren and their driver were abducted at gunpoint by three masked kidnappers and buried underground in a large tomb from which they later escaped. The driver had seen the license plate on one of the vans that the kidnappers had used and had tried to memorize the numbers. However, he was unable to recall the numbers until he was hypnotized and told to visualize the van as if it were in a TV documentary. At one point during the hypnotic session, he suddenly called out a license plate number he remembered seeing. Except for one digit, the number was correct and expedited the capture of the three culprits, who were later convicted and sentenced to life in prison.

Forensic applications of hypnosis continue at a rapid pace. Thousands of law enforcement officers have been trained to use forensic hypnosis, and there are a number of books devoted to the topic (e.g., Hibbard & Worring, 1981; Kline, 1983; Reiser, 1980; Udolf, 1983). An International Society for Investigative and Forensic Hypnosis as well as an International Association for Forensic Hypnosis have been formed. Is all this effort worthwhile for crime detection? Does hypnosis of witnesses pose special dangers?

What Is Hypnosis?

Hypnosis is an ancient technique, practiced at least as early as 500 B.C. in the sleep temples of Greece, where followers of Aesculapius pursued miraculous cures revealed to them through mystical dreams and visions. The French physician Anton Mesmer (1743–1815) was most responsible for bringing hypnotism to the attention of the Western world. He called the technique *mesmerism* and practiced it in a flamboyant manner that resembled magic and spiritual ecstasy more than natural science. Throughout the 19th and 20th centuries, several physicians experimented with hypnosis as a treatment procedure and tried to salvage it from the occult connotations that Mesmer lent it. James Braid, an English physician, coined the term *hypnotism* in 1843.

Everyone is aware of hypnosis, and perhaps you have been hypnotized yourself. During the past two centuries, hypnotism has been used to treat a vast range of psychological and physical disorders (including obesity, smoking, addictions, pain, fears, asthma, and stress disorders) despite inconsistent findings about its effectiveness (Wadden & Anderton, 1982). In fact, many different explanations exist for what occurs during a hypnotized state, as well as for the essential ingredients of hypnosis.

Explanations of hypnosis fall into one of two categories. First, some investigators think of hypnosis as a procedure delivered by a skilled practitioner who induces a special mental state in subjects, known as the *trance*, that provides them with unique mental abilities. The second perspective focuses on subjects' *suggestibility*, which is maximized during hypnotic inductions. For our purposes, we define hypnosis as a state of *extreme suggestibility*. The hypnotized subject is very relaxed, very attentive to incoming stimuli, and very responsive. In effect, the subject agrees to suspend critical judgment, to dispense with logic and evaluation even though still "in control." Hypnosis often heightens attention and imagination. Later, imagined memories and memories of real events may become confused.

Hypnosis and Crime: A Brief History

The relevance of hypnosis to the legal system was recognized in the 19th century when concerns were expressed that immoral or criminal behavior might be coerced through hypnotic suggestions (Laurence & Perry, 1983). Conn (1981) describes the demonstrations of M. Liegois, an adventurous professor of law at Nancy, France, who once hypnotized a Mrs. G. at a party and then suggested that she:

> kill with the revolver a Mr. P., an old magistrate, who was present. Without hesitation Mrs. G. fired a shot (from the unloaded pistol, of course) at Mr. P. Immediately questioned by the police inspector, who was in the room, she acknowledged her crime with the utmost indifference. She had killed P. because he did not please her. They might just as well arrest her; she knew very well what punishment she would get; if they took her life, she would go to the other world, like her victim. . . . She was asked if she had not received the idea of murder from (someone else). No, she had done it from her own impulse; she alone was guilty; she was resigned to her fate . . . (Tinterow, 1970).

Gravitz (1983) reports the first use of hypnosis to solve a crime. In this case, originally published in the 1845 *St. Louis Magnet*, a clairvoyant woman was hypnotized at the request of a shopowner who wanted to know the identity of a thief who had taken four dollars from the store's cash drawer. Under hypnosis the woman described a 14-year-old boy as the criminal and proceeded to trace his actions after he left the store. When ultimately located and confronted with the woman's allegations, the "rogue" confessed his crime and promised to repay the money.

Laurence and Perry (1983) cite two 19th-century American cases in which defendants successfully (*State v. Gray*, 1895) and unsuccessfully (*People v. Worthington*, 1894) used hypnotic influence as a defense against charges of murder. Experts of that day, including Bernheim and Janet, cautioned that a person's testimony under hypnosis could contain illusions and distortions. As early as 1897, in *People* v. *Ebanks*, the supreme court of California ruled that evidence uncovered by hypnosis was not admissible (Laurence & Perry, 1983).

In *On the Witness Stand*, Munsterberg (1908) devoted one chapter to "Hypnosis and Crime," in which he first warned that hypnosis was "certainly not a plaything" and then discussed, with considerable skepticism, the following possible uses or abuses of hypnosis in the legal arena: (1) unveiling "hidden truths" from witnesses, (2) exonerating wrongfully accused persons, (3) coercing otherwise innocent people to commit crimes, and (4) preventing crime through posthypnotic suggestions to inhibit criminal obsessions.

Decades of research have confirmed Munsterberg's opinion that forensic hypnosis is neither as powerful nor as reliable as its practitioners have often claimed. Despite this evidence, hypnosis is frequently used by law enforcement officials and government agencies. The two goals for which forensic hypnosis is most often used are: (1) to generate investigative leads that can then be pursued through other means and subjected to independent confirmation and (2) to refresh the memories of witnesses, victims, or defendants who have forgotten important details of events about which they might testify in court. Although the methods used to reach these two goals are basically identical, the legal status and professional evaluations of them need to be distinguished.

Dangers of Hypnosis as a Memory Refresher

How the police use hypnosis. The use of hypnosis to refresh memories usually follows one of two approaches. The first involves *age regression*, in which the hypnotized subject is asked to relive past events, even some that might have taken place years earlier. Age-regressed subjects often talk and act in a manner that is supposedly typical of them at the time to which they are regressed. They also report vivid, detailed memories of the past, sometimes with very strong, and apparently appropriate, emotions. Although age-regressed subjects often appear compellingly credible, experimental research has failed to support the conclusion that their recollections are accurate portrayals of the past (Orne, 1979).

The second memory-enhancement technique, and the one favored by many hypno-investigators, involves hypnotic suggestions to subjects, through the use of some metaphor like a television, blackboard, blank screen, or tape recorder, that they will be able to recall past events clearly. The pioneer of this method is Dr. Martin Reiser, Director of the Los Angeles Police Department's Behavioral Science Service. Reiser (1980) favors the *television technique* of retrieval. The subject is told, before being hypnotized, that memories are stored in the subconscious mind and that this level of consciousness can be reached through hypnosis. After hypnosis is achieved, subjects are asked to imagine that they are watching a televised documentary about the events to be recalled. They are instructed that their documentary can be slowed down, sped up, reversed, stopped, or played back and that close-ups of the people or objects involved are possible. The sound can be turned up so that everything can be heard clearly. The subject is told that the television will depict everything of importance vividly and accurately; however, even though what is shown on the screen might have been upsetting when it happened, the subject will remain calm and detached while watching it so that he or she will now have an accurate memory of what took place.

Reiser attributes the effectiveness of this technique to the fact that all perceptions are stored faithfully at a subconscious level and that these memories can be reactivated with hypnosis. He claims that over a four-year period involving more than 300 cases, L.A. police hypno-investigators elicited additional information from 80% of the subjects they hypnotized; this information was considered valuable in 65% of the cases that had been solved (Reiser & Nielson, 1980). Other investigators (e.g., Kroger & Douce, 1980) report comparable figures regarding the frequency with which hypnosis has proven helpful in eliciting new information in a series of cases. However, these studies are plagued by numerous methodological difficulties, so the validity of their claims is not certain (Greene, 1986).

Effects of Hypnosis on Memory: Memory Aid or Altered Memory?   Few professionals find fault with forensic hypnosis when it is restricted to generating new leads for a police investigation that has stalled. However, the situation is different when hypnosis is used to help a witness recall details that may later be testified to in court or when hypnosis is used to help witnesses choose between conflicting versions of events that they have provided on different occasions. In these situations, many hypnosis researchers contend, the technique is fraught with so many problems and potential abuses that its use to refresh memories of witnesses should be allowed only under the strictest of safeguards or should be banned altogether (Diamond, 1980; Orne, 1979; Smith, 1983).

What are the dangers of hypnosis as an enhancer of memory? Critics point to seven difficulties with hypnosis of potential witnesses. These objections reflect a theory of memory that is very different from that proposed by practitioners of forensic hypnosis. This view of memory is based on research (e.g., Loftus, 1979) that depicts memory as constantly changing and as being subject to reconstruction so that it "fits" with recently acquired information. From this perspective, memory is rewritten in a manner that helps preserve existing knowledge and mental structures. Memories are created and revised rather than faithfully stored and reproduced in "their pristine form" (Orne, 1979). The major concerns about the effects of hypnosis on memory are as follows:

1. Subjects often remember more material when hypnotized than when they are in a nonhypnotized state, an effect known as *hypermnesia*. However, the additional material consists of a mixture of accurate and inaccurate recollections (Dywan & Bowers, 1983). Recall of new facts is purchased at the price of adding falsehoods to one's memory. These false "recollections" can be implanted through suggestions from the hypnotist, or they can originate in other ways that are not yet completely understood. This addition of false information to accurate recollections is called *confabulation*. For example, an Illinois man was charged with first-degree murder after an eyewitness, under hypnosis, described his license plate. The witness claimed to have seen the car at a distance of 230 feet, at night, with lights shining directly in his eyes. The charges were dropped, however, after an ophthalmologist testified that a person could not see more than 30 feet under such conditions.

2. One reason why confabulation occurs under hypnosis is that subjects relax their standards for reporting information. They become less critical about what they report and accept approximations of memory as "accurate enough." These approximations are then added to accurate memories to yield a version of events that is part fact and part fabrication. A second factor that contributes to confabulation

is that hypnotized subjects are extremely suggestible and want to please the hypnotist by giving as full a report as possible. This motive encourages subjects to fill in the gaps in their memory with plausible details or with information they believe the hypnotist is expecting.

3. The greatest danger of confabulation is that persons who have been hypnotized find it very difficult to separate actual memories from those generated under hypnosis. This problem can be compared to that of the basketball fan who watches a controversial play at an arena and then that same night goes home to watch TV replays of the same play. This fan will develop a clear "picture" of the play in memory but will be unable to separate which parts of the picture are from the actual viewing of the game and which come from the TV replay.

4. After being hypnotized, witnesses not only find it difficult to distinguish their original memories from those brought out under hypnosis, but they also tend to become more confident about their recall despite the fact that it might contain a number of false recollections (Sheehan & Tilden, 1983). This confidence often persists long after the hypnosis session has ended. Hypnosis can translate beliefs or expectations into "memories," a process that has been called *memory hardening*.

5. It is not just hypnotized subjects who find it difficult to separate accurate from confabulated recall—hypno-investigators have the same problem. Even the most experienced of hypnotists can be misled to accept confabulated recollections or to believe that a subject is hypnotized when in fact he or she is faking it.

6. Several studies have shown that hypnotized subjects are more responsive to the biasing influence of leading questions. For example, Zelig and Beidleman (1981) showed experimental subjects a short film of several bloody workshop accidents. After watching the film, the subjects were asked leading and nonleading questions about it while either hypnotized or not hypnotized. Hypnotized subjects made more mistakes on the leading questions, but they did not differ from the nonhypnotized subjects on the nonleading questions. Similar results have been reported by Putnam (1979) with a film depicting an accident between a car and a bicycle. But a more recent experiment contrasting hypnotized with nonhypnotized witnesses found no evidence that hypnosis increased the degree to which witnesses were misled by leading questions (Spanos, Gwynn, Comer, Baltruweit, & de Groh, 1989).

7. Posthypnotic testimony of witnesses in the courtroom is likely to affect the evaluation and weight given to this testimony by jurors. For example, Diamond (1980) warned that formerly hypnotized witnesses would become so confident about their testimony that they would be invulnerable to cross-examination, although what little data are available on this matter suggest that this danger may be minimal (Spanos et al., 1989; Spanos, Quigley, Gwynn, Glatt, & Perlini, 1991). If hypnotically refreshed testimony is going to be presented to juries, it is important to learn what general attitudes people hold about hypnosis and how these beliefs compare to the scientific evidence on the effects of hypnosis.

Orne, Soskis, Dinges, and Orne (1984; cited in Greene, 1986) reported that 96% of a sample of college students believed that hypnosis could help people remember material they otherwise could not recall. Wilson, Greene, and Loftus (1986) also found that substantial proportion of a collegiate sample endorsed common "myths" about the power of hypnosis; however, these same students indicated that they would place *less* rather than *more* faith in the testimony of a witness who had been hypnotized. On the basis of additional mock jury research, Greene (1986) concludes " . . . it appears that hypnotic testimony is viewed by jurors with a certain amount of skepticism." Concerns that jurors will be overawed by hypnosis in the courtroom have not been supported by preliminary research, but questions remain about the possible effects of "hypnotically elicited testimony, perhaps presented in an authoritative manner and bolstered by expert testimony as is often the case in the courtroom" (Wilson et al., 1986).

Legal Status of Hypnotically Refreshed Testimony

What if, as a result of being hypnotized, a victim apparently becomes able to identify her attacker—for example, by remembering his name or the license number of his car? Can such information be introduced at a trial?

The legal status of hypnotically induced testimony is rapidly changing (Scheflin & Shapiro, 1989), but the courts can be roughly divided into the following four camps concerning the admissibility of hypnotically refreshed testimony.

1. Up to about 1980, the majority view was that hypnotically assisted testimony was admissible (Diamond, 1980). According to advocates for this position, which is identified with the Maryland case of *Harding v. State* (1968), the fact that a witness has been hypnotized should apply to how much weight a jury should give that person's testimony and not to whether the testimony is admissible at trial. In *Harding*, Mildred Coley, a victim of a shooting and attempted rape, initially said she was attacked and stabbed by three black men. During a second interrogation, she remembered being in a car with two males and another woman, being shot by one of the men, and then being put out of the car. Finally, she was hypnotized and was then able to recall James Harding as her assailant. She identified him at his trial, and he was convicted of assault with attempt to rape and assault with

attempt to murder. In its review of the case, the Maryland supreme court reasoned that hypnosis was not that different from other memory aids and ruled that the jury could hear Coley's testimony and evaluate its accuracy before reaching a verdict.

A number of courts followed *Harding*'s line of thinking and ruled that hypnotically aided recall could be permitted in court but that the jury should consider the many problems of hypnosis when deciding how much weight to give such testimony. Wyoming, Tennessee, and Idaho are a few of the states still following this approach.

2. The second camp, taking what is sometimes known as the "guidelines approach," requires that hypno-investigators follow specific precautions or guidelines if hypnotically aided testimony is to be admitted. These guidelines are usually based on the recommendations of Dr. Martin T. Orne, a University of Pennsylvania psychiatrist and widely recognized expert on hypnosis. The lead opinion in this category is *State v. Hurd* (1981), a case decided by the New Jersey supreme court. *Hurd* attempts to prevent most dangers of hypnotic memory refreshment by requiring the following safeguards: (1) the hypnosis should be conducted by a psychiatrist or psychologist with special training in hypnosis; (2) the hypnotist should be independent of the prosecution, the police, or the defense; (3) information given to the hypnotist prior to the hypnosis session should be written and retained so that it can be examined by other parties in the case; (4) the entire hypnosis session should be tape-recorded, preferably by video; (5) only the hypnotist and the subject should be present during any phase of the hypnosis, including the posthypnosis interview; and (6) all of the subject's prehypnosis memories for the events in question should be carefully recorded and preserved. In addition to New Jersey, the guidelines solution is followed

in states such as Texas, Oregon, Ohio, New Mexico, and Wisconsin.

3. The third position is represented by decisions such as *People* v. *Hughes* (1983), in which the New York court of appeals awarded a new trial to a defendant who had been convicted of rape after having been identified by a victim who had undergone hypnosis to improve her memory. On May 19, 1978, a man broke into a married woman's apartment, dragged her from bed, beat her, and raped her in the yard behind the apartment. When the woman's husband returned home from work, he found his wife lying naked outside their apartment. He called the police, who took his wife to the hospital, where she stayed several days. She was interviewed by police on numerous occasions and at one time while in the hospital spoke with her sister about the crime. Although her recall was not clear, she seemed to remember that her assailant was "Kirk" (the defendant's first name). In an attempt to improve her memory, the woman was hypnotized numerous times by a psychologist and a psychiatrist, who also administered sodium pentothal to her at the hospital. During one of the hypnosis sessions, which was videotaped, she identified Kirk Hughes as her attacker. Following this session, she gave an affidavit to the police indicating that Hughes was the man who beat and raped her. At the trial, the woman testified to the events as she recalled them both before and after the several sessions of hypnosis. Based in part on her identification of Hughes, the jury convicted him of rape, burglary, and assault.

On hearing the defendant's appeal, the New York court stopped short of completely banning a hypnotized witness from testifying, ruling that "the pretrial use of hypnosis does not necessarily render the witness incompetent to testify to events recalled prior to being hypnotized." The court concluded that decisions about the admissibility of prehypnotic

recollections should be made on a case-by-case basis as courts evaluate whether the hypnosis was conducted in a way likely to contaminate prehypnotic memories.

4. The fourth, and most restrictive, position is that a witness who has been hypnotized to refresh recall in a criminal investigation cannot testify about either prehypnotic or posthypnotic recollections in the prosecution of that case. This view became increasingly popular in the 1980s beginning with the case of *State* v. *Mack* (1980), in which the supreme court of Minnesota, relying on the *Frye* test (discussed more fully in Chapter 8's description of the polygraph), ruled that hypnosis had not been generally accepted by the scientific community as a reliable method for enhancing accurate recall and that such recall was to be excluded from the trial (see Box 7-4). This position has been adopted by several states, including California, North Carolina, Massachusetts, Missouri, Nebraska, Indiana, New York, Arizona, Pennsylvania, and Maryland, which overruled its earlier *Harding* decision with *State* v. *Collins* (1983).

The most influential case in this group is *People* v. *Shirley* (1982), which disallowed all testimony by a witness on any events that were a subject of hypnotic sessions. (However, the California legislature passed a law in 1984 allowing witnesses to testify on matters they had recalled before hypnosis, if the hypnosis was conducted by a psychiatrist.) This decision by the California supreme court relied extensively on a 1980 *California Law Review* article by Dr. Bernard Diamond (1980), a psychiatrist and University of Southern California law professor. Diamond, a vigorous opponent of the use of hypnosis with witnesses, contends that "after hypnosis [a] subject cannot differentiate between a true recollection and a fantasized or suggested detail."

The most recent chapter on this topic was written with the 1987 U.S. Supreme Court decision of *Rock* v. *Arkansas* (see Box 7-5 for a summary of the facts of this case), in which it was decided that an automatic ban against hypnotically refreshed testimony violated previously hypnotized criminal defendants' rights to testify on their own behalf. What effect the *Rock* decision will have on the use of hypnosis in the courtroom is not clear. By holding that hypnotically aided testimony is not to be automatically excluded, the *Rock* court came to a conclusion that is similar to the *Hurd* approach, in which each case is examined on the merits of how the hypnotic refreshment was conducted.

Certainly we can expect law enforcement officials and victims of crime to argue that it is fundamentally unfair to permit defendants to have their memories refreshed by hypnosis but deny this opportunity to the state. At the same time, the evidence about the potentially biasing effects of hypnosis on memory is becoming more and more persuasive; so it would be surprising to see a large swing in the direction of relaxing the admissibility standards for hypnotically aided testimony. In fact, in the case of *Little* v. *Armontrout* (1987), the U.S. Court of Appeals for the Eighth Circuit ruled that an indigent defendant was entitled to a court-appointed expert to assist him in challenging the validity of hypnotically enhanced testimony against him by two prosecution witnesses.

In summary, hypnosis makes recall less accurate, although it generates more information that the police can check out. But, given the inconsistent rulings, what can we say about the wisdom of relying on hypnotically aided memory?

The best use of hypnosis is during the early stages of a criminal investigation in which police

---

Box 7-4 | *Questioning under Hypnosis*

The Minnesota case of *State* v. *Mack* (1980) illustrates the problems that have led courts to restrict the use of hypnosis as a memory refresher for witnesses. In this case the victim, at first, remembered nothing about her attack, other than waking up in a pool of blood (apparently she had been drunk when attacked). However, six weeks later, when hypnotized, she remembered several vivid details of the crime. She recalled her male companion telling her to get on a bed and strip. Then he pulled a switchblade, threatened to kill her, and stabbed her repeatedly, to "get even with you for running out on me" (Ritter, 1985).

After these memories were revealed through hypnosis, the woman repeated them in an affidavit. She also recalled—for the first time—that she had danced with the man and that she had, indeed, run out on him. On these grounds, the police arrested a suspect.

But the woman had remembered too much under hypnosis, including several incidents that could not possibly have taken place (Serrill, 1984). She said she had eaten pizza at a restaurant that didn't serve it. She described the defendant's motorcycle as a black Yamaha, when it actually was a maroon Triumph. She danced with someone the night of the attack, but it was someone else, not the defendant. And although, under hypnosis, she remembered being stabbed repeatedly, there was only a single wound (Ritter, 1985).

Because of these discrepancies, the Minnesota appeals court decided that hypnotically refreshed recall was too inaccurate to be accepted as evidence. The probative value of the testimony (that is, its usefulness as evidence) was outweighed by the risk of distorted recollections and unjustified confidence by the witness in the accuracy of these recollections.

otherwise lack information. Hypnosis can help witnesses provide clues: a license number, a piece of clothing, a description of a gun. These leads, even if they sometimes don't pan out, are better than no clues at all. At the first stage of a criminal investigation, inaccurate "facts" are not as damaging as they are at a trial.

Less desirable is the use of hypnosis by the police to *verify* previously obtained information, especially if such verification requires the use of leading questions. Even riskier—in fact, an undesirable practice—is to hypnotize a witness who has given several different stories, in order to learn the "true" story. This step will

---

Box 7-5 | Hypnosis and Defendants

All the court decisions and changes in state laws described in the text refer to the hypnosis of witnesses, usually victims of a crime. What if a defendant who is charged with a crime claims he or she cannot remember what happened at a crucial time? Then, if the defendant is hypnotized before the trial and "remembers" facts that would help prove his or her innocence, should this testimony be admitted into evidence?

The U.S. Supreme Court faced this question in the case of *Rock v. Arkansas* (1987). Vicki Lorene Rock had been convicted of manslaughter in the shooting of her husband, Frank, in 1983 and sentenced to ten years in prison. After the shooting, she could remember that she and her husband had been arguing, that he pushed her against a wall, and that she wanted to leave the house but he wouldn't let her. She recalled clutching the gun because she thought it would keep him from hitting her again. She also recalled phoning the police, who arrived to find Frank lying on the floor, a bullet in his chest.

Only after Vicki had been hypnotized was she able to recall that she had *not* put her finger on the gun's trigger, that her husband had grabbed her from behind, that they struggled, and that the gun went off by accident. As a result of this new information, Vicki's attorney hired a gun expert to examine the handgun. This investigation revealed that the weapon was defective and prone to fire when hit, even without the trigger being pulled.

The judge at Mrs. Rock's trial, following the law in Arkansas, refused to let her tell the jurors anything she remembered as a result of being hypnotized. In her appeal, she contended that this ruling (which was upheld by the Arkansas supreme court) had denied the jury of hearing testimony crucial to her defense.

Note the dilemma facing the U.S. Supreme Court: On the one hand, hypnosis "is not generally regarded by the scientific community as reliable" (to quote the Arkansas attorney general, responding to Mrs. Rock's appeal), and recent

rulings and legislation had restricted its application. On the other hand, a defendant has a Fourteenth Amendment constitutional right to due process, and in this case the defendant's defense depended on the recollection of events that she could not remember before she was hypnotized.

The Supreme Court ruled, in a 5-to-4 decision, in favor of Mrs. Rock and struck down the Arkansas law prohibiting *all* hypnotically refreshed testimony. Mrs. Rock was to be granted a new trial. In the majority opinion, Justice Harry Blackmun acknowledged that hypnosis may produce "incorrect recollections" but said that the Arkansas court decision excluding all hypnotically refreshed testimony per se was "arbitrary." However, the decision did not open the floor to *all types* of hypnotically enhanced testimony; Blackmun wrote: "We express no opinion on the admissibility of previously hypnotized witnesses other than criminal defendants."

simply fix in the witness's mind one particular version of the testimony, which he or she then will faithfully produce on demand.

If a witness is hypnotized during the investigatory phase, whatever is learned from that procedure should not be used as evidence in a trial. The American Medical Association has advocated the position that hypnotically induced memories are not accurate enough to be allowed on the witness stand. An AMA committee reported that it found "no evidence to indicate that there is an increase of only accurate memory during hypnosis" (Ritter, 1985). This seems a wise conclusion.

A recent proposed substitute for hypnosis is the procedure called *context reinstatement* (Geiselman, Fisher, MacKinnon, & Holland, 1985). Instead of a standard interview ("Tell me what happened"), witnesses participate in cognitive interviews in which they are encouraged to mentally recreate the scene and report everything they can remember. The interviewer may ask them to think about the surroundings, the smells and sounds, the temperature, the location of the furniture, or anything else about the event that may elicit memories they couldn't otherwise recall. The interviewer may suggest that they recall events in a reverse order or that they try to reexperience the moods they originally felt. All these activities help reinstate the context in which the crime occurred. Preliminary analyses show that a cognitive interview that emphasizes context reinstatement leads to more recall than a standard interview does (O'Rourke et al., 1989), with fewer confabulations than in hypnosis (Fisher & Quigley, 1989; Leary, 1988).

SUMMARY

Evidence produced by eyewitnesses often makes the difference between an unsolved crime and a conviction. In the early stages of a crime investigation, eyewitness accounts can provide important clues and permit suspects to be identified.

But witnesses often make mistakes, and mistaken identifications have led to the conviction of numerous innocent persons. Errors can occur at the moment the crime is committed or at any of the three phases of the memory process—encoding, storage, and retrieval. Furthermore, subsequent questioning or new experiences can alter what has been remembered from the past. Errors can also result from unconscious transference or focus on a weapon.

Psychological tests of eyewitnesses' accuracy conclude that there is much error present, although rates of accuracy depend on many factors—some environmental, some personal, and some related to the interval between the crime and the recall. Despite these limitations, jurors are heavily influenced by the testimony of eyewitnesses, and they tend to overestimate the accuracy of such witnesses.

To alert jurors to these problems, two types of interventions have been tried. Some trial judges permit psychologists to testify as expert witnesses about the problems in being an accurate eyewitness. Laboratory evaluations of mock juries find that such testimony generally reduces conviction rates when the only significant evidence comes from an eyewitness. But often courts will not permit a psychologist to testify as an expert witness. The other intervention, encouraged by the U.S. Supreme Court and several state courts, is for the judge to give the jurors a "cautionary instruction," sensitizing them to aspects of the testimony of eyewitnesses that they should especially consider.

Often eyewitnesses are not able to remember everything that happened during a crime. The police have used hypnosis as a way of enhancing memory. Hypnosis creates a state of extreme suggestibility, in which the subject is very relaxed and cooperative. Although hypnosis increases the amount of information remembered, it also produces some erroneous memories. The courts in the various states have taken different positions about the admissibility of hypnotically induced testimony. Three cautions seem paramount: the hypnosis should be carried out by a psychiatrist or a psychologist (not a police officer) who is not aware of the facts of the case, the procedures should be recorded so that they can be scrutinized by others, and the products of such a hypnosis during the investigation of a crime should not be used as evidence during a trial. A context-reinstatement procedure has recently been suggested as a substitute for hypnosis.

8

Identification and Evaluation of Criminal Suspects

In Chapter 7 we discussed how psychological findings and techniques contributed to two important areas of crime investigation: assessment of the accuracy of eyewitness reports and the use of hypnosis to enhance the memory of witnesses and to uncover new leads in criminal investigations. In this chapter we discuss three other areas in which psychology can assist law enforcement: the profiling of criminal suspects, the use of polygraphy in evaluating the truthfulness of suspects, and the evaluation of confessions from suspects. The common thread that ties these topics together is the assumption that psychological theory and techniques can be used to improve police officers' identification or evaluation of criminal suspects.

These contributions occur in a logical sequence. Psychological profiling is usually performed at the beginning of a criminal investigation, when the police need help focusing their investigation on certain types of people who might be the most likely suspects. Once suspects have been identified, law enforcement officials use other procedures to determine which, if any, of these suspects should be charged. The police may encourage suspects to confess, because confessions make it more likely that suspects will be bound over for trial (and eventually convicted). But confessions may be coerced; individual rights may be submerged in the quest for conviction. Courts have tried to clarify when a confession is truly voluntary, but, as we see in this chapter, psychological findings often conflict with the courts' evaluations of confessions—again reflecting the final dilemma described in Chapter 1.

The police may also suspect specific people of criminal behavior but lack firm evidence of their lawbreaking. Hence the police may create situations in which these suspicious persons have the opportunity to commit crimes. Often when lawbreakers are caught in such actions, they claim *entrapment* as a defense. There is confusion in the legal world over the meaning of this term, and further problems become evident when entrapment is examined from a psychological perspective, as we do later in this chapter.

Suspects are often given so-called lie detection tests to provide more information about their guilt or innocence and, sometimes, to encourage them to confess. Here again, the legal system's belief about the efficacy of lie detection procedures conflicts with some psychological findings about their accuracy. Some states permit the results of a lie detection test to be admitted into evidence, whereas many psychologists question the objectivity of the procedure as usually administered and hence the validity of its results. Thus, a consistent theme throughout this chapter is the conflict between the legal system and psychological science regarding ways of gaining knowledge and obtaining truth. A subsidiary conflict is the subordination of the goal of truth to the desire to resolve conflict and maintain the stability of the system.

PROFILING OF CRIMINAL SUSPECTS

Do criminals commit their crimes or choose their victims in distinctive ways that leave clues to their psychological makeup—much as fingerprints point to their physical identity or ballistics tests reveal the kind of gun they used? Evidence is accumulating that psychological characteristics are linked to behavioral patterns and that these links can be detected by a psychological analysis of crime scenes. Criminal profiling is used by behavioral scientists and police to narrow an investigation to suspects who possess certain behavioral and personality features as revealed by the way a crime was committed. Profiling does not identify a specific suspect. Instead, profilers sketch a general biographical description of the most likely type of suspect so that the police can concentrate their investigation of difficult cases in the most profitable directions. (Profiles are also developed to help investigators search for persons who fit descriptions known to characterize hijackers, drug couriers, and illegal aliens; Monahan & Walker, 1990).

Many famous fictional detectives are excellent profilers because they can interpret the meaning of a small detail or find a common theme among seemingly unrelated features of a crime. Lew Archer, the hero in Ross MacDonald's famous series of detective novels, often begins his search for a missing person (usually a wayward wife or a troubled daughter) by looking at the person's bedroom, examining her reading material, and rummaging through her closet in order to discover where her lifestyle may have misdirected her. And Helen McCloy's Dr. Basil Willing, the psychiatrist/detective featured in novels such as *The One That Got Away*, boasted: "Every criminal leaves psychic fingerprints and he can't wear gloves to hide them."

One of the earliest cases of criminal profiling involved the 1957 arrest of George Metesky, otherwise known as the Mad Bomber of New York City. Over an eight-year period, police had tried to solve a series of more than 30 bombings in the New York area. They finally consulted Dr. James Brussel, a Greenwich Village psychiatrist, who examined pictures of the bomb scenes and analyzed letters that had been sent by the bomber. Based on these data, Brussel advised the police to look for a heavyset, middle-aged, Eastern European, Catholic man who was single and lived with a sibling or aunt in Connecticut. Brussel also concluded that the man loved his mother and was very neat. He predicted that, when the man was found, he would be wearing a buttoned double-breasted suit. When the police finally arrested Matesky, this composite turned out to be uncannily accurate—even down to the right type of suit.

Not all early profiles were so useful. For example, a committee of experts charged with the task of profiling the Boston Strangler predicted that the killer was not one man but two, each of whom lived alone and was a schoolteacher. They also suggested that one of the men would be homosexual. When Albert DeSalvo ultimately confessed to these killings, police discovered that he was a married construction worker who lived with his wife and two sons and was not homosexual (Porter, 1983).

The major source of research and development on criminal profiling is the FBI's Behavioral Science Unit, which has been working on criminal profiles since the 1970s. This unit (now a part of the National Center for the Analysis of Violent Crime) is composed of special agents with training in behavioral science as well as consultants from the mental health professions; it has amassed large amounts of data on the backgrounds, family characteristics, current behaviors, and psychological traits of various types of criminal offenders. The unit has concentrated on the study of violent offenders, especially those who commit bizarre or repeated crimes (Jeffers, 1991). Special attention has been given to rapists (Ressler, Burgess, & Douglas, 1988), arsonists (Rider, 1980), sexual homicides (Hazelwood & Douglas, 1980), and mass and serial murderers (Porter, 1983). A key element in this research is interviews with known offenders of a given type aimed at discovering how they select and approach their victims, how they react to their crimes, what demographic or family characteristics they share, and what personality features might predominate among them. For example, as part of its study of mass and serial killers, the FBI has conducted detailed interviews with some of this country's most notorious killers—among them Charles Manson, Richard Speck, and David Berkowitz—in order to determine the similarities among them.

Douglas, Ressler, Burgess, and Hartman (1986) divide the FBI's profiling strategy into five stages, with a final, sixth stage being the arrest of the correct suspect. This five-stage model is illustrated in Box 8-1. The five phases, as they evolve in a murder investigation, are as follows:

1. *Profiling inputs.* The first stage involves collecting all information available about the crime, including physical evidence, photographs of the crime scene, autopsy reports and pictures, complete background information on the victim, and police reports. The profiler does not want to be told about possible suspects at this stage, because such data might prejudice or prematurely direct the profile.

2. *Decision process models.* In this stage the profiler organizes the input into meaningful questions and patterns along several dimensions of criminal activity. What type of homicide has been committed? (See Box 8-1 for a discussion of different styles of murder.) What is the primary motive for the crime—sexual, financial, personal, or emotional disturbance? What level of risk did the victim experience, and what level of risk did the murderer take in killing the victim? What was the sequence of acts before and after the killing, and how long did these acts take to commit? Where was the crime committed? Was the body moved, or was it found where the murder was committed?

3. *Crime assessment.* Based on the findings of the previous phase, the profiler attempts to reconstruct the behavior of the offender and the victim. Was the murder *organized* (suggesting a killer who carefully selects victims against whom to act out a given fantasy) or *disorganized* (indicating an impulsive, possibly psychotic killer)? Was the crime *staged* to mislead the police? What motivation was revealed by such details as cause of death, location of wounds, and position of the body? For example, as general profiling rules, (1) brutal facial injuries point to killers who know their victims, (2) murders committed with whatever weapon happens to be available are more impulsive than murders committed with a gun and may reveal a killer who lives fairly near the victim, and (3) murders committed early in the morning seldom involve alcohol or drugs.

4. *Criminal profile.* In this stage, profilers formulate an initial description of the most likely suspects. The typical profile includes the perpetrator's race, sex, age, marital status, living arrangements, and employment history; psychological characteristics, beliefs, and values; probable reactions to the police; and past criminal record, including the possibility of similar offenses in the past. As shown in Box 8-1, this stage also contains a feedback loop whereby profilers check their predictions against stage-2 information to make sure that the profile fits the original data.

5. *Investigation.* A written report is given to investigators, who concentrate on suspects matching the profile. If new evidence is discovered in this investigation, a second feedback process is initiated, and the profile may be revised.

6. *Apprehension.* The intended result of these procedures, arrest of a suspect, allows profilers to evaluate the validity of their predictions. The key element in this validation is a thorough interview of the suspect in order to assess the influences of background and psychological variables.

Is there any evidence about the validity of psychological profiling? Are profilers more accurate than other groups in their descriptions of suspects, or is this activity nothing more than a reading of forensic tea leaves? Do profilers use a different process in evaluating information than other investigators?

A study by Pinizzotto and Finkel (1990) provides initial data on the effectiveness of criminal profiling. In this investigation, four different groups of subjects evaluated two criminal cases—a homicide and a sex offense—that had already been solved but that were completely unknown to the subjects. The first group consisted of four experienced criminal profilers who had a total of 42 years of profiling experience and six police detectives who had recently been trained by the FBI to be profilers. The second group consisted of six police detectives

with 57 years of total experience in criminal investigations but with no profiling experience or training. The third group was composed of six clinical psychologists who had no profiling or criminal investigation experience. The final group consisted of six undergraduates drawn from psychology classes.

All subjects were given, for each case, an array of materials that profilers typically use. These materials included crime-scene photographs, crime-scene descriptions by uniformed officers, autopsy and toxicology reports (in the murder case), and descriptions of the victims. After studying these materials, subjects were asked to write all the details of each crime they

---

Box 8-1 | The Changing American Murderer

Experts agree that the contemporary American murder scene is changing. Historically, most murders have been committed by killers who were well acquainted with their victim, had a personal but rational motive, killed once, and were then arrested. In the past two decades, however, new patterns of homicide have emerged involving killers with irrational or bizarre motives who kill strangers and who are much less likely to be apprehended than in former days. Many of these murderers kill several victims, either at one place and time or at different locations and over a longer period of time.

Mass murderers have become a favorite subject of lurid true-crime books such as *The Only Living Witness* (Ted Bundy), *The Co-Ed Killer* (Edmund Kemper), and *Killer Clown* (John Gacy), as well as of more scholarly, comparative studies of multiple homicides (Levin & Fox, 1985; Leyton, 1986; Ressler, Burgess, & Douglas, 1988). On the basis of such studies, multiple killers have been classified into one of three categories, based on the pattern of their murders.

The mass murderer kills four or more victims in one location during one period of time that lasts anywhere from a few minutes to a few days. Most mass murderers are mentally disturbed people (although not necessarily psychotic) whose problems build to the point that they erupt against whoever happens to be in the vicinity. Charles Whitman, who shot and killed 16 people and wounded more than 30 others from a tower on the University of Texas campus, and James Huberty, who murdered 21 people, most of whom were children, at a San Diego McDonald's restaurant, are examples of mass

murderers. Mass murderers are sometimes divided into those who kill only members of their family and those who kill victims to whom they are not related.

Spree killers murder victims at two or more different locations with no "cooling-off" interval between the murders. The killing constitutes a single event, although it can last either a short or a long time.

Serial murderers kill three or more victims, each on separate occasions. Unlike mass and spree types, serial killers usually select a certain type of victim who fulfills a role in the killer's fantasies. There are cooling-off periods between serial murders, which are usually better planned than mass or spree killings. Some serial killers (e.g., Ted Bundy) travel continually and murder in several locations; others (e.g., Wayne Williams, the man could recall and to indicate the importance of these details to completing a profile. Three tests of profiling quality were used: all subjects prepared a profile of a suspect in each case, they answered 15 questions about the identity (e.g., gender, age, employment) of the suspects, and they were asked to rank-order a written "line-up" of five suspects from most likely to least likely to have committed each of the crimes.

The results indicated that, compared with the other three groups, the profiler group wrote longer profiles that contained more specific predictions about suspects, included more accurate predictions, and were rated as more helpful by other police detectives. Although they did not

differ substantially in the way they thought about the evidence, profilers were more accurate in answering specific questions about the sex-offense suspect than the other groups; the groups did not differ in their accuracy about the homicide suspect. Similar results were found with the "line-up" identification task; profilers were the most accurate for the sex offense, whereas there were no differences for the homicide case.

This early evidence suggests that profilers can produce more useful and valid criminal profiles, even when compared to experienced crime investigators. This advantage may be limited, however, to certain kinds of cases or to the types of information made available to investigators.

convicted of killing the Atlanta children) are geographically stable and kill within the same area.

Because they plan their murders, often travel long distances between their crimes, kill for idiosyncratic reasons, and frequently wait months between killings, serial murderers are difficult to apprehend. However, social scientists have gained some knowledge about these criminals, who may number as many as 100 in the United States. In general they are white males, aged 25–34, of at least average intelligence, and often charming in nature. Many were illegitimate and experienced abuse as children. They tend to select vulnerable victims of some specific type who gratify their need to control people. They prefer to kill with "hands-on" methods such as strangulation and stabbing. They are often pre-

occupied with sadistic fantasies involving domination and control of their victims; these fantasies often are sexualized, as was the case with Jeffrey Dahmer. Many serial killers are impressed with police work and like to associate with the police. Although the incidence of murder has been disproportionately higher in the South, serial killers are not likely to hail from southern states. Over the course of their criminal careers, their murders may become less organized and more poorly planned.

Ronald Holmes, a criminologist at the University of Louisville who specializes in the study of serial murder, has identified four subtypes of serial killers (Holmes & DeBurger, 1988). The *visionary* type feels compelled to murder because he hears voices or sees visions ordering him to kill certain

kinds of people. The visionary killer is often psychotic. The *mission-oriented* type seeks to kill a specific group of people who he believes are unworthy to live and without whom the world would be a better place. He is not psychotic; in fact, his everyday acquaintances frequently will describe him as a fine citizen. The *hedonistic* type kills for the thrill of it. Such killers simply enjoy the act of killing. Sexual arousal associated with killing is common with this type of murder. Finally, the *power-oriented* type kills because he enjoys exerting ultimate control over his victims. These murderers are not psychotic, but they are obsessed with capturing and controlling their victims and forcing them to obey their every command.

"LIE DETECTION" THROUGH USE OF THE POLYGRAPH

Throughout history, many societies have assumed that criminals can be detected by the physical effects of their denials. Ever since King Solomon tried to discover which of two women who claimed to be the mother of an infant was lying by watching their emotions when he threatened to cut the baby in half and divide it between them, people have believed that the body will reveal in some way that the mind is lying when the mouth protests innocence. Who knows how many children have been scared into truthfulness by the prospect that their noses, like Pinocchio's, will give away their deceits.

The ancient Hindus forced suspects to chew rice and to spit it out on a leaf from a sacred tree. If the rice was dry, the suspect was considered guilty. The Bedouins of Arabia required conflicting witnesses to lick a hot iron; the one whose tongue was burned was thought to be lying (Kleinmuntz & Szucko, 1984). Both these procedures reflect activity of the sympathetic nervous system (under emotional states, salivation usually decreases) and thus are crude measures of emotion, though not necessarily of lying. But emotion and lying are not the same, even if they are correlated to some extent (Saxe, 1991). The failure to appreciate this distinction is at the root of many of the mistaken ideas about the polygraph, as well as its unacceptably high rate of misclassifying persons as honest or deceitful.

Emergence of the Polygraph

Despite this long history, the polygraph, or "lie detector," was not developed until around 1917, with the work of William Moulton Marston, a complex and colorful figure who origi-nated the term *lie detector*. Marston had studied at Harvard University with Hugo Munsterberg, who directed the experimental psychology laboratory there. Marston claimed that he could detect lying by noting increases in systolic blood pressure when subjects told untruths. And he was an avid publicist for his new technique; he even tried to get permission to test Bruno Hauptmann, the alleged kidnapper of the Lindbergh baby, on his new lie detector machine (Lykken, 1981).

Marston's technique was the procedure under question in the landmark *Frye* v. *United States* case (1923) that we discussed in Chapter 7. In this case, James Frye appealed his murder conviction on the ground that the trial judge did not allow a polygrapher to testify about the results of a physiological deception test that supported Frye's claim of innocence. The appeals court upheld Frye's conviction and stated the now-famous "*Frye* test" for admitting expert testimony into evidence: "while courts will go a long way in admitting expert testimony deduced from a well-recognized scientific principle or discovery, the thing from which the deduction is made must be sufficiently established to have gained general acceptance in the particular field in which it belongs." (Many courts have moved away from relying on *Frye* to decide whether an expert may testify; instead, they increasingly rely on the criterion of whether the expert's testimony will be relevant and will help fact finders reach an appropriate decision.) Because of his extravagant claims, Marston was repudiated not only by the courts but also by serious investigators. (Marston was a man of many talents; using the name "Charles Moulton," he created the comic strip *Wonder Woman*.)

A solid step forward in the use of the polygraph was taken by John A. Larson of the Berkeley, California, Police Department (Larson, 1932). He built a forerunner of the modern polygraph that could measure pulse rate, blood pressure, and respiratory changes during questioning. Here we see the origins of the *polygraph* concept (*poly* meaning "many"). What is commonly called the lie detector does not measure lies as such; it measures *emotion*. It is more properly called a polygraph because it employs several physiological measures—usually blood pressure, heart rate, breathing rate, and the galvanic skin response (or skin resistance to an electrical current). Unfortunately for Marston, Larson, and others who sought a specific "lie response," the *physiological* manifestations of various negative emotions—fear, guilt, anger—are all very similar (physiological differences between positive and negative emotions are more apparent; Zajonc & McIntosh, 1992).

Larson also developed the first systematic way of questioning suspects. The R/I procedure (standing for *relevant/irrelevant*) intersperses "relevant" questions about the crime under investigation ("Did you steal Mrs. Riley's cow?") with "irrelevant" questions that are unrelated to the crime and are not stressful ("What did you do on your last birthday?"). Larson compared suspects' physiological reactions on these two types of questions to determine whether greater emotion was shown in response to the relevant questions. He assumed that truthful subjects would respond with equivalent reactions to all questions, whereas guilty, and dishonest, subjects would react more to the relevant questions.

Because one negative emotion can't be reliably distinguished from another on physiological grounds, Larson was forced to *infer* lying. But such an inference is unacceptable. Simply being a *suspect* in a crime, even if you are innocent, may generate a great deal of surplus emotion, but that should not be taken as a sign of guilt. Regardless of whether you are guilty or

innocent, you are more likely to be aroused by relevant questions; these questions are obviously related to the crime being investigated, whereas the irrelevant questions are just as obviously unrelated to it. Despite these problems, the polygraph procedure, during the 1930s and later, was enthusiastically and uncritically employed by law enforcement officials. In fact, during the first *half-century* after 1915, Larson himself was the only investigator to report an objective study of the diagnosis of deception using polygraph recordings obtained from criminal suspects (Lykken, 1985).

The Control Question Test. A further refinement was made by criminologists associated with the Northwestern University Law School. In the 1930s the Keeler polygraph, the prototype of current instruments, was developed by Leonarde Keeler and his colleagues. During the middle of this century, lie detectors were quite the topic of interest. In the movie *Northside 777*, it was Keeler himself who administered the R/I test to Richard Conte in Joliet Prison, proving what reporter Jimmy Stewart had suspected all along: that Conte was innocent of the crime for which he had been imprisoned. Such media portrayals contributed to the public's belief that lie detectors were infallible measures of honesty and dishonesty.

While at Northwestern University, Keeler met Fred Inbau and John Reid. Reid had also developed a polygraph, and they established schools to train investigators to use polygraph techniques. Most present examiners have been trained through outgrowths of these schools.

In the 1940s, John Reid pioneered the Control Question Test, which became the most popular approach to polygraphic examinations. The exam begins with an interview in which the examiner gathers biographical information from the subject and attempts to impress upon the subject that he or she must be honest at all times during the test. The examiner tries to convince the subject that the polygraph is an infallible instrument; this strategy is meant to threaten guilty subjects at the same time that it reassures the innocent. Polygraphers often use a *stim test* to instill respect for the instrument (see Box 8-2 for a description of the stim test).

Next the subject is asked a series of two kinds of questions. *Relevant questions* inquire about the crime under investigation, such as "Did you steal the law school's TV set?" *Control questions* are not directly concerned with the crime under investigation but are calculated to induce an emotional reaction because they cover common misdeeds that almost all of us have committed at some point—for example, "Have you ever stolen anything?" or "Prior to the age of 21, did you ever try to hurt someone you disliked?" Most polygraphers consider these "known lies." They are assumed to have occurred, but subjects will deny them, thereby providing a characteristic physiological response to a lie. Guilty subjects should be more aroused by the relevant questions (to which they must lie to maintain their innocence), whereas innocent subjects should be more aroused by the control questions (because they will worry that admitting to a past misdeed might make them look more like a criminal at the present time). Therefore, this procedure works best when innocent subjects lie to the

---

Box 8-2 | Using Intimidation to Elicit Confessions

Some polygraph examiners will readily acknowledge that a basic goal in giving the test is to encourage lawbreakers to confess. Reid and Inbau (1966), leading experts in the development of the procedure, advise:

> After the subject's questions, if any, about the instrument and test procedure have been answered . . . he should be told something like the following: "You know, of course, that we're checking on the death of John Jones at First and Main Street the other night. . . . If you did do this thing . . . , I'm going to know about it as soon as this investigation is over. If you did do this, therefore, I suggest you tell me about it now, before the test" [1966, p. 13].

Examiners will use tricks to intimidate suspects and to convince them that the machine is infallible. A favorite is the "stim test." The subject is shown seven playing cards and told to take one, look at it, and put it back in the deck without showing it to the examiner. Reid and Inbau write: "After the selection is made, the examiner proceeds to shuffle the cards and instructs the subject to answer 'no' to each question concerning the cards, even when asked the number of the card he selected. In other words, the subject's answer to one of the questions will be a lie" (1966, p. 27).

At the end of this exercise, the examiner tells the subject which card he or she picked, leaving the implication that the apparatus detected lying. But Reid and Inbau advise examiners that "the cards are arranged and shown to the subject in such a way that the examiner will immediately know which card has been picked by the subject" (1966, p. 27). Another variant of this shoddy procedure is to use a deck of 52 replications of the same playing card (Lykken, 1981).

Reid and Inbau even acknowledge that the polygraph is not completely accurate; one of the reasons for the card-trick deception is that "the [polygraph] record itself may not actually disclose the card 'lie'" (1966, p. 27).

control questions (or at least show greater emotional turmoil over them) and the guilty subject lies (and becomes more emotionally aroused) to the relevant questions.

Reid also introduced "guilt complex" questions. In this procedure, the examiner pretends to be equally interested in whether the suspect is also guilty of some fictitious crime. Since this other crime is imaginary, the examiner knows that the suspect's denial is truthful and therefore can compare the subject's physiological responses to the "guilt complex" questions with the responses to the questions about the actual crime. However, the "measurement" of lying still rests here on a shaky assumption—that differences in intensity of physiological reactions are based on guilt.

The final step in the Control Question Test is to interpret the polygraphic charts. Most polygraphers reach a conclusion about the subject's honesty on subjective grounds that include the physiological record as well as the interviewers' observations of the subject's behavior throughout the test. A second approach, known as the *zone of comparison* method (Backster, 1974), involves a quantified comparison of physiological reactions to the relevant and control questions.

The Guilty Knowledge Test. The *Guilty Knowledge Test* was developed by David Lykken (1981), a University of Minnesota psychologist who has also been one of the staunchest critics of standard procedures such as the Control Question Test. Both the procedure and the purposes of this method are fundamentally different from the Control Question approach. The goal is to detect the presence of guilty knowledge in the suspect's mind, not to detect lying. The procedure relies on the accumulation of facts that are known only by the police, the criminal, and any surviving victims. For example: In what room was the victim's body found?

What was the murder weapon? What strange garment was the victim wearing? What was clutched in the victim's hand?

A series of multiple-choice questions is created, based on this information, and the suspect is presented with each question in order and asked to respond to each choice. "Was it the bedroom? Was it the kitchen? Was it the living room?" Although each alternative would appear equally plausible to an innocent person, the true criminal will be revealed by physiological reactions that accompany recognition of guilty knowledge. Imagine that the suspect has been asked five questions about the crime, each of which has five choices, and that on question 1 his physiological reaction is much stronger to the "correct" response than to any of the others. Just by coincidence that would happen 20% of the time—that is, one time out of five choices. So we can't make any strong inference about his knowledge of the crime from his responses to just one question. But let us say further that for each of the five questions his emotional reaction to the correct response is much greater than to the other choices. By coincidence, this set of reactions would be unlikely; its probability is $1/5 \times 1/5 \times 1/5 \times 1/5 \times 1/5$, or 1/3125. One in 3125 is a probability of .00032, or very, very unlikely by chance. If this pattern of reactions occurs, we can be confident that the suspect has detailed and accurate *knowledge* of the crime. That, in itself, is suggestive, but not direct, evidence that the suspect *committed* the crime.

Notice that the goal of the Guilty Knowledge Test is not to detect emotions that might accompany deception; rather, it is to detect knowledge possessed by subjects. The underlying assumption is that people are more physiologically aroused when they perceive a meaningful stimulus. This well-established pattern is known as the *orienting response* (Ben-Shakhar, Bar-Hillel, & Lieblich, 1986).

Obviously, this technique can be used only

when the details of the crime have been kept from the public. Even then, it is conceivable that the suspect is not the perpetrator but, rather, was told about the crime by the true criminal and therefore possesses "guilty" knowledge. Moreover, it is possible that some guilty subjects pay so little attention to the details of their crimes that they actually lack the requisite knowledge of them that this method requires.

Validity of Polygraph Procedures

Advocates of polygraph procedures claim very high rates of accuracy. Reid and Inbau asserted that their success rate was 99%. F. Lee Bailey proposed on national television that, out of every 100 polygraph tests administered, 96 are accurate, 3 are inconclusive, and only 1 will be in error (quoted in Lykken, 1985, p. 96). Critics of the polygraph argue that most of the techniques are based on implausible psychological assumptions and that errors of classification are too frequent. Within psychology this debate has been waged vigorously by David Lykken (1981, 1985), who strongly criticizes most polygraphic techniques, and David Raskin (1982, 1989), a University of Utah psychologist who argues that the polygraph yields valid indications of deception when used correctly.

Before summarizing the results of empirical studies of polygraphic accuracy, we highlight five problems that complicate scientific study of criminal polygraphy and that must be kept in mind when evaluating evidence about the polygraph.

1. Clearly, the polygraph is useful in inducing suspects to confess their crimes. This outcome, produced presumably by suspects' beliefs that the polygraph will ultimately detect their guilt and that they can best mitigate their sentences by confessing their crimes, is no small accomplishment. But false confessions can and do occur. Therefore, the *utility* of the polygraph

in prompting confessions should not be confused with its *accuracy* in determining truth versus deceit. This latter issue is at the heart of the validity question.

2. A vexing problem in evaluating polygraph results is the difficulty of finding a decisive criterion of accuracy, sometimes known as *ground truth*. In some studies, ground truth is defined by a panel of judges who review all the evidence in a case and conclude who is the guilty culprit. In other studies, ground truth is established through subsequent confessions. A third choice is to use the official judicial outcome (e.g., jury verdict) as the criterion. All these alternatives have some methodological limitations.

3. In the context of criminal investigations, detecting a liar is a *true positive* and believing a truthful suspect is a *true negative*. Believing a liar is truthful is a *false negative*, whereas disbelieving a truthful subject is a *false positive*. The frequency of these errors depends on both the accuracy of the technique and the *base rate* (how often something happens) of liars and honest subjects among a tested sample. The following example illustrates this relationship. Assume that the overall accuracy of the polygraph is 80%; also assume that the base rate of guilt and accompanying deception among criminal suspects is 75% (a reasonable figure if we grant that the police usually arrest and charge the right suspects). If 1000 people are arrested, 750 will be guilty in our example. The polygraph will catch 600 (750 x .80), but it will make 150 false negatives. Of the 250 innocent suspects, the polygraph will exonerate 200, but it will falsely implicate 50 persons. Given a constant level of polygraphic accuracy, as the base rate of liars increases, false negatives also increase. More false positives will occur when the base rate of lying by suspects is low. The problem of base rates also indicates how a claim of "96% correct" can be misleading. Let us say a major theft has occurred in a factory with 50

employees. One is the thief; 49 are honest. The polygrapher gives a lie detection test to each of the employees; each employee denies being the thief. The polygrapher misclassifies one of the innocent people as the thief (false positive). He also fails to detect lying in the true thief (false negative). So he has erred in two cases, but he has been correct in classifying the 48 others as truthful. His accuracy rate is 48 out of 50, or 96%. But he has still erred on the crucial determination; despite the inflated overall "accuracy rate," his basic test result is invalid.

4. *Field studies* of the polygraph are based on real-life investigations of subjects who have a large stake in being cleared of suspicion. *Analog studies* involve investigations of "mock" crimes staged by an experimenter who also arranges for some subjects (often, college students) to be "guilty" and others to be "innocent." Field studies face the problem of locating ground truth, but their use of subjects who are motivated to avoid detection is a methodological advantage (Kircher, Horowitz, & Raskin, 1988). In addition, analog studies may overestimate polygraphic accuracy because "innocent" analog subjects will probably not experience the emotional arousal that a vulnerable but innocent subject feels in a real crime investigation.

5. A final threat to the polygraph is that deceptive subjects will "beat" the test by using countermeasures to avoid detection. Deliberate physical movements, drugs, and cognitive or psychological maneuvers have all been suggested as possible countermeasures. Effective countermeasures should increase false negatives, but they should have negligible effects on false positives. In fact, there is little evidence that countermeasures have any consistent distorting effects on polygraph results (Raskin, 1989).

The most thorough review of the polygraph's validity was a report in 1983 by the Office of Technology Assessment (OTA), directed by Leonard Saxe and entitled *Scientific Validity of*

Polygraphic Testing: A Research Review and Evaluation. A brief version of OTA's report by Saxe, Dougherty, and Cross (1985) reported that, of 250 empirical studies of polygraphic testing, only 10 field studies met adequate scientific standards. All 10 studies investigated the Control Question Test (CQT). The average rate of false negatives across these 10 studies was 11.5% (ranging from 0–23%). The average range of false positives was 18.3% (range: 0–53%). Saxe et al. (1985) interpret these outcomes as follows: "on average, in field studies polygraphic test results reduced 64% of the error of chance prediction" (p. 360), "although the data also suggest that substantial rates of false positives, false negatives, and inconclusives are possible" (p. 364). Since the OTA review, a major field study of the polygraph using U.S. Secret Service examiners indicated that, across a three-year period, these examiners correctly identified 95% of the 76 deceptive suspects and 96% of the truthful subjects they polygraphed (Raskin, 1989).

Twelve analog studies of the CQT met adequate scientific standards and showed an average 47% reduction in errors from chance predictions. OTA located no field studies of the Guilty Knowledge Test (GKT). However, Lykken (1985) argues that analog evaluations of the GKT are acceptable since this procedure does not rely on the emotional arousal that can be dependably elicited only in the field. For eight analog studies of the GKT cited by Lykken (1985), 88.2% of 161 "guilty" subjects were detected, whereas 96.7% of 152 "innocents" were cleared.

Even severe critics of the polygraph, such as Lykken, acknowledge that the technique has overall accuracy rates of 65% or better. But is this figure high enough to permit polygraphic data as evidence at a trial or high enough to base a prosecution of a suspect on it as the primary evidence? We think not. The best use of the polygraph remains at the investigatory stages of a criminal prosecution and as a "stage prop" to encourage confessions from suspects against whom other incriminating evidence has been gathered.

Other "Lie Detection" Methods

In recent years, as controversy about the polygraph has continued to swirl, other "lie detection" procedures have been advocated. The *psychological stress evaluator (PSE)* uses the speaking voice as the determinant of lying. Advocates of the PSE claim that it can measure variations in emotional stress—that it can distinguish words and phrases spoken in periods of high and low stress. Despite claims of accuracy by its users, no evidence has been published in any scientific journal showing that the psychological stress evaluator is effective (Lykken, 1985). A second approach is to judge lying on the basis of facial, bodily, or vocal cues. For example, when subjects lie, their voice pitch tends to increase, they illustrate their language with gestures less frequently, and they may attempt to lengthen the time they gaze at persons to whom they lie (Ekman, 1985). However, the ability of observers to use this information to "catch" liars is fairly limited (Ekman & O'Sullivan, 1991).

Admissibility of Polygraph Records

Because of the controversies surrounding the polygraph, many courts do not allow polygraph examiners to testify in trials about their conclusions. In about 20 states, however, such examiners may testify if both parties in the trial *stipulate* or agree that the evidence can be used (Morris, 1989). And in Massachusetts and New Mexico they may testify even over the objection of one side. This would seem to be a dangerous procedure, for the examiner's testimony goes directly to the issue of the defendant's truthfulness.

How do juries react to such testimony? Do they blindly accept polygraph evidence? Cavoukian and Heslegrave (1980) conducted two studies to find out. In the initial study, mock jurors reacted to one of three versions of a trial. In the first version, they were given a summary of the major points in the case and the judge's instructions. In the second, they also had polygraph evidence showing the defendant to be innocent. In the third, they had these materials plus an additional instruction from the judge that polygraph tests were about 80% accurate and so jurors should be cautious in deciding verdicts on the basis of such tests. The percentages of jurors who acquitted the defendant in the three conditions were 48%, 72%, and 60%, respectively. The judge's cautionary instruction reduced some of the effect of the polygraph evidence. And even when the polygraph results were presented, the subjects did not follow them blindly. In a second study, using a different case, Cavoukian and Heslegrave (1980) found that the judge's cautionary instruction was even more influential; it reduced the acquittal rate below what it was without any polygraph evidence at all.

Recently, the legality of the polygraph has been challenged in another way. The administration of a polygraph examination as part of an employment application has been outlawed in the case of most jobs; see Box 8-3. The Federal Employee Polygraph Protection Act of 1988 prohibits most private employers from using polygraphs (as well as PSE machines) to screen employees for honesty or past offenses. Ironically, most firms that previously used polygraph examinations are now using other devices, especially "integrity tests," to detect potentially dishonest employees. These paper-and-pencil tests are intended to measure employees' attitudes toward thefts or other crimes, but the evidence to date indicates that such tests are probably inferior to the polygraph as "honesty tests." They appear to be easily faked, to be trivially related to actual honest or dishonest behavior, and to produce high false-positive rates (Guastello & Rieke, 1991).

USE OF CONFESSIONS

Throughout history, confessions have been accorded enormous importance. Confession is valued as an indicator of truth and also as an act that benefits confessors because it relieves them of guilt and earns them forgiveness from their fellow citizens. Many religions maintain that confession is the first step toward redemp-

tion and have evolved special rituals to encourage it.

When the police capture suspects, one of their first acts is to encourage them to confess to the crime. A confession will, of course, permit a district attorney or grand jury to bring charges. Even if the suspect later denies the confession and pleads not guilty to charges, the confession can be introduced into evidence at the trial.

Disputed "confessions" by defendants occur more often than most of us would guess; Kalven and Zeisel's classic study *The American Jury* (1966) states that they surface in one-fifth of all cases that go to trial. And we read of them frequently in the press. U.S. Marine Sergeant

---

Box 8-3 | *The Lie Detector and Job Applications*

This chapter has focused on polygraph techniques in criminal investigations, but until recently more polygraph examinations were administered in employment screening than in criminal cases. Probably 80% of the 2 million tests given each year in the United States were job related. Beginning in December 1988, however, the use of the polygraph as part of a job interview was banned for all private businesses except those manufacturing or dispensing drugs or those employing security guards or doing sensitive work on government contracts. However, the law did not prohibit federal, state, or local governments from continuing to use preemployment polygraph tests.

Before this law, whenever a crime occurred in a business, its

management might routinely administer polygraph tests to all employees. Some companies would randomly test some employees each month, even if a crime had not occurred. According to the new law, an employer can ask a current employee to take the test only if the employer, in a written statement, provides reasons for suspecting the worker was involved in a theft or other crime and the employee had access to any missing materials. Furthermore, an employee may not be fired *solely* on the basis of the results of a polygraph examination.

Given the void created by this important law, some firms have begun to use "integrity tests" as a substitute in the employment process. These are paper-and-pencil personality questionnaires that try to assess

the honesty of the job applicant. In 1990 an estimated 5.5 million integrity tests were administered. Firms like Stop 'N Go stores and certain of the Kentucky Fried Chicken restaurants are requiring all their applicants to take integrity tests (Caprino, 1989). Questions elicit self-reports about shoplifting, drug use, drinking, petty theft, and financial problems, as well as behaviors less obviously related to honesty on the job. These straightforward questions (Example: "Have you ever taken something from a store without paying for it?") are quite easy to fake, but adherents of integrity testing claim that many job applicants will freely reveal their past transgressions (Gorman, 1989). However, the validity of integrity tests is yet to be proved.

Arnold Bracy initially confessed that he had let KGB spies into the code room of the American Embassy in Moscow; he later denied it. Johnny Wilson, a mentally retarded man, confessed to the murder of a 79-year-old woman after a six-hour, late-night interrogation. He later said that he confessed so he could go home and avoid an abusive police questioner. He was sentenced to life in prison, even though a convict in another state has since claimed responsibility for the crime (Spivak, 1989).

If jurors hear a police detective testify about a confession by the defendant—even though they know the defendant now is pleading not guilty—their eventual verdicts often are affected by the incriminating testimony, whatever happens later. A simple study demonstrates the power of such evidence (Miller & Boster, 1977). All the mock jurors in this study received a brief description of Smith's relationship to Jones and of Smith's murder. One-fourth were told of testimony from an eyewitness to the murder who was not acquainted with Smith or Jones; one-fourth received testimony from an eyewitness who knew both Smith and Jones; a third group was apprised only of circumstantial evidence; and the remaining fourth learned that Jones had confessed and that this confession was introduced as evidence at the trial. Those mock jurors who received information about the confession were most likely to judge the defendant guilty—more so even than the jurors who knew that an eyewitness had identified the defendant.

THE VOLUNTARINESS OF CONFESSIONS

Knowledge of a prior confession often pushes a juror's verdict in the guilty direction. But are confessions always valid? Some "confessions" do not come spontaneously from the defendant; rather, they result from intensified questioning by the police—interrogation that may involve promises, threats, harassment, or even brutality. Do the police ever go too far? Are there safeguards against going too far?

When Is a Confession Not a Confession?

The courts have ruled that a confession must be voluntary for it to be admitted into evidence. But it is not always easy to categorize a confession as voluntary or involuntary. Box 8-4 proposes a continuum of voluntariness.

Confessions ought to be voluntary. The truthfulness of an involuntary confession is questionable, and therefore the confession is not trustworthy evidence for jurors who are mandated to assume the innocence of the defendant and to require the prosecution to *prove* guilt. Illustrating one of the dilemmas of Chapter 1, this standard conflicts with practices that allow government officials to question an accused person and introduce into evidence statements that the accused has made under possibly coercive conditions.

Four hundred years ago, that dilemma was not considered a legitimate question. All confessions were routinely admitted into evidence. In fact, a confession was treated as a plea of guilty—that is, as a criminal pleading rather than as a matter of evidence (Wigmore, 1970). One statement, in 1607, pointedly said "A confession is a conviction." Even confessions extracted by torture—and they were numerous—were accepted into evidence without question.

We have come a long way since then, but, as this section will show, jurors' evaluations of confessions are still problematic. Slowly over the centuries, the place of confessions in the legal system shifted. In the mid-1600s, the right against self-incrimination emerged in English common law. A century later, in Rudd's case, the admissibility into evidence of ordinary confessions was first limited. By the middle to late 18th century, coerced confessions began to be excluded as evidence because, as the case of *Hopt* v. *Utah* (1884) held, the trustworthiness of a confession was lost when it was obtained through threat or inducement. A general viewpoint developed that a confession should be "reliable" (in other words, an accurate representation of the truth) before it is used in evidence. A few judges therefore began to scrutinize confessions more carefully: What is the nature of the witness who testifies that a confession occurred? Is the witness a paid informer? An overzealous police officer? But, in reality, few confessions were excluded from evidence during this time period.

By the late 1800s, judicial opinions tended to agree that confessions vary in their trustworthiness but that they should be admitted as evidence and then left to the jury for an evaluation of their utility. This laissez faire approach, however, did not suffice. In the early 1900s, courts in the United States were increasingly faced with cases of black defendants who had "confessed" to crimes after being beaten by the police. *Brown* v. *Mississippi*, a Supreme Court decision in 1936, was a landmark decision on this matter. This case involved three black defendants who had been convicted of the murder of a white man entirely on the basis of "confessions" procured after one of the defendants had been severely whipped and hung twice from a tree and the other two defendants had been stripped naked and beaten until they signed a confession the police had written. The Supreme Court reversed these convictions on the ground

---

Box **8-4** | *What Is a Voluntary Confession?*

How can we tell whether a particular confession is voluntary and hence likely to be truthful, or whether it is involuntary, coerced, and hence possibly false? Some cases lead to subjective opinions, but we could probably agree generally to the relative position of the following specific examples on a continuum of voluntary-to-involuntary confessions.

COMPLETELY VOLUNTARY

X Comes in to the police station and turns himself in, for a crime for which he wasn't even a suspect.

X Is stopped by police and questioned for a specific crime and then confesses.

"GRAY" AREA—
VOLUNTARY OR
INVOLUNTARY?

X Confesses after he is promised a lenient sentence if he confesses.

X Confesses after he is threatened with severe punishment if he fails to confess and is still convicted.

X Questioned in a cell for 24 hours, without sleep. Only after that does he confess.

X Has broken ankle, is in pain, and is denied treatment until he confesses.

X Beaten, tortured, kept without sleep or food for several days. Only then confesses.

COMPLETELY INVOLUNTARY

that the police had violated the defendants' rights to due process of law; the Court ruled that evidence procured through torture must be excluded from trials.

What emerged after *Brown* was a distinction between coerced confessions—hence, involuntary ones—and voluntary confessions. The courts said that coerced confessions could not be included as evidence for three reasons. First, coerced confessions were untrustworthy. Second, their use would offend the community's sense of fair play and decency. Third, the exclusion of coerced confessions from evidence would, it was hoped, reduce the use of brutality and other undue pressures when police question suspects (Wigmore, 1970, p. 324). What constituted "coercion" remained a thorny question. As early as the Supreme Court case of *Bram* v. *United States* (1897), the courts recognized that sheer physical brutality was not the only means of coercion. Other factors that were considered were drugs (*Townsend* v. *Swain*, 1963), sleep deprivation (*Ashcraft* v. *Tennessee*, 1944), lack of food (*Reck* v. *Pate*, 1961), and prolonged interrogations (*Davis* v. *North Carolina*, 1966).

A case-by-case approach to assessing the voluntariness of confessions proved difficult for many reasons. The task was highly subjective, and it resulted in countless "swearing contests" between police and suspects about what went on behind the closed doors of interrogation rooms. The case of *Miranda* v. *Arizona* (which we discuss more in the next chapter) was in part an attempt to remedy the above problems by creating a rule, based on the Fifth Amendment privilege against self-incrimination, that any confessions obtained without suspects having been advised of their legal rights to obtain counsel and to remain silent were inadmissible at trial.

However, *Miranda* does not solve all problems about the voluntariness of confessions.

A suspect could be read his Miranda rights, waive these rights, and then give a statement that is still coerced through any number of influences. For their part, the police may believe that a waiver of Miranda rights gives them greater latitude in how they question suspects. The result may be a statement that the defendant later claims should not be admitted because it was coerced. Finally, there are suspects whose intellectual disability or psychological instability renders them especially vulnerable to certain tactics of interrogation. Although an individual's special vulnerabilities must be considered in assessing voluntariness, the Supreme Court has stated, in *Colorado* v. *Connelly* (1986), that a suspect's mental or psychological problems alone are not sufficient for concluding that a confession was involuntary.

The Supreme Court, in *Jackson* v. *Denno* (1964), made explicit the exclusion of confessions obtained against the will of the accused. In fact, the Court in this case held that criminal defendants are entitled to a pretrial hearing that determines whether any confession they have made to officials was voluntarily given and not the outcome of physical or psychological coercion, which the U.S. Constitution forbids. Only if the fact finder (usually the judge) at this hearing determines that the confession was in fact voluntary may it then be introduced at the trial to the jury.

Judging the Voluntariness of a Confession: What Should Be the Standard of Proof?

Requiring a judge or other fact finder to screen confessions is a sensible idea—as well as a life-saving one for some defendants. But did that rule take care of the problem? No. Left unclear in *Jackson* v. *Denno* was the question of what should be the standard of proof by which the fact finder judges voluntariness. Some states adopted the stringent criterion that voluntariness must be proved "beyond a reasonable doubt." In contrast, other states approved lesser standards, including proof of voluntariness by a mere "preponderance of the evidence." The Supreme Court resolved this discrepancy in the case of *Lego* v. *Twomey* (1972) by ruling that only a preponderance of the evidence in the direction of voluntariness was necessary to admit a confession into evidence. This decision was a blow for defendants and defense attorneys, who had hoped a more rigorous threshold would be required before such potentially damaging testimony could be introduced to the jurors.

In *Lego* v. *Twomey*, the Supreme Court reasoned that the aim of the previous *Jackson* v. *Denno* decision was to exclude the evidence because it was illegally obtained and hence violated the individual's right to due process; it was not excluded because of the possible untruthfulness of a coerced confession. The Supreme Court, in fact, assumed that jurors can be trusted to use potentially inaccurate confessions cautiously. Specifically, the Court stated: "Our decision was not based in the slightest on the fear that juries might misjudge the accuracy of confessions and arrive at erroneous determinations of guilt or innocence. . . . Nothing in *Jackson* questioned the province or capacity of juries to assess the truthfulness of confessions" (*Lego* v. *Twomey*, 1972, p. 625).

Guided by this faith in jurors' capacities, the Supreme Court thus justified a lower threshold by which the fact finder may consider a confession whose voluntariness is in some question. Much as in the matter of assessing the accuracy of eyewitness identifications (described in Chapter 7), the courts assumed that jurors would be able to disregard testimony if they questioned the motivations behind it.

Do Jurors Really Discount a Possibly Coerced Confession?

Is that assumption by the Supreme Court well founded? This is another problem in attribution, which, as we indicated earlier, is a topic central to social psychology. Jurors are confronted with a behavior (a confession) whose cause is unclear (is it sincere and self-initiated, or is it a response to coercion?). If a defendant confesses while under severe threat during an interrogation, that confession may be viewed either as a reflection of the defendant's true guilt or as a means of avoiding the negative consequences of silence. Ideally, jurors would employ what a leading attribution theorist (Kelley, 1971) has called the *discounting principle:* they would have more doubts about the truth and reliability of a confession elicited by threat than about one made in the absence of threat. In other words, they would "discount," or give less weight to, the confession—and perhaps even disregard it—because it was generated by threat of force.

But discounting doesn't always occur. A number of social-psychological studies have reported that, when making attributions about the causes of another's behavior, most people do not give sufficient importance to the external situation as a determinant; instead, they believe the behavior is caused by stable, internal factors unique to the actor (Jones & Nisbett, 1971). Thus, in the present situation, they would conclude: "He confessed, so he must be guilty." In a series of experiments, Jones and Harris (1967) had subjects read an essay or hear a speech presumably written by another student. These speeches and essays reflected certain attitudes. In one study, subjects read an essay in which the communicator either supported or criticized the unpopular Castro regime in Cuba. Some subjects were told that the communicator had freely chosen to advocate this position; others were told that the communicator had been assigned to endorse the position by a political science instructor. But even when subjects thought the communicator had no choice about what to write in the essay, their impressions about the communicator's true beliefs were still markedly influenced by the particular position espoused. *It seems that what you say is more influential than why you say it.*

The parallels between this research procedure and the coerced confession are striking. In both, observers (subjects or jurors) are faced with a verbal behavior, which they may attribute either to the actor's true attitude or to the pressures emanating from the situation. Yet, although the Supreme Court assumed that jurors would reject an involuntary confession as not to be trusted and thus would not allow it to guide their decisions, the program of research by Jones and Harris suggests that jurors might not reject the confessions when considering the actor's true guilt.

Are Threats and Promises of Leniency Equivalent Determinants of Involuntariness?

But the problems do not stop there. To complicate matters further, the legal system defines coercion as either the *threat* of harm and punishment or the *promise* of leniency and immunity from prosecution (LaBuy, 1963; refer to Box 8-4). The courts view these as equivalent conditions for determining involuntariness. In fact, jurors are sometimes provided this legal definition in the judge's charge. Moreover, most states follow what is known as the "orthodox rule": once the judge decides to admit a confession, the jury is never told that its voluntariness was ever questioned. Consequently, jurors receive no special instruction on the matter. However, a few states provide that, even after the judge has admitted this evidence, he or she must also instruct the jury that it must also

decide the issue of voluntariness before rendering a verdict. In states that use this latter procedure, two forms of the approved instruction are available (Mathes & Devitt, 1965). One type simply asks the jurors to determine voluntariness and reject the confession if they conclude it is coerced; the other operationally defines coercion as either a positive or a negative inducement and explains the reasons for the confession's unreliability.

Unfortunately, the assumption that positive and negative inducements are equivalent conflicts with empirical findings that observers attribute more responsibility and freedom to a person who takes actions in order to gain a positive outcome than to a person who takes similar actions in order to avoid punishment (Bramel, 1969; Kelley, 1971). These findings have clear implications for how jurors evaluate different kinds of coerced confessions. We would expect jurors to perceive a confession made to a promise of leniency—that is, a positive inducement—as more voluntary and hence more indicative of guilt than one that followed a threat of punishment, or negative constraint.

In a program of research on jurors' reactions to coerced confessions, Kassin and Wrightsman tested this prediction and clarified some of the ambiguities resulting from court decisions. In the first two of their studies (Kassin & Wrightsman, 1980, 1981), mock jurors read a detailed transcript of a criminal trial in which testimony revealed that the accused had confessed to the arresting officer, either on his own initiative or in response to an offer of leniency or a threat of punishment. (For a fourth group of subjects, no evidence of a confession was included in the transcript.) Subjects' individual verdicts showed that they saw a confession induced by a threat of punishment as essentially involuntary; that is, they treated it as no confession. Confessions induced by threats of punishment also led to low rates of conviction.

When the confession was induced by a promise of leniency or favored treatment, however, subjects responded inconsistently: *they conceded that the defendant had confessed involuntarily, but they judged him to be guilty anyway.* They were unable or unwilling to disregard the confession. Consistent with previous research (Jones & Harris, 1967), then, these subjects accepted the defendant's confession as probative (that is, as useful evidence) despite acknowledging that it had been induced through a promise of leniency.

More subtle forms of obtaining confessions show similar effects. When confessions are "noncoercively" encouraged by interrogators who sympathetically attempt to minimize the severity of the charges or the culpability of suspects while questioning them, subjects show the same strong *positive coercion bias:* they are willing to vote guilty even when they see the confessions as being involuntary (Kassin & McNall, 1991).

Another interpretation for these results is possible: maybe jurors associated the differences between positive and negative *kinds* of constraint with differences in the perceived *degree* of cause. People often assume that punishment is a more powerful form of behavioral inducement than reward (Wells, 1980). For example, threatening a child with a spanking if she doesn't clean her room is usually seen as a stronger motivator than offering her money if she *does* clean her room. In the above studies, subjects may have accepted the leniency-induced confessions not simply because the constraint was positive but because a promise of leniency or suggestion of sympathy seemed like a relatively weak inducement.

Judge's Instructions as an Effort to Rectify Matters

How might the courts deal with this inconsistency between the legal assumptions and the empirical findings? It would seem that the courts should exercise special caution when a confession has apparently resulted from an offer of a lighter sentence or some other form of leniency. One way to try to curb this bias is through the use of a judge's instruction. As indicated earlier, some states provide the opportunity, after the confession has been admitted into evidence, for the judge to instruct the jurors that they, too, should determine the voluntariness issue before rendering a verdict.

Hence a third study in Kassin and Wrightsman's program of research tested the effects of two forms of judicial instruction that have actually been used in different jurisdictions (Kassin & Wrightsman, 1985). The researchers measured whether, in the mock jurors' opinion, threats of punishment and promises of leniency differed in how strongly they induced a suspect to confess. Further, subjects received from the judge either a brief confession-related instruction or a more detailed instruction or no instruction at all. After reading the trial transcript, subjects judged the voluntariness of the confession, rendered their verdicts, and answered other case-related questions.

Subjects' responses verified the findings of earlier studies. When confronted with a defendant who had confessed in response to a threat of harm or punishment, subjects discounted the confession. They viewed *that* confession as involuntary, just as the Supreme Court in *Lego* v. *Twomey* expected them to. They rarely said the defendant was guilty. But, once again, subjects evaluating a leniency-induced confession did not fully discount the confession. They rated it as coerced more often than not, but they still used the confession as evidence and voted guilty more often than did subjects who were told the confession was unsolicited. In short, confessions produced through the promise of lenient treatment constitute an evidentiary problem for the courts.

But the primary question posed by this

third study was whether an instruction by the judge could effectively curb the jurors' use of the positively coerced confession. As it turned out, the manipulation of instructions had two interesting effects. First, compared with the uninstructed subjects, those who had received the elaborate judicial instruction generally conceded that more pressure to confess had been exerted on the suspect. Yet the instruction did not affect a more practically important variable: judgments of voluntariness. Second—and perhaps more disturbing—these instructions also had no influence on verdicts even though subjects *claimed* they had been influenced by the instruction. This pattern thus reveals a fascinating discrepancy between the actual impact of the judge's charge and subjects' self-reported beliefs about that effect.

Overall, these results suggest that a judge's instructions do not dissipate the positive coercion bias. It is premature, however, to dismiss totally the potential utility of instructions, since they did affect certain reactions by the mock jurors. Instead, it would be helpful to speculate about why they failed and to explore how they could be improved.

"Unfairness" and "Untrustworthiness" of Coerced Confessions—Which Is More Influential?

Recall two of the reasons why coerced confessions are deemed inadmissible as evidence: (1) they are unconstitutional and unfair to the accused, and (2) they are unreliable and untrustworthy. A close look at the elaborate, or long-form, judge's instruction shows that it emphasizes the latter and neglects to advance the "fairness" justification. Yet Kalven and Zeisel (1966), citing real-world examples, sug-

gest that "the jury may not so much consider the credibility of the confession as the impropriety of the method by which it was obtained" (p. 320). This observation implies that one promising approach to improving the elaborate instruction is to shift its emphasis. Perhaps an argument that emphasizes what Kalven and Zeisel call the "sympathy hypothesis" rather than the "credibility hypothesis" might prove effective.

Hence Kassin and Wrightsman (1985) conducted a fourth experiment in this series, in order to evaluate and compare a "sympathy instruction"—that is, one that emphasizes the unfairness of the coerced confession. Specifically, mock jurors read the transcript of a hypothetical assault case that included testimony about either an unconstrained confession or a confession induced through the promise of lenient treatment; then the subjects received either the standard credibility instruction about evaluating the truthfulness of the confession, an instruction pointing out the unfairness of a coerced confession (a "sympathy instruction"), or a judge's instruction that encompassed both arguments. The remaining fourth of the subjects received no judge's instructions.

For the fourth time in a row, there emerged the conflicting influence of a confession induced through a promise of leniency; that is, even though subjects acknowledged that the leniency-induced confession was relatively involuntary, they did not disregard that evidence when rendering their verdicts. The sympathy appeal, presented either alone or combined with other instructions, significantly increased the mock jurors' perceptions that the defendant had been unfairly treated. But it failed to lower the conviction rate. Here again, mock jurors are unduly influenced by the "what" of behavior rather than the "why."

Jurors' Inability to Fulfill the Court's Expectations

Throughout the last four centuries, the legal definition of coercion has progressed through a series of stages: (1) negative/physical pressure, (2) negative/physical or psychological pressure, (3) positive or negative/physical or psychological pressure. But Kassin and Wrightsman's program of research suggests that the layperson, the potential juror, is stuck at the second stage. Subjects readily acknowledge that a mere threat, even without signs of physical brutality, is coercive enough to elicit an untruthful confession. Yet they seem unable or unwilling to excuse defendants whose confessions are propelled by a promise or hint of a lighter sentence—this despite the recognition that accused persons might plausibly have "confessed" to acts they had not committed.

Clearly, up to this point, efforts to use judicial instructions to reduce the positive coercion bias have not been totally successful. Subjects' responses to some questions are affected by which instructions they are given, but not on the most important variable—verdicts.

An alternative strategy for improving the instruction might be to bolster the credibility argument. Since positive forms of coercion appear to be problematic partly because people underestimate their power to induce compliance in general and confessions in particular, judges might address this misconception. Wells (1980) found, for example, that this bias can be eliminated by providing subjects with information about the actual base rates for compliance. An instruction that is designed to convey to jurors the fact that many people confess in response to a reward might conceivably decrease the credibility and hence the persuasiveness of a confession so

elicited. But this specific prediction remains to be tested.

ENTRAPMENT

In their zeal to catch criminals, do the police go overboard and sometimes encourage criminal activity in order to then stifle it? Does the use of police officers disguised as "prostitutes" or "drug dealers" tempt otherwise law-abiding persons to commit criminal acts? More basically, we might ask, as Katz does: "When a sting operation is used to bring to the surface a personal weakness that might never have surfaced otherwise, are we really punishing the criminal act or the criminal disposition?" (1987, p. 4).

Twice in recent years, highly publicized cases have caused critics to examine the activities of the police and the FBI in order to determine whether entrapment occurred. In this section we examine these cases, the legal definitions of entrapment, and the psychological interpretation of the phenomenon. In doing so, we note similarities between coerced confessions and entrapment.

The Supreme Court (in *Sherman* v. *United States*, 1958) has equated entrapment and positive coercion of confessions in that they both coax individuals into self-incriminating behaviors. But the courts have differed on how to define entrapment. When is it acceptable for a defendant to claim entrapment as a defense? That is, when should a judge or jury rule that the defendant is not guilty because he or she was lured into committing a crime? There are two positions.

The minority view uses the "objective test" to define entrapment. It focuses entirely on the propriety of investigative methods, maintaining that entrapment occurs when the conduct of law enforcement officials is compelling enough to *instigate* a criminal act, even by an individual who is not otherwise ready and willing to commit it.

In contrast, the "subjective test" is considered the majority view, because it is the law in most states and the federal government. Here the emphasis is on the defendant's state of mind. If the defendant was behaviorally predisposed, then the police are said merely to have afforded the opportunity to commit the offense. What procedure the authorities used is irrelevant. Within this framework the jury is responsible for evaluating the credibility of entrapment as a defense. If the defendant was not predisposed, the fact finders should conclude that entrapment was present, and the defendant should be found not guilty. In fact, in the federal courts, once the defense has raised the claim of entrapment, the government must disprove entrapment beyond a reasonable doubt (Kassin & Wrightsman, 1985).

How do average citizens react to the defense of entrapment? First, they have difficulty understanding the judge's instructions about the definition of entrapment, especially when the "objective" definition is used (Borgida & Park, 1988). Second, if the subjective definition is used, and the defendant has a prior conviction, this admission heightens the likelihood of guilty verdicts (Borgida & Park, 1988). In general, laypersons react harshly to an entrapment claim. They respond as jurors do to a confession elicited by positive coercion. They say "He got caught, so he must be guilty." Moreover, use of entrapment as a defense usually doesn't work. Jurors have a hard time believing that otherwise honest people could be so easily induced into criminal behavior.

The Abscam Trials

In the early 1980s, the FBI, in an operation designed "to test the faith of those in high echelons of government," contrived opportunities to tempt U.S. senators, members of the U.S. Congress, and local officials to commit acts of corruption. The FBI claimed that it chose only elected officials for whom there was already some indication of previous receptivity to bribes. FBI agents and Melvin Weinberg (who had been convicted of mail fraud) posed as representatives of two wealthy Arab sheiks (see Box 8-5). In this so-called Abscam operation, every public official who succumbed to the temptation was found guilty and sentenced to prison. Whenever a defendant tried to use entrapment as a defense, the jury rejected it.

All the government officials filed posttrial motions requesting that the judge set aside their convictions. Different judges ruled in inconsistent ways on these claims, an outcome resulting partly from the different definitions of entrapment. This inconsistency also reflects the discretion granted to judges by the legal system, reflecting one of the overriding dilemmas in the legal system.

Several congressmen/defendants urged the presiding judge, George Pratt, to use an objective standard of entrapment to evaluate the government's conduct. The judge declined; the defendants, he said, "could simply have said 'no' to the offer" (quoted in Gershman, 1982, p. 1575) and avoided criminal liability. In particular, he rejected the contention that the inducements offered by the government were overwhelming, since "no matter how much money is offered to a government official as a bribe or gratuity, he should be punished if he accepts" (quoted in Gershman, 1982, p. 1576). The judge also noted that one representative, Edward Patton of New Jersey, and one senator, Larry Pressler of South Dakota, had declined all bribe offers.

At his trial, Senator Harrison Williams used the subjective defense of entrapment, arguing that he was not predisposed to accept the government agents' bribes. The jury rejected his claim. Judge Pratt also sustained this verdict and noted that although there was no clear-cut evidence showing that Williams had engaged in prior corrupt activity, there was proof that Williams "had earlier sought to use his influence to obtain a permit for casinos, that Williams was willing to receive cash as 'expense money' as long as it did not pass to him directly, and that Williams sought to conceal his involvement in the titanium mine by use of a blind trust" (quoted in Gershman, 1982, p. 1577, footnote 56).

With a different judge, Congressman Richard Kelly fared better. Judge William Bryant of the District of Columbia set aside his conviction. Although recognizing the need for covert investigations to discover crimes, this judge was unwilling to allow the government to pursue that goal without restraints. He believed that the federal government had unleashed Abscam on Kelly without "the remotest suspicion" of prior, ongoing, or imminent criminal activity on his part. In fact, Judge Bryant labeled Abscam "governmental manufacture of crime" and said its testing should have ended after Kelly rejected the first bribe offer. He noted that, in a return visit to Kelly, the "sheiks" had spread $25,000 in $100 bills on the desk in front of him. They told him that, if he didn't help them, they would make their investments in another congressional district (Katz, 1987).

Compared with these judicial reactions, the treatment of the two Philadelphia officials, Harry Jannotti and George Schwartz, was equally inconsistent but in a different way. After a jury had found them guilty, Judge John Fullam set aside their convictions, expressing concerns like those of Judge Bryant. In this particular scam, the government agents had insisted to the Philadelphia officials that a hotel

---

Box 8-5 | The "Sting" in the Abscam Operation

Both national and local officials were approached by FBI agents supposedly representing Arab sheiks. They were told that the sheiks wanted to emigrate to the United States and invest in real estate. Two congressmen from Pennsylvania accepted $50,000 for assistance in these efforts; one used the entrapment defense and one didn't, but they were both found guilty. Two other congressmen, one from New York and one from New Jersey, were tried jointly. They had both eventually taken payments of $50,000, although one of them had refused the money at the initial meeting with the supposed representatives of the Arabs. Neither of these raised entrapment as a defense. A Florida congressman also refused—several times—before accepting a $25,000 bribe.

Senator Harrison Williams of New Jersey met with the "sheiks" at least seven times over a year. They offered financial assistance for a business venture of his in exchange for his promise to obtain government contracts for them. Williams used the entrapment defense, but the jury found him guilty of bribery, conspiracy, receiving a criminal gratuity, and interstate travel for unlawful activity. They concluded that he had either received or agreed to receive stock in a titanium-mining venture and financing from the sheik in return for his commitment to help obtain government contracts for the titanium mine. Two Philadelphia city officials apparently were told that the Arab way of doing business was to establish friendships first and that the sheiks' concept of making friends meant paying them money. These officials were found guilty also.

project would be dropped unless Jannotti and Schwartz accepted the sheik's gesture. The judge ruled that no factual evidence had been presented that showed the defendants were predisposed.

But the Court of Appeals for the Third Circuit reversed Judge Fullam's ruling and reinstated the jury verdicts. This court ruled that the jury properly could have found that acceptance of the money by the defendants, even if they did not originate the scheme, showed predisposition. Two of the circuit court judges strongly disagreed with the majority opinion and called the prosecutions "classic models of the type of entrapment that our society emphatically condemns." They even compared the government to the Gestapo of Nazi Germany.

The John DeLorean Trial

In his cocaine-trafficking trial, John DeLorean used the defense of entrapment. In contrast to the Abscam defendants, DeLorean was found not guilty by the jury. In his instructions to the jury, the judge included the subjective definition of entrapment. Jurors, questioned after their decision was announced, gave several reasons for acquitting DeLorean (Brill, 1984). Some said the government had not proved its case or met, in the words of one juror, its "hellacious burden of proof"; others said that the undercover investigation had sometimes slipped over the line into entrapment. "Without the entrapment," said one man on the jury, "there would have been a hung jury."

It does seem true that the government presented a weak case. As one example, a government agent who had impersonated a dishonest banker admitted to rewriting some of his investigative notes. Another government agent, posing as a drug dealer, had backdated some forms. More important, the government's key witness, James Timothy Hoffman, was quoted in court testimony as promising government officials: "I am going to get John DeLorean for you guys."

DeLorean's guilt or innocence became largely irrelevant for the jurors, and several legal experts have observed that the jury decided the case using an *objective* definition of entrapment, even though the judge instructed them to use the subjective standard. The jury's focus was on the morality of the government's actions—that is, the objective standard. Alan Dershowitz, the Harvard law professor we encountered in Chapter 3 and a self-proclaimed defender of unpopular defendants, was quoted as saying "There's not a court or judge in the country that would have acquitted DeLorean on the basis of the evidence. DeLorean's guilt or innocence played no role in this. All the attention was focused on the government, and he was presented as the victim" (quoted in Margolick, 1984).

Limitations of the Entrapment Doctrine

There is a fundamental incoherence in the entrapment doctrine, which arises at the core of the defense. "Predisposition" is very difficult for jurors to assess, and "inducement" is never defined with respect to its limits. As Katz (1987) observes, the law punishes us for criminal acts, not for criminal dispositions. Entrapment loads the dice too heavily in the direction of punishing some of us for dispositions that may reside in most of us.

In regard to "predisposition," the prosecution often tries to demonstrate a prior criminal inclination on the defendant's part. This could include the defendant's bad reputation, past criminal conduct, or even rumored bad activities. In cases involving drug trafficking or prostitution, these procedures are often applicable, because such defendants often have past criminal records. But politicians like Marion Barry usually do not. Barry, the former mayor of Washington, DC, was videotaped by the FBI using cocaine in a Washington, DC, hotel room, after being lured there by a female acquaintance.

But even when this procedure is applicable, it still is inconsistent with criminal law generally. Nowhere else does criminal law entitle a prosecutor to prove culpability (that is, show blame) for an act simply on the basis of the defendant's previous criminal acts. Even worse, in the case of several of the congressmen, the fact that they readily accepted cash payments was found to constitute sufficient evidence that they had a preexisting intention to take a bribe. This is circular reasoning; there is no independent test of their predisposition, and that creates a major problem.

In addition, Abscam probably stretched the concept of "inducement" to its psychological limits (Gershman, 1982). Huge amounts were offered. Senator Williams was promised $170 million to finance his mining venture. Of this, $10 million was his anticipated profit. A total of $150 million was offered to the Philadelphia city officials to finance the hotel project. Ordinarily, one would expect that the inducements tendered by the government should match, in amounts or value, those that the target person has been exposed to in his or her previous criminal acts. When offers are so incredibly large, they prevent a fair assessment of the presence of predisposition. Similarly, in the case of *Jacobson* v. *United States* (1992), the Supreme Court ruled that inducements offered by postal authorities to a Nebraska farmer to order child pornography were too persistent; therefore the Court reversed the man's conviction.

In summary, entrapment is a doctrine riddled with ambiguity and inconsistency. Psychologically it is very difficult for jurors to operationalize. Lawyers, judges, and social scientists need to work together to clarify it. Box 8-6

presents several recent proposals. So far, none of them has been adopted.

SUMMARY

The police use a variety of devices to increase the likelihood that suspects will be prosecuted and convicted. Among these are criminal profiling, the so-called lie detector (technically, the polygraph technique), and procedures to induce confessions. Police may even create crime situations to tempt suspects to commit new crimes. When the latter is done, the accused may claim entrapment as a defense against the charge.

Criminal profiling is an attempt to use what is known about how a crime was committed in order to infer what type of person might have committed it. Preliminary evidence about profiling suggests that it may have some validity as a means of narrowing police investigations to the most likely suspects.

Lie detection has a long history but a short career as a standardized technique. Early attempts to be rigorous still confused "lying" with the display of any emotion. No measure of physiological reactions can precisely distinguish between guilt and other negative emotions, such as fear, anger, or embarrassment. Nevertheless, examiners using the Keeler polygraph (which measures pulse rate, breathing rate, and electrical resistance of the skin) claim high rates of accuracy (96–99%) in distinguishing between subjects who are lying and those who are not. There are several problems in accepting such claims, including the lack of real followups, the question of adequate criteria, and the misleading nature of "accuracy rates." There is also the problem of lack of consistency in the conclusions of different examiners. Critics of the procedure acknowledge, however, that the polygraph has accuracy rates of 65% or higher.

The best use of the polygraph appears to be during the investigatory stages of a criminal prosecution. Its results may excuse some suspects; however, polygraph examiners often use

---

Box **8-6** | *Trying to Define Entrapment*

A U.S. Senate committee has proposed a limited objective entrapment defense that reads as follows: "The defendant would be acquitted if he could prove by a preponderance of the evidence that he was induced by government agents to commit an offense and that the government used methods that more likely than not would have caused a normally law-abiding citizen to commit a similar offense."

This guideline contains two matters of note. First, "a preponderance of the evidence" standard probably benefits defendants. Second, jurors are given as a comparison the question "Would a normal law-abiding citizen have 'bitten,' given the same inducement?" This creates a problem of its own, for jurors do not agree on what "normal" citizens will and will not do. Some people are cynical about human nature; others are more trusting and optimistic.

A second proposal has been advanced by Bennett L. Gershman (1982), a law professor. He defines unlawful entrapment as the following:

A law enforcement official or his agent commits unlawful entrapment if for the purpose of obtaining evidence for a criminal prosecution he induces any person to engage in criminal activity by methods that are unreasonable or undertaken in bad faith, or that cause or threaten substantial harm to individuals or society, or that [induce] a non-disposed person to engage in criminal activity [1982, p. 1587].

A third proposal, suggested by a psychology professor and a law professor, includes the following in its instruction to the jury:

When you decide whether the method used here was unfair, do not base your decision on whether the method would persuade you to commit the crime, or whether it would persuade an average, ordinary person to commit the crime. Decide whether it would be likely to persuade someone who had a weakness for the crime but who would not normally commit the crime.

The question here is whether the agent used unfair methods, not whether the defendant was ready and willing to commit the crime. Sometimes it may be necessary to take into account what the defendant said and did in deciding whether the agent used unfair methods. However,

remember that the final issue is whether the agent used unfair methods, not whether this defendant already was willing to commit the crime before the agent made contact with him. For example, suppose that in a narcotics case an agent threatened the defendant by telling him that his wife would be arrested unless the defendant sold him drugs. That would be an unfair method, and it would not matter whether the defendant was already ready and willing to sell drugs to the agent before the threat was made.

It is not unfair for an agent merely to give a suspect an opportunity to commit a crime. For example, in a narcotics case, it is not unfair for an agent merely to ask for drugs as a part of his undercover work. However, if an agent goes beyond merely asking, then the jury must decide whether the agent has used unfair methods. If you find that the agent used unfair methods, then you should return a verdict of not guilty [Borgida & Park, 1988, pp. 38–39].

This last proposal is based on an objective definition of entrapment.

the technique to intimidate their subjects and trick them into confessing. In some states, polygraph examiners are allowed to testify about the results of their examinations. This appears to be a dangerous procedure if jurors are convinced of a defendant's guilt on the basis of this testimony alone.

Recently the use of polygraph examinations as part of screening for employment in private businesses has been outlawed.

The police encourage suspects to confess. Sometimes after a suspect "confesses" to the police, he or she will later deny this; recanted confessions occur in about 20% of all criminal cases. Therefore, it is important to assess the voluntariness of a confession, because the Supreme Court has ruled that the prosecution can introduce a confession into trial evidence only if it was truly voluntary (that is, not coerced).

But jurors have difficulty evaluating confessions that were elicited by a promise of lenient treatment. Many jurors still judge the defendant guilty in these circumstances.

Entrapment, as a defense to charges of lawbreaking, rests on two different legal standards. The objective test of entrapment focuses entirely on the propriety of investigative methods. It asks whether the actions of the authorities were so compelling that they elicited a criminal act in a person not otherwise ready and willing to commit it. In contrast, the subjective standard (used in most states and by the federal government) emphasizes the defendant's state of mind—whether he or she was predisposed to commit an offense. Jurors have not generally been sympathetic to a defendant's claim of entrapment; they react much like jurors who are evaluating a coerced confession.

CHAPTER 9

The Rights of Victims and the Rights of the Accused

A fundamental task of our society, extending from the dilemmas of Chapter 1, is to balance the claims of individuals to just treatment and presumed innocence against organized society's expectation that public order will be maintained. During the last 30 years, the U.S. Supreme Court has been the battleground for continuing efforts to achieve both goals. The Supreme Court in the 1960s, led by Chief Justice Earl Warren, believed that a number of earlier Court decisions had abused the rights of accused persons. So the Warren Court tried to redress the balance by making a number of influential decisions affecting suspects and defendants. The first section of this chapter reviews some of these decisions. With the shift in the membership of the Supreme Court in the early 1970s and again in the late 1980s and early 1990s, more recent decisions have shifted toward the crime-control model described in Chapter 1.

A psychological analysis of these Court decisions is appropriate because these judgments, either directly or indirectly, reflect current values in American society. As we will see later in this chapter, in some recent cases the Supreme Court has recognized the difficulty in achieving a balance between the competing goals identified at the beginning of this book.

DECISIONS THAT PROVIDED MORE RIGHTS TO THE ACCUSED

The decade of the 1960s unleashed permissive and democratic forces that influenced the Supreme Court in its decision making. The following six examples of decisions that changed the treatment of suspects by law enforcement authorities have been selected as the most in-fluential and reflective of the spirit of those times.

Mapp v. *Ohio* (1961): The Exclusionary Rule

Although the *Mapp* case began as a bombing investigation, it led to the conviction of Dolree Mapp on a charge of possession of obscene materials. The case is now known because of its effect on the methods police may use for obtaining evidence. On May 23, 1957, seven Cleveland, Ohio, police officers forcibly opened a door to Ms. Mapp's house after she refused to admit them because they had no search warrant. A paper, purported to be a warrant, was held up by one of the officers. Ms. Mapp grabbed it and placed it "in her bosom" (to use the phrasing of the Supreme Court). A struggle ensued, the police retrieved the paper, and they handcuffed Ms. Mapp because she was being "belligerent." They then searched the entire house, including her child's bedroom, and eventually found the obscene materials leading to her conviction. (There was no indication that she knew anything about the bombing.) At her trial, no search warrant was produced by the prosecution; nor was the failure to produce one explained. Still, she was found guilty.

What if the police exceed the limits of the law in their law enforcement activities and yet, in doing so, discover evidence of criminal behavior? Should evidence, such as a murder weapon or stolen property, obtained during an illegal search and seizure be admitted in court? In its decision in *Mapp* v. *Ohio* (1961), the Warren Court said no, that it was inadmissible in both state and federal courts. Until this decision, about half the states had admitted illegal evidence into testimony.

The *Mapp* case deals with the *exclusionary rule*—that is, what must be excluded from the evidence admitted in court. As we will see later

in this chapter, the broadening of the exclusionary rule is one of the decisions by the Warren Court under greatest attack by the Supreme
Court in the last decade.

The exclusionary rule was first adopted by
the Supreme Court in 1914, as a countermea-
sure against police officers who violated constitutional protections against invasions of privacy, who coerced confessions from suspects, and
who ignored the right of the accused to an attorney. It reflects the language of the Fourth
Amendment of the U.S. Constitution, which
guarantees to citizens the right "to be secure in
their persons, houses, papers, and effects,
against unreasonable searches and seizures."

Mapp v. *Ohio* is considered a landmark case
because the Supreme Court ruled that the exclusionary rule is part and parcel of the Fourth
Amendment and also because it stated that the
Fourteenth Amendment to the Constitution
"incorporated" the provisions of the Fourth
Amendment and thus made binding on the
states all the provisions of the Fourth Amendment (Kerper, 1972). This aspect of the *Mapp*
decision is reflected in subsequent cases discussed in this section.

Gideon v. Wainwright (1963): The Right to Counsel during a Trial

Clarence Earl Gideon, a 51-year-old white man,
was tried for breaking and entering the Bay Harbor Pool Room in Panama City, Florida, and
stealing money from a cigarette machine and a
jukebox. He was convicted and was serving a
five-year term in a Florida prison in 1963, when
the Supreme Court ruled on his appeal. It was
not his first offense; Gideon had served time on
four previous occasions, mostly for burglary. He
was a small-town thief who lived on the fringes of
society; yet Gideon's case made legal history.

At his trial, several years before, Gideon had
asked the judge to appoint an attorney to defend him, because he had no money to pay for
one. The judge, in accordance with the laws in
Florida, had refused. Free attorneys were provided only if there were special circumstances in
the case—if, for instance, the offense was a very
serious one or if the defendant's mental abilities were limited.

So Gideon did not have a lawyer during his
trial. He lost, as we have seen, and eventually—
from his prison cell—he filed a pauper's appeal
to the U.S. Supreme Court. His contention,
laboriously printed in pencil, was that the U.S.
Constitution guaranteed the right of every defendant in a criminal trial to have the services
of a lawyer. Gideon's effort was a long shot; well
over 1500 paupers' appeals are filed each term,
and the Supreme Court agrees to consider only
about 3% of them.

Furthermore, 20 years earlier, in the case of
Betts v. *Brady* (1942), the Supreme Court had
rejected the very proposition that Gideon was
making by holding that the right of poor defendants to free counsel existed only under "special circumstances"—if, for example, the defendant was very young or illiterate or mentally
ill. (Thus the *Brady* decision was similar to the
Florida position.) Although the Sixth Amendment to the U.S. Constitution guarantees that
all defendants in criminal trials should have
"assistance of counsel," the courts had interpreted that provision to apply only in federal
trials, not in state-court cases like Gideon's.

Yet, over the two decades since its adoption,
the doctrine of *Betts* v. *Brady* had come under
increasing criticism from legal authorities as inconsistent and unjust. When the Supreme
Court agreed to hear Gideon's appeal, four of
the justices had already declared, in commenting on recent cases, their belief that *Betts* v.
Brady should be overturned.

When Gideon's case was argued before the
Supreme Court in January 1963, he was represented by Abe Fortas, a Washington attorney lat-

er named a Supreme Court justice. Fortas argued that it was impossible for defendants to have a fair trial unless they were represented by a lawyer. He also observed that the "special circumstances" rule was very hard to apply fairly.

On March 18, 1963, the Supreme Court ruled unanimously that Gideon had the right to be represented by an attorney, even if he could not afford one. Justice Hugo Black's opinion stated: "That the government hires lawyers to prosecute and defendants who have the money hire lawyers to defend are the strongest indications of the widespread belief that lawyers in criminal cases are necessities, not luxuries" (*Gideon v. Wainwright*, 1963, p. 344). Although *Gideon* applied only to defendants accused of felonies, nine years later the Supreme Court extended the right to counsel to persons accused of misdemeanors (*Argersinger v. Hamlin*, 1972).

Once more, as in *Mapp v. Ohio*, the Supreme Court applied the Fourteenth Amendment guarantee of due process of law to state cases. But it stopped short of advocating Justice Black's long-standing belief that all the Bill of Rights provisions are binding on the states.

Nearly two years after he was sentenced, Clarence Gideon was given a new trial. With the help of a free, court-appointed attorney, he was found not guilty. The simple handwritten petition of a modest man had changed the procedures of criminal trials, perhaps forever. Gideon lived the rest of his life almost free of legal tangles; his only subsequent difficulty came two years later, when he pled guilty to a charge of vagrancy in Kentucky. He died in 1972.

Escobedo v. Illinois (1964): The Right to Consult a Lawyer during Questioning by the Police

After the *Gideon* decision, on virtually an annual basis over the next few years, the Warren Court expanded the rights of suspects. The

next petitioner to become a test case was Danny Escobedo, a 22-year-old Mexican-American laborer living in Chicago, who was accused of murdering his sister's husband. A few hours after the killing, he was arrested without a warrant and interrogated. While being questioned by the police, he asked repeatedly to see his lawyer but was refused. The police told him his lawyer "didn't want to see him." Meanwhile, his lawyer was trying to contact him during the interrogation, which lasted almost 20 hours.

Escobedo was tricked into admitting his guilt (or at least he so claimed) during this long period of intensive questioning, and his confession was used against him at his trial. (This case, in the early 1960s, antedated some of the court decisions on voluntariness described in Chapter 8.) The jury found Escobedo guilty; he was sentenced to prison for 20 years to life.

Were his rights violated when the police denied his request for a lawyer who could have advised him during his interrogation? The Supreme Court, in June 1964, said yes: because the police did not warn Escobedo of his right to remain silent as guaranteed under the Fifth Amendment and denied him the aid of a lawyer in violation of the Sixth Amendment, statements of his that the police elicited during the questioning should not have been introduced into evidence against him at his trial. Accordingly, now in the absence of a confession that was admissible in court, Escobedo's conviction was overturned and he was released. The prosecutors concluded that they did not have a strong enough case against him without the confession.

In the *Escobedo* decision, the Supreme Court broadened the application of the Fifth and Sixth Amendments, thus giving suspects greater legal protections at earlier stages in a criminal investigation. This ground-breaking decision passed by the narrowest of margins, 5 to 4.

Danny Escobedo's life did not proceed

swimmingly from that point on, even though he was set free. He later claimed that he was constantly harassed by the Chicago police. He was arrested 16 more times, most of the charges eventually being dropped. Then he was convicted of conspiracy to sell amphetamines and spent five years in prison. And two days before Christmas in 1983, he was charged with sexually abusing a 13-year-old child while living with her and her mother; he was convicted and sentenced to 12 years. Two years later, in 1985, having been freed on bond while appealing the indecent-liberties conviction, he was charged with two counts of attempted murder during a shooting in a Southside Chicago tavern.

Miranda v. Arizona (1966): The Right to Remain Silent

At the time of this decision, many people thought *Escobedo* would require lawyers to be in police cars or at the police station because language in the decision implied that the Sixth Amendment right to counsel began at the moment of arrest. In the famous case of *Miranda v. Arizona* (1966), however, the Court made it clear that the Sixth Amendment right to counsel begins with the commencement of formal proceedings—usually with the filing of a complaint or an indictment (*Brewer* v. *Williams*, 1977).

To deal with the general problem of coerced confessions, the Supreme Court agreed to hear four cases that were similar in content. The test case, *Miranda v. Arizona*, is the most famous of all the cases considered during the 1960s because it generated the "*Miranda* warning."

The "*Miranda* case" started in an all-too-typical fashion with an all-too-disturbing outcome. Late on a Saturday night, May 2, 1963, an 18-year-old woman finished her job at the refreshment stand at the Paramount Theater in downtown Phoenix, Arizona. After taking the

bus to near her home, she started walking the remaining distance. But a man grabbed her, dragged her to a parked car, tied her hands behind her, laid her down in the back seat, and tied her ankles together. He told her to lie still. She felt a cold, sharp object—she was never sure what it was—at her neck. Her abductor drove her to the desert, where he raped her. Then, as he waited for her to get dressed, he demanded whatever money she had. She gave him the four $1 bills from her purse.

The young woman was one of 152 reported rape victims in Phoenix in 1963. There had been only 123 the previous year and even fewer, 109, in 1958. By 1970 more than 300 were being reported every year. These figures are a microcosm of those, countrywide, that eventually contributed to reversing the direction charted by the Warren Court decisions.

But national implications of a court decision were far from the minds of the Phoenix police when they had the victim look at a lineup on Sunday morning. She had described her attacker as a Mexican-American male, 27 or 28, 5'11", and weighing 175 pounds. He was slender, she said, and had a medium complexion, with black, short hair. She remembered him as having a tattoo and wearing Levis, a white T-shirt, and dark-rimmed glasses. The police composed a lineup of likely looking choices, but the victim failed to identify anyone. She was very shy; apparently of limited intelligence, she had dropped out of school after failing for several years.

But the victim's brother-in-law, a week after the rape, spotted a car like the one she had described. He pointed it out to her and she said yes, it did look like it. As the car sped away, they were able to remember enough of the license plate for the police to trace it. The car was registered to a young woman who had a friend named Ernest Miranda. He fit the description; he was a Mexican American in his early twenties.

When the police located the car, they saw a rope strung along the back of the front seat, just as the young woman had described it. Police records also confirmed that Miranda had several previous criminal convictions, including one for assault with intent to commit rape. A man with a long criminal history, back to age 14, he had been charged with attempted rape at the age of 15.

So the police put together a new lineup. They chose three Mexican Americans, all about the same height and build, to stand with Miranda. But he was the only person wearing a short-sleeved T-shirt; he was the only one with eyeglasses; and he was the only tattooed man in the lineup. Still, the young woman couldn't identify her assailant, although she felt that number 1—Miranda—had a similar build and features.

Frustrated, the police then took Miranda to an interrogation room. "How did I do?" Miranda asked. "You flunked," a police officer replied and then he began to question Miranda about the rape of the young woman. No attorneys were present, or witnesses, or tape recorders. The police later reported that Miranda voluntarily confessed, that he "admitted not only 'that he was the person who had raped this girl' but that he had attempted to rape another woman and to rob still another" (Baker, 1983, p. 13).

But Miranda described the interrogation differently:

> Once they get you in a little room and they start badgering you one way or the other, "You better tell us . . . or we're going to throw the book at you;" . . . that is what was told to me. They would throw the book at me. They would try to give me all the time they could. They thought there was even a possibility that there was something wrong with me. They would try to help me, get me medical care if I needed it. . . . And I haven't had any sleep since the day before. I'm tired. I just got off my work, and they have me and they are interrogating me. They mention first one crime, then another one, they are certain I am the person. . . . Knowing what a penitentiary is like, a person has to be frightened, scared. And not knowing if he'll be able to get back up and go home [quoted in Baker, 1983, p. 13].

Whichever story one believes, Ernest Miranda emerged from the questioning a confessed rapist. Since the young woman had been unsure of her identification, the police summoned her to the interrogation room to hear Miranda's voice. As she entered, one of the officers asked Miranda "Is that the girl?" "That's the girl," he replied, believing that she had already identified him in the lineup.

Miranda was brought to trial in June 1963. The jury of nine men and three women convicted him of rape and kidnapping, and he was sentenced to 20 to 30 years for each charge. But after Miranda appealed his conviction all the way to the U.S. Supreme Court, the Court—again by a 5-to-4 vote—concluded that his right against self-incrimination had been violated. Henceforth, they stated, the police must warn suspects of certain rights before starting a custodial interrogation. If these procedures are not followed, any damaging admissions made by suspects cannot be used by the prosecution in a trial. These "*Miranda* rights" are the following:

1. Suspects must be warned that they may remain silent, that anything they say may be used against them, that they have the right to have a lawyer present during questioning, and that a lawyer will be appointed if they cannot afford one.
2. If suspects waive their right to counsel and later change their minds, all questioning must stop until the lawyer arrives.
3. If suspects waive their right to an attorney and then confess, the prosecution must show that they knew what they were doing when they waived their rights.

By unintentionally giving his name to the warning that police officers must give suspects, Ernest Miranda became a footnote to history. His own history took an ironic twist, as Box 9-1 illustrates.

In re Gault (1967): The Rights of Juvenile Offenders

A 15-year-old boy named Gerald Francis Gault was committed to a state industrial school in Arizona for six years, for making lewd remarks over the phone. (The Court opinion described these as being "of the irritatingly offensive, adolescent sex variety.") If he had been an adult in Arizona and had done the same thing, he could have been jailed for no more than two months and fined from $5 to $50. Should children be punished more than adults for the same violations?

Moreover, the boy had not been advised of his right to a lawyer or his right to remain silent when questioned by police officers. Initially his parents were not informed that he had been detained. When the decision was appealed to the Supreme Court, the attorneys for the state of Arizona explained that juvenile offenders were not given these and other criminal safeguards because they were not formally charged with crimes.

For years the juvenile courts had been given wide freedom to disregard the standard procedures used in trials of adults, supposedly so that these courts could concentrate on rehabilitation rather than punishment of wayward children. (See Chapter 17 for elaboration of this point.) But the Warren Supreme Court acted to stop such practices. In the majority opinion, Abe Fortas declared that juveniles had the rights to a lawyer, to cross-examination of witnesses, and to protection against self-incrimination. The way things were then, wrote Justice Fortas, "the child

---

| Box **9-1** | *What Ever Happened to Ernest Miranda?* |

Ernest Miranda was given a new trial as a result of the Supreme Court's ruling in his appeal. But, even though his confession was excluded, he was convicted again in 1966, because the prosecution had uncovered new evidence against him.

Between that time and 1976, Miranda served some prison time, was released, but had several further run-ins with the law. At the age of 34 he was an ex-con, an appliance-store delivery man, and, probably, a drug dealer. On the night of January 31, 1976, he was playing poker in a flophouse section of Phoenix. A drunken fight broke out, involving two illegal Mexican immigrants. As he tried to take a knife away from one of them, Miranda was stabbed in the stomach and again in the chest. He was dead on arrival at the hospital.

Miranda's killer fled, but his accomplice was caught. Before taking him to police headquarters, two Phoenix police officers read to him—one in English, one in Spanish—from a card:

You have the right to remain silent.

Anything you say can be used against you in a court of law.

You have the right to the presence of an attorney to assist you prior to questioning and to be with you during questioning, if you so desire.

If you cannot afford an attorney, you have the right to have an attorney appointed for you prior to questioning.

Do you understand these rights?

Will you voluntarily answer my questions?

Thus ironically ended the life, but not the legacy, of Ernest Miranda.

receives the worst of both worlds; he gets neither the protections accorded to adults nor the solicitous care and regenerative treatment postulated for children" (*In re Gault*, 1967, p. 1428). The only significant right denied to children after *Gault* is the right to a jury; juveniles are tried by judges. The ability of juveniles to understand and exercise their legal rights is a separate matter that we consider in Chapter 11.

Jackson v. Denno (1964): The Right to Have a Confession Judged Voluntary or Involuntary

As noted in Chapter 8, a defendant often makes and then withdraws an out-of-court confession. The legal admissibility of such a confession into evidence has been controversial. In the sixth major decision of the Warren Court, *Jackson v. Denno* (1964), the Supreme Court held that a criminal defendant is entitled to a pretrial determination that any confession he or she made to officials was given voluntarily and was not the outcome of physical or psychological coercion, which the Constitution forbids. Only if the fact finder (usually the judge) determines at the hearing that a confession was in fact voluntary may it then be introduced at trial to the jury. As noted in Chapter 8, the problems in the jury's psychological interpretations of confessions do not stop there, but *Jackson v. Denno* at least reflected the Warren Court's view of the dangers of confessions.

THE RIGHTS OF VICTIMS AND POTENTIAL VICTIMS

As suspects were being granted more rights, society began to question whether victims were being treated fairly. This concern came partly from greater awareness of crime rates in the United States. On an annual basis approximately one out of every four households in the United States is a target of a violent crime or theft. In a recent year, 37 million Americans were crime victims. Among these, 2 million were victims of violent crime—rape, robbery, assault, attempted murder. Advocates of "law and order" and critics of court rulings in the late 1960s and early 1970s claimed that the government offered innocent victims little or no support, even though ostensibly the criminal justice system was established to serve them (Karmen, 1984).

Increasingly, victims are perceived as forgotten "third parties" at an investigation or a trial. Crimes are often thought of somewhat abstractly as hostile acts against the state, which represents *all* the people, rather than as events that hurt a specific person. As Ellison and Buckhout (1981) note, the victim of a crime is known as the "complaining witness" and sometimes assumes the status of a bit player or even a piece of evidence.

Victims are often dissatisfied with the criminal justice system and have begun to express their frustration. A study released by the National Institute of Justice asked 249 victims of major crimes in six cities how satisfied they were with the handling of their cases (Meddis, 1984a). It discovered that 77% said the courts were "too slow" and wasted time; even more, 86%, felt that offenders weren't punished enough. In contrast, only 30% felt that the courts care about victims' needs. Increasingly, legislators, prosecutors, and court systems are trying to respond to the legitimate concerns of crime victims. Box 9-2 summarizes some recent developments in this area.

Compensating the Victim

Some states provide compensation to victims of crimes. About three-fourths of the states now have such programs, but many are woefully underfunded. New York will pay victims unlimited medical costs (beyond those reimbursed by insurance) and up to $20,000 in lost wages, at a rate of up to $250 weekly. New Jersey limits financial aid to $10,000. Kansas has a small fund administered through a Victims Reparation Board. California now has what is called a "reverse *Miranda* law," in which the police must inform victims that they have the right to apply for state assistance.

The federal government has also provided assistance to victims. President Reagan signed the Victims of Crime Act of 1984, establishing a Crime Victims Fund, which provides federal assistance to the states' crime-victim compensation programs. The fund is financed through fines collected from prisoners convicted of federal offenses.

More recent, and more radical, programs have been developed to respond to the needs of crime victims, including programs that seek a reconciliation between victims and criminals. Some of these are described in Box 9-3.

THE SHIFT IN SUPREME COURT DECISIONS

As the constituency of the Supreme Court shifted in the 1970s to reflect appointees of presidents Nixon and Ford, so did the direction of the Court's decisions. Although the Supreme Court headed by Warren Burger was less

---

Box 9-2 | The Victim as a "Third Party"

In addition to the trauma they suffer from being the targets of crime, victims have historically been neglected by the criminal justice system. Their role as witnesses is time consuming. Their privacy is necessarily invaded by police as they investigate the crime, by prosecutors as they develop a case against the defendant, and by defense attorneys as they cross-examine the victims. Many of these proceedings are public and may be reported in the media. Crime victims have often felt as if they have little voice in the criminal justice system, and they are usually frustrated over the long delays prior to a final verdict being reached in their case.

As a result of these problems, several changes have recently been introduced in the criminal justice system to increase the sense of influence and voice by crime victims. For example, modern statutes typically provide the following:

1. Notice to victims of all judicial proceedings such as bail hearings and preliminary hearings.
2. A say—although rarely a veto—in the plea-bargaining process.
3. The right to make a "victim impact statement" for a judge to consider in sentencing a convicted defendant.
4. The right to testify in the sentencing phase of capital cases (a right recently upheld by the Supreme Court in the case of *Payne* v. *Tennessee*, 1991).

5. An opportunity to be heard when the defendant is considered for parole.
6. A requirement that the defendant make restitution, if possible, in cases in which the victim has suffered monetary losses.

It is safe to say that few prosecutors, particularly elected prosecutors, will take actions in a case that go against the active opposition of the crime victim. Although in theory prosecutors owe their allegiance to the justice of the "system," in practice they increasingly try to represent the victims of crime.

Adapted from Ellison and Buckhout (1981).

ideologically consistent than the Warren Court, one of its primary emphases was to provide victims more safeguards under the law. Chief Justice Burger wrote: "I refuse to join in what I consider an unfortunate trend of judicial decisions in this field which strain and stretch to give the guilty not the same but vastly more protection than the law-abiding citizen." Appointment by President Reagan of three justices (O'Connor, Scalia, and Kennedy) and by President Bush of two (Souter and Thomas) gave second wind to restrictions on the rights provided suspects and defendants by the Warren Court.

Changes in the direction of Court decisions do not happen by chance. A psychological analysis of the causes of this shift in judicial decisions focuses on the values, attitudes, and behavior of individuals. One reason why the Supreme Court has moved toward restricting the rights of the accused over the last 20 years is that its newer members reflect the conservative political values of the presidents who chose them (Nixon, Ford, Reagan, and Bush). But, at another level, those presidents were elected—and hence were able to make the appointments—because of shifts in the concerns of individual voters and society at large. Crime, particularly street crime, became a highly publicized issue in the United States in the late 1960s and early 1970s. "Law and order" was the rallying cry during the presiden-

---

Box 9-3 | Reconciliation between Crime Victims and Criminals

A number of alternatives have recently been tried in efforts to respond to victims' needs and to rehabilitate lawbreakers. Several states have victim/offender reconciliation programs (VORPs), in which volunteer mediators bring together the two parties to try to work out a suitable restitution or some substitute. For example, a Kansas City man got his stolen ten-speed bicycle back and now meets regularly with the youth who stole his bike. The two discuss the young man's progress in school and the reasons for turning to crime. In another case, five teenagers who vandalized a house and stole $9000 worth of valuables did lawn service, landscaping, and other household duties for the victim's

*Pope John Paul II
with Mehmet Ali Agga*

family. The victims have met with the offenders several times. "I wouldn't take a million dollars for those meetings with those boys," the victim said; "they even call from time to time to see how I'm doing and offer to work around our place. I learned a lot, and those boys have made a complete turn-

around" (quoted in Penn, 1985, p. B2).

The most publicized and dramatic illustration of a VORP was the meeting in an Italian prison between Pope John Paul II and the man who had tried to kill him. That meeting reflected two goals and values of such programs. One is the view of crime as an interaction involving conflict between two parties—a position that leads to reliance on conflict resolution rather than on punishment as the preferred way of intervention. The other is the VORP's goal of reconciliation, or an emphasis on mutual understanding and acceptance by the two persons (Green, 1984).

tial campaign of 1968. The election of Richard Nixon as president in that year symbolized a shift in the sympathies of the general population. More than two decades later, crime remains a prime concern of U.S. citizens. In the 1988 presidential campaign, George Bush effectively used the fact that his opponent, Michael Dukakis, when governor of Massachusetts, had furloughed a criminal, Willie Horton, who then raped a woman. Reactions of approval for the "subway vigilante," Bernhard Goetz, reflect the public's fear and condemnation toward criminal behavior (see Box 9-4). The decisions described in this section exemplify how the Court has reflected and reacted to the public outcry over the last two decades.

As early as 1968, the courts began to redress the perceived imbalance between suspects' rights and society's rights. In that year the U.S. Supreme Court upheld the authority of the police to stop and frisk suspicious-looking people; however, the police officer had to have a "reasonable and articulable" suspicion, supported by objective facts, that the suspect was about to commit a crime or had just done so.

Thus the Burger Court replaced adherence to the exclusionary rule with a cost/benefit analysis in which the possibility of freeing a "clearly guilty" offender was balanced against the effect of excluding evidence because of misconduct by police (Schwartz, 1988). This process reflects the crime-control orientation described in Chapter 1 and puts more value on efficient police action than on deterring police from making mistakes. This emphasis fits with the basic cognitive processes of most people; Casper, Benedict, and Kelly (1988) found, as an example, that mock jurors' decisions about whether police acted inappropriately in

---

Box 9-4 | *Reactions to the "Subway Vigilante"*

A few days before Christmas in 1984, newspaper reports began to appear about a New York City subway incident that seemed to resemble the action in a Charles Bronson movie. Eventually, Bernhard Goetz came forward as the white man who had shot and wounded four black youths when they approached him and asked for five dollars. One of the young men was shot in the back. The case became news throughout the country and the world.

Polls taken by the *New York Daily News* two weeks after the confrontation on the subway train

Bernhard Goetz

found that 49% of respondents approved of Goetz's shooting the youths and 31% disapproved (Lichtenstein, 1985). Only 28% felt that he should be charged with attempted murder; 58% disapproved of his being charged. Other polls produced similar results: about twice as many respondents supported his actions as criticized them. Bernhard Goetz became a mythic hero for many Americans, despite the fact that he was to stand trial on four counts of attempted murder and on criminal possession of an unregistered gun. In keeping with this sentiment, Goetz's jury found him guilty only of the gun possession, not of attempted murder. He was sentenced to one year in prison.

search-and-seizure cases depended on whether they actually found anything illegal during their warrantless search, a tendency known as the *hindsight bias*. Courts also appear to be influenced by hindsight bias in that they may be more likely to approve of questionable police procedures when those procedures uncover important evidence of criminal activity (Saks & Kidd, 1986).

Even though the basic principle of the *Gideon* decision remains affirmed 30 years later, the Court recently made it clear that the constitutional right to free counsel does not apply beyond the trial and one appeal (Kamisar, 1988). Many (but not all) states still provide attorneys for what are termed "collateral attacks"—that is, efforts to get appellate courts to reverse convictions that have become final—but they are no longer required to according to the current Supreme Court.

Miranda v. *Arizona* (confessions) and *Mapp* v. *Ohio* (searches) are the most important of the "individual rights" cases of the 1960s. After 30 years of attention by a more conservative Supreme Court, the principles established by those cases reflect a tenuous balance between individual and collective rights. First let's look at the current state of *Miranda*:

1. *Miranda affects only cases in which the prosecution seeks to use the defendant's confession to prove the defendant committed the crime.* Prosecutions not involving confessions are not affected by *Miranda*. In his career as public defender, one of the authors occasionally represented clients laboring under the misimpression that *Miranda* warnings are required in all prosecutions.
2. *Miranda affects only the admissibility of confessions used to prove commission of the crime.* Confessions that violate *Miranda* may be used to *impeach* a defendant. Suppose a person confesses when arrested, and the confes-

sion is taken in violation of the *Miranda* warnings. If the defendant testifies to his innocence at trial, the prosecutor may use the confession to show that the defendant should not be believed (*Harris* v. *New York*, 1971).
3. *Confessions of defendants who don't fully understand the warnings may still be admissible.* *Miranda* holds that the privilege against self-incrimination requires that, before custodial interrogation begins, an accused must be advised:

   a. You have the right to remain silent.
   b. Anything you say may be used against you.
   c. You have the right to speak with an attorney before answering questions and to have an attorney present during questioning.
   d. An attorney will be appointed for you if you cannot afford one.

To validate a subsequent confession, it is enough that the police give the warnings and the defendant responds affirmatively when asked if he or she wishes to make a statement. Although *inability* to understand the warnings, as a result of low IQ or mental illness, is reason to suppress a confession, misimpression or incomplete understanding by a suspect of normal intelligence will not invalidate a confession. Thus the police can take advantage of a suspect who thinks that an oral confession is not admissible (*North Carolina* v. *Butler*, 1979). Similarly, the police need not tell the defendant that they suspect him of additional crimes and plan to question him about those matters if he agrees to be questioned about the crime with which he is charged (*Colorado* v. *Spring*, 1987).

4. *Defendants can change their minds about confessing.* *Miranda* held that, if a defendant changes his or her mind about talking, the interrogation must stop. It also must stop if the suspect asks for a lawyer, and the police

cannot later initiate a conversation to get a confession from someone who has asked for a lawyer (*Edwards* v. *Arizona*, 1981). If the defendant initiates the conversation, however, any resulting confession is admissible (*Oregon* v. *Bradshaw*, 1983).

5. *Miranda does not apply unless the suspect is in the custody of the police.* The Court has treated "custody" as a term of art, with recent decisions emphasizing the evils that *Miranda* was designed to prevent: stationhouse questioning, in which the accused fear they are subject to indeterminate isolation and interrogation. Thus, roadside questioning of a motorist stopped for drunk driving is noncustodial, even though the motorist is not free to go (*Berkemer* v. *McCarty*, 1984). "Stop and frisk" questioning is usually viewed as noncustodial, because such questioning accompanies temporary detentions in public places. Confessions obtained through "jail plants" do not implicate *Miranda* because the defendant, though incarcerated, believes he or she is talking to a fellow inmate (*Illinois* v. *Perkins*, 1990).

6. *Miranda does not apply unless the defendant is being interrogated.* A volunteered confession is always admissible. Suppose the police arrest a robbery suspect and decide, for whatever reason, not to interrogate him. On the way to the station, however, the accused volunteers that he wouldn't have been caught if he'd kept his mask on. This confession is admissible because it was not in response to police questioning.

7. *Miranda warnings are not required in situations in which the safety of the public might be endangered by giving the warnings.* In *New York* v. *Quarles* (1984) a woman told the police that she had been raped by a man with a gun who had just run into a supermarket. Officer Kraft entered the market and spotted Quarles running to the rear of the store. Officer Kraft gave chase and caught him in the storage area. After frisking Quarles and finding no gun, Officer Kraft asked where the gun was. Quarles nodded in the direction of some empty cartons and said "The gun is over there." The police found the gun, and Quarles was prosecuted for criminal possession of the weapon (the rape charge was not pursued). The New York courts suppressed the defendant's statement (and the gun) because Quarles had not been given the *Miranda* warnings. The Supreme Court used the case to create a "public safety" exception to *Miranda*; warnings do not have to be given when police questioning is reasonably motivated by a concern for public safety.

Remember that *Mapp* v. *Ohio* (1961) held that suppression of illegally obtained evidence would deter police from violating the Fourth Amendment. Although controversial, because it may result in reliable evidence not being used, this exclusionary rule has not been overruled by the Burger/Rehnquist Court. It has, however, been modified:

1. *The "good faith" exception.* In *United States* v. *Leon* (1984) the Court held that the interests protected by the Fourth Amendment are not advanced by excluding evidence obtained by officers acting in reasonable reliance on a search warrant issued by a neutral judge, when the warrant is ultimately found not to be supported by probable cause.

2. *The standing requirement.* To object to an illegal search or seizure, the defendant must have "standing"—that is, a "legitimate expectation of privacy" in the place searched (*Rakas* v. *Illinois*, 1978) or a possessory interest in the thing seized (*United States* v. *Payner*, 1980). No matter how outrageous the police conduct, there will be no exclusion if the defendant lacks standing. In

Payner, FBI agents illegally removed private papers from the briefcase of a bank official and used them to prosecute Payner, one of the bank's customers. The Court held that Payner could not object because he owned neither the briefcase nor the papers.

3. *The inevitable discovery exception. Nix* v. *Williams* (1984) holds that illegally seized evidence need not be excluded if it would inevitably have been found by legal means.

Williams, by the way, is an unusual case, one that has become known as the "Christian burial speech" case. On a Christmas Eve in 1968, a former mental patient named Robert Williams abducted a 10-year-old girl in Des Moines, Iowa. Williams's car was found abandoned in Davenport, 160 miles away. The day after Christmas, Williams's lawyer arranged for Williams, then in Davenport, to surrender to local police, who would turn him over to Des Moines detectives for the return trip to Des Moines. The detectives agreed that they would not question Williams during the trip.

Knowing that Williams was deeply religious and a former mental patient, the detectives used the return trip to work on Williams's psyche. One of them began engaging Williams in a wide-ranging conversation. Addressing Williams as "Reverend," the detective said:

> I want to give you something to think about while traveling down the road. . . . Number one, I want you to observe the weather conditions. It's raining; it's sleeting; it's freezing; driving is very treacherous; visibility is poor; it's going to be dark early this evening. They are predicting several inches of snow for tonight, and I feel that you yourself are the only person that knows where this little girl's body is, that you yourself have only been there once, and if you get a snow on top of it you yourself may be unable to find it. And, since we will be going right past the area on the way into Des Moines, I feel that we could stop and locate the body, that the parents of this little girl

should be entitled to a Christian burial for the little girl who was snatched away from them on Christmas Eve and murdered. And I feel we should stop and locate it on the way in rather than waiting until morning and trying to come back out after a snow storm and possibly not being able to find it at all.

He then stated:

> I do not want you to answer me. I don't want to discuss it any further. Just think about it as we're riding down the road.

As the car approached Grinnell, Williams asked whether the girl's shoes had been found. When the detective said he wasn't sure, Williams directed the officers to a service station where he said he had left the shoes; a search for the shoes was unsuccessful. As they continued toward Des Moines, Williams asked whether the police had found the blanket and directed them toward a rest area where he said he had disposed of the blanket. Nothing was found. They continued toward Des Moines, and, as the car approached Mitchellville, Williams said he would show the officers where the body was. He then directed the police to the body of the 10-year-old girl.

Ultimately the Supreme Court held that the "Christian burial speech" violated Williams's right to counsel, since the police had employed trickery to coerce a confession in violation of their agreement with Williams's lawyer (*Brewer* v. *Williams*, 1977). The question then was whether the evidence connected with the body had to be suppressed, since the body was discovered as a result of Williams's illegally obtained statement. At the second trial the prosecutor convinced the judge that the body would have been discovered anyway, in essentially the same condition as it was found, because the search teams were moving toward the area at the time Williams led the police to the body. This holding was upheld by the Supreme Court in *Nix* v. *Williams* (1984) and stands for the "inevitable discovery" exception to the exclusionary rule.

What is an *unreasonable* search or seizure within the meaning of the Fourth Amendment? Although this is an enormously complex subject, the following generalizations may be useful:

1. *The accused must have a legitimate expectation of privacy, which was violated by the search or seizure.* A legitimate expectation of privacy is one that society is willing to protect, but the Supreme Court defines what society is willing to protect. The average person might be surprised to learn that the Court does not believe there is a legitimate expectation of privacy in bank records (*United States* v. *Miller*, 1976), fenced fields (*Oliver* v. *United States*, 1984), or a backyard visible (as all backyards are) to low-flying planes (*California* v. *Ciraola*, 1986). In general, the Court has refused to recognize a legitimate expectation of privacy when the item seized could be seen or handled by strangers. Recently, the Court held that there is no legitimate expectation of privacy in garbage that is bagged and set out at a curb (*California* v. *Greenwood*, 1988).

2. *More protection is afforded in the home than elsewhere.* Except in emergencies, police must have a warrant to enter a home without consent. A warrant is an authorization signed by a judge on the basis of an affidavit that establishes *probable cause* to believe that criminal evidence is in the home. Warrants are generally not needed to stop and search cars, boats, or planes. "Probable cause" is an illusive concept but generally is thought to imply at least a 50% probability.

3. *"Reasonable suspicion" will support a temporary detention or protective search.* In *Terry* v. *Ohio* (1968), the Court upheld a "stop and frisk" of three men apparently preparing to rob a jewelry store, on the basis of the officer's *reasonable suspicion* that criminal activity was afoot. This principle is central to day-to-day law enforcement. The police cannot stop a car or pedestrian based on a mere "hunch," but they *can* stop a car or pedestrian if there are factors, which can later be explained to a skeptical judge, supporting a reasonable suspicion of criminal activity. Once stopped, the officer may frisk the person (or conduct a limited search of the car) if there is reasonable suspicion that the person is armed. There may be a brief period of detention to gather additional information. A DUI ("driving under the influence") stop illustrates these principles. A weaving car gives the officer "reasonable suspicion" that the driver is intoxicated. The officer pulls the car over, thereby "seizing" car and driver. The officer further detains car and driver to perform sobriety tests and check the car's registration. A "frisk" of the driver or a search of the driver's seat would be necessitated if the driver threatened bodily harm to the officer.

4. *The general principles are complicated by special "rules" that affect certain kinds of searches and seizures.* Although they are beyond the scope of this chapter, the reader should be aware that the Court has treated differently searches and seizures incident to arrest (*United States* v. *Robinson*, 1973), pursuant to a legitimate inventory (*Illinois* v. *Lafayette*, 1983), pursuant to a health and safety regulation (*New York* v. *Burger*, 1987), at the border (*United States* v. *Montoya de Hernandez*, 1985), of schoolchildren (*New Jersey* v. *T.L.O.*, 1985), and of parolees (*Griffin* v. *Wisconsin*, 1987).

As the Court moves through the 1990s, with Reagan/Bush appointees giving Chief Justice

Rehnquist a solid law-and-order majority on most issues, the Court's lack of sympathy for the privacy interests protected by the Fourth Amendment is obvious. In *Florida* v. *Bostick* (1991), for example, the Court held that the Fourth Amendment is not violated by a police officer boarding a bus, arbitrarily picking out a passenger, and asking for permission to search the passenger's bag. The Court said the passenger had not been "seized," because he was "free" to leave the bus or otherwise refuse the officer's request. Would the Court have been more sympathetic if the passenger had been a middle-aged businessman and the confrontation had taken place on a plane waiting for takeoff?

In the view of the present Supreme Court, a person loses a substantial amount of personal privacy on stepping into an automobile. Warrants are not required to search a car on probable cause (*United States* v. *Ross*, 1982). In *California* v. *Acevedo* (1991) the Court eliminated the warrant requirement with regard to containers found in a car. Suppose the police have probable cause to believe that an arriving airline passenger's bag contains cocaine. As the passenger walks down the airport corridor, any search of the bag requires a search warrant. As soon as the passenger puts the bag in the trunk of a car, however, the police may swing into action and seize and search the bag without a warrant. Furthermore, the Court has recently said that, when a person consents to the search of a car, it may be assumed that he or she has consented to the search of anything—a briefcase, for example—found in the car (*Florida* v. *Jimeno*, 1991).

The police conduct searches without warrants when, for example, a third party (such as a landlord, a spouse, or a roommate) consents to let them search an area that the third party controls or shares with the suspect. The courts have assumed that people who share space with others yield their expectation of privacy with respect to the shared space. Therefore the third party can consent to a police search of this space even over a suspect's objection.

Is there any validity to these assumptions? Do people commonly believe that they relinquish their rights to privacy when they share space with others? For that matter, do people's expectations of privacy decrease when they sit in their cars, discard objects in their garbage, or place items in their backyards? The courts have not been shy about basing their decisions on their assumption that people have different privacy expectations in different situations. However, judges have seldom considered scientific research on these topics despite the availability of pertinent studies. Psychologists have conducted empirical research on these questions, and their preliminary results challenge many of the courts' assumptions (Kagehiro, Taylor, & Harland, 1991).

For example, Kagehiro, Taylor, Laufer, and Harland (1991) asked college students about whether they believed one coresident in a condominium could consent to the police searching for evidence against a suspect (the other coresident) without a warrant. Depending on the experimental condition, subjects read that (1) the suspect just happened to be absent during the search, (2) the police had waited to search the condo until they knew the suspect had left, or (3) the suspect was present during the search and was protesting it. Half of the subjects read that the search uncovered the incriminating evidence the police were after; the other half read that the police did not find incriminating evidence. Results indicated that people hold more complex expectations about privacy in shared living arrangements than the courts have assumed. When incriminating evidence was discovered, subjects were more likely to believe that the consenter had a right to allow the police search when the suspect was gone just by chance (92%) than when the suspect was present and protested the search (67%). When the police discovered no evidence, subjects were more likely to believe that the consenter could permit a police search when the suspect was present and protesting (83%) than when the suspect happened to be absent by chance (42%). Additional research on how citizens rate the intrusiveness of different types of searches and seizures (Slobogin & Schumacher, in press) suggests that the courts consistently underestimate the intrusiveness of many search-and-seizure methods, at least as they are perceived by the public. (See Box 9-5 for an extension of warrantless searches to the use of drug-runner profiles.)

As noted before, the decisions of the Burger Court did not go as consistently in one direction as the Warren Court's decisions did in the other. For example, the Burger Court not only reaffirmed the *Gideon* decision but extended it by ruling in *Ake* v. *Oklahoma* in February 1985 that poor defendants must be given free psychiatric help in preparing an insanity defense if a serious question about their sanity has arisen (Turkington, 1985). The Burger Court even overturned a death sentence in its ruling. Glen Burton Ake had been convicted of the 1979 murder of an Oklahoma minister and his wife. Although the state had been permitted to introduce testimony by a psychiatrist who had concluded that Ake was sane, defendant Ake

---

Box 9-5 | Drug Couriers' Profiles and the Exclusionary Rule

As the United States tries to deal with its increasing drug problem, some people have begun to advocate drastic measures such as declaring martial law, scrubbing civil liberties, and replacing civilian courts with military tribunals (Beck, 1989). These proposals affect interpretations of the Fourth Amendment protection against unreasonable search and seizure. What is "unreasonable"? University of Chicago law professor Geoffrey Miller (quoted in Beck, 1989, p. 21) says: "An argument could be made that what is unreasonable in ordinary circumstances becomes reasonable when facing a plague of drug violence."

An example comes from the decision in *United States* v. *Sokolow*

(1989). When David Sokolow arrived at Honolulu International Airport after a 48-hour trip to Miami and back, agents from the Drug Enforcement Administration (DEA) were aware that he had paid $2100 for tickets with $20 bills from a roll containing possibly twice that amount; that the name he used for his airline tickets did not match the name under which his telephone number was listed; that Miami, a source city for cocaine, was his earlier destination; that he appeared nervous; and that he did not check his baggage (Cutler, 1989).

So the DEA agents stopped Sokolow, searched him, and arrested him for possession of 1063 grams of cocaine. After he tried

unsuccessfully to have the evidence suppressed, he was tried and convicted.

Was the use of a "drug courier profile" sufficient to stop Sokolow? Or should there be evidence of "ongoing criminal activity" to warrant reasonable suspicion? On review, the U.S. Supreme Court held that the search was justified. Chief Justice Rehnquist in the majority opinion advocated consideration of "the totality of the circumstances—the whole picture" and observed that, just because some of the contributions to a conclusion of "reasonable suspicion" came from a "profile," they shouldn't be denied probative value.

had been denied the opportunity to have other psychiatrists assist in his defense.

Ake's sole defense was insanity. Four months before the trial, a state psychiatrist had found him not competent to stand trial and had recommended that he be committed to a state mental hospital. But he was found competent to stand trial a month later, after sedation with large doses of Thorazine three times a day.

The Supreme Court observed that the testimony of a psychiatrist or a psychologist as an expert witness for the defense was a "virtual necessity" if the plea was to have any chance of success. Thurgood Marshall, writing the majority opinion, stated: "Without the assistance of a psychiatrist to conduct a professional examination on issues relevant to the defense, to help determine whether the insanity defense is viable, to present testimony, and to assist in preparing cross-examination of a state's psychiatric witnesses, the risk of an inaccurate resolution of sanity issues is extremely high" (quoted in Turkington, 1985, p. 2). The sole dissent was offered by Justice William Rehnquist, who observed: "A psychiatrist is not an attorney, whose job it is to advocate."

At Ake's second trial in 1986, a court-appointed psychiatrist testified that he had diagnosed Mr. Ake as a paranoid schizophrenic who had been hearing voices since 1973. He said that Mr. Ake had gone to the victims' home in an attempt to find the source of the voices and make them stop. Despite this testimony, the jury in the second trial also found the defendant guilty, and Mr. Ake was sentenced to life in prison.

Ake is significant because it establishes the principle that an indigent defendant is entitled not only to an attorney at the state's expense but also to the assistance of experts at the state's expense if there are grounds to believe that testimony by experts is necessary for a fair determination of the facts at trial. Unfortunately, it is not clear that the Ake decision is being followed in a conscientious manner in most courts (Perlin, 1992).

ADVANTAGES TO THE PROSECUTION AND TO THE DEFENSE IN A CRIMINAL TRIAL

As society continues to struggle over the appropriate balance between the rights of victims and the rights of the accused, it is meaningful to consider the advantages to each side in a criminal trial. Although full coverage of trials will be deferred until Chapters 12, 13, and 14, a listing of the elements relevant to the balance between the two sides is warranted now because it is part of the continuing tension between the rights of individuals and society's needs for public safety.

Advantages to the Prosecution

The state, in its efforts to convict wrongdoers and bring justice to bear, has several benefits:

1. It has the full resources of the government at its disposal to carry out a prosecution. Detectives can locate witnesses and subpoena them. The state can call on expert testimony from chemists, fingerprint examiners, medical examiners, psychiatrists, photographers, or whoever is an appropriate expert.
2. The prosecution can produce its evidence in a virtually unfettered way if a grand jury system is used to bring down indictments. (Chapter 10 describes the operation of the grand jury.)
3. In the trial itself, the prosecution presents its evidence before the defense does, getting "first crack" at the jury. In presenting open-

ing statements, which are not evidence but do provide a structure for the entire trial, the prosecution always goes first. And at the end of the trial, when both sides are permitted closing arguments (again, not part of the evidence), the prosecution usually gets to go first and then is permitted to offer a last-word rebuttal to the defense attorney's closing argument.

Advantages to the Defense

The courts also provide defendants certain safeguards in addition to those described earlier in this chapter:

1. The defense is entitled to "discovery"; the prosecution must turn over exculpatory evidence, but the defense does not have to turn over incriminating evidence.
2. The defense may waive the right to a jury trial (although the prosecution must approve).
3. If a trial is before a jury, the defense may have more peremptory challenges—that is, opportunities to remove potential jurors without giving a reason (see Chapter 12)—than the prosecution.
4. Defendants do not have to take the stand as witnesses in their own behalf. In fact, they do not have to put on any defense at all; the burden of proof is on the prosecution to prove beyond a reasonable doubt that the defendant is guilty of the crime.
5. If a defendant is found not guilty, he or she can never be tried again for that specific crime. For example, Claus von Bulow was, in his trial, found guilty of the attempted murder of his wife. But the Rhode Island court of appeals ruled that some of the procedures used by the prosecution were inappropriate, and thus the conviction was overruled and

von Bulow was entitled to another trial. In his second trial he was found not guilty, and that decision will stand. No appeal may reverse a not-guilty decision.

THE FUTURE OF THE DILEMMA

Times change. Matters are never settled in a complex society. The constant quest continues for fairness to all parties—to crime victims and to criminal suspects, who are assumed to be innocent until proven guilty. Although it is futile to expect that the issues examined in this chapter will ever be completely resolved, we should be encouraged that the quest continues.

In the mid-1990s, the balance weighs in one direction; Chief Justice Rehnquist wants to overturn *Mapp* v. *Ohio*, describing the decision as a "basic unconstitutional mistake." The public and the courts strongly favor the prosecution and the police. But a decade or two from now, the balance may have shifted again. There is always conflict and reconciliation.

Despite the differences, society benefits ultimately from the continued quest to guarantee the rights of the accused and the rights of victims. We should seek to avoid an extreme "either/or" orientation, in which the rights of one group are pitted against the rights of the other. Civil liberties activists, concerned that suspects receive their due rights, and conservatives, threatened by Warren Court decisions, both are assisted by the scrutiny devoted to this issue. Rights that are won by the "unworthy" are won for all of us (Lewis, 1984). As Karmen notes, "What the critics of the civil liberties movement fail to appreciate is the contribution these reforms have made toward easing the plight of crime victims" (1984, p. 21). Likewise, by increasing the professionalism and the responsibility of the police, we are all better off; the Warren Court decisions led to better training, closer supervision, and higher qualifications for police officers. As a result, all of us—suspects or victims—are more likely to receive nonsexist, nonracist treatment and effective responses from the police. In addition, we are all better off because these court decisions have extended guarantees of equal protection of the law to types of victims who were formerly neglected (Walker, 1982). Victims who were previously ignored because they were powerless—the poor, minorities, women—now have greater access to the law enforcement system.

By the same token, civil libertarians need to view recent modifications of the exclusionary rule as votes of confidence for the police. A Columbia University law professor (Uviller, 1988) spent his sabbatical leave with the police on patrol in the crime-ridden Ninth Precinct in Manhattan. He reports that, even though many police officers don't like some of the rules, they have learned to live with them. He observed occasional violations by the police—for example, when officers would casually question suspects in the back of the police car, saving the reading of their *Miranda* rights for the police station (T. Jacoby, 1988). But sometimes the police were even more scrupulous than the court authorized with regard to respecting rights of suspects.

SUMMARY

Assuring both the rights of suspects and the rights of crime victims and potential victims is one of the most challenging tasks of any complex society. Suspects are assumed to be innocent until proven guilty; yet, as shown in previous chapters on the inducement of confessions and the use of the polygraph to intimidate suspects, the opposite assumption has often been made in the law enforcement system.

During the 1960s the Supreme Court of the United States, led by Chief Justice Earl Warren, made a number of pivotal decisions that extended the rights accorded to suspects and defendants. Among these were (1) *Mapp v. Ohio* (1961), which restricted state courts from admitting into a trial evidence that had been obtained by the police through illegal means; (2) *Gideon v. Wainwright* (1963), which provided indigent defendants with an attorney during any criminal trial; (3) *Escobedo v. Illinois* (1964), which permitted suspects to consult an attorney during questioning by the police; (4) *Miranda v. Arizona* (1966), which permitted suspects to remain silent after being arrested and also established that the police must demonstrate that suspects are aware of their rights; (5) *In re Gault* (1967), which extended many rights of adult suspects and defendants to minors; and (6) *Jackson v. Denno* (1964), which required that any confession the police claim to have obtained be independently assessed to determine whether it was voluntary before it is admitted into evidence.

As a result of publicity over these decisions—but, more important, as an outcome of citizens' increasing concern over the crime rate—the Supreme Court in more recent years has tended to relax some restrictions on the activities of police officers as they apprehend criminals. These relaxations have dealt primarily with the exclusionary rule and *Miranda* rights.

Rights of defendants and victims are also illustrated through the advantages given respective sides in a criminal trial. For example, the prosecution, seeking to convict the defendant, has the advantage of access to extensive government resources. At the trial it "goes first," thus providing the initial structure for jurors. In the closing arguments at the end of the trial, the prosecution has both the first word and the last word. In contrast, defendants enjoy special rights during the trial phase. Defendants are entitled to know whether the prosecution has uncovered evidence that supports a conclusion of innocence; also, defendants may choose to have their case decided by a judge rather than a jury. No defendant is required to testify; in fact, the defense is not required to present any evidence.

Between Arrest and Trial

Chapters 6 through 9 presented psychological perspectives on the actions of law enforcement officials as they investigate crimes and make arrests. Between these events and the eventual trial of a suspect are several other steps with psychological implications. These steps also reflect the dilemmas posed in Chapter 1.

The grand finale in our adversary system of justice is the trial, a public battle waged by two combatants (prosecution versus defense or plaintiff versus defendant), each fighting for an outcome favorable to his or her side. To the victors go the spoils of this contest; criminal defendants seek their freedom through an acquittal, and civil plaintiffs seek compensation for wrongs they have suffered. Although the trial may be the most dramatic conflict in our system, many skirmishes come before it that play large, if not decisive, roles in determining victors. In the adversary system, both sides seek numerous tactical advantages and favorable ground rules before they fight the trial/battle. Attorneys wage these struggles vigorously because they know they are crucial in shaping the contours of the adversarial contest.

In this chapter and the next, we concentrate on these pretrial proceedings. This chapter examines four pretrial activities with psychological significance: (1) bail setting, (2) grand jury actions, (3) plea bargaining, and (4) change of venue. Then, in Chapter 11, we discuss the legal concept of *competence*. Competence refers to the capacity to understand and participate meaningfully in legal proceedings; it covers mental and psychological abilities that the criminal justice system requires of defendants in order for court actions to be applied to them. Questions of competence are usually raised between the time of arrest and the formal trial, and they typically are concerned with two issues: competence to plead guilty and competence to stand trial.

Before we discuss bail, the grand jury, plea bargaining, and change of venue in detail, we provide a framework for these topics by describing the usual sequence of pretrial activities in the criminal justice system.

Steps between Arrest and Trial

If the police feel that probable cause exists to believe that a suspect committed a crime, they will in all likelihood arrest the suspect. However, being arrested for a crime and being charged with a crime are two different events. A person may be arrested without being charged; the police may arrest a drunk in order to detain him and sober him up. Charging implies a formal decision to continue with the prosecution, and that decision is made by the prosecuting attorney rather than the police.

The Initial Appearance

The *initial appearance* is an important step in the criminal process that must be taken soon after arrest—usually within 24 hours. Important players—the judge and the defense counsel—enter a process in which the defendant has been substantially in the control of the police and prosecutor. In the United States, prolonged police detention of those charged with a crime violates the Fourth Amendment proscription against "unreasonable" seizures (*Gerstein* v. *Pugh*, 1975), and thus defendants must be taken promptly before a judge or released.

This appearance is not an occasion for testifying or challenging the state's proof but, rather, an organizational meeting in a judicial setting. The purposes of this meeting are for the judge to do the following:

1. Inform suspects of the charges against them.
2. Review the evidence summarized by the prosecutor to determine if there is probable cause for believing that the suspects committed the crimes charged (the Supreme Court has held that this *probable cause determination* must be held within 48 hours of a person's arrest; *Riverside County* v. *McLaughlin*, 1991).
3. Inform suspects of their constitutional rights, especially their right to counsel and their privilege against self-incrimination.
4. Inform suspects that they have a right to free counsel. If they cannot afford a lawyer, either the public defender's office will provide a lawyer or the judge will recruit a private lawyer to represent the accused at a modest compensation by the state. (See Box 10-1 for a discussion of public defenders versus private defense attorneys.)
5. Consider the issue of whether suspects should be kept in custody or released from jail while they await their trial. If the judge decides to release a suspect, he or she will usually set conditions on the release designed to protect the community and ensure that the suspect will appear in court when required. These conditions usually involve a "setting of bail," in which suspects must arrange for a sum of money to be deposited with the court as security to ensure subsequently required appearances.
6. Schedule further court proceedings as required.

The Preliminary Hearing

The next step after the initial appearance is the *preliminary hearing*. The preliminary hearing serves to filter out those cases in which the prosecution's proof is insufficient. At a preliminary hearing the prosecution must offer some evidence on every element of the crime charged.

Hearsay is admissible, meaning that one witness may summarize what another has said. Thus a victim's account of a crime can be presented through the testimony of the investigating officer. The judge must decide if the prosecutor has presented evidence sufficient to support a finding of probable cause on all elements of the crime. Cross-examination by defense lawyers is limited to the issue of probable cause. No jury is present, and the judge has no authority to choose between competing versions of the events.

For these reasons the defendant rarely testifies or offers any evidence at a preliminary hearing. Furthermore, defense attorneys often waive the preliminary hearing because they are afraid that the publicity accompanying the hearing will harden community attitudes against their clients and make it more difficult to seat an impartial jury. At times, however, the preliminary hearing serves as an opportunity to glimpse the prosecution's case and size up its chief witnesses.

At the preliminary hearing, the judge will bind the defendant over to the grand jury if the judge finds there is probable cause to believe the defendant committed the crimes charged. It is also possible that the judge will reduce the charges, either because he or she believes the evidence does not support the level of crime charged by the prosecutor or because of a plea bargain between the prosecutor and the defense attorney. Generally, the judge also reconsiders the amount of bail originally set, if the defendant is still being held in custody. (A later section of this chapter describes bail setting in detail.)

The Grand Jury

Consisting of citizens drawn from the community, those chosen for the grand jury meet in secret with the prosecutor to investigate criminal activity and return indictments. In theory, the grand jury functions as a "sword," issuing subpoenas and compelling reluctant witnesses to testify, and as a "shield," protecting those accused of crime from unjust prosecution.

About one-third of the states require that felony prosecutions be preceded by grand jury review, and several additional states require an

---

Box **10-1**

Public Defenders versus Private Attorneys on Assignment by the State

Today one-third of the counties in the United States have a system of public defenders (Neubauer, 1988). Fourteen states have established statewide programs.

Casper (1972), interviewing convicts in prison in Connecticut, asked "Do you think your attorney was on your side?" The responses were as follows:

- Those who had a public defender: 10 of 49 (20%) said yes.
- Those who retained a private lawyer: 12 of 12 (100%) said yes.
- Those who had a Legal Aid attorney (furnished by the Office of Economic Opportunity): 7 of 10 (70%) said yes.

Defendants are often suspicious of public defenders; some of them even see public defenders as tools of the judge or the district attorney. Since public defenders are paid by the state, many defendants believe the state will control them.

Some defendants do not see public defenders as legitimate attorneys. One defendant said "If I'm going to real jail, I want a real lawyer." Anything with *public* in its title sounds phony to them. This attitude is unfortunate, because most public defenders are competent and sincerely motivated to achieve their clients' welfare. It is true that they have large caseloads; in New York City they average 70 to 100 *active* cases each (Kunen, 1983). But they specialize in criminal law (most private attorneys do not), and they know the preferences and predispositions of judges and prosecutors. They also stay informed on changes in the relevant laws.

Public defenders are not paid by the case or by the hour. They are paid poorly, usually on a salaried basis. Their major occupational problem is burn-out. James Kunen, a former public defender, has written eloquently about the problems in an aptly titled book, *How Can You Defend Those People?* (1983):

> You get tired of the exertions of the practice, having to be in court—several courts—every single day. And you get tired of the pressure—someone's freedom always riding on you. And you get tired of what the exertion and the pressure is all about; you're defending the Constitution, you're defending *everybody's* rights, but you're also, more often than not—*much more often than not*—defending a criminal. That needs to be done, but it doesn't need to be done *by you*, not all your life. After a while, it's somebody else's turn.
>
> The job takes a toll of your emotions. Of course, you feel sympathy for the victims, but you suppress it. It gets in the way. Nor can you afford a lot of sympathy for the clients. Some of them earn the courthouse epithet "dirtball," but most of them are likable enough when you're trying to help them, and you'd have to be a moral moron not to see that they are victims, too. It's just that too much sympathy for the clients gets in the way of doing your job. You have to sell them on the advantages of doing five years instead of ten. You have to watch the iron doors closing behind them all the time. Even now, I know, exactly, to within a couple of hundred feet, where they are every minute of every day for the next 10, 12, 15 years. I hardly ever think about it. You don't get worn out from all the pain and sadness. You get worn out from *not feeling* the pain and sadness. You get tired of not feeling.
>
> And you leave because you want to make some money [pp. 142–143].

indictment in capital offenses. The remaining states permit the prosecutor to proceed either by grand jury indictment or by *information*—for example, a complaint prepared and signed by the prosecutor describing the crime charged.

In states that require grand jury review, the prosecutor schedules those cases that have been "bound over" from preliminary hearings for consideration by the grand jury. The grand jury meets secretly and listens to the witnesses called by the prosecutor (who may relate what other witnesses said) and votes whether to indict and, if so, for what offenses. The grand jury may call witnesses on its own initiative if it is dissatisfied with the witnesses presented by the prosecutor and may vote to indict or not to indict for any reason. Its decision is not appealable to a court, although a prosecutor disgruntled over a jury's refusal to indict may resubmit a case to a second grand jury.

If the grand jury decides that sufficient evidence exists to justify the defendant's being tried, it issues an *indictment*, signed by the foreperson of the grand jury. The indictment is a written accusation by the grand jury, accusing one or more persons of one or more crimes. Its function is to clearly inform defendants of the nature of the charges against them, so that they have the opportunity to prepare a defense.

Arraignment

A grand jury gives its indictments to a judge, who brings those indicted to court for *arraignment* on the indictment. At the arraignment the judge makes sure that the defendant has an attorney and appoints one if necessary. The indictment is then read to the defendant, and the defendant is asked to plead guilty or not guilty. It is customary for defendants to plead not guilty at this time, even if they contemplate ultimately pleading guilty. The reason is to provide opportunities both for *discovery* (which means that the defendant's attorney gets a look at the evidence against the defendant) and for plea bargaining. At arraignment the judge again reviews the issue of pretrial release (bail) and sets a date for the trial. Often the judge will also fix a date by which pretrial motions must be filed.

Discovery and Pretrial Motions

Defendants and their attorneys want to be aware of the materials the prosecution will use to form its case. In civil trials, discovery is a well-formed prerogative of each side; in criminal trials, just how much of its case the prosecution has to reveal to the defense is controversial. Some states require prosecutors to turn over all reports, statements by witnesses, and physical evidence to the defense. Most states, however, require only that the prosecutor share certain evidence, such as laboratory reports, and evidence that is *exculpatory*—i.e., that tends to show the defendant to be not guilty as charged. In the case of *Brady* v. *Maryland* (1963), the U.S. Supreme Court ruled that the prosecution must disclose to the defense evidence in its possession that is favorable to the defendant. The American Bar Association has endorsed this position and has urged prosecuting attorneys to disclose, as soon as possible, all information about their witnesses (including the witnesses' testimony before the grand jury and their criminal records), the reports prepared by experts and consultants, the documents and material possessions taken from the accused, and any statements made by the accused. Beyond the constitutional obligation to disclose exculpatory evidence (called *Brady* material), however, the extent to which discovery occurs in criminal cases is determined by local statutes, not constitutional right.

In many cases, the prosecution provides "open file" discovery even though not obligated to do so, primarily to induce guilty pleas. The prosecutor, knowing that defense counsel will find it difficult to recommend a guilty plea without knowing the strength of the prosecution's case, will turn over most evidence, expecting that defense counsel, made aware of the prosecutor's firepower, will talk sense to the defendant and encourage a guilty plea. At the same time, prosecutors must remain sensitive to witnesses who may not want their identities or statements given to defense counsel.

Discovery is a two-way street. In general, states require the defense to turn over materials that the prosecution is required to turn over. If the prosecution is required to reveal laboratory reports, the defense will likewise be required to share such reports. In many states the defense is required to notify the prosecution if it intends to rely on certain defenses, notably insanity and alibi defenses. The reason for requiring such pretrial notice is to give the state an opportunity to investigate the claim and avoid being surprised at trial. The Supreme Court has upheld the constitutionality of pretrial notice requirements, provided the state is required to notify the defendant of witnesses it would call to refute an alibi (*Williams v. Florida*, 1970).

During the discovery phase of the case, pretrial motions are filed by both sides. The defense will often move for dismissal of the charges. Both sides will seek favorable rulings on the admissibility of evidence. Both sides will explore the possibility of a negotiated plea—a plea bargain. Although it is impossible to list all pretrial motions, the following are the most common:

1. *Defense motion for separate trials.* When two or more defendants are jointly indicted, one of them can be counted on to move for a separate trial, claiming that a joint trial would be prejudicial. When some of the prosecution's evidence is admissible against one defendant but not against the other, the motion is often granted.

2. *Defense motion to sever counts.* Suppose the indictment charges the defendant with robbing a convenience store on February 15 and burglarizing a house on April 15. The defendant may move for separate trials on these offenses. A defendant will argue that it is prejudicial for the same jury to hear evidence about separate crimes because the jury will be tempted to combine the evidence introduced on the separate crimes to find the defendant guilty of each crime.

3. *Defense motion for change of venue.* The defendant may move for a change of venue on the ground that community opinion, usually the product of prejudicial pretrial publicity, makes it impossible to seat a fair-minded jury. We discuss the involvement of psychologists in such motions in a later section of this chapter.

4. *Defense motion to dismiss on speedy trial grounds.* The Sixth Amendment of the U.S. Constitution guarantees defendants a right to a "speedy trial." A delay in trial is cause for dismissal if the prosecutor was attempting to obtain an unfair advantage and the defendant was harmed by the delay—as would happen if a crucial defense witness died (*Barker v. Wingo*, 1972). Dismissals *with prejudice* are rarely granted. The term "with prejudice" refers to a dismissal that bars any subsequent attempt to reinstate the prosecution; a dismissal "without prejudice" allows reprosecution.

5. *Defense motion to dismiss on grounds of selective prosecution.* Generally speaking, indictments will not be dismissed simply because the defendants were *selected* for prosecution. Effective use of limited resources often requires that police and prosecutors direct their efforts toward the most culpable offenders or those whose convictions will best deter others (*Wayte v. United States*, 1985), as, for example, in drug-trafficking crimes. Selective enforcement and

prosecution is unconstitutional, however, when the selection is made on racial or sexual grounds or when the selection impermissibly interferes with First Amendment rights. For example, it would be unconstitutional for the police to give speeding citations only to out-of-state motorists, because such a selection would interfere with the First Amendment right to travel freely within the United States. Dismissal on this ground is rare, because the defense must prove that others similarly situated were not prosecuted, that the selection was purposeful, and that the selection was for an impermissible reason.

6. *Defense motion to dismiss on double-jeopardy grounds.* The Fifth Amendment to the U.S. Constitution states that no person shall be "subject for the same offense to be twice put in jeopardy of life or limb." The Court has interpreted this clause to mean that the state is entitled to one, but only one, "fair chance" to convict the defendant. If the state loses—or if the trial is aborted without reason—the defendant cannot be retried. Most litigation over the double-jeopardy clause involves the question of whether the second charge is for the "same offense" as the one for which the defendant previously was tried (*Grady v. Corbin*, 1990).

7. *Defense motion to suppress evidence on Fourth Amendment grounds.* The *exclusionary rule*, which we discussed in Chapter 9, requires courts to suppress evidence obtained in violation of a defendant's right under the Fourth Amendment to be free from unreasonable searches and seizures. An exception to the exclusionary rule is made if the officers were operating in a good-faith belief that the search or seizure was in accord with the Fourth Amendment (*United States v. Leon*, 1984).

8. *Defense motion to suppress a confession or other statement by the defendant.* The Fifth Amendment protects against self-incrimination, the due-process clauses of the Fifth and Four-

teenth Amendments protect against the use of confessions extracted by duress or promise, and the Sixth Amendment forbids the use of a statement taken in violation of the right to counsel. One or more of these constitutional provisions is implicated any time the prosecution offers a confession or other statement by a defendant as evidence of guilt. Typically, defense counsel files a motion alleging that the confession was obtained in violation of the defendant's constitutional rights, the prosecutor files a written response, and the court holds a hearing at which the defendant and police give their versions of the circumstances under which the confession was obtained. The judge hears the testimony without a jury and decides the issue based on what was said and the credibility of the witnesses. Questions of credibility are usually resolved in favor of the police.

9. *Discovery motions.* When disputes arise in the discovery process, either side can ask the trial court for assistance. The typical dispute involves a sweeping defense request (for example, a request for the names of all persons who saw the robbery) and a prosecutor who resists the request because the prosecutor has decided to give the defense lawyer only what is required to be turned over.

10. *Motions in limine.* Perhaps the most common pretrial motions are those that seek advance rulings on evidentiary issues that will arise at trial. Suppose, for example, that the defendant was previously convicted of burglary; it is within the discretion of the court whether to allow the conviction into evidence in order to discredit the defendant if he chooses to testify. The defendant obviously wants a pretrial ruling on this issue in order to plan the questioning of the jurors and to decide whether to testify. Similarly, the prosecutor may want a pretrial ruling on the admissibility of a certain piece of evidence in order to plan the opening statement (a cardinal sin of trial practice is to

refer to a matter in the opening statement that is later deemed inadmissible). A *motion in limine* is simply a request for a pretrial ruling. Although judges are not constitutionally required to grant such a request, most trial judges are happy to cooperate with counsel who are trying to avoid midtrial problems.

Finally, there is the trial, designed to determine guilt or innocence. Only then can a person be "proven guilty." "Finally" is appropriate, for the whole process between initial appearance and trial—and beyond, if there are appeals—can take years. The James Richardson trial, described in the next paragraphs, is a sadly typical story of how justice is often delayed in our courts (Phillips, 1977).

At about 5:00 P.M. on June 28, 1972, a workday, James Richardson was on his way to work as a night-shift admissions clerk in a New York City hospital. At the same time, James Skagen, a New York subway police officer, was on his way home to the Bronx. He was not in uniform; he had been in Manhattan testifying at a trial.

Their paths crossed at the toll-booth level of a crowded Manhattan subway. Something about Richardson caught Skagen's attention. Drawing his off-duty revolver and his badge, he approached Richardson, yelling "I'm a cop! Get your hands up and get against the wall!"

Richardson meekly complied; he turned his back and slowly extended his hands until they touched the station walls. The subway police officer stepped forward to frisk Richardson. But suddenly there was a blur of action, and for a split second the two men stood facing each other with guns in their hands. Four shots rang out. Two of them hit Skagen in the shoulder; another creased Richardson's groin; the fourth ricocheted around the subway station walls, miraculously missing the masses of commuters.

Richardson began to run; he darted through the exit gate and up the stairs to the street. Meanwhile, Skagen, staggered by his injuries, fell backward but then recovered and began to give chase. Outside, on the street, two police officers were writing out a ticket for a peddler who was selling flowers without a license. They heard the shots, pulled their guns, and ran toward the subway entrance. When they got there, they saw James Richardson running up the stairs at full speed, shouting "He's shooting! A crazy man is shooting at me!"

At that instant Skagen arrived at the bottom of the stairs. He fired a single shot, which hit Richardson above the right shoulder blade. Despite the injury, Richardson kept running.

From the top of the stairs, Patrolman Wieber saw Skagen fire his gun, so he aimed his gun down the stairs, pulled the trigger, and kept on firing until the gun was empty and Skagen had fallen.

Richardson ran right into the arms of the other police officer, Patrolman Jacobsen. The two tumbled to the ground together, but Richardson got up first, drew his gun and briefly pointed it at the police officer, and then started running again. He was caught several blocks away.

After Patrolman Wieber shot Skagen, he ran down the stairs to where Skagen lay. Skagen pulled the badge out of his pocket, said "I'm a cop," and then fainted. He died on the way to the hospital.

Richardson was taken into custody but also taken to a hospital for treatment of his groin wound. He told police detectives: "We had words which I can't remember and the guy pulled his gun and shield and I pulled mine—a chrome-plated .32-caliber snub-nosed revolver. I had my gun tucked inside my pants up front. Then the cop shot me right here (indicating low right groin) and I shot him." He claimed that Skagen looked "run-down, dingy." Richardson wasn't impressed by the badge, perhaps because he had one himself, stolen from a female police officer.

The prosecutor decided to bring charges against Richardson, and the grand jury issued an indictment, accusing Richardson of committing seven crimes:

1. Murder ("The Defendant, while engaged in the commission of a felony, Escape in the Second Degree, caused the death of John Skagen").
2. Manslaughter in the second degree ("The Defendant recklessly caused the death of John Skagen").
3. Attempt to commit the crime of murder.
4. Escape in the second degree ("The Defendant, having been arrested for a felony, escaped from custody").
5. Possessing a weapon as a felony (Richardson's gun was not registered to him; in fact, it was a stolen gun).
6. Reckless endangerment in the second degree ("recklessly engaged in conduct which created a substantial risk of serious physical injury to one John Jacobsen, a police officer").
7. Criminal possession of stolen property in the third degree (the police badge).

One reason for the overlapping charges was the difficulty in ascertaining the exact cause of Skagen's death. The autopsy revealed that five bullets had hit Skagen, including three from Officer Wieber's gun.

Bail setting was scheduled for July 11, 1972, two weeks after the incident. The judge set bail at $50,000; Richardson's attorney appealed, and a week later another judge reduced the bail to $40,000. Richardson's attorney now appealed to the New York Supreme Court, which reduced the bail to $25,000 on August 2. Five months later, after another appeal, bail was reduced to $15,000. Because of publicity and community support for the defense fund, enough money was collected to pay Richardson's bail bond, and he was released from custody on February 13, 1973, after spending seven months in jail.

But the trial would not take place until September 1974. The average delay in homicide cases in New York City is 24 months, but this one was even longer, mostly because of the unavailability of Richardson's attorney, William Kunstler, who was representing the defendants in the Wounded Knee trial at the time.

During the jury trial the prosecution tried to discredit Richardson's claim of self-defense. Ballistics indicated that Skagen's revolver had been fired only once, as Richardson was running up the stairs. Richardson had done all the firing on the subway toll-booth level; two of the shots went into Skagen's shoulder, a third into the air, and the fourth (actually the first) into his own groin as he pulled the gun out of his pants. Given that, what was the cause of death? Neither the shoulder wounds nor the abdominal wounds (from Wieber's gun) were necessarily fatal. Skagen had bled to death. But the wounds from Wieber's gun were more serious.

The jury reached a compromise verdict; it found Richardson not guilty of the murder or attempted murder of Skagen but guilty of manslaughter. He was also found guilty of illegal possession of a weapon and of the police badge.

Richardson was sentenced to prison on December 13, 1974, for not more than ten years for manslaughter and not more than seven years, concurrently, for the weapons possession. The stolen-property (badge) conviction was discharged. But Richardson's attorney appealed, and on April 13, 1976, the Appellate Division of the New York State Court unanimously reversed the manslaughter conviction, ruling that the causal link between Richardson's recklessness and Skagen's death had not been established.

On May 27, 1976, Richardson was resentenced to three years in state prison. So ended the processing on an action that had occurred one month short of four years before.

THE DECISION TO SET BAIL

As we have already described, judges often must decide whether to keep defendants in custody throughout the sometimes lengthy period between arrest and trial. There are three options: defendants can be kept in jail without bail, given the opportunity to be free on bail, or released on their own recognizance (i.e., on their promise that they will return). In fact, bail setting evolved in the American legal system as an attempt to resolve the basic conflict between individual and societal rights (the first dilemma discussed in Chapter 1).

The Purposes of Bail

The bail decision determines whether defendants are detained or released before trial. When bail is higher than defendants can afford, they have no choice but to remain in jail. And often bail can be quite high. In the case of John Emil List, who was arrested after his crimes of 17 years before were portrayed on the TV program *America's Most Wanted*, the judge set bail at $5 million. A similar amount was set for Imelda Marcos's bail, after she was charged with fraud and embezzling $100 million from the Philippine government.

Defendants have no absolute right to pretrial release. The Eighth Amendment to the U.S. Constitution says that excessive bail shall not be required, but the Supreme Court has ruled that this provision does not guarantee a right to bail; it simply requires that bail, if any, should not be excessive (*United States* v. *Salerno*, 1987). In 1988, of the approximately 350,000 inmates held in local jails throughout the United States, almost 50% were in custody waiting to be arraigned, to be tried, or to have their trials conclude (Maguire & Flanagan, 1991).

They were in jail not because they had been convicted of a crime, but because either they had been denied bail or they had not been able to raise the bail that had been set for them. Is this fair, given the fundamental value in U.S. society that defendants are innocent until proven guilty? What considerations affect the decision whether to set bail?

Traditionally, the justification has been the degree of risk that the defendant will not appear for his or her trial. Defendants who are believed not to pose this risk are often released on their own recognizance (called ROR); those for whom there is some doubt are allowed to post a bail bond as a kind of insurance that they will appear; and those who are considered very high risks are kept in custody. Sometimes this justification is unnecessary. John Emil List was recognized by neighbors from a 17-year-old photograph, and Imelda Marcos was so well known as to have even been caricatured on *Saturday Night Live*. Furthermore, studies of jurisdictions where defendants are given ROR reveal that very few defendants fail to appear (Ares, Rankin, & Sturz, 1963; Feeley, 1983).

Should the dangerousness of the defendant or his or her likelihood of committing other crimes in the interim also be a consideration? Around 1970 a push began for legislation that would legitimate preventive detention. Asked whether they approve of this, most citizens say yes, opting for society's need to be protected over the rights of individual suspects to be presumed fully innocent until proven guilty.

The Bail Reform Act of 1984 was introduced by Congress in part to ensure that community safety from potentially dangerous persons was considered by judges when they set bail for criminal defendants. Despite challenges to the constitutionality of the preventive detention authorized by this act, it has been upheld by the U.S. Supreme Court. In the 1987 case of *United States* v. *Salerno*, the Court upheld the provision in this law permitting the detention of defendants charged with serious crimes if prosecutors could establish probable cause that the defendants committed the crimes charged and could convince the judge that "the safety of any other person and the community" would be jeopardized if the defendants were released on bail (Taylor, 1987a). (The standard to be used was "clear and convincing evidence.") Thus, preventive detention on the grounds of perceived dangerousness—not only a federal law, but on the books (in some form) in many states—was reaffirmed. Reflecting the dilemma in Chapter 1 between individual rights and society's needs, Chief Justice Rehnquist wrote: "We have repeatedly held that the Government's regulatory interest in community safety can, in appropriate circumstances, outweigh an individual's liberty interest" (quoted by Taylor, 1987a, p. 9). Crucial to the Court's opinion, however, was the assumption that the defendant would be tried promptly in accord with the Federal Speedy Trial Act.

Preventive detention requires two procedures: (1) determining which persons pose threats of additional crimes if released from jail and (2) detaining these persons prior to their trials. In practice, preventive detention assumes that valid predictions of future dangerous conduct can be made, an assumption that is uncertain at best (Monahan, 1984). In fact, although psychologists might be able to make valid predictions of future dangerousness for about 50% of the persons they evaluate (Slobogin, 1984), this level of accuracy (or inaccuracy) has led some scholars to argue that mental health professionals simply should not make such predictions because they lack scientific validity (Ewing, 1991).

Psychologists and other social scientists can play a helpful role in this area by conducting research on the determinants and fairness of bail-setting decisions (Goldkamp & Gottfredson, 1979). Among the topics that psychologists have evaluated are the following: (1) What factors most strongly influence whether defendants released from pretrial custody appear when they are required—ties to the local community or the amount of money posted as bond? (2) Can defendants who pose a high risk of fleeing if they are released from pretrial custody be identified at the time of bail setting? (3) What effect does pretrial detention have on the outcomes of defendants' trials? (4) What criteria influence a judge's decision to set bail?

Does Bail Ensure Defendants' Appearance, and Is It Discriminatory?

Across many studies in several different communities, researchers have discovered that ROR as a form of release is as effective in guaranteeing defendants' return for trial as requiring them to post bail. In these studies the "skip rate" for defendants released ROR has averaged less than 10% (Ares et al., 1963; Feeley, 1983; Nietzel & Dade, 1973). One reason why the decision about custody versus cash bail versus release on recognizance is important is the possibility that the setting of bail unjustly discriminates against certain types of people, particularly if bail is not essential for ensuring required appearances. If the judge sets bail at $15,000, the defendant must come up with this amount of money as a security deposit or remain in jail until the trial is completed. (The defendant receives this security deposit back when he or she appears for trial.) The more affluent the defendant, the more capable he or she will be to provide the money and obtain temporary freedom. This difference conflicts with our society's goal that people be treated equally before the law, regardless of their occupation, income, or status.

In many communities, bonding agents (colloquially called "bail bondsmen") serve as intermediaries between courts and defendants. For a given percentage of the bail—usually 10%—the bonding agent provides the total bail as a surety bond. If the defendant fails to appear for trial, the agent pays the entire amount of the bail to the court. The 10% is the fee paid by defendants for their freedom. If bail is set at $15,000 and the defendant hires an agent, the defendant does not have to post the $15,000 to get his freedom—often an impossible task—but he is out the $1500 fee, even if he does appear in court. Furthermore, most bonding agents require the defendant to provide collateral (personal property such as jewelry, a car, antiques, or a mortgage on real estate); if the defendant fails to appear, the agents use this property to recoup some of their loss. So bail is costly to defendants, especially those who can least afford it. (See Box 10-2 for an interview with a bonding agent.)

Can High-Risk Defendants Be Identified?

The major concern about defendants released from pretrial custody is that they will commit more crimes once they are released or will fail to return for trial as required. If those defendants who pose the greatest risk for new offenses following their release could be accurately predicted, guidelines could be developed for judges to use in their bail-setting decisions. In one recent study (Goldkamp & Gottfredson, 1988, cited in Monahan & Walker, 1990), the researchers followed the status of 2200 persons who had been arrested for felonies and were then released from custody prior to their trial. Within 90 days of their release, 17% of these defendants had been arrested either for a new crime or for failing to appear as required in court. Among the factors that predicted new offenses or failure to appear were the following: the defendant lived alone, the original criminal charge was for robbery or a property offense, the defendant previously had

---

Box 10-2 | *An Interview with a Bonding Agent*

The term *bail bondsman* is imprecise as well as sexist, for in Lawrence, Kansas, one of the two bonding agents is female. Vanessa Mock says that most of her business comes from repeat customers. "Basically I just have regular clients. There are some people who, no matter what they do, they can't seem to stay out of trouble," she says.

She reports that she gets called down to the county jail in the middle of the night at least two or three times a week. "If you get called twice in one night, that's hard," she says. Although she won't reveal her income, she reports "I've made enough money to pay off my car, make my house payments, and go on vacation." She also wears several pieces of collateral, including reset jewelry; "I prefer jewelry as collateral," she says.

At the same time, the job has its costs. "There aren't a whole lot of people who want to work 24 hours a day seven days a week," she says; "I could be in the movies on a date and get beeped out and just have to leave." And a couple of her clients have taken swings at her; she excuses them for it, though, acknowledging the stress they feel from getting arrested and jailed. "I'm the last person who gets to them, and by the time I get there they're already crazy," she observes.

Adapted from Coleman (1984, p. 5).

failed to show up for a required court appearance, and the arresting police officer noted factors at the time of arrest suggesting a risk of fleeing. Based on these factors, defendants were classified into four groups, representing increasing levels of risk. The failure rates (defined as a new offense or a failure to appear) of these four groups were 6%, 12%, 23%, and 30%. Many courts now use similar empirical guidelines in denying bail to defendants or setting different levels of bail. (Note, however, the large number of false positives represented among the highest-risk group; 70% of the persons in group IV did not commit a new crime or fail to appear after being released.)

Does Pretrial Release Affect Trial Outcomes?

What if the defendant cannot provide bail and is forced to remain in jail until the time of trial? Does this make any difference in the trial's outcome? Clearly, yes. Those defendants who are detained in jail are more likely to be convicted and to receive higher sentences than those who can afford bail, even when the seriousness of their offenses and the evidence against them are the same (Goldfarb, 1965). An accused person who is out on bail finds it easier to gather witnesses and prepare a defense. Jailed defendants cannot meet with their attorney in the latter's office, have less time with their attorney to prepare for trial, and have less access to records and witnesses. In addition, pretrial detention is likely to cost defendants their jobs, making it harder for them to pay attorneys. Detention also corrodes family and community ties. Casper's (1972) interviews with convicted defendants who were serving prison sentences revealed that, for many of them, the time spent in local jails prior to trial was worse than the time in prison; the conditions were terrible, there was nothing to do, and the treatment by guards was hostile.

Civil libertarians oppose pretrial detention because it conflicts with our society's fundamental assumption that a defendant is innocent until proven guilty. The Supreme Court recently has taken a somewhat different view—that the "presumption of innocence" refers to the rule of trial procedure that places the burden of demonstrating a defendant's guilt on the government, and that pretrial detention is not a punishment but rather a regulation (like a quarantine) for the public's protection. A law professor, Robert Nagel (1989), notes: "[the rule] hardly requires that, before trial, society must shut its eyes to all available proof of wrongdoing" (p. 14). Regardless of the interpretation, numerous surveys (reported in Goldfarb, 1965) have shown that many defendants in pretrial detention because they could not pay bail were later found not guilty of any crimes. In Philadelphia, of 1000 people who were detained an average of 33 days, two-thirds were later acquitted or, if convicted, not given any prison sentences. Another survey of 114,653 people in pretrial detention reported that only 27% were later convicted and given jail or prison sentences. A partial explanation for these outcomes is that charges are sometimes dismissed (or the defendant is credited with time already served in jail) when the prosecutor believes that the pretrial incarceration has been sufficient punishment for the crime.

What Factors Determine Judges' Bail-Setting Decisions?

Faced with a bail determination, judges must balance two concerns: that society's interest in the defendant's appearing in court is satisfied and that the defendant's rights will be protected. Ordinarily the judge hears the prosecuting attorney and the defendant's lawyer each recommend different amounts of bail—or even different actions, because bail recommendations can be conceptualized along a monetary continuum from zero (accused is released on ROR) to infinite (accused is held in jail without bail).

Social psychologists Ebbe Ebbesen and Vladimir Konecni (1975) studied the decision processes that judges use in setting bail. They conducted two studies, with differing outcomes. In the first, 18 municipal and superior court judges in San Diego, California, participated in what was described to them as a "social psychology class project." Each judge was given eight fictitious case records. Some aspects of these records were consistent; they all involved robberies, and the accused was always an unmarried white male between the ages of 21 and 25 who claimed he was innocent. The type of stolen property differed, but its value was always between $850 and $950.

In contrast to these constant factors, Ebbesen and Konecni varied four aspects of the record from case to case. These became the independent variables that the researchers manipulated in order to determine their relative weights in judges' decisions about the appropriate bail:

1. *Prosecuting attorney's recommendation.* In actual robbery cases in San Diego, the average recommendation for bail by the district attorney had been $2850. The researchers established three levels of recommended bail for different case records: low ($1500–$1700), medium ($2000–$2500), or high ($5000–$7500).
2. *Recommendation of the defense attorney.* In actual cases the average recommendation by defense attorneys was $747. Again, three levels were established, but, as you would expect, they were lower than the prosecutor suggested: low ($0—that is, ROR), medium ($500–$600), or high ($1000–$1200).
3. *Prior record.* In actual bail hearings, prose-

cuting attorneys usually refer to the prior criminal record of the accused to bolster their recommendations; two levels were embedded in the district attorney's statement. In one, the defendant had no prior record; in the other, he had a past history of felony convictions and was currently on probation.
4. *Local ties.* Defense attorneys, trying to make the best possible case that their clients deserve less bail, often portray them as responsible persons. One means is to refer to the defendant's local ties: he has lived in that city for a long time, or he is employed there. Two extremes were created: the defendant had either strong local ties (he had lived in San Diego for four to six years, he was employed there, and his family was also living in San Diego) or weak ones (he had lived in San Diego only one or two months, he was unemployed, and his family lived several hundred miles away).

Thus there were 36 possible combinations of these four factors—that is, 3 x 3 x 2 x 2. Each judge reviewed eight cases; this meant that each of the 36 cases was reviewed by four judges. Judges were asked what amount of bail they would set for each case they reviewed. Table 10-1 presents the average decisions. Judges were influenced most by the degree to which the defendant was tied to the area and by a previous criminal record. Weak local ties led to higher bail amounts, as did presence of a criminal record.

But remember that this was a simulation study. Judges were aware that these were not real cases, and some of the judges even commented that certain combinations of the four factors would never occur in real bail hearings. Consequently, Ebbesen and Konecni decided to observe actual bail-setting hearings.

In this second study, trained observers at-

Table **10-1** **Mean Bail Set by Judges in a Controlled Simulation of the Bail-Setting Situation**

District attorney's recommendation	Prior record	Defense attorney's recommendation					
		$0		$550		$1100	
		Strength of local ties					
		Strong	Weak	Strong	Weak	Strong	Weak
$1600	No	$ 687	$2775	$ 937	$1550	$2000	$1550
	Yes	2500	2125	1312	1900	2550	2550
$2250	No	1625	2375	750	2312	1750	2625
	Yes	1250	2375	1387	3000	1750	2875
$6250	No	1125	3250	2125	2875	1550	3300
	Yes	2750	5687	3125	3375	1600	4250

Source: Ebbesen and Konecni (1975, Table 1, p. 809).

tended the hearings of five judges. Decisions involving 106 defendants, including four charged with homicide, were studied. The observers recorded information about five independent variables:

1. *Severity of the crime,* divided into six categories: (a) homicide; (b) violent crimes not resulting in death (kidnapping, rape, and assault); (c) crimes with the potential of violence or death (armed robbery or possession of a deadly weapon); (d) nonviolent but major crimes with specific victims (sale of drugs or robbery); (e) nonviolent minor crimes with unspecified victims (forgery); and (f) victimless crimes, such as possessing drugs or being AWOL.

2. *Prior record.* Four levels of the accused's previous criminal record could be distinguished: (a) none; (b) only traffic violations; (c) a moderate record (no more than one prior felony conviction, and that for a nonviolent crime); or (d) a severe prior record (consisting of more than one felony conviction or one violent-crime felony conviction).

3. *Local ties.* Three levels of local ties were distinguished, based on whether the defendant

was employed and had relatives in the San Diego area and on how long he or she had lived there.

4. *Defense attorney's recommendation.* The actual monetary recommendations were recorded. These ranged from $0 to $25,000 (in one murder case).

5. *Prosecutor's recommendation.* The actual monetary recommendations from the district attorney's office for these 106 cases ranged from $0 to $100,000.

The researchers used a statistical procedure called "multiple regression" to determine how the five independent variables interacted to affect the judges' decisions about bail. In combination, the five independent variables accounted for 80% of the variance in the judges' decisions.

The district attorney's recommendation was the single strongest predictor of the judge's decision. One reason is that this recommendation incorporated aspects of two of the other four variables (severity of crime and prior record). For example, when the crime was more severe and there was a prior record, the prosecutor suggested higher bail. Interestingly, local ties did not play a consistent role in the prosecuting attorney's recommendation; in fact, when the crime was severe, the attorney proposed that higher bail be set when there were strong local ties.

The mean bail amount set by the judges ($2162 without the murder cases) fell between the district attorneys' ($2820) and the defense attorneys' ($583) mean recommendations. And although the defense attorney's recommendation did influence the judge, it had less influence than the prosecutor's. In fact, Ebbesen and Konecni (1975) concluded:

> From an applied point of view, the results of the present research portray a rather unfortunate picture of the way bail gets set in the San Diego (and possibly many other) felony courts. Even though a hearing is held in which both attorneys make a major point of discussing the prior record and local ties of the accused, the judges set bail almost in complete accord with the district attorney's recommendations. This decision strategy seems inconsistent with the traditional claim that the accused is presumed innocent until proven guilty, especially since in the adversary system the district attorney's goal is to prove that the accused is guilty. . . . Furthermore, since the district attorneys always seem to recommend a higher bail than the defense attorneys, following the former's recommendations is more likely to lead to discrimination against the poor [p. 820].

A later survey in Philadelphia, using a larger number of cases (Goldkamp & Gottfredson, 1979), also concluded that community ties had very little impact on bail setting. Seriousness of the offense was most important, accounting for 29% of the variance in judges' decisions to release defendants on their own recognizance. But, in contrast to Ebbesen and Konecni's study, Goldkamp and Gottfredson concluded that much of the variance in their judges' deci-

sions was unexplained by the variables suggested to judges in prescriptive guidelines.

THE ROLE OF THE GRAND JURY

In the federal system and in many states, a defendant cannot be convicted of a felony unless a grand jury has first returned an indictment. In theory, the grand jury should therefore serve as a shield against unwarranted prosecutions. But, although the grand jury can serve as a buffer against hasty prosecution of innocent suspects, it also can be used by prosecutors as a tool to implement their wishes to "put criminals behind bars." Sometimes the grand jury can be used for the political aims of the prosecuting attorney, who, for various reasons, does not want to indict a suspect. After Mary Jo Kopechne drowned in Senator Ted Kennedy's car off Chappaquiddick Bridge in July 1969, the grand jury—according to its foreperson, Leslie Leland—was denied access to witnesses and the transcript of the inquest. "I felt I had been set up by the D.A. so that they could claim there was a grand jury investigation; we had been used," Leland is quoted as saying (Kunen, Mathison, Brown, & Nugent, 1989, p. 36). A grand jury can thus be used as a "dumping ground" by prosecutors who don't want "to take the heat" for a decision not to prosecute.

Historically, the grand jury arose out of a struggle between King Henry II of England and the Roman Catholic Church. In the year 1164, the church reluctantly agreed to accept an organization that represented the earliest forerunner of the modern grand jury. At this point the grand jury served as an instrument of the king; "grand jurors were . . . penalized if they failed to return an indictment against someone considered indictable by the Crown" (Clark, 1975, p. 9). An equivalent concern, that the grand jury serves as a "rubber stamp" for the prosecutor, remains today. Clark (1975) observes, for example, that "in periods of severe political stress, or when a locality or the nation has been caught up in some intense ideological struggle, the grand jurors have shared the political sympathies of the prosecuting agent, and unpopular accused people have not been protected against improper or politically inspired charges" (p. 26).

At the same time, the grand jury can serve as a useful investigative tool. The grand jury can subpoena witnesses to give testimony, and it can require that documents be brought forth. The grand jury has been extremely effective in gathering evidence in cases involving organized crime, in conspiracy cases such as Watergate, and in others of equal importance.

Problems with the Grand Jury

Because public procedures could injure the reputations of innocent parties (people bound over to the grand jury but ultimately not indicted) and inhibit potential witnesses, grand jury procedures are conducted in secret. Furthermore, they are one-sided in that those people facing possible indictment have no right to be present or to cross-examine witnesses. The grand jury can consider any evidence it chooses to hear, including hearsay and evidence produced by illegal searches. These practices have led to problems with the way some grand juries have functioned, causing them at times to be more of a threat to, than a protector of, the innocent.

Ordinarily, during a grand jury inquiry, the prosecutor—not the jurors—does the questioning. (Grand jury members can furnish questions.) Suspects do not have a right to testify in their own behalf (although they may be permitted to do so), nor do they have the right to have their attorneys present while they are questioned by the prosecuting attorney. (Suspects may refuse to answer, and they may excuse themselves temporarily to consult their attorneys, who have to remain outside the hearing room.)

These procedures reflect a current view that the grand jury hearing is more of an inquest than a trial (Frankel & Naftalis, 1977). For example, the suspect might have information that would help the grand jury decide whether to indict, leading some commentators (Frankel & Naftalis, 1977) to suggest that suspects should be entitled to propose other witnesses to be called.

Controversy also exists over the representativeness of the grand jury. The Jury Selection and Service Act of 1968 proclaims: "The policy of the United States is that all litigants in federal courts entitled to trial by jury shall have the right to grand and petit [that is, trial] juries selected at random from a fair cross-section of the community in the district or division wherein the court convenes." It also states that "no citizen shall be excluded from service as a grand or petit juror on account of race, color, religion, sex, national origin, or economic status," but in many jurisdictions, grand jurors are chosen because they are leading citizens of the community, "the best and the brightest." They do not represent a true cross-section of the populace.

States also differ on whether the suspect is permitted access to the minutes of the grand jury deliberations. Some permit ready access; others (and the federal government) do not consider this necessary, concluding that, once indicted, "a defendant is adequately protected by the requirement of proof beyond a reasonable doubt before a unanimous trial jury may convict" (Frankel & Naftalis, 1977, pp. 24–25).

Use of the Grand Jury as a Political Weapon

During the administration of President Richard Nixon (1969–1974), the executive branch of the federal government used federal grand juries as weapons against political opponents. Leroy D. Clark, a law professor and observer of the process, noted at the time that "there are strong indications that the Justice Department has used the grand jury to gather intelligence against groups deemed 'radical,' to harass and deplete the resources of political opponents, and generally to discredit and intimidate people from continuing to support and participate in groups that the administration differs with politically" (1975, p. 6). When people refused to tell these grand juries about their friends and associates, they were jailed for contempt.

PLEA BARGAINING

No better example exists of the dilemma between truth and conflict resolution as goals of our legal system than the extensive use of plea bargaining in the criminal justice system of the United States. Most criminal cases—at least 80%—end between arrest and trial, when the defendant pleads guilty to *some* charge, usually in exchange for a concession by the prosecutor. For example, between March 27 and April 21, 1989, the largest county in New York State disposed of 1256 felony cases. A total of 82.5% were plea-bargained; 6.8% were resolved through jury trials; 9.1% were dismissed; and the remaining 1.6% had other dispositions (Lee, 1989). In a comprehensive study of Connecticut's system from the 1800s to the late 1970s, guilty pleas accounted for about 90% of the criminal case dispositions in most of the years studied (Heumann, 1978). Not all guilty pleas are reached through bargaining; some defendants plead guilty with no promise of leniency because they choose to end the process as quickly as possible and get on with serving their sentences. However, most defendants plead guilty as a result of a negotiation process that leads them to expect a concession or benefit from the prosecutor in exchange for not contesting guilt. This process is known as plea bargaining.

The defendant's part of the bargain requires an admission of guilt. This admission relieves the prosecutor from any obligation to prove that the defendant committed the crimes charged. This admission usually takes the form of a formal plea of guilty to a judge, who, if he or she accepts the plea, imposes a sentence. In addition, most states allow *deferred prosecution* for minor crimes, in which first-time offenders who admit guilt are placed on probation and have the charges against them dismissed if they stay out of trouble during probation. By admitting guilt—either through a guilty plea or through a deferred-prosecution agreement—the defendant saves the prosecution the time, expense, and uncertainty of a trial.

The prosecutor's part of the bargain may involve an agreement to allow the defendant to plead guilty to a charge less serious than the evidence supports. Manslaughter is a lesser charge to murder, and many murder prosecutions are resolved by a plea of guilty to manslaughter. In Brooklyn in a recent year, of 6621 people charged with narcotics felonies, 2983 charges were ultimately reduced to misdemeanors (Kurtz, 1988).

In another type of "charge bargaining," the prosecutor drops some charges in return for a plea of guilty. Charge bargaining may lead prosecutors to charge the defendant with more crimes or a more serious crime than they could prove at trial as a strategy for motivating guilty pleas (see Box 10-3). The defendant who engages in this type of bargaining may win only hollow victories. Cases in which prosecutors offer to drop charges are likely to be ones for which judges would have imposed concurrent sentences for the multiple convictions anyway. Judges and parole boards also tend to pay more attention to the criminal event itself than to the formal charge when making sentencing decisions.

Plea bargaining may also take the form of "sentence bargaining," in which prosecutors recommend reduced sentences in return for guilty pleas. Since sentencing is the prerogative of judges, judges vary in their willingness to follow prosecutors' recommendations. Judges can "rubber-stamp" prosecutorial sentencing recommendations, and some judges do just that. On the other hand, judges should consider many factors when imposing a sentence— seriousness of the crime, harm to the victim, background of the offender, to name a few—

Box 10-3 | An Example of Overcharging

A New Jersey man reports that a male adult came up behind him as he was opening the door to his apartment, stuck something—"I think it was a gun"—in his back, pushed him inside, and ordered him to give over his money. The victim handed over his wallet, which contained $25 in cash and five credit cards. The perpetrator took it and left. The victim turned around in time to catch a glimpse of him going down the stairs. He called the police.

A suspect was arrested when he tried to use the victim's credit card to buy gas. A gun was found in his jacket pocket.

Charges against this suspect might include (with penalties):

Charge	Maximum fine	Maximum sentence
Robbery	$5000	15 years
Assault with a deadly weapon	2000	7 years
Unlawful use of dangerous weapon	5000	10 years
Carrying concealed weapon	1000	3 years
Unlawful entry	2000	7 years
Possession of stolen property	2000	7 years
Attempted fraud (misuses of credit card) (5 counts)	1000	3 years (each count)

Because evidence against the suspect is strong, his attorney, with the suspect's consent, may work out a "bargain" with the prosecutor: the suspect will plead guilty to carrying a concealed weapon and attempted fraud, and the other charges will be dropped. The prosecutor will suggest to the judge that the defendant be given a maximum sentence of ten years in prison. Usually the judge accepts the suggestion—even though he or she is not legally bound by it. A trial is averted.

Source: New Jersey Police Manual, 1962; reprinted from Ellison and Buckhout (1981, p. 29).

and some judges believe that simply going along with every recommendation from the prosecutor compromises their duty to consider these factors sufficiently. In general, most defendants can expect that judges will usually follow the sentences that have been recommended by a prosecutor. Prosecutors can promote this expectation and earn the trust of judges by recommending sentences that are reasonable and fair.

Defendants try to negotiate a plea in order to obtain a less severe punishment than they would receive if they went to trial and were convicted. But why do prosecutors plea-bargain? What advantages do they seek, given that they hold the more powerful position in this bargaining situation? Prosecutors are motivated to plea-bargain for one of five reasons: (1) to dispose of cases in which the evidence against the defendant is weak or the defense attorney is a formidable foe; (2) to obtain the testimony of one defendant against a more culpable or infamous codefendant; (3) to expedite the flow of cases for an overworked staff and a clogged court docket; (4) to maintain a cordial working relationship with defense attorneys from whom the prosecutor may want certain favors in the future; or (5) to avoid trials that might be unpopular because the defendant is a well-liked figure in the community or the crime charged might be seen as morally justified.

Evaluations of Plea Bargaining

Plea bargaining remains a controversial procedure. During the 1970s, two national commissions reviewed its value; one concluded that it was a necessary device for keeping cases moving through the courts, but the other called for its abolition. Plea bargaining has been practiced in the United States since the middle of the 19th century, although some states purport to forbid (Alaska) or restrict (California) the practice. The Supreme Court has upheld plea bargain-

ing, calling it "an essential component of the administration of justice" (*Santobello* v. *New York*, 1971). However, several rules must be followed for guilty pleas to be valid. First, as we discuss in the next chapter, pleas of guilty must be voluntary, intelligent, and knowing. A plea of guilty is voluntary even if it is induced by a promise of leniency, as long as the defendant is represented by an attorney (*Brady* v. *United States*, 1970). Likewise, a plea can be voluntary even if encouraged by the threat of additional charges should the defendant insist on trial. In *Bordenkircher* v. *Hayes* (1978), the Court held that forcing a defendant to choose between unpleasant alternatives (e.g., pleading guilty or facing a trial in which a more severe sentence would be sought) does not mean that the choice is involuntary, provided that the choices advance legitimate social goals and do not impose unconstitutional restrictions on the defendant. However, some pressures will not be tolerated. In *Bordenkircher*, for example, the Court expressed reservations about offers not to prosecute third parties in exchange for a guilty plea from a defendant. Also, prosecutors cannot renege on their "deals" and require a more severe sentence than their original negotiated offer (*Santobello* v. *New York*, 1971).

Plea bargaining has been defended as a necessary and useful part of the criminal justice system (American Bar Association, 1978), and it has been condemned as a practice that should be abolished from our courts (Alschuler, 1968; Kipnis, 1979; Langbein, 1978; National Advisory Commission on Criminal Justice Standards and Goals, 1973). Advocates cite the following justifications for the procedure: (1) the defendant's admission of guilt is the important first step in rehabilitation; (2) guilty pleas relieve the backlog of cases that would otherwise engulf the courts; (3) outcomes are reached promptly and with a sense of finality; (4) other criminal justice participants benefit from the process—from the police officer who doesn't have to spend hours in court testifying to the victim who is spared the trauma of trial; and (5) the defendant's cooperation may facilitate prosecution of others.

Critics urge the abolition of plea bargaining on the following grounds: (1) improper sentences—somtimes too harsh but, more often, too lenient—are likely; (2) the process encourages defendants to surrender their constitutional rights; (3) prosecutors exert too much power in negotiating guilty pleas; (4) the process is private and encourages "shady" deals not available to all defendants; (5) innocent defendants might feel coerced to plead guilty because they fear the more severe consequences of being convicted by a jury.

Data on these contentions are limited, but what evidence exists suggests that plea bargaining is not as evil as the abolitionists claim or as essential as its defenders believe. Rates of plea bargaining are surprisingly consistent across rural and urban jurisdictions as well as across understaffed and well-funded prosecutors' offices (Heumann, 1978; Silberman, 1978). After Alaska ended plea bargaining in 1975, defendants continued to plead guilty at about the same rate, court proceedings did not slow down, and a modest increase in the number of trials occurred—though not as great as had been feared (Rubinstein, Clarke, & White, 1980). On the other hand, when El Paso, Texas, abolished plea bargaining in 1975, it experienced a serious backup of cases; this occurred largely because defendants perceived no benefit of pleading in comparison to waiting for their trials in the hopes that witnesses would not be available or other weaknesses in their case would develop, making acquittal more likely (Greenberg & Ruback, 1984). The risk of innocent parties pleading guilty is uncertain; however, experimental data from college "simulators" suggest that "guilty" parties are more likely to

plea-bargain than are the "innocent" (Gregory, Mowen, & Linder, 1978). Experimental research also suggests that "defendants" (college students or prisoners asked to imagine themselves plea bargaining) prefer to participate in the bargaining process themselves and perceive it as being more fair when they do (e.g., Houlden, 1981).

Plea bargaining serves the need of the defense attorney to appear to gain something for his or her client and the need of the prosecutor to appear fair and reasonable. Both prosecutors and defense attorneys believe they are making the "punishment fit the crime" by individualizing the law to fit the circumstances of the case, and both are comfortable with a system in which most cases are resolved without a clear winner or clear loser. Experienced prosecutors and defense attorneys teach plea bargaining to the rookies in their offices, and lawyers from both sides engage in a ritual of give and take, with changing facts and personalities but with the same posturing and rationalizations. In fact, the procedures are so well known that in some cases no formal bargaining even takes place; everyone involved—prosecutor, defense attorney, defendant, and judge—knows the prevailing "rate" for a given crime, and, if the defendant pleads guilty to that crime, the rate is the price that will be paid.

Defense attorneys appeal to prosecutors' inclination to bargain through two approaches. First, they try to offer something of benefit to the prosecutor, enhancing the value of the benefit as much as possible without misstating facts. Benefits for prosecutors have already been described, but one constant advantage of guilty pleas is that they eliminate the uncertainty of trials (a benefit whenever the prosecutor believes an acquittal is possible because of weak evidence). The second strategy is to offer the prosecutor the chance to "do the right thing" for a client who deserves a break. The duty of prosecutors is to "seek justice, not merely to convict" (ABA Standards for Criminal Justice, 1978, 3-1.1). Many prosecutors are open to alternatives to incarceration and will look for opportunities to mitigate the harshness of punishments that could be imposed if a defendant stood trial and was convicted. Community service and compensation to victims are attractive dispositions, particularly when related meaningfully to the offense. When the crime results from mental illness, supervised probation coupled with therapy for the offender can be an appropriate resolution.

Of course, there is a "dark side" to plea bargaining when dispositions are not commensurate with the gravity of the offense. When these "errors" are in the direction of sentencing leniency, they often are attributed to a perceived overload in the prosecutor's office or the courts. It is wrong for a defendant to be able to plead to a greatly reduced charge simply because the criminal justice system lacks the resources to handle the case. However, the answer to problems of unwarranted leniency is not the abolition of plea bargaining; rather, adequate funding must be provided for the court system as well as for the correctional system so that, when severe penalties are necessary, severe penalties can be given. In the long run, if plea bargaining serves primarily as a method for balancing the underfunded budgets of our courts and correctional systems, it will cease to be a bargain in the larger sense and will become, instead, too great a price for our society to pay.

Ethical Issues in Plea Bargaining

Plea bargaining may work against the long-range goal of achieving justice. When some lawbreakers bargain a guilty plea, the agreement may permit other lawbreakers to escape prosecution.

Sidney Biddle Barrows, a 33-year-old New York socialite, was arrested on charges of running a 20-woman prostitution ring from a brownstone house on Manhattan's Upper West Side. In mid-1985 she pleaded guilty to promoting prostitution. Her penalty: a $5000 fine and no prison sentence. As a result of the plea bargain, she was not required to reveal the names of the 3000 clients of her "escort service." If, in fact, Barrows was operating a house of prostitution, her customers were breaking the law too.

Plea bargaining also may prevent the families of victims from seeing the defendants "get justice" or hearing them acknowledge full responsibility for their offenses. In the so-called Preppie Murder Case, Robert Chambers agreed to plead guilty to a lesser charge of manslaughter *while the jury was deliberating* whether to convict him of the 1986 murder of Jennifer Levin (Taubman, 1988). The family of Ms. Levin was not consulted, although ordinarily the victim or his or her family has a say in plea bargaining.

Another problem in plea bargaining involves the use of criminals as prosecution witnesses, which occurs when lawbreakers turn state's evidence to avoid prosecution or to reduce their own penalties. The following example illustrates this controversy.

On September 21, 1976, Orlando Letelier and a companion were killed by a bomb that had been planted under their car. Letelier was a former Chilean diplomat, exiled from Chile; his car was boobytrapped, and he was murdered as he drove to work from his home on Embassy Row in Washington, DC. This monstrous crime was planned by agents of the Chilean DINA (Chile's equivalent of the CIA) and a U.S. citizen, Michael Townley, and carried out by Cuban exiles.

Townley was permitted to plead guilty to a single count of conspiracy to murder a foreign official. Even though his involvement in the murders was probably more serious than that of the actual assassins, the U.S. government placed him in the role not of defendant but of star witness (Dinges & Landau, 1980, p. 346). Townley's testifying as a prosecution witness was tied to an apparent agreement between the Chilean and U.S. governments that served to shield the Chilean government and the DINA from exposure and blame—a kind of plea bargaining between *nations.*

During the trial of the assassins, Townley refused to answer questions about the internal workings of the DINA and about other crimes he had allegedly committed in its service. His refusal was sanctioned by the *prosecuting* attorney, who passionately supported him and defended the right of the DINA to remain a secret operation. The judge even scolded the prosecutor, saying "It sounds like you are representing Mr. Townley" (Dinges & Landau, 1980). (In actuality, the prosecution had even given Townley access to its office and phone.)

In accordance with the plea bargain signed more than a year before, Townley, in exchange for his testimony, was sentenced to ten years in prison, with credit given for his time already served (Freed & Landis, 1980). Under the federal witness protection program, he received a new identity and was confined in an undisclosed medium-security prison.

The trial of the Letelier assassins may not be a representative example of the dangers of plea bargaining. But it illustrates the pervasiveness of the practice, even with respect to relationships between nations.

PRETRIAL PUBLICITY: CHANGE OF VENUE AND OTHER REMEDIES

Two cherished rights guaranteed by the U.S. Constitution are freedom of speech (the First Amendment) and the right to a speedy, public trial before an impartial jury (the Sixth Amendment). The right to free speech applies to the written as well as the spoken word. It also applies to the institution of the press, not just to individuals. The press is expected to be the government's watchdog, a role encouraged by constitutional protection. The right to an impartial jury and a fair trial is also a fundamental expectation of Americans. The fairness of our adversarial system of justice rests in large part on the decision making of an unbiased group of jurors.

In the vast majority of cases, the liberties ensured by the First and Sixth Amendments are compatible and even complementary. The press informs the public about criminal investigations and trials, and the public not only learns the outcomes of these proceedings but often gains increased appreciation for both the justness and the foibles of our system of justice.

For a few trials, however, the First and Sixth Amendments clash. The press publishes information that, when disseminated among the public, threatens a defendant's right to a trial by impartial jurors. These problem cases can involve defendants and/or victims who, because of their fame or infamous acts, gain a national reputation. The trials of Wayne Williams, William Kennedy Smith, John Hinckley, and Mike Tyson are examples. A more common problem occurs when local media release incriminating information about a defendant that is later ruled inadmissible at trial. Once made public, this information can bias opinion about the defendant. Examples include publication of details about a prior criminal record, a confession made by the accused, or unfavorable statements regarding the defendant's character. In general, local news coverage of trials exerts a greater impact in small towns than in large cities because in small towns a larger percentage of the population knows the parties; also, serious crimes occur less frequently in smaller towns, thereby increasing attention and rumor when they do occur.

In cases with extensive pretrial publicity, the courts must answer two basic questions. First, does the publicity threaten the fairness of a defendant's trial? Second, if the answer to this question is yes, what steps should be taken to remedy the situation? Psychologists have conducted research on both queries and can offer guidance to judges who are willing to listen.

Court Decisions on Pretrial Publicity

The history of the "free press/fair trial" controversy divides into three phases, differing in the ways the courts assessed pretrial publicity and the steps they favored to remedy any prejudice that was created (Loh, 1984). Phase One began with the famous trial in 1807 of Aaron Burr, third vice president of the United States, who was charged with treason. Burr claimed that he could not get a fair trial because inflammatory newspaper articles had prejudiced the public against him. Chief Justice Marshall ruled that the law did not require a jury "without any prepossessions whatever respecting the guilt or innocence of the accused" and that finding such a jury would be impossible anyway. However, the Court did consider "those who have deliberately formed and delivered an opinion on the guilt of the prisoner as not being in a state of mind to fairly weigh the testimony, and therefore as being disqualified to serve as jurors in the case" (*United States* v. *Burr*, 1807). In Phase One, the question of pretrial publicity was evaluated in terms of the effects jurors reported it to have on their minds.

In Phase Two, the Supreme Court began to question whether jurors' own assurances of impartiality in the face of massive amounts of prejudicial publicity constituted a sufficient protection for defendants subjected to this publicity. *Irvin* v. *Dowd* (1961) was the first case in which the U.S. Supreme Court struck down a state conviction on the ground of prejudicial pretrial publicity. In this case, six murders had been committed around Evansville, Indiana, between December 1954 and March 1955. The defendant, Leslie Irvin, was arrested on April 8, 1955. Shortly thereafter the prosecutor and local police issued extensively publicized press releases saying that Irvin had confessed to the present crimes as well as to 24 other burglaries; that he had been previously convicted of arson, burglary, and AWOL charges; and that he was a parole violator, a bad-check artist, and a remorseless and conscienceless person. Irvin's attorney obtained a change of venue to adjoining Gibson County, which was found to be saturated by the same publicity that tainted the original venue. He petitioned to have the trial moved again, but this motion was denied. At Irvin's trial, 430 prospective jurors were examined; 268 were excused because they were convinced of Irvin's guilt. Eight members of the jury that was seated admitted that they thought he was guilty prior to his trial. At the trial Irvin was convicted of murder and sentenced to death.

Following *Irvin*, the Supreme Court considered several cases in which defendants claimed that their right to an impartial jury had been destroyed by inflammatory pretrial publicity. In *Murphy* v. *Florida* (1965), the defendant was the well-known "Murph the Surf," who contended that widespread news accounts of his prior conviction denied him a fair trial. The Court held that jurors need not be totally ignorant of a defendant's past, especially if the jurors swear that such knowledge would not interfere with their impartiality in deciding the case; consequently, Murphy's conviction was upheld.

On the other hand, exposure to news that includes information strongly pointing to the defendant's guilt in the case at trial has been found to violate due process, regardless of jurors' assurances of their fairness. In *Rideau* v. *Louisiana* (1963), a local TV station broadcast at three different times a 20-minute clip of Rideau, surrounded by law enforcement officials, confessing in detail to charges of robbery, kidnapping, and murder. A request for a change of venue was denied, and Rideau was convicted and sentenced to death by a jury, of which at least three members had seen the televised confession. The Supreme Court reversed this decision.

In *Sheppard* v. *Maxwell* (1966), the Court reviewed the famous trial of Dr. Sam Sheppard, a prominent Cleveland physician charged with the murder of his wife. News coverage of this trial was unrestrained and turned the proceeding into a media carnival. The Court overturned Sheppard's conviction, concluding that "where there is a reasonable likelihood that prejudicial news prior to a trial will prevent a fair trial, the judge should continue the case until the threat abates, or transfer it to another county not so permeated with publicity" (p. 363). The Court also discussed several options to prevent a trial where "bedlam reigned at the courthouse." This attention to remedies for adverse publicity heralded the beginning of Phase Three.

Phase Three, spanning the 1970s and 1980s, was concerned with various preventive or remedial techniques for adverse pretrial publicity. It is important to recognize, at the outset, that some of these methods will almost certainly be rejected by the courts. One such measure is for a judge to order the press not to publish pretrial information likely to be prejudicial, a procedure known as "prior restraint," or "gag rule." The leading case is *Nebraska Press Association* v. *Stuart* (1976), in which the Supreme Court ruled that a trial judge could not order the press to not publish information likely to be prejudicial to a defendant unless it could be shown that a fair trial would be denied the defendant without

such prior restraint. The Court has yet to encounter such a showing in any trial.

Likewise, the press cannot be barred from attending and reporting a trial, because the First Amendment guarantees public access to criminal trials (*Richmond Newspapers, Inc.* v. *Virginia*, 1980). However, the press can be excluded from pretrial hearings in which potentially prejudicial material may be at issue (*Gannett Co.* v. *DePasquale*, 1979). The press can also volunteer to put off publishing incriminating information, and responsible members of the media often will limit their disclosures, especially when the police are investigating possible suspects in unsolved crimes.

We would prefer that the history of the free press/fair trial debate end with Loh's Phase Three. Such is not the case, however. There is a Phase Four, initiated by the 1984 Supreme Court case of *Patton* v. *Yount*. The *Patton* case represents a return to the standards of *Burr*—or even something less than this standard.

In 1966 Jon Yount confessed that he had killed Pam Rimer, an 18-year-old Pennsylvania high school student. His confession was published in two local papers and was admitted into evidence at Yount's trial, where, despite his plea of temporary insanity, he was convicted. However, his conviction was overturned because his confession had been obtained in violation of *Miranda*. A second trial was held in the same county in 1970. Yount moved for a change of venue because of the continuing publicity about the case, including his confession, which was not going to be admissible at the second trial. The motion for a change of venue was denied. Of 163 prospective jurors questioned, all but two said they had heard about the case, and 77% admitted they had an opinion about Yount's guilt. Eight of the final jurors acknowledged having at some time formed an opinion as to Yount's guilt. Yount did not testify at the second trial; nor did he claim insanity.

The jury convicted him of murder and sentenced him to life imprisonment.

Yount appealed, claiming that he was not tried by an impartial jury because the publicity had made a fair trial impossible in the venue county. Nonetheless, by a 5–2 majority, the Supreme Court held that the passage of time between the two trials had cured the prejudice that existed at the first trial and that there was not a "wave of public passion" that made a fair trial unlikely by the second jury. In addition, the Court reasoned that a "presumption of correctness" should be given to the trial judge's opinion on this matter because, being present at the trial, he was in a better position to evaluate the demeanor, the credibility, and, ultimately, the competence of prospective jurors. Unless the record shows that the judge made a "manifest error," reviewing courts should defer to the trial judge.

From a psychological standpoint, real deficiencies exist in this decision. The Court trusted the passage of time to erase bad memories. It speaks of time as "softening or effacing opinion." As a matter of fact, remembering and forgetting are enormously complex phenomena that depend on several factors, including how well new information is integrated with old knowledge, what new learning takes place in intervening periods of time, what type of contexts surrounded the initial learning and later retrieval, what emotional state a subject was in when the material was originally learned, what state the subject is in at the time of attempted recall, and what type of material is to be remembered (facts, attitudes, sensations, or feelings). Time can dull a memory. Time can also enlarge it until a person "remembers" more than he or she learned in the first place. Time can enable memories to be reconstructed to fit new information, a process almost certain to work to the detriment, not the advantage, of a person being

tried for the same crime a second time. Our prior discussions of hypnotically aided recall and the vagaries of eyewitness testimony also illustrated this problem.

A second problem with this decision was the Court's willingness to accept, at face value, what jurors say about their own opinions. The problem is not that jurors lie about their beliefs (although some probably do). The issue is that there are many reasons why people might not admit the full measure of their prejudice in public. People might not recognize the extent of their biases; even if completely aware, they might not disclose them in an open courtroom before a judge who encourages them to be fair and open minded. In the case of *Mu'Min* v. *Virginia* (1991), the Supreme Court compounded this problem by holding that defendants do not have a constitutional right to ask prospective jurors about the pretrial publicity to which they have been exposed. Under such circumstances, it is difficult to know how much trust to place in jurors' assurances that they are impartial, but the Supreme Court concluded that such assurances are all that the Constitution requires. This is the reason why there are better remedies for ensuring fair trials in light of heavy pretrial publicity. (We discuss these remedies later in this chapter.)

Effects of Pretrial Publicity

Does pretrial publicity influence public opinion? Does adverse publicity produce negative opinions about defendants? If so, do these negative opinions continue despite efforts to control them?

Carroll et al. (1986) surveyed the social science research on these questions and concluded: "it is surprising that so little is known." Others (e.g., Fulero, 1987) reviewed the same evidence and concluded that "the body of research taken as a whole demonstrates an adverse effect of pretrial publicity on jurors."

Serious crimes attract extensive news coverage, typically from the prosecutor's view of the case. A number of studies have examined effects of pretrial publicity by polling samples of people exposed to varying media coverage about actual crimes. These studies, whether surveying opinions about notorious crimes (McConahay, Mullin, & Frederick, 1977; Rollings & Blascovich, 1977) or cases with only local fame (Constantini & King, 1980; Nietzel & Dillehay, 1982), consistently find that persons exposed to pretrial publicity are more likely to believe defendants are guilty before their trials and are more knowledgeable of incriminating facts that would be inadmissible at the trial. For example, prior to the rape trial of William Kennedy Smith, a number of newspapers published reports by unnamed earlier victims; the judge did not allow this information to be presented at the trial.

Carroll et al. (1986) question the significance of these studies, claiming, first, that there is no proof that preformed opinions are related to actual verdicts and, second, that it is possible that proprosecution persons simply read/watch the news more often and remember more. Their first objection is irrelevant. The law does not require bias to be translated into actual verdicts; biased persons are not qualified to serve as jurors. The second claim could be tested; but, even if true, how does a person become proprosecution in a given case? Could it be from reading and hearing news unfavorable to the defendant? In fact, when persons are asked what has most influenced their opinions about a given crime, they reliably report the leading sources to be what they read in the papers and what they discuss with other people (Nietzel & Dillehay, 1982).

Additional evidence on the harmful effects of pretrial publicity comes from "mock jury" studies. There are several such studies (see Carroll et al., 1986, for a review) in which subjects (usually college students) are first exposed (or not exposed) to some form of prejudicial publicity, shown a brief videotape or written transcript meant to simulate a trial, and then asked their opinions about a verdict. Some studies examine whether problems of pretrial publicity can be prevented by warnings to subjects not to consider it (Sue, Smith, & Gilbert, 1974), by use of voir dire (Sue, Smith, & Pedroza, 1975), by continuance of the trial to a later date (Kramer, Kerr, & Carroll, 1990), or by group deliberations (Kramer et al., 1990). Other researchers have looked at what type of pretrial information is the most harmful and discovered that reports of a confession and of a prior criminal record are the biggest problems (Hvistendahl, 1979; Tans & Chaffee, 1966).

Mock jury studies often have serious limitations. They frequently lack realism, employ methods that have little resemblance to actual court proceedings, use subjects who are often very different from jurors, and request opinions that have no real-world importance (Dillehay & Nietzel, 1980). Nonetheless, the best of these studies repeatedly find an adverse effect of pretrial publicity on subjects. Mock jury studies should not be ignored, especially when they agree with the survey evidence collected from real cases (e.g., Moran & Cutler, 1991).

We agree with Fulero (1987) that, despite some gaps and methodological weaknesses, the available research indicates to "a reasonable degree of scientific probability" that pretrial publicity adversely affects the impartiality of prospective jurors.

Remedies for the Effects of Pretrial Publicity

If pretrial publicity adversely affects juror impartiality, the next question is what procedures should be used to restore the likelihood of a fair trial for the defendant? Basically, four alternatives are available.

1. *Continuance.* The trial can be postponed until a later date with the expectation that the passage of time will lessen the effects of the prejudicial material. This view remains in vogue with the current Supreme Court. However, research indicates that, although continuances may decrease jurors' recall of factual evidence, they do not dampen jurors' recall of emotionally biasing information (Kramer et al., 1990).

2. *Expanded voir dire.* The most popular method for rooting out pretrial prejudice is to conduct a thorough voir dire (questioning) of potential jurors. Standard 8-3.5 of the American Bar Association's (1978) *Fair Trial and Free Press* recommends that, in cases in which jurors have been exposed to prejudicial publicity, an intensive, thorough questioning of each prospective juror be conducted, outside the presence of other chosen and prospective jurors. Although thorough voir dire can be a valuable protection against partiality, it may not always be adequate. Jurors may not recognize their own biases, and they can hide their true feelings from an examiner if they so choose.

3. *Imported jurors.* Prospective jurors can be imported to the venue from another county "whenever it is determined that potentially prejudicial news coverage of a given criminal matter has been intense and has been concentrated primarily in a given locality in a state . . . " (ABA, 1978). These *foreign venires* allow the trial to be conducted in the original venue but before a group of jurors presumably less affected by prejudicial material than local jurors would be.

4. *Change of venue.* A change of venue involves the most extreme remedy for pretrial prejudice. Changing venue requires that the trial be conducted in another geographical jurisdiction altogether and that the jurors for the trial be drawn from this new jurisdiction. Because venue changes are expensive, inconvenient, and time consuming, courts are reluctant to use them. Venue changes can result in significant variations in characteristics of the communities involved, as was illustrated by the change of venue from Los Angeles to Simi Valley, California, for the trial of the L.A. police officers charged with assaulting Rodney King. In the wake of the acquittal of these police officers, some jurisdictions are considering new laws that would require a judge to consider the demographic characteristics of the original venue and the proposed community to which the trial would be moved.

According to the ABA Standards:

A motion for change of venue or continuance shall be granted whenever it is determined that, because of the dissemination of potentially prejudicial material, there is a substantial likelihood that, in the absence of such relief, a fair trial by an impartial jury cannot be had. This determination may be based on such evidence as qualified public opinion surveys or opinion testimony offered by individuals, or on the court's own evaluation of the nature, frequency, and timing of the material involved. A showing of actual prejudice shall not be required [ABA, 1978, Standard 8-3.3(c)].

Psychologists can be enlisted to support a lawyer's motion for one or more of the above protections against pretrial prejudices by testifying about the psychological evidence that pertains to each one. When pretrial contamination is extensive, a professionally conducted public opinion survey is the technique of choice for evaluating the degree of prejudice in a community. Public opinion surveys gauge how many people have read or heard about a case, what they have read or heard, whether they have formed opinions, what these opinions are, and how they affect the way the case is perceived.

Change of Venue Surveys

There is a growing literature on ways to conduct venue surveys, as well as on the practical, methodological, legal, and ethical issues involved in them (Arnold & Gold, 1978–1979; Constantini & King, 1980; Hans & Vidmar, 1982; Nietzel & Dillehay, 1982; Pollock, 1977). In this section we outline the steps involved in these surveys.

1. *Planning the survey and designing the questionnaire.* Scripts for the survey questionnaires are written for telephone interviews, which usually take about 15 minutes to complete. The content is based on an analysis of the media to which the community has been exposed, and the wording of the survey questions is aligned with the key words and phrases used repeatedly in the media.

2. *Training the interviewers.* The persons who conduct the telephone interviews are trained to administer the questionnaire in a standardized fashion. Interviewers should be "blind" to the purpose of the survey as much as possible. Therefore the callers do not construct the questionnaire or interpret the results.

3. *Drawing the sample.* Respondents to venue surveys must be drawn at random for the results to be valid. Usually persons are surveyed in at least two jurisdictions—the original venue county and at least one other "comparison" county. Data about the differences between the surveyed counties are then presented to show the relative levels and effects of pretrial influence in the different jurisdictions.

4. *Presenting the results.* Survey results are presented in one of two ways. The expert can prepare an *affidavit*, which is a written report sworn to be truthful. A stronger presentation results when the expert testifies about the design, results, and meaning of the survey at a change-of-venue hearing. Such testimony is subject to cross-examination by the opposing side.

Public opinion surveys are time consuming, hectic activities that often demand more resources than the typical client can afford. However, they usually yield valuable information. Obtaining a change of venue for a highly publicized case is probably the most effective procedure available for improving the chances for a fair trial. Moreover, even if the venue is not changed, the results of the survey can often be used to assist the defense in jury selection. Because of the multiple purposes for which they can be used, public opinion surveys are a popular tool among litigation consultants. We discuss some of these additional uses in the next chapter.

SUMMARY

The following steps take place between arrest and trial:

1. An initial appearance, at which defendants are informed of the charges, of their constitutional rights, and of future proceedings.

2. A preliminary hearing, in which the judge determines whether there is enough evidence to hold the defendant for processing by the grand jury. This hearing can result in anything from dismissal of the charges to a decision to bind the defendant over to the grand jury. In the latter case, the judge must decide whether to set bail.

3. Action by the grand jury, which decides whether there is sufficient evidence for the defendant to be tried; if so, it provides an indictment, or statement of accusations.

4. An arraignment, involving a formal statement of charges. and an initial plea by the defendant to these charges.

5. A process of discovery, requiring that the prosecutor reveal to the defense certain evidence, and pretrial motions, or attempts by both sides to win favorable ground rules for the subsequent trial.
6. A trial to determine guilt or innocence.

In determining whether to release a defendant between the indictment and the trial, the judge is supposed to consider the risk that the defendant will not show up for his or her trial. Many citizens believe that dangerousness of the defendant should be another consideration. The Supreme Court has upheld legislation authorizing preventive detention.

If defendants cannot provide the money for their bail, they are kept in jail until the trial. Bail can discriminate against poor defendants; it has been found that those who are detained in jail are more likely to be found guilty and to receive higher sentences than those who can afford bail, even when the seriousness of their charges and the evidence against them are the same. Pretrial detention violates the spirit of our legal system—that a person is innocent until proven guilty.

A simulation study of the determinants of the amount of bail, using fictitious materials but real judges as subjects, found that judges were influenced the most by the degree to which defendants were tied to the local area and by whether they had a previous criminal record. But, in observing judges' bail setting in actual cases, the researchers concluded that the district attorney's recommendation was the single strongest predictor.

The grand jury theoretically operates to shield citizens from unwarranted prosecutions, but it sometimes risks being a rubber stamp for prosecutors who seek community endorsement for their recommendations. Many questionable procedures are allowed in the operation of the grand jury.

Plea bargaining is an excellent example of the conflict between truth and conflict resolution as goals of our legal system. At least 80% of criminal cases end between arrest and trial with the defendant pleading guilty to some (often reduced) charges. Prosecutors claim that the system would break down if all cases went to trial. In one jurisdiction that abolished plea bargaining (El Paso, Texas), the delays did become intolerable, although in another jurisdiction (Alaska) the processing of court cases actually speeded up.

Plea bargaining poses risks for both defendants and prosecutors. Defendants accept some penalty and give up the chance that, after a trial, they might be acquitted of all charges. Prosecutors want to "win," but they realize that frequent plea bargains allow their prosecution skills to deteriorate.

The rights to a free press and a fair trial are usually complementary, but some criminal trials generate extensive publicity to the point that the defendant's right to an impartial jury is jeopardized. Psychologists have studied the effects of pretrial publicity on potential fact finders and have also evaluated different mechanisms for curbing or curing the negative effects of pretrial publicity.

11
Competence in the Legal System

The question of a defendant's *competence* is the psychological issue most frequently addressed in the criminal justice system. Concerns about a defendant's competence are tied to one fundamental principle: criminal proceedings should not continue against a person who is not able to understand their nature and purpose. This rule holds at every stage of the criminal justice process, but it is most often applied at pretrial hearings concerned with two topics: competence to plead guilty and competence to stand trial.

What does the law mean by "competence"? Why is it an important doctrine in our system?

Competent defendants must have the ability to understand the charges and the proceedings against them so that they can participate in these proceedings in a meaningful way. Because competence refers to an understanding of legal proceedings, it follows that the criteria for competence differ depending on the proceeding to be understood. For example, Box 11-1 describes several different competencies that mental health experts are asked to evaluate in defendants. Different questions are involved in these evaluations because the requirements of the different tasks facing defendants vary. (Of course, several questions

---

Box **11-1** | *Other Competencies*

Because questions about competence can be raised at any point in the criminal justice process, there are several other competencies (besides competence to plead guilty and competence to stand trial) that address a defendant's capacity to participate knowingly in different functions. Competence for any legal function involves: (1) determining what functional abilities are necessary; (2) assessing the context in which these abilities must be demonstrated; (3) evaluating the implications of any deficiencies in the abilities that are required in particular contexts; and (4) deciding whether the deficiencies warrant a conclusion of incompetence (Grisso, 1986).

Here are some types of competencies that mental health professionals might be asked to evaluate (this material is discussed extensively in Melton et al., 1987, Chapter 5):

1. *Competence to confess.* Discussed previously in Chapter 8, competence to confess requires that defendants, once in custody of the police, make a confession only after having waived their *Miranda* rights—knowingly, intelligently, and voluntarily. A mental health professional's assessment of this ability is difficult because, in most cases, the waiver and confession occur months before the professional's evaluation, requiring many assumptions about the defendant's psychological condition at the time. As a result of these difficulties, professional evaluations of competence to confess are given less weight than evidence about the police methods used to obtain the confession.

A special topic for research has been whether young defendants or defendants in general are able to understand the *Miranda* warnings and appreciate their meaning.

(This theme will be discussed in more detail when we consider the competence of children and adolescents.)

2. *Competence to waive the right to an attorney.* Can defendants decide they do not want a lawyer to represent them at trial? The Supreme Court has held that defendants have a constitutional right to waive counsel and represent themselves at trial, providing that this decision is made competently (*Feretta* v. *California*, 1975). The standard for this competence is that the defendant waives the right to counsel with understanding and while voluntarily exercising informed free will. Defendants do not have to convince the court that they possess a high level of legal knowledge, although some knowledge of this type is probably essential. Melton et al. (1987) recommend that the evaluation for this competence "should proceed as in

about competencies arise in civil law; we discuss these in later chapters.)

The law requires defendants to be competent for several reasons (Melton, Petrila, Poythress, & Slobogin, 1987). First, legal proceedings are more likely to arrive at accurate results with the participation of competent defendants. Second, punishment of convicted defendants is morally acceptable only if these defendants understand the basis for their punishment. Finally, the perceived fairness of our adversary system of justice requires participation by defendants who have the capacity to defend themselves against the charges of the state. As Grisso and Siegel (1986) observed,

"there is no honor in entering a battle in full armor with the intention of striking down an adversary who is without shield or sword" (p. 146).

COMPETENCE TO PLEAD GUILTY

When defendants plead guilty, they waive several important constitutional rights—the right to a jury trial, the right to confront their accusers, the right to call favorable witnesses, and the right to remain silent. The Supreme Court has

an evaluation of competency to stand trial, with special emphasis on the functions that legal counsel performs" (p. 100).

3. *Competence to refuse the insanity defense.* In cases in which there is a likelihood that the defendant was insane at the time of the offense, can the defendant refuse to plead insanity? If there is evidence that a defendant was not mentally responsible for criminal acts, do courts have a duty to require the defendant to plead insanity when he or she does not want to do so? The courts are divided on this question. In some cases they have suggested that society's goal of punishing only mentally responsible persons requires the imposition of an insanity plea even on unwilling defendants (*Whalen v. United States*, 1965). Other decisions (*Frendak v. United States*, 1979) approach this question within the general framework of

competency; if the defendant understands the alternative pleas available and the consequences of those pleas, he or she should be permitted to reject an insanity plea. This latter approach recognizes that an acquittal on grounds of insanity is not always a "better" outcome for a defendant than a conviction and criminal sentence.

4. *Competence to be sentenced and punished.* For legal and humanitarian reasons, convicted defendants are not to be sentenced to punishment unless they are competent. In general, the standard for this competence is that the defendant can understand the punishment being imposed and the reasons it is being imposed. It is a more straightforward question for the clinician to evaluate than competence to plead guilty or stand trial, which involves more complex issues of interaction with counsel and appreciation of alternative

courses of action.

The most controversial aspect of this question is determining whether a defendant is competent to be executed. The U.S. Supreme Court decided, in the case of *Ford v. Wainwright* (1986), that the Eighth Amendment ban against cruel and unusual punishments prohibits the execution of defendants while they are incompetent. Therefore, mental health professionals will at times be called upon to evaluate inmates waiting to be executed to determine whether they are competent to be put to death. The ethical dilemmas involved in these evaluations are enormous and are discussed in a rapidly growing literature (Heilbrun, 1987; Mossman, 1987; Susman, 1992). We will consider this problem at greater length in Chapter 18.

held that a waiver of such important rights must be "knowing, intelligent, and voluntary" (*Johnson v. Zerbst*, 1938), and trial judges are required to question defendants about their plea in order to establish clearly that these defendants understand that they are waiving their constitutional rights by pleading guilty. The concept of a "knowing, intelligent, and voluntary" guilty plea also involves an understanding of the charges and the possible penalties that can be imposed and requires the judge to examine any plea bargain to ensure that the plea is "voluntary" in the sense that it represents a considered choice among constitutionally permissible alternatives. For example, although prosecutors can offer a lighter sentence to a defendant in exchange for a guilty plea, they cannot offer money to the defendant to encourage a guilty plea.

The accepted test for one's *competence to stand trial* is a "sufficient present ability to consult with his attorney with a reasonable degree of rational understanding, and . . . a rational, as well as factual understanding of the proceedings against him" (*Dusky v. United States*, 1960). Logically, *competence to plead guilty* requires an understanding of the alternatives the defendant faces and an ability to make a reasoned choice among them. *Such a capacity, theoretically at least, is more exacting than competence to stand trial.* Defendants standing trial need only be aware of the nature of the proceedings and be able to cooperate with counsel in order to present the defense. Defendants pleading guilty, on the other hand, must understand the possible consequences of pleading guilty instead of going to trial and be able to make a rational choice between the alternatives.

Although several courts have recognized the difference between competence to stand trial and competence to plead guilty (*United States v. Masthers*, 1976), the majority use the *Dusky* standard (cited above) for both competencies.

There are two reasons for this tendency. First, a separate standard for competence to plead guilty cuts too fine by requiring distinctions between types of legal understanding that are difficult for mental health professionals to make. Second, a separate standard could create the difficult situation of having a class of defendants who are competent to stand trial but incompetent to plead guilty and who thereby could not participate in the possibly advantageous plea-bargaining process.

The American Bar Association's (1989) position on this question, as stated in the ABA Criminal Justice Mental Health Standards (Box 11-2), reflects a compromise between those who say that the tests for competence to stand trial and competence to plead guilty are the same, and those who would require a separate finding of competence to plead guilty. Criminal Justice Mental Health Standard 7-5.1 (ABA, 1989) provides:

a. No plea of guilty or nolo contendere should be accepted from a defendant who is mentally incompetent to enter a plea of guilty.

  I. Ordinarily, absent additional information bearing on defendant's competence, a finding made that the defendant is competent to stand trial should be sufficient to establish the defendant's competence to plead guilty.

  II. The test for determining mental competence to plead guilty should be whether the defendant has sufficient present ability to consult with the defendant's lawyer with a reasonable degree of rational understanding and whether, given the nature and complexity of the charges and the potential consequences of a conviction, the defendant has a rational as well as factual understanding of the proceedings relating to entry of a plea of guilty.

Although this latter test is different from the test to stand trial, ordinarily a judge could rely on a finding that a defendant is competent to stand trial and would not routinely order a second competency examination before accepting a guilty plea.

| Box **11-2** | *The American Bar Association Standards for Criminal Justice* |

In 1963 the American Bar Association began the ambitious task of formulating guidelines for the administration of criminal justice. Committees were formed to address specific functions (for example, the role of the prosecutor, jury trials), and the committee reports were sent to the House of Delegates of the American Bar Association for approval. The first ten reports were approved in 1968, three more in 1970, two in 1971, and one each in 1972 and 1973, with approval of the final report completing work on the first edition. The 17 reports became the 17 chapters of the ABA Standards, with each chapter following the same format: "standards" (guidelines), followed by explanatory text. A standing committee was appointed to monitor developments and recommend changes.

In 1976 the standing committee was authorized to begin work on a second edition, and the revised edition was released and approved in 1978 and 1979. A lengthy chapter on mental health (insanity, competency, etc.) was added in 1984, and the standing committee has continued to supplement existing chapters.

The ABA Standards are not intended to serve as rules but rather as guidelines for those involved in the administration of criminal justice. There are over 500 approved standards, covering almost every aspect of the criminal justice system. The Standards provide guidance on subjects as diverse as political activity of police officers (Standard 1-6.2) and note taking by jurors (15-3.2).

Although the Standards are not designed to be adopted as a set of rules, they are influential in shaping rules made by courts and legislatures. According to the introduction to the second edition of the Standards, as of 1979 the Standards had been cited by the appellate courts of the United States over 7500 times, and at least 36 states had used the Standards in overhauling their criminal codes. The relatively new (1989) Mental Health Standards, which we refer to repeatedly throughout this and later chapters, hold great potential for improving the way in which the criminal justice system deals with problems of mental illness and retardation.

In commenting on the Standards, then Chief Justice Warren Burger said in 1974 that:

The Standards are a balanced, practical work intended to walk the fine line between the protection of society and the protection of the constitutional rights of the accused individual. Taken as a whole, they can be utilized by the various states and the federal system to elevate criminal justice to a new level—one that is reasonable, workable, and above all fair. They are valuable tools to undertake the massive task of overhauling the entire criminal justice system. They need not be accepted on an "all or nothing" basis but may be used as a resource for improvement.

The Standards are not "minimum" standards (that adjective was dropped in 1969) but aspirational, with no deference to the baser aspects of the criminal justice system. The Standards do not "allow" police to harass, prosecutors to pursue publicity, defense lawyers to cut corners, or mental health specialists to shade their testimony. We believe the Standards have exerted a positive effect on the evolution of criminal justice in the United States.

The Standards also require prosecutors and defense attorneys to alert the court if they have information that bears on the defendant's competence to plead. Imposing this requirement on defense attorneys may work to the defendant's detriment, but the Standards reason that attorneys have an obligation of candor to the court that overrides loyalty to the client. Thus, lawyers must inform a trial judge that their clients may lack the competence to plead guilty, even though the client does not want to raise the issue and even though a lengthy period of incarceration could result from a competency evaluation. This principle has been invoked to censure a defense attorney who hid evidence of his client's mental illness because neither the client nor the lawyer wanted a competency evaluation (*State v. Johnson*, 1986).

In evaluating competence to plead guilty, the mental health professional should focus on several topics, such as the nature of the existing criminal charges, the defendant's reasons for wanting to plead guilty, his or her understanding of the charges and any possible defenses, and his or her understanding of the possible outcomes of going to trial and of relinquishing specific rights by pleading guilty. If the evaluator believes the defendant is competent, this opinion and the reasons for it will be stated in a written report. If the evaluator believes the defendant is incompetent to plead, the report should also discuss possible treatments that might render the defendant competent to plead.

The evaluator's report should be not be changed at the request of an attorney, although it may be supplemented in response to questions or comments from an attorney. In the real world of the criminal justice system, attempts by attorneys to influence the content, style, or conclusions of these reports are not uncommon.

COMPETENCE TO STAND TRIAL

Jamie Sullivan was a 24-year-old grocery clerk charged with arson, burglary, and murder in connection with a fire he had set at a small grocery store in Kentucky. The evidence in the case indicated that, after closing hours, Sullivan had returned to the IGA store where he worked and forced the night manager, Ricky Ford, to open the safe and hand over the $800 in cash left in the safe. Sullivan then locked Ford in a small back-room office, doused the room in gasoline, and set the store on fire. Ford was killed in the blaze. Police arrested Sullivan within hours at his grandmother's apartment on the basis of a lead from a motorist who saw him running away from the scene. If convicted on all charges, Sullivan faced the possibility of a death sentence.

Jamie Sullivan was mentally retarded. He had dropped out of school in the eighth grade, and a psychologist's evaluation of him at that time reported his IQ to be 68. He could read and write his name and a few simple phrases, but nothing more. He had a history of drug abuse and had spent several months in a juvenile correctional camp at the age of 15 after he had vandalized five homes in his neighborhood. The Army refused his attempt to volunteer for service because of his limited intelligence and his drug habit. His attorney believed that Sullivan's mental problems might render him incompetent to stand trial and therefore asked a psychologist to evaluate him. After interviewing and testing Sullivan and reviewing the evidence the police had collected on the case, the psychologist found the following: Sullivan's current IQ was 65, which fell in the mentally retarded range; he did not appear to suffer any hallucinations or delusions, but he expressed strong religious beliefs that "God watches over his children and won't let nothing happen to them." The psychologist asked Sullivan a series of questions about his upcoming trial:

Q: What are you charged with?
A: Burning down that store and stealing from Ricky.
Q: Anything else?
A: They say I killed Ricky too.
Q: What could happen to you if a jury found you guilty?
A: Electric chair, but God will watch over me.
Q: What does the judge do at a trial?
A: He tells everybody what to do.
Q: If somebody told a lie about you in court, what would you do?
A: Get mad at him.
Q: Anything else?
A: Tell my lawyer the truth.
Q: What does your lawyer do if you have a trial?
A: Show the jury I'm innocent.
Q: How could he do that best?
A: Ask questions and have me tell them I wouldn't hurt Ricky. I liked Ricky.
Q: What does the prosecutor do in your trial?
A: Try to get me found guilty.
Q: Who decides if you are guilty or not?
A: That jury.

At a hearing to determine whether Jamie Sullivan was competent to stand trial, the psychologist testified that Sullivan was mentally retarded and that, as a result, his understanding of the proceedings was not as thorough as it might otherwise be. However, the psychologist also testified that Sullivan did understand the charges against him as well as the general purpose and nature of his trial. The judge ruled that Jamie Sullivan was competent to stand trial. A jury convicted him on all the charges

and sentenced him to life in prison rather than to death by execution.

It is estimated that, much like Jamie Sullivan, as many as 25,000 defendants are evaluated annually to determine their competence to stand trial (Steadman, Monahan, Hartstone, Davis, & Robbins, 1982). Of the almost 32,000 mentally disordered offenders committed to nonfederal hospitals in 1980, the largest category—almost 58% of those admitted—consisted of defendants being evaluated or already judged incompetent to stand trial (IST) (Steadman, Rosenstein, MacAskill, & Manderscheid, 1988).

As we have already discussed, the standard for competence to stand trial was defined by the U.S. Supreme Court in *Dusky* v. *United States* (1960) as: "whether (the defendant) has sufficient present ability to consult with his lawyer with a reasonable degree of rational understanding—and whether he has a rational as well as factual understanding of the proceedings against him." With some minor modifications, this standard is used in all American courts. It establishes the central criterion of competence as the capacity to know or do the things that a trial requires of a defendant. The criterion refers to *present* abilities rather than the psychological state of the defendant at the time of the alleged offense, which is the focus for evaluations of a defendant's sanity (see Chapter 16).

A problem with the *Dusky* standard is that it does not specify *how* the evaluator judges the sufficiency of rational understanding, ability to consult, or factual understanding when making a competency decision. A number of courts and mental health groups have tried to "put some meat on *Dusky*'s bones" by listing more specific criteria related to competency. For example, the Florida Rules of Criminal Procedure require consideration of the following 11 factors:

1. Defendant's appreciation of the charges.
2. Defendant's appreciation of the nature and range of penalties.
3. Defendant's understanding of the adversary nature of the legal process.
4. Defendant's capacity to disclose to attorney pertinent facts surrounding the alleged offense.
5. Defendant's ability to relate to attorney.
6. Defendant's ability to assist attorney in planning defense.
7. Defendant's capacity to realistically challenge prosecution witnesses.
8. Defendant's ability to manifest appropriate courtroom behavior.
9. Defendant's capacity to testify relevantly.
10. Defendant's motivation to help himself in the legal process.
11. Defendant's capacity to cope with the stress of incarceration prior to trial.

Raising the Issue of Competence

The question of a defendant's competence can be raised at any point in the criminal process, and it can be raised by the prosecutor, the defense attorney, or the presiding judge. The issue is typically raised before trial by the defense attorney, although it was common, prior to the 1970s, for prosecutors to question a defendant's competence, because up until that time it was not unusual for defendants found incompetent to be confined in mental hospitals for excessive periods of time. (Sometimes such confinements were even longer than their sentences would have been had they stood trial and been convicted.) However, this practice was stopped, *at least in theory*, in 1972, when the U.S. Supreme Court decided the case of *Jackson* v. *Indiana*. In this decision the Court held that defendants committed because they were IST could not be held "more than a reasonable period of time necessary to determine whether there is a substantial probability that (they) will attain that capacity in the foreseeable future." As a result of the *Jackson* decision, most states revised their procedures to limit the length of time a defendant found incompetent could be confined; however, a number of states still permit indefinite periods of commitment for incompetent defendants (Roesch & Golding, 1987).

Once the question of incompetence is raised, the judge is obligated to order an evaluation of the defendant if a "bona fide doubt" exists that the defendant is competent. The circumstances of each case and the behavior of each defendant are considered when judges make this determination. However, any time the question of competence is raised, an examination will usually be conducted. As Melton et al. (1987) suggest, because it is relatively easy to obtain such evaluations, attorneys seek them for reasons other than a determination of competence, such as to discover information about a possible insanity defense, to bring about the lengthy incarceration of a potentially dangerous person without going through the more cumbersome procedures of involuntary civil commitment (see Chapter 16), to deny bail, and to delay the trial as one side tries to gain an advantage over the other (Berman & Osborne, 1987).

The Evaluation of Competence

After a judge orders a competency examination, the defendant is typically taken to a special hospital or forensic facility for observation and examination. Most competency evaluations are conducted on an inpatient basis, despite the fact that inpatient exams are more costly, require more time, and are seldom clinically necessary compared to local, outpatient evaluations. In fact, several commentators (Melton, Weithorn, & Slobogin, 1985;

Roesch & Golding, 1987) have recommended that competency evaluations be performed on an outpatient, local basis whenever possible. Most defendants could have their competence evaluated on an outpatient basis.

In most states, physicians, psychiatrists, and, increasingly, psychologists and social workers are authorized to examine the defendant and prepare a report on their findings. Preliminary data suggest that competency evaluations by nonmedical professionals are equivalent, if not superior, to those prepared by physicians (Petrella & Poythress, 1983).

Prior to 1970 the usual evaluation of a defendant's competency involved a standard psychiatric or psychological examination consisting of assessment of current mental status, psychological testing, and social history taking. If the examiner diagnosed a serious disorder such as schizophrenia or a paranoid state, or if the defendant was seriously mentally retarded, the expert would often conclude that the defendant was IST. The problem with this approach was that it ignored the legal definition of competency as the capacity to understand and function as a defendant. Psychosis or mental retardation may or may not render a defendant IST. The crucial question is whether the psychological disorder impairs a defendant's ability to participate knowingly and meaningfully in the trial and to cooperate with the defense attorney. A psychotic defendant might be competent to stand trial in a relatively simple, straightforward case but be incompetent to participate in a complex trial that would demand more skill and understanding. As we saw in the case of Jamie Sullivan, his mental retardation did not make him incompetent, because he was able to understand the charges against him and the basic nature of his trial.

Current competency evaluations focus on the defendant's present ability to function adequately in the legal process. This focus has been aided by the development of structured assessment instruments specifically aimed at measuring competence to stand trial. Increasingly, competency examinations use one or more of three specially designed competency assessment instruments; these are described in the following paragraphs.

Competency Screening Test (CST). Developed by A. Louis McGarry, Paul Lipsitt, and their colleagues at the Harvard Laboratory of Community Psychiatry, the CST is a 22-item sentence-completion task designed as an initial screening test for incompetence (Lipsitt, Lelos, & McGarry, 1971). Because the vast majority of defendants referred for competency evaluations are later determined to be competent (Nicholson & Kugler, 1991; Roesch & Golding, 1987), an instrument that is able to quickly distinguish competency would be useful because it would save the time and expense of many unnecessary, detailed evaluations in a hospital.

In the CST, the defendant answers each of the 22 sentence stems (see Box 11-3), and each response is then scored as a 2 (a competent answer), a 1 (a questionably competent answer), or a 0 (an incompetent answer). Total scores can range from 0 to 66; generally a score of 20 or less suggests possible IST.

Despite widespread use, the CST has been criticized on several grounds. First, the scoring of the sentence completions reflects what some observers (Roesch & Golding, 1987) claim is a naively positive view of the legal process. For example, on the item "Jack felt that the judge _____," the answer "would be fair to him" would be scored a 2, whereas a response of "would screw him over" would be scored a 0. In reality, however, defendants might have encountered judges for whom the second answer was more accurate than the first; thus their answer should not be regarded as a sign of incompetence. A second difficulty is that the CST produces a large number of false positives (defendants called incompetent who, with fuller evaluations, are judged to be competent). On the one hand, a false positive is less serious than the error of mistakenly forcing to trial a defendant who is incompetent (a false negative). But too many false positives would rob the CST of its claim to be an effective screening instrument. Finally, despite evidence that interrater reliability coefficients on the CST are generally .85 or better (Lipsitt et al., 1971; Randolph, Hicks, & Mason, 1981), Melton et al.

(1987) caution that such levels of agreement between raters appear to require extensive training and experience with the instrument.

Competency Assessment Instrument (CAI). Also developed by the Harvard group, as a more in-depth instrument for assessing competence in those defendants with suggestive findings on the CST, the CAI is a structured interview, lasting about one hour, that covers 13 functions relevant to competent functioning at trial (Laboratory for Community Psychiatry, 1974; see Box 11-4). A defendant is rated on each function

---

Box 11-3 | Competency Screening Test

1. The lawyer told Bill that _____
2. When I go to court, the lawyer will _____
3. Jack felt that the judge _____
4. When Phil was accused of the crime, he _____
5. When I prepare to go to court with my lawyer _____
6. If the jury finds me guilty, I _____
7. The way a court trial is decided _____
8. When the evidence in George's case was presented to the jury _____
9. When the lawyer questioned his client in court, the client said _____
10. If Jack had to try his own case, he _____
11. Each time the DA asked me a question, I _____
12. While listening to the witnesses testify against me, I _____
13. When the witness testifying against Harry gave incorrect evidence, he _____
14. When Bob disagreed with his lawyer on his defense, he _____
15. When I was formally accused of the crime, I thought to myself _____
16. If Ed's lawyer suggests that he plead guilty, he _____
17. What concerns Fred most about his lawyer is _____
18. When they say a man is innocent until proven guilty _____
19. When I think of being sent to prison, I _____
20. When Phil thinks of what he is accused of, he _____
21. When the jury hears my case, they will _____
22. If I had a chance to speak to the judge, I _____

From Lipsitt, Lelos, and McGarry (1971).

with a score from 1 (total incapacity) to 5 (no incapacity). A specific cutoff score has not been used, although a substantial number of scores of 3 or less is cause for concern. Few studies of the reliability of the CAI have been conducted, but Roesch and Golding's (1980) study of North Carolina defendants evaluated with the CAI revealed adequate interrater agreements on the separate functions and a 90% agreement with separate decisions about competence rendered after a lengthy hospital evaluation.

Interdisciplinary Fitness Interview (IFI). Golding and Roesch's IFI is a semistructured interview that evaluates a defendant's abilities in specific legal areas (5 items). It also assesses 11 categories of psychopathological symptoms. Each area is rated from 0 to 2 in terms of the degree of capacity the defendant demonstrates. Evaluators also rate each item on the weight they attached to it in reaching their decision about competency. These weights will vary depending on the nature of the defendant's case; for example, whereas hallucinations might impair a defendant's ability to participate in some trials, they might have minor effects in others and would therefore be given slight weight. The IFI is designed to be administered jointly by a mental health professional and an attorney, although it often is administered only by a mental health professional.

Golding, Roesch, and Schreiber (1984) found that interviewers using the IFI agreed on final judgments of competency in 75 of 77 cases evaluated. These judgments agreed 76% of the time with independent decisions about competency made later at a state hospital. Although additional research on this instrument is necessary, it looks like a promising tool, particularly in "close-call" cases.

Other specialized competency tests are available (Nicholson, Robertson, Johnson, & Jensen, 1988; Wildman et al., 1978), but their use is not widespread. Moreover, most evaluations that use a specialized instrument also include the CST, CAI, IFI, or some local variation of one of them.

Following the collection of assessment data, evaluators communicate their findings to the judge. Often a written report is submitted that summarizes the evidence pertaining to IST as well as the likelihood of restored competence through appropriate treatment. In more controversial or strongly contested cases, like the Jamie Sullivan trial, a formal competency hearing might be held at which the experts will testify and be questioned by attorneys from both sides. The proper content of such testimony and of written reports is a hotly debated topic. Some (Morse, 1978) believe that experts should restrict their comments to a description of the referral questions and the techniques used to answer these questions, followed by a thorough summary of the findings and a discussion of the defendant's mental difficulties and the possible consequences of these impairments. This camp also contends that the expert should not offer an opinion on the ultimate question of whether the defendant is IST, because it is the court's responsibility to make that legal decision. On the other hand, many courts require the expert to state just such a conclusion, believing, along with some mental health experts, that no one is better suited for such a judgment than a qualified mental health professional (see Poythress, 1982; Rogers & Ewing, 1989).

Results of Competency Evaluations

About 70% of defendants referred for evaluation are ultimately found competent to stand trial (Nicholson & Kugler, 1991); when very rigorous examinations are conducted, the rate of defendants found competent approaches 90%. Judges seldom disagree with clinicians' decisions about competence (Steadman, 1979), and opposing attorneys often will stipulate (agree without further examination) to clinicians' findings (Melton et al., 1987). As a result, mental health professionals exert great—perhaps excessive—influence on this legal decision.

What sort of person is most often judged to be incompetent? In his study of more than 500 defendants found IST, Steadman (1979) found them often to be "marginal" men who were undereducated and deficient in job skills, with long histories of involvement in both the legal and the mental health systems (see also Williams & Miller, 1981). Problems of substance abuse were common. Minorities were overrepresented. Other researchers report relatively high percentages of psychosis and lower intelligence among IST defendants (Roesch & Golding, 1980; Nicholson, Briggs, & Robertson, 1988). One other consistent finding is that IST defendants are charged with more serious crimes than defendants in general. After an extensive review of competency research, Nicholson and Kugler (1991) described the typical defendant found IST (1) to have a history of psychosis for which previous treatment had been received; (2) to exhibit symptoms of current serious mental disorder; (3) to be single, unemployed, and poorly educated; and (4) to score poorly on the assessment instruments designed specifically to evaluate incompetence.

Box 11-4 | Competency Assessment Instrument (CAI)

1. *Appraisal of available legal defenses:* This item calls for an assessment of the accused's awareness of his possible legal defenses, and how consistent these are with the reality of his particular circumstances.
2. *Unmanageable behavior:* This item calls for an assessment of the appropriateness of the current motor and verbal behavior of the defendant, and the degree to which this behavior would disrupt the conduct of a trial. Inappropriate or disruptive behavior must arise from a substantial degree of mental illness or mental retardation.
3. *Quality of relating to attorney:* This item calls for an assessment of the interpersonal capacity of the accused to relate to the average attorney. Involved are the abilities to trust and to communicate relevantly.
4. *Planning of legal strategy including guilty pleas to lesser charges where pertinent:* This item calls for an assessment of the degree to which the accused can understand, participate, and cooperate with his counsel in planning a strategy for the defense that is consistent with the reality of his circumstances.
5. *Appraisal of role of:*
   a. Defense counsel
   b. Prosecuting attorney
   c. Judge
   d. Jury
   e. Defendant
   f. Witnesses
   This set of items calls for a minimal understanding of the adversary process by the accused. The accused should be able to identify prosecuting attorney and prosecution witnesses as foe, defense counsel as friend, the judge as neutral, and the jury as the determiners of guilt or innocence.
6. *Understanding of court procedure:* This item calls for an assessment of the degree to which the defendant understands the basic sequence of events in a trial and their import for him—e.g., the different purposes of direct and cross-examination.
7. *Appreciation of charges:* This item calls for an assessment of the accused's concrete understanding of the charges against him, and to a lesser extent the seriousness of the charges.
8. *Appreciation of range and nature of possible penalties:* This item calls for an assessment of the accused's concrete understanding and appreciation of

If a defendant referred for a competency evaluation is found competent, the legal process resumes and the defendant again faces the possibility of trial. If the defendant is found IST, the picture becomes more complicated. For crimes that are not serious, the charges might be dropped, sometimes in exchange for requiring the defendant to receive treatment. If the charges are serious, the defendant usually will be sent to an institution to be treated for restoration of competence (which, if successful, will result in the return of the defendant for trial). Outpatient treatment of incompetent defendants is seldom practiced, even though it might often be justified.

The real dilemma for IST defendants occurs when treatment is not successful in restoring competence and holds little promise of success in the future. At this point all options are problematic. Theoretically, *Jackson* prohibits the indefinite commitments that were common in the past; as a result, many states limit the period of treatment to restore competence to six months (four months in the federal system), after which a reevaluation of competence is conducted. If the defendant is still found IST, a single six-month extension of treatment is usually permitted. One solution to the problem of permanently incompetent defendants is to have them committed to a hospital through involuntary civil commitment

---

the conditions and restrictions that could be imposed on him and their possible duration.

9. *Appraisal of likely outcome:* This item calls for an assessment of how realistically the accused perceives the likely outcome, and the degree to which impaired understanding contributes to a less adequate or inadequate participation in his defense. Without adequate information on the part of the examiner regarding the facts and circumstances of the alleged offense, this item would be unratable.

10. *Capacity to disclose to attorney available pertinent facts surrounding the offense including the defendant's movements, timing, mental state, and actions at the time of the offense:* This item calls for an assessment of the accused's capacity to give a basically consistent, rational, and relevant account of the motivational and external facts.

11. *Capacity to realistically challenge prosecution witnesses:* This item calls for an assessment of the accused's capacity to recognize distortions in prosecution testimony. Relevant factors include attentiveness and memory. In addition there is an element of initiative. If false testimony is given, the degree of activism with which the defendant will apprise his attorney of inaccuracies is important.

12. *Capacity to testify relevantly:* This item calls for an assessment of the accused's ability to testify with coherence, relevance, and independence of judgment.

13. *Self-defeating versus self-serving motivation (legal sense):* This item calls for an assessment of the accused's motivation to adequately protect himself and appropriately utilize legal safeguards to this end. It is recognized that accused persons may appropriately be motivated to seek expiation and appropriate punishment in their trials. Of concern here is the pathological seeking of punishment and the deliberate failure by the accused to avail himself of appropriate legal protection. Passivity or indifference does not justify low scores on this item. Actively self-destructive manipulation of the legal process arising from mental pathology does justify low scores.

From Laboratory of Community Psychiatry (1974).

proceedings (see Chapter 17). Standards for this type of commitment are stricter than those for ISTs, however. The state must show that the person is mentally ill and either imminently dangerous to self/others or so gravely disabled as to be unable to care for self. Furthermore, civil commitments cannot generally last longer than one year, although they can be renewed by holding new commitment hearings when necessary.

If an incompetent defendant cannot meet the criteria for a civil commitment, what happens? One possibility is that permanent incompetence might immunize this person from standing trial for future crimes. In response to this fear, it appears that, despite *Jackson*, some states simply continue to confine incompetent defendants for indefinite periods. Although this "solution" might appease the public, we believe it jeopardizes defendants' due-process rights and results in lengthy periods of punishment (disguised as treatment) without a trial.

Several alternative procedures have been proposed to solve this "Catch-22," including proposals to abolish the IST concept altogether (Burt & Morris, 1972) or to allow defendants to make a valid waiver of their right to be competent under certain circumstances (Fentiman, 1986). One solution that we think is promising has been proposed by the American Bar Association (1989). Under this plan, a provisional trial would be held for a defendant who is likely to be declared permanently incompetent. This hearing would decide the question of guilt or innocence. If the defendant is found not guilty, he or she is formally acquitted and could be further confined only through civil commitment. If proven guilty, the defendant would be subject to a special form of commitment that would recognize society's needs for secure handling of these persons.

Other Competence Issues

Amnesia and Competence to Stand Trial. Are amnesiac defendants IST? Not necessarily.

Loss of memory might render a defendant incompetent, but the law does not presume that amnesia per se is incapacitating. Most courts believe this question should be answered on a case-by-case basis, with consideration given to the severity of the amnesia and the extent to which it interferes with preparation of a defense. A leading decision in this area, *Wilson* v. *United States* (1968), listed six factors to be considered when deciding whether amnesia produces IST.

1. The extent to which the amnesia affected the defendant's ability to consult with and assist counsel.
2. The extent to which the amnesia affected the defendant's ability to testify at trial.
3. The extent to which evidence could be reconstructed by others in view of the defendant's amnesia. Such evidence would include evidence relating to the crime itself and any reasonable alibi.
4. The extent to which the government assisted the defendant and counsel in that reconstruction.
5. The strength of the prosecution's case. For example, if there is any substantial possibility that the accused could, but for the amnesia, establish an alibi or other defense, it should be presumed that (s)he would have been able to do so.
6. Any other facts and circumstances that would indicate whether the defendant had a fair trial.

Most judges are skeptical about claims of amnesia, believing that it can easily be faked. Consequently, in light of *Wilson*, claims of amnesia will not usually lead to a finding of incompetence, but they might result in the prosecution's having to cooperate more with the defense attorney in reconstructing the events of the offense and exploring possible alibi defenses.

Competent with Medication, Incompetent Without? For most defendants found IST, psychoactive medication has been the treatment of choice because it is assumed to be the only intervention with much chance for bringing the defendant to a level of competence in a reasonable period of time. Can incompetent defendants refuse this treatment? If medicated, will defendants be found competent to stand trial, even though the medication, through its temporarily tranquilizing effects, might undercut a defense like insanity? Few courts have considered the first question, but most of those that have done so have affirmed compulsory treatment to restore competence. The answer to the second question has usually been yes. In one interesting case on this topic, the New Hampshire supreme court, recognizing the possible tactical disadvantages faced by a medicated (and therefore artificially subdued) defendant claiming insanity as a defense, ruled that "defendants should be allowed to appear at trial without medication, provided they are medicated and competent when they make the decision to appear at trial unmedicated, thereby insuring a valid waiver of their right to be tried while incompetent" (Melton et al., 1987, p. 78, commenting on *State v. Hayes*, 1978).

In 1992 the U.S. Supreme Court considered the case of *Riggins v. Nevada*. In this case the defendant, David Riggins, was being tried for murder and robbery. As he awaited trial, Riggins started to hear voices and have trouble sleeping. A psychiatrist prescribed Mellaril for Riggins, who was then found competent to stand trial. However, Riggins asked that the Mellaril be stopped during his trial so that he could show the jurors his true mental state, thereby bolstering the credibility of his insanity defense. The trial judge refused his request. However, the Supreme Court ruled that forcing Riggins to receive the antipsychotic medication violated his Sixth and Fourteenth Amendment rights *unless* it could be shown that the medi-

cine was medically appropriate and was necessary to ensure Riggins's safety or the safety of others or that a fair trial could not be conducted unless Riggins was medicated. This finding requires that, before a defendant can be medicated against his or her will, the court must find the treatment to be medically appropriate and necessary for accomplishing an "essential state interest."

The development of nonmedical "treatments" for incompetence to stand trial may solve some of the above problems. Psychoeducational, problem-solving approaches that try to teach incompetent defendants how to communicate effectively with their attorneys and how to understand and participate better in legal proceedings show promise in improving competence skills (Siegel & Elwork, 1990).

LEGAL COMPETENCE OF CHILDREN AND JUVENILES

The legal system presumes that adult witnesses are competent to testify and that they will do so honestly, under oath to tell the truth, in response to nonleading questions posed on direct examination and to confrontive, even hostile, questions during cross-examination. When children are slated to testify, however, special questions about their competence to do so may be raised. In addition, in certain circumstances the procedures for questioning child witnesses may be modified in order to facilitate their testimony (Bulkley, 1988).

For many years, American courts have been skeptical about whether children under a certain age are competent to testify in court (Perry & Wrightsman, 1991). Contributing to this belief are doubts about whether young children can separate truth from falsehood, whether they understand their duty to tell the truth on the witness stand, whether they comprehend the consequences of not telling the truth, and whether they have the cognitive and memory skills necessary to give reliable, trustworthy testimony. As a consequence, most states *presumed* a child of less than a given age to be incompetent, although there now is a trend away from this presumption (Bulkley, 1988; Quinn, 1988). The age below which a child has been presumed incompetent varies. Case law set the limit at 7, but several states have passed statutes that make 10 or 14 the critical age.

Even if there is a presumption of incompetence for child witnesses of young age, this presumption can be overcome by evidence that the child can testify competently. This decision is made by the judge, usually after questioning the child about his or her ability to tell the difference between truth and lies, to understand the need to tell the truth at a trial, and to appreciate what happens if the truth is not told. In effect, statutes that set age guidelines for child witnesses are mandating that the judge make an individualized competency assessment of each child under that age. This approach is reflected in the 1895 Supreme Court decision of *Wheeler* v. *United States*, in which a 5-year-old boy whose father had been killed was judged to be a competent witness. The Court based its decision, in part, on the boy's answers to the judge's examination of him:

> The boy . . . said among other things that he knew the difference between the truth and a lie; that if he told a lie the bad man would get him, and that he was going to tell the truth. When further asked what they would do with him in court if he told a lie, he replied they would put him in jail. He also said that his mother had told him that morning to "tell no lie," and in response to a question as to what the clerk said to him,

when he held up his hand, he answered, "don't you tell no story."

Four factors bear on a child's competence to testify (Melton, 1981). First, does the child know the difference between truth and falsehood and appreciate the need to tell the truth? Second, does the child have the cognitive abilities to understand the events that he or she witnessed and to describe them accurately at a later point in time? Third, does the child have sufficient memory skills to testify in court about past events? Fourth, can the child maintain these three skills under the stress and psychological pressures of the courtroom, or is he or she too vulnerable to the powers of suggestibility or the stress of the courtroom to be trusted as a witness?

Recognizing and Telling the Truth.   Melton (1981) has concluded that "there is . . . little correlation between age and honesty." Although judges are often preoccupied with assessing a child's attitude toward the truth, available evidence suggests that children, at least of school age, are no more prone to disregard the truth than are adults—although their reasons for telling the truth change as they mature (Colby, Kohlberg, Gibbs, & Lieberman, 1983).

Cognitive Capacity to Understand and Describe Events.   Does a young child have the cognitive maturity to understand complex events and to organize them so that his or her later description of these events is trustworthy? This question is concerned with the child's competence to conceptualize events at the time they occur. A number of principles of cognitive development point to some egocentric and illogical qualities in children's thinking before the age of 7 (Bjorklund & Green, 1992).

Immature cognitive abilities pose a problem

in evaluating the testimony of young children, but they may not be so severe as to render the testimony incompetent (Melton, 1981). First, even though the child's account may be egocentric, adult jurors could in many cases reconstruct a fairly objective picture of the events that the child describes. Second, even if a child does not fully understand the meaning of all that he or she is describing, the testimony might still be "good enough" to show that some critical event occurred. This "good enough" principle is illustrated in cases in which sexual abuse of children is alleged. The child need not have a complete understanding of human sexuality to be able to describe the acts that took place in response to questions that use language appropriate to the child's age.

Memory Abilities. The laboratory research on children's ability to remember events has led to some surprising findings. In a study by Marin, Holmes, Guth, and Kovac (1979), subjects, differing in age from 5 years to adulthood, witnessed a 15-second argument. After time delays of varying lengths, the subjects were asked to remember what had happened through the use of free recall, direct questions, leading questions, and a photographic identification. Adults did better than children only on the free-recall tasks. The youngest children equaled the adults in correctly answering objective questions.

A number of studies have shown that, although young children recall less information about witnessed events than do adults, they are also less likely to make errors of commission—that is, they are less prone to "recall" information that was not present (Goodman & Reed, 1986; Marin et al., 1979). Few studies have included children as young as 3, but eyewitness memory abilities appear to decline among 3-year-olds relative to 6-year-olds (Goodman & Reed, 1986). However, even these 3-year-olds made few errors of commission, and the errors

they did make were so irrelevant that jurors would be able to identify them as false and not be misled by them. Goodman and Reed conclude that, with events that the children are able to understand and with proper questioning techniques, "even 3-year-olds might be accurate witnesses."

The amount that children can remember is related to the type of material being recalled and the way memories are being assessed. For example, children's memory for familiar stimuli can actually surpass that of adults (Lindberg, 1980). In addition, Goodman and Hahn (1987) report research showing that the use of props to aid reports enhances young children's recall abilities. So too should questions that are worded to account for children's vocabulary and cognitive abilities.

Children's Suggestibility. The major controversy about the competence of child witnesses is that, assuming they are able to understand the original events they witness, to remember them adequately, and to realize they must tell the truth about them, will they be so suggestible to the deliberate or unintended influences of parents, lawyers, and judges that their testimony about these events will be compromised? A host of biasing influences are possible—from outright attempts to coerce the child to testify falsely to subtle suggestions in the form of leading questions or misleading information after the critical event has occurred.

Research comparing children's and adults' suggestibility produces conflicting results. With some exceptions (e.g., Duncan, Whitney, & Kunen, 1982; Marin et al., 1979; see also Loftus & Davies, 1984), most researchers have found that younger children are more vulnerable to suggestive or misleading influences than older children and adults. These differences have been demonstrated for preschoolers versus primary school children (Ceci, Ross, & Toglia, 1987;

Goodman & Reed, 1986), preschoolers and primary schoolers versus adults (Goodman & Reed, 1986), and 9-year-olds versus 12-year-olds and college students (Cohen & Harnick, 1980).

These results are consistent with the tendency of potential jurors to undervalue the testimony of children, in part because they believe younger children are more suggestible (Goodman, Golding, & Haith, 1984) and in part because children's testimony is generally regarded with greater skepticism. However, the meaning of this research for children's testimony must be regarded with caution. First, the experimental procedures used to assess the biasing effects of postevent suggestions influence the size of the effects (Bulkley, 1988)—in some cases, reducing them considerably even for 3-year-olds (Ceci et al., 1987). Second, the effects of suggestion on younger children appear to occur largely on peripheral information rather than on the central activity that had been observed; this is an important distinction when considering the nature of most courtroom testimony (Quinn, 1988).

Implications of Research on Children

Because of increased prosecutions of adult sexual abusers in cases in which the child/victim is the critical witness, and because research has shown that children's testimony is probably reliable enough in most cases to be admitted into evidence, courts' assumptions about the competence of child witnesses are changing. Several jurisdictions have shifted from a presumption of incompetence to a presumption of competence for the child witness, in line with Rule 601 of the Federal Rules of Evidence, which provides that "every person is competent to be a witness, except as otherwise provided in these rules." Judges may still interview a child if his or her competence is challenged, but the burden of proof falls on the challenger under this revision.

Some scholars (Melton, Bulkley, & Wulkan, 1985) even question whether judges' screening of young witnesses is necessary in most cases, citing advice from legal experts as far back as Wigmore (1940/1970) that: "Recognizing on the one hand the childish disposition to weave romances and to treat imagination for verity, and on the other the rooted ingeniousness of children and their tendency to speak straightforwardly what is in their minds, it must be concluded that the sensible way is to put the child upon the stand and let the story come out for what it is worth" (p. 601). Others (e.g., Underwager & Wakefield, 1992) argue that the research on children's ability to testify competently and on their reactions to the courtroom is not thorough or realistic enough to base legal policy on it; instead, Haugaard (1988) suggests that psychologists play a larger role in the screening process for determining the competence of an individual child witness. This latter recommendation is dubious; there is no research showing that psychologists are any better at making this kind of decision than judges or laypersons who have the opportunity to observe the child on a regular basis.

Another development relating to acceptance of young children as competent witnesses is the use of special procedures for protecting children from the trauma of testifying in court. These protections are most often used when the child is testifying about alleged sexual abuse suffered from a defendant. (We discuss these procedures extensively in Chapter 17.)

Competence and Juveniles

Turning from the use of children as witnesses to the status of juveniles as defendants, we encounter another concern about whether limited cognitive or intellectual skills might render juveniles incompetent to fully understand the procedures of the criminal justice process. In 1967 the Supreme Court extended to juveniles many of the procedural rights that had been accorded adults (*In re Gault*, 1967). Prior to *Gault* the courts had treated juvenile defendants differently from adults under the theory that the state should assume a parental interest in rehabilitating youthful offenders rather than punishing them. In exchange for this benevolent interest and presumably less adversarial attitude (known as the theory of *parens patriae*), the juvenile relinquished some constitutional rights given to an adult defendant because they were deemed not necessary. The *Gault* decision replaced the former parental stance toward juveniles with a more adversarial posture in which juveniles were to be accorded many of the same constitutional protections given to adults. Of course, constitutional rights need to be understood if they are to fully protect accused persons. A major question is whether juveniles possess adequate psychological capacities to knowingly, intelligently, and voluntarily waive their *Miranda* rights and make a confession during police interrogation.

Thomas Grisso (1981), the leading expert on juvenile comprehension of *Miranda* warnings, describes two approaches to evaluating the competence of a juvenile's waiver of *Miranda* rights. First, the *totality of the circumstances* surrounding the waiver can be considered. Included in such an evaluation would be the juvenile's age, intelligence, and prior experience in criminal proceedings as well as the methods used by the police in obtaining the waiver and in questioning the youth. A second strategy, known as the *per se* approach, assumes that juveniles are limited in their understanding of these matters and requires that they be provided special assistance from an interested adult to help them grasp the meaning of the rights and the implications of waiving them. If such assistance were not given, regardless of the court's assessment of the totality of circumstances, the waiver would be judged incompetent.

The totality approach prevails in most American courts, although some states follow the per se approach. The leading case in this area is *Fare* v. *Michael C.* (1979), in which the Supreme Court adopted the totality approach as the constitutional standard. In *Fare*, the defendant was a $16\frac{1}{2}$-year-old boy taken into custody by police and questioned about the murder of a man in Van Nuys, California. The boy had a long record of legal trouble and had been on probation in juvenile court since he was 12. Before questioning him, the police read Michael C. the *Miranda* warnings, but they then refused his request to see his probation officer. He finally agreed to talk to them about the murder without an attorney being present, and he went on to make statements and draw pictures that incriminated him in the murder. The Supreme Court held that "the totality of the circumstances surrounding the interrogation" made it clear that Michael had knowingly and voluntarily waived his rights and that the statements and pictures he made could be admitted into evidence against him. The Court based its decision partly on the fact that Michael had an extensive prior police record and would therefore, the Court assumed, possess sufficient knowledge about police methods.

In order to evaluate adults' and juveniles' comprehension of *Miranda* warnings, Grisso (1981) conducted a series of studies that measured subjects' understanding of (1) the vocabulary and phrases used in the warnings and (2) the significance or purpose of the rights involved. He also examined the correlations between these measures and several background characteristics of the juveniles. Grisso developed three different measures of vocabulary and phrase comprehension: a 12-item true/false test, a test requiring subjects to paraphrase the important *Miranda* concepts, and a test requiring subjects to define six critical words in the warnings (*consult, attorney, interrogation, appoint, entitled,* and *right*). In addition, subjects' perceptions of the function and significance of the warnings were assessed through a structured interview in which they described their understanding of three drawings—one of the police questioning a suspect, one of a suspect consulting with an attorney, and one of a courtroom.

The juvenile subjects included residents of a boys' town, residents of a correctional school, and recently arrested juveniles. They ranged in age from 10 to 16, with an average age of 14.6 years; 59.4% were males; 73.3% were white and 26.7% were black; average IQ was 88; 32.7% had at least one prior felony. Two samples of adults were also evaluated: 203 offenders on parole and 57 volunteers drawn from custodial and maintenance crews. For the offender group, average age was 25.5 years; 79.3% were male; 41.9% were white and 58.1% were black; average IQ was 89; 65.7% had at least one prior felony. For the adult volunteers, average age was 27.1 years; 43.9% were male; 28.1% were white and 71.9% were black; average IQ was 92; they were assumed not to have a prior record.

Subjects were tested about their understanding of the following form of the *Miranda* warning, which was read and shown to them:

You do not have to make a statement and have the right to remain silent. Anything you say can and will be used against you in a court of law. You have the right to consult an attorney before interrogation and to have an attorney present at the time of the interrogation. If you cannot afford an attorney, one will be appointed for you.

Among the most important results of this research were the following discoveries:

1. At least one of the four crucial elements of *Miranda* was inadequately paraphrased by 55.3% of the juveniles versus 23.1% of the adults.
2. At least one of the six crucial vocabulary words was completely misunderstood by 63.3% of the juveniles versus 37.3% of the adults.
3. The majority of juveniles younger than 15 years had significantly poorer comprehension of the significance or function of the warnings than did adults.
4. Among juveniles with IQs lower than 80, blacks had poorer comprehension than whites.
5. Prior court experience was not related to an understanding of the vocabulary and phrases in the warnings, but juveniles with more court experience had a better appreciation of the significance of *Miranda* rights.

Based on these results, Grisso (1981) concluded that juveniles younger than 15 do not understand all of their *Miranda* rights and that they therefore would require assistance to waive these rights knowingly. He recommends a per se approach that would rely on one of four special protections: (1) using a simplified *Miranda* warning appropriate for juveniles, (2) requiring a preinterrogation screening of the juveniles to assess whether they comprehend the warnings adequately, (3) requiring the presence of an interested adult during the interrogation to advise the juvenile, or (4) requiring that an attorney for the juvenile be present during interrogation. Grisso prefers the last alternative.

Although juveniles 15 or older comprehended better than younger juveniles, they still showed gaps in their *Miranda* understanding (as did substantial percentages of the adults).

Therefore a per se approach even for older juveniles may be justified, especially if we heed *Gault's* advice that the courts give the "greatest care" to evaluating juveniles' waivers of rights. On the other hand, if priority is to be given to efficient, vigorous police investigation of crime, courts' general satisfaction with the totality standard will continue. Currently, unless the suspect is so severely retarded or mentally disordered that he or she couldn't understand what a waiver meant, or unless it can be shown that the police took improper advantage of a suspect's psychological disorder in their interrogation methods, a waiver of *Miranda* rights will probably be judged competent, even if the suspect is a juvenile.

One's preference for a per se versus totality standard will also reflect the personal emphasis one places on the competing values embodied in the dilemma we introduced in Chapter 1: the belief that extra protections are owed people who have special needs, even if these protections handicap society in certain ways, versus the belief that individual rights must sometimes give way to society's interest in identifying criminals and protecting itself from them.

SUMMARY

The most frequently asked psychological question in the criminal justice system is whether a criminal defendant is competent to stand trial. Competence to stand trial has been defined as having a sufficient present ability to consult with one's attorney with a reasonable degree of rational understanding and with a rational, as well as factual, understanding of the proceedings.

When mental health professionals are asked to evaluate a defendant's competence to stand trial, they usually use one of several structured interviews designed specifically for the purpose of assessing how well a defendant understands the charges and potential proceedings. These structured interviews have proven useful in accurately identifying possibly incompetent defendants, and they have made competency evaluations more objective and systematic. Determinations of a defendant's competence are often complicated by such factors as whether amnesia is sufficient to render a defendant incompetent and whether incompetent defendants can be treated against their will in order to restore their competence.

Questions about competence can also be raised at several other points in the criminal justice system. Examples include competency to plead guilty, to confess to a crime, to waive the right to an attorney, to refuse to plead insanity as a defense, and to be executed. Psychologists have been asked to evaluate each of these different competencies. These evaluations require the psychologist to know the proper legal standard that covers each separate competency.

The legal system has become increasingly concerned about the competence of children and juveniles. Do young persons fully understand their legal rights? If not, what special protections do they need? Are children competent to be witnesses in trials? Do they have sufficient memory for events about which they are to testify, and do they appreciate the need to describe these events truthfully in the courtroom? The legal system has gradually become more willing to presume that children can be competent witnesses. This conclusion is supported by psychological research suggesting that children have "good enough" abilities to process and retain information to be accepted as competent witnesses.

The Trial Process

Even though the trial occurred 60 years ago, people still talk about it, books are still being published about it, and one of the jurors is still alive and available to be interviewed about it. The act that led to it was called "the crime of the century." The violent treatment of the victim sickened the nation, which then sought revenge and retribution.

Sometime during the night of March 1, 1932, the young son of Colonel Charles A. Lindbergh was kidnapped from a crib in the nursery of his parents' estate in Hopewell, New Jersey. Lindbergh, called "Lucky Lindy," was the quintessential American hero; in 1927, piloting the *Spirit of St. Louis,* he had become the first person to complete a solo flight from the United States to Europe.

A month after the baby's kidnapping, Col. Lindbergh, through a go-between, paid $50,000 to a shadowy figure in a Bronx, New York, cemetery; Lindbergh had been assured that the child would then be returned unharmed. But he was not. On May 12, 1932, two months after the kidnapping, the baby's body was found in a shallow grave about five miles from Lindbergh's home. His skull had been bashed in, probably on the night he was kidnapped.

For more than two years, the police and the FBI sought the criminal. They found several physical clues, including ransom notes, footprints under a first-floor window, and a makeshift ladder apparently used to climb to the second-floor nursery. On September 19, 1934, police arrested Bruno Hauptmann and charged him with the crime.

Bruno Richard Hauptmann, 34 at the time of his arrest, was German-born and in the United States illegally. Through dogged persistence he had entered the United States without money, passport, or source of income and successfully adapted to a new country and a new language.

The trial began in Flemington, New Jersey, the day after New Year's in 1935. Public interest was unquenchable; hundreds of reporters crowded into the small courthouse to cover the trial. Some media representatives went beyond calm, objective reporting; "no harmless rumor was too wild to print, no conjecture too fantastic to publish" (Whipple, 1937, pp. 46–47). Radio stations retained well-known attorneys daily to broadcast their opinions about the progress of the case and about Hauptmann's likelihood of conviction.

The public hoped the chances were good; the whole country seemed to harbor a deep-felt desire that the defendant be convicted and executed. And he was. After a trial that lasted 40 days, the jury unanimously voted that Bruno Richard Hauptmann was guilty of murder; there was no recommendation of mercy from the death sentence. After several unsuccessful appeals, he was electrocuted on April 3, 1936.

Was Bruno Hauptmann guilty? Box 12-1 presents the arguments and evidence used by each side in his trial. What do you think?

WHAT IS THE PURPOSE OF A TRIAL?

Every trial, civil or criminal, presents two contrasting versions of the truth, just as the Hauptmann trial did. Both sides try to present the "facts" of the event in question in order to convince the fact finder (the judge or the jury) that these facts are the truth. The fact finder must render judgments on the probable truth or falsity of these factual statements.

If we were asked what the purpose of a trial is, our first response would be "to determine the truth, of course." Conflicts over the purposes of the legal system, however, raise the question whether this is the prime function of a trial. In fact, trials serve many purposes in our society. In line with one of the dilemmas described in Chapter 1, trials also serve the function of providing a sense of stability and a way to resolve conflicting issues so that the disputants can get some satisfaction. Miller and Boster (1977) have identified three images of the trial that reflect these contrasting conceptions.

The Trial as a Rational, Rule-Governed Event

Many people see a trial as a "rational, rule-governed event involving the parties to a courtroom controversy in a collective search for the truth" (Miller & Boster, 1977, p. 23). This view assumes that what really happened can be clearly ascertained, that witnesses are capable of knowing, remembering, and describing events completely and accurately. Although

this image of the trial recognizes that the opposing attorneys present only those facts that buttress their positions, it assumes that the truth will emerge from the confrontation of conflicting facts. It also assumes that judges or jurors, in weighing these facts, can "lay aside their prejudices and preconceived views regarding the case and replace such biases with a dispassionate analysis of the arguments and evidence" (Miller & Boster, 1977, p. 25).

The Trial as a Test of Credibility

The image of the trial as a rational, rule-governed event can be challenged on several grounds. Chapter 7 questioned the assumption that eyewitnesses are thorough and accurate

---

Box **12-1** | *The Trial of Bruno Richard Hauptmann*

In the Lindbergh kidnapping trial, the prosecution presented the following evidence and arguments:

1. One of the ransom bills was found in a bank deposit from a gasoline station. In examining the bill, the FBI discovered written on it an automobile license plate number—that of a car registered to Hauptmann.
2. A thorough search of Hauptmann's garage revealed $14,600 of the Lindbergh ransom money secreted in an extraordinary hiding place.
3. Written on a strip of wood in a closet in Hauptmann's house was the telephone number of the man who served as an

Charles Lindbergh

intermediary in the transport of the ransom money.

4. When the police dictated to Hauptmann the contents of the ransom notes, he misspelled certain words, just as the author of the notes had. (The wording

of the notes—such as "The child is in gut care"—implied that they had been composed by a German-speaking person.)
5. Hauptmann stopped work on the very day the ransom was paid and never thereafter resumed steady employment. He bragged to friends that he could live without working because he knew how to beat the stock market, although in actuality he was losing money (Whipple, 1937).
6. Wood from the makeshift ladder could have come from a portion of the floorboards of Hauptmann's attic that had been removed.

reporters, as we would like to believe they are. Sections of Chapters 13, 14, and 18 review the limitations of jurors and judges as they seek to put aside their own experiences and prejudices. Although this image remains as an aspiration, other images need to be considered.

A second conception, that the trial is a test of credibility, acknowledges that facts and evidence are always incomplete and biased. Hence the decision makers, whether judge or jury, "must not only weigh the information and evidence, but must also evaluate the veracity of the opposing evidential and informational sources" (Miller & Boster, 1977, p. 28). They must focus on the *way* evidence is presented, the qualifications of witnesses, the omissions from a body of testimony, and the inconsistencies between witnesses. Competence and trust-

worthiness of witnesses take on added importance in this image.

These two images share the belief that the primary function of a trial is to produce the most nearly valid judgment about the guilt of a criminal defendant or the responsibility of a civil defendant. The difference between the two images is one of degree, not of kind; Miller and Boster (1977) observe that "where the two images diverge is in the relative emphasis they place on weighing information and evidence per se as opposed to evaluating the believability of the *sources* of such information" (p. 29).

This image of the trial also has problems. Fact finders often make unwarranted inferences about witnesses and attorneys based on race, gender, mannerisms, or style of speech. Judges' and jurors' judgments of credibility may be

---

The defense presented the following responses:

1. Several witnesses testified that they saw Hauptmann in the Bronx, New York, the night of the kidnapping, implying that he could not have kidnapped the baby.
2. Expert witnesses claimed that the wood on the makeshift ladder did not match that from the attic.
3. The ransom money in his garage, he said, had belonged to his friend Isidor Fisch. Fisch had returned to Germany and then died, and so Hauptmann had kept the money safely hidden.
4. He claimed that, when the po-

Bruno R. Hauptmann

lice had dictated the ransom notes to him, they insisted that he spell the words as they were spelled in the notes. He knew, for example, that *boat* was not spelled *boad,* as it was on the notes.

Hauptmann proclaimed his innocence to the day he died; so does his wife, who is still alive and still seeks to reverse the decision. As recently as 1985 the Third U.S. Circuit Court of Appeals rejected her request to reinstitute a lawsuit against the state of New Jersey for wrongfully trying and convicting her husband. In that same year a book by Ludovic Kennedy (1985) concluded that the prosecution withheld unfavorable evidence, perjured its witnesses, and capitalized on the public mood in order to frame Hauptmann.

based more on stereotypes, folklore, or "common-sense intuition" than on the facts.

The Trial as a Conflict-Resolving Ritual

The third image shifts the function of the trial from determining the truth to providing a mechanism for the truth to emerge. Miller and Boster (1977) express it this way: "At the risk of oversimplification we suggest that it removes primary attention from the concept of *doing justice* and transfers it to the psychological realm of *creating a sense that justice is being done*" (p. 34).

Chapter 1 posed the dilemma between two needs of society: achieving truth and providing a way to resolve conflicts. This third image gives priority to maintaining a shared perception that "our legal system provides an efficient means of resolving conflict peacefully" (p. 34). Truth remains a goal, but participants in the trial process also need both the opportunity to have their "day in court" and the reassurance that, whatever the outcome, "justice was done."

In 1935 the nation wanted to know the identity of the Lindbergh baby's kidnapper. Did Bruno Hauptmann really do it? But the nation also needed to know that the killer had been captured, tried, and convicted. The nation could not tolerate, indefinitely, any uncertainty in this matter. So trials serve to stabilize society, to provide answers and give closure so that people can resume their normal business. They are necessary rituals in our process of ensuring that evils are punished in a just manner. This stabilizing function is worthless, of course, if the public doubts that justice was done in the process. (In 1935 there was very little doubt about that matter; only more recently have provocative questions been raised about the accuracy of Hauptmann's conviction.) The quality of individual verdicts remains important in this image

of the trial, but the shift in priorities favors *perceptions* of reality.

These three contrasting images are guideposts for interpreting the findings presented in this chapter and in the next two chapters. Truth is elusive, and in the legal system all truth seekers are subject to human error, even though the system seems to assume that they approach infallibility. The failure to achieve perfection in our decision making will become evident as the steps in the trial process are reviewed.

STEPS IN THE TRIAL PROCESS

The usual steps mandated for a trial are sketched out here, as a framework for issues to be evaluated in this and the next two chapters.

Preliminary Actions

In Chapter 10 we discussed *discovery*, the pretrial process by which each side tries to gain vital information about the case held by the other side. This information includes statements by witnesses, police records, documents, material possessions, experts' opinions, and anything else that is relevant to the case.

In carrying out discovery, particularly in civil cases, attorneys may collect *depositions* from witnesses expected to testify at trial. A deposition is usually an oral statement by a potential witness, given under oath in the presence of a court reporter and attorneys from both sides. (A judge is seldom present.) It is taken in question-and-answer form, like testimony in court, with the opportunity for the opposing lawyer (or "adversary") to cross-examine the witness. Statements from parties involved in the case may also be taken in written form, called *written interrogatories.* These do not permit cross-examination, however.

Before the trial, the decision must be made whether a judge or a jury will hear the evidence and render the verdict. The U.S. Constitution provides criminal defendants with the right to have charges against them judged by a jury of their peers, but defendants sometimes choose to waive a jury trial and, if the prosecutor agrees, have a judge decide their case. Does it make any difference? We answer this important question in a later section of this chapter.

Civil lawsuits may also be decided by either a jury or a judge, depending on the preferences of the opposing parties. Many states have revised the size and *decision rule* from the traditional 12-person jury requiring a unanimous verdict. In some states, for some kinds of cases, juries as small as six persons and decision rules requiring only a three-fourths majority are in effect. We assess the history of these changes and their psychological impact in Chapter 14.

Jury Selection

If the trial is before a jury, the jury must be selected. This is a two-step process. The first step is to draw a panel of prospective jurors, called a *venire,* from a large list (usually based on voter registration lists).

Once the venire for a particular trial has been selected—this may be anywhere from 30 to 200 people, depending on the customary practices of that jurisdiction and the nature of the trial—a process known as *voir dire* is employed to select the actual jurors. (Voir dire, in French, means "to tell the truth.") In actuality, prospective jurors who reveal biases and are unable to be open minded about the case are dismissed from service, so that the task is one of elimination rather than selection. Prospective jurors who appear to be free of these limitations are thus "selected." Voir dire can have impor-

tant effects on the outcome of the trial; the process is described in detail in Chapter 13.

The Trial

At the beginning of the trial itself, lawyers for each side are permitted to make *opening statements.* These are not part of the evidence (if the trial is before a jury, the jurors are instructed that these opening statements are not to be considered evidence), but they serve as overviews of the evidence to be presented. The prosecution or plaintiff always goes first, as this side is the one that brought charges and bears the burden of proof. Attorneys for the defendant, in either a criminal or a civil trial, can choose to present their opening statement immediately after the other side's or wait until it is their turn to present evidence.

After opening statements, the prosecution or plaintiff calls its witnesses. Each witness testifies under oath, with the threat of a charge of *perjury* if the witness fails to be truthful. That witness is then cross-examined by the adverse counsel, after which the original attorney has a chance for *redirect questioning.* Redirect questioning is likely if the original attorney feels that the opposition has "impeached" his or her witness; *impeach* in this context refers to a cross-examination that has effectively called into question the credibility (or "reliability") of the witness.

The purpose of redirect examination is to "rehabilitate" the witness, or to salvage his or her original testimony. The defense, however, has one more chance to question the witness, a process called *recross* (for "re-cross-examination").

After the prosecution's or plaintiff's attorneys have presented all their witnesses, it is the defense's turn. The same procedure of direct examination, cross-examination, redirect, and recross is used.

After both sides have presented their witnesses, one or both may seek to introduce additional evidence and witnesses and petition the judge's permission to do so—that is, to present *rebuttal evidence,* which attempts to counteract or disprove evidence given by an earlier adverse witness.

Once all the evidence has been presented, each side is permitted to make a *closing argument,* also called a *summation.* Although jurisdictions vary, ordinarily the prosecution or plaintiff gets the first summation, followed by the defense, after which the prosecution or plaintiff has an opportunity to rebut. The order of presentation, with the plaintiff going both first and last, has psychological implications that we assess in Chapter 14.

The final step in the jury trial is for the judge to give instructions to the jury. (In some states, instructions precede the closing statements.) The judge informs the jury of the relevant law. For example, a definition of the crime is given, as well as a statement of what elements must be present for it to have occurred—that is, whether the defendant had the motive and the opportunity to do so. The judge also instructs jurors about the standard they should use to weigh the evidence (see Box 12-2). With criminal charges, the jurors must be convinced "beyond a reasonable doubt" that the defendant is guilty before they vote to convict. Although the concept of "reasonable doubt" is difficult to interpret, generally this standard means that jurors should be strongly convinced (but not necessarily convinced beyond all doubt). Each of us interprets such an instruction differently, and as Chapter 14 illustrates, this instruction is a source of confusion and frustration among jurors.

In a civil trial, in which one party brings a

Box 12-2 | An Example of the Judge's Instructions to the Jury

Before the jury is adjourned to deliberate, the judge gives instructions regarding the law in the case. In a typical criminal case these instructions will include such matters as the functions of the judge and the jury, the presumption of innocence, the burden of proof, a definition of the offense (including the elements that must be proved to exist), defenses that are proper in the case (for example, insanity plea, entrapment claims), and the procedures to be followed in the jury room. Many of these instructions are quite brief or inexplicit. For example, the definition of reasonable doubt may be as follows:

In this action the plaintiffs have the burden of establishing beyond a reasonable doubt all facts necessary to prove their case.

Reasonable doubt is defined as follows: It is not a mere possible doubt, because everything related to human affairs, and depending on moral evidence, is open to some possible or imaginary doubt. It is that state of the case which, after the entire comparison and consideration of all the evidence, leaves the minds of the jurors in that condition that they cannot say they feel an abiding conviction, to a moral certainty, of the truth of the plaintiff's case.

If the evidence presented does not establish the plaintiff's case beyond a reasonable doubt, then your verdict must be for the defendant.

A great deal of research has been conducted on ways to make jury instructions clearer so that jurors will understand them accurately and use them properly. This research is discussed in Chapter 14.

claim against another, a different standard is used. The *preponderance of the evidence* is all that is necessary to find in favor of one side. Usually judges and attorneys translate this to mean "Even if you find the evidence favoring one side to be only slightly more convincing than the other side's, rule in favor of that side." "Preponderance" is often interpreted as meaning at least 51% of the evidence.

The jury is also given instructions on how to deliberate, but these are usually sketchy. Jurors are excused to the deliberation room, and no one—not even the bailiff or the judge—can be present or eavesdrop on their deliberations. When the jury has reached its verdict, its foreperson informs the bailiff, who informs the judge, who reconvenes the attorneys and defendants (and plaintiff in a civil trial) for the announcement of the verdict.

Sentencing

If the defendant in a criminal trial is judged guilty, at some later point a punishment must be decided. In many jurisdictions the judge makes this decision, but in some states the jury is reconvened, evidence relevant to the sentencing decision is presented by both sides, and the jury deliberates until it agrees on a recommended punishment. (See Chapter 18 for aspects of this process.)

THE ADVERSARIAL SYSTEM

American trial procedure—whether in criminal or civil cases—is fundamentally adversarial in nature. Exhibits, evidence, and witnesses are introduced by one side or the other for the purpose of convincing the fact finder that that side's viewpoint is the truthful one. The choice of what evidence to present is left, within broad limits, to the discretion of the parties in dispute and their attorneys (Lind, 1982). Judges rarely call witnesses or introduce evidence on their own. Judges seldom ask questions of witnesses, and they usually do not permit jurors to do so, despite evidence that (1) allowing jurors to ask questions increases the jurors' own satisfaction that witnesses have been thoroughly examined, and (2) questioning by jurors is not impractical or disruptive of the trial process (Heuer & Penrod, 1988). The adversarial system is derived from English common law.

This approach contrasts with the *inquisitorial approach,* which is used on the continent of Europe (but not in Great Britain). Lind (1982) describes the procedure in France, for example, as follows:

> The questioning of witnesses is conducted almost exclusively by the presiding judge. The judge interrogates the disputing parties and witnesses, referring frequently to a dossier that has been prepared by a court official who investigated the case. Although the parties probably have partisan attorneys present at the trial, it is evident that control over the presentation of evidence and arguments is firmly in the hands of the judge [p. 14].

In the inquisitorial system, the two sides do not have separate witnesses; the witnesses testify for the court, and the opposing parties are not allowed to prepare the witnesses before the trial (Sheppard & Vidmar, 1980).

The adversarial model has been criticized on the ground that it promotes a competitive atmosphere that can distort the truth about a dispute (Lind, 1982). Jurors have to choose between two versions of the truth, both of which are probably inaccurate in some ways and are certainly incomplete at best. But the effects of the adversary system intrude before the jury's decision-making step. Sheppard and Vidmar (1980) found that witnesses who were interviewed by a lawyer with an adversarial orientation biased their reports in favor of the lawyer's client. Chapter 2 described the dilemma that even expert witnesses face in this regard.

However, research on these contrasting approaches reveals several benefits of the adversarial model. A research team led by a social psychologist, John Thibaut, and a law professor, Laurens Walker (Thibaut & Walker, 1975; Thibaut, Walker, & Lind, 1972; Walker, La Tour, Lind, & Thibaut, 1974), carried out a program of research whose conclusion was that the adversary system led to less biased decisions and to decisions that were more likely to be seen as fair by the parties in dispute. One possible explanation for this more favorable evaluation of the adversary system is that it is the system that American subjects are accustomed to. But a study by Lind and his associates (Lind, Erickson, Friedland, & Dickenberger, 1978) found that subjects from countries with nonadversary systems (France and West Germany) also rated the adversary procedure as fairer. Why? Perhaps because the adversarial system motivates attorneys to try harder to identify all the evidence favorable to their side. Especially when student/attorneys believed that the weight of the information and evidence favored the other side rather than their client, they conducted more thorough investigations of the case. Thus, when the case was presented to the judge, the arguments appeared less unbalanced than the original distribution of facts would warrant (Lind, 1975; Lind, Thibaut, & Walker, 1973).

A primary advantage of the adversarial system is that it gives participants a full opportunity to present their version of the facts so that they feel as if they have been treated fairly (Lind & Tyler, 1988); Sheppard and Vidmar (1983) point out that any method of dispute resolution that produces this belief is more likely to be viewed favorably than alternatives that do not.

As new methods of dispute resolution that do not involve formally adversarial court hearings are attempted, this principle would appear to be an important influence on the extent to which these new methods will be accepted and used by the public. For example, psychologists have recently investigated litigants' responses to alternative dispute resolution methods such as mediation (a neutral third party helps the disputants discuss, develop, and agree on a resolution to their conflict) or arbitration (the parties in conflict formally agree to submit their dispute to a neutral third party who arrives at a binding resolution). These techniques are increasingly being used in divorce actions, child custody cases, and personal injury disputes because they purportedly save time and reduce some of the stress associated with adversary techniques.

In fact, researchers have found that litigants sometimes view these supposedly nonadversarial methods as more coercive and less adequate than proponents have assumed (Vidmar, 1992). The degree to which people comply with the law, seek formal remedies through the legal system, and accept legally mandated resolutions of disputes as final may depend to a great extent on their belief that the *process* by which decision outcomes are reached is fair, is open, and conveys a "perception that the dispute is treated with dignity, neutrality, and importance" (Vidmar, 1992).

JUDGES' DECISIONS VERSUS JURIES' DECISIONS

As noted earlier, defendants in criminal trials ordinarily opt for a jury to decide their guilt or innocence, but they can choose a judge (called a *bench trial*). In 1989, Carl Stokes, formerly mayor of Cleveland and now a municipal court judge, was charged with stealing a 20-pound bag of dogfood from a pet store in Shaker Heights, Ohio. Stokes had been involved in an earlier incident; six months before, he had acknowledged absentmindedly taking a $2.39 screwdriver from a Bedford, Ohio, store and putting it in his pocket.

Stokes denied any guilt in the second case and specifically requested a jury trial. The jury found him not guilty.

Why do defendants choose to have their case decided by a jury or by a judge? And does it make any difference? A recent survey (MacCoun & Tyler, 1988) found that citizens believe a jury decision offers more procedural fairness (i.e., greater thoroughness, better representation of the community, fewer personal biases affecting decisions) than a decision by a judge. We know that juries and judges sometimes disagree, but we don't know how frequently. When they do disagree, can we say which made the better decision? After all, jury verdicts are not systematically compared against some "correct," back-of-the-book answer—even if there were one. Jury verdicts are rarely overturned on appeal, and not-guilty verdicts are final, regardless of their "validity." So we must rely on the social sciences and survey data to get some estimate.

Harry Kalven and Hans Zeisel (1966), professors at the University of Chicago, carried out the most extensive survey of the outcomes of jury trials. It is a classic application of the methods of social science to the understanding of juries' decisions. Kalven and Zeisel asked each district court judge and federal judge in the United States to provide information about recent jury trials he or she had presided over. Of approximately 3500 judges, only about 500 responded to a detailed questionnaire. But some judges provided information about a large number of trials—some, more than 50 trials—so that the database for this analysis consisted of approximately 3500 trials. Although one might wonder about judges' ability to recall accurately the details of 50 different cases, the Kalven and Zeisel study remains the most thorough investigation of judge/jury agreement that has been conducted.

Of basic concern were the following two questions: What was the jury's verdict? And did the judge agree? By looking at the frequency of agreement, we can get hints about the extent of juries' deviations from application of the law.

In criminal trials, the judges reported that their verdict would have been the same as the jury's actual verdict 75% of the time (see Table 12-1 for detailed results). Thus, in three-fourths of the trials, two independent fact-finding agents would have brought forth the same result. Similar consistency was found for civil trials, as illustrated in Table 12-2. Although each of us may have our own reaction

Table 12-1 *Agreement of Verdicts of Jury and Judge Based on 3576 Trials (in Percentage of All Trials)*

| | Jury | | | |
Judge	Acquits (%)	Convicts (%)	Hangs (%)	Total, judge (%)
Acquits (%)	**13.4**	2.2	1.1	16.7
Convicts (%)	16.9	**62.0**	4.4	83.3
Total, jury (%)	30.3	64.2	5.5	100.0

Adapted from Kalven and Zeisel (1966, p. 56). Figures in bold show judge/jury agreements on verdict.

Table **12-2**   *Agreement of Judges' and Juries' Decisions in Civil Cases (in Percentage of All Trials)*

Judge finds for:	Jury finds for:		Total, judge (%)
	Plaintiff (%)	Defendant (%)	
Plaintiff (%)	**47**	10	57
Defendant (%)	12	**31**	43
Total, jury (%)	59	41	100

Adapted from Kalven and Zeisel (1966, p. 63). Figures in bold show judge/jury agreements on verdict.

to the adequacy of this degree of agreement, it does suggest that jurors are not deviating to an inappropriate degree from the narrow mandate to follow the judge's instructions about the law and use only that information plus the actual evidence to reach their verdict.

In fact, we might speculate on what *is* an optimal degree of agreement between judge and jury. What if they agreed 100% of the time? That would be undesirable, indicating that the jury was a rubber stamp of the judge. But if they agreed only 50% of the time, given only two possible outcomes of guilty and not guilty (putting aside "hung" juries momentarily), it would reflect no real agreement at all. (Two independent agents, choosing yes or no at random, would agree 50% of the time by chance alone.) Appropriately enough, the 75% level of agreement is halfway between chance and a too-perfect agreement. More important, all this speculation after the fact should not obscure the basic conclusion that *in the vast majority of cases, juries base their verdicts on the evidence and the law* (Visher, 1987).

Among the 25% of the criminal cases in which there was disagreement, 5.5% resulted in hung juries; that is, the jury members could not agree on a verdict. Thus it is more appropriate to say that in 19.5% of the criminal cases the jury provided a guilty verdict where the judge would have ruled not guilty, or vice versa.

"Vice versa" needs to be emphasized because in most of these discrepant decisions, the jury was more lenient than the judge. The judge would have convicted the defendant in 83.3% of these cases, whereas the jury convicted in only 64.2% of them. For every trial in which the jury convicted and the judge would have acquitted, there were almost eight trials in which the reverse was true. In only 2% of the cases would the judge have ruled not guilty when the jury found the defendant guilty; in contrast, in 17% of cases the opposite was true.

Judge/Jury Differences and Types of Charges

The foregoing results would lead to a conclusion that, other things being equal, defendants are better off putting their case in the hands of a jury. But we need to remember that Kalven and Zeisel's conclusions were drawn only from those trials in which the defendants had chosen the jury to hear their case. To verify the conclusions, it would be necessary to deny defendants the choice between a jury trial and a bench trial, randomly assign them to one versus the other, and then see for a large sample of trials whether juries were still more lenient. Such a study is, of course, not legally possible, given the rights that society, appropriately, provides to defendants.

There are other qualifications to a conclusion of overall jury leniency. For example, the jury is *much* more lenient than the judge in certain types of cases—mostly minor offenses such as gambling or hunting-law violations. In contrast, juries in libel trials are more likely to find the defendant (for example, a newspaper or a television station) at fault than judges are; one survey found that, when such cases were tried before juries, the media lost almost nine out of every ten (Associated Press, 1982). In serious crimes, such as murder or kidnapping, the judge and the jury were in closer agreement. This is a useful finding because often, in trials for capital offenses, the prosecuting attorney will remind the jury that its standard of reasonable doubt should not be looser just because a guilty verdict would determine the rest of a defendant's life—or death. In actuality, juries in cases involving serious or capital crimes seem to adjust their standard of reasonable doubt so that it is more in keeping with the judge's.

Determinants of Discrepancies

Type of case aside, what else accounts for the discrepancies between judge and jury? For their sample of cases, Kalven and Zeisel unfortunately have only one source to answer this: the judge's opinion. Yet on this basis they offer a classification of cases. Through an analysis of these cases, we may be able to shed more light on the subject (see also Box 12-3).

A few of these discrepancies—about 2% of all the trials—apparently resulted from facts

---

Box **12-3** | *Judges and Juries—Experts and Novices*

An unfortunate interpretation of the findings in Kalven and Zeisel's survey is that, when judge and jury disagree, the jury is "at fault" or "in error." This conclusion is enhanced by a tendency to distinguish between experts and novices. The "expert/novice" distinction has recently achieved prominence in the literature of experimental psychology (Chi, Glaser, & Farr, 1988). Experts are described as better able to perceive large meaningful patterns in their domains of expertise, they are faster than newcomers at performing the skills of their domain, and they see and represent a problem in their domain at a deeper level than do novices, who tend to represent a problem at a superficial level (Glaser & Chi, 1988).

But several factors counteract a conclusion that judges necessarily render "more valid verdicts." First, a judge is only one person; juries are composed of 6 to 12 persons, and a consistent research finding in social psychology is that decisions by groups are often more accurate than those by an individual (Forsyth, 1990), although situational factors can complicate this finding (for example, very cohesive groups, led by a strong leader and debating complex problems, can sometimes reach extremely poor decisions, a process called *groupthink*—Janis, 1982). The process of identifying and discussing individual judgments, especially without any time pressures as is the case with jury deliberations, usually leads to a group outcome that is more accurate than the majority of the initial individual judgments of the members. Group discussions (here, deliberations) provide an enhanced opportunity for detecting errors and rejecting incorrect interpretations.

A second reason to soft-pedal the implications of the expert/novice distinction is that, although judges are experts on the procedures of the courtroom and the law, they may not possess any more expertise on the specific evidence of the case than the jurors. Third, there is no evidence that judges can evaluate the credibility or honesty of witnesses any better than can jurors; indeed, the evidence that any experts are superior on this task is limited. And, finally, judges may disagree among themselves regarding the verdict in a specific case—a point elaborated in Chapter 18.

that one party knew but the other did not. For example, in several cases the judge was aware of the defendant's prior arrest record (a matter not introduced into evidence) and hence would have found him guilty, but the jury acquitted him. Or, especially in a small community, a member of the jury might share with fellow jurors some information about a witness or the defendant that was not part of evidence and not known to the judge at the time. In cases like this, it is hard to make a blanket indictment of the jury for basing its verdict on something beyond the evidence. One or more of the jurors may possess knowledge that the only eyewitness to the crime is a known liar in the community. Judgments of the credibility of witnesses are legitimate parts of the jury's function.

A second source of judge/jury discrepancies was the relative effectiveness of the two attorneys. In about 1% of Kalven and Zeisel's sample of trials, the jury was swayed by this factor and produced a verdict that was, at least in the judge's opinion, contrary to the weight of the evidence. If this is a generalizable finding, it is a matter of some concern. At the same time, it is not surprising that some portion of jury verdicts would have such determinants, in light of findings on the impact of nonevidentiary aspects (to be described in the next two chapters).

But the more frequent reasons for jury/judge differences get more to the heart of the trial decision; they are, first, disagreements over the evidence and, second, what Kalven and Zeisel called "jury sentiments." It is inevitable that, in cases in which the evidence is balanced and the decision rests on the evidence (that is, issues of law are straightforward), the judge may occasionally disagree with the jury. Kalven and Zeisel (1966, p. 165) conclude that the jury often relies on sentiment to resolve the issue when evidence is relatively inconclusive—that is, when the evidence could support either verdict.

Consider a case of theft in which there is a solitary eyewitness and the accused person claims mistaken identity. In a "barebones" case like this, the issue boils down to: whom do you really believe? The judge may trust the eyewitness more; the jurors, though initially in disagreement, may eventually come to give the defendant the benefit of their collective doubt. In such cases, judge and jury may differ in their estimates of the probability that the defendant committed the crime or in their standards of reasonable doubt or in both. And on such matters there can be honest disagreement. (In fact, two judges could disagree over these issues.) Although *any* inconsistency between judge and jury may, to some, imply unreliability in the fact-finding process, this type of disagreement seems to rest on differences in standards for the acceptability of evidence. Judge/jury discrepancies based on "Whom do you believe?" are of less concern to us than are some of Kalven and Zeisel's other explanations.

Jury "Sentiments"

In fact, jury "sentiments," as an explanation, seem more fundamental, partly because they account for about half of the disagreements (9% of Kalven and Zeisel's sample of trials) and partly because the label "sentiments" seems possibly prejudicial. Kalven and Zeisel, after reviewing the multitude of discrepancies, used this term to cover all trials in which, in the judge's view, the jury's verdict was detrimentally determined by factors beyond the evidence and the law. (There is an implicit assumption here that the judge's decision was free of sentiment—a dubious claim given that some judges admitted favoring conviction for defendants who the judge, but not the jurors, knew had a prior conviction!)

Sometimes, the judge concluded, the jurors felt that the "crime" was just too trivial for *any* punishment or at least for the expected punishment, and hence they found the defendant not guilty, thus making sure that he or she would not be punished. In one case, a man was brought to trial for stealing two frankfurters. Since this was his second crime, if he had been convicted, it would have been considered a felony conviction and he would have been sentenced to prison. Whereas the judge would have found him guilty, the jury voted 10 to 2 for acquittal.

In other cases the jury seemed to believe that a law was unfair and hence voted to acquit. In trials for the sale of beer and liquor to minors who were military servicemen, juries have concluded that there was minimal social harm. Apparently they felt that, if a young man can be forced to die for his country, "he can buy and consume a bottle of beer" (Kalven & Zeisel, 1966, p. 273).

In actuality, jury sentiments surfaced in many types of cases involving "unpopular" crimes—for example, in small misdemeanors such as gambling or in "victimless crimes" such as prostitution. Often the jurors' brusque announcement of a not-guilty verdict, when technically the defendant most certainly had committed a crime, was their way of expressing frustration. "Why waste our time over such minor affairs?" they might have been thinking.

More relevant to the question of whether jury sentiments are sources of jury error or expressions of a different definition of justice are cases in which the jury, after due deliberation, concluded that the defendant had already been sufficiently sanctioned and that punishment by the legal system was hence unnecessary. Here are two examples.

In one case the defendant had fired a shot into the family home of his estranged wife. The judge would have found him guilty of shooting with the intent to kill; the jury convicted him only on the lesser charge of pointing and discharging a firearm. The decisive circumstance appears to be that, although the defendant's shot hadn't hurt anyone, his brother-in-law had shot back in self-defense and had seriously injured the defendant.

In a second example, the pivotal circumstances were unrelated to the crime. In a case of income tax evasion, the following series of misfortunes plagued the defendant between the crime and the trial: "His home burned, he was seriously injured, and his son was killed. Later he lost his leg, his wife became seriously ill, and several major operations were necessary . . . his wife gave birth to a child who was both blind and spastic" (Kalven & Zeisel, 1966, p. 305). The jury found the defendant not guilty of income tax evasion, apparently concluding that he had already suffered divine retribution. The judge would have found him guilty.

Jury Sentiments and Jury Nullification

Do juries have the right to disregard the judge's instructions and disobey the law when they render their verdicts? What if they conclude that the victim's rights take precedence over the law? Box 12-4 presents a fictional treatment of this issue, but there are numerous real-life examples.

A trial introduced earlier, in Chapter 3, reflects the problem. Lester Zygmanik was brought to trial in New Jersey for the murder of his brother George. As George lay in agony in his hospital bed, paralyzed from the neck down, he made Lester swear that he would not let George continue in such a state of pain. Lester shot his brother in the head. Minutes later he turned himself in and acknowledged that he had done it as an act of love for his brother (Mitchell, 1976). With no laws regarding mercy killing on the books in New Jersey, the state felt that a case could be made for charging Lester with first-degree murder.

If we focus on the relationship between the state and the defendant, as our system of justice traditionally does, Lester Zygmanik was clearly guilty, for his action fit all the elements that the law required for guilt to be proven.

But the jurors saw matters from a contrasting perspective. After deliberating less than three hours, they found Lester Zygmanik not guilty. Their focus, apparently, was on the relationship between Lester and his brother, and they concluded that Lester had been overcome by grief, love, and selflessness. In rendering

their decision, they implicitly acknowledged that commitments to care for others were more important to them than the strict guidelines of the law.

The Zygmanik case makes us aware that different conceptions of justice make different demands on, and ask different questions of, the evidence. The traditional approach deals with concepts of planning and implementation. It asks about the defendant's "intent" in a way that isolates intent from the relationship of the actor and the recipient of the act. In the legal system, Lester's altruistic motivation is irrelevant if the procedural elements of the crime can

---

Box 12-4 | *The Jury's Verdict: Based on the Law or on Its Sentiments?*

The film *The Verdict*, for which Paul Newman received an Oscar nomination, was potent courtroom drama. Even though the cards were stacked against attorney Frank Galvin (Newman) and his client, justice triumphed in the end. Or did it?

The Verdict is, of course, a work of fiction. As a representation of fact, it contains at least 15 major legal flaws (Ostroff, 1983; Press, 1983b). But the author of the novel on which the film was loosely based is a Boston attorney, Barry Reed, who specializes in representing patients in medical malpractice cases. In 1978 his firm won the then-highest jury verdict ever in a medical malpractice case in the United States—$5.8 million.

An example of art imitating life, *The Verdict* also involves a medical

Paul Newman as Attorney Frank Galvin in The Verdict

malpractice case. A prominent Catholic hospital in Boston and some of its doctors are sued for negligence in the treatment of a young woman who had been admitted for the delivery of a child. While on the operating table, the young woman vomited in her surgical mask, and that triggered respiratory and cardiac arrest. As a result, she is brain-damaged. In fact, she is a living corpse.

As Frank Galvin, Paul Newman plays a down-and-out attorney who is hired by her family to represent the young woman. Not only does he seek vindication for his client, but a victory would represent a self-renewal for him.

The doctors and the hospital authorities produce the admissions form, which indicates that the woman had not eaten for nine hours prior to the operation. They claim, therefore, that, when they gave her a general anesthetic, they had no idea that there was food in her stomach or that they ran the risk of asphyxiation. (Administering a general anesthetic on a full stomach often brings about vomiting; if the person is unconscious, the vomiting can impair breathing.) Hence, they claim, they should not be be associated with his actions. So the court asks: Did he show behaviors that indicated prior planning? Were his actions before and during the event deliberate? A contrasting approach (Gilligan would describe it as *feminine*) asks different questions: What evidence is there that this was intended as a harmful or malicious act? What was the relationship of the actor to the victim? Does the evidence indicate that his actions before and during the event reflected an ethic of care for others?

There is a way to resolve this inadequacy in the U.S. legal system. In fact, it is already available in three states, Indiana, Maryland, and Georgia, which provide for a judge's instruction called, rather confusingly, *jury nullification* (Scheflin, 1972; Scheflin & Van Dyke, 1980). As currently conceived, "jury nullification is a mechanism, and a defense, which allows the jury, as representatives of the community, to disregard both the law and the evidence and acquit defendants who have violated the letter, but not the spirit, of the law" (Horowitz, 1985, p. 25).

The concept of jury nullification reflects society's awareness that we have juries for two reasons. Not only do they resolve the facts and apply the law, but they also represent the

held liable for the regrettable outcome.

Only as the jury trial nears its completion does attorney Galvin track down the most important witness on behalf of his client. The admissions nurse who prepared the form is now long gone from Boston, and it takes some time and detective work for Frank Galvin to locate her in New York City and persuade her to return to Boston to testify. But, reluctantly, she does. And reticently she testifies that on the admissions form she recorded the woman's report that she had last eaten *one hour* before admission, thus leaving the clear implication that the form was later tampered with by the doctors. In fact, the ex-nurse also testifies that one of the doctors on trial later insisted that she change the number on the form. She refused, and that is why she is no longer a nurse. She even

produces a photocopy of the original form, showing "1 hour." Here, it seems, is clear-cut devastating documentation of the doctors' culpability.

But the judge does not allow the former admissions nurse's rebuttal testimony to be allowed into evidence, ruling that this rebuttal testimony is not related to direct evidence. He pointedly instructs the jury to disregard all testimony of the former nurse. Galvin appears to have lost his one chance for victory and vindication.

Interestingly enough, in the novel on which the screenplay was based, the judge admits this testimony into evidence. The book, written by an attorney, is legally more valid than the movie—it is unlikely that the judge would strike such evidence *on the spot, if at all*—but the movie packs more drama.

The climax of the movie is, of course, the jury's verdict. The jury finds the hospital and the doctors negligent. Galvin and his client win. On the basis of the sense of relief and pleasure expressed by audiences, we can say that justice has been done.

But had the jurors obeyed the law, in this rather contrived trial, they would not have had any basis for such a verdict. The judge could even have instructed them to bring down a directed verdict absolving the hospital and doctors of any negligence. Is it right for jurors to disregard the judge's instructions? And do juries operate from a higher standard of justice—or at least a different definition of justice—than that provided by the law?

breadth of community values. This latter function manifests their historical role of serving as the conscience of the community (Becker, 1980). Even though most juries in the United States are instructed that their task is only to evaluate the facts and then apply the law as described by the judge, for several centuries there has existed the opportunity to apply a community perspective, even if it ignores or "violates" the law.

For example, in a precedent-setting trial during colonial times, the printer John Peter Zenger was charged with printing material that had not been authorized by the government; hence he had committed sedition. The British law stated that the truth of the unauthorized material was irrelevant (Alexander, 1963). But Zenger's attorney, Andrew Hamilton, told the jurors that they "had the right beyond all dispute to determine both the law and the facts." They did; they went against the judge's instructions and acquitted Zenger. The philosophy of "the jury as the judge," at least in criminal cases, was very prominent in post-Revolutionary America, partly in keeping with the resentment felt toward Crown-appointed judges (Rembar, 1980, p. 362).

The concept of jury nullification withered away in the United States during the 19th and early 20th centuries. The most recent Supreme Court case dates back to 1895 (*Sparf and Hansen* v. *United States*); at that time the Court ruled against the use of the nullification doctrine in federal trials. But, as Horowitz (1985) notes, the controversy resurfaced in the turbulent 1960s and early 1970s, when the federal government sought to prosecute anti–Vietnam War activists, usually on charges of conspiracy. Defense lawyers sought ways that jurors could, within the law, consider the morality of such actions. Several such cases reached the federal appellate level, although none progressed as far as the Supreme Court

for review. However, in a 1968 decision (*Duncan* v. *Louisiana*), the Supreme Court recognized the jury's power to displace the law by appeal to conscience as a characteristic so "fundamental to the American scheme of government that a state violates due process of law in eliminating a jury trial" (Kadish & Kadish, 1971, p. 204).

In *United States* v. *Dougherty* (1972) the appeals court in the District of Columbia reviewed a 1970 case in which several members of the Catholic clergy had been found guilty of ransacking the Dow Chemical Company's offices to protest the company's manufacture of napalm. The trial judge had refused their attorney's request that he instruct the jury that they could acquit the defendants whether or not there had been a violation of criminal law. The U.S. Court of Appeals, by a 2-to-1 vote, upheld this decision by the trial judge. In the majority opinion, Judge Harold Leventhal suggested that the jurors "already 'knew' of their nullification powers from informal sources and to institutionalize these powers in routine judge's instructions to the jury would alter the system in unpredictable ways" (Horowitz, 1985, p. 27).

Jurors clearly have the *power* to nullify. That is, in criminal cases they can do as they please in favor of the accused. They do not have to prove that their verdict corroborates the facts or follows the law. But most courts have held that they do not have the express *right* to nullify.

As Rembar (1980) notes, this is a strange state of affairs. Juries can thumb their noses at the judge, but ordinarily they aren't told they can. Would explicit nullification instructions to the jury affect their decisions and lower conviction rates? In an important study on this matter, the researcher, Irwin Horowitz (1985), thoughtfully included several types of cases with the expectation that community standards might apply to them differently. Several mock juries of six persons each listened to an audiotape of a criminal case—either a mercy killing, a murder, or a drunk-driving case that resulted in a pedestrian's death. In all three cases the weight of the evidence indicated that the defendant was guilty.

Some mock jurors were given nullification instructions, either those available in Maryland or a more radical version based on a proposal by Van Dyke (1970). The latter version included three points; these jurors were told (1) that "although they are a public body bound to give respectful attention to the laws, they have the final authority to decide whether or not to apply a given law to the acts of the defendant on trial before them"; (2) that "they represent the community and that it is appropriate to bring into their deliberations the feelings of the community and their own feelings based on conscience"; and (3) that, despite their respect for the law, "nothing would bar them from acquitting the defendant if they feel that the law, as applied to the fact situation before them, would produce an inequitable or unjust result."

This radical nullification instruction had a dramatic effect. In the euthanasia case, in which a nurse was tried for the "mercy killing" of a terminal cancer patient, the jurors who heard this instruction were much less likely to find the defendant guilty. However, when faced with a drunk driving case involving vehicular homicide, the jurors with radical nullification instructions were *more* likely to find the defendant guilty. For the third case, the murder of a grocery store owner during a robbery, the presence of these instructions had no effect on the verdicts.

In contrast to the juries with radical jury nullification instructions, those with the Maryland instruction behaved no differently than juries that were unaware of the nullification proce-

dure. The Maryland instruction is brief and is considered by some to be rather vague. In its entirety, it reads as follows:

> Member of the Jury: this is a criminal case and under the constitution and the laws of the state of Maryland in a criminal case the jury are the judges of the law as well as the facts in the case. So whatever I tell you about the law, while it is intended to be helpful to you in reaching a just and proper verdict in the case, it is not binding upon you as members of the jury and you may accept or reject it. And you may apply the law as you apprehend it to be in the case.

Jury nullification instructions encourage the application of "sentiments," to use Kalven and Zeisel's term, in the jury's decision making. But they are not without their problems, of course (Rembar, 1980). For example, prosecutions of police officers for using excessive force in the course of their duties are an example of charges that are often unpopular and prone to nullification. The 1992 acquittal of four Los Angeles police officers charged with the assault of black motorist Rodney King is vivid proof that some jurors are reluctant to convict police officers for actions that they see as "just part of the job" of fighting crime. In fact, verdicts like the ones rendered in the King beating case might be one cause for judges' hesitation to formally recognize or encourage nullification. Confident judgments about "what happened" in the King case are also complicated by possible racial influences. King was beaten by four white police officers, and the first jury, which deliberated the charges for seven days, contained no black persons.

An instruction that explicitly permits jurors to disregard the law puts an additional burden of responsibility on them. And if jurors have a license to acquit despite the facts and the law, do they equivalently have the license to convict when the facts and the law fail to support that decision? We all know of cases in which the defendant was convicted for the wrong reasons. If the nullification procedure is ever implemented countrywide, it must be available only in cases in which a jury wants to acquit in the face of law and evidence to the contrary; it should not be available to a jury that vindictively wants to convict even though the evidence would lead to acquittal.

SUMMARY

Every trial presents two contrasting views of the truth. Although on first glance the purpose of a trial is seen as determining truth, it has also been argued that agreed-on conflict resolution is an equally valid purpose. This debate is exemplified by three contrasting images of a trial: (1) as a rational, rule-governed event, (2) as a test of credibility, and (3) as a conflict-resolving ritual.

When a case is brought to trial, the legal system employs a series of steps. Pretrial procedures include discovery, or the process of obtaining the information about the case held by the other side. Interviews of potential witnesses, called depositions, are a part of the discovery procedure. Before the trial, attorneys may make motions to exclude certain witnesses or testimony from the trial. The decision whether a judge or jury will render the verdict is also made at this point.

After the jury, if any, is selected (a process called voir dire), the following sequence of steps unfolds in the trial itself:

1. Opening statements by attorneys for the two sides (prosecution or plaintiff goes first).
2. Direct examination, cross-examination, and redirect and re-cross-examination of wit-

nesses, with prosecution witnesses first, then defense witnesses.
3. Presentation of rebuttal witnesses and evidence.
4. Closing statements, or summations, by the two sides, usually in the order of prosecution, then defense, then prosecution again.
5. Judge's instructions to the jury (in some jurisdictions, these come before the closing statements).
6. Jury deliberations and announcement of verdict.
7. If guilty, determination of the punishment.

The trial process that the United States adopted from England is called the "adversary model" because all witnesses, evidence, and exhibits are presented by either one side or the other. In contrast, in the inquisitorial model used on the continent of Europe, questioning of witnesses is done almost entirely by the judge. Although the adversarial model has been criticized for instigating undesirable competition between sides, in empirical studies it has been judged to be fairer and to lead to less biased decisions.

The question of whether juries' and judges' verdicts differ significantly has been answered in a massive empirical study by Harry Kalven and Hans Zeisel. In actual trials, 75% of the time the jury came to the same verdict that the judge would have. With respect to the discrepancies, in 5.5% of the cases the jury was hung. In the remaining 19.5% the judge and jury disagreed. In the vast majority of these disagreements, especially those involving minor offenses, the jury was more lenient than the judge would have been.

Among the sources of the discrepancies were facts that the judge possessed and the jury did not (accounting for a small percentage of disagreements), the relative effectiveness of the two attorneys (again, a small percentage), disagreements over the weight of the evidence, and what Kalven and Zeisel call "jury sentiments," or factors beyond the evidence and the law.

The doctrine of jury nullification (now in effect in Indiana, Maryland, and Georgia) provides a way to justify the decision to acquit a defendant in, for example, a mercy-killing case, even when the evidence would lead to a conviction. Jury nullification instructions give the jurors the explicit right to disregard the weight of the evidence and the law if, in their judgment, community standards argue for compassion.

13
Jury Trials:
I. Jury Representation
and Selection

The year 1974 remains significant in U.S. political/legal history because it saw the resignation that August of an incumbent president, Richard Nixon. In the spring of that year, at the height of the publicity over the break-in of the Democratic party headquarters at the Watergate Hotel, John Mitchell and Maurice Stans were tried in federal court in New York City, charged with conspiracy to impede a Securities and Exchange Commission (SEC) investigation of Robert L. Vesco, a financier and fugitive from justice. The prosecution claimed that Mitchell, former chairperson of President Nixon's reelection campaign in 1972, and Stans, the campaign treasurer, had received a $200,000 contribution from Vesco, targeted for use in the campaign.

THE MITCHELL/STANS TRIAL AS AN ILLUSTRATION OF JURY SELECTION

The Mitchell/Stans trial is by no means typical of all trials with respect to the jury's selection and its deliberations, but it still merits a detailed review as an illustration of how juries are composed and how they can function in our justice system. Beyond that, the trial's surprising outcome is fascinating, resulting from one ironic twist after another.

Rumor has it that, before their trial, Mitchell and Stans told their assistants to approach some prominent social scientists for help in selecting their jury. The procedure of so-called *scientific jury selection* had been publicized only a year before, when social scientists assisted the Berrigan brothers and their codefendants in the "Harrisburg Seven" trial (see Box 2-2). But these social scientists were willing to offer their free services only to those activist and protest groups that they believed were the targets of political trials aimed at suppressing dissent. Other early examples of social scientists aiding jury selection also concentrated on cases involving politically unpopular defendants, such as Black Panther leader Huey Newton (Blauner, 1972), the "Attica brothers" (Levine & Schweber-Koren, 1976), and the Wounded Knee defendants (Christie, 1976).

Rebuffed by the social scientists, Mitchell and Stans hired a public relations firm to conduct a survey and then advise their attorneys about selecting a jury. (Box 13-1 clarifies some jury "selection" procedures.)

In attempting to identify the "best" jurors, the public relations firm also wanted to determine just whom to exclude. It therefore developed a profile of persons who would seem to be most prejudiced against defendants Mitchell and Stans. This profile of the "worst possible juror" included the following: a liberal Democrat, Jewish, who read the *New York Times* or *New York Post,* who watched the TV news with Walter Cronkite (then the most influential of TV anchorpersons), who was interested in political issues, and who was well informed on Watergate.

The defense team had a challenging task: to try to compose a jury of 12 residents of New York City who were not well educated, who were not Jewish, and who—in 1974—had never heard of Watergate! Thanks to the detailed analysis of this case's jury selection procedures by social scientists Hans Zeisel and Shari Seidman Diamond (1976), on whose report we have heavily relied, we can evaluate the defense team's success.

Drawing a Panel, or Venire

Jury selection begins with the drawing of a panel, or venire, of prospective jurors. In this case an unusually large number—196 persons—was included. But the presiding judge quickly excluded

85 of these prospective jurors for "hardship" reasons, including job demands, poor health, and presence of small children in the home. Hence, even if the original panel had been drawn in a manner that would have made it representative of the community, the exclusion of 43% of its sample threatened the representativeness of the remainder.

As a result of additional questioning, 38 more jurors were excused because they appeared prejudiced or had conflicts of interest. Then the judge excused 21 more in order to have a net pool of 52, a figure he deemed sufficient to cover the peremptory challenges he had granted to each side. Note that this net figure of 52 was only about one-fourth of the original venire.

However, the government's attorneys did not appear especially concerned with making selections from within this group; they used only 6 of their allocated 8 challenges of jurors and none of the 3 they were allowed for alternates. In contrast, the defense team for Mitchell and Stans

capitalized on every opportunity; it used all 20 of its peremptory challenges for the 12-person jury and its 3 for the 6 alternate jurors. From the defense team's perspective, its efforts were highly successful. Of the original 196 members of the venire, 45% had some college education; only 1 (or 8%) of the actual 12 jurors did—and only one year of college at that! Thirty-two percent of the original jury panel described themselves as "well informed" about Watergate; only 1 of the 12 final jurors did. None of the jurors or alternates had a Jewish name. Thus the defense team had been able to compose a jury largely of clerical workers with a high school education who seemed to care little about Watergate.

Did the Jury Selection "Work"?

Not only were the demographic characteristics of the original venire dramatically different from those of the final jury, but the actual jurors matched the defense team's criteria almost

---

Box 13-1   *Peremptory Challenges and Challenges for Cause*

Technically, opposing counsel do not *select* a jury; rather, the judge gives them the opportunity to *exclude* a certain number of potential jurors from the eventual jury without having to give any reasons. These exclusions are called *peremptory challenges*; their number, determined in advance by the judge, varies from one jurisdiction to another. In the Mitchell/Stans trial, the judge allowed each defendant ten peremptory challenges, or a total of 20 potential jurors to be

excluded, plus three more for alternate jurors. The government, as the prosecution, was furnished only eight plus three for alternates.

In addition, in any trial each side can claim that particular jurors should be excluded from service *for cause* because they are inflexibly biased or prejudiced or because the relationship of the prospective juror to the parties or the issues seems to raise the *appearance* of bias. (For example, a relative or business associate of a party will be

excused for cause.) Additionally, the judge may excuse a panelist for cause without a request to do so from either attorney. In contrast to the finite number of peremptory challenges, the number of challenges for cause is theoretically unlimited. However, in real life, few prospective jurors are excused for prejudice. In a survey of New Mexico courts over a three-year period, only about one out of every 20 jurors was dismissed for cause (Hans & Vidmar, 1986).

perfectly. So how well did the strategy work? One of the delicious ironies of this case is that it would not have worked, except for an accidental event that the defense team even tried to prevent.

Newspaper reporters and local courtroom habitues predicted that Mitchell and Stans would be found guilty. Although conspiracy is a hard charge to prove, the government had accumulated impressive evidence. And despite the one-sidedness of the jury's composition, the inclination of most jurors, once they began their deliberations, was to find the defendants guilty. A *New York Times* reporter, Martin Arnold (1974), interviewed some jurors after the trial and reconstructed the process of deliberations. He learned that the first informal vote by the jury was 8 for conviction and 4 for acquittal. Even given the requirement of a unanimous verdict, it was very likely that this jury would eventually have convicted the defendants—unless special circumstances intervened.

We can state this expectation because Kalven and Zeisel (1966) examined the first ballot and the final verdict in 225 actual trials that used 12-person juries. They reported that, when the number of guilty votes on the first ballot was between 7 and 11—recall that here it was 8—the final outcome was a unanimous verdict of guilt in 86% of the trials. The same trend exists when an initial majority favors a not-guilty verdict, as another famous trial, held in 1992, indicated. According to newspaper accounts, a large majority of the jurors in the first trial of the policemen charged with assaulting Rodney King were inclined to acquit on all counts from the beginning. The three or four dissidents were overwhelmed by the majority; one of the holdouts recounted that she fasted and prayed to no avail and ultimately followed the "lead of other jurors who had prior jury service," after "being mocked when she asked to see the videotape again" (*New York Times,*

May 9, 1992, p. A7). In only one trial out of 20 does an initial vote that is split strongly toward conviction lead to an eventual acquittal. In about 10% of trials such vote splits lead to hung juries; in the first Rodney King trial there was a hung jury on one count.

You may have seen the staple of late-night TV, the film *Twelve Angry Men,* in which Henry Fonda singlehandedly converts all his fellow jurors to his viewpoint. At the beginning of the deliberations, he is the only juror unwilling to convict the young defendant; eventually he persuades all remaining 11 jurors to vote not guilty. Of such outcomes is high drama made, but Kalven and Zeisel's data indicate that, in this case, life does not *ordinarily* imitate art.

But such a turnaround did happen in the Mitchell/Stans trial, because a special circumstance intervened in the form of Andrew Choa, an alternate juror. He appears to have been the main cause for the shift of the majority from conviction to acquittal—for, despite its original vote leaning toward guilt, the jury eventually, unanimously, acquitted the defendants. (Both Mitchell and Stans were later found guilty of other Watergate-related crimes, however.)

One irony stemming from this special circumstance is that Choa would not have served on this jury had not one of the jurors become ill several weeks into the trial. Most certainly he was not what the defense team wanted on the jury: Andrew Choa was a vice president of the First National City Bank (the second largest in the United States), he was a college graduate, he read the *New York Times* every day, and he probably knew as much about Watergate as anyone else in the original venire of 196. In fact, the defense team had even tried to have him removed for cause (that is, prejudice) because he was "too" well informed about Watergate, but the judge had refused.

What the defense team did not know was that Choa was a dedicated supporter of Richard

Nixon. And, although he did not reveal his allegiances to his fellow jurors at the beginning of the deliberations, he gradually became an open advocate for the acquittal of Mitchell and Stans. He also ingratiated himself with the other jurors by breaking the monotony of the long evenings during sequestration. (Because of the publicity accorded this case before and during the trial, the judge had sequestered, or isolated, the jurors in a local hotel to shield them from outside influences.) Choa bestowed a lot of "perks" on the other jurors. For example, when the jurors wanted to see the St. Patrick's Day parade but were not allowed to mingle with the street crowds, Choa arranged for them to watch it from one of the branch offices of his bank. Occasionally he took the other jurors to movies in the private auditorium of the bank. Choa paid minor expenses for other jurors and served as a kind of social director for the group. Could the other jurors resist feeling appreciative toward the man who used his social position to make the ten long weeks of their sequestration more bearable (Zeisel & Diamond, 1976)? And could they resist being influenced by him?

Not only was Choa ingratiating, but he also seemed to understand the tactics necessary to influence others. During the deliberations he was initially circumspect. He later told the *New York Times* reporter that he purposely chose a seat that would ensure his being called on last. Even while declaring "I did not want to influence my fellow jurors," he may have known that the person who speaks last carries an extra measure of influence. All these actions swung the tide. Zeisel and Diamond write:

> We know that Choa was one of the four jurors who from the outset voted for acquittal and, one must presume, began the arduous task of converting the majority to his view. We know no details, but are told that he persuaded the jury at several points to have testimony as well as judge's instructions reread. We do not know what testimony, but are told that these requests were drafted by Choa for the forelady's signature. When it came to the jury's appraisal of the memorandum written by Vesco (or an associate) to Nixon's brother, in which Vesco threatened to disclose his secret $200,000 cash contribution unless the SEC dropped his case, Choa said he considered it "trash"—and the jury seemed to have agreed [1976, p. 166].

Put yourself in the other jurors' shoes. Choa was successful, he was well informed on governmental and financial matters, and he seemed to be a very helpful person. Whether he intended to or not, it would have been difficult for Andrew Choa not to have influenced his juror colleagues. And simply because of his accidental inclusion on the jury, the defense team triumphed—despite its efforts to select a completely uninformed jury!

When William Kennedy Smith was accused of raping a woman on the grounds of Senator Edward Kennedy's Florida estate, he employed a team of jury experts, who developed jury questionnaires and assisted counsel in the jury selection process. As reported in the *American Bar Association Journal* (April 1992, p. 29), husband-and-wife consultants Cathy Bennett and Robert Hirschhorn later explained their techniques to an audience of lawyers, saying that "some of the least promising prospects on paper went on to become some of their favorite candidates for the jury."

> Take the 44-year-old married man who said he was a church-going Catholic with children the same age as the daughter of Smith's accuser, for example. On his questionnaire, the man also indicated that a member of his family was in law enforcement and his daughter had been the victim of a crime.
>
> Based on his answers to the questionnaire, a majority of the audience said they would have quickly rejected the man as a juror for the defense in the Smith trial. But the consultants revealed how the man . . . won them over during voir dire.

Under questioning, the man came across as sensitive, warm, and caring, they said. He spoke softly and looked directly at Smith in a nonjudgmental way. And he said he admired his own father because his dad worked hard and never quit on his family.

The defense team spent nearly four weeks helping to select the jury; the jury spent only 77 minutes in deliberations before acquitting William Kennedy Smith.

GENERAL PROBLEMS IN FORMING A JURY PANEL

Was the selection procedure used in these trials fair? Were the outcomes just? The Mitchell/Stans trial highlights some of the challenges to the legal system's goal of forming juries that are both representative *and* fair. When implementing this first step of forming a venire, each state—as well as the federal government—has its own procedures about how the sample of prospective jurors is to be drawn. But each method shares the goal of not systematically eliminating or underrepresenting any subgroups of the population. To encourage representativeness, U.S. Supreme Court cases going back to 1880 (*Strauder* v. *West Virginia*, 1880) have forbidden systematic or intentional exclusion of religious, racial, and other *cognizable* groups from jury panels. Despite these rulings, until about 30 years ago it was clear that customary venire composition did not achieve this goal and that middle-aged, better-educated white men were overrepresented (Beiser, 1973; Kairys, 1972). In some cities and counties, *every* jury was exclusively composed of white men.

Furthermore, 30 years ago no consistent standard for composing the jury pool existed. In 1961, according to the Department of Justice,

92 federal courts employed 92 different methods of establishing the venire (Hyman & Tarrant, 1975). In some local jurisdictions, representativeness was totally ignored or defined in a way foreign to the foregoing criteria. It was the custom in some towns to use as jurors those retired or unemployed men who hung around the courthouse all day.

Judicial and Legislative Reforms

In a series of decisions, the Supreme Court and the U.S. Congress established the requirement that the pool from which the jury is selected must be a representative cross-section of the community. One of the most noteworthy of these decisions, the Jury Selection and Service Act of 1968, led federal courts to seek uniform criteria for determining what groups are to be excused from jury service.

These decisions were propelled by two policy concerns, each of which entails a psychological assumption (Hans & Vidmar, 1982). First, the government assumed that, if the pools from which juries are drawn represent a broad cross-section of the community, the resulting juries will be more heterogeneous. The courts believed that this diversity would produce two benefits: (1) heterogeneous juries would be better fact finders and problem solvers, and (2) juries composed of a diverse collection of people would be more likely to include minority-group members, who might discourage majority-group members from expressing prejudice.

This second assumption seems valid on a logical basis; casting a wider net will yield members of smaller religious and ethnic groups. But the first expectation—that more heterogeneous juries are better problem solvers—is an empirical question.

Extensive research on the dynamics of groups studied in the psychological laboratory shows that, other things being equal, groups composed of people with differing abilities, personalities, and experiences are better problem solvers than groups made up of people who share the same background and perspective (Hoffman, 1965). The first type of group is more likely to evaluate facts from different points of view and will have a richer discussion. But the tasks carried out by these laboratory groups are very different from the jury's task. For the lab groups the task usually permits a solution that can be judged as clearly correct or incorrect; in the case of the jury the correctness of the decision is difficult to assess. In addition, the speed of solution is often used as a measure of superior decision making in laboratory groups. Although almost everybody in the courtroom would prefer juries to hold speedy deliberations, few would argue that speed should substitute for accuracy.

In summary, the initial reason the legal system offers for requiring representative venires seems justified, both logically and empirically, although the applicable psychological findings must be highly qualified.

The second policy reason for the Court's and Congress's decisions on representativeness is more concerned with the *appearance* of legitimacy than with the jury's actual fact-finding and problem-solving skills (Hans & Vidmar, 1982). Juries should reflect the standards of the community. When certain components of the community are systematically excluded from jury service, the community is likely to reject both the criminal justice process and its outcomes as invalid. Someone has said that "justice must not only be done; it must be seen to be believed," and the different elements of the community must see that they are well represented among the dispensers of justice—that they have a voice in the process by which disputes are resolved (Hans, 1992).

The violent aftermath of the first trial of four white Los Angeles police officers who were acquitted of assault charges for their role in beating black motorist Rodney King illustrates this problem more dramatically than any event in our nation's history. The panel eventually selected for the trial of these officers contained no black jurors (Box 13-2). After the jury found the police officers not guilty, the black community rejected the validity of the verdict and angrily challenged the legitimacy of the entire criminal justice system for black people. Shaken by the surprising verdicts and shocked by the ensuing riots, many Americans, regardless of their race, questioned the fairness of the jury's decision, in part because of the absence of black citizens from its membership.

So, too, might defendants reject the fairness of decisions made by juries whose members share few if any social or cultural experiences with them. Consider, for example, the likely reaction of a college sophomore, on trial for possession of marijuana, who is found guilty by a jury composed entirely of people in their fifties and sixties.

Representative juries not only preserve the legitimacy of the legal process, but they also solidify participants' positive feelings toward the process. If members of underrepresented groups—the poor, the elderly, blacks, youth—do not serve on juries, they are more likely to become angry and impatient with the legal process. Almost always, the net result of serving on a jury is an increased appreciation for the jury as a worthwhile institution.

Devices Used for Drawing a Pool

So representativeness is an eminently worthwhile goal. Given the guidelines from the federal courts and the legislature, how should local courts go about drawing representative pools? (It is important to note that these laws do not require any one pool to be representative; they require that a series of jury pools drawn over a period of several years be representative of the community's composition; Farmer, 1976.) The 1968 law required that voter registration lists be used as "the primary source" for jury pool selection. But such lists underrepresent certain segments of the community. Compared with the general population, people who have recently reached voting age are less likely to have registered to vote; people who move frequently may not have registered; smaller percentages of the poor, blacks, and other minorities register to vote. Consequently, representative pools will require that voters' lists be supplemented by other sources, such as lists of licensed drivers, persons receiving public assistance, and unemployment lists (Kairys, Kadane, & Lehoczky, 1977). Unfortunately, the Jury Selection and Service Act of 1968 did not make these recommendations into

requirements. Even though some jurisdictions have used additional sources, recent studies indicate that unrepresentative pools are still common. For example, a study conducted almost a decade after the new law was passed documented continued use of outdated voter registration lists, failure to contact those who had not returned their questionnaires, and very liberal application of exemptions (Alker, Hosticka, & Mitchell, 1976). In its examination of jury panel composition in one division of the U.S. District Court for the District of Massachusetts, this study found that the process discriminated against the poor, the young, racial minorities, and persons who had either very little or a great deal of education.

Box 13-2 | **The Jury in the Rodney King Beating Trial**

The first trial of four white Los Angeles police officers accused of the videotaped beating of black motorist Rodney King was moved from urban Los Angeles to neighboring Ventura County as a result of pretrial publicity. The demographics of Ventura County favored the defense—suburban, white, a bedroom community with over 2000 police families, a place to which people move to escape urban problems. It could be expected that jurors would empathize with the defendants—the "thin blue line" regarded by many as protecting the citizenry from drugs and gang violence—rather than with Rodney King, a large, black, drunk driver. As one legal specialist put

The Videotaped Beating of Rodney King

it, "I think the case was lost when the change of venue was granted. I don't think Terry White (the prosecutor) had a chance, and it doesn't do a lot of good to debate whether they should have called Rodney King and all that stuff, because I think from that point on these people approached the case with a mindset" (*National*

Law Journal, May 11, 1992, p. 15).

The six-man, six-woman jury, whose verdict of acquittal sparked one of the worst riots in this nation's history, consisted of ten whites, one Hispanic, and one Asian, but no African Americans. The median age of the jurors was 50 years. Five jurors were registered as Republicans and five as Democrats, one did not indicate a party preference, and one was not registered. Three were members of the National Rifle Association, and two others had law enforcement backgrounds. Most of the jurors were married and owned or were purchasing their own homes.

Furthermore, *some* local courts have ruled that underrepresentation of such groups—in a 1973 test case in Louisiana, it was the poor—does not violate the purpose of the Jury Selection and Service Act (Handman, 1977). The courts have still not agreed about what "representativeness" means in practice.

Exclusions and Exemptions: Threats to Representativeness?

Once a pool of potential jurors has been drawn, they are each sent a questionnaire in order to assess their qualifications and ability to serve. Some people may be excluded by law because of certain personal limitations, although these restrictions are changing. For example, deaf people have recently been permitted to serve on juries in several jurisdictions. Although the rationale for prohibiting the service of certain groups (the visually impaired, those who do not speak English, people who have felony convictions) may be justified, a number of decisions during this phase have further eroded the representativeness of the eventual jury. For example, there is a lower return rate of the questionnaire by some segments of the community (the highly mobile, the less educated), and in some jurisdictions this failure to respond results in these people being excluded from jury service (Macauley & Heubel, 1981). The courts play an indirect role in these exclusions when they fail to recruit such people zealously.

In contrast to the exclusions or disqualifications required by law, many prospective jurors avoid service by claiming personal hardship. In small communities the judge will naturally exempt anyone (a physician, for example) whose jury service might inconvenience the community. Many judges are also sympathetic to claims of ill health, business necessity, vacation plans, and the like. Since only those who ask to be are excused, the result is a winnowing out of many who don't want to serve. Does this change the representativeness of the pool? Intuitively, it would seem that those who remain are more likely to regard jury service as a civic responsibility important enough for them to endure personal inconvenience.

Until 1979, Missouri offered *all* women an automatic exemption, which allowed them to opt out of jury service simply by signing their name at an appropriate place on the jury questionnaire. Before this policy was changed, women constituted only about 15% of the jurors in the Kansas City, Missouri, area. A ruling by the Supreme Court in 1979, stating that the procedure violated the aspiration of the jury to be a "fair cross-section of the community," has led to a fourfold increase in the percentage of Missouri jurors who are women (Mills, 1983; see also Box 13-3).

Thus, even before the formal "jury selection" in a trial is underway—that is, choosing from among the people who are physically present in the courtroom—the selection process has already begun with the removal of some people from the panel of prospective jurors from which the final jury will be drawn. These removals will distort the representativeness of panels whenever certain groups of people are overrepresented among those removed. As Hans and Vidmar state after reviewing the evidence, "The ideal of a jury panel as a representative cross-section of the community is seldom realized" (1982, p. 46).

VOIR DIRE: A REASONABLE PROCESS WITH UNREASONABLE OUTCOMES?

As if the previous steps in the jury-empaneling procedure had not already compromised the representative nature of the jury, the voir dire process may accentuate the resulting jury's bias, as we saw in the Mitchell/Stans jury. Paradoxically, the purpose of the voir dire questioning is to *eliminate* biased jurors. As part of the constitutional right to be tried by a "fair and impartial" jury, a defendant is afforded the opportunity to screen prospective jurors in order to determine whether any of them are prejudiced (*Dennis* v. *United States,* 1966). (See Box 13-4 for examples of questions posed to potential jurors during the voir dire.)

As for procedures, the ways in which voir dire is conducted are almost as numerous as the judges who hold trials (Bermant, 1982). Who asks the questions, what questions are asked and how they are phrased, how long the questioning goes on, and whether the questions are posed to individual jurors or to jurors as a group are all matters left to judges' discretion. In federal courts, judges tend to interrogate jurors themselves and to direct their questions to the entire group rather than to individuals (Bermant, 1977, 1982). Some federal judges will accept additional questions from the opposing attorneys. But even here there is variation; in three federal courts, all in Pennsylvania, by local custom the judge is not even in the courtroom while the attorneys or the deputy court clerk carries out the questioning (Bermant & Shapard, 1978). In state courts, judges are more likely to permit the attorneys to

---

Box 13-3 | *Are Women a "Cognizable" Group?*

Women were not allowed on juries anywhere in the United States until 1898, when Utah did so. Prior to 1920, only four other states had granted this right to women. Connecticut did not do so until 1937! This discrimination against women was tolerated for many years by the courts; the 1880 *Strauder* v. *West Virginia* decision ruled that jury selection could not discriminate on the basis of race but that it was acceptable to limit jury service to men.

In 1966 the Mississippi supreme court wrote: "The legislature has the right to exclude women so they may contribute their services as mothers, wives, and homemakers, and also to protect them from the filth, obscenity, and noxious atmosphere that so often pervades a courtroom during a jury trial" (quoted by Hans & Vidmar, 1986, p. 53).

It was not until 1975 (in *Taylor* v. *Louisiana*) that the Supreme Court ruled that jury service could not be confined to men and that the use of special exemptions for women resulted in depriving a defendant of a fair and impartial jury. This decision also forbade a practice like that used in New York, in which the court refused to pay women for jury service but did pay men.

Subtle discrimination of women persisted, however. In the early 1980s in New York City, a prospective juror named Carolyn Bobb was asked during voir dire whether there was a "Mr. Bobb" and, if so, what his occupation was. She refused to answer, saying that it was her perception that only female members of the jury panel had been asked questions about their spouse, and hence the procedure reflected sex discrimination. The municipal court judge sentenced Ms. Bobb (an attorney) to one day in jail for refusing to answer the question.

The principles of *Batson* v. *Kentucky* (1986) and *Powers* v. *Ohio* (1991) have not yet been extended to gender; a lawyer can still peremptorily challenge a female juror just because she's a woman. However, several cases appealing this issue are just now beginning to be decided in the courts.

ask the questions; some local judges may offer only minimal supervision. Examination of jurors is usually conducted in open court, but, if very sensitive topics are raised, the questioning may be done at the judge's bench or in the judge's chambers.

Voir dire varies in other important aspects as well, such as how long the process takes and how the peremptory challenges are applied. As noted in Box 13-1, the questioning may reveal that certain prospective jurors are biased and hence should be excluded from jury participation for cause. A prospective juror is excused from jury duty on a specific case if the judge accepts the challenge for cause; this "stricken"

juror will be eligible for potential jury service on other cases.

Use of Peremptory Challenges

Potential jurors who are prejudiced against either party in a trial should be stricken from service, and that is the purpose of judges granting challenges for cause. But additionally, as Box 13-1 explained, each side may exclude a designated number of prospective jurors "without a reason stated, without inquiry, and without being subject to the court's control" (*Swain* v. *Alabama,* 1965). The purpose of providing this opportunity is to make sure

---

Box 13-4   *Examples of Voir Dire Questions*

Among the questions that prospective jurors in a criminal trial might be asked in voir dire are the following:

- "Have you ever served on a jury before, either in a criminal or a civil case, or as a member of a grand jury, either in federal or state courts?"
- "Have you or any members of your family or close friends ever been the victims of this type of charge?"
- "Can you set aside any personal beliefs or feelings and any knowledge you have obtained outside the court and decide this case solely on the evidence you hear from the witness stand?"
- "Do you have any opinion at this time as to the defendant's guilt or innocence?"

- "Do you understand that all the elements of the crime must be proven beyond a reasonable doubt, and, if any element is not proven, would you then vote not guilty?"

Notice that most of these questions can be answered with a simple "yes" or "no." These are the types of "close-ended" questions attorneys are taught to ask in the courtroom. They are effective in controlling the answers of witnesses, but they are not very useful in learning about jurors' beliefs and attitudes. This goal requires "open-ended" questions that encourage jurors to talk more about their feelings and experiences. Psychologists who aid attorneys in voir dire often teach them to use open-ended questions when they need to dis-

cover a juror's true feelings about something. Examples of these questions are the following:

- "When you read about these crimes in the paper, what did you think about the person accused of committing them?"
- "What experiences have you had in your life that caused you to believe that a person was being discriminated against because of the color of his skin?"
- "If there were evidence that Mr. Wallace had been drinking alcohol that night, how would that affect your ability to listen to the rest of the evidence about his behavior?"

that the jurors will decide on the basis of the evidence placed before them, not on irrelevant factors that either side might believe will color the opinion of a given juror (*Swain* v. *Alabama*, 1965). The number of these *peremptory challenges* allowed to each side varies not only from one jurisdiction to another but also on the basis of the type of case (civil or criminal) and the seriousness of the charge. In criminal trials the defense will have either the same number or a greater number than the prosecution. In civil litigation the defense and the plaintiff are granted the same number of peremptories, which is usually less than that granted in criminal trials in the same jurisdiction. For example, in a capital (death penalty) case, California gives each side 26 peremptory challenges, but Virginia gives only 4 to each side. In felony cases the federal government gives the prosecution 6 challenges and the defense 10, but the defense can be awarded more if special circumstances warrant.

Peremptory challenges are the vehicle that attorneys use to challenge jurors who they believe will not be sympathetic, for whatever reason, to their client. Their use raises an interesting dilemma. Are *only* truly biased panelists eliminated from service during voir dire, or do opposing attorneys manage to obtain jurors who might be *biased in their favor*? Most attorneys seek to build a jury of individuals who are sympathetic to their side of the case. For such lawyers the goals of voir dire are threefold: (1) to identify and eliminate—preferably through challenges for cause but, if need be, through peremptory challenges—those prospective jurors unfavorable to their side and to "select" those they think will look favorably on their arguments; (2) to indoctrinate prospective jurors and influence those who ultimately will make up the actual jury; and (3) to create positive impressions about themselves and their client.

Do these goals match the legal system's goals for voir dire? Basically these latter goals are threefold: (1) to determine whether a prospective juror meets the statutory requirements for jury service, (2) to discover any grounds for a challenge for cause, and (3) to discover information that can lead to the intelligent exercise of peremptory challenges (*United States* v. *Dellinger*, 1972). These goals direct voir dire to one overall aim: ensuring that an impartial jury is empaneled. However, lawyers are well aware that jury selection, as practiced in an adversary system, permits them to achieve other goals. Their law school textbooks in trial practice and trial advocacy instruct them that jurors are prejudiced in one way or another and hence that attorneys should try to capitalize on jurors' biases. These texts, plus lawyers' workshops and the use of trial consultants, many of whom are psychologists, provide advice about how to indoctrinate those jurors who are chosen. For example, Holdaway (cited in Blunk & Sales, 1977, p. 44) gives the following example of how counsel can introduce a question that will acquaint the juror with rules of law or facts expected to arise in the case but introduce it in such a way that it allies the juror with the attorney's position. The question is "Do you agree with the rule of law that requires acquittal in the event there is reasonable doubt?" The real purpose of this question is, of course, to alert the prospective juror right from the start that reasonable doubt could exist in the case and to make the juror aware of the rule in the hope that he or she will thus look for reasonable doubt and then vote to acquit.

The *Batson* Decision

As a result of a series of Supreme Court decisions, it is forbidden to exercise peremptory challenges solely on the basis of a juror's race.

In *Batson* v. *Kentucky*, decided in 1986, the Court held that a black defendant was denied his Sixth Amendment right to a jury of his peers by the prosecution's strikes against black members of the venire. In *Holland* v. *Illinois*, a 1990 case, the Court held that a *white* defendant could also complain about the exclusion of blacks because the principle of representativeness was violated by the arbitrary exclusion of any racial group. Finally, and most significantly, the Court in 1991 held that striking jurors solely on the basis of race violates the Equal Protection rights of the *jurors* (*Powers* v. *Ohio*; *Edmonson* v. *Leesville Concrete Co.*). *Edmonson* makes it clear that race-based peremptory strikes are forbidden in civil cases, and in the 1992 case of *Georgia* v. *McCollum*, the Supreme Court also applied the principle to forbid race-based strikes by defense counsel in criminal cases.

In a case in which a peremptory challenge is exercised against a black juror, the judge may ask the attorney for an explanation. The attorney must then advance a race-neutral explanation for the strike—for example, that the juror has a brother in prison or has filed a suit against the police. The judge must then determine whether the explanation is genuine, considering the jurors who were not struck by the attorney. For example, if an attorney were to explain that she struck a black juror because he had been robbed, the judge would want to know why she had not struck a white juror who also had been robbed (Box 13-5).

At present *Batson*, *Powers*, and the other cases have not been extended to strikes based on cognizable group characteristics other than race. Since prospective jurors are protected by the Equal Protection Clause, however, it is likely that future court decisions will decide that attorneys should not be permitted to strike jurors on the basis of religion, gender, or national origin.

Lawyers' Theories: Stereotypes in Search of Success

Do the trial strategies of attorneys conflict with the goal of having unprejudiced fact finders? Do they perpetuate or extend the bias inherent in the prior selection procedures? Before we answer these questions, we need to answer a more basic one: how do lawyers go about selecting or excluding jurors, and do their strategies work?

In everyday life, our impressions about others are governed largely by what psychologists have termed *implicit personality theories*. An implicit personality theory is a person's organized network of preconceptions about how certain attributes are related to one another and to behavior. Trial lawyers often apply their implicit personality theories to jury selection. For example, William J. Bryan (1971) advised prosecutors to "never accept a juror whose occupation begins with a P. This includes pimps, prostitutes, preachers, plumbers, procurers, psychologists, physicians, psychiatrists, printers, painters, philosophers, professors, phoneys, parachutists, pipe-smokers, or part-time anythings." We know of another attorney who vowed to always use a peremptory strike against any prospect who wore a hat indoors. Implicit personality theories lead to stereotypes when the person believes that all members of a distinguishable group (such as a religious, racial, sexual, age, or occupational group) have the same attributes. They also produce assumptions that two qualities are associated—for example, when a lawyer assumes that slow-talking jurors are also unintelligent.

We all tend to link qualities together and form our own implicit personality theories. Sometimes these judgments are rationally based; we may have had enough consistent experiences to draw a firm conclusion about the relationship. Other theories, however, like the examples above, are only intuitive or based on very limited experiences and probably coincidental relationships. But of such material are stereotypes often formed.

Even though implicit personality theories can stem from snap judgments, they can become well developed, detailed, and entrenched. An example comes from a book, published in 1920, entitled *Characterology: An Exact Science,* which related individuals' character to their head shape, body shape, coloring, facial features, and the like. The author concluded, for

example, that small ears indicate a poor memory, whereas bushy eyebrows are a sign of a harsh, inflexible mentality.

These examples may sound exaggerated and almost charmingly outdated. But the emergence of implicit personality theories is almost inevitable when we form impressions of others and make interpersonal decisions. After all, human behavior is very complex. We must simplify it in some way. Richard "Racehorse" Haynes, a highly successful lawyer, was once defending

---

Box 13-5 | *Peremptories after Batson: Discriminatory or Race-Neutral?*

In *Branch* v. *State* (Ala. 1986), decided soon after *Batson*, the court accepted as genuine the prosecutor's explanations for striking six black jurors:

HARRIS: One of the prosecutors had participated in a "bust" five months before, at a home close to Harris's residence, and saw Harris during the "bust"; he could not recall Harris's relationship to the person arrested, so he thought it best to strike him. Moreover, Harris was similar in age and physical appearance to Branch.

MANOR: As an employee of Gold Kist, Manor was not desirable as a juror because it was the prosecutors' general experience that Gold Kist's employees had not been attentive as jurors and because a number of employees were being investigated for a variety of crimes.

MEADOWS: Meadows's back-ground as an unemployed former student was not attractive, and she "appeared . . . to have kind of a dumbfounded or bewildered look on her face, as if she didn't know why she was here, or what she was supposed to do."

MONTGOMERY: Being a scientist, Montgomery's presence on the jury would have put too great a burden on the prosecution, considering the background of the case and "knowing the problems with one hundred percent mathematical aspects of a case like this"; the prosecutors did not want "a scientific application in the decision."

PARMER: Parmer's general appearance was unkempt. Moreover, he worked in "credit management," and, because the prosecutors were not able to question him about his specific job, they deemed it too risky to leave Parmer on the jury. Parmer appeared to be a gruff collector, and the prosecution did not want a juror who would be at odds with anyone else on the jury.

KELLEY: As a single female who was about the same age as Branch, Kelley "might feel as though she were a sister, or that type thing and have some pity on the person." Moreover, Kelley was observed frowning and the prosecutors did not want, on the jury, a person who was in a bad mood. Finally, her response to defense counsel was much more favorable than her response to the prosecutors.

Do the *Branch* results indicate that a judge will always accept a lawyer's "race-neutral explanation" for striking a juror? If so, *Batson* is a paper tiger.

two white Houston police officers charged with beating a black prisoner to death. Like all lawyers, Haynes had his ideas about the kind of juror who would be sympathetic to his police-officer clients, but his candor may be a surprise. After the trial was over, Haynes was quoted as saying "I knew we had the case won when we seated the last bigot on the jury" (Phillips, 1979, p. 77).

Lawyers must choose which prospective jurors to strike with their quota of peremptory challenges. Hence their own implicit personality theories come into play. Typically, their decisions are based on little information beyond the juror's race, sex, street address, appearance, and occupation (Hawrish & Tate, 1974–1975). Even if they are allowed to question jurors individually, lawyers cannot know for certain if they are being told the truth. By necessity, they fall back on their own impressions.

What attributes do lawyers find important? Textbooks and journal articles on trial advocacy provide a wealth of folklore about jurors' characteristics; even phrenology and astrology have been relied on to identify "good" jurors. Not surprisingly, characteristics that are visible or easily determined—age, sex, race, religion, occupation, country of origin—receive special attention, as Box 13-6 illustrates.

In addition to applying their own theories of personality to juror selection, some attorneys use their understanding of group structure. For example, they play hunches about which jurors will emerge as dominant figures during the deliberations. Who will be selected as foreperson (if, as in most jurisdictions, that choice is left up to the jury)? What cliques will form? Although such awareness of group dynamics is more sophisticated than simple stereotypes of individual jurors, lawyers who use such conceptions are still relying on their own assumptions about human behavior. Keeton (1973) has noted that a significant number of lawyers

maintain a simple "one-juror verdict theory"— that is, they believe that the final group decision is usually determined by the opinions of one strong-willed, verbal, and influential juror. Lawyers who adhere to this explanation of jury behavior look for one juror who is likely to be both sympathetic and influential and then concentrate their influence attempts during the trial on that individual. In pursuing this search for a "key juror," the typical attorney follows one basic rule of thumb: "In general, an individual's status and power within the jury group will mirror his status and power in the external world" (Christie, 1976, p. 270).

Finally, some attorneys follow the "first 12 called" rule. Frustrated by their past attempts to predict how jurors will behave based on their background, they simply accept the first prospects called to the jury box, sometimes deliberately drawing jurors' attention to their willingness to believe that everyone is fair and can therefore be trusted to decide the case "correctly."

Do Lawyers' Theories Work?

Trial attorneys must make informed guesses about which prospective jurors will be more favorable to their side. They are ethically bound to defend their client "zealously." Given their task, the nature of the adversary system, and the ample availability of peremptory challenges, failure to make choices may well reflect lawyers' inflated opinion of their own persuasiveness. But two questions need to be answered. First, does any evidence exist for the accuracy of lawyers' implicit personality theories? And, second, do lawyers' selection strategies work?

Demographic characteristics of jurors appear to be related to their verdicts only part of the time, and even then the relationships are weak and there is inconsistency from one type of trial to another (Feild, 1978b; Fulero & Penrod,

1990; Penrod, 1979). The relationships that emerge are usually very minor; they may permit researchers to claim "There's something there!" but they offer a scant guarantee of success to the practicing attorney who deals with only a few individuals and one trial at a time.

For example, research on the relationship between jurors' gender and their verdicts has yielded results that focus on the type of crime. Simon (1967) had subjects listen to a simula-

tion of a trial for either housebreaking or incest. She found that women were more lenient toward the housebreaking defendant than men but somewhat harsher toward the incest defendant than men. But the most consistent gender difference is a matter of style rather than content; men play a more active role in the jury room than women. A man is more frequently selected as foreperson (Dillehay & Nietzel, 1985; Strodtbeck, James, & Hawkins, 1957),

---

Box 13-6 │ *A Lawyer's Stereotypes about Jurors*

This is how the master attorney Clarence Darrow expressed his advice about what he looked for in jurors:

> I try to get a jury with little education but with much human emotion. The Irish are always the best jurymen for the defense. I don't want a Scotchman, for he has too little human feelings; I don't want a Scandinavian, for he has too strong a respect for law as law. In general, I don't want a religious person, for he believes in sin and punishment. The defense should avoid rich men who have a high regard for the law, as they make and use it. The smug and ultra-respectable think they are the guardians of society, and they believe the law is for them [quoted in Sutherland & Cressey, 1974, p. 417].

Perhaps the most pungent summary of the state of the art is by

Clarence Darrow

Keith Mossman, currently a trial attorney:

> As a young practicing attorney, I used to get advice from experienced trial lawyers who agreed that potential jurors could be chosen on the basis of occupation. Cabinetmakers and accountants, the adage went, should be avoided because they require everything in a case to fit together neatly. Carpenters, on the other hand, were said to be more likely to accept the de-

fendant's case, since they are accustomed to making do with available materials. Like successful poker players and other gamblers, most criminal trial lawyers have acquired some "superstitions" in their attitude toward jury selection. A nationally known trial lawyer once told me that he would not accept any left-handed jurors. Along with occupational criteria, some of the old men of the trade thought that nationality played a crucial role in jury selection. According to the maxim, jurors of Southern-European descent tended to be more sympathetic to a defendant than did more exacting jurors with German or Scandinavian blood. In all my years of practice in Iowa, however, I have yet to encounter the ideal juror—a Spanish carpenter [Mossman, 1973, p. 78].

and men speak more often during deliberations (James, 1959). Men seem to be chosen more often to head the jury for two reasons: they are more likely to make a personal statement about their status by choosing the end seat at the deliberation table, and they are seen by other jurors as more experienced in such decisions (Strodtbeck & Lipinski, 1985).

Jurors' socioeconomic status and occupational level are related to their verdicts in only a very general way. In a survey of how jurors voted in 100 criminal trials, Adler (1973) found that jurors who voted to convict the defendant were of higher socioeconomic status (as indicated by income, occupational level, education, and similar variables) than those who voted for acquittal. This tendency for "well-off" jurors to be harsh on defendants has been confirmed in controlled laboratory studies (Simon, 1967). And, like men, jurors of higher economic status are more likely to be elected foreperson (Strodtbeck et al., 1957). One demographic variable—education—has been shown to predict antilibertarian attitudes that are in turn associated with a tendency to convict defendants (Moran, Cutler, & Loftus, 1990).

Attempts to relate jurors' ethnic origin to their verdicts have led to some conclusions— for example, jurors of German and British descent favor the government, whereas those of Slavic and Italian descent favor the defense (Broeder, 1959)—but these generalizations must be viewed with *great* caution. Other factors play a role here; for example, socioeconomic differences among ethnic groups may provide a better explanation for their different reactions. When other demographic characteristics are studied (such as race, level of education, or place of residence), they are often found to interact so much with ethnicity, with one another, and with characteristics of the case that it is impossible to make even the most tentative of conclusions about the influence of any one

variable. Some psychologists have concluded that their research shows black jurors to be more lenient than whites, but such sweeping conclusions seem unwarranted. Rather, leniency of the verdict is affected by the interaction of characteristics of jurors, such as their race and social class, with aspects of the trial, such as the type of crime, race of the defendant, and race of the victim. Simon (1967) reported that black mock jurors were more likely than white mock jurors to acquit defendants who used an insanity defense. On the other hand, upwardly mobile black middle-class jurors may, in fact, be harsher toward black defendants in violent crimes such as murder and rape than white jurors (Nietzel & Dillehay, 1986).

Personality Characteristics of Jurors

If demographic qualities have an uncertain relationship to jury verdicts, what about the personality characteristics of the individual juror? Do attorneys' implicit personality theories and stereotypes work here? A number of studies have concluded that enduring aspects of personality *may* influence a person's courtroom decisions, but usually only to a modest degree. Many commentators suggest that personality factors do not usually predict more than 10% of the variance in jury verdicts, but other researchers claim that in certain cases these variables can account for as much as 30% of the variance (Moran et al., 1990).

Psychological research using simulated juries in laboratory settings has indicated that certain personality attributes of mock jurors, such as level of authoritarianism, internal or external locus of control, and belief in a just world, may at times be related to verdicts in a jury simulation. Lawyers have a slight chance of improved outcomes when they select jurors on those dispositions. But we need to remember that the trials used in these studies were "close calls";

that is, the evidence for each side was about equally persuasive, and it is in such cases that individual juror characteristics may have their greatest influence (Hepburn, 1980; Nietzel & Dillehay, 1986; Penrod, 1990). In the real world, the evidence is often so conclusive for one side that the jurors' personality dispositions have no appreciable impact. And equally important—yet often overlooked—is the interaction between the jurors' personality characteristics and aspects of the trial.

Authoritarianism is the personality characteristic of jurors most predictive of their verdicts. However, when highly authoritarian jurors find a symbol of authority in the defendant, their usual tendencies to punish the defendant are reversed (Nietzel & Dillehay, 1986). The relationship between personality and behavior is not always smooth or even discernible (Kassin & Wrightsman, 1988). Jury research has shown that authoritarian subjects are more likely to vote for conviction (Narby, Cutler, & Moran, in press) and impose more severe sentences than less authoritarian jurors (Bray & Noble, 1978). Psychologists measure authoritarianism using the California F Scale, which distinguishes people who rigidly adhere to traditional values, identify with and submit to powerful figures, and are punitive toward those who violate established norms. In fact, about the only time that more authoritarian mock jurors were not more conviction-prone occurred in a trial in which the defendant was a police officer. In this case, apparently the more authoritarian jurors identified with the powerful and punitive image of the officer.

Beliefs about the sources of our outcomes in life form another personality variable that sometimes has an effect on jurors' verdicts. Clinical psychologist Julian Rotter (1966) proposed that people differ in their beliefs about whether their lives are controlled by internal factors, such as their own skills and effort, or external factors, such as luck, fate, or the actions of others. Research has shown that this internal/external dimension (or I-E, as it is abbreviated) is a potent determinant of behavior in a variety of settings (Phares, 1976). In their verdicts, jurors seem to project their own orientations on the behavior of defendants; jurors with an internal locus of control (those who see themselves as responsible for their own outcomes) tend to perceive defendants as more responsible for their predicaments, especially when the evidence is ambiguous (Phares & Wilson, 1972). Hence they may be harsher jurors than those who hold external beliefs; the latter are more likely to attribute criminal acts to forces beyond the defendant's control.

A third possibly relevant personality characteristic of jurors is called "belief in a just world" (Lerner, 1970). As indicated in Chapter 3, individuals differ in the extent to which they believe that people get what they deserve (and deserve what they get) in life. A person who believes in a just world has a need for explanation and justification; it is threatening to such a person to face the possibility that events happen by chance. Imagine that someone is killed in what appears to be a completely coincidental accident; he is walking along a downtown sidewalk when a truck careens out of control and runs him down. Those who believe in a "just world" are so threatened by the idea that the victim died just by chance that they will conclude that he must somehow have deserved such a fate—that he *must* have done something wrong to cause his misfortune. Relatives and friends of rape victims, instead of providing sympathy, often will derogate them on the assumption that, if they got raped, they must somehow have provoked, invited, or caused it. Consistent with this view, researchers have found that persons who believe in a just world, in order to maintain their belief system, will then berate the victim of a crime or be tougher on the defendant (Gerbasi, Zuckerman, & Reis, 1977; Moran & Comfort, 1982).

One final juror characteristic that has been linked to jury outcomes is not a personality variable at all; it is the amount of prior experience the juror has had deciding other cases. Although the results of studies about the effects of prior juror experience on jury verdicts are inconsistent, most criminal defense attorneys prefer jurors who have never served on a jury before, whereas attorneys for civil defendants prefer experienced jurors (Bailey & Rothblatt, 1985; Belli, 1954). In an effort to learn whether prior jury service influences latter verdicts, Dillehay and Nietzel (1985) studied 175 consecutive criminal trials across one calendar year in Lexington, Kentucky. Because jurors in this jurisdiction are "on call" for service for 30-day terms, they have the opportunity to serve on several trials in one month. Two indices of juror experience correlated with a greater likelihood of conviction: the number of jurors per jury who had served on at least one prior jury and the total number of juror experiences represented on each jury. Guilty verdicts increase when a majority of jurors on a given case have had prior jury experience. Although a follow-up study of 169 trials in the next 18 months did not find any relationship, a third study (Himelein, Nietzel, & Dillehay, 1991) of these cases found that juries whose members were more experienced jurors handed down more severe sentences than did inexperienced juries (Kentucky is one of the few states where jurors sentence convicted defendants).

Although most psychologists doubt that personality and demographic characteristics can predict *individual jurors'* verdicts sufficiently well to be useful, many legal experts persist in their opinions (Gayoso, Cutler, & Moran, in press). With a few exceptions, practicing attorneys and authors of trial advocacy textbooks state that a case can be won or lost during voir dire. After Joann Little was acquitted of the murder of her jail guard in 1975, her attorney boasted that he had "bought" the verdict with a large defense fund, which was used in part to determine what kind of jurors to select (Bermant & Shapard, 1978).

Many attorneys take pride in their skills in selecting a proper jury. For example, a recent president of the Association of Trial Lawyers in America wrote: "Trial attorneys are acutely attuned to the nuances of human behavior, which enables them to detect the minutest traces of bias or inability to research an appropriate decision" (Begam, 1977, p. 3). Yet Kalven and Zeisel (1966), two experts on jury decision making, suggest that, in general, lawyers overestimate their own abilities to turn a jury verdict in a favorable direction. Others are even more skeptical about how much lawyers can accomplish in voir dire. One social scientist observed the jury selection process in 23 consecutive trials in a federal court in the Midwest and concluded that "the *voir dire* was grossly ineffective not only in weeding out 'unfavorable' jurors but even in eliciting the data which would have shown particular jurors as very likely to prove 'unfavorable'" (Broeder, 1965, pp. 505–506).

In a recent set of studies (Olczak, Kaplan, & Penrod, 1991), experienced trial attorneys were observed to use juror selection strategies that were not different from, nor better than, those of inexperienced college and law students asked to evaluate the favorability of mock jurors. As with other comparisons of "experts" and novices, trial attorneys do not appear to think any more accurately when making person judgments than do nonprofessionals. Even when asked to perform a more realistic task—rating jurors from the videotapes of a previous voir dire—attorneys were not able to do better than chance in detecting jurors who were biased against them (Kerr, Kramer, Carroll, & Alfini, 1991).

A few other findings are a bit more favorable to attorneys. In one experiment involving a simulated personal injury case, a social scientist (Strodtbeck, reported in Zeisel & Diamond, 1978) asked experienced civil attorneys to rank jurors according to the size of the damage award that each might advocate in the jury deliberations. He then compared their rankings with the actual awards proposed by these jurors. Both plaintiff and defense attorneys were good at predicting the variations in awards. Another study by a team of psychologists and lawyers (Padawer-Singer, Singer, & Singer, 1974) also concluded that the voir dire served its purpose for the attorneys; compared with jurors who were not questioned by attorneys those selected were more sympathetic about mitigating circumstances, less influenced by negative pretrial information, and more concerned about following the law set forth by the judge.

In a more sophisticated study, two social scientists (Zeisel & Diamond, 1978) assessed lawyers' selection skills by looking at how prospective jurors who were challenged and excused *would have* voted. For 12 criminal trials conducted at the U.S. District Court of Northern Illinois, the researchers had those venire members who had been excused remain as "shadow jurors," watch the trial from the spectator section of the courtroom, and then render their own verdicts. In this way the researchers could compare the decisions of actual juries composed solely of those who had survived the voir dire with the verdicts of hypothetical juries composed simply of the first 12 venire members. (The latter, reconstituted juries were thus made up of both real jurors and those who had been excused.) Zeisel and Diamond estimated that, in 3 of the 12 cases, the actual verdicts were affected by the defense attorney's effective use of peremptory challenges. They concluded that trial attorneys apparently do win some of their cases because of their decisions during the

voir dire. Interestingly, defense attorneys seem to exercise more peremptory challenges than do prosecutors, even when the number granted to each side is equal; this "zealous" representation of their client may be one reason for their relative effectiveness in the preceding survey (Van Dyke, 1977).

"SCIENTIFIC JURY SELECTION": DOES IT WORK ANY BETTER?

As this chapter has noted, for years trial lawyers have selected jurors on the basis of their own theories about how people behave. To the extent that these gut-level hunches, superstitions, and stereotypes have validity—and sometimes they do—the process can increase attorneys' chances of winning some cases they might have lost if decided by a jury with a different composition.

Many attorneys, convinced of the importance of jury selection, but skeptical of their ability to do it well or limited in the time they can devote to it, have hired social scientists as jury selection consultants. These consultants try to use empirically based procedures, including systematic ratings of prospective jurors and surveys of the community, to detect bias, thereby earning this innovation the label of "scientific" or "systematic" jury selection. Although these techniques were first used to aid defendants in several highly publicized "political" trials, they are now frequently practiced in the full range of criminal and civil trials. (Box 2-2 illustrated the use of scientific jury selection in a high-profile case.)

Jury consultants also attempt to predict the power structure and sociometric network within the eventual jury; that is, they try not only to eliminate the "wrong" individuals but also to arrange the composition of the jury so that their preferred individual is elected foreperson. In the trial of the Gainesville Eight, described in Chapter 2, the defense team was able to do just that, and the jury voted unanimously for acquittal.

Earlier, in considering whether lawyers' strategies "work," we concluded that they do, to a slight degree, when the legal evidence is equivocal. Similarly, when the defense in criminal trials has relied on the more empirically grounded "scientific jury selection," it has often been victorious. At first glance the procedure seems to work, but it has been observed that the success rate may be inflated by any of the following factors: (1) many of the more widely discussed cases involved weak evidence against defendants; (2) the cases often involved conspiracy charges, with no direct evidence that the defendants committed unlawful acts; and (3) attorneys who make the extra effort to enlist jury consultation resources may also be more diligent and thorough in other areas of their case preparation.

How does scientific jury selection compare to traditional attorney methods when the two approaches are used to select jurors for the same trials? Horowitz (1980) carried out one empirical comparison, using four criminal cases. Conventional jury selection methods used by attorneys, including reliance on their past experience, interactions with similar jurors in recent trials, and conventional wisdom, were pitted against social science methods. Neither approach was superior to the other for all four trials. Scientific jury selection was more effective in those cases in which there were clear-cut relationships between personality or demographic variables and jurors' votes, but, when these relationships were weak, scientific selection lacked accuracy and precision.

In an attempt to evaluate the effectiveness of the defense's use of jury consultants in a series of death penalty cases, Nietzel and Dillehay (1986) examined the 35 outcomes of 31 capital trials (some trials had two defendants). Juries recommended the death sentence 61.1% of the 17 verdicts in trials in which consultants were not employed by the defense versus 33.3% of the verdicts in trials with defense jury consultants. The correlation between use of a consultant and an outcome other than the death penalty was .26. The small number of cases in the sample rendered this correlation statistically nonsignificant. Of course, these cases differed on many variables besides the use of consultants, so it is not possible to conclude that any differences were due to their presence alone. But the results are consistent with claims that jury consultants might be effective in cases in which jurors' attitudes are particularly important, as they are when a jury is asked to choose between life and death.

Recognizing that jurors' demographic and personality characteristics do not correlate strongly with verdicts in general, jury consultants have shifted their focus in recent years to the intensive study of specific cases (Smith & Malandro, 1986; Vinson & Anthony, 1985). This new strategy emphasizes the following methods:

1. Public opinion surveys, small-group discussions (or "focus groups"), and jury simulation studies in which subjects hear abbreviated versions of the evidence, discuss it, and make individual and group decisions about it as the consultant watches and listens to their deliberations. The consultant tries to discover whether any individual characteristics of these subjects are systematically related to the different reactions they have to the evidence. If so, these relationships will guide the use of peremptory challenges in the subsequent trial.

2. Analysis of how different jurors form a narrative or private story that summarizes the evidence into a coherent, compelling account

(Pennington & Hastie, 1986, 1988). This analysis is followed by an attempt to relate the narratives to the demographic characteristics, personality traits, and attitudinal differences of subjects.

3. Development of a consistent case theme suggested by the results of the study groups used in steps 1 and 2. This theme is then reinforced by voir dire questions, evidence presentation, opening statements, and closing arguments so that the most salient psychological factors of the case are repeatedly presented to the jurors in a manner that best supports the attorney's desired interpretation of the facts.

LAWYERS, PSYCHOLOGISTS, AND ETHICS: PROBLEMS WITH JURY SELECTION

The legal system promulgates an idealized assumption that all members of the community will have an equal chance of serving on juries. Prevalent practices prevent that. All segments of the community are not fairly represented in the jury pools of many jurisdictions across the nation. Attorneys do not seek unbiased and neutral jurors; they seek those favorable to their own side. Proponents of the current system acknowledge this tendency but assume that, if both parties reject those who are unfavorable to them, their respective challenges will balance out. In theory, both extremes will be eliminated, leaving those who are less biased, more neutral, and more open-minded.

This assumption is required by the logic of our adversary system, which holds that fair process and just outcomes are achieved when two opponents work zealously to win outcomes favorable to themselves. But, unfortunately, actual trials don't usually work out that way. Because some lawyers don't really care about jury selection ("Give me *any* 12 people and I'll convince 'em!")

and because others are inept in their selection of favorable jurors, this theoretical balance is seldom if ever achieved. The use of jury consultants by one side but not the other probably adds to the imbalance. In effect, when one of the attorneys is more motivated or more capable at jury selection, the outcome is equivalent to giving that side a larger number of peremptory challenges. Of course, this imbalance is not restricted to adversarial systems; resources are not equally distributed in education, medicine, government, or any of our other social institutions. But the adversary system may magnify the impact of unequally qualified participants; when opponents are not evenly matched, the superior one will win more often.

It is paradoxical that the legal system insists that jurors first be drawn so as to be typical of their communities and then at the last minute allows this representativeness to be undone. As we saw with the Mitchell/Stans case at the beginning of this chapter, the jury selection process can conflict with the goals of representativeness. The "12 good 'men' and true" who found John Mitchell and Maurice Stans not guilty were themselves not representative of their community. But then, representativeness as a goal may have its limits. In cases in which the local community is biased but a change of venue is not granted, justice is sacrificed in order to fulfill the goal of representativeness. And although the legal system seeks with equal fervor to achieve both representativeness and fairness, it fails to recognize that these ideals may be incompatible.

SUMMARY

Among its goals for juries, the legal system seeks that they be representative and unbiased. Each of these goals is hard to achieve. The jury selection process in the conspiracy trial of John

Mitchell and Maurice Stans reveals how the selection process can create an unrepresentative jury.

Reforms have generally not been successful in creating juries that are representative of the adult populations. Too many people are excused from service.

The process of selecting a jury from the panel of prospective jurors is called the voir dire. The institutional goal is to end up with a jury that is unbiased. Each side may discharge a certain number of prospective jurors without giving any reasons; these are called "peremptory challenges." Prospective jurors who have biases or conflicts of interest are "challenged for cause" and discharged. Questioning of the prospective jurors is done at the discretion of the judge. In most local courts the attorneys do the actual questioning; in federal courts, judges typically interrogate the jurors. When questioning jurors, most attorneys will also try to sway jurors to their viewpoint through various ingratiation and indoctrination techniques.

In choosing jurors, lawyers often base their decisions on their implicit personality theories and stereotypes of what is a "good" juror. There are a few personality characteristics of jurors that are somewhat related to their verdicts: authoritarianism, locus of control, and belief in a just world.

Whether lawyers' choices of jurors actually improve their chances of winning is controversial. Clearly the relative weight of the evidence is the most important determinant of the jury's verdict. Initially, practitioners of "scientific jury selection" used community surveys to determine which demographic characteristics of jurors were related to their being sympathetic to one side or the other in trials. More recently, trial consultants have concentrated on studying how specific individual characteristics may be related to the psychological themes and interpretation of evidence in a specific case. There is some proof that science-oriented consultation may be useful in cases in which the evidence is equivocal or jurors' attitudes about the evidence are important.

14
Jury Trials:
II. Assumptions
and Reforms

More than one-fourth of all American adults report that they've served on a jury (Gallup Organization, 1989). Three million U.S. citizens are called for jury duty every year. At the very least, they experience a disruption of routine, and for many jurors their participation demands major sacrifices of income, time, and energy. More than 300,000 jury trials are held annually, each of which decides an important issue for the contesting parties.

The ancient Greeks had a form of citizen-jury. Antecedents of the contemporary jury system stretch back to English law established 700 years ago, and even beyond. Throughout its history the jury, as a system, has been under attack; today is no exception. Recent juries have made some very unpopular decisions. In an ABC News poll carried out within 24 hours of the jury's verdict that John Hinckley was not guilty by reason of insanity of the attempted murder of President Ronald Reagan, 75% of the viewers thought the decision was unjust (Kassin & Wrightsman, 1988). A *Newsweek* poll, taken days after a jury found four Los Angeles policemen not guilty of the assault of Rodney King, reported that 73% of white Americans and 92% of African Americans thought the verdict was not just. American citizens had strongly polarized opinions about the jury's acquittal of William Kennedy Smith, who was charged with the rape of a Florida woman on the grounds of the Kennedy estate in Palm Beach, and considerable controversy greeted the jury's decision in 1992 to convict boxing champion Mike Tyson of the rape of a young woman in Indianapolis.

In personal injury cases, responsive juries have made mind-boggling awards to plaintiffs, such as more than $200,000 to a Chicago couple who were "bumped" from a flight to Florida, causing them the "humiliation, indignity, and outrage" of missing *the birth of a horse.* Another jury awarded $425,000 to a Long Island woman who bit into a squirming beetle while eating a cup of Dannon yogurt.

And in civil suits between large corporations, juries have made awards beyond the comprehension of the average person; a Texas jury awarded Houston's Pennzoil Company $10.53 *billion* plus interest in its lawsuit against Texaco.

Furthermore, the jury system has been described as an expensive and time-consuming anachronism. Some critics want to restrict the use of juries; others would prefer to abandon them. Advocates of radical revision of the jury have even included former Chief Justice Warren Burger of the U.S. Supreme Court, who publicly questioned the abilities of jurors to understand and sort out the complexities of protracted civil cases, such as the one between Pennzoil and Texaco.

Not all the criticism comes from the outside. From the perspective of jurors themselves, the satisfaction of doing their civic duty often does not overcome their apprehensions or discomforts about jury service. In the Wayne Williams murder trial in Atlanta (Williams was charged with killing a number of children), many potential jurors were reluctant to serve because they feared public censure if they were to find the defendant not guilty. Some trials challenge human endurance; the Los Angeles trial concerning the sexual abuse of children in the McMartin preschool took more than three years to complete. Jurors are sometimes housed in hotels during the trial (or at least during deliberations); they are prevented from contacting family or friends and are denied access to television and newspapers. After their verdict in the first Rodney King police brutality trial was announced, the jurors were warned not to open their mailboxes because officials feared that bombs might have been placed inside them.

The right to a trial by jury is protected by state constitutions and by the Sixth Amendment to the U.S. Constitution. Furthermore, the trial jury is an institution that routinely, on every working day, draws ordinary citizens into the decision-making apparatus of the justice system. It consumes human resources and government expenditures in massive doses. Although many states have instituted changes in the jury procedure over the last two decades—such as reduced size and decision rules other than unanimity—the jury system has received little systematic evaluation from the legal system. However, psychologists have frequently evaluated the need for, and in some cases the effects of, these recent changes. In fact, the study of juror behavior and jury variables is one of the clearest examples of the dilemma posed in Chapter 1 of psychology challenging the law's methods for establishing legal procedures. Hence it is legitimate and timely for psychology to examine the effectiveness of the jury as an institution. Are the criticisms justified? What, specifically, do the courts expect from juries? Are these expectations usually met? If not, can the legal system do anything to improve the functioning of juries?

ASSUMPTIONS ABOUT JURORS AND JURIES

Court procedures reveal a number of assumptions about the performance of juries. Perhaps the most fundamental of these is that jury decisions are determined by the evidence presented in court, not by the defendant's background or appearance or by what jurors read in the newspapers. But other assumptions are reflected in the ways the legal system treats jurors. Another assumption, that jurors are representative of their communities, was evaluated in Chapter 13.

Certainly not all judges and attorneys believe that these assumptions are met; in fact, many do not believe them. Still, these assumptions dictate courtroom procedure; they specify how jurors are to behave and what juries are expected to do and not do. And if they are violated, no one necessarily knows the difference. For example, some jury decisions may be based on irrelevant considerations rather than on the evidence. But checking on the reasons for a verdict following a trial is done only very infrequently, and the real reasons for a verdict are often impossible to assess.

THE ASSUMPTION OF A TABULA RASA

Jurors are assumed to enter the trial as *tabulae rasae*, or "blank slates," free of overwhelming biases; that is, the courts assume that they can put aside any preconceptions about the guilt of a criminal defendant or the merits of civil defendants and plaintiffs when forming their judgments. If they cannot, they should be excused for cause. (In criminal cases the "blank slates" should be tinted by a presumption that the defendant is innocent of the charges at the outset.)

A frequent question during voir dire takes the form "Sir, do you believe that you, as a juror, can set aside any negative feelings you might have toward the defendant because he is [black or a police officer or a used-car salesman—whatever the group membership that possibly elicits prejudice] and make a judgment based on the law and the facts of this case?" If the prospective juror says yes, the judge usually believes him, and he is allowed to serve as a juror.

Some prospective jurors have discernible and resolute prejudices or vested interests in the outcome of the case; they can be identified and dismissed. But what can be done about prospective jurors who, during the jury selection process, consciously or unconsciously misrepresent their views? One of the jury pool members in the Harrisburg Seven trial (described in Chapter 2) was a man in his fifties who owned two grocery stores. When questioned by the attorneys, he said that he "couldn't be against hippies because I have sons who look like that" (Schulman, Shaver, Colman, Emrich, & Christie, 1973). On the Vietnam War, he stated: "More could be done and should be done to end the war. . . . I don't know whether we should be there or not." A Lutheran, he felt that priests and nuns *should* oppose the war. Would you have chosen this juror? As you might expect, the defense team believed that he was sympathetic to its side, and the consulting psychologists greeted with enthusiasm his selection as an actual juror.

But his behavior during the deliberations completely contradicted these pronouncements and expectations. In fact, during the seven days of deliberations, he was one of the two jurors who held out for a conviction. As a result, the jury was declared "hung," with a vote of two guilty, ten not guilty. At the very beginning of the deliberations, the grocery store owner pronounced the defendants "guilty by the will of God," shouting that it was necessary to convict them "to satisfy God's will and to save the children and grandchildren of America." Ranting and raving, he banged on the table for emphasis, causing a marshal outside the door to come in and quiet him. Apparently this juror's mind had been made up long before the deliberations began, and it is conceivable that he deliberately misrepresented his views during the jury selection so that the defense team would see him as an attractive choice.

The courts assume that individual jurors can divest themselves of any improper "leaning"

toward one side or the other and that through detailed, sometimes time-consuming, jury selection procedures the ideal of open-minded jurors can be achieved. Because prospective jurors whose preconceptions would affect their verdicts are identified and dismissed, the trial can begin with the expectation that the jury will reach a fair verdict. But this aspiration faces at least four types of challenges. First, attorneys are motivated to select jurors who are favorable to their own side, rather than those who are neutral and unpredictable. Second, as we discuss in detail later, it is impossible for anyone to be completely uninfluenced by past experiences and resulting prejudices. Third, as seen in the above example, if people systematically misrepresent their views during jury selection, no sure way exists to detect it. And, finally, as illustrated in Chapter 13, trial lawyers often deliberately attempt to bias the panel through the use of suggestive questions during voir dire.

Inevitability of Juror Bias

Bias is an inevitable human characteristic. But even though the word *bias* conjures up many unfavorable associations, we should not focus exclusively on its negative qualities. Rather, bias is simply part of the human condition, and as such it colors all our decisions, including jury verdicts.

"Bias," as used here, refers to a human predisposition to make interpretations based on past experience—to try to fit new stimuli and information into one's already developed system for looking at the world. When we are exposed to a new event, we respond to it by relying on past experiences. For example, when we view a traffic accident, it is hard to separate our perceptions from our interpretations. We may make judgments that one car was going too fast or that another car was in the wrong lane. We may assume a particular driver was at fault simply because we happen to have a negative stereotype about, for example, teenage drivers or drivers from a particular city or state.

Bias in our responses to the actions of others is inevitable because people account for so many outcomes in our lives, and we must make assumptions about the causes of their behavior. Why was Emily so abrupt when she spoke to me this morning? Why did Juan decide to buy a new car? Why did the defendant refuse to take a lie detection test? Every day we make decisions based on our assumptions about other people. Criminal defense lawyers make recommendations to their clients on how to plead, based on their expectations about the reactions of prosecuting attorneys, judges, and jurors. College administrators decide who will be admitted as students on the basis of applicants' credentials and academic promise. Choices are always necessary, and our expectations about the outcomes of our choices rest partly on our biases.

Why do we have expectations? We probably could not tolerate life if people were constantly surprising us. We need assumptions about people to help in predicting what they will do. Our expectations often help us simplify our explanations for people's behavior.

Such processes apply to the behavior of jurors, too. Virtually all the legal and psychological conceptions of how a juror makes decisions in a criminal case propose that verdicts reflect the implicit operation of two judgments on the part of jurors.

One judgment is an estimate of the probability of commission—that is, how likely it is that the defendant actually committed the crime. Most jurors base their estimates of this probability mainly on the strength of the specific evidence, but their previous beliefs and experiences also have an impact on how they interpret the evidence. Although jurors must arrive at subjective estimates of this probability,

they are reluctant to use more objective probabilities about the occurrence of the events in question to guide them to a conclusion (Cohen, 1986). Psychologists have begun to study the reasons why people in general are hesitant to use "naked statistical evidence" to answer questions of liability or causation (Wells, 1992).

A second judgment by the juror concerns "reasonable doubt." Judges instruct jurors in criminal cases that they should bring back a verdict of not guilty if they have any reasonable doubt of the defendant's guilt. Yet the legal system has difficulty defining and operationalizing reasonable doubt; a common, but not very informative, definition is that it is a doubt for which a person can give a reason. Jurors apply their own standards for the threshold of certainty deemed necessary for conviction.

On the basis of these factors, many jurors can be classified as having a proprosecution bias or a prodefense bias. (These generally resemble, respectively, the crime-control model and due-process model described in Chapter 1.) Jurors with a proprosecution bias view the conflicting evidence through the filter of their own past experiences and beliefs, which make them more likely to think that the defendant committed the crime. Consider, for example, the statement "Any suspect who runs from the police probably committed the crime." Agreement with this statement reflects a bias in favor of the prosecution. But persons with prodefense biases also filter the evidence as a result of *their* past experiences and reactions. For example, agreement with the statement "Too many innocent people are wrongfully imprisoned" reflects filters leading to biases sympathetic to the defense.

Even if we accept the proposition that bias is inevitable, we must still ask whether such biases color the judgments of jurors. That is the bottom line.

To determine whether bias affects one's verdicts, Kassin and Wrightsman (1983) measured potential jurors' biases by having them complete a 17-statement attitude inventory containing statements like those given as examples above. Later these mock jurors—college students and people recruited from jury lists—watched videotapes of reenacted actual trials or read transcripts of simulated trials. Five types of criminal trials were used. After being exposed to the trial, each mock juror was asked to render an individual verdict about the defendant's guilt or innocence. Jurors voting guilty were then compared with those voting not guilty to see whether their preliminary biases differed. In four of the five cases they did. Even though everyone was exposed to the same evidence and judge's instructions, mock jurors holding a proprosecution bias were more likely to find the defendant guilty. The average rate of conviction was 81% for the prosecution-biased jurors, compared with only 52% for defense-biased ones. It appears that, at least in a majority of cases, each juror's reaction to the evidence is filtered through personal predispositions. Pretrial beliefs and values may influence or even overwhelm the evidence presented in court.

But in one of the five cases, pretrial bias did not influence eventual verdicts. In the trial for rape, jurors predisposed to favor the defense were just as likely to find the defendant guilty as jurors who were predisposed to favor the prosecution. This failure to find a difference demands an explanation. It is possible that prodefense jurors, who are relatively liberal in their political views, generally favor the victim when the crime involves a sexual assault. Thus their general bias in favor of the defendant—which they manifested in the other cases—is countervailed when the charge against the defendant is rape. (See Chapter 15 for elaboration.) Such an explanation for the results in

this one case seems more likely than a conclusion that juror bias manifests itself in only a few situations.

Recommended Reforms: Can We Achieve Both Representativeness and Fairness?

Chapter 13 and this chapter offer both empirical evidence and logic to show that unrepresentative juries are often selected in the legal system. Furthermore, tendencies to be biased in one direction or the other are inevitable influences on jurors' decisions. What can be done about unrepresentative juries? Would any reforms be of help?

Continued broadening of the procedures used to select the venire seems warranted. The names of potential jurors should be drawn from several different sources. In a nation in which only about half of those eligible to vote do so, sources other than voter registration lists should be used, such as driver's license registrations, city directories, and welfare lists.

Voir dire procedures need reexamination also. Some commentators have recommended that the judge carry out the questioning directly, rather than allowing opposing counsel to do so (Bermant, 1985). Although each side could submit questions, the judge would scrutinize these before asking them, in order to eliminate attempts by the attorneys to persuade the jurors. However, other social scientists believe that questioning by the judge inhibits frankness of response (Padawer-Singer, Singer, & Singer, 1974), because jurors feel more pressure to give the "proper" answer when interrogated by a judge than by an attorney. Observational research by Nietzel and Dillehay (1982) led them to conclude that intensive questioning by attorneys on a sequestered basis (that is, with each potential juror questioned individually, away from the other jurors) is a very effective way to uncover potential biases. Richard Christie, in comparing the results of several well-publicized trials, found that, when prospective jurors were questioned individually by both the judge and the attorneys and a wide latitude of questioning was permitted, the greatest numbers were excused for cause (cited by Hans & Vidmar, 1986, p. 72). Box 14-1 lists other arguments for each procedure.

Taking account of the arguments from many perspectives, we doubt that totally unrestricted lawyer-administered voir dire is in the best interests of justice. As Bermant and Shapard note, defenders of this procedure claim that "because adversary advocacy works on the principle that fairness emerges from the confrontation of well-matched, highly skilled opponents, a lawyer helps to seat an impartial jury by trying to gain one biased in the client's favor" (1978, p. 8). But they go on to note that the assumption that this approach produces impartiality "is part of what may be called the 'advocacy myth,' which frees each side to pursue its own cause with a relative

lack of concern about the fairness of the outcome of the other side" (p. 8).

In contrast, a study (described in Chapter 13) that looked at the actual verdicts of dismissed prospective jurors (Zeisel & Diamond, 1978) led to a conclusion that the most significant obstacle to the formation of an unbiased jury was "the inconsistent performance of attorneys. Occasionally, one side performed well in a case in which the other side performed poorly, thereby frustrating the law's expectation that the adversary allocation of challenges will benefit both sides equally" (p. 529).

We would recommend the following methods. On routine matters, such as whether jurors know the attorneys or the parties at trial, the voir dire questions should be posed to the panel of prospective jurors by the judge. On more sensitive matters, such as jurors' knowledge about the case or the nature of any past experiences that might affect their judgments, jurors should be asked to identify their concerns to the judge. Then, to enhance the accuracy and

---

Box 14-1   Judge-Administered versus Lawyer-Administered Voir Dire

Currently, in most federal courts the judge questions potential jurors, whereas in most local courts judges relinquish this responsibility to the attorneys but retain supervisory responsibility. Which is a better procedure? Bermant (1985) lists the following reasons why the Association of Trial Lawyers of America (ATLA) advocates that attorneys do the questioning:

1. Judges do not know how to ask questions in a way that encourages candid replies.
2. Potential jurors will lie to a judge or misrepresent themselves during voir dire.
3. Judge-conducted voir dire may encourage invasion of jurors' privacy.
4. Judges don't know as much about the case as the lawyers do.

Each of these reasons is speculative. There is little empirical evidence to support them, and, for

some, one could as well argue the opposite (for example, prospective jurors might be more honest in answering a judge than an attorney because they have more fear of the consequences of deceiving a judge). Of course, one reason why the ATLA advocates attorney-conducted voir dire is because its attorney members want to begin to persuade the jury at the earliest possible time.

candor of these jurors' answers, additional questioning should be carried out with one prospective juror at a time, by both the judge and attorneys in the judge's chambers.

Granted, jury selection would then take much longer than is currently customary. The average time for voir dire has recently been about one hour in civil trials and about two hours in criminal trials (Hans, 1982), but the range is immense. In one jurisdiction the *average* time for jury selection is 18 minutes; however, in the highly publicized "Hillside Strangler" trial in Los Angeles, the voir dire alone took 49 court *days*, and in the "Pontiac 10" case it took five *months* (Cox, 1989). Although few cases need this much time, the recommended procedure would be more expensive. The trade-off is between increases in time, court costs, and impatience and an increase in fairness. As Bermant and Shapard observe, "It is difficult to discern how more than the most superficial characteristics can be ascertained during the very brief time (usually) allotted" (1978, p. 26). After all, just how effective in unearthing bias is a directive, posed to 12 or 28 prospective jurors sitting together in a jury box, to "raise your hand if you feel that you are prejudiced against Iranians and that would stand in your way of being fair in this case"? In a group setting, few people will publicly acknowledge socially unacceptable feelings. Rather, one usually answers with whatever is the socially correct way to respond. More open-ended questioning of individuals in the judge's chambers will be more revealing. It also keeps jurors from witnessing their predecessors' responses and rehearsing their own.

If bias is inevitable, selection of an actual jury that is representative of varying viewpoints in a community will mean that different biases will be present within the decision-making body. To facilitate this result, we offer another recommendation for voir dire: prohibit the use of an excessive number of peremptory challenges by either side. In some trials, attorneys have been allocated an almost unlimited number of peremptory challenges. This approach allows attorneys to go "juror shopping," searching only for ideal jurors and peremptorily challenging anyone who fails to meet their standards. Voir dire should not be a search for perfect jurors. Prospective jurors who show evidence of conflicts of interest or prejudice should be excused for cause. Judges need to be vigilant in identifying biased jurors during this phase. In fact, if judges are not scrupulous in evaluating challenges for cause and granting them whenever justified, any curtailment of peremptory challenges could cause a great disservice to litigants. On the other hand, one could argue that, with current voir dire procedures, judges are somewhat hesitant to grant challenges for cause because they assume the attorneys can and will use their allotted peremptory challenges to remove questionable juror prospects.

Why permit attorneys on each side to engage in any "free" strikes, in challenges often based, in the words of Supreme Court Justice Byron White, "on the sudden impressions and unaccountable prejudices we are apt to conceive upon the bare looks and gesture of another" (in *Swain v. Alabama*, 1965, p. 220)? The rationale for peremptory challenges was best articulated by Barbara Babcock in a 1975 article in the *Stanford Law Review*. Peremptory challenges reassure litigants who fear, for whatever reason, that certain prospective jurors are hostile to them. They also are necessary to remove jurors who will not admit obviously held biases, and they avoid the necessity of "trafficking in the core or truth of common stereotypes."

[H]uman experience, common sense, psychological studies, and public opinion polls tell us that it is likely that certain classes of people statistically have predispositions that would make them inappropriate jurors for particular kinds of cases. But to allow this knowledge to be expressed in the evaluative terms necessary for challenges for cause would undercut our desire for a society in which all people are judged as individuals and in which each is held reasonable and open to compromise.

By using peremptory challenges, attorneys can, without confrontation and embarrassment, excuse jurors who appear biased. On the other hand, attorneys sometimes fool themselves into thinking they can "pick a jury." Former Supreme Court Justice Thurgood Marshall (who, in the case of *Batson* v. *Kentucky*, 1986, advocated the elimination of peremptories) told the story of a young lawyer, defending a black client, who struck a prospective juror because she was white. The woman remained in the courthouse to watch the trial. After the defendant was convicted, the woman came up to the defense lawyer and the following conversation took place:

"Mr. Dobbins, you remember me?"
"Of course," he said.
"Why did you strike me from the jury?" she said.
"Well, . . . " he said.
"Because I am white?" she said.
"Well, if you want to say it, that is the reason. That was the reason, because you're white," he said.
"For your information, I am not white, and I would never have convicted your man. Goodbye!" she said.

Justice Marshall told this story to illustrate his belief that lawyers would do well to take the first 12 persons in the jury box, because you can never tell what is on someone's mind.

In recent federal trials in the United States, as many as 120 peremptory challenges have been awarded the defense (Cox, 1989). A comparison with procedures in Great Britain is instructive (Hans, 1982). In 1977 Britain's Criminal Law Act reduced the number of peremptory challenges available to the defense from seven to three. The prosecution—that is,

the Crown—has *no* peremptory challenges, in a technical sense, but the Crown may instead ask prospective jurors to "stand by for the Crown." This means that, if the jury can be composed with other panel members, such jurors are then excused. But they may remain eligible if the jury cannot be completed from the remaining panel members. This "standing by for the Crown" is the functional equivalent of a peremptory challenge (Hans, 1982, p. 288). Challenges for cause in the British system are theoretically possible but are *very* rare. One judge commented "I have never seen this done" (quoted in Clarke, 1975, p. 47). The reason why challenges for cause are uncommmon is that an English barrister has no right to question a juror in court until a *prima facie* case for a challenge is provided by other evidence (Cornish, 1968; Hans, 1982).

More surprising is that peremptory challenges are used in only a minority of trials in Great Britain. One survey reported that they were exercised in only 24 trials out of 341; another survey, done in 1975, found that, in 370 trials in Birmingham, only 101 challenges were made (Baldwin & McConville, 1979, 1980). Although there is some indication that British defense barristers have increased their use of peremptory challenges in the last few years, especially in highly publicized trials, the fact is that, in the system closest to the one in the United States, the formation of a jury proceeds with a much more limited removal of prospective jurors (Hans & Vidmar, 1986).

THE ASSUMPTION OF AN EVIDENTIARY FOCUS

Jurors, in forming their verdicts, are assumed to use the evidence and disregard that which is not evidence. They are expected to obey instructions to base their verdict only on the evidence and to consider as evidence only that information that comes through the testimony of witnesses and through exhibits. Is this assumption justified?

Effects of Pretrial Publicity

One of the tasks of the voir dire is to determine whether publicity about the case has caused potential jurors to form preconceptions that would impair their ability to be impartial jurors. Does massive and inflammatory pretrial publicity preclude open-mindedness among jurors? Psychologists, because of their knowledge of the power of first impressions, are more concerned than judges about the detrimental effects of pretrial publicity. What evidence is there that the voir dire process eliminates jurors who have formed an irrevocable opinion because of exposure to publicity before the trial?

A few empirical findings shed some light on this question. Nietzel and Dillehay's (1982) demonstration of the effectiveness of sequestered voir dire leads us to believe that questioning of jurors on an individual basis would help. Other research suggests that extensive voir dire can neutralize the effects of general confusion about legal concepts but that it has little effect on prejudice specifically created by pretrial publicity (Dexter & Cutler, 1991). Furthermore, there is consistent evidence from reactions to real cases that people who have greater knowledge about a case, gleaned from the mass media, are more likely to assume the defendant is guilty (Constantini & King, 1980; Moran & Cutler, 1991; Vidmar & Judson, 1981). (This is because most news stories—detailing arrest of the defendant, a "confession," and other incriminating evidence—report proprosecution information.)

It has also been shown in a controlled experiment (Padawer-Singer & Barton, 1975) that exposure to media information that is detrimental to a criminal defendant leads to a greater likelihood of a guilty verdict. Of the mock jurors—adults drawn from jury rolls—who had been exposed to newspaper articles about the defendant's prior criminal record and his retracted confessions, 47 of 60 (78%) decided that the defendant was guilty after listening to an audiotape of the trial; only 33 out of 60 (55%) decided he was guilty after reading newspaper accounts that omitted the presumably prejudicial information. A second experiment by the same authors, using juries rather than individual jurors, produced similar results. The exposure treatment had an effect even though jurors in both conditions then listened to a complete replay of the trial and heard the judge's instructions.

What is of special concern is that further studies show that effects of pretrial publicity persist even when a host of remedies are attempted to erase or limit these effects. Research with mock jurors exposed to different types of pretrial publicity consistently indicates that traditional remedies, such as continuance of the trial to a later date, jury deliberations, and explicit instructions by the judge to disregard pretrial publicity, are ineffective solutions, particularly for publicity that is emotionally arousing (Carroll et al., 1986; Kassin & Wrightsman, 1988; Kramer, Kerr, & Carroll, 1990).

In summary, the empirical evidence suggests that voir dire does not reliably eliminate jurors with publicity-influenced pretrial opinions from the panel, even though extreme forms of pretrial publicity can influence their verdicts.

It is disheartening that the Supreme Court of the United States ignores this evidence and assumes that jurors can "set aside" opinions formed on the basis of pretrial publicity and "try the case solely on the basis of the testimony from the witness stand." In *Patton* v. *Yount*

(1984) the Court denied a defendant's appeal in a case in which his confession (inadmissible at trial because it was taken in violation of *Miranda*) was widely publicized in the local media, in which all but 2 of 163 venire members had heard of the case, and in which 126 of 163 venire members admitted that they had formed opinions prior to trial. The Court was willing to accept at face value the assertions of the prospective jurors that they could "set aside" what they had read and heard and be *tabulae rasae* for the trial. The defendant's conviction was affirmed.

Further research is needed to distinguish among effects of different types of pretrial publicity. For example, Kramer et al. (1990) have demonstrated that effects of emotional publicity accentuating the grisliness or sensationalism of a crime are more prejudicial and difficult to eliminate than the influence of factual publicity linking the defendant to the criminal act. Type of crime and size of community also may be factors (Carroll et al., 1986).

Finally, certain types of jurors may be especially sensitive to biasing effects of pretrial publicity because of how they process information. People who are very active in the way they think about information and who make extra efforts to evaluate information carefully may be more susceptible to the biasing effects of initial (i.e., pretrial) information (Kassin, Reddy, & Tulloch, 1990).

Impact of Opening Statements

As part of a trial, the attorneys for the two sides are allowed to make opening statements, which usually take the form of pledges to show certain facts and conditions. In some courts the statement must be limited to a general outline; in others, counsel are permitted to recite in detail the evidence that will be put forth by each of their witnesses. Judges have discretion to permit wide diversity in both the content and the length of opening statements; in the first trial of Juan Corona (charged with and ultimately convicted of murdering 25 derelicts and drifters within a 3-square-mile area in California), the prosecution's opening statement took a day and a half!

In a civil trial the person or organization filing charges (that is, the plaintiff) is permitted to make the first opening statement. In a criminal trial the prosecution makes the initial statement, and the defense then has the option of either giving its overview immediately or waiting until the other side has presented its evidence. Textbooks on trial advocacy differ on which of these is the wiser procedure. Some argue that the defense should make its opening statement immediately after the other side's, in order to try to negate any one-sided bias; but others argue that it is better not to "show your hand" to the opposition until the last minute. Regardless of when the defense chooses to make its opening statement, it would seem that the prosecution or plaintiff has several psychological advantages by presenting its side first.

Even though opening statements are not evidence, they can exert great influence on jurors, occurring as they do at the beginning of the trial. As we know, the legal system insists that jurors should not form their decisions on the basis of opening statements. Judges will often instruct the jury that "statements and arguments of counsel are not evidence. They are only intended to assist the jury in understanding the evidence and the contentions of the parties" (LaBuy, 1963, p. 41).

Is this kind of instruction necessary? Are counsels' statements and arguments a significant source of nonevidentiary influence? Apparently so. In a Miami trial, two lawyers disagreed over a point of law, right after the completion of the opening statements and before the introduction of any testimony. The judge asked the jury to leave the courtroom while the legal point was discussed. When, a few minutes later, the jury was brought back, the foreperson announced "We've arrived at a verdict, Your Honor" (quoted in Kassin & Wrightsman, 1988, p. 105). Trial lawyers often believe that a case may be won or lost on the basis of their statements and arguments to the jury. Louis Nizer has written: "By a skillful presentation of what he intends to prove . . . [the attorney] can convert a mere informative exercise into a persuasive plea . . . the opportunity to condition the jury favorably is as limitless as the attorney's art" (1961, p. 42). The psychological findings support these claims—to a disturbing degree.

An early study (Weld & Danzig, 1940) showed that individual mock jurors' predispositions toward guilt or innocence fluctuated throughout the trial after they heard one or both opening statements. A more recent set of studies (Pyszczynski, Greenberg, Mack, & Wrightsman, 1981; Pyszczynski & Wrightsman, 1981; Wells, Miene, & Wrightsman, 1985) demonstrates that opening statements can even overrule evidence.

In one study, mock jurors from the community watched an hour-long videotape of a case involving a charge of transporting a car across state lines. Some mock jurors were shown brief opening statements by either or both sides; in these, the attorneys only introduced themselves and whatever witnesses they had and then promised that their evidence would be convincing. Other mock jurors heard, from either or both sides, much more extensive opening statements, which consisted of a full preview of what the attorney expected the evidence to be and the way he believed the evidence should be interpreted. Then all the mock jurors watched the same evidence and closing arguments. Half of the jurors were asked for their individual verdicts at 12 points during the trial presentation, as well as at the end.

This device illustrated the process of decision making. In fact, it indicated that mock jurors were predisposed to favor one side or the other very early in the trial, and they maintained this predisposition throughout the course of the trial. Certainly their midcourse verdicts changed somewhat in light of the most recent evidence; they waxed and waned, but only within a limited range. Only when both sides' opening statements were brief was there any *substantial* shift in preferences for a verdict over these 12 data points. When jurors did not have extensive opening statements from either side, they seemed to give the defendant the benefit of doubt and hence started out leaning toward a not-guilty verdict. After hearing the prosecution's first witness testify, however, they began to shift toward a guilty verdict and stayed there until the conclusion of the trial.

It was clear that extensive opening statements had a strong impact on verdicts, but it was the first extensive one that really mattered. Most jurors who heard an elaborate statement from the prosecution began by believing the defendant to be guilty, and they maintained that verdict throughout the trial presentation. If the defense made an extensive opening statement, the jurors responded with verdicts of not guilty *only* if the prosecution had made only a brief introduction. Nowhere is the power of first impressions more clearly demonstrated than in these differences. In fact, a follow-up study (Wells et al., 1985) found that, if the defense was permitted to make its opening statement *before* the prosecution's (a procedure not allowed by the rules), jurors were most likely to find the defendant not guilty.

Why does the first strong opening statement carry such impact? Consider the juror's situation. Called for jury service, the prospective juror is anxious and yet conscientious. Most prospective jurors dread the responsibility; they fully expect that they will be serving in some sleazy murder trial, and they abhor the task of deciding another's fate. Some also fear retaliation from disgruntled defendants. Yet they are attracted to the suspense and the importance of the jury trial. Most jurors want to do a good job; they take their responsibilities seriously. All these concerns combine to make jurors very eager to "get a handle" on the case. The judge may have told them a little about the charge; during voir dire there may have been hints about the evidence and the witnesses. But it is not until the opening statements that they get their first systematic overview of the nature of the case.

All of us reject ambiguity to one degree or another. We seek explanations for behavior. The opening statements provide these; they create what social psychologists have called a thematic framework, or schema (Lingle & Ostrom, 1981), which guides jurors in their processing and interpretation of actual testimony that is presented later in the trial. Jurors apparently use the theories developed by the attorneys in extensive opening statements as plausible scenarios of what took place on the day of the crime. These frameworks assist jurors in their attempts to make sense of the rather disjointed array of information that is presented in a typical trial.

Experimental psychologists have demonstrated the usefulness of thematic frameworks in memory. For example, recall of sentences and of prose is improved when the material is preceded by a thematic title (Bransford & Johnson, 1972). After exposure to a list of 15 common, everyday behaviors, participants who had been asked to form an impression of a hypothetical target person who enacted those behaviors recalled more of the behaviors than did participants who had been instructed to memorize the list (Hamilton, Katz, & Leirer, 1980).

The oft-repeated conclusion that first impressions affect later reactions reflects the operation of thematic frameworks. In a typical study (Langer & Abelson, 1974), subjects listened to a tape of two men interacting. Half the subjects had been told that the tape was of a job interview and the other half that it was of a psychiatric intake interview. Subjects who believed the tape to be of a psychiatric interview reported more pathology in the interviewee's behavior; they distorted background information to make it fit better with their impressions. Thematic frameworks affect not only the encoding of information and its retrieval from memory but also the interpretation that is placed on that information (Brewer & Nakamura, 1984; Taylor & Crocker, 1981). This is especially true when the thematic framework is concrete rather than abstract (Pryor, McDaniel, & Kott-Russo, 1986), such as the description of the criminal as wearing a certain type of shirt or having a mustache.

But how far should lawyers go in opening statements? Lawyers are often faced with a situation in which they are not sure exactly what the testimony of a particular witness will be. Should they run the risk of promising more than can be delivered? If so, how might a jury react? Would the lawyer who promised too much lose all credibility?

From an information-processing viewpoint, the dangers of making too extensive an opening statement may not be as great as some observers have assumed. Social psychologists using the concept of thematic frameworks argue that, in most situations, people's inferences and verdicts are affected more by their initial judgments in response to an informational set than by the set itself. After hearing a persuasive, extensive opening statement, jurors may make tentative decisions about guilt or responsibility and begin to view the evidence in light of these early "hunches." Even if the subsequent evidence is not exactly as promised, these initial impressions may strongly influence the final verdicts.

To test these ideas, Pyszczynski and his colleagues compared the effects of three versions of a trial transcript. In one, the defense attorney, in his opening statement, claimed: "we will provide evidence that will show conclusively that Ron Oliver could not possibly have stolen the car. Specifically, we will present testimony proving that he was seen at the Sundown Motel in Murray, Kentucky, at the very time the crime was taking place. Since Ron was seen at the Sundown Motel at the time the theft occurred, there is certainly no way he could have stolen the car" (Pyszczynski et al., 1981, p. 437). However, *no such evidence was presented to any of the jurors.*

In a second version of the transcript, other mock jurors not only were given this claim in the opening statement but also were reminded by the prosecution at the end of the trial that the defense had not fulfilled its promise. The prosecutor said:

> Whatever became of the much-touted evidence showing that Mr. Oliver was at a motel at the time of the theft? No such testimony was introduced in this courtroom. I ask you, ladies and gentlemen, what became of this evidence? Clearly the defense never had any such evidence. If such evidence had existed, surely the defense would have presented it. Ladies and gentlemen of the jury, beware! The defense has tried to pull the wool over your eyes with a cheap ploy [p. 437].

The remaining third of the mock jurors were exposed to a trial transcript that contained neither a promise from the defense nor a reminder from the prosecution. The actual evidence was the same for all three types of jurors.

Of course, the greatest danger to the attorney who makes a promise that cannot be fulfilled is for the opposing counsel to make the jury aware of the discrepancy, as was done here.

And it had the expected effect. Jurors exposed to the opposing attorney's reminder apparently began to question other aspects of the overzealous attorney's case; they were more confident that the defendant was guilty than were subjects who had not been exposed to this unfulfilled promise.

But, more important, if the jurors were given an unfulfilled promise and were never reminded of it by the opposition, they were *more likely* to acquit the defendant than if they had not been given such a false promise. A completely unsubstantiated claim worked.

These disturbing results need to be qualified. First, the respondents were mock jurors, not true ones; second, they did not engage in any deliberation. The process of deliberating may weaken any tendency of individual jurors to give precedence to the opening promise over the actual evidence, although some research suggests that deliberations do not force jurors to focus on the evidence. And, in real trials, any opposing attorney who is at all alert will remind the jurors of his or her adversary's omission.

Even though we doubt that a blatant lie in an opening statement could be an effective strategy, some attorneys may opt to take the risk to make the strongest, most extensive opening statement that is plausible. By so doing, the attorney may provide a favorable framework that jurors will use to interpret later evidence. Even if this later testimony does not fully substantiate the lawyer's claims, the final verdicts may not be less favorable than if such strong claims had not been made. Indeed, in their closing arguments, clever defense attorneys could even admit that such factors as capricious witnesses may have prevented them from fulfilling their claims, thereby eliminating the opportunity for prosecutors to discredit those claims.

Of course, an ethical dimension also needs to be considered in this area. An attorney who deliberately refers to inadmissible or unavailable evidence violates the codes that govern the profession—the Model Code of Professional Conduct and the Model Rules of Professional Responsibility. This practice may lead to censure by the trial court or reversal by an appellate court. In one such case the prosecutor said in his opening: "Officer Lines didn't see the men coming out. . . . Townsend saw them coming out and I'm sorry he can't be here but Lines at least will testify." For this reference to unavailable evidence, the prosecutor saw the conviction reversed (*Hall* v. *State* [Georgia, 1987], as recounted in Underwood & Fortune, 1988, p. 314).

Effect of Instructions to Disregard Inadmissible Evidence

Research on inadmissible evidence is also relevant to the assumption that jurors can separate evidence from nonevidence. All fans of *Perry Mason* are familiar with the attorney's "I object." If the judge sustains an objection, the opposing attorney's objectionable question or the witness's objectionable response will not be recorded, and the judge will instruct or admonish the jury to disregard the material. But are jurors able to do so?

Most of the empirical evidence indicates not only that they are not but—even more disturbing—that a judge's admonition to disregard inadmissible evidence may boomerang (Tanford, 1990). For example, Sue, Smith, and Caldwell (1973) found that, when the initial evidence against a defendant was ambiguous, additional testimony introduced by the prosecution, but ruled inadmissible, biased mock jurors toward finding the defendant guilty (in comparison with a condition in which the critical testimony was never introduced). Broeder (1959) reports an experiment in which mock jurors in a civil trial learned either that the defendant had insurance or that he did not. Half

the subjects who were told that he had insurance were admonished by the judge to disregard that information. Juries composed of subjects believing that the defendant had no insurance awarded damages to the plaintiff in an average amount of $33,000. Juries believing that he did have insurance awarded an average of $37,000. But those juries that were aware of the insurance but had been admonished to disregard it gave the highest award, $46,000.

This last finding implies that admonishments to disregard certain testimony serve instead to sensitize the jurors to the inadmissible evidence. In terms of *reactance theory* (Brehm, 1966), instructions to disregard evidence may threaten jurors' freedom to consider all available evidence. This interpretation is supported by the results of a study by Wolf and Montgomery (1977), who found that, when the judge specifically admonished the jurors to disregard the inadmissible testimony, their verdicts were influenced in the direction of that testimony. In fact, those jurors reported a significantly greater desire to be allowed to consider the inadmissible testimony than did jurors who had not been admonished.

Not all the empirical evidence indicates such a boomerang effect (Kagehiro & Werner, 1977; Mitchell & Byrne, 1972; Simon, 1966). But the overall pattern of findings makes us very suspicious of an assumption that jurors are able to disregard inadmissible evidence, especially when such evidence would lead to conviction of the defendant (Thompson, Fong, & Rosenhan, 1981). One prominent illustration of this problem is "impeachment" evidence, which is evidence that the defendant is guilty of some prior conduct suggesting dishonesty. Jurors are instructed that they should use such evidence only for the purpose of assessing the defendant's credibility, not for making judgments about the defendant's propensity to commit crimes in general or about guilt for the specific crime at trial. However, the research clearly indicates that jurors are likely to use this evidence to evaluate a person's tendency to commit crimes and that judges' instructions are generally ineffective in preventing them from doing so. After a very thorough review of the experimental evidence, Tanford (1990) concluded: "the empirical research clearly demonstrates that instructions to disregard are ineffective in reducing the harm caused by inadmissible evidence and improper arguments" (p. 95).

Inadmissible evidence thus is information that has been ruled legally irrelevant, but it still has potentially great influence on jurors' opinions. There are many other irrelevant factors in the trial presentation that could influence the jury's decision. They include the gender, race, age, physical appearance, and attractiveness of the litigants and other witnesses, the personal style and credibility of attorneys, and the order of presentation of evidence. For example, Zebrowitz and McDonald (1991) discovered that, as civil plaintiffs increased in physical attractiveness, they were more likely to win their case; defendants who appeared more baby-faced were more likely to win cases when they were charged with intentional wrongdoing but less likely to win when they were charged with negligent conduct.

Are jurors able to eliminate such irrelevant considerations from their decisions about verdicts, sentencing, and damage awards? Space does not permit a discussion of all the issues and empirical findings, but a thorough review by Gerbasi, Zuckerman, and Reis (1977) provides a summary: "Some degree of generalizability seems cautiously appropriate. It appears that extraevidential factors, such as defendant, victim, and juror characteristics, trial procedures, and so forth, can influence the severity of verdicts rendered by individual jurors" (p. 343).

Reforms

The findings in this section offer serious challenge for those who want to reform jury procedures so that jurors do pay attention only to the evidence, as they are assumed to do. In their current form, instructions and admonishments by judges do not seem to work.

To deal with the effects of inadmissible evidence, a radical reform has been proposed: to videotape the whole trial before the jurors are present, edit out any references to inadmissible evidence, and then play it for jurors. But such a procedure—providing the jury with a filmed presentation rather than a "live" one—has limitations of its own: jurors may be less motivated to do a conscientious job, and the tape restricts their freedom to observe what they want to (such as watching the defendant's face when the victim's widow testifies). In addition, practical problems involving excessive expense and court time make this reform problematic.

Other reforms involve drafting instructions to jurors using clear, comprehensible language rather than the legal jargon that now typifies many instructions (Elwork, Sales, & Alfini, 1977; Tanford, 1990). If jurors cannot even understand their instructions, their behavior will not be guided by them. Here's an example of how jurors are instructed about the meaning of "proximate cause," an important concept in civil trials: "a cause which, in a natural and continuous sequence, produced damage, and without which the damage would not have occurred." If you were a juror, would you now be confident that you know the meaning of that term? Instructions could also be made more comprehensible if they were written and copies were then given to jurors rather than merely having the judge read them aloud. Finally, several studies have shown beneficial effects on jurors' comprehension for instructions when the instructions are given repeatedly throughout a trial (Tanford, 1990).

THE ASSUMPTION THAT JURORS ARE ACCURATE AND COMPLETE INFORMATION PROCESSORS

The legal system assumes that jurors can understand and retain all important information, even in complex trials that extend for weeks and months. The mass of isolated facts must be assimilated and comprehended. The fact that jurors are still prevented from taking notes during the trial presentation in many jurisdictions is an indication of the court's view of jurors as able to attend, perceive, understand, and remember (Flango, 1980). (Box 14-2 reports on one jury trial that questions this assumption, and Box 14-3 presents a possible procedural change that could be used to make complex cases less difficult.)

One reform would be to provide jurors with pens and notepads and encourage them to take notes, but many judges fear that notetaking would cause jurors to miss some of the testimony and would give undue advantage during deliberations to those jurors who had chosen to take notes (Urbom, 1982). These concerns could be alleviated if the jury were given a complete transcript of the trial—or, even better, a videotape—just as it begins to deliberate. Many judges already grant requests by jurors to have portions of testimony read back to them (or, in the case of a videotape trial, shown to them).

One of the major obstacles to jurors' being satisfactory information processors is that seemingly relevant information is not provided to them. Jurors often express frustration that significant facts about the case were not introduced during the trial. Why did the defendant have some of the marked bills in her possession? Has anyone located her supposed accomplice? Increasingly, judges permit jurors to ask questions during the trial. Usually these are submitted to the judge in writing at the end of the testimony of a given witness. The judge eliminates those that are inappropriate and gives each attorney a chance to object outside of the hearing of the jury; then the judge asks the question of the witness. Allowing questioning by jurors should increase their satisfaction with the verdict and occasionally might unearth significant new evidence.

In a carefully designed field experiment, Heuer and Penrod (1988) determined some of the effects of allowing jurors to ask questions or take notes, after gaining permission to do so from judges in Wisconsin circuit courts. No evidence surfaced that those jurors who had chosen to take notes were more influential during deliberations. Notetaking jurors were more satisfied with their participation than were jurors in other trials who were not permitted this behavior. In contrast, when jurors in other trials were allowed to ask questions, their satisfaction with the trial process was not affected; nor did the questioning uncover any new issues. But the opportunity to question did alleviate the jurors' doubts about trial testimony, and it gave the attorneys useful feedback about how the jurors saw the trial.

Another helpful reform is to vary the timing of the judge's instructions about the trial. Although the judge may instruct the jury at any point in the proceedings, the general charge is typically read at the close of the trial, after the evidence has been presented and just before the jury retires to deliberate. In a survey on the feasibility of instructing jurors about the law at the beginning of the trial (Smith, 1990), a group of California judges was divided into those who favored such pretrial instructions (42%) and those who opposed them (57%). Judges who favored preinstructions did so because they believed jurors' ability to process trial information and to integrate these facts with the law would be improved. Judges who opposed preinstructions believed they would not improve jurors' performance; moreover, they claimed that they could not know before the trial what instructions would be appropriate because they had not heard the evidence.

In most jurisdictions the judge's instruc-tions come at the close of the trial—when the evidence is complete and it is clear what in-structions are needed for the jury to decide the case. Instructing the jury at the conclusion of the trial reflects a belief in the "recall readi-ness" hypothesis (Jones & Goethals, 1971). This hypothesis predicts a recency effect, sug-gesting that the judge's instructions will have

---

Box 14-2 | *Remembering All the Evidence:*
The Case against Procter & Gamble

In the early 1980s the phenome-non of "toxic shock syndrome" drew national attention. The use of Rely tampons apparently caused the death of several women and the injury of many others. More than 400 lawsuits were filed against Procter & Gamble, the manufac-turer of this product. In one of these suits, Deletha Dawn Lamp-shire, age 18, of Denver, claimed that, as a result of using the tampons, she suffered a near-fatal bout with toxic shock syndrome, experiencing such symptoms as high fever, low blood pressure, swollen mucous membranes, peel-ing skin, and scarlet rash. Her at-torney reported that the cellulose chips used only in the Rely brand of tampon broke down into simple sugars when moist, encouraging the growth of the bacterium thought to cause toxic shock syn-drome. Ms. Lampshire asked for $5 million in compensatory damages and $20 million in punitive dam-ages against Procter & Gamble.

The trial, in March 1982, in-volved 11 days of highly technical testimony from scientists and med-ical experts. During its three days of deliberations, the jury of three women and five men requested a reading of part of the transcript covering the testimony of a partic-ular physician witness. The jurors had disagreed about what the wit-ness had said. Jurors are usually not allowed to take notes during a trial, and the opportunity to have a re-reading of the testimony during de-liberations could compensate for misperceptions and forgetting. But in this instance, U.S. District Court Judge Sherman Finesilver denied the request and told the jurors that they must use their col-lective memories.

The jury's verdict in this case was rather bewildering. The jurors ruled that Procter & Gamble was negli-gent in selling Rely tampons, but they refused to award Lampshire any damages, despite her claims that the illness had severely altered her personality and that she had spent $4000 in medical expenses. Apparently, they were unconvinced that Lampshire's condition was se-vere enough or long-lasting enough to warrant any damages.

The confusing outcome of this trial cannot necessarily be attribut-ed to the judge's failure to provide the jury with a rereading of part of the testimony. But this case high-lights another assumption about jury behavior—that, through their collective memory, jurors will recall all the testimony, arguments, and instructions that unfold during the trial. And, if they can't, they will know they can't.

There is no built-in provision for assessing when a jury is unable to retrieve relevant information. It is as if the courts designed a proce-dure based on an assumed ideal of how people perform and then left it to run itself regardless of the reality of the assumption. Even when the jury is aware that it lacks informa-tion or disagrees over what was said, judges are not required to pro-vide the jury with a rereading of the transcript. The Rely tampon trial is an example of the court's proce-dures gone awry, with the jury suf-fering the consequences.

a more powerful impact on a jury's decision when they are given late in the trial, after the presentation of evidence. The reasoning behind the recall readiness hypothesis reflects an assumption that immediate past events are generally remembered better than more remote ones, especially when the earlier events have unfolded over a longer period of time. Presenting the instructions after the evidence should thus increase the salience of the instructions and make the judge's charge more available for recall during deliberations. Hav-

ing just heard the judge's charge, deliberating jurors would have it fresh in their minds and be more likely to make references to it, thus multiplying its potential impact.

Questioning the Recall Readiness Hypothesis

Logical as the recall readiness hypothesis might seem, it has been questioned by a number of authorities. Two lines of reasoning guide such criticisms.

Box 14-3 | *Jury Decision Making in Complex Trials*

Many critics of our justice system claim that juries are especially prone to faulty decisions in complicated, lengthy cases that involve technical information or that require many decisions as part of the verdict. Civil cases can be particularly difficult when several plaintiffs join together to sue the manufacturer of a product they charge was defective and caused all of them injury. Suits against drug companies are a common example of this type of litigation. In these cases a jury must decide several issues within the same deliberation: Did the product cause harm to the plaintiffs? Was the manufacturer responsible for a defect in the product that produced the harm? If the answers to the first two questions are yes, how much should plaintiffs be compensated?

In order to simplify the tasks for juries in these complex cases, some

courts have divided or *bifurcated* the trials into separate parts. For example, the jury first hears evidence about causation and decides if the product was faulty. If the jury concludes the product was faulty, it then hears evidence on the other issues and deliberates to a decision about them. If the jury initially concludes that the product was not faulty, the trial would end at that point; no evidence about manufacturer liability or damages to plaintiffs would be heard.

Do bifurcated trials affect jury decisions? Some commentators have suggested that a bifurcated structure might favor civil defendants, because the plaintiffs do not have an opportunity to influence causation and liability decisions through the accompanying presentation of evidence that would increase jurors' sympathies about plaintiffs' injuries and damages.

Horowitz and Bordens (1990) investigated this possibility by randomly assigning adult volunteers to one of 128 mock juries that heard a taped trial in which a group of plaintiffs were suing a chemical company for dumping chemicals improperly and polluting their water and food supplies. These juries differed on the structure of the trial presentation they heard. Some heard all the evidence and rendered verdicts on causation, liability, and damages in the same trial; others heard evidence about the different issues separately and rendered verdicts unique to the separate evidence. As expected, juries in the "unitary" trials were more likely to return a verdict for the plaintiff, but this tendency was offset by the unexpected finding that "unitary" juries returned smaller awards to the plaintiffs than did the "separate" juries.

First, Roscoe Pound, former dean of the Harvard Law School, and others have proposed what is essentially a "schema" theory—that jurors should be instructed *before* the presentation of testimony because this gives them a set to appreciate the relevance or irrelevance of testimony as it unfolds and thus to make selective use of the facts. This line of reasoning gains support from research findings in experimental psychology showing (1) that people learn more effectively when they know in advance what the specific task is and (2) that schematic frameworks facilitate comprehension and recall (Bartlett, 1932; Neisser, 1976).

Second, a number of judges (such as Frank, 1949) have objected to the customary sequence on the ground that instructions at the end of the trial are given after the jurors have already made up their minds. Research (Kalven & Zeisel, 1966) has shown that, despite cautionary instructions, jurors often form very definite opinions before the close of the trial. This argument is an example of the "primacy" hypothesis, and Judge E. Barrett Prettyman's position reflects it:

> It makes no sense to have a juror listen to days of testimony only then to be told that he and his conferees are the sole judges of the facts, that the accused is presumed to be innocent, that the government must prove guilt beyond a reasonable doubt, etc. What manner of mind can go back over a stream of conflicting statements of alleged facts, recall the intonations, the demeanor, or even the existence of the witnesses, and retrospectively fit all these recollections into a pattern of evaluations and judgments given him for the first time after the events; the human mind cannot do so [1960, p. 1066].

So there is a clear-cut contrast between the recall readiness hypothesis and the primacy hypothesis concerning predicted effects if the judge's instructions are delayed to the end of the trial. Psychologists believe this leads to an empirical question: at what point in the trial proceedings should the judge instruct the jury in order to maximize the jurors' adherence to that instruction?

Empirical Tests of Contrasting Hypotheses

In an attempt to answer this question, Kassin and Wrightsman (1979) varied the timing of the "requirement of proof" instruction. From the perspective of defendants, this directive is perhaps the most crucial of the mandatory instructions. Specifically, criminal defendants are entitled to a statement to the jury that they are presumed innocent, that the burden of proof is on the prosecution, and that all elements of the crime must be proved to a constitutional standard of "beyond a reasonable doubt." In this experiment, subjects watched a one-hour videotape of an auto-theft trial. The trial itself consisted of three phases: the attorneys' opening statements; the direct, cross-, and redirect examination of witnesses; and the closing arguments by the counsel. The judge's instruction, based on those in current use, represented a fourth part of the study whose presence or absence and timing were varied. In one condition the instructions appeared before the introduction of evidence (that is, between phases one and two). In a second condition they appeared after the closing arguments (that is, after phase three). In a third condition no instruction was given the jurors. After the trial presentation, the subjects gave their verdicts, were tested for recall of the facts brought out in testimony, and answered several case-related questions. Additionally, so that the researchers could examine the mock jurors' evaluations of the evidence as it unfolded, half the subjects in each condition made judgments of guilt or innocence at various points during the trial presentation.

The results clearly supported the primacy hypothesis espoused by Judge Prettyman and others. Only 37% of subjects who received the judge's instructions *before* the evidence voted to convict the defendant, compared with 59% when the instruction came at the end of the trial. In fact, the conviction rate for this group, 59%, was not significantly different from the conviction rate—63%—for mock jurors who did not receive any instructions. In other words, *the judge's instructions affected mock jurors' verdicts when they were delivered before the testimony but not when presented afterward.* Furthermore, the midtrial judgments made by half the subjects showed that presenting the instructions before the evidence produced a lowered conviction rate *immediately*—even from the first decision point, assessed after the direct examination of the first witness. Finally, when subjects were instructed after the evidence, they recalled significantly *fewer* case-related facts than when the instructions were delivered before the evidence or not at all. This last result is particularly impressive when coupled with previous findings (Elwork et al., 1977) that subjects do not recall the instruction better when it is presented at the close of the trial.

From these findings we conclude that the timing of instructions may influence jurors' mid- and posttrial judgments. Instructions about general propositions of law, such as burden of proof, have a dramatic impact when they precede testimony; however, when they follow it, their effect is minimal. When the instructions come before the evidence, jurors filter their judgments through the threshold of "reasonable doubt"; they may, in their hearts, believe that it is likely that the defendant committed the act but still think that the prosecutor did not produce enough evidence to prove guilt beyond a reasonable doubt.

What practical applications can be drawn from these findings? A number of states give their judges discretion as to when they instruct the jury. Indiana goes further; its state supreme court requires the presentation of a preliminary instruction on the manner of weighing testimony. The jury is then advised that it will receive further instructions at the close of the trial. In Missouri the state supreme court's committee on jury instructions recommended:

> that the jury be instructed before the trial begins about its duty to determine the facts solely from the evidence, how it shall determine the believability of evidence, and its obligation to give each party fair and impartial consideration without sympathy or prejudice. The committee believes that it is better to draw the jury's attention to these matters before the trial rather than waiting until after the jurors may have reached a decision.

As part of their evaluation of reforms in court procedures, Heuer and Penrod (1989) compared the results of 67 Wisconsin trials in which the judges randomly assigned the cases to a preinstruction or no-preinstruction condition. In 34 trials, judges preinstructed the juries on procedural law and any substantive issues they thought would be helpful. In the other 33 trials, no preinstructions were given. Based on the judges' evaluations of these methods, there was little if any evidence that preinstructions disrupted the trial or produced any other disadvantages that judges have often predicted. Preinstructions did have some advantages; they increased jurors' satisfaction with the trial process, and they helped jurors evaluate the evidence according to correct legal principles.

These examples are, unfortunately, the exception rather than the rule; judicial use of preinstructions is vastly underutilized. There is no reason why general instructions about the law (e.g., burden of proof, assessment of the credibility of witnesses) should not be given at both the beginning and end of trials; instructions that depend on the specific evidence in a trial could be given at the end.

THE ASSUMPTION THAT JURORS CAN SUSPEND JUDGMENT

Jurors are presumed to be able to withhold judgment until all the evidence is presented. Or, at the very least, the ideal represents the juror as someone who, though swayed by the evidence first in one direction and then the other, treats these facts as separate inputs, not influenced by their order. But certain kinds of courtroom happenings may challenge the validity of this assumption; the following report, describing the voir dire in the first Claus von Bülow trial, is one example.

Prospective jurors typically do not know the nature of the case when they first appear in the courtroom. Unless the impending trial has been highly publicized in their community, their first glimpse of the facts surrounding the crime is usually provided by the presiding judge's brief introductory statement or by lawyers' jury selection questions. Jurors are instructed to keep an open mind and not to form or express an opinion or reach a conclusion until they have heard all the evidence, arguments, and relevant instructions. But can they avoid doing so? Is it possible to suspend all judgment while listening to a persuasive communication?

Being unable to interview jurors as the trial progresses makes it hard to provide pure examples of early, inflexible opinion formation. But sometimes jurors reveal themselves by their actions.

When jury pool members were called for trial service in Newport, Rhode Island, on January 11, 1982, they were told to arrive at the courthouse at 7:30 A.M. As they shivered outside in the windy 2° temperature until the doors were opened (30 minutes later!), most of them prob-

ably already knew that they might participate in the trial of socialite Claus von Bülow, charged with the attempted murder of his wife. Eventually the pool of 100 or so was narrowed to 35, from whom 16 (12 jurors and 4 alternates) were chosen for the actual jury. Each person was interrogated by the opposing attorneys as the judge, spectators, and numerous reporters watched.

Speculation and publicity about the von Bülow case had swirled before the trial began. But the existence of a love affair between the defendant and a television star had not been widely discussed, so when the defense attorney—yes, von Bülow's own attorney—raised the question during jury selection, the impact on prospective jurors was like a dash of cold water thrown in their faces.

Jury pool members heard the defense attorney, Herald Fahringer, ask: "It might come out during the trial that Mr. von Bülow had an affair with another woman while married to Mrs. von Bülow. Would that affect your opinion of Mr. von Bülow or your ability to judge him fairly in this case?" A reporter on the scene observed:

> It was fascinating to see the effect of this "other woman" on female jurors. They all echoed the male panelists in assuring Fahringer that von Bülow's infidelities would not affect their judgment, but with almost every woman the mention of his having an affair while married produced a visible tightening of the facial muscles or a set to the jaw. . . . While vocally claiming indifference, female panelists gave off waves of outrage that permeated the courtroom [Wright, 1983, p. 181].

Was this tightening of the facial muscles associated with a closed opinion about the defendant's guilt? Did this admission by von Bülow's attorney prematurely fix the eventual outcome? We cannot say. The jurors—seven men and five women—did unanimously find von Bülow guilty, although it took six days for them to reach that decision. By then they were aware that their verdict was to be based on *all* the evidence. Certainly none of them would have said something like "I knew he was guilty from the moment I heard he was cheating on his wife," even if thinking it. Yet for many people—and possibly some of the jurors—such an admission by von Bülow's own attorney would be so powerful that it would inevitably distort interpretation of all subsequent evidence. (Von Bülow's conviction was appealed, and the Rhode Island supreme court ruled that certain procedures and evidence in the first trial were improper. In his second trial, in 1985, he was found not guilty.)

In many ways, the juror's task is like that of the reader of a mystery story. The juror is bombarded with many pieces of evidence, often incomplete and conflicting, just as the mystery reader is tantalized by hints, clues, and coincidences. The joy of reading a mystery comes from savoring each clue, bouncing it off prior clues, and then evaluating its significance in the overall puzzle of who committed the crime. That is how most jurors operate. They form a *schema*, a mental structure that aids in the processing and interpretation of information. As indicated earlier, such schemata—precisely because they provide a cognitive framework—can produce a skewed perception and recall of reality. Just like mystery readers who remember those clues that fit their hypothesis and forget others that do not, jurors construct their own private stories about the evidence so that it makes sense to them (Pennington & Hastie, 1988); in the process they pay inordinate attention to certain pieces of evidence while ignoring others.

The courts expect something different. They envision a juror who does not form hunches and is not unduly influenced by the "early re-

turns" but instead passively processes all incoming information without immediate interpretation until finally instructed by the judge to decide. Are human beings capable of such detached information processing? Can they separate the acquisition of information from its evaluation? Should the court's ideals and procedures be revised to bring them in line with jurors' actual abilities? The studies previously described in this chapter discourage viewing jurors as dispassionate information processors and encourage modifications such as built-in review periods, in which each attorney summarizes his or her case so far.

THE ASSUMPTION THAT JURY DELIBERATIONS ARE UNAFFECTED BY GROUP PRESSURES OR PERSONAL WISHES

Deliberating juries are assumed to be decision-making groups that produce objective and fact-based outcomes. Generally ignored is the possibility that they are subject to the group pressures or irrational impulses that operate in some groups when they make decisions. The courts disregard the likelihood that the content of jury deliberations may involve matters (personal anecdotes, opinions about the trial attorneys, and so on) other than the evidence and the law.

Whether the ideal of objectivity is achieved is difficult to assess because we have so little information about jury deliberations. The few actual trials for which we have a detailed recon-

Box **14-4**

The Supreme Court's Decisions on Jury Size and Decision Rule

It is instructive to review the process by which two "reforms" of jury procedure were instituted. These changes—the decisions that six-person juries and nonunanimous decision rules are acceptable for certain types of cases—were claimed by the Supreme Court to be based on research findings. But the legal system's conception of what is empirical evidence falls far short of what social scientists would accept. In fact, the difference is so great that it qualifies as a further example of the theme of "law and psychology in conflict" described in Chapter 1.

Why 12 persons on a jury, rather than some other number? The number may be based on Christ's 12 apostles; we are not sure. The requirement of a unanimous decision, we know, was established in England in the 14th century. Both regulations were extended to North America as part of the British colonization.

These procedures were never really challenged or modified until 1966, when, in Great Britain, the jury's decision rule was changed so that only a majority of 10 out of 12 was required. In response to a challenge from the state of Florida, the U.S. Supreme Court, in 1970 (in the case of *Williams* v. *Florida*), ruled that juries numbering as few as six persons were constitutionally acceptable. Soon after that, a more profound innovation was authorized. In two 1972 cases (*Johnson* v. *Louisiana* and *Apodaca, Cooper, and Madden* v. *Oregon*), the Supreme Court, by a narrow major-

ity, affirmed that decision rules as thin as 9 out of 12 were sufficient. At present all the states have the option of reducing the size of the jury and the decision rule to at least the levels noted by the Supreme Court.

In the case of *Williams* v. *Florida*, the majority opinion of the Supreme Court was that 6-person juries could function as successfully as 12-person juries. A portion of the opinion is worth quoting:

The performance of this role is not a function of the particular number of the body that makes up the jury. To be sure, the number should probably be large enough to promote group deliberation, free from outside attempts at intimidation, and to provide a fair possibility for obtaining a representative cross-section of the community. But we find little reason to think that these goals are in any meaningful sense less likely to be achieved when the jury numbers six, than when it numbers twelve—particularly if the requirement of unanimity is retained. And, certainly the reliability of the jury as a fact finder hardly seems likely to be a function of its size [*Williams* v. *Florida*, 1970, pp. 100–101].

The Supreme Court opinion went on to state that the available research findings—using trials of civil cases—"indicate that there is no discernible difference between the results reached by the two

different-sized juries" (*Williams* v. *Florida*, p. 102). But the six "research findings" on which this conclusion was based were "primarily expressions of opinion based, if on any evidence at all, upon uncontrolled observations that might be likened to clinical case studies" (Saks, 1977, p. 9). (Saks, 1977, p. 10, describes these studies; all were published in legal journals rather than in social science journals.) One of the six is a mere assertion without any evidence; three are casual observations; another simply reported that a smaller-sized jury had been used; and the last described the economic advantages of a smaller jury, without even considering jury functioning. As Zeisel has written, these studies offer "scant evidence by any standards" (1971, p. 715)—legal or scientific!

The Court's justification for a nonunanimous decision rule is even more disturbing, for it misinterpreted a basic social science finding: in the *Williams* decision *the Court invoked Solomon Asch's conformity experiment as support* for its conclusion that the majority juror in a 5-to-1 split was under no more pressure to change than a minority juror in a 10-2 split (McConahay, 1978). Asch (1956) placed subjects individually in a line-judging experiment in which all the other subjects differed with them. He found that subjects who were confronted with unanimous disagreement with their responses changed their answers one-third of the time. Surely a label of "law and psychology in conflict" seems appropriate when a legal decision is based partly on a misreading of research results.

Subsequent empirical studies have failed to produce large differences in outcome, but, still, in many of these studies the size of the jury and the decision rule had effects on the deliberation process. Saks (1977) summarized these differences as follows:

Large juries, compared to small juries, spend more time deliberating, engage in more communication per unit time, manifest better recall of testimony, induce less disparity between minority and majority factions in their rating of perceived jury performance and in sociometric ratings, and less disparity between convicting and acquitting juries in number of arguments generated, facilitate markedly better community representation, and, though not achieving statistical significance, tend to produce more consistent verdicts [p. 105].

With regard to the effects of the decision rule, Saks concludes that "unanimous juries, in comparison to quorum juries, deliberate longer [and] are more likely to hang" (p. 105). Juries with a requirement of, say, a three-fourths majority as sufficient for a verdict do not continue deliberating once this degree of agreement has been achieved. Saks sees this as a detrimental procedure; he concludes that "only in unanimous juries could the minority effectively alter the course set by the majority" (p. 106).

What conclusion can we draw from this pattern of findings? Can it be that the Supreme Court made an appropriate decision based on inappropriate evidence?

First, even if outcomes would not be affected by the modifications in the unanimous decision rule, the psychological process most certainly is. The courts are concerned that appropriate deliberations occur, but their desire to increase efficiency and reduce costs has tampered with this deliberative process.

Second, not all the evidence is in. The familiar slogan that "further research is needed" is appropriate here. For example, Louisiana recently operated under a three-level system (see Louisiana Code of Criminal Procedure, Article 782). Capital crimes were tried before 12-person juries in which unanimity was required; serious noncapital crimes were tried before 12-person juries with a requirement that only 9 must concur; and lesser crimes were tried before 5-person unanimous juries. The appellant in the *Johnson* v. *Louisiana* (1972) case argued that his trial under a 9-of-12 decision rule had given him less protection from conviction than defendants with 12-of-12 or 5-of-5 decision rules receive. The Court chose to ignore the possible interactive effects of group size and decision rule, but social scientists have not. For example, Saks and Ostrom (1975) developed a model that permits computation of the probability that a verdict will be reached for any level of certainty of defendant's guilt in a jury of any size, operating under any decision rule. According to their model, the 12-of-12 jury is least likely to reach a verdict, the 5-of-5 more likely, and the 9-of-12 most likely. Thus the appellant, Johnson, apparently was correct; a conviction would have been less likely had he had a 12-of-12 or 5-of-5 decision rule.

The Louisiana procedure was modified somewhat by a U.S. Supreme Court decision in 1978, involving a Georgia case (*Ballew* v. *Georgia*). Claude Ballew, the operator of an "adult theater" in Atlanta, had been convicted of obscenity by a five-person jury after he showed the movie *Behind the Green Door*. The U.S. Supreme Court ruled that five-person juries were too small; six was the acceptable minimum.

Maintenance of the requirement of a unanimous verdict forces a further resolution of disagreements and leads to a binding together of all opinions within the jury, a conclusion that can be inferred from the detailed study of jury deliberations by Hastie et al., (1983). Then, too, the necessity for unanimity may sometimes lead to a verdict opposite to that resulting from an initial majority vote.

struction of deliberations suggest that at least some of the time is spent on such side issues as the motivations of the defense attorney or the relative amounts of education of different jurors.

One of these accounts—a remarkable book by Villasenor (1977)—deals with the first trial of Juan Corona, charged with the serial murder of 25 people. Villasenor observed the trial presentation, which dragged on over a period of five months. From numerous interviews with each of the jurors, Villasenor claims to have reconstructed not only statements made and questions raised during the deliberations themselves but also many of the feelings, incidental actions, and other minutiae that took place during this eight-day period.

If one accepts the content of Villasenor's book as factual, then reading it produces respect and admiration for the way the Juan Corona jury performed in one of the most challenging cases ever presented. The task was initially unstructured, even to the point of whether a separate verdict should be decided for each murder; there were 117 witnesses and 980 exhibits to review; all the evidence was circumstantial, and the government had bungled part of its presentation. At the same time, the jury deliberations illustrate the nonrational, unpredictable side of jury behavior. A record of the votes may suffice to prove these claims.

After finally deciding to deal with guilt or innocence collectively for all 25 murders, the jury took its first vote on the morning of the second day; it was five for guilty and seven not guilty. (The votes were anonymous and recorded on slips of paper.) But two of the seven who voted not guilty did so in order to prevent the jury from reaching a premature decision. To quote one: "I voted innocent, too. But not because I have any doubts that Corona isn't guilty. I was just afraid we might've convicted

him on the first ballot and I don't think that's right. I think we should do all kinds of talking and explaining before we convict a man of murder" (Villasenor, 1977, p. 58).

Although the eventual verdict was unanimous for guilt, the pattern of votes (see Table 14-1) was not a constantly increasing one. There was a waxing and waning of predispositions toward guilt. Jurors wanted to separate the flamboyant style of the defense attorney from the evidence he presented. They were concerned about what reasonable doubt meant. Finally, as the group realized that there was one holdout juror, they wondered whether her final shift in vote reflected a sincere change of opinion. In fact, at one point the holdout juror said "Please, I'll change my vote. Just don't hate me. I'll change my vote so you can go home to your wife." However, the next day she told the rest of the jury: "I think I've changed my mind. Yesterday you gave me a day's rest and I relaxed and I saw things differently. . . . Basically, I now think you people are right and I do think Corona is guilty" (Villasenor, 1977, p. 213). Did she shift her vote out of conviction, or was it in response to her awareness of the other jurors' feelings or even the knowledge that her sister could no longer remain at her house to feed her cats? We do not know.

Some general findings and some reports of individual trials have provided information about juror interaction. For example, the selection of the jury's foreperson is not a random procedure; high-status, older, and better-educated males are most likely to be selected by their colleagues (Dillehay & Nietzel, 1985; Strodtbeck, James, & Hawkins, 1957). Communication within the jury is also influenced by gender and socioeconomic status. Jurors of higher socioeconomic status make more comments than those of lower status (Strodtbeck & Mann, 1956). The individual judgments of male and high-status jurors have a greater effect on the jury's verdict (Hastie, Penrod, & Pennington, 1983; Strodtbeck et al., 1957).

Limited evidence on the content of jury deliberations also runs counter to an assumption that the majority of time is spent evaluating the evidence or procedural matters. Rita James Simon (James, 1959) reports that in her studies about 50% of the jurors' comments were expressions of opinions or recounting of personal experiences. Only 15% of the time was spent on testimony; a great percentage (25%) was allocated to discussing procedural issues. (The remaining 10% was spent on judge's instructions.)

The courts themselves have tried to revise (if not reform) the deliberative process. Two changes approved by the U.S. Supreme Court in the 1970s—the use of fewer than 12 persons on a jury and the acceptance of a decision rule of less than unanimity—are evaluated in Box 14-4 (pp. 332-333).

THE JURY: AN INSTITUTION LONG ON TRADITION BUT SHORT ON EVALUATION

The American trial jury is a remarkable institution—and, in important ways, almost a unique one. Four fifths of all the criminal-case jury trials in the world are held in the United States. Kalven and Zeisel make the following comments about the jury system:

> It recruits a group of twelve lay [people], chosen at random from the widest population; it convenes them for the purpose of a particular trial; it entrusts them with great official powers of de-

cision; it permits them to carry out deliberations in secret and report out their final judgment without giving reasons for it; and, after their momentary service to the state has been completed, it orders them to disband and return to private life [1966, p. 3].

The remarkable use of average citizens to determine outcomes for rich or politically powerful figures such as Patty Hearst or John DeLorean or Leona Helmsley manifests our country's commitment to egalitarian values. It is no exaggeration to claim that the trial jury is sanctified as one of our fundamental democratic institutions; to many, it should be above scrutiny. So when a group of University of Chicago researchers tape-recorded actual jury deliberations in Wichita, Kansas, in the mid-1950s—with the permission of the judge but without the knowledge of the jurors—the public clamor was overwhelming. It was the only time in recorded history that the American Civil Liberties Union and the conservative radio commentator Fulton Lewis, Jr., ever agreed on something! So did the courts, and now a federal law makes it illegal to observe, listen to, or record the deliberations of a federal jury.

This prohibition deprived social scientists and legal scholars of the most direct means of observing the jury decision-making process and discouraged fruitful research for several decades. But because the institution of the jury trial did not diminish in importance, researchers were challenged to develop other methods and paradigms by which to gain relevant information about juries. As a result of these innovative techniques and the continued interest in the institution, we now possess a systematic body of knowledge about jury functioning and about possible reforms that could improve jury functioning.

Table 14-1 Pattern of Votes by the Jury in the First Juan Corona Trial

	Guilty	Not guilty
1st vote—2nd day (A.M.)	5	7
2nd vote—2nd day (P.M.)	9	3
3rd vote—2nd day (P.M.)	11	1
4th vote—2nd day (late P.M.)	8	4
5th vote—3rd day (A.M.)	7	5
6th vote—3rd day (late P.M.)	9	3
7th vote—5th day (A.M.)	10	2
8th vote—5th day (A.M.)	10	2
9th vote—5th day (late P.M.)	9	3
10th vote—6th day (early A.M.)	9	3
11th vote—6th day (A.M.)	10	2[a]
12th vote—6th day (A.M.)	11	1
13th vote—8th day (early A.M.)	12	0

[a]On Victim #1 only.

SUMMARY

The right to a trial by jury is one of our fundamental liberties, but it is currently under attack and intensified scrutiny. Five assumptions about the jury, made implicitly by the legal system, are each of questionable validity when evaluated by psychological research. These are:

1. The assumption that jurors act without bias.
2. The assumption that jurors base their verdict only on the evidence and the law.
3. The assumption that jurors are accurate and complete information processors.
4. The assumption that jurors can suspend judgment.
5. The assumption that jury deliberations are based on the law and the evidence and are unaffected by group pressures or personal wishes.

Both empirical research and case histories of actual trials question these assumptions. In light of these findings, we have proposed a number of reforms, including the following:

1. Increase the representativeness of the jury by severely restricting jury exemptions. Expand the jury pool base beyond the usual voter registration lists to include city directories, welfare rolls, and lists of people with driver's licenses.
2. Avoid an excessive number of peremptory challenges awarded to each side in a criminal trial. In voir dire, encourage the questioning to be performed in a manner that encourages jurors' candor and decreases attorneys' ingratiation techniques. Judges could routinely be responsible for some of the questioning, but attorneys may need to ask other questions. On sensitive matters, the questioning should be done of individual jurors, outside the presence of the rest of the panel.
3. A proposed reform for curtailing the biasing effects of inadmissible evidence is to videotape the trial, edit it to remove objectionable material, and then play it for the jury. The practical problems with such a reform are a major impediment to this procedure.
4. During deliberations, if practical, the jury should be provided with a transcript or videotape of the trial, which it could examine whenever questions arise.
5. Jurors, during the trial, should be permitted to take notes or to refer questions to the judge for presentation to witnesses.

6. The information-processing demands placed on jurors should be simplified. More clearly worded instructions, in written as well as oral form, delivered at the beginning and at the conclusion of the trial, would be helpful. In complex trials in which multiple verdicts must be decided, organizing the questions that jurors must answer into a logical sequence of separate verdicts should improve the decision-making.

15

Rape: Rapists and Victims

D
r. John Huntington Story was, for a time, the leading citizen of the small town of Lovell, Wyoming. Although a short, mumbling fellow described by some as "a pluperfect geek," he was a physician of unassailable reputation, a staid family man, and founder of the ultraconservative Lovell Bible Church (Jones, 1989). But, during his 26 years as a family doctor, in the privacy of his examining room, he raped or otherwise sexually molested somewhere between 150 and "over a thousand" girls and women (Olsen, 1989). His known rape victims ranged in age from 10 to 68; he chose them carefully in the hopes (largely successful) either that they would not know what he was doing behind the sheet draped over their knees, or that they would be too docile to report him. Many women who did bring accusations against him were ridiculed by town and church officials. But he was eventually brought to trial, convicted, and, at the age of 60, sent to prison (Jones, 1989; Olsen, 1989).

The dilemmas confronted throughout this book, especially the quest to preserve both the rights of suspects and the rights of victims (as exemplified in Chapter 9), are highlighted when we consider the crime of rape. Society, until recently, has denied rape victims their legitimate rights; among victims of various crimes, rape victims have been singled out for misunderstanding, harassment, and neglect. For example, if a rape victim does not resist, people may incorrectly assume that she wanted to be raped; in contrast, people never raise the question of whether a robbery victim wanted to be robbed, even when he or she didn't resist (Scroggs, 1976). Furthermore, society struggles over the proper treatment of convicted rapists. Is rape a sexual crime or an act of violence? Is it the act of a disordered mind or a normal one?

Rape, among serious crimes, is perhaps the most appropriate for psychological analysis. Myths abound about the nature of rapists and their relationship to the victims. Rape is a crime in which the interaction between the criminal and his prey is central in attributions of intention and responsibility. And the last two decades have seen an explosion of psychological research directed toward the understanding of sexual assaults (Blader & Marshall, 1989; Ellis, 1991; Hall & Hirschman, 1991). For these reasons, we devote a separate chapter to the crime of rape and its victims. The focus of the chapter is female rape victims, but the fact that men are also raped should not be overlooked, even though the law has only recently recognized them as victims.

MYTHS ABOUT RAPE

Brownmiller (1975), among others, has noted the profusion of myths and incorrect stereotypes about rape, rapists, and rape victims in our society. These take three general forms: (1) women cannot be raped against their will, (2) women secretly wish to be raped, and (3) most accusations of rape are faked. For example, we are told: "Only bad girls get raped." (But we are also told: "All women want to be raped" and "Women ask for it.") We also learn that "Any healthy woman can resist a rapist if she really wants to" and that "Women 'cry rape' only when they've been jilted."

These falsehoods create a climate hostile to rape victims, portraying them as often willing participants in or even instigators of furtive sexual encounters. In fact, these attitudes often function as self-serving rationalizations and excuses for blaming the victim. In a survey of a cross-section of American adults, 50% agreed with the statement "A woman who goes to the home or apartment of a man on the first date implies she is willing to have sex."

Examples of Rape Attitude Surveys

In providing a much-needed scientific perspective on forcible rape, psychologists can offer a number of methodological skills and theoretical constructs. Rape means many different things to many different people, and these differing attitudes and perceptions affect behaviors toward both offenders and their victims (Feild, 1978a). Some respondents feel more empathy toward rape victims than others do; some feel empathy toward defendants charged with the crime of rape (Deitz, Blackwell, Daley, & Bentley, 1982; Deitz, Littman, & Bentley, 1984; Deitz, Russell, & Hammes, 1989). Thus the conceptualization and measurement of attitudes about rape can help clarify what different people believe about this crime, its victims, and its perpetrators.

In his ground-breaking efforts here, Herbert S. Feild (1978a, 1979; Barnett & Feild, 1977; Feild & Barnett, 1978; Feild & Bienen, 1980) hypothesized that attitudes about rape are multidimensional rather than unidimensional; that is, a person's view on rape cannot be summarized simply by one score on a single scale. Rather, Feild proposed that a number of separate components, or "factors," make up attitudes about rape. After constructing a 75-item Attitudes toward Rape questionnaire and analyzing responses to it, he concluded that a number of specific attitude clusters contribute to our overall perspective. Field identified these factors as the following:

1. *Women's responsibility in rape prevention.* Sample items are "A woman should be responsible for preventing her own rape" and "A raped woman is a responsible victim, not an innocent one." Individuals scoring high on this factor explain a rape as partly the result of the woman's acquiescence. In its extreme form, this perspective sees *consent* as an inherent part of the interaction. This attitude permits potential rapists to indulge their desires while not having

to think of themselves as rapists. People with this attitude, if serving as jurors, would be less likely to convict an alleged rapist.

2. *Sex as motivation for rape.* Sample attitude items are "The reason most rapists commit rape is for sex" and "Rape is the expression of an uncontrollable desire for sex." A high score reflects a traditional view that the motive for rape is sexual release. The fact that this cluster of statements emerges as a separate factor means that it is largely independent of the first factor; that is, a person who believes that rapists are sexually motivated may or may not feel that a woman should be held responsible for preventing her own rape.

3. *Severe punishment for rape.* Sample items are "A convicted rapist should be castrated" and "A man who has committed rape should be given at least 30 years in prison." High scores reflect a belief in strong retribution against rapists. This factor is not necessarily correlated with scores on the first two factors.

4. *Victim precipitation of rape.* Sample item: "Women provoke rape by their appearance and behavior." Alhough it appears related in content to factor 1, this attitude cluster concentrates on beliefs about the instigation of the rape and the supposition by some that women's "flirtatious" behavior or "scanty" dresses are the real cause of rape.

5. *Normality for rapist.* Sample item: "Rapists are 'normal' men." Characterizations of the degree of mental illness of rapists are separate attitudes from the preceding factors.

6. *Favorable perception of a woman after rape.* This factor is concerned with the perceived attractiveness of a woman after her rape. A sample item is "A woman should not feel guilty following a rape."

7. *Resistance as women's role during rape.* A high score here indicates the belief that a woman should try to resist a rapist's attack—a matter to which we will return later in this chapter.

For some of these factors it is possible to characterize a high score as reflecting either a prorape or an antirape attitude. But on factors 2, 5, and 6, this is not possible—which offers further evidence for the multidimensionality of our attitudes toward rape.

What Accounts for Stereotypes and Myths about Rape?

Despite the multitude of components, several of these factors reflect an attitude that may be characterized—in its virulent form—as unsympathetic to victims and tolerant of rape, since it excuses rapists from being responsible for their actions. (Feild labeled high scores on these factors as "prorape.") For people possessing such attitudes, belief in the myths described earlier would justify their attitudes. Burt (1980) has proposed that such persons have developed a broad ideology of values and beliefs that encourages the acceptance of myths about rape. Among the aspects of this ideology are the following:

1. *Sexual conservatism.* This attitude emphasizes restrictions on the appropriateness of sexual partners, sexual acts, and circumstances under which sexual activity should occur. Burt observes: "Since many instances of rape violate one or more aspects of this conservative position, a sexually conservative individual might feel so strongly threatened by and rejecting of the specific circumstances of rape that he or she would overlook the coercion and force involved, and condemn the victim for participating" (1980, p. 218).

2. *Adversarial sexual beliefs.* This component refers to the belief that sexual relationships are fundamentally exploitive—that each participant in them is manipulative, sly, unfaithful, opaque to the other's understanding, and not to be trusted. To a person holding this ideology, "rape might seem the extreme on a continuum of exploitation, but not an unexpected or horrifying occurrence, or one justifying sympathy or support" (Burt, 1980, p. 218).

3. *Acceptance of interpersonal violence.* Another important part of the ideology is the belief that force and coercion are legitimate ways to gain compliance, especially in intimate and sexual relationships. This ideology approves of men's dominating women and overpowering passive partners with violence and control.

4. *Sex-role stereotyping.* The last component of Burt's ideology limits the expectations for the two genders, especially females (who are placed in an inferior and passive role). It casts each gender into the traditional mold of behaviors and denies the possibility of androgyny.

Burt constructed a set of attitude statements and administered them to a sample of 598 Minnesota adults in order to determine whether each of these components contributed to acceptance of myths about rape. Examples of the attitude statements can be found in Box 15-1.

When subjects' responses on the attitude-ideology clusters were compared with their answers to a scale measuring beliefs in myths about rapes, Burt found that three of the four clusters had an impact (sexual conservatism did not). The strongest predictor of believing the myths was the acceptance of interpersonal violence. The subjects, both men and women, who felt that force and coercion were acceptable in persuading others were the ones who agreed with items like "Women who get raped while hitchhiking get what they deserve" and "Any healthy woman can successfully resist a rapist if she really wants to."

Another pattern of characteristics related to attitudes about rape has been labeled the "macho personality constellation" or hypermasculinity (Mosher & Sirkin, 1984). The Hypermasculinity Inventory measures three components: calloused sexual attitudes toward women, a belief that violence is manly and desirable, and a view of danger as exciting. Males scoring high on this inventory also report higher levels of drug use, dangerous driving following alcohol consumption, aggressive behavior, and delinquent behavior during childhood. Mosher and Anderson (1986) found a positive relationship between scores on this macho personality constellation and a history of aggressive sexual behavior.

FACTS ABOUT RAPE

As we have seen, mistaken beliefs about rape reflect underlying values that relate to general attitudes about law and crime. But what are the facts about rape?

Rape in the United States

The United States has the highest rate of forcible rape (distinguished from statutory rape) of any industrialized country; 80 forcible rapes are reported annually to the police for every 100,000 females. This rate—one rape reported every five minutes—is three times that of England or West Germany, five to ten times that of France or Japan, and twice that of Canada (Kutchinski, 1988; Quinsey, 1984; Russell, 1984). The frequency of rape in the United States reflects the relatively high incidence of all types of violent crime in this country. The rate of reported sexual assaults against adults increased 600% between 1933 and 1973 (Hindelang & Davis, 1977) and has quadrupled since 1971. According to the FBI *Uniform Crime Reports*, 102,555 rapes were reported to U.S. law enforcement agencies in 1990, an

---

Box 15-1 | *Sample Items from Burt's Ideology Components*

Sexual conservatism:
1. People should not have oral sex.
2. A nice woman will be offended or embarrassed by dirty jokes.
3. A woman shouldn't give in sexually to a man too early or he'll think she's loose.
4. A woman who initiates a sexual encounter will probably have sex with anybody.

Adversarial sexual beliefs:
1. In a dating relationship a woman is largely out to take advantage of a man.
2. A man's got to show the woman who's boss right from the start or he'll end up henpecked.

3. Most women are sly and manipulating when they are out to attract a man.
4. Women are usually sweet until they've caught a man, but then they let their true self show.

Acceptance of interpersonal violence:
1. Sometimes the only way a man can get a cold woman turned on is to use force.
2. Being roughed up is sexually stimulating to many women.
3. Many times a woman will pretend she doesn't want to have intercourse because she doesn't want to seem loose, but she's really hoping he will force her.

Sex-role stereotyping:
1. A woman should be a virgin when she marries.
2. A wife should never contradict her husband in public.
3. It looks worse for a woman to be drunk than for a man to be drunk.
4. A man should fight when the woman he's with is insulted by another man.

From Burt (1980, p. 222).

increase of 9% over the previous year. However, experts estimate that reported rapes are only a minority of all those that occur (Reeves, 1989; Warshaw, 1988). Estimates are that between 20% and 30% of females in the United States will experience at least one rape or rape attempt (Ellis, 1989; Koss & Oros, 1982; Muehlenhard & Linton, 1987). But the *percentage* of rapes that *are* reported is probably increasing. More and more rape victims are, in the words of Maureen Dowd (1983), "refusing to withdraw into a silent scream."

Just what percentage of rapes are reported? Russell's (1984) survey found a report rate of only 9.5%. An earlier study by Russell (1975) had estimated that, when both reported and unreported rapes and attempted rapes are included, over 1.5 million attacks occurred in one year. Blader and Marshall (1989) estimate that 2000 sexual assaults take place in the United States each day.

Given this apparent epidemic of assaults, why the low report rates? Feldman-Summers and Ashworth (1981) speculate about reasons: the woman believes that reporting "won't do any good," she will suffer further embarrassment as a result of reporting, and she will not be believed by law enforcement officers. Many victims are afraid that the attacker will retaliate if charges are made; rapists often promise their victims that they will come back. Some of these expectations are often fulfilled. According to FBI figures, only about half of reported rapes result in an arrest. And if a suspect is charged and the victim is a witness at his trial, his defense attorney may ridicule her testimony and impugn her character.

A major study of rape published in 1992 has provided valuable data on the frequency of rape and women's reactions to it. This study, known as the National Women's Study, was organized and funded by several governmental agencies and crime-victim organizations. A nationwide,

stratified sample of 4008 adult women were interviewed over the telephone about their experiences as victims of sexual aggression. Because children and adolescents were excluded from the sample, the figures will, of course, underestimate the total number of rapes, but they do give us a picture of the magnitude of the problem with adult women. Among the study's findings are the following:

1. Based on the sample of women surveyed, an estimated 683,000 women were raped during 1990; this is more than six times as many rapes as were reported to the police during the same year.
2. Among rape victims, over two-thirds reported that they received no physical injuries during the rape, 24% reported minor injuries, and 4% reported serious physical injuries.
3. An estimated 12.1 million women in the United States have been raped at least once in their lifetime.
4. Among rape victims, 61% report having been raped before the age of 18.

In an interview study dealing with hypothesized reactions to rape, Feldman-Summers and Ashworth (1981) found that women (not actual rape victims) who were members of minority groups (blacks, Chicanos, Chinese Americans) were less likely than white women to say they would report a rape. Minorities tend to be distrustful of and alienated from public agencies in this country; moreover, Asian women are reluctant to talk about sex.

As Russell (1984) notes, females of all ages, social classes, and ethnic groups are vulnerable to rape. In 1989 five New Jersey teenage boys, including co-captains of the local high school football team, were charged with raping a 17-year-old mentally retarded girl (Hanley, 1989). In Georgia a 46-year-old man was charged with raping a 4-year-old girl. According to the

National Women's Study, the high-risk age groups are children and adolescents, but other surveys report that between 1% and 12% of victims are over 50 years of age. Of those men arrested for rape, almost half are under the age of 25.

Motivations for Rape

In our society, the stereotype is that rapists are sex-starved or insane or both. Most experts now regard rape primarily as a crime of violence, not of sexual arousal (Dowd, 1983). Although rape uses the sexual act for its fulfillment, its instigation is usually not sexual tension. Most rapists are not sexually deprived; they have other outlets for their sexual needs. Many rapists are married (Melani & Fodaski, 1974). Furthermore, many rapists are unable to maintain an erection without assistance from the victim, and some cannot ejaculate. Instead, other motives are important. One rapist told an interviewer: "You know, I could get all the sex I wanted because my brother ran a chain of massage parlors. But if they were giving it to me, I wasn't in control. I wanted to take it" (quoted in Dowd, 1983, p. 27). Another was asked why, if it was sex he wanted, he didn't patronize prostitutes. In essence, his reply was that the macho thing to do was to get sex free (Rowland, 1985). Such comments illustrate Russell's conclusion in *The Politics of Rape* (1975, p. 260) that rape is not so much a deviant act as an overconforming one; that is, rape represents an extreme acting out of the qualities that are seen as masculine in this and many other societies: aggression, force, power, strength, toughness, dominance, and competitiveness.

Not all rapists have the same motives. Rape involves diverse combinations of aggressive and sexual motivation and deviant lifestyles for different offenders (Barbaree & Marshall, 1991). Experts have developed typologies of rapists,

some proposing as many as nine types (Prentky & Knight, 1991), some as few as two or three (Groth, 1979). Most typologies have emphasized four factors that distinguish different types of rapists: (1) What amount and type of aggression does the rapist use? (2) If the level of aggression is high, does it heighten sexual arousal, in a classically sadistic manner? (3) Does the offender show evidence of psychopathy or antisocial personality disorder? (4) Does the offender have deviant sexual fantasies accompanied by high sexual arousal?

Recent theories of sexual aggression attempt to combine several causal factors into an integrated scheme that accounts for the different types of rapists. For example, Hall and Hirschman (1991) propose different combinations of four factors, similar to those identified above, to describe most rapists: (1) high levels of sexual arousal that are not inhibited by aggression, (2) attitudes and beliefs about women that justify aggressiveness toward females, (3) loss of control over negative emotions such as anger and hostility, which are "acted out" in sexual aggression, and (4) long-standing antisocial personality disorder arising out of parental abuse or neglect or familial criminal history.

In a different approach, Ellis (1989) has identified three theories of rape: the feminist theory, emphasizing rape as a pseudosexual act of male domination and exploitation of women; the social-learning approach, suggesting that sexual aggression is learned through observation and imitation; and the evolutionary theory, holding that natural selection favors men who use forced sexual behavior. Ellis (1991) also suggests that high levels of testosterone increase the proclivity to rape by increasing a man's sexual urges and by decreasing the man's sensitivity to aversive outcomes such as a victim's suffering.

These different approaches illustrate that rape cannot be easily explained by any one label or theory. However, every one of these classification systems still fails to some degree to capture the full spectrum of behavior and motivations that typify rapists. Some of these systems are limited, too, by the fact that they are based on studies of *convicted* rapists who have been sentenced to prison. The majority of rapists are never imprisoned for their offenses.

Characteristics of Rapists

Russell's critique alerts us to another set of myths. Just as we have stereotypes and myths about the nature of rape, so too do we have about the characteristics of rapists. Often they are *not* strangers; it is estimated that as many as 70%–80% of rapes are carried out against victims who know their assailants (Koss, 1985; Warshaw, 1988). Most rapists are not sex-crazed deviants who exist on the margins of society. In fact, it is hard to consistently distinguish all rapists from other men on many physiological, sociological, or psychological variables (Blader & Marshall, 1989; Hall, 1990). The research also finds that the link between sexually aggressive behavior and psychopathology is inconclusive (Koss & Leonard, 1984). Finally, attempts to show that convicted rapists are more pathological than other criminal offenders have proved futile (Marolla & Scully, 1982).

Acquaintance Rape and "Date Rape"

As noted, over three-fourths of rapes are committed by acquaintances, and these are the hardest for women to report (Dubrow, 1984). Sometimes these actions are not even interpreted as rape. Kanin (1957, 1971) found that, over a 20-year period, between one-fourth and one-fifth of college women he had surveyed reported forceful attempts at sexual intercourse by their dates, during which the women resorted to such reactions as screaming, fighting, crying, and pleading. But usually they did not label the event as attempted rape. More recent surveys make similar conclusions; 22% of college females in Yegidis's (1986) survey reported being a victim at least once of an attempted or a completed rape; 25.3% of a sample of undergraduates in New Zealand reported being raped or having a rape attempted against them (Gavey, 1991). Muehlenhard and Linton (1987) reported that 15% of females had experienced at least one date rape and that 70% of males had committed this offense in their lifetime. But if we broaden the label to include any unwelcome sexual initiative during a date, the reported figures increase to 78% of females and 57% of males. Even among college males, 6% in one study reported having been sexually assaulted at least once (Lott, Reilly, & Howard, 1982).

"Date rapes" and acquaintance rapes are increasingly being reported on college campuses. In one campus survey, at the University of South Dakota, almost half of the women said they had been touched, held, or kissed against their will, and about 10% had been beaten or physically abused in one or more relationships (Associated Press, 1985a). The 1992 National Women's Study reported that only 22% of rapes were committed by strangers to the victim; 29% were committed by nonrelative acquaintances; 27% by a relative; 9% by a boyfriend or former boyfriend; and 9% by a husband or former husband. In general, date rapes differ from sexual assaults by a stranger in several ways. They tend to occur on weekends, between 10:00 P.M. and 1:00 A.M., and they usually take place at the assailant's home or apartment. An interview study by Gail Abarbanel (quoted in Seligmann, 1984) found that they last longer than sexual violations by strangers—sometimes for hours. But they are less likely to involve use of weapons; instead, the date rapist employs verbal threats and physical prowess to overpower his victim.

Cross-Cultural Rape Rates

Sexual abuse is much more frequent in some cultures than in others. In *rape-prone* societies, rape is often a ceremonial act, or it is a device by which men threaten or punish women. In such cultures it may be allowed, or at least overlooked, by law enforcement officials. Women are especially powerless in these societies; they do not participate in public decision making. Earlier we described the macho personality constellation; Reiss (1986) has found that, in societies with a high incidence of rape, the macho personality is more likely to be endorsed as the appropriate one for males.

An example is the Bantu-speaking Gusii tribe in southwestern Kenya, in Africa. LeVine (1959) estimates that the annual rate of rapes is 47.2 or more per 100,000 *total population* (recall that the annual rate in the United States is about 80 per 100,000 *women,* so the Gusii rate is actually higher than ours). A Gusii proverb is "Those whom we marry are those whom we fight" (Brownmiller, 1975, p. 7). In the Gusii culture it is considered normal for sexual intercourse to cause a woman pain. "When a bride is unable to walk after her wedding night, the groom is considered by his friends to be a 'real man' and he is able to boast of his exploits, particularly if he has been able to make her cry" (Sanday, 1981, p. 10).

Of 156 cultures throughout the world, Sanday has classified 18% as "rape-prone," 35% as having rape statistics too low for the society to be considered rape-prone, and 47% as "free of rape." In rape-free societies women are treated with respect, and prestige is attached to female reproductive roles. Also, in rape-free societies interpersonal violence is

minimized, and people's attitude toward the natural environment is one of reverence.

Why are some societies rape-prone? Such cultures embrace a configuration of values that includes interpersonal violence, male dominance, and separation of the sexes. Brownmiller (1975) has proposed that rape is the means by which men subjugate women: "It is nothing more or less than a conscious process of intimidation by which *all men* keep *all women* in a state of fear" (p. 5). This description seems characteristic of many of these rape-prone societies. By limiting women's freedom and making them dependent on men for protection, the threat of rape provides support for a social system based on male dominance. Thus the link between a society's treatment of women in a possessive, dominating, and demeaning manner and that society's tendency to be rape-prone provides support for feminist and social-learning theories of rape, both of which emphasize the learning of sexist and aggressive behaviors.

ARE ALL MEN POTENTIAL RAPISTS?

Feminist writings often portray the male gender as rape-prone. The New York Radical Feminists (1974, p. 1) ask: "Is it possible that the *average* male is programmed to be a rapist?" Melani and Fodaski (1974) answer this question by saying "We live in a culture that, at best, condones and, at worst, encourages women to be perennial victims, men to be continual predators, and sexual relations to be fundamentally aggressive" (p. 84).

In what ways does the culture condone rape? A decade ago television soap operas began to portray rapists as heroes. When Luke raped

Laura on *General Hospital,* not only did she refuse to report the attacker, but she eventually fell in love with him and married him (Waggett, 1989). Romance novels, which are highly popular in our country, often capitalize on a rape scene. One author, Jude Deveraux, had a manuscript returned to her by her editor because it contained no such scene. "I was told that I had to have the hero rape somebody— preferably the heroine—to prove he's virile," she said (quoted by Kayle, 1989, p. 69).

How do men view themselves in this regard? Malamuth (1981) asked male college students at the University of California at Los Angeles, the University of Manitoba, and Stanford University to indicate the likelihood that they would personally rape if they could be assured of not being caught or punished. They were asked to respond on a 5-point scale, from 1 = not at all likely to 5 = very likely. About 35% of the men indicated some likelihood that they would carry out a rape (that is, 2 or above on the scale). About 20% of the men—one out of five—indicated even higher likelihoods (3 or above on the scale). In interpreting these figures, it should be noted (Russell, 1984) that the word *rape* was specifically used in the questionnaire; the percentages might be even higher if the wording were something like "willing to use or threaten force in order to obtain intercourse." A survey of 97 males enrolled in introductory psychology classes at the University of Kansas (Weir & Branscombe, 1989) found that 13% reported some likelihood that they would rape if assured of not getting caught, 15% admitted a likelihood of forcing a woman to have intercourse, and 32% acknowledged actually having attempted to "strongly persuade" a female into intercourse despite being told she did not want to.

At least three types of responses do discriminate between some rapists and the general population of men. First, rapists are more likely to have been sexually aggressive on prior occasions; past sexual aggression is a good predictor of future sexual aggression (Hall & Proctor, 1987). This difference may extend back to the offender's having himself been a victim of sexual aggression; sexually aggressive boys are more likely to have been sexually abused in the past than are normal boys or delinquent, but not sexually aggressive, boys (Friedrich, Beilke, & Urquiza, 1987, 1988).

Second, there is some indication that rapists can be distinguished from men who do not rape on the basis of specific psychological concepts. Let us return to Malamuth's one-item self-report (which he called the likelihood-of-rape or LR measure) to see whether propensity to rape is related to any other attitude or behavior measures.

Men's responses on the LR scale were correlated with those from the two scales developed by Burt (mentioned earlier in this chapter). Self-reported likelihood of committing a rape correlated +.60 with the Rape Myth Acceptance Scale and +.54 with the subscale measuring Acceptance of Interpersonal Violence.

Research consistently shows that those who report they are likely to rape or that they have engaged in sexual coercion also tend to believe rape myths (Briere & Malamuth, 1983; Malamuth, 1981). More recent research (Weir & Branscombe, 1989), however, emphasizes the importance of hypermasculinity components such as attraction to danger, calloused sexual attitudes, Machiavellianism, and similar cognitive and personality measures that reflect acceptance of exploitation of others.

Oros, Buk, and Koss (cited in Malamuth, 1981) administered a sexual experiences survey to male undergraduates. This questionnaire included items such as "Have you ever obtained sexual intercourse with a woman who didn't want to, by using some degree of physical force (twisting her arm, holding her down, etc.)?"

On the basis of their responses, these students were classified by level of sexual aggressiveness. In a later session, subjects were presented with a scenario of an interaction between a man and a woman that ended with the man using force to have intercourse. Each subject was asked to describe his perception of the events. Subjects' reactions were found to be related to their level of sexual aggressiveness; the more aggressive men were more likely to believe that the woman knew the man would use force. In addition, these men were less likely to believe that the man's actions would result in a rape conviction. Another, even more impressive, indication of the validity of the LR self-report measure is found in Box 15-2.

Rapists are also more likely to hold callous attitudes about women and sexual violations (part of the macho personality constellation) and to endorse rape myths. They believe women *want* to be raped, and after a sexual assault they are likely to say to the victim, with great sincerity, "You enjoyed that, didn't you?" Burt (1980) argues that acceptance of rape myths

plays an important role in causing rape. She hypothesizes that rapists use such beliefs as justifications of their behavior and as "psychological releasers or neutralizers, allowing potential rapists to turn off social prohibitions against injuring or using others when they want to commit an assault" (quoted in Malamuth, 1981, p. 43). When these beliefs are the primary motivation for rape (as opposed to a personality disorder or out-of-control anger), the rapist may be less likely to use brutal aggression and therefore to be reported by victims and apprehended by police (Hall & Hirschman, 1991). Paradoxically, the low rate of reporting of these offenders may actually strengthen the rapists' belief that their victims enjoyed the aggression.

The third difference between rapists and other men is that some rapists show a tendency to experience relatively high levels of sexual arousal in response to depictions of rape. One rapist told an interviewer: "I went to a porno bookstore, put a quarter in the slot, and saw this porn movie. It was just a guy coming up from behind a girl and attacking her and raping

---

Box 15-2 | *Propensity to Be a Rapist and Conditions Leading to Sexual Arousal*

Malamuth and Check (reported in Malamuth, 1981) compared men who were low and high on the LR self-report scale of rape likelihood. Several days after doing their self-ratings, the subjects listened to one of three tapes: (1) a rape depiction in which the victim continuously abhors the assault (Rape Victim Abhorrence condition), (2) a rape depiction in which the rapist perceives that the victim involun-

tarily becomes sexually aroused (Rape Victim Arousal condition), or (3) a depiction of a mutually consenting sexual activity with a willing, sexually aroused partner (Consenting condition). The authors report the effects of these different audiotapes on two measures of sexual arousal, a self-report measure and a measure of erection of the penis, separately for men high in rape likelihood and those low in

likelihood. For example, men who are classified as high in likelihood of rape report much greater sexual arousal while listening to the Rape Victim Arousal tape than when listening to the Consenting tape. In contrast, men who are low on the LR scale are no more sexually aroused by one of these tapes than by the others.

her. That's when I started having rape fantasies. When I seen that movie, it was like somebody lit a fuse from my childhood on up. . . . I just went for it, went out and raped" (quoted in Beneke, 1982, pp. 73–74).

Because sexual offenders often lie about their sexual preferences and behavior, forensic investigators have developed special physiological measures of their sexual arousal that are supposedly less easily faked. A typical laboratory method involves playing audiotapes or videotapes for a subject that depict different types of erotic behavior, some of it deviant and some of it nondeviant. While the subject watches or listens to these tapes, a strain-gauge attached to his penis records changes in penile circumference. It is assumed that greater erectile responses to sexually aggressive material signal greater levels of sexual arousal. Several studies have shown sex offenders to have equal or greater arousal to rape stimuli than to scenes of consenting sexual activity (Hall, 1990). In contrast, men who are not rapists usually show less sexual excitation when watching or listening to scenes of rape. Recent work on reactions to violent pornography, described in the following paragraphs, elaborates on this important finding.

Pornography is often distinguished from other erotic material as being explicitly degrading and abusive in its content (Longino, 1980). During the past two decades, pornographic material combining sex and violence has become so commonplace that people can rent videotapes of this nature in suburban stores. What effect do scenes of rape and coercive acts have on violent behavior toward women? An answer comes from the extensive research program of Edward Donnerstein and his colleagues (Donnerstein, 1982; Linz, Donnerstein, & Penrod, 1984, 1987a, 1988; Malamuth & Donnerstein, 1982). These studies and similar ones by Feshbach and Malamuth (1978) *consistently*

show that men who are exposed to violent pornographic materials (in either a print or a film medium) are more aggressive toward women in subsequent interactions.

In a typical study (Donnerstein & Berkowitz, 1981), male college students were led to believe that they were participating in an experiment on the effects of stress on learning. They were told that they would be paired with either a male or a female student. During an early part of the experiment, the partner gave the subject a high number of electrical shocks, indicating that the partner didn't think much of an essay the subject had written. In the next part of the experiment, the subject was exposed to one of four films: a neutral talk-show interview, an erotic film depicting sexual intercourse with no violent content, or one of two pornographic films that combined aggression and sexual behavior, depicting a woman being slapped and sexually assaulted. One of these pornographic films ended with the woman smiling at her attackers; in the other version, the woman was clearly suffering at the end of the film. Then the subject was given a chance to be aggressive toward his partner by administering electrical shocks. Both pornographic films increased the male subject's level of aggression with a female partner but not with a male partner.

Research findings such as these are being used to support proposals in several communities to restrict the availability of obscene and pornographic materials. The report of the Attorney General's Commission on Pornography (or "Meese Commission"), published in July 1986, singled out pornography as a factor in aggression. As noted in Chapter 5, shortly before he was executed, serial murderer Ted Bundy claimed that childhood exposure to sexual violence in the media had influenced his later development, and the wide publicity given his interview has increased efforts to restrict the availability of pornographic material. These proposals are, of course, controversial (Page, 1989; Wilcox, 1987); they exemplify the conflict from Chapter 1 between individuals' rights and society's needs. The researchers on whose work the generalizations are founded are reluctant to see censorship or restrictions on pornography based only on their research (Linz, Donnerstein, & Penrod, 1987b). They propose that research in nonlaboratory settings and longer time frames are needed. They *resist* the conclusion that "this type of pornography is at the root of much of the rape that occurs today" (Malamuth, 1989, p. 580).

Another problem with research on the sexual arousal of rapists is that the expected patterns of specific deviant arousal are not found consistently enough to ensure validity. Some men with no history of sexual offense are sexually aroused by rape stimuli; also, many rapists are more aroused by nondeviant stimuli than by coercive sexual stimuli (Hall, 1990). In addition, investigators using the strain-gauge methods often assume that the act of rape is *in response* to deviant arousal, when clinical evidence suggests that many rapists initially want their victims to consent to sex with them rather than to resist it. The distinguishing physiological pattern for rapists may be that their sexual arousal is not inhibited by aggression, as is the case for other men (Blader & Marshall, 1989). At this point in time, most experts caution that physiological measures of sexual arousal should still be regarded as experimental in nature rather than as absolute indications of sexual aggression (Hall, 1990).

In summary, although it is true that men rape for a number of reasons (and sexual release is not the primary cause), men who rape may be differentiated from nonrapists on three factors: (1) they have a history of prior sexual aggression as victims or perpetrators or both; (2) they show a hostile disrespect for women and a propensity for aggressive ways of resolving

conflicts; and (3) their sexual arousal may not be inhibited by aggression in the way that other men's is.

RESPONDING TO RAPE VICTIMS

Chapter 9 described some of the rights recently provided by the courts and legislatures to victims of violent crimes. The focus in this section is on providing psychological assistance to the victim, which is an equally important goal. Rape victims suffer physical hurt, emotional pain and humiliation, and sometimes severe psychological aftereffects. Recovery from the trauma of rape can be very slow. The plight of rape victims has received increased attention through of a number of highly publicized cases in which females have come forward to report their sexual harassment and rape experiences. As these cases have unfolded in the public eye, sexual aggression has become a topic of unprecedented discussion among men and women. The gang rape of the "Central Park Jogger" during a "wilding" spree, Anita Hill's explosive charges of sexual harassment against Supreme Court nominee Clarence Thomas, Patricia Bowman's claim that she was raped by William Kennedy Smith after meeting him in a bar, and Desiree Washington's rape charges that resulted in the conviction of former heavyweight boxing champion Mike Tyson—all have focused this nation's attention as never before on matters of sexual conduct and on the plight of the victims of sexual aggression.

One key feature of this focus has been a debate about whether the names of victims of sexual assault should be made public. The tradition of the media in this country has been to protect the identity of rape victims by not using their names in media coverage. However, in the trial of William Kennedy Smith, both NBC News and the *New York Times* broke with this tradition and published the name of Smith's accuser: Patricia Bowman. Defenders of this decision argued that not naming rape victims perpetuates the stigma, making it more difficult in the long run for victims to come forward and confront their attackers. Critics of the practice claimed that publishing the victim's name invaded her privacy and perhaps ruined her future because she will forever be "branded" as a rape victim. The results of the previously described National Women's Study indicate that most rape victims prefer to *not* have their names published; 86% of the women surveyed said they would be less likely to report a rape if they knew their names would be made public.

The Rape Trauma Syndrome

How do women react to being raped? King and Webb (1981) note: "Some women become very tearful, hysterical, and severely upset. Others remain much more in control, never displaying a great deal of emotion, emotional upheaval, or distress" (p. 95). But all rape victims share one common outcome: the experience takes a mighty psychological toll on every survivor (Ellis, 1983).

Burgess and Holmstrom (1974, 1979) described a collection of symptoms that are experienced by most rape victims regardless of their *style* of expression; they labeled this the *rape trauma syndrome*. It contains three categories of reactions: emotional responses, disturbances in functioning, and changes in lifestyle.

Among the emotional responses are fear, including fear of being left alone and fear evoked by situations similar to the one in which the rape occurred (Calhoun, Atkeson, & Resick, 1982). Even the most general of associations with the rape or rapist may trigger an emotional response. Judith Rowland (1985), a deputy district attorney, describes a reaction of a white rape victim, Terri Richardson, as the trial of her alleged attacker began. Her attacker was a black man.

> Now, in the summer of 1979 the San Diego Municipal Court had one black judge among its number. As it happened, . . . his chambers were next door. As Terri and I stood . . . while the bailiff scurried out to reassemble the jury, this lone black judge was also preparing to take the bench. I was aware of him standing in his doorway, wearing his ankle-length black robes. It was only when his bailiff held the courtroom door open for him and he was striding toward it that Terri saw him. In less than the time it took him to get through the door, Terri had bolted from the corridor, through the courtroom, and into the main hallway. By the time I got to the outside corridor, I found only a group of startled jurors. I located Terri in a nearby ladies' room, locked in a stall, crying. With a bit more comforting, she was able to regain her composure and get through both my direct and the defense's cross-examination with only minor bouts of tears, particularly while describing the attack itself [pp. 166–167].

And this response by the victim occurred seven months after the attack.

Guilt and shame are also frequent emotional responses. Victims may blame themselves: "Why was I at a bus stop in a strange part of town?" "Did I check that the back door was locked that night?" They may also feel that they didn't resist strongly enough.

The victim also feels a sense of loss, including the loss of autonomy and control over her body. She may also experience diminished trust in others, a loss that may never be fully repaired throughout her lifetime. One victim describes the feeling this way: "I never feel safe. I couldn't stand the apartment where I lived, but I'm so afraid to be alone anywhere. I never was like that before. I carry things with me, like kitchen knives and sticks, when I go out" (quoted in Rowland, 1985, p. 146).

The second general type of reaction, a disturbance in functioning, is also frequent among rape victims. Specific disturbances include changes in sleeping patterns (insomnia, nightmares, and early awakening), social withdrawal, problems in sexual functioning, and changes in appetite. One victim reports:

> At first, I had no appetite. I didn't eat anything for three whole days. It hurt to swallow for some reason. Then I began to eat a lot, you know, and gained weight. I don't think I slept for the same three days that I didn't eat. I remember not even going to bed the first two nights. After that I couldn't sleep more than a couple of hours at a time for a week or so, and that still happens two or three times a week. I've had nightmares, but I can't remember what they are. Only that I wake up feeling like I'm about to be hurt. Very scary, afraid [quoted in Rowland, 1985, p. 146].

Feldman-Summers, Gordon, and Meagher (1979) studied the impact of rape on victims' sexual satisfaction. Although the sample was small, consisting of 15 white victims, the study did include a comparison group of women who had not been sexually assaulted. Compared with them, the rape victims reported no difference in frequency of sexual behavior or degree of satisfaction with sexual activities before the rape. However, on a majority of the interview questions the victims reported less satisfaction one week after the rape than during the period before the rape. "Interestingly, the only activities that were not rated as less satisfying during the post-rape period were those involving masturbation and primarily affectional behaviors such as holding hands, hugging, and talking with or being held by one's partner" (Kilpatrick, Resick, & Veronen, 1981, pp. 108–109). The level of dissatisfaction diminished somewhat over the next two months, but wom-

en who had been raped did not, during this period, approach the level of sexual satisfaction they had experienced before the attack.

The reports of individual victims confirm this pattern and illustrate that irrevocable changes in sexual relationships can occur as a result of being raped. Judith Rowland (1985, p. 259), a prosecutor, described her questioning of a victim:

> "Jill, . . . how is your relationship with Alan now, and since the assault?"
> "We broke up about four months later."
> I learned that she had slept with no one but Alan for over a year before the rape, but had not been able to have satisfactory intercourse with him, or anyone else, since. She never attempted it again in her own apartment, and at his place she had cried the two or three times they had gotten close to making love; so they stopped trying, and their relationship had deteriorated through the summer.
> "Alan was kind to me, but I couldn't let him back in, emotionally or physically."

Changes occur not only in emotions and in general functioning but also in lifestyle. Some victims report obsessively checking doors to make sure they are double-locked; one of the victims whose attacker was prosecuted by Rowland (1985) took 45-minute showers two or three times daily, trying to remove the rapist's odor from her body. Other women make major changes in lifestyle, breaking up with their boyfriends (as we saw earlier), changing jobs, and moving to new residences. Women with more than one sexual victimization across their childhood and adult years are more likely to report unplanned and aborted pregnancies (Wyatt, Guthrie, & Notgrass, 1992). These reactions are exacerbated by the beliefs and comments of friends who assume "it's all in her head" if she can't adjust. Victims face real problems of disbelief; male companions, feeling that the women are damaged goods, may abandon them, and friends may subscribe to the rape myths described earlier in this chapter.

Crisis Reactions

These poignant descriptions of trauma imply that changes differ over time, also. In fact, observers (Burgess & Holmstrom, 1974; Ellison & Buckhout, 1981, p. 54; Joshua Golden, cited in Rowland, 1985) have described the typical rape victim's response as a crisis reaction that follows a series of discrete phases.

The acute crisis phase begins with the attack and lasts a few hours or a day. Among its components are:

1. *Denial*—for example, "This couldn't be happening to me."
2. *Disruption,* or an initial stage of disorganization in which normal coping mechanisms don't work.
3. *Regression* to a state of helplessness or dependency.
4. *Guilt or hostility* and blame toward others.
5. *Distorted perceptions.*

Veronen, Kilpatrick, and Resick (1979) reported the following responses checked by 25 rape victims:

"Scared"—96% agreed.
"Worried"—96% agreed.
"Terrified"—92% agreed.
"Having racing thoughts"—80% agreed.
"Trembling"—96% agreed.
"Pain"—72% agreed.
"Numbness"—60% agreed.

During this acute phase, the victim's needs are for understanding what is happening, regaining control over her life, being able to predict what will happen next, and ventilating her feelings to someone who will listen without passing judgment (Ellison & Buckhout, 1981).

At this point, police officers investigating the crime can either help or hinder the victim. For example, a pelvic examination and the collection of any foreign hairs and semen samples are necessary at this point; it is unlikely that the suspect can be prosecuted otherwise. But the examination may cause a resurgence of the initial feelings of disruption, helplessness, hostility, and violation.

A secondary crisis phase may lead to false optimism. Within a few hours or days of the attack, most victims slip into a period of false recovery. Denial occurs: "I'm okay; everything is the same as before." Then a secondary crisis reaction occurs—a sort of "flashback"—in which some of the symptoms of the acute crisis phase, particularly phobias and disturbances in eating and sleeping, return (Ellison & Buckhout, 1981, p. 59). This phase may last for hours or days before another "quiet period" emerges.

There are usually long-term effects, too (Kilpatrick, Best, & Veronen, 1984). Depending on the severity of the attack and injury, the person may never be the same, not only physically but also psychologically. The sense of security has been torn away, and a feeling of chronic vulnerability has replaced it.

Because of increased public awareness of the needs of rape victims, rape crisis centers have been established in many cities. (They first appeared in the early 1970s, as isolated grassroots organizations in several cities.) They provide crisis counseling to victims. Most follow up with at least one further interview (usually by phone), and a third of their clients have from two to six follow-up interviews. The crisis center also checks for pregnancy and venereal disease.

Long-Term Effects

Long-term counseling is more difficult to provide, because of the lack of staff at rape crisis centers and, in some cases, a feeling that it is not needed or is of no use. Burgess and Holmstrom (1979), in a follow-up of their earlier sample, found that 74% of rape victims felt themselves to be recovered—that is, back to normal—four to six *years* after the rape. But 26% *did not*. Dean Kilpatrick, who tested the psychological adjustment of 204 rape victims at different periods up to four years later, concluded that most of the improvement came in the first three months (cited in Sperling, 1985).

A longitudinal study of 20 rape victims (Kilpatrick et al., 1981) measured the personality and mood of these victims and of a matched control group at three time intervals: one month, six months, and one year after the rape. These researchers employed a model from social-learning theory that "views rape as an in vivo classical conditioning situation in which the threat of death and/or physical damage to the victim serves to elicit strong autonomic arousal—fear. The fear reaction is an unconditioned response to the life-endangering situation the victim finds herself in and includes anxiety responses that are cognitive and behavioral as well as psychological" (p. 110).

Thus, any kind of stimulus present during the rape—a specific neighborhood or type of automobile, a man of a particular appearance—becomes associated, through the process of classical conditioning, with the fear response. This cue then becomes a conditioned stimulus that can evoke the same anxiety and fear response in other situations.

The researchers note:

> In the days and weeks that follow the assault, the victim may experience a very similar fear reaction upon encountering any of the cues that were present during the assault. In order to reduce her fear, the victim may then engage in operant avoidance behavior such as avoiding being alone, [not] interacting with men she does know, or leaving the lights on at night [p. 110].

Because of these reactions, Kilpatrick et al. found that, even at a one-year follow-up, victims continued to suffer emotional effects of sexual assault. Among major problems were fear and anxiety. Victims scored higher than control subjects on a paranoia scale and psychoticism scale (indicating confusion and flashbacks). About one-quarter of the victims reported being symptom-free after one year.

Rape Trauma Syndrome in Court

Psychologists, along with psychiatrists and other physicians, are beginning to testify as expert witnesses in rape trials, especially about the rape trauma syndrome as a reaction of victims (Frazier & Borgida, 1985). As an acute stress reaction, the syndrome is an example of a posttraumatic stress disorder, similar to that experienced by veterans of combat, survivors of natural disasters, and women who are battered by their partners. The psychologist is of special use to the prosecution in those trials in which the defendant admits that sexual intercourse took place but claims that the woman was a willing participant; evidence of rape trauma syndrome can corroborate the complainant's version of the facts (Frazier & Borgida, 1985). In addition, jurors are often not familiar with the reactions that rape victims frequently experience (Borgida & Brekke, 1985), and so psychological experts can educate the jury. Courts around the country are divided, however, on the admissibility of such testimony, and the resulting controversy has generated legal debates (R. Lawrence, 1984; Ross, 1983).

The argument against admitting expert testimony on the rape trauma syndrome is as follows: The psychological responses of rape victims are not unique to rape and are not uniform; thus it is impossible to say with certainty that a woman exhibiting any given set of responses has been raped. Therefore a psychologist should not be allowed to testify that a woman is suffering from rape trauma syndrome, because to do so in effect tells the jury that she has been raped, which is a matter for the jury to decide. As of this writing, most courts reject expert testimony on the rape trauma syndrome on the ground that the reliability of the syndrome has not been established.

LEGISLATION AND COURT DECISIONS

Throughout history rape has had a rather uncertain status within whatever moral and legal system was in effect. Laws about rape in the United States, rooted in English common law, changed little for three centuries (Harper, 1984). Implicit in this long tradition was the assumption that women were inferior in the eyes of the law—and even that they were property. For example, the first American law about rape, created in Massachusetts, imposed the death penalty on the rapist *except* when the victim was unmarried, reflecting a view that women belonged to their husbands (Estrich, 1987). But in the last decade legislation about rape has undergone dramatic review and revision. Since Michigan initiated reform in 1974, most of the other states have modified their rape statutes or passed new ones. These changes are correlated with our increased knowledge about rape, generated by social science research and publicized by feminist groups. As Harper (1984) notes, these revisions have encompassed both form and substance, transforming the legal view of rape from "a violent expression of sex to a sexual expression of violence" (p. B-16). They also

reflect a greater acceptance of the credibility of women as victims and witnesses.

Despite these changes—which will be reviewed in subsequent paragraphs—the basic definitional element of rape remains the absence of consent by the victim. How do we distinguish between rape and a consensual sexual act? No single standard defines what is meant by *nonconsent*; feminists would prefer an explicit statement to the effect that "if a woman chooses not to have intercourse with a specific man and the man chooses to proceed against her will, that is a criminal act of rape" (Brownmiller, 1975, p. 8).

Shifts in Rape Laws

The nature of the victim's conduct has been a matter for legal reform, even if the definition of consent has not been fully resolved. How much does the victim's behavior contribute to the determination of "nonconsent"? Is resistance relevant or necessary? Wallace Loh, a psychologist and law professor, writes:

> If the actor's conduct (physical force or threat of force) is the legal criterion, then evidence pertaining to the victim's prior unchastity is mostly irrelevant for providing that element. But if the victim's conduct (resistance) is determinative, past sexual conduct can be material. Thus, different forcible rape laws can be ordered along a continuum of victim-actor orientation. Common-law statutes are at the victim's end because they typically require some degree of resistance. Reform statutes such as Michigan's . . . which define crime exclusively in terms of the actor's conduct, are at the opposite end of the continuum. Washington's reform legislation takes both parties' conduct into account and therefore can be located in the middle [1981, p. 30].

As of the late 1980s, about four-fifths of the states still imposed a resistance standard in their definition of rape (Largen, 1988). But most of them have expanded their definition of force to include coercion or intimidation by the alleged rapist, so the standard of resistance has been weakened.

Loh has identified an important continuum, both for its measurement possibilities and for its categorization of shifts in state laws. For example, the previous Washington law was completely at the attacker's end of the continuum: if the victim did not resist or did not possess fear of immediate and great bodily harm, no rape supposedly took place, even though force was used. Similarly, a Texas court stated that, if the alleged victim " . . . does not put forth all the power of resistance which she was capable of exerting under the circumstances, it will not be rape" (*Perez v. State*, 1906). As long as "overcoming resistance" is included as a requirement and is not defined, some jurors will define it in extreme ways. One Kansas juror, before that state's law was changed, told the other jurors that, to her, "resistance" meant fighting to the limit of death; since the victim had not died, she had not adequately resisted, and hence this juror could not find the defendant guilty of rape.

A second shift in rape laws has been to divide rape into several crime levels. Previously, some states found that, with only one degree of offense, which carried possibly severe penalties, juries found the sentence (which could be life in prison) to be too extreme for some cases; hence they opted for not-guilty verdicts. The new Washington State law, for example, divides rape into three degrees according to the extent of force or threat:

1. *First-degree rape*: Sexual intercourse (with a nonspouse) by forcible compulsion under aggravated circumstances (for example, using a deadly weapon or kidnapping the victim). Punishable with a minimum sentence of 20 years and a minimum confinement period of 3 years.
2. *Second-degree rape*: Requires only sexual intercourse by forcible compulsion. Penalty: maximum of 10 years.
3. *Third-degree rape*: Defined as sexual intercourse without consent or with threat of substantial harm to property rights. Penalty: not more than 5 years.

Many states, in shifting to a levels approach, have done away with the term *rape* in the charge and have substituted *sexual assault* in hopes that victims will be more likely to report the crimes. The use of *assault* also eliminates any lingering requirements that the state provide corroborating evidence for the victim's testimony, and it devotes more attention to the extent of physical and psychological injury inflicted on the victim.

Among other recent modifications of state laws is a broadening of the definition of *rape* to include other acts besides insertion of the penis into the vagina. In some states, rape laws also deal with acts between two men or acts with a man as the victim. And most states have altered the laws to include *spousal rape*; as of mid-1993, all but three states had some regulations about husbands raping their wives.

In Florida in 1984, a 41-year-old man was found guilty of kidnapping and raping his wife. He was the first man to be convicted of a sexual battery that occurred while the couple were married and living together. Previous convictions for spousal rape had involved couples who had divorced or were living apart.

The Rape Victim as a Trial Witness

Shifts in the rape laws have also addressed a persistent problem in the trials of alleged rapists. Their defense attorneys often have tried to make the rape victim look like the instigator of the sexual act. Nowhere in criminal trials has the defense been given such free rein to discredit an opposing witness. Although there have been instances in which women have claimed a rape after consenting to a sexual act or even when no act took place, the overriding effect of this cross-examination strategy has been to punish a multitude of innocent victims for asserting their rights to bring charges and to testify against their alleged attackers.

Some defense attorneys use the cross-examination to attack the victim's truthfulness and her general morality. These attorneys, through relentless questioning, try to portray the victim as sexually promiscuous by graphically inquiring about her past sex life and even bringing forth a string of past lovers to testify about the breadth and frequency of her sexual experiences. Jurors are influenced by such testimony, especially about the woman's character, reputation, and lifestyle (Lee, 1985). In one savage rape, the victim's jaw was fractured in two places, but the jury acquitted the defendant because it found that there may have been sexual relations on previous occasions and the two persons had been drinking together on the night of the incident (Kalven & Zeisel, 1966, p. 251). As a result of this type of problem, most states have adopted *rape shield* laws to provide victims more protection as trial witnesses. Also, the Privacy Protection for Rape Victims Act of 1978 has amended the federal rules of evidence with regard to the admissibility of testimony on the victim's sexual history with parties other than the defendant.

Although these laws differ from jurisdiction to jurisdiction (Borgida, 1981), they usually rule out any arbitrary inquiry about the victim's previous sexual conduct unless it can be shown to be relevant to specific issues of the case. In Connecticut, for example, testimony about prior sexual activity may be admissible only if it does one of the following:

1. Raises the issue of consent by showing prior sexual conduct between the victim and the defendant.
2. Shows that the defendant was not the source of semen, pregnancy, or venereal disease.
3. Attacks the victim's credibility, provided she has testified on direct examination about her past sexual conduct.
4. Is otherwise so relevant and so material to a critical issue in the case that excluding it would violate the defendant's constitutional rights.

An example (from another jurisdiction) of evidence "so relevant and so material" that exclusion would violate the defendant's constitutional rights is *Commonwealth* v. *Wall* (1992). A child victim had been placed in an aunt's home following a sexual assault by her mother's boyfriend. The child was unhappy in the aunt's home and allegedly fabricated a sexual-assault claim against her uncle in an attempt to be removed. The Pennsylvania court held that it was very relevant to the defense to introduce evidence of the earlier sexual assault.

Despite these court decisions, wide latitude is still allowed in questioning rape victims; in some jurisdictions, rape shield laws may not shield the victim from very much. Borgida (1980, 1981) has classified these laws into three categories, based on the extent to which evidence is excluded, and has determined how adult mock jurors react to different versions of a rape-trial reenactment that reflect these modifications. Consider, for example, the following:

The complainant testifies that she met the defendant at a singles bar, danced and drank with him, and accepted his offer to drive her home. She testifies that at the front door he refused to leave, forced his way into her apartment, and raped her. The defendant wants to prove that the complainant had previously consented to intercourse with casual acquaintances she had met at singles bars. Is the evidence relevant [Borgida, 1981, p. 234]?

According to what Borgida calls moderate reform statutes, this evidence would probably be admitted; the judge would likely rule that the evidence of the victim's past liaisons is material to the fact at issue. But, under the more restrictive "radical reform" statutes of some states (Borgida, 1981, p. 213), such evidence would probably be excluded. These states have concluded that such evidence would be prejudicial (against the victim), and Borgida's (1981) jurors affirmed this expectation. They were reluctant to convict the defendant when testimony was introduced regarding the victim's past sexual relationships with other men.

After initially passing rape shield legislation, a few states (e.g., Iowa, Hawaii, and North Carolina) have since repealed these laws, largely as a result of concerns that the constitutional rights of defendants to fully confront their accusers were being violated by the legislative shields. Even if stringent rape shield laws are in force, some jurors will continue to doubt the testimony of rape victims on the witness stand or will use aspects of the testimony to make attributions about the witnesses' honesty. For example, mock jurors who are relatively lacking in empathy for rape victims are less likely to see an attacker as responsible for a rape (Deitz, Littman, & Bentley, 1984). Mock jurors who are low on rape-victim empathy will take the fact that an alleged victim stares intensively at the defendant throughout her testimony and conclude from that that she is lying (Weir, Willis, & Wrightsman, 1989; Weir & Wrightsman, 1990).

One experience that seems to increase empathy for rape victims is to be personally acquainted with a woman who has been raped. In a laboratory study in which subjects read written summaries of witness testimony and then were asked to rate the responsibility of a man charged with rape, men and women who themselves knew a rape victim were twice as likely to find the accused guilty of rape as were men and women who did not personally know a rape victim (Wiener, Wiener, & Grisso, 1989).

PREVENTING RAPE

Rape is an act of violence and humiliation; short of homicide, rape is the "ultimate violation of the self" (a term coined by White-Ellison and Bard, quoted in Rowland, 1985, p. xiii). The goal of concerned citizens, law enforcement officials, and social scientists should be the prevention of rape through the formulation of multipronged prevention strategies (Chappell, 1989). Two methods are reviewed here: (1) actions by potential victims and (2) punishments of and interventions with convicted rapists or potential rapists.

Rape Avoidance for Potential Victims

If a woman finds herself in a situation in which a man begins to sexually assault her, what should she do? Should she scream and cry out? Should she fight back? Or should she try to reason with him? Some have suggested that she tell him she has herpes or is having her menstrual period. Others have counseled submission, especially if he has a weapon—all the while trying to notice as many identifying features of the attacker as possible.

There is no uniformly correct response, just as there is no one type of rapist. However, on the issue of passive compliance, a Justice Department survey of over a million attacks (quoted in Meddis & Kelley, 1985) found that women who did not resist a rape attack were twice as likely to suffer a completed rape as women who tried to protect themselves.

An unusual study by Pauline Bart (1981) identified actions that deflect rape attempts. Bart interviewed 13 women, each of whom had been raped but also had avoided being raped when attacked on another occasion. All the women were adults when both attacks occurred; 15% were under the age of 25. For 8 of them, the rape occurred before the attempted rape; for 5, the sequence was reversed.

Women were more likely to avoid rape under the following circumstances:

1. When they were attacked by strangers rather than men they knew, especially men with whom they had a prior sexual relationship. Of the 13 women, 9 avoided rape with strangers, compared with 4 who avoided it with acquaintances.
2. When the assault took place away from, rather than in, their own homes.
3. When their primary concern was to avoid being raped, in contrast to when their primary concern was to avoid being killed or mutilated.
4. When there was no force or threat of force. Threat of force was present in only 3 of 13 avoidances, compared with 6 of 13 rapes.
5. When they used multiple strategies, screamed, and physically struggled, as opposed to only talking and pleading. Struggling occurred in 10 of 13 avoidances but in only 5 of 13 rapes. Screaming occurred in 8 of 13 avoidances but in 3 of 13 rapes, and talking was used in 7 of 13 avoidances but in 11 of 13 rapes.

But there is an irony here. Branscombe and Weir (1989) found that, when subjects were told that a potential rape victim had resisted both physically and verbally (in the latter case, screaming obscenities at the attacker), they found her behavior to be inappropriate. Women who violate our stereotyped norms of female passivity and dependence are penalized, even when they are rape victims.

Interventions with Rapists

In some states, men convicted of sex crimes are required to complete a sex-offender program before being considered for parole. In such programs the offender must acknowledge responsibility for his actions and participate in exercises designed to modify behavior. More radically, some convicted rapists have been offered treatments with physical or medical procedures. In Europe, psychosurgery and surgical castration have been used on rapists, but their effectiveness is unclear. Because of the ethical controversies that surround these procedures, few experts advocate their use in the United States (Marshall, Jones, Ward, Johnston, & Barbaree, 1991). A South Carolina judge sentenced three convicted rapists to their choice of 30 years in prison or surgical castration. (Even though all three men chose the castration, they were instead sentenced to the prison term; the state supreme court had ruled that castration violated constitutional safeguards against cruel and unusual punishment.)

In a different type of intervention, *anti-androgen drugs* have been given to sex offenders to reduce their sex drive, a procedure described as *chemical castration*. The most common treatment involves giving offenders a synthetic female hormone, MPA, which is manufactured by the Upjohn Company under the tradename Depo-Provera. MPA decreases the level of testosterone in the body, thereby decreasing sexual arousal in most men. Its use with sexually aggressive offenders has met with mixed success (Marshall et al., 1991). But the drug has also been associated with a number of negative side effects, including weight gain, hair loss, feminization of the body, and gall bladder problems.

In some cases, men were told they would not have to serve any time in prison if they agreed to submit to drug treatments. In 1983 Joseph Frank Smith, 30, of San Antonio, Texas, became the first convicted rapist to actually receive drug treatments as a condition of his ten-year probation. Both feminists, on the one side, and defense attorneys, on the other, have raised a number of questions and criticisms regarding this procedure. For instance, its effectiveness has yet to be fully assessed, even though one of its advocates, Dr. Fred Berlin of Johns Hopkins Hospital in Baltimore, claims an 85% success rate in reducing sex drive in more than 100 men he has treated in an experimental program begun in 1979 (Thompson, 1984).

Antiandrogen treatments have problems other than negative side effects. The rate of men dropping out of treatment prematurely is very high. Of greater concern is the fact that the treatment does not always reduce sexual arousal and sexual offenses. In some men, arousal is not dependent on their level of testosterone, so the drugs have minimal effects on their sexual behavior. This point relates to the fact that rape is an act of violence, not of inappropriate sexual arousal; consequently, drugs aimed at reducing sexual desire may be pointing at the wrong target. Even if the drugs inhibit sexual appetites, they may not control violent outbursts (Thompson, 1984). Hence they would not truly rehabilitate these offenders. But as Professor Susan Estrich has said, "There is a sense that judges continue to view rape in some large respects as different from other crimes. They have to deal with the fact it is not crime of sexual desire but brutal violence of the worst sort short of murder" (quoted in Goodman, 1983).

Another major approach to treating aggressive sexual offenders involves combining several behavior therapy techniques into an integrated treatment package designed to increase offend-ers' self-control, improve their social skills, modify their sexual preferences, and teach them how to prevent "relapses" of their offenses. These programs are usually situated in institutions because of the prison sentences imposed on offenders, but they have also been implemented in the community. Some programs are run in a group format; others rely on individual treatment.

These integrated programs employ a wide range of treatment techniques. Sex education and directed training in social skills are common ingredients because of the widespread belief that sex offenders are often socially incompetent. Biofeedback and different forms of aversive conditioning are often used to decrease inappropriate sexual arousal and replace it with arousal to nonaggressive sexual cues. Existing programs appear to be able to produce short-term decreases in recidivism (Quinsey, Chaplin, Maguire, & Upfold, 1987), but longer-term improvements have been difficult to achieve. As a result, relapse-prevention techniques (which have proven useful in the treatment of drug addictions and cigarette smoking) have been added to some programs.

DETECTING THE RAPIST

The previous sections have demonstrated the difficulty of bringing convictions against alleged rapists. Do any means exist to prove whether a given suspect committed a rape? The late 1980s saw the introduction of a device that initially was acclaimed as the greatest advance in the science of crime detection in a century (Lohr, 1987).

The technique, called *genetic fingerprinting*, relies on genetic X-ray analyses of DNA samples, which produce patterns for each of us as distinctive as our fingerprints. The DNA (or deoxyribonucleic acid) samples can be taken from any kind of biological material, including hair or skin, as well as from substances such as blood, saliva, and semen. Geneticists have claimed that the identifying patterns are absolutely specific for each individual (quoted in Lohr, 1987, p. 5).

The procedure was used in a highly publicized case in Great Britain, which has been described in a nonfiction book by Joseph Wambaugh, *The Blooding* (1989). On separate occasions three years apart but in the same location, two 15-year-old girls were sexually assaulted and strangled to death. For several years, despite intensive efforts by the police, no killer was found. But with the development of genetic fingerprinting, the Leicestershire police decided to obtain blood samples from every possible perpetrator of the crimes and compare these with the analyses of the semen taken from the bodies of the victims. All men living in the vicinity who had been born between 1953 and 1970—that is, thousands of men—were asked asked to present themselves for a "blooding"; if they did not appear, officers searched them out. Despite the absence of civil liberties, and even though the killer tried to cheat, the police found their man (Walker, 1989). When confronted, the murderer (named "Pitchfork") confessed.

Genetic fingerprinting has become a growing industry in the United States. The FBI uses the procedure in its crime lab. Genetic-fingerprinting results were admitted into evidence in a Florida rape trial, and their admissibility was upheld when the defendant's conviction was upheld. Colorado now requires genetic profiling of people convicted of sex offenses before they are released (Malcolm, 1989), a step being considered by several other states.

However, there is cause for concern about genetic fingerprinting, even beyond civil rights aspects. For example, the crime laboratory at the Orange County, California, sheriff's department sent about 50 blood and semen samples drawn from about 20 people to each of three labs. The labs were asked to identify which specimens came from the same people. One lab was wrong on one of the 44 matches it found; a second was wrong on one out of 50. The third, more cautious, lab offered no conclusions on about 14 of the samples but got all 37 of its reported matches correct (M. Thompson, 1989). Across the board, the accuracy rate was 98%, but not absolutely perfect. It may be that current technology is unable to secure a perfect match, or it may be that assumptions about the underlying characteristics being independent of each other are false (Thompson & Ford, 1989).

SUMMARY

Rape is a humiliating and degrading crime; for its victims it is the "ultimate violation." Yet until recently society has denied rape victims their legitimate rights, and it was only a decade ago that extensive social science research on rapists and rape survivors began to influence public consciousness and legal reform.

Myths about rape still abound. One reason for their prevalence is that they are congruent with a multidimensional set of attitudes that foster rape or at least show tolerance for it. People who endorse these myths and "prorape" attitudes have an ideology, or integrated set of values and beliefs, that includes adversarial sexual beliefs, acceptance of interpersonal violence, and sex-role stereotyping.

In contrast to the myths, the following are some of the facts about rape:

1. The United States has the highest incidence rate of reported forcible rape of any industrialized country.

2. Even at that, most rapes in the United States are never reported to the police.

3. Rape is more a crime of violence than of sexual arousal. Among the frequent motives for rape are anger, power, and sadism. Most rapists are not sexually deprived.

4. About three-fourths of rape victims know their assailants. Acquaintance rape and "date rape" are increasingly recognized as major manifestations of sexual assault in our society. Between one-fourth and one-fifth of college women have reported forceful attempts at sexual intercourse by their dates.

5. Rape is far more frequent in some societies than in others. In rape-prone societies it is often a ceremonial act or a means by which men threaten or punish women. In rape-free societies, women are treated with considerable respect, and prestige is attached to females' reproductive roles.

Although feminist writing frequently portrays all men as rape-prone, research on rape propensity indicates individual differences in the areas of attitudes toward women, prior sexual aggression both as a victim and as a perpetrator, and sexual arousal patterns. About one-third of college men indicate some likelihood that they would carry out a rape. Rape-prone men subscribe to myths about rape and to the ideology that permits rape to occur (such as disrespect for women and acceptance of violence as a way of getting what they want).

A consequence of rape for its victims is rape trauma syndrome, or disturbances in three major types of reactions: emotions, functioning, and lifestyle. Among the emotional reactions are fear, guilt, shame, and a sense of loss of autonomy and control. Sexual functioning is often disrupted. Reactions of rape survivors fall into a series of phases, beginning with an acute crisis phase (lasting up to a day) that includes denial, disruption, regression to a younger style of adjustment, guilt, and distorted perceptions. Rape crisis centers are useful in providing counseling, especially at the acute crisis phase. Even with such counseling, about one-fourth of rape victims report that they are not fully recovered even as long as four to six years later.

In the last decade, state legislatures and the courts have begun to rewrite, modify, or reinterpret long-standing laws about rape. One general type of shift is to deemphasize resistance as a requirement in showing that a rape took place. A second shift is to divide rape into several degrees of offense, permitting juries to bring down more guilty verdicts. Some states now permit a husband to be charged with rape against his wife; most states now have rape shield laws that restrict the defense attorney's questioning of the victim about her previous sexual conduct.

Prevention of rape has taken two routes. One is to try to determine what responses by potential victims are most effective in warding off a sexual assault. The other is to vary the treatment of convicted rapists. Antiandrogen drugs, which reduce sex drive, and a combination of various behavior-therapy techniques have shown limited effectiveness as treatments for convicted rapists.

Technological advances like "genetic fingerprinting" have been advocated as procedures for detecting rapists. Some courts now admit genetic data as evidence against defendants, but controversy still surrounds the procedure. Because it is not infallible but nevertheless carries such a strong presumption of accuracy, its use as evidence in criminal trials must be evaluated carefully.

Insanity and the Law

The issue of insanity intensifies each of the dilemmas of Chapter 1. Any society that respects the rights of individuals recognizes the possibility that some of its citizens cannot comprehend the consequences or the wrongfulness of their actions. Yet the highly publicized "success" of defendants (such as John Hinckley) who claimed insanity as an explanation for their actions has caused lawmakers to introduce new legislation intended to make it more difficult for jurors to acquit defendants by reason of insanity.

The quest for equality is also threatened by great discretion in the application of the insanity defense. It is *much* harder to find a defendant not guilty by reason of insanity in some states than in others. About half the states use an entirely different legal definition of insanity from that of the remaining states. Three states have abolished insanity as a defense. And the federal government has revised its definition of this defense three times in the last 40 years.

Likewise, truth is an ideal that is very hard to implement when insanity is adopted as the defendant's explanation for his or her actions. The jury or judge must answer the question "*Why* did he fire the gun?" rather than "Did *he* fire the gun?" How can we determine whether a defendant is truly insane? Can we know what the perpetrator's state of mind was when he committed his antisocial act? The task of truth finding becomes even more formidable when we acknowledge that the fact finders—juries and judges—must determine not whether the person is currently insane but, rather, whether he or she was insane at the time of the crime, possibly months or years before.

Another reason why truth is so elusive in cases of alleged insanity stems from the conflict between law and behavioral sciences as alternative pathways to knowledge. As noted in Chapter 1, insanity is a legal entity, not a medical or psychological one. In many states a defendant could be hallucinating, delusional, and diagnosed as schizophrenic, but, if the individual knew the difference between right and wrong, he or she would be classified as legally sane. Thus, psychiatrists and clinical psychologists are called on as expert witnesses to make absolute judgments about a concept that is beyond their professional/scientific framework. Their goals—diagnoses that necessarily are qualified and complex—compete with the legal system's demand for a straightforward yes-or-no answer. Furthermore, psychiatrists and other mental health experts can assist the trial process by giving names to disorders, but their contributions do not make the jury's task any easier or its decision any more accurate (Winslade & Ross, 1983).

Some mental health professionals would even argue that the law and the behavioral sciences are incompatible (Winslade & Ross, 1983). The law assumes that we are free agents; so, if we act illegally, we should be punished. The behavioral sciences assume that behavior is caused—either by conditions within the person or by the environment acting on the person. As the juvenile delinquents proclaim in the song *Gee, Officer Krupke!* from *West Side Story*, "We're depraved on accounta we're deprived." With such an assumption, "responsibility" becomes a much-diluted concept. If you're depraved because you're deprived, what's the justification for punishment?

RATIONALE FOR THE INSANITY DEFENSE

Why do we have laws about insanity at all? Wouldn't it be simpler to do away with insanity in the legal system? As Footlick notes, "The insanity defense exists as a legal compromise to a moral dilemma" (1978, p. 108). The provision for a criminal defendant to plead not guilty by reason of insanity reflects a fundamental belief: a civilized society should not punish persons who do not know what they are doing or who are incapable of controlling their conduct. Thus, on occasion, the state must tell the victim's friends and family that, although it abhors the defendant's acts, some offenders deserve compassion and treatment rather than punishment. Before it can do that, however, a judgment about whether such persons were responsible for their actions must be made.

In most cases in which an insanity defense is used, another decision must be reached first. As we discussed in Chapter 11, if the defendant cannot understand the trial proceedings or cannot participate meaningfully in his or her own defense, the offender is declared incompetent to stand trial, and the trial is delayed until the defendant is found competent to proceed. Holmes (1991) discusses the circumstances surrounding a *competency hearing*:

> Andrew was arrested for stealing a car. Before his trial, his attorney discovered that Andrew had a serious thought disorder that made it difficult or impossible for Andrew to understand the legal proceedings or to testify accurately. (Andrew was suffering from schizophrenia.) When this was confirmed by a psychologist, the judge ruled that Andrew was incompetent to stand trial, and Andrew was committed to a hospital for treatment until he was judged to be competent. The incompetence ruling protected Andrew from an unfair trial, but there was still a problem because his confinement for treatment might be longer than his confinement would be if he stood trial and were convicted [p. 504].

A judgment that the defendant is not competent to stand trial does not relieve the individual of responsibility for an illegal act; it only delays the determination. Under the rule of *Jackson* v. *Indiana* (1972), defendants cannot

be committed or otherwise ordered to undergo treatment if there is "no substantial probability that they will attain that capacity in the near future." Thus, in Andrew's case, the judge and the defense lawyer should monitor the commitment to ensure that he is not confined for an unreasonable period. Also, remember that competence refers exclusively to the defendant's mental abilities at the time of the proceeding, whereas insanity relates to the defendant's mental state at the time the offense was committed.

In trying to define insanity, back in the 1700s, the courts used phrases like "did not know what he did" or "(did not know more) than an infant, than a brute, or a wild beast." By the 1800s, "knowing the difference between right and wrong" was the predominant legal definition. At that time it was assumed that juries could clearly identify whether a defendant was truly insane without the help of professional witnesses. But the more we know about psychological disorder and the more sophisticated we have become, the more difficult we find the task to be.

As noted earlier, *insanity* is a legal term, not a scientific one. What is the legal standard for responsibility? How is *insanity* defined? There is no one answer. The following sections describe several definitions currently in use. Although the legal standards used to define criminal responsibility vary considerably from state to state, the defendant is presumed to be responsible for his or her alleged act. Therefore defendants, if pleading insanity, have the duty to present evidence that would disprove the presumption of criminal responsibility in their case—a requirement known as an *affirmative defense* . Central in the law is the assessment of *mens rea*, or the mental state accompanying a forbidden act. To be a criminal offense, the act must not only be illegal but also be accompanied by the necessary mental state.

THE MCNAUGHTON RULE—AN EARLY ATTEMPT TO DEFINE INSANITY

In 1843 an Englishman named Daniel McNaughton—variously spelled M'Naughten, McNaughten, M'Naghten, and Macnaghten—shot and killed the private secretary of the British prime minister. Plagued by paranoid delusions, McNaughton believed that the prime minister, Robert Peel, was part of a conspiracy with the Tory party against him. At first McNaughton sought to escape his imagined tormentors by traveling the continent of Europe. But when that didn't work, he stalked the prime minister and, after waiting in front of the prime minister's residence at No. 10 Downing Street, shot the man who he thought was Peel.

McNaughton was charged with murder, and his defense was to plead not guilty by reason of insanity. Nine medical experts, including the American psychiatrist Isaac Ray, testified for two days about his mental state, and all agreed that he was insane. On instructions from the lord chief justice, the jury brought forth a verdict of not guilty by reason of insanity without even leaving the jury box to deliberate. McNaughton was committed to the Broadmoor asylum for the insane, where he remained for the rest of his life.

But the public was infuriated, as was Queen Victoria, who had been the target of several attempts on her life. She demanded a tougher test of insanity. Subsequent debate in the House of Lords led to the presentation of five questions, not to medical experts but to 15 high court judges. Their replies constitute what has come to be called "the McNaughton rule." So the split between science and the law over the definition of insanity began 150 years ago. The rule was announced in 1843, long before *psychi-*atry became a household word. "Even so," notes Post, "the high court judges established a nonscientific test of insanity which a jury of 12 good and true men of varied intelligence and widely differing backgrounds were to apply after hearing medical evidence from both sides" (1963, p. 113).

The McNaughton rule defined insanity in the following manner:

> The jury ought to be told in all cases that every man is to be presumed to be sane, and to possess a sufficient degree of reason to be responsible for his crimes, until the contrary be proved to their satisfaction; and that to establish a defense on the grounds of insanity it must be clearly proved that, at the time of committing the act, the accused was laboring under such a defect of reason, from disease of the mind, as not to know the nature and quality of the act he was doing, or, if he did know it, that he did not know what he was doing [was] wrong [quoted in Post, 1963, p. 113].

The McNaughton rule, which became the standard for defining insanity in Great Britain and the United States, thus "excuses" criminal conduct if the defendant, as a result of a "disease of the mind": (1) did not know what he was doing (for example, believed he was shooting an animal rather than a human); or (2) did not know that what he was doing was wrong (for example, believed killing unarmed strangers was "right"). In some jurisdictions an *irresistible impulse* test was added, to try to deal with individuals who might have known that an act was wrong but lacked the willpower to avoid performing it. For example, in *Smith* v. *United States* (1929), the Court of Appeals of the District of Columbia declared:

> The accepted rule . . . is that the accused must be capable, not only of distinguishing between right and wrong, but that he was not impelled to do the act by an irresistible impulse, which means

before it will justify a verdict of acquittal that his reasoning powers were so far dethroned by his diseased mental condition as to deprive him of willpower to resist the insane impulse to perpetrate the deed, though knowing it to be wrong.

Defining an irresistible impulse has proven difficult. Can we distinguish between an irresistible impulse and an impulse that simply is not resisted? The American Psychiatric Association described the line between an irresistible impulse and an impulse not resisted as "no sharper than that between twilight and dusk" (APA Statement on the Insanity Defense, 1982). One proposed solution has been called the "police at the elbow test" because it asks, in effect: would the impulse have been so overwhelming that the individual would have committed the crime even if a police officer had been standing at his or her elbow, thereby assuring that he or she would be caught? Neither legal experts nor forensic clinicians are satisfied with the concept, and it is now used in very few statutes defining insanity (Rogers, 1986).

The McNaughton rule remains the standard for defining insanity in approximately 20 states, but it has constantly been criticized by mental health professionals, who contend that the definition is too restrictive and that the relevant issue is more a motivational question—being able to control wrongful actions—than a cognitive one—distinguishing right from wrong (Melton, Petrila, Poythress, & Slobogin, 1987). Thus modifications were inevitable.

THE DURHAM RULE

Monte Durham had little going for him, as Box 16-1 illustrates. He was in and out of mental hospitals and prisons, and in 1954 his case provided the impetus for a change in the standard for insanity used in the U.S. federal courts.

When Durham was originally tried, his defense was that he "was of unsound mind" (that is, insane) when he robbed a house on July 13, 1951. But the judge rejected this defense, saying "I don't think it has been established that the defendant was of unsound mind as of July 13, 1951, in the sense that he didn't know the difference between right and wrong or that even if he did, he was subject to an irresistible impulse by reason of derangement of mind" (Durham v. United States, 1954, pp. 865–866). Durham was found guilty.

But Durham's lawyer appealed his conviction, claiming that the existing standards of criminal responsibility were obsolete and should be replaced. Some judges would have held to the precedents of previous decisions, but Judge David Bazelon of the U.S. Court of Appeals, District of Columbia Circuit, chose to respond to the increasing agitation for reform of the McNaughton rule.

In his decision, Judge Bazelon reviewed the century-long history of the right/wrong test and presented the opinions of scientists, physicians, and various commissions. He quoted one of the founders of the American Psychiatric Association, who called knowledge of right and wrong a "fallacious" test of criminal responsibility. He cited Supreme Court justices' complaints about the standard ("Everyone concedes that the present [legal] definition of insanity has little relation to the truths of mental life"). And he summarized the report of the Royal Commission on Capital Punishment, which stated that the McNaughton test "is based on an entirely obsolete and misleading conception of the nature of insanity."

Before Judge Bazelon's decision in 1954, there had been judicial opinions questioning the use of the McNaughton standard. In Holloway v. United States, in 1945, the opinion had argued: "The modern science of psychology . . . does not conceive that there is a separate little man in the top of one's head called reason whose function it is to guide another unruly little man called instinct, emotion, or impulse in the way he should go."

Thus the U.S. Court of Appeals overturned the conviction of Monte Durham and ordered a new trial in which the standard for determining insanity would not be the right/wrong test. Instead, in keeping with psychological advances, the court specified the rule to be "that an accused is not criminally responsible if his unlawful act was the product of mental disease or mental defect." This became known as the Durham rule or the *product rule*; it was adopted by the federal courts in 1954. Mental health professionals approved of it initially; in fact, it led to an influx of psychiatrists and clinical psychologists into the courtroom as expert witnesses.

But many judges and prosecutors did not like the Durham standard. Some felt that it permitted the testimony of psychiatrists to usurp the jury's fact-finding function. In fact, evidence exists that some judges in Washington, DC, did not appreciably modify their instructions after the Durham rule was instituted there. Arens and Susman (1966) studied the transcripts of trials between 1960 and 1962 in which the insanity

---

Box 16-1 | *Monte Durham—Was He Insane?*

In 1945, when he was 17, Monte Durham was discharged from the U.S. Navy after a psychiatric examination had diagnosed a "profound personality disorder" that left him unfit for military service. Two years later he was convicted of stealing a car and was placed on probation for up to three years. He attempted to commit suicide and was committed to St. Elizabeth's Hospital in Washington, DC (where John Hinckley currently resides). But after two months he was released.

A year later, in 1948, Durham was found guilty of passing bad checks, his probation was revoked, and he began serving his prison sentence for the earlier car theft. In prison he behaved so bizarrely that he was given another mental examination. Found to be of "unsound mind," he was sent back to St. Eliz-abeth's Hospital, where he was diagnosed as suffering from "psychosis with psychopathic personality." After a little over a year, he was discharged as "recovered" and sent back to prison to complete his sentence. Released on parole, he almost immediately violated one of the conditions by leaving the District of Columbia.

Finally captured—and having passed some more bad checks while he was a fugitive—Durham was once more diagnosed as being of unsound mind and once more, in February 1951, admitted to St. Elizabeth's. Three months later he was discharged for the third time. On July 13, 1951, he was arrested for housebreaking. The police had discovered him in an apartment; when they entered, he was cowering in a corner with a T-shirt over his head, and he had stolen property worth about $50 in his pockets (Maeder, 1985). Again he took a psychiatric examination, and again it was concluded that he should be committed to a mental hospital. But after being there for 16 months, he was judged competent to stand trial. Durham claimed the defense of insanity, but the judge refused to admit such testimony, and Durham was convicted.

Was Monte Durham insane? It depends on the standard of insanity. The appeals court found the prevailing standard inadequate, and that is why Durham's case took on more than local interest. Ironically, Durham was tried three times for this same crime of housebreaking, because of appeals. At his third trial he pleaded guilty (Maeder, 1985).

defense was used. Judges tended to retain the language of the McNaughton instructions, perhaps passively reflecting their disapproval of the Durham rule. Furthermore, alcoholics and drug addicts charged with crimes could claim that their acts were the result of a mental disease and they should thus be ruled insane. A former jewelry store manager claimed the insanity defense in a case involving the theft of $500,000 worth of diamonds. He insisted that, being a compulsive gambler, he couldn't help himself. Although adopted for the federal courts, the Durham rule was never accepted by more than a few states (currently, only New Hampshire uses a product rule for insanity). In 1972 the Bazelon court unanimously repealed the Durham standard in the federal system and replaced it with the Brawner rule.

THE BRAWNER RULE, STEMMING FROM THE MODEL PENAL CODE

In response to problems with the Durham rule, a committee of legal scholars sponsored by the American Law Institute (ALI) developed the Model Penal Code, which led to what is now called the Brawner rule (or ALI rule). This rule states that a defendant is not responsible for criminal conduct who, "at the time of such conduct as a result of mental disease or defect, (lacks) substantial capacity either to appreciate the criminality [wrongfulness] of his conduct or to conform his conduct to the requirements of the law."

This standard, or a variation of it, is now used in about half the states; in a drastically altered form (which we will describe later), it is also used in all federal courts. It may be the best solution yet, because the key words are general enough to allow the jury some latitude and yet solid enough to provide ground for the testimony of expert witnesses. It differs from the McNaughton rule in three substantial respects: (1) By using the term *appreciate*, it acknowledges the emotional determinants of criminal actions. (2) It does not require a total lack of appreciation by offenders for the nature of their conduct—only a lack of "substantial capacity." (3) It includes *both* a cognitive element and a volitional element, making defendants' inability to control their actions an independent criterion for insanity.

In theory, varying rules for insanity should influence jurors to come to different verdicts, but psychologists have questioned whether the typical juror can comprehend the legal language of these definitions and then apply them as intended by the courts. (Further evaluation of the effectiveness of the judge's instructions to the jury can be found in Chapter 14.) Elwork, Sales, and Suggs (1981) found jurors only 51% correct on a series of questions testing their comprehension of instructions regarding the McNaughton rule. Arens, Granfield, and Susman (1965) and Ogloff (1991) obtained similar results: regardless of what insanity rule was used, college students showed very low rates of accurate recall and comprehension of crucial components in various insanity definitions.

The limited empirical evidence indicates that different standards of insanity make little difference in verdicts. Simon (1967) presented mock juries with re-creations of two actual trials in which the insanity defense had been used; one was a charge of housebreaking, the other incest. A third of the juries received the McNaughton rule, a third the Durham rule, and a third no instructions about how to define insanity (although they knew the defendant was using this as his defense). In both trials, jurors operating with the McNaughton rule were less likely to vote for acquittal (although the differences between conditions were not large). The Durham rule seemed to produce verdicts more in keeping with the jurors' "natural sense of equity," as reflected in their judgments without any instructions at all. Interestingly, at least half the uninstructed and the Durham juries brought in the defendant's ability to distinguish between right and wrong—the McNaughton standard—during their deliberations.

This latter finding suggests that, although instructions have some effect on jury decision making in insanity cases, they tell only part of the story—and perhaps a minor part at that (Finkel, 1989, 1991; Ogloff, 1991; Roberts & Golding, 1991; Roberts, Golding, & Fincham, 1987). Equally or probably more important than formal instructions are jurors' own views or schemata through which they interpret and filter the evidence they hear and then reach verdicts that are compatible with their own personal sense of justice. This decision process is yet another example of how jurors are prone to interpret "facts" in the context of a personal story or narrative that "makes the most sense" to each of them subjectively. Differences among jurors in the individual narratives they weave about the same set of trial "facts" may be related in turn to the different attitudes they hold about the morality of the insanity defense and the punishment of mentally ill offenders (Roberts & Golding, 1991).

In general, it appears that jurors are more likely to find a defendant not guilty by reason of insanity when they (1) believe the defendant is seriously mentally ill, to the point of lacking the capacity to plan his or her acts or to think logically about his or her behavior; (2) hear expert testimony, uncontradicted by a prosecution expert, about the defendant's mental illness; and (3) find no other evil motive for the defendant's actions. In addition, jurors appear to be flexible in their use of such personal constructs, emphasizing different variables in different

cases rather than seeing all insanity cases in the same way.

FAMOUS TRIALS AND THE USE OF THE INSANITY PLEA

Is the insanity plea a frequent problem in the American criminal justice system? Are many defendants getting off "scot free" by using it? One reason for the congressional action to shift the federal standard was the public perception, precipitated largely by the verdict in John Hinckley's trial, that criminals are escaping punishment through this defense. Several surveys over the last 20 years have concluded that most U.S. citizens view the insanity defense as a legal loophole through which many guilty people escape conviction (Bower, 1984; Hans & Slater, 1983). A survey of 665 physicians by *MD* magazine in 1983 found them overwhelmingly opposed to the insanity plea; even the psychiatrists in the sample were split about evenly on this issue (Bower, 1984). Before reporting on the actual frequency and effectiveness of attempts to use the plea, we will review the results of several highly publicized trials that have molded public opinion about insanity pleas.

Trials in Which the Insanity Plea Failed

Among murder defendants who have pleaded insanity as a defense were Jack Ruby, whom millions saw kill Lee Harvey Oswald, President John F. Kennedy's alleged assassin, on television; Sirhan Sirhan, charged with the assassination of Robert F. Kennedy; and John Wayne Gacy, who was convicted of killing 33 young boys in Chicago. All these defendants were found guilty of murder despite their pleas of insanity.

More recently, the sensational case of Jeffrey

Dahmer (described in Chapter 5) was one in which jurors rejected a plea of insanity as a defense against murder charges. Dahmer admitted killing and dismembering 15 young men over about a ten-year period, but his attorney, Gerald Boyle, claimed that Dahmer was insane at the time: "This is not an evil man, this is a sick man." Predictably, prosecutor E. Michael McCann disagreed, arguing that Dahmer "knew at all times that what he was doing was wrong." After listening to two weeks of evidence and expert testimony about Dahmer's mental condition, the jury ruled, by a 10-2 margin, that Jeffrey Dahmer was sane. He was subsequently sentenced to life in prison for his crimes.

Wisconsin defines insanity with the ALI rule; consequently, to have found Dahmer insane, the jury would have had to be convinced that he suffered a mental disorder or defect that made him unable either to know right from wrong or to control his conduct as required by the law. The jury rejected both conclusions, perhaps because of evidence that Dahmer was careful to kill his victims in a manner that minimized his chances of being caught: this cautiousness suggested that he appreciated the wrongfulness of his behavior *and* could control it when it was opportune for him to do so.

In the case of Herbert Mullin there seemed to be some basis for an acquittal on the ground of insanity, but the jury convicted him nonetheless (Lunde & Morgan, 1980). Between October 1972 and February 1973, Mullin, aged 26, killed 13 persons in the environs of Santa Cruz, California. There was no pattern to the murder victims: a derelict, a hitchhiking young woman, a priest in a church, four teenaged campers, a family. Mullin reported hearing voices. For example, the day he was caught, before delivering a load of wood to his parents, he was "instructed" to kill a man he had never seen before.

Mullin had a history of hospitalizations (one in 1969, another in 1970) and diagnoses of schizophrenia. A social psychologist, David Marlowe, had administered a personality inventory, the Minnesota Multiphasic Personality Inventory, and found that Mullin scored at very high levels on six out of ten clinical scales, suggesting a severe psychological disorder. Marlowe concluded that Mullin suffered a "schizophrenic reaction, paranoid type."

But at Mullin's trial a psychiatrist, Joel Fort, testified for the prosecution that Mullin was legally sane at the time of the killings. Fort stated "He knew the nature and quality of his actions and did specifically know that they were wrong" (quoted in Lunde & Morgan, 1980).

On the third day of its deliberations, the jury found Mullin guilty of two counts of first-degree murder and eight counts of second-degree murder. The judge sentenced him to concurrent life terms for the first-degree murders and imposed consecutive sentences of five years to life for the eight second-degree murder convictions. He will be eligible for parole in the year 2020. Today he is in San Quentin State Prison, although, at those times when his condition deteriorates and his conduct becomes bizarre, he is transported to the state prison system's medical facility at Vacaville to be sedated until his symptoms subside (Lunde & Morgan, 1980).

Another defendant who claimed insanity was Richard Herrin, the Yale graduate who brutally murdered his college sweetheart, Bonnie Garland, by splitting her head open with a hammer as she slept at her parents' home. Herrin claimed a "transient situational reaction," which his psychiatrist said was so split off from his otherwise normal and integrated personality that the jury should not hold him responsible for the murder (Gaylin, 1982). Although the jury rejected his plea, it found him guilty of manslaughter, not of murder—a verdict that left persons on both sides frustrated with the outcome (Meyer, 1982).

Richard Herrin's trial points up a salient dilemma of the insanity defense. Herrin was a good person—modest, tolerant, and good humored. He had risen above his illegitimate birth and his upbringing in an East Los Angeles barrio to graduate from Yale University. When Bonnie Garland, his sweetheart for almost three years, told him that she wanted to date other men, he suddenly decided to kill her and then commit suicide. Afterward he could describe the act with amazing precision, but he reported no emotion while committing it and no understanding of why he had done it.

As Paul Robinson notes, excerpts from Herrin's letters and interviews with him "leave an indelible impression of a winning young man in love far beyond his psychological means" (1982, p. 38). To many people Herrin's behavior was incomprehensible; "he must have been crazy" is a gut reaction to the bludgeoning. Some kind of psychiatric explanation is almost inevitable. But in succumbing to the temptation to always define extreme behavior in psychological terms, we lose sight of the legal responsibility that juries have to address the matter of criminality and provide justice (Robinson, 1982). Thousands of seriously mentally ill people live disoriented and disrupted lives, but they have never murdered anyone. Yet, when we think of their behavior exclusively in psychological terms, we are tempted to sympathize. Madame de Staël wrote: "*Tout comprendre, c'est tout pardonner*" ("To understand is to forgive"). And, if we forgive, it is harder to punish.

Several other famous defendants who might have attempted to escape conviction through use of the insanity plea did not do so. Among these are the "Son of Sam" serial murderer David Berkowitz, the cult leader Charles Manson, and Mark David Chapman, who killed John Lennon.

Trials in Which the Insanity Plea "Succeeded"

Sometimes when the insanity plea appears to "work," the defendant spends more time in an institution than he or she would have in prison if found guilty. Anthony Kiritsis found that to be true. He was an Indianapolis businessman who in 1977 strapped a shotgun to the head of a mortgage banker who was planning to foreclose on Kiritsis's real estate project. Kiritsis was found not guilty of kidnapping by reason of insanity and committed to the hospital ward of the Indiana State Reformatory at Pendleton. As of last report, Kiritsis remained in the state institution; he regards himself as a "political prisoner." Had he been convicted of kidnapping or plea-bargained for a lesser charge, it is likely he would be a free man today.

Ed Gein, another serial killer from Wisconsin, was acquitted by reason of insanity on multiple charges involving the mutilation, skinning, and murder of at least two women in the 1950s around Plainfield, Wisconsin. Gein admitted to other atrocious crimes, including robbing bodies from graves; he later made the corpse parts into ornaments and clothes that he wore to recreate the image of his dead mother. Gein, who was the real-life "inspiration" for several Hollywood films (including *Psycho* and *Silence of the Lambs*), was committed to a state psychiatric hospital, where he remained until his death in 1984.

The trial of John W. Hinckley, Jr., is, of course, the single case that triggered much of the court reform and legislative revision regarding the insanity plea. Everyone has seen television replays of his March 30, 1981, attempt to kill President Ronald Reagan. When Hinckley came to trial 15 months later, his lawyers didn't dispute the evidence that he had planned the attack, bought special bullets, tracked the president, and fired from a shooter's crouch. But he couldn't help it, they claimed, for he was only responding to the driving forces of a diseased mind. (Box 16-2 summarizes the details of the defense's case.) Dr. William Carpenter, one of the defense psychiatrists, testified that the assailant did not "appreciate" what he was doing; he had lost the ability to control himself.

Even though the Hinckley case is one in which the insanity defense was successful in the narrow sense of the word, that outcome was largely a result of a decision by the presiding judge regarding the burden of proof. Judge Barrington Parker instructed the jury in accord with then-existing federal law, which required the prosecution to prove the defendant sane beyond a reasonable doubt, rather than with the law of the District of Columbia (which has its own penal code), which would have placed the burden on the defendant to prove insanity. Since Hinckley was charged with both federal and DC crimes, Judge Parker seems to have made the correct decision.

After listening to two months of testimony, the Hinckley jury deliberated for 4½ days before finding the defendant not guilty by reason of insanity. Afterward several jurors said that,

---

Box **16-2**   *The Defense of John W. Hinckley, Jr.*

The defense in John Hinckley's trial made several claims:

1. Hinckley's actions had reflected his pathological obsession with the movie *Taxi Driver*, in which Jodie Foster starred as a 12-year-old prostitute. The title character, Travis Bickel, is a loner who is rejected by Foster; he stalks the president and engages in a bloody shootout as part of a rescue attempt. It was reported that Hinckley had seen the movie 15 times and that he so identified with the hero that he had been driven to reenact the fictional events in his own life (Winslade & Ross, 1983).

2. Although there appeared to be planning on Hinckley's part, it was really the movie script that provided the planning force. The defense argued: "A mind that is [so] influenced by the

John Hinckley, Jr.

outside world is a mind out of control and beyond responsibility" (Winslade & Ross, 1983, p. 188).

3. The expert witnesses provided somewhat different diagnoses, but they agreed that generally Hinckley was suffering from schizophrenia.

4. The defense tried to introduce the results of a CAT scan—an X-ray of Hinckley's brain using computerized axial tomography—to support its contention that he was schizophrenic. The admissibility of this evidence became a controversy within the controversy of the trial. The prosecution objected, claiming that all the apparent scientific rigor of this procedure—the physical evidence, the numerical responses—would cause the jury to place undue importance on it. The prosecution also contended that there are no grounds for concluding that the presence of shrunken brain tissue necessarily denotes schizophrenia. Initially the judge rejected the request to admit this testimony, but later he reversed the decision on the ground that it might be relevant.

given the instruction that it was up to the government prosecutors to prove Hinckley sane, the evidence was too conflicting for them to agree. They thought his travel meanderings raised some question about his sanity, and both sides' expert psychiatric witnesses had testified that he suffered from some mental disorder.

What types of defendants use the insanity plea successfully? The public tends to assume such people are of three types: "mad killers" who attack victims without provocation; "crafty cons" who fake symptoms to escape conviction; or "desperate defendants," aware of the strength of the evidence, who use the insanity defense as a last resort (Sales & Hafemeister, 1984). The empirical data do not support these assumptions. The insanity defense is not used only for murder or attempted murder charges, as assumed (Pasewark & Pantle, 1981); in Oregon and Missouri only one of ten such pleas is for the crime of murder (Sales & Hafemeister, 1984). Usually the charges do involve violent crimes, but this is not always the case.

The "crafty con" charge is also questionable. Available research consistently suggests that the majority of defendants found not guilty by reason of insanity (NGRI) have been diagnosed as psychotic, suggesting severe and probably chronic mental impairments (Melton et al., 1987). Insanity acquittees do not appear to be especially "crafty"; in fact, one study revealed that defendants found NGRI had significantly lower IQ scores than men who pled insane but were convicted (Boehnert, 1989).

Another approach to the "crafty con" question is to study how often criminal defendants being assessed for insanity try to fake a mental disorder. On the basis of his research, Rogers (1986, 1988) estimates that about one out of four or five defendants being assessed for insanity engages in at least moderate malingering of mental disorders. Although this figure suggests that crafty conning is not rampant, it occurs

frequently enough to cause concern. As a result, psychologists have developed a number of assessment methods to detect persons who are trying to fake a mental disorder. These methods include special structured interviews (Rogers, Gillis, Dickens, & Bagby, 1991), individual psychological tests (Wetter, Baer, Berry, Smith, & Larsen, 1992), and batteries of different tests (Schretlen, Wilkins, Van Gorp, & Bobholz, 1992).

In several laboratory studies these techniques have shown promising results in differentiating between subjects who were trying to simulate mental illness (in order to win monetary incentives for being the "best" fakers) and those who were reporting symptoms truthfully. In a careful study that was limited to the court records of a single county, Steadman, Keitner, Braff, and Arvanites (1983) were able to compare defendants who were successful and unsuccessful in their pleas of insanity. The factor most strongly associated with success was the outcome of a court-authorized mental examination before the trial. When this evaluation concluded that the defendant was insane, in 83% of cases the charges were dismissed or the defendant was later found at a trial to be not guilty by reason of insanity. If the mental examination concluded that the offender was sane, in only 2% of the trials did the insanity defense "work." Box 16-3 lists several other characteristics that are typical of defendants who have been acquitted on the basis of an insanity defense.

FACTS ABOUT THE INSANITY PLEA

The American public has repeatedly expressed its dissatisfaction with the insanity defense.

After John Hinckley was found NGRI for the shooting of President Reagan and four other men in 1982, a public opinion poll conducted by ABC News showed that 67% of Americans believed that justice had not been done in the case; 90% thought Hinckley should be confined for life, but 78% believed he would eventually be released back to society.

The public's disapproval of the insanity defense appears to be stimulated by trials (such as Hinckley's) that receive massive publicity. Melton et al. (1987) found the following four beliefs to be prevalent among the public: (1) a large number of criminal defendants use the insanity defense; (2) most of those defendants who use the insanity defense are acquitted by juries who are too gullible about it; (3) those defendants found NGRI are released back to society shortly after their trials; and (4) persons found insane are extremely dangerous.

How accurate are these views? Are they myths or realities? We'll now review data concerning each of these questions.

How Often Is the Plea Used, and How Often Is It Successful?

The plea is used a lot less than people assume. A 1979 study in Wyoming showed that people assumed that the insanity plea was a ploy used in nearly half of all criminal cases and that it was successful in one out of five cases (Pasewark & Pantle, 1981). The actual figures: it was pleaded by only 102 of 22,102 felony defendants (about 1 in every 200 cases) and was successful only once in those 102 times. In California in 1980, only 259 of 52,000 criminal defendants were acquitted on a plea of insanity. Lunde and Morgan (1980, p. 131) estimate that only about 2% of murderers are ever found insane in U.S. courts. Juries are especially reluctant to find violent offenders NGRI out of fear that they will be released and repeat their violence. Although few individual states have kept records on the use of the insanity plea and its relative success, we may safely conclude that the number of acquittals represents an extreme-

---

Box **16-3** | *Characteristics of Insane Defendants*

On the basis of research studies, we are beginning to replace misconceptions about defendants found NGRI with more accurate portrayals of this group of defendants. This research paints the following picture of the typical insane defendant:

1. Most NGRI defendants have a record of prior arrests or convictions, but this rate of previous criminality does not exceed that of other felons (Boehnert,

1989; Cohen, Spodak, Silver, & Williams, 1988).

2. Most NGRI defendants come from lower socioeconomic backgrounds (Nicholson, Norwood, & Enyart, 1991).

3. Most NGRI defendants have a prior history of psychiatric hospitalizations and have been diagnosed with serious forms of mental illness, usually psychoses (Nicholson et al., 1991).

4. Most NGRI defendants have

previously been found incompetent to stand trial (Boehnert, 1989).

5. Although most studies have concentrated on males, female defendants found NGRI appear to have similar socioeconomic, psychiatric, and criminal backgrounds to their male NGRI counterparts (Heilbrun, Heilbrun, & Griffin, 1988).

ly small percentage of those on trial (Melton et al., 1987; Sales & Hafemeister, 1984).

What Happens to Defendants Who Are Found NGRI?

People mistakenly assume that defendants who are found NGRI go "scot free." We have seen Anthony Kiritsis's situation. It is doubtful that John Hinckley will be released from custody in the near future. Teddy Roosevelt's assassin was confined to a mental hospital for 31 years, until he died. Steadman and Braff (1983) found that defendants acquitted on the basis of the insanity plea in New York had an average hospital stay of 3½ years. During the period studied, the average length of hospitalization was increasing. These researchers also found a clear trend for longer detentions of defendants who had committed more serious offenses. After reviewing several studies conducted in New York, Michigan, Illinois, Connecticut, and New Jersey on this topic, Melton et al. (1987) concluded:

> In some jurisdictions persons found NGRI spend significantly shorter time in confinement than do felons. But this differential is obviously not the case everywhere . . . [and] it does not by itself signify that there is a problem with the insanity defense. . . . Only if NGRI individuals *need* to be confined for longer periods of time would these data merit such a conclusion [p. 114].

One reason why insanity acquittees do not usually serve shorter terms of confinement than those convicted of comparable crimes is that many states have followed a procedure of automatically committing persons found NGRI to a mental institution and then releasing them only when they convince a judge that they can be released safely. A problem with these procedures is that the criteria for release are often more restrictive than those for the usual civil commitment—perhaps intentionally so in or-

der to guarantee longer confinements. In the 1992 case of *Foucha* v. *Louisiana*, however, the Supreme Court held that it is unconstitutional for a state to continue to hold a defendant who is no longer mentally ill and dangerous. This is the usual test for civil commitments.

How Dangerous Are Defendants Found NGRI?

Because most defendants who are found NGRI are quickly committed to an institution following their acquittal, it is difficult to assess how dangerous they are at that time. In addition, they are likely to receive treatment in the hospital to which they are committed, further complicating the question of how dangerous they would have been without this treatment. What evidence is available on this question points to either no difference in recidivism rates between NGRI defendants and "regular" felons or slightly *lower* recidivism rates among the NGRI group (Cohen et al., 1988; Melton et al., 1987). Nicholson et al. (1991) collected data on 61 defendants found NGRI in Oklahoma; this group constituted the entire population of NGRI defendants over a five-year period who had been treated in the state forensic hospital. Follow-up of persons released from custody indicated that, within 2½ years, half of the discharged patients had been either rearrested or rehospitalized. Thus, insanity acquittees continue to have legal and/or psychiatric problems, but their overall rate of criminal recidivism falls in the range found for criminals in general. Whether the period of hospital commitment and treatment following an acquittal has any benefits for persons found NGRI is not certain; some studies show that individuals who complete a treatment program do better than those who go AWOL from the institution (Nicholson et al., 1991), but another study reported no differences between regularly discharged acquittees and those who escaped from the institution (Pasewark, Bieber, Bosten, Kiser, & Steadman, 1982).

CURRENT CRITICISMS OF THE INSANITY DEFENSE

Even if the defense is not as effective as presumed, legitimate concerns remain about its continued use. Several of these will now be evaluated.

It Sends Criminals and Troublemakers to Hospitals and Then Frees Them

An example: At age 18, Thomas Vanda, the oldest child of a suburban Chicago family, was found guilty of stabbing a teenager as she lay in her bed. Soon after that, while on probation and while receiving psychiatric care, he was charged with killing a 15-year-old girl with a hunting knife. Vanda was first declared mentally unfit to stand trial but then was tried and found not guilty by reason of insanity (Footlick, 1978). In less than a year, psychiatrists at a mental hospital declared his psychosis in remission, and—despite objections from the judge and even from his own defense counsel—he was released. At age 25 he was again charged with shooting a woman to death. Within a two-year period, at least five Chicago-area murders were attributed to people previously acquitted because of insanity pleas (Footlick, 1978).

Another example: E. E. Kemper III murdered his grandparents and then spent five years in a California hospital for the criminally insane. He was released in 1970; three years later he petitioned to have his psychiatric records sealed. After psychiatrists examined Kemper and found him sane, the judge agreed to the request. The authorities were not aware that, since his release, he had murdered his mother and seven other women—one of them only three days before the court decision. Most of the bodies had been dismembered. Kemper, it was later claimed, had memorized the responses to 28 standardized psychological tests so that he could appear to give "well-adjusted" answers (Gleick, 1978, p. 23).

Psychopathic killers can try to capitalize on the insanity plea to escape prison and eventually get released from the hospital. How often this happens is unknown, but, as we have already discussed, what data are available indicate that persons found NGRI tend to be no more or no less dangerous following their release than non-NGRI felons (NGRI persons who *escape* from the hospital may pose a higher risk of dangerousness to the community). Some would say that, even if the preceding examples were the only ones, they would be too many. The real problem with such incidents is that they contribute to the public's perception that these outcomes "happen all the time" and that the insanity defense is therefore a constant threat to justice. Such incidents do not happen all the time; in fact, they are very rare. Further, if all NGRI defendants were kept hospitalized until they no longer showed symptoms of mental illness, in the interest of protecting society, then society would have to be willing to violate the rights of many mentally ill persons to protect against the violence of a few.

It Is a Defense Only for the Rich

San Francisco lawyer/psychiatrist Bernard Diamond is quoted as saying "You shouldn't murder anyone unless you have $100,000" (Footlick, 1978, p. 108). The parents of John W. Hinckley, Jr., spent between $500,000 and $1,000,000 on psychiatric examinations and expert psychiatric testimony in their son's trial—an amount that contributes to the perception of the insanity defense as jail-dodge for the rich.

Of all the criticisms leveled at the insanity defense, this one is perhaps most contradicted by the data. A long line of studies have failed to find socioeconomic or racial bias in the use or the success of the insanity defense (Boehnert, 1989; Howard & Clark, 1985; Nicholson et al., 1991; Pasewark & Pantle, 1981; Steadman et al., 1983). In addition, this criticism is further weakened by the Supreme Court's 1985 ruling, in the case of *Ake* v. *Oklahoma,* that poor defendants who plead insanity are entitled to psychiatric assistance at state expense in pursuing this defense. It still may be the case that defendants who can afford more than one expert are more likely to benefit from raising the issue of insanity, but this is not a problem unique to the insanity defense. Defendants who can afford to hire ballistic experts, chemists, and their own private detectives also have an advantage over poor defendants, but no one suggests that a defense relying on ballistic evidence, blood analyses, or mistaken identity should be prohibited because of the expense.

It Relies Too Much on Psychiatric Experts

There are several issues here. One criticism is that testifying about insanity forces psychiatrists and clinical psychologists to give opinions about things they are not competent or trained to do—for example, to express certainty rather than probability about a person's mental condition, to predict future dangerous behavior, and to claim greater knowledge about the relationship between psychological research and legal questions than is justified.

Psychologists themselves are sharply divided on these matters. Their debate centers on three related questions. First, can clinicians reliably and validly diagnose mental illness? Second, will these diagnoses permit accurate opinions about a defendant's criminal responsibility for acts committed in the past? And, finally, *assuming* that the answers to the first two questions are yes, are psychologists any more expert or capable of answering these questions than nonprofessionals? A growing number of respected psychologists are skeptical about psychology's expertise on these issues and have challenged their forensic colleagues to provide whatever supporting evidence they have (Dawes, Faust, & Meehl, 1989; Ziskin & Faust, 1988).

Additionally, critics are concerned over the intrusion of psychiatry into the decision-making process. They want to reserve the decision making for the judge or jury, the fact finder in the trial. This criticism is an example of the general concern (discussed in Chapter 2) over the use and willingness of experts to answer legal questions for which they possess limited scientific evidence. Again, some psychologists vigorously oppose the courts' reliance on mental health experts' opinions about a defendant's status as insane or sane (Bonnie & Slobogin, 1980; Morse, 1978). In general this opposition is grounded on the belief that psychology has not established its scientific expertise on the three questions described above. Obviously, if one cannot show expertise, one should not testify as an expert. But, even if we were to grant special expertise to psychologists, critics raise the additional objection that questions about a defendant's criminal responsibility for an act are properly answered only by jurors, not by expert witnesses.

One remedy often proposed to solve this problem is to prevent experts from giving what is often called "ultimate opinion" testimony; that is, they could describe a defendant's mental condition and the effects it could have had on his or her thinking and behavioral control, but they could not state conclusions about whether the defendant was sane or insane. As we discuss next, the federal courts, as part of their reforms of the insanity defense, now prohibit mental health experts from offering ultimate opinion testimony about a defendant's insanity. But does this prohibition solve any problems, or is it, in the words of Rogers and Ewing (1989), merely a "cosmetic fix" that has few effects?

In a study designed to answer this question (Fulero & Finkel, 1991), subjects were randomly assigned to read one of ten different versions of a trial, in all of which the defendant was charged with murdering his boss and was pleading insanity at the time of the offense. For our purposes, the comparisons among three different versions of the trial are of greatest interest: some subjects read transcripts in which the mental health experts for both sides gave only *diagnostic* testimony (that the defendant suffered a mental disorder at the time of the offense); a second group read a version in which the experts gave a diagnosis and then also offered differing *penultimate* opinions about the effects this disorder had on the defendant's understanding of the wrongfulness of his act; a final group read a transcript in which the experts offered differing diagnoses, penultimate opinions, and *ultimate opinion* testimony about whether the defendant was sane or insane at the time of the killing.

Did ultimate opinion testimony affect the subjects' verdicts? Not in this case; subjects' verdicts were not significantly different regardless of the type of testimony they received. The lack of difference could be interpreted as evidence that the prohibition of ultimate opinion testimony is unnecessary, or it could indicate that the ban streamlines the trial process without sacrificing any essential information. Of course, as Box 16-4 discusses, psychologists and psychiatrists offer ultimate opinions about many other topics in the justice system.

Finally, there is the feeling that the process holds mental health professionals up to ridicule. When the jury sees and the public reads about a parade of mental health experts representing one side and then the other, their confidence in the behavioral sciences is jeopardized (Slater & Hans, 1984). Patty Hearst's trial saw two expert witnesses on each side; the Hinckley trial had even more. Further, some experts, in an effort to help the side that has retained them, offer explanations of such an untestable nature that their profession loses its credibility with jurors and the public. In a recent trial in which a young man was charged with the rape and murder of an 80-year-old woman, a psychiatrist testified that, during the murder, the defendant suffered from a "brief reactive psychosis" as a result of severe stress. The specific determinants and components of the "diagnosis" made one wonder whether it was a convenient label and nothing more.

RECENT AND PROPOSED REVISIONS AND REFORMS

Several reforms in the rules and procedures for implementing the insanity defense have been introduced in recent years. They have led to mixed outcomes.

Proposals have ranged from complete abolition of the insanity defense (as has already been done in three states), to provision of a "guilty but mentally ill" verdict, to reform of insanity statutes, to maintenance of the present procedures. Three proposals will be reviewed in this section.

The Guilty But Mentally Ill (GBMI) Verdict

Since 1976 about a quarter of the states have passed laws allowing juries to reach a verdict of

Guilty But Mentally Ill (GBMI) in cases in which a defendant pleads insanity. These GBMI rules differ from state to state, but generally they give a jury the option of finding a defendant who is pleading insanity the following verdict alternatives: (1) guilty of the crime, (2) not guilty of the crime, (3) NGRI, or (4) GBMI. Typically a judge will sentence a defendant found GBMI exactly as he or she would the same defendant found guilty of the same offense. The intent is for the prisoner to start his or her term in a hospital and then be transferred to prison after treatment is completed.

Proponents of GBMI verdicts hoped that this compromise verdict would decrease the number of defendants found NGRI. Whether insanity acquittals have actually decreased as a result of GBMI legislation is highly questionable. Mock jury research consistently reveals that adding the GBMI option decreases NGRI verdicts (Roberts & Golding, 1991). But GBMI statutes have not produced decreases in NGRI verdicts in South Carolina or Michigan, although decreases were noted after GBMI laws were enacted in Georgia (Callahan, McGreevey, Cirincione, & Steadman, 1992) and Pennsylvania (see Roberts & Golding, 1991, for a discussion of the effects of this legislation on jury decisions).

Other problems have provoked a "second look" at the GBMI reform, leading to growing skepticism about its value. If regular insanity

---

Box 16-4 | *Topics for Expert Testimony*

The prohibition against ultimate opinion testimony on insanity by experts highlights one paradox about expert testimony: experts *are* permitted to give ultimate opinions on a host of other psychological questions that juries must consider. These questions span criminal trials, civil litigation, and domestic disputes. Experts testify on these matters much more frequently than they do about criminal defendants' claims of insanity; the fact that the same restrictions do not apply is a further indication of the intense political controversy the insanity plea generates.

Below is a list of questions on which psychological testimony is most often sought in legal proceedings. Experts will be permitted to testify about these topics if they meet a set of four requirements that are used in most courts: (1) the expert must be qualified by virtue of special training, knowledge, or experience in the area of expertise in which testimony is sought; (2) the testimony should meet standards of scientific reliability, which is often interpreted to mean that the methods upon which it is based are generally accepted in the relevant scientific community; (3) the testimony should be helpful to fact finders in their consideration of the issues; and (4) the testimony should not be unduly prejudicial (see Frazier & Borgida, 1992; Heilbrun, 1992).

1. Insanity defense	What is the relationship between the defendant's mental condition at the time of the alleged offense and the defendant's responsibility for the crime with which he or she is charged?
2. Competence to stand trial	Does the defendant have an adequate understanding of the legal proceedings?
3. Sentencing	What are the prospects for the defendant's rehabilitation? What deterrent effects do certain sentences have?
4. Eyewitness identification	What are the factors that affect the accuracy of eyewitness identification? How is witness confidence related to witness accuracy?
5. Trial procedure	What effects are associated with variations in pretrial and/or trial procedures?

instructions are confusing to jurors, the GBMI verdict only adds to the confusion by introducing the very difficult distinction for juries to make between mental illness that results in insanity and mental illness that does not. Also, the claim that the GBMI option will make it more likely that mentally ill offenders will receive treatment is largely a bogus promise. Overcrowding at hospitals in most states has impeded implementation of this part of the GBMI option. In one Michigan study, 75% of GBMI offenders went straight to prison with no treatment (Sales & Hafemeister, 1984).

In Kentucky, in spite of a statute that appears to promise treatment to those found GBMI, the chair of the parole board filed an affidavit in 1991 stating that "from psychological evaluations and treatment summaries, the Board can detect no difference in treatment or outcome for inmates who have been adjudicated as 'Guilty But Mentally Ill,' from those who have been adjudicated as simply 'guilty'" (Runda, 1991). Finally, the opportunity to be found GBMI and then treated (in states where there is a difference in treatment opportunities) is available only to defendants who themselves first raise an insanity defense. An equally disturbed defendant who does not claim insanity cannot be found GBMI.

Somewhat similar to the GBMI concept is the diminished-capacity defense, which is discussed in Box 16-5.

6. Civil commitment	Does a mentally ill person present an immediate danger or threat of danger to self or others that requires treatment no less restrictive than hospitalization?
7. Psychological damages in civil cases	What psychological consequences has an individual suffered as a result of tortious conduct? How treatable are these consequences? To what extent are the psychological problems attributable to a preexisting condition?
8. Psychological autopsies	In equivocal cases, do the person's personality and circumstances under which he or she died indicate a likely mode of death?
9. Negligence and product liability	How do environmental factors and human perceptual abilities affect an individual's use of a product or ability to take certain precautions in its use?
10. Trademark litigation	Is a certain product name or trademark confusingly similar to a competitor's? Are advertising claims likely to mislead consumers?
11. Class-action suits	What psychological evidence is there that effective treatment is being denied or that certain testing procedures are discriminatory against minorities in the schools or in the workplace?
12. Guardianship and conservatorship	Does an individual possess the necessary mental ability to make decisions concerning living conditions, financial matters, health, etc.?
13. Child custody	What psychological factors will affect the best interests of the child whose custody is in dispute? What consequences are these factors likely to have on the family?
14. Adoption and termination of parental rights	What psychological factors affect the best interests of a child whose parents' disabilities may render them unfit to raise and care for the child?
15. Professional malpractice	Did defendant's professional conduct fail to meet the standard of care owed to plaintiff?
16. Social issues in litigation	What are the effects of pornography, violence, spouse abuse, etc., on the behavior of a defendant who claims that his or her misconduct was caused by one of these influences?

Based on Nietzel and Dillehay (1986).

The Insanity Defense Reform Act

In the wake of the John Hinckley trial, the U. S. Congress enacted the Insanity Defense Reform Act (IDRA) in 1984. The main purpose of this law was to limit the insanity defense so that fewer defendants would be able to use it successfully. The law did not abolish the insanity defense, but it changed the way the defense could be used in the federal system in the following three ways:

1. It did away with the so-called volitional prong of the Brawner rule. Lack of behavioral control because of mental illness is no longer a criterion for insanity. The definition of insanity in the federal system is now restricted to the cognitive portion of the defense; that is, as a result of mental illness the defendant lacks the capacity to appreciate the nature and quality or the wrongfulness of his or her acts. Without the volitional part of the defense, the test is now essentially a restatement of McNaughton. The volitional prong was abolished because of the prevailing beliefs that it was the bigger loophole through which defendants were escaping and that it could not be assessed as reliably as the cognitive part of the defense. Both beliefs are contradicted by empirical data, but here is a case where political considerations are more influential than empirical data. (Both the Ameri-

---

Box 16-5 | "Diminished Capacity" and the Dan White Case

Many states allow a defense of *diminished capacity*, which is a legal doctrine that is applicable if the defendant lacks the ability to "meaningfully premeditate the crime." Like the insanity defense, diminished capacity often involves evidence that the defendant suffers a mental disorder. It differs from insanity in that it focuses on whether defendants had the capacity to "premeditate"—that is, to think through the consequences of their contemplated actions—not on whether they knew the crime was wrong or whether they could control their behavior. Suppose that McNaughton knew that murder was wrong but, because of his mental condition, wasn't thinking clearly at the time he shot Peel's secretary. Under these conditions

George Moscone   *Harvey Milk*

he would not be insane, but he would lack the *mens rea* for first-degree murder; so he probably would have been convicted of second-degree murder or manslaughter.

The rationale for this defense is simple: the offender should be convicted of the crime that matches his mental state, and expert testimony should be offered on the issue of his mental state. Even if the

diminished-capacity defense "works," it still usually leads to a prison sentence.

In 1979 the Dan White trial brought national publicity to the plea of diminished capacity. Dan White was tried for killing George Moscone, the mayor of San Francisco, and Harvey Milk, a San Francisco city supervisor. The killings were clearly premeditated. White had resigned his $9600-a-year supervisor position because of its low pay and then decided he wanted it back, only to learn from the mayor that it was no longer available. Several days later (on November 27, 1978), he loaded the .38 Smith & Wesson revolver that he had owned since his days on the police force, wrapped ten extra bullets in a handkerchief, and headed for the can Psychiatric Association (1982) and the American Bar Association (1989) are also on record as favoring the abolition of the volitional prong.)

2. It prohibited experts from giving ultimate opinions about a defendant's insanity. The rule states: "no expert witness testifying with respect to the mental state or condition of a defendant in a criminal case may state an opinion or inference as to whether the defendant did or did not have the mental state or condition constituting an element of the crime charged or of a defense thereto. Such ultimate issues are matters for the trier of fact alone." We have already seen that this prohibition may have little effect on jurors,

but the reformers believed it would prevent expert witnesses from usurping the province of the jury.

3. The burden is on the defendant to prove insanity by clear and convincing evidence, rather than on the prosecution to disprove insanity.

What little research that has been conducted on the Insanity Defense Reform Act suggests that it does not accomplish either what its proponents envisioned or what its critics feared. At least in mock jury studies, verdicts do not significantly differ regardless of whether the jurors have heard IDRA instructions, ALI (Brawner) instructions, or no instructions (Finkel, 1989).

mayor's office. He slipped through a city-hall window to avoid a metal detector at the main entrance. He pumped nine bullets into Moscone and Milk, his opponent on the board. Some shots were fired point-blank as White leaned over their prostrate bodies.

Although Dan White did not take the witness stand in his own defense at his murder trial, his attorneys argued that his mental faculties had been impaired, that his steady diet of junk food had produced a chemical imbalance in his brain—the so-called Twinkie defense. He was also depressed, they said, because of his financial status and the political maneuvering. His "diminished capacity" left him unable to premeditate, deliberate, or harbor malice. Therefore he lacked the *mens rea,* or criminal intent, necessary to be convicted of first-

Dan White

degree murder. Four psychiatrists and one psychologist testified to this effect.

After the jury found him guilty of voluntary manslaughter—the least-serious charge possible— there were angry protests, especially in the homosexual community, for which Harvey Milk had been an advocate. Citizens even tried to charge White with violating the civil rights of the mayor and the

supervisor by denying them a chance for reelection, but the Justice Department decided not to prosecute.

White was sentenced to seven years and eight months in prison, but he served less than five years. He was released from Soledad Prison on January 6, 1984, and ordered to live in Los Angeles County (and avoid San Francisco) during his one-year parole. (Had he been found guilty of premeditated murder, his actual time served in prison would probably have been about 13 years.) White committed suicide in October 1985.

In June 1982 a proposition to abolish the diminished-capacity defense was overwhelmingly passed by the voters of California. That state still permits defendants to use the insanity defense, however.

Elimination of the Insanity Plea

Winslade and Ross (1983) reviewed seven recent trials (mostly for murder) in which the insanity defense was used and psychiatric testimony was introduced to justify it. They conclude that the possibility of an insanity defense often leads to injustice, for the following reasons:

1. Juries are asked to decide questions that predispose them to make arbitrary and emotional judgments because of either overidentification with or alienation from the defendant;
2. Psychiatrists and other mental health professionals are encouraged to parade their opinions, guesses, and speculations under the banner of scientific expertise; and
3. Society's views about criminality and craziness are so intertwined that an insanity defense to a crime does not make much sense [p. 198].

On the basis of their detailed analysis of the outcomes of these trials, Winslade and Ross recommend that the insanity defense be phased out. They write:

A workable solution would require the elimination of the insanity plea; the elimination of any testimony by psychiatrists about the actual or theoretical state of the defendant's mind at the time of the crime; the elimination of psychiatric expert witnesses in the guilt phase of the trial; and the requirement of a [two-phase] trial that would, in its first phase establish guilt or innocence of the commission of the crime with no concern for the individual's state of mind in terms of mental illness at the time the crime was committed. The second phase of the trial, if guilt were found, would address itself to the appropriate disposition of the defendant [1983, p. 219].

In the second part of the trial, if a defendant claimed mental illness, he or she would be required to testify. The judge would permit psychiatrists to testify as expert witnesses, but only to report on previous clinical assessments, not to predict the defendant's future behavior. Psychiatrists representing state institutions would also be required to testify about the likelihood of rehabilitating the defendant; they would be asked to specify at least a minimum duration of treatment. Combinations of hospitalization and incarceration, in Winslade and Ross's proposal, would be based on the defendant's amenability to treatment.

Arguments against Eliminating the Plea

At the opposite end of the continuum is the position of James Kunen (1983), a former public defender, who proposes that "guilty but mentally ill" is logically impossible. He explains his opposition to states that have adopted the additional option of a "guilty but insane" verdict, such as Michigan (the first, in 1975) and Georgia:

Such legislation represents a radical departure from Anglo-American legal tradition, which for centuries has required that to convict someone of a crime, the prosecution must prove not only that he did a particular act—such as pulling a trigger—but that he did it with a particular state of mind. . . . "Guilty but insane" is a contradiction in terms, because insane means not capable of forming a criminal intent, not responsible, and, therefore, not guilty [p. 157].

Kunen's comments are especially useful in distinguishing between *commission of an act* and *guilt.* Winslade and Ross confound these terms when, in their proposal quoted earlier, they advocate an initial phase of a trial in order to "establish guilt or innocence of the commission of the crime with no concern for the individual's state of mind" (1983, p. 219). As Kunen notes, we cannot talk about guilt without bringing in the person's "state of mind." If a defendant slashes his victim's throat, thinking that he is slicing a cucumber, we say that he committed an act but not that he was guilty of the intent to commit a crime.

There *are* some offenders who are truly "not guilty by reason of insanity"; they do not know the "nature and quality of their acts"—they literally do not know what they are doing. Harvard law professor Alan Dershowitz has said: "I almost would be in favor of abolishing the insanity defense, except there really are a few genuinely crazy people who believe they're squeezing lemons when they're actually squeezing throats" (quoted in Footlick, 1978, p. 108). The actual number of such people is much smaller, of course, than the number who employ the NGRI defense.

We believe the NGRI plea should be maintained as an option, and modifications of the system should be restricted to those that clarify the rule and later evaluate those for whom it is successful. For example, the federal government has already acted to change the law that formerly put the burden of proof on the prosecution to prove beyond a reasonable doubt that John Hinckley was not insane. If an act similar to Hinckley's were committed today in a federal jurisdiction, the defendant, not the prosecution, would bear the responsibility of proving his plea; otherwise he would be found guilty.

It is legally acceptable for an NGRI defendant to be confined to a hospital longer than a guilty defendant remains in prison for the same crime. Michael Jones was accused of shoplifting a coat in 1974; he "successfully" used the NGRI defense. He was still in St. Elizabeth's Hospital in 1983 when the Supreme Court, hearing his appeal, ruled that such commitments in excess of the maximum sentence are legal. States should carefully monitor people committed after NGRI verdicts, to ensure that they are not released while still mentally ill and dangerous. All indications are that this is being done. In Washington, DC, a survey of St. Elizabeth's Hospital showed that patients committed after NGRI verdicts spent 39 months locked up before being allowed to even walk the grounds, while the average period of incarceration for those found guilty on similar charges was 32 months (cited in Kunen, 1983). In fact, it is likely that many NGRI defendants are now unconstitutionally locked up, because they are no longer mentally ill and dangerous (*Foucha v. Louisiana*, 1992).

SUMMARY

Any civilized society tries to deal humanely with those citizens who are incapable of comprehending the consequences of their criminal actions. The competency hearing and the insanity plea are two of our system's major responses to this challenge.

Several definitions of insanity are used currently. The McNaughton rule defines *insanity* as not knowing the difference between right and wrong: "To establish a defense on the grounds of insanity it must be clearly proved that, at the time of committing the act, the accused was laboring under such a defect of reason, from disease of the mind, as not to know the nature and quality of the act he was doing, or, if he did know it, that he did not know what he was doing was wrong." In some jurisdictions an "irresistible impulse" test has been added to the McNaughton rule.

In response to criticism of the McNaughton rule, the federal government, from 1954 to 1972, used the Durham rule: "that an accused is not criminally responsible if his unlawful act was the product of mental disease or mental defect." The Durham rule was supplanted by an extension that closed some of its unanticipated loopholes; this revision, called the Brawner rule, states that a person is not responsible for a criminal act if, as a result of mental disease or defect, the person lacked "substantial capacity either to appreciate the criminality of his conduct or to conform his conduct to the requirements of the law."

The Brawner rule or a variation of it is the standard in about half the states. Until 1984 it was also the federal standard, but the federal system now requires the defense to show that, as a result of a severe mental disease or defect, the defendant was unable to appreciate the nature and quality or the wrongfulness of his or her acts. Three states have outlawed insanity as a defense, although these states do allow a defendant to prove he lacked *mens rea*. Some highly publicized trials, especially that of John W. Hinckley, Jr., have led to "successful" use of the insanity defense. But several others who used this defense were nevertheless found guilty; these defendants include John Wayne Gacy, Jeffrey Dahmer, and the convicted killers of Robert Kennedy and Lee Harvey Oswald.

The insanity plea is used much less frequently than people assume; it is tried in only about 1 out of every 200 cases, and it rarely succeeds. If it does succeed, there is no guarantee that the defendant will be released from the hospital any sooner than he or she would have been paroled from prison. Yet some examples of early release of NGRI defendants have led to justified criticism of the procedure. Other criticisms are that insanity cannot be reliably and validly assessed and that the insanity defense relies too much on psychiatric testimony.

Recent reforms include the Insanity Defense Reform Act and the adoption in several states of a "guilty but mentally ill" verdict, resulting (at least in theory) in the defendant's being treated in a state hospital until releasable and then serving the rest of the sentence in prison. A number of states also allow the diminished-capacity plea, a partial defense based on mental condition. But it also has been controversial, and at least one state (California) that formerly allowed the defense no longer does so.

The Rights of Special Groups

The two little girls were walking home from school through a small wooded area in Essex Junction, a small town in Vermont. They were stopped by two males, brandishing knives. Both girls were sexually violated several times. They were cut up with a knife. One was killed; the other, left for dead, managed to survive the ordeal and, eventually, to identify her attackers. The girls were both 12 years of age.

The two males were 15 and 16 years old; both boys lived in the area. Vermont had a law that children under age 16 could not be tried for crimes like adults; thus, instead of being charged with a law violation, the boys were given a hearing by the juvenile justice system. At these hearings, any juvenile found to have committed an illegal act would be sent to a state institution until age 18. That meant that the 15-year-old boy—who had forced a 12-year-old girl to perform fellatio on him and who had tortured her and carved an X on her chest—would be given his freedom in slightly over two years, *with no criminal record by his name.*

When the community learned that this was the state law, the outrage was so great that Vermont's governor called an expensive special session of the state legislature, with only one task: to reform the laws about the age at which minors could be prosecuted as adults. At this session, legislators proposed to reduce the age at which juveniles would be treated as adults by the state courts.

Is this appropriate? If a 10-year-old commits a heinous crime, should he or she be given a different treatment from adult offenders? Or should the child be subject to the same punishments? Do children possess any special rights to differential treatment?

And what of the little girl who survived this ordeal? As the sole material witness to the crime, she was especially valuable to the police in their investigation and to the district attorney in his prosecution. Even though she could barely talk about the attack, they wanted her to pick out her attackers from a lineup and identify the 16-year-old at his trial. Is this appropriate—to put a 12-year-old through the agony of reliving an experience that none of us would want to suffer even once? Do the needs of justice outweigh her rights as a child to be free of such terror?

Throughout history, certain types of people have been provided special rights because of their age, past experience, or condition. But society has not always agreed on what rights these identifiable groups possess, and many matters remain controversial. Any of us who have flown on a commercial airplane know that "persons needing assistance," including blind people, are permitted to board before the other passengers. But do blind passengers have the right to sit in any row of the plane, including those rows with the emergency exits? The recent controversy over this specific question reflects the fact that society is often paternalistic in its granting of rights to special groups. It treats them as "special" by granting them some rights but denying them others that are automatically granted to other people in our society.

Other groups of people, such as homosexuals or the elderly, have been denied rights but are beginning to demand them. The issue is so reflective of basic dilemmas introduced in Chapter 1—such as equality versus discretion and the rights of individuals versus the needs of society—that this chapter is devoted to the rights of four "special groups" within the legal system: children, psychologically disturbed persons, mentally retarded persons, and prisoners.

CHILDREN'S RIGHTS IN SOCIETY

The assumption that children even have rights—and, if they do, that these rights may differ substantially from those of adults—is a fairly recent conception (Aries, 1962; Farson, 1974). From Roman times to the late Middle Ages, children were abandoned throughout Europe in great numbers, by parents at every socioeconomic level (Boswell, 1989). The philosopher Thomas Hobbes once wrote that "like the imbecile, the crazed and the beasts, over children there is no law" (cited in Worsfold, 1974). We may look on such attitudes as historical oddities, but, even as late as the early 20th century, children were for the most part still regarded as extensions of their parents, with no legal status per se. The prevailing legal and societal assumption has been, and for the most part continues to be, that the interests of a child are adequately protected by his or her parents (Rodham, 1973). It was not until the middle of this century that any of the rights guaranteed adults by the Constitution were applied to children as well (*Haley* v. *Ohio*, 1948). Chapter 9, in reviewing the rights of defendants, described one of the most important cases, *In re Gault* (1967), that dealt with children's rights to legal assistance.

Two important issues that have not been fully resolved, however, are the following: (1) Under what circumstances should the state (police, social workers, etc.) take action *for* the child but *against* the wishes of the parents? (2) What decisions should children be allowed to make? (Box 17-1 describes a recent Supreme Court decision on child abuse.)

Box 17-1

Child Abuse—When Does the State Have a Duty to Rescue?

Early in 1989 the Supreme Court announced that the U.S. Constitution does not obligate state or local government officials to protect citizens, including children, against harm from private individuals. In a 6-to-3 vote, the Court decided that the failure of a public social welfare agency in Wisconsin to protect a boy from his father's brutal acts did not violate the child's constitutional rights.

Joshua DeShaney had been beaten by his father for two years. By the age of 4, he had suffered severe brain damage and hence was mentally retarded and had to be institutionalized. His father was convicted of child abuse but served less than two years of prison time.

His mother then brought suit against the Winnebago County, Wisconsin, Department of Social Services, claiming that its social workers had reason to suspect that the boy (who was in his father's custody) was in danger. But the social workers failed to intervene. Did this failure to act violate Joshua's 14th Amendment right not to be deprived of life or liberty without due process of law?

The Court said no; Chief Justice Rehnquist's majority opinion stated that the purpose of the 14th Amendment's due-process clause "was to protect the people from the State, not to insure that the State protected them from each other" (*DeShaney* v. *Winnebago County*, 1989). The Court acknowledged that the social agency staff might have known that the boy was in danger. Periodically it had been reported that he was being abused; at one point the agency took custody. And states could, continued the opinion, enact laws that placed liability on such officials under similar circumstances, "but they should not have it thrust upon them by this Court's expansion of the Due Process clause."

In a dissenting opinion, Justice William Brennan wrote: "My disagreement with the Court arises from its failure to see that inaction can be every bit as abusive of power as action, that oppression can result when a State undertakes a vital duty and then ignores it."

Advocacy for Children's Rights

Children's rights advocates were outraged by the decision described in Box 17-1. Why, they asked, do we hold bars legally responsible for continuing to serve liquor to intoxicated customers and yet not hold the state accountable when it has been warned that a child is in peril? Society, in part goaded by the child advocacy movement, seeks to clarify the rights of children. Yet for every advocate of liberalization, someone else wishes to keep children in their present status or place further restrictions on them. Whereas in the last decade groups have been formed for the protection of children against abuse and violence from parents and other adults, there has also been new shrillness to the demands for corporal punishment in the schools. And although 18 is the legal age of "majority" (adulthood) in most states, in response to threats from the federal government to curtail funds, all states have fixed 21 as the legal drinking age.

Consider the matter of the right to an abortion. With regard to whether minors have a constitutional right to abortions, the Supreme Court has relied on psychological assumptions but has ignored relevant psychological research (Melton, 1987; Melton & Russo, 1987). For example, although some potential differences in the decision-making abilities of minors and adults exist, available research indicates that minors, at least as young as 15, do not show any substantial differences from adults in their legal competence to consider a decision like abortion (Ambuel & Rappaport, 1992). But most states require either parental consent or approval by a judge before an adolescent can obtain an abortion.

Clearly our society holds strong, yet conflicting, attitudes toward the rights of children. The topic is multifaceted and complex: one child's advocate may focus on one area, such as nutrition, even as another is concerned only with the legal rights of children. Another advocate may work for the expansion of services to children, while another emphasizes children's achieving the freedom to determine their own outcomes. As Rodham puts it, "children's rights" is a slogan in search of definition; it lacks any "coherent doctrine regarding the status of children as political beings" (1973, p. 487).

Two Contrasting Conceptions of Children's Rights

Given the diversity of opinions and approaches to the topic, psychologists can help by developing a schema, or taxonomy, for classifying children's rights. Annas and Healey (cited in Beyer, 1974) suggest that the most helpful way to conceptualize the various meanings of the term *right* is to place them on a continuum: at one end, the recognized legal rights; somewhere near the middle, those rights that probably would be recognized as such by a court of law if the occasion arose; and at the other end, philosophical or political statements of what the law ought to be. This approach distinguishes between rights already granted and potential rights that have been advocated on behalf of children by various individuals and groups.

The literature on children's advocacy embodies two differing orientations toward the extension of children's rights (Rogers & Wrightsman, 1978).

The first, labeled the *nurturance* orientation, stresses the provision by society of supposedly beneficial objects, environments, services, and experiences for the child. The nurturance orientation is essentially paternalistic, in that what is good or desirable is determined not by children themselves but by society or some subset of society. For example, an amendment to the Fair Housing Act that took effect in 1989 bars sellers or renters from discriminating against families with children under age 18, and many states now have laws prohibiting adults-only apartment complexes (Sanders, 1989).

The second view, labeled the *self-determination* orientation, stresses those rights that would allow children to exercise control over their own environments, to make their own binding decisions about what they want, and to have autonomous control over various facets of their lives. For example, does a teenager have a right to seek an abortion without her parents' knowledge or permission? Some teenagers ask: "Why should a younger person have any less of a right to privacy than an older person?" As the 1990s began, 38 states had either parental-notification or judicial review laws covering adolescents' rights to an abortion, though many of the state laws had been enjoined by court decisions (Greenberger & Connor, 1991). The U.S. Supreme Court has recently handed down rulings that uphold statutes requiring minors to obtain either parental consent or judicial approval before they can have an abortion (*Planned Parenthood* v. *Casey*, 1992). The nurturance orientation may be simplistically described as "giving children what's good for them" whereas the self-determination orientation may be thought of as "giving children the right to decide what's good for themselves."

The distinction between nurturance and self-determination parallels one that Farson (1974) made between two classes of child advocates: those interested in protecting children and those interested in protecting children's rights. It also relates to Worsfold's (1974) distinction between the paternalistic view of children and children's rights to fair treatment.

Measurement of Attitudes toward Children's Rights

Rogers and Wrightsman (1978) sought to measure these conceptions of children's rights.

Their expectation was that each of the two orientations would be a unique domain; that is, instead of conceptualizing them as endpoints on some continuum, the researchers favored Kerlinger's (1958, 1961, 1967) criterial referents approach. Usually, when two criterial referents exist, they are hypothesized to be independent of each other—unrelated—thus allowing someone to be in favor of both, or of neither, or of one but not the other. In regard to attitudes toward children's rights, this distinction was troublesome; traditionally the denial of self-determination rights to children has been justified on the ground that children are too immature to understand where their self-interests lie, so society must protect them from themselves (a nurturance orientation). The researchers resolved this difficulty by narrowing their original definition of the nurturant orientation to exclude all nurturant activities that rested on a denial of the child's rights to make his or her own decisions.

Although the conceptual distinction between self-determination rights and nurturant rights was of paramount importance to Rogers and Wrightsman, they expected that attitudes toward the rights of children might vary according to the subject-matter topic. For example, an individual might support giving them the right to make choices in the area of education and yet oppose giving them the right to make choices about health care. Relying especially on Farson's (1974) and Maurer's (1974) typologies, the researchers identified five basic content areas: (1) health, (2) education and information, (3) economic, (4) safety and care, and (5) legal/judicial/political. Within each of these content areas are dimensions of nurturance and of self-determination, resulting in a 2 × 5 framework for classifying the specific rights advocated for children. Table 17-1 gives examples of rights within each category.

With this conceptualization as a blueprint,

Table **17-1**   *Examples of Children's Rights*

Content area	Conceptual dimension	
	Nurturance	*Self-determination*
Health	Free health care	Choice to refuse or accept treatment; right to abortion
Education and information	Quality education	Choice not to attend school
Economic	Equal pay for equal work	Right to enter into binding contracts
Safety and care	Products designed to be safe; a drug-free pregnancy	Choice of where to live; hairstyles; clothing
Legal/judicial/political	Due process	Choice of legal counsel

Source: Rogers and Wrightsman (1978, p. 63).

Rogers and Wrightsman (1978) developed an attitude scale designed to cover each of the ten combinations. A total of 300 attitude-scale items were created, forming the Children's Rights Attitude Scale. People from four different groups (high school students, undergraduate education majors, undergraduate liberal arts majors, and adults) completed the scale.

The most striking difference among the groups on the nurturance subscales was that, on three of the five subscales (health, safety and care, and education and information) and on the overall nurturance scale, high school students held the *least favorable* attitudes toward extending nurturant rights to children. This finding could reflect a residual resentment toward the paternalistic societal policies directed at them. Holt (1974) suggests that "most young people, and at earlier and earlier ages, begin to experience childhood not as a garden but as a prison" (p. 133). In contrast, the undergraduate education majors were the most favorable of the groups toward extending nurturant rights to children.

High school students were most in sympathy with children's self-determination rights. A possible interpretation of these data is that older children (as these subjects are) will be more supportive of self-determination rights than will other groups, primarily because they are re-

sponding in terms of what they want (but do not have) for themselves, whereas other types of respondents support the extension of self-determination rights to a currently dependent and powerless class of individuals. Education majors also supported the viewpoint that children should have the right to determine their own outcome.

Males and females revealed different attitudes toward children's rights on most of the nurturance subscales; wherever there was a statistically significant gender difference, women were more nurturant than men. This probably reflects gender differences in role socialization. The traditional roles of women and men with regard to children are that the woman plays the nurturer and the man plays the economic provider.

But perhaps more important than any group differences is the finding that respondents more strongly favored extending nurturant rights to children than extending self-determination rights. This pattern was found regardless of respondents' gender, group membership, or content area. Across all participants, the average response to self-determination items was "neither agree nor disagree," whereas the average response to nurturant items fell midway between the "agree somewhat" and the "agree strongly" levels. Apparently we are more willing to try to make the dependent status of children more comfortable than to grant children freedom.

Rights of Children in the Legal System

Children *are* different from adults, in contemporary society's view, when they participate in the legal system. This section discusses legal and psychological issues that arise when children become involved in custody disputes between divorcing parents, when they are asked to testify as witnesses in a trial, and when they themselves are charged with illegal acts. In each of these three matters the law has been in a state of rapid change.

Children's Rights in Custody Decisions

Historically, when parents decided to divorce, the child's rights were of no consequence in the decision to assign custody to one parent or the other. Until the early 1900s, children were treated as property and automatically assigned to their fathers. Then, throughout the first two-thirds of the 20th century, mothers, by virtue of their traditional roles as primary caretakers of children, usually received custody of children following a divorce. But since about 1970 another shift has occurred, placing the child's best interests at the forefront. A child is now treated as a distinct person and is to be accorded, by law, individual rights in the child custody proceedings (Woody, 1977).

Who determines what is "in the best interests of the child"? Custody is awarded to the mother, still, in the majority of cases (Reppucci, 1984). Yet a more objective evaluation of the father's potential for custody is emerging. Psychologists are now consulted by the courts in custody decisions and are asked to carry out evaluations about the child's best welfare (Skafte, 1985).

At least 20 states permit children beyond a specified age to state which parent they prefer for custody. But judges have tremendous discretion over such decisions. For example, when one New Jersey couple decided to divorce, the only matter on which they agreed was the custody of their two daughters: the girls would live with their mother, and the father would visit. But the judge decided that it would be best for the couple to share their children; the girls would switch homes every four months (Press, 1983a). An even more radical plan, instituted by a Michigan judge, is described in Box 17-2.

The majority of states have adopted some sort of joint-custody plan (Buie, 1988), although the definitions of *joint custody* differ widely from state to state. In some instances, the amount of time the child is in the physical custody of each parent is split relatively equally; in other cases, the child lives mainly with one parent, but both parents retain legal rights over decisions about the child's education, health, and welfare. Joint custody is not, as originally hoped, a panacea for difficult custody decisions. Such procedures work best when the parents still live near each other, agree on most aspects of raising the child, and maintain the semblance of a relationship. In fact, joint custody was described by Michigan law professor David Chambers as the "pet idea" of the decade of the 1980s, perhaps because it promised something for everyone. Children could maintain their relationships with both parents, divorced fathers could have more influence over the lives of their children, and mothers could avoid the burden of being the sole custodial parent (Press, 1983a). In some states, joint custody is the determination in as many as 80% of the cases (Byczynski, 1987).

Early evaluations of joint-custody arrangements tentatively concluded that most participants were more satisfied than were those in arrangements in which one parent had exclusive custody. But a study by Susan Steinman (1981) discovered less consistent reactions. Steinman interviewed 24 families, all of whom had agreed to a joint-custody arrangement. Most of the parents and children thrived under this system, but about one-fourth of the 32 children reported having a difficult time shifting back and forth between two homes. Some critics also view a judge's decision to award joint custody as a "cop-out," an avoidance of making an unpopular choice between contesting parties. As noted earlier, some judges have ruled for joint custody even when neither parent has requested it (Spindler-Cruden, 1983), and one judge ruled that custody of a nursing infant would alternate every two weeks between mother and father.

More recent research concludes that sometimes joint custody is helpful for children and sometimes it is harmful. If the parents have an amicable relationship, joint custody seems to have no adverse effect on the emotional health of the children (Kline, Tschann, Johnston, & Wallerstein, 1989). But it can be detrimental to the children if the parents have a continuing conflict-riddled relationship. If one parent keeps tearing down the other, it's not advisable for the adversaries to share the responsibilities of making major decisions for the child; the better solution in such cases is probably for one parent to have legal custody and the other parent to have generous visitation rights. Several recent studies suggest that custody arrangements are less influential on children's adjustment than parents' emotional stability and the amount of continuing conflict between them (Grych & Fincham, 1992). Box 17-3 also deals with the impact of divorce on children.

Children as Witnesses in Court

Sometimes a child is the only witness to a crime—or its only victim. Even in some civil cases, the only dispassionate observers to accidents may be children. Is it appropriate for children to testify? There are two distinguishable problems here: one deals with the accuracy of children as witnesses in court, and the other

---

Box **17-2** | *An Innovative Custody Decision*

A judge in Traverse City, Michigan, made an unusual decision "in the best interests of the children" in a custody case. He awarded three adolescent boys the custody of their house, with their mother and father alternating month-long visits. Everybody seemed to accept the decision; the three boys, aged 11, 13, and 15 at the time, wouldn't have to change schools or move their belongings back and forth. The family lived in a small town, Interlochen (population 4000), and each parent would live close by when not living at the house.

But, in the long run, is such a decision "best" for all parties? What if one of the parents decides to remarry? Would the new spouse be willing to cycle from one domicile to another on a month-by-month basis? In addition, would this shared-residence solution work with parents who were still having conflicts with each other?

relates to threats to their well-being by subjecting them to the stress of testifying.

At what age can children distinguish between fact and fantasy? Do young children know what it means to take an oath to tell the truth? In keeping with the initial dilemma posed at the beginning of this book, society's desire for criminals to be prosecuted and punished demands that all relevant witnesses be allowed to testify, but defendants also have the right not to be convicted on the basis of inaccurate testimony. Accusations of sexual abuse of children by adults have increased dramatically in the last few years; children now appear to be reporting a much higher percentage of such violations. But this increased awareness has had detrimental as well as beneficial effects; it has led to false accusations by some children. For example, in the small Minnesota town of Jordan, 24 adults were charged with molesting 41

Box 17-3   *Divorce—Not "in the Best Interests of the Child"?*

For most couples, if relations are so acrimonious that a divorce seems like the only solution, the separation itself must come as a relief. With respect to the children affected by a divorce, a longitudinal study of 131 children and adolescents from 60 divorced families in Marin County, California (Wallerstein & Blakeslee, 1989) concludes that the outcome is more complex. The comfortable assumption that "children are resilient; they eventually will get over it" is challenged in this 15-year follow-up study. Only 10% of the subjects in this study felt relieved when quarreling parents separated, and these tended to be older children who had been the recipients or observers of physical violence. Judith Wallerstein, one of the authors of the study, states: "Almost half of children of divorces enter adulthood as worried, underachieving, self-deprecating, and sometimes angry young men and women" (quoted by Toufexis, 1989, p. 61).

Wallerstein and Blakeslee describe a "sleeper effect" on females: many of them seem to have adjusted to their parents' divorce admirably well into adulthood, at which point they suffer "an intolerable level of anxiety about betrayal." They may drop out of college, become promiscuous, or trap themselves in unsatisfactory relationships—all, according to the authors, because of a wish to protect themselves from rejection, abandonment, and betrayal. Wallerstein and Blakeslee (1989) report that this reaction occurred in two-thirds of the women between the ages of 19 and 23.

Of children whose mothers remarried, half said they did not feel welcome in the new family. Ten years after the divorce, more than one third reported having poor relationships with *both* parents.

One problem with this study is the lack of a control group of intact families to whom the divorced families could be compared. Without this type of control, we cannot be certain that the effects reported by the children in the divorced families are due, in fact, to the divorce, rather than to some other factor.

A recent review of 95 studies that compared children from divorced and intact families found that the children from divorced families had slightly poorer adjustment, particularly in the areas of aggression and interpersonal relationships, than the children from the intact families. Longitudinal studies indicated "that behavior problems are common at the time of divorce but generally diminish as time passes after the divorce" (Grych & Fincham, 1992, p. 436). Moreover, several studies of divorce indicate that it may not be the divorce per se that is harmful to children; factors such as the amount of hostility between the parents and the consistency of their discipline of the children are stronger predictors of children's adjustment than divorce itself.

children. But the two adults who were tried were acquitted, and charges against the remaining defendants were dropped. The main witness, a boy, admitted that he had been lying. For this and other reasons, children as witnesses in court may not be seen as credible by jurors. And, as Melton and Thompson (1987) remind us, jurors are the ultimate arbiters of the credibility of every witness, child or adult.

Despite the publicity given to false accusations, our limited empirical evidence suggests that children rarely make up events of such serious magnitude. Jones (1985) investigated 576 sexual abuse cases reported to the authorities in Denver. Of these, about 8% were concluded to be fictitious, and the vast majority of these were based on false allegations by adults. Less than 2% of the reports of sexual abuse were false allegations that children had initiated; of those (about 10 out of 576), all were made by adolescent girls who had been sexually abused on previous occasions. Other research (Haugaard, Reppucci, Laird, & Nauful, 1991) confirms that most children as young as 4 know that telling something that is untrue, even if prompted to do so by a parent, is a lie.

The second conflict also falls under the category of society's needs versus individuals' rights, but the focus is the child's right not to be abused again by the legal system. It is legitimate to ask, as Berliner and Barbieri (1984, p. 128) do, "Will the child as witness suffer more than the child as victim?" As these authors note, a major barrier to prosecuting defendants in child sexual assault cases is that the child will experience further suffering and psychological injury in the legal process. Children are forced to remember and even describe to others, in a public setting, the intimate atrocities they long to forget. In a typical case, for example, a young child may be forced to tell the jury about an attacker inserting his penis into her vagina and the pain she experienced in the process.

Both these issues—the credibility of child witnesses and their rights to avoid further distress—are illustrated in a Colorado case described by Gail S. Goodman (1984a, p. 1):

In the summer of 1983, three-year-old Lori Poland was playing in the front yard of a neighbor's home when a man pulled up in an orange Datsun and ordered her inside. Several children playing near Lori at the time reported later to the police that the man said, "Take your pants off and get in the car," and Lori did. Three days later, she was found in the pit of a deserted mountain outhouse—crying, bruised, and suffering from exposure. When found, she was able to tell the police that the "bad man" hit her and put her "in the hole." After a day of recovery in the hospital, the police, working on a lead, showed Lori a 12-person photo lineup that included a suspect. With a gasp, Lori quickly identified the suspect as her abductor.

The prosecutor now faced the decision of whether to bring the suspect to trial. Can an identification by a 3-year-old be introduced in court? In this case the judge did not have to decide whether to admit the child's testimony into evidence; a week before the trial, the man whom Lori had identified confessed. His statement to the police bore out her account of what had happened.

As we described in Chapter 11, the presumption that young children (under age 10) are not competent to testify has been replaced by a presumption that young children can testify if they meet the following criteria: (1) they know the difference between truth and falsehood, (2) they understand and can describe the events they witnessed, (3) they have sufficient memory for these events, and 4) they are able to testify in court about what they remembered and witnessed.

As rigid age barriers have been removed, the child's level of intelligence and "appreciation of the difference between truth and falsehood, as well as his duty to tell the former" (*Wheeler* v. *United States*, 1895, pp. 524–525), have become more salient. The child's demeanor is also taken into account. Judges—who have discretion about admitting the child's testimony—usually interview the child and may decide that he or she is competent to testify on some issues but not others.

In Atlanta during the spring of 1988, someone kidnapped a 4-year-old girl from a parked car as she waited for her mother to visit a friend. The kidnapper brutally raped the child, injuring her so severely that reconstructive surgery was required. Luckily, the child lived and was able to identify her assailant from a group of photos. Then began the hard task of acclimating the child to the courtroom, trying to prepare her to testify and respond to cross-examination. Assisted by a counselor, the female prosecutor worked for a month with the child, chatting and playing with her, trying to break down her reluctance to talk about the rape. They worked with coloring books, toys, and anatomically correct dolls and finally took the young girl to court to face the accused. After three other witnesses testified, the judge and the lawyers questioned the little girl to determine her competency as a witness. She responded well when questioned by the prosecutor, reflecting the trusting relationship developed over the course of many counseling sessions, but clammed up when questioned by the defense lawyer, a man she had never seen before. When the child twice refused to answer his questions, the judge had no choice but to find her to be not a competent witness. The prosecutor then, crying openly in court, had no choice but to ask that the charges against the defendant be dismissed.

If the judge allows a child to testify, the same rules apply to the child as to an adult witness, with at least one important exception (Goodman, 1984b). Leading questions—ones that suggest an answer to the witness—are permitted during direct examination, as well as in cross-examination. (With adult witnesses, leading questions can be used only by the opposing attorney, on cross-examination.)

As discussed in Chapters 7 and 11, asking leading questions enhances the possibility that a person's suggestibility can affect responses detrimentally; this effect may be particularly strong if the suggestive questions are asked by someone who was actually a participant in the original event (Haugaard et al., 1991). Misleading information in a leading question may meld with the original memory, leading to an altered and incorrect response (Ceci, Toglia, & Ross, 1988). Leading questions have limits, however, on how much bias they can create. This conclusion is supported by a finding (Goodman, Aman, & Hirschman, 1987) that children are less susceptible to suggestion when questioned about important events than about peripheral aspects.

Two reasons are often given for denying children—especially young children—the right to testify. First, compared to adults, children are assumed to notice less, omit more, and forget faster. Second, children are assumed to make more errors of commission than adults.

A review of the literature (Johnson & Foley, 1984) concludes that, although there are qualifications, on memory tasks involving recall, children do make more errors of omission than adults. One reason is that young children have not yet developed the organizational strategies that adults use to aid in remembering.

The evidence is less clear on the issue of whether children notice less. Neisser (1979) found that a higher percentage of first-graders than fourth-graders or adults remembered *irrelevant* information when watching a ballgame on TV. Such seemingly unimportant details may become vital in a courtroom prosecution.

Likewise, the assertion that forgetting occurs

more rapidly in younger children is not supported by the available evidence. Belmont and Butterfield (1969) found the rate of loss of information in short-term memory tasks to be comparable across age levels. Simple and straightforward information is acquired and retained by children; an age difference occurs when complex stimuli must be remembered, requiring the use of organizational processes. These processes develop with age. For example, Goodman and Reed (1986) used exposure times of 5 minutes rather than the 10–30 seconds that is typical of laboratory experiments and found that 6-year-olds were as accurate in their identifications of photographs as were adults, even after delays of four to five days. But 3-year-olds did poorly under these conditions. Similarly, children are less skilled than adults in providing a free narrative description of what they observed (Marin, Holmes, Guth, & Kovac, 1979). But this is a reporting difficulty, not a perceptual or a memory deficit.

The second concern about children's memory is that they are prone to make more errors of *commission* than adults. As Johnson and Foley (1984) note, "The extreme wariness about children's testimony reflected in legal literature and practice originates from [assumptions that] children are often supposed to have more trouble than adults in distinguishing real from imagined events and to be especially susceptible to errors produced by uncritical embellishment of memory and to errors produced by suggestion" (p. 34). But a program of research by these authors on what they call "reality monitoring" suggests that children have difficulty with some, but not all, such situations. Their summary concludes:

A good deal of developmental theorizing would lead us to expect that children are generally unable to identify the sources of their memories.

These studies demonstrate, however, that this is not necessarily the case. How confused young children appear depends on the nature of the discrimination called for. Children as young as 6 years were as able as older subjects to separate memories originating from different perceptual sources. . . . More importantly, children as young as 6 or 8 were at no disadvantage in relation to older subjects in discriminating between memories originating from internal and external classes of experience (e.g., imagined and perceived pictures; imagined and perceived words). These findings indicate that children do not have a general deficit in discriminating the origin of information in memory. However, it would be a mistake to conclude that children are never more confused than adults about reality and fantasy. When children are asked to distinguish memories for ideas realized in action from memories of ideas only . . . , they were at a marked disadvantage [p. 44].

What about the effects on young children of being scrutinized by the courts? Do child witnesses have any rights? "The law is more concerned with protecting the legal rights of defendants than with protecting the mental health of children who testify," states Spencer Eth, a child psychiatrist who has interviewed more than 50 children who were victims of or witnesses to violence (quoted by Goleman, 1984, p. B-5). When the crime is a sexual assault on the child, there is a real danger that the child will be further distressed by involvement in the legal process (Berliner & Barbieri, 1984). Eth notes: "Children who have undergone extreme trauma, such as watching the murder or rape of a parent, can be retraumatized by having to act as a witness in court months or years later" (quoted by Goleman, 1984, p. B-7).

Furthermore, a trial may stretch the limits of the child's capacity for physical exertion. In preparation for a case involving sexual assault in a Los Angeles preschool, prosecutors asked children an average of 400 questions a day, and children were required to testify for many hours. Protracted cases like this one can disrupt the child's normal healing processes (see also Box 17-4).

Additionally, having to describe atrocities in a public setting increases the trauma for many children. Some children can, in private sessions, describe in graphic detail how they were sexually abused. They can demonstrate, with anatomically correct dolls, what happened to them. But when these children are put in a courtroom full of strangers, a judge in a long black robe, a jury, and even the person accused of attacking them, they often become speechless, evasive, or immobilized (Leech, 1985). They feel that they are being made victims all over again. Especially when children know their abuser, they experience tremendous conflict. They are often frightened about an attacker who has threatened them with further abuse. Defense lawyers may try to intimidate the child. Some district attorneys report that, out of concern for the child or out of fear that the child's testimony on the witness stand will not reflect the true state of affairs, they decide not to prosecute. As a result, known child molesters are encouraged to act again, confident that the courts will find it hard to convict them (Lawrence, 1984).

What possible solutions are there to this dilemma? One strategy, allowed in many states and approved by the Supreme Court, is to excuse the child from testifying and to introduce the evidence of abuse through hearsay testimony by a physician, psychologist, teacher, police officer, or social worker who repeats the out-of-court statements that the child has previously made about the attack. Another approach, developed by a number of states during the 1980s, allows a child's testimony to be videotaped, with only the judge and attorneys from both sides present. Then the videotape is shown in court.

Defense attorneys have objected to the videotaping of child witnesses' testimony. They see the potential for abuse of another kind: abuse of the Sixth Amendment rights of defendants to confront their accusers in a court of law (Leech, 1985). Often the jury, too, wants to see the defendant and the victim in the same room together, in order to judge whether the child is being truthful.

Some recent legislation has tried to protect defendants' rights by allowing the defense to file objections to videotaping in some cases. Also, having the defense attorney present during the videotaping permits cross-examination of the child, as in a normal courtroom procedure. The noted trial attorney F. Lee Bailey has said on this topic: "As a defense attorney, I don't think I'd object to videotaped testimony as long as I could be there to ask questions" (1985).

Another innovation in some states has been the placement of a one-way screen in front of the defendant so that he can't be seen by a child testifying against him. For example, the state of Iowa passed a law permitting the use of this device when the alleged victim was under the age of 14, in order to safeguard the child from emotional trauma.

This type of screen was used in the recent trial of John Avery Coy, who was convicted of sexually assaulting two 13-year-old girls while they were sleeping outdoors in a tent. At the trial a screen was placed in front of Coy when the two girls testified. (He was able to see the girls, but they could not see him.) Coy appealed his conviction on two grounds: (1) that the presence of the screen caused the jury to presume that he was guilty and (2) that the screen deprived him of the opportunity to confront the girls face to face. In a 1988 decision, the Supreme Court agreed with Coy about the second claim; by a 6-to-2 vote, it overturned his conviction, saying that the defendant's Sixth Amendment constitutional right to confront his accusers face to face was not outweighed "by the necessity of protecting the victims of sexual abuse" (*Coy v. Iowa*, 1988).

Justices Blackmun and Rehnquist dissented; they stated that the right to cross-examination (which Coy still had) was central to the Sixth Amendment's confrontation clause, whereas the right to a face-to-face confrontation was only peripheral (Hans, 1988). Their minority opinion reflected their interpretation of psychological research that child victims could be psychologically injured even more by having to testify as they faced their alleged abusers. The dissent also noted that such concerns "may so overwhelm the child as to prevent the possibility of effective testimony, thereby undermining the truth finding function of the trial itself."

In the *Coy* decision, the Court left the door open for a state to use one-way closed-circuit television to present the testimony of a child unable to testify in open court. In the 1990 case of *Maryland* v. *Craig*, the Court upheld a Maryland law permitting such a procedure when the trial court has found that the child is likely to suffer significant emotional distress not just by testifying in court but specifically by being in the presence of the defendant. *Craig* thus modifies the rule of the *Coy* case.

One strategy that may reduce the trauma of testimony is to have the child visit the courtroom several times, sit in the witness chair, meet the judge and the bailiff, and become familiar with the surroundings and procedure (Perry & Teply, 1985). Goodman and Helgeson (1986) suggest that providing children with toys, crayons, and paper or asking about their hobbies can help establish a more relaxed atmosphere. Some judges bend the rules a bit; in one Seattle trial, a 5½-year-old witness was permitted to sit on her mother's lap (Beach, 1983).

As professionals learn more about the extent of sexual abuse of children and the effects on them of testifying, we may expect additional

---

Box 17-4 | The McMartin Preschool Trial

The longest criminal trial in U.S. history stemmed from charges of sexual abuse of children, directed at Raymond Buckey and his mother, Peggy McMartin Buckey, who were teachers at the family-owned McMartin Preschool in Manhattan Beach, California.

The case began in 1983, when a mother complained that her toddler had been sexually abused by "Mr. Ray" (Raymond Buckey). Originally, seven teachers, including the wheelchair-bound founder of the school, Virginia McMartin, were arrested and charged with 207

Raymond Buckey

counts of conspiracy and child molestation.

After a preliminary hearing that stretched over a year and a half,

charges against five of the teachers were dropped because of insufficient evidence.

The trial itself began in April 1987. Jury selection took 40 days, and opening statements weren't given until July of that year. One of the defendants, Raymond Buckey, spent five years in jail, until supporters were able to raise the money for his $3 million bail bond; he was released in February 1989, while the trial was in progress. Finally, in July 1989, Buckey took the stand in his own behalf; he repeatedly denied that he had trial procedures designed to protect children while trying to maintain the rights of defendants. For example, some courts permit expert witnesses to describe typical behaviors observed in abused children, such as not telling anyone right away that they have been abused or recanting their testimony when they are challenged about it. Jurors may interpret these behaviors as signs that the child is lying when, in many cases, delays and recantations are common reactions among abused children. Courts are divided on whether to allow expert testimony on "child abuse accommodation syndrome" (Levine & Battistoni, 1991). But they are usually very reluctant to let an expert testify about the credibility of a specific child, since credibility is thought to be an issue that the jury can decide as well as the expert.

Laws that facilitate testimony by children have an additional, less obvious, benefit. Although testifying has the potential for harm, it can also provide a beneficial therapeutic experience for the child, who can feel a sense of control over events and can gain some satisfaction if the defendant is found guilty. As an example, one 15-year-old girl said "If I, as a young person, were a victim of a sexual abuse or rape case, I would *want* to testify before a full court. I might be scared at first or a little embarrassed, but I'd want to be present to make my assailant look like a complete fool. I'd want to *see* him convicted—with my own eyes. It would make me stronger" (quoted in Gunter, 1985, p. 12A).

These developments have generated a number of research questions for psychologists to try to answer. Grisso (1985) notes three examples: (1) Does a policy that permits lawyers to ask leading questions of child witnesses affect the accuracy of their testimony or jurors' perceptions of its accuracy? (2) Does closed-circuit televising or videotaping of the testimony of children deprive jurors of cues that they would use if the child testified in the courtroom?

sodomized children, played any naked games with them, or taken pornographic photographs of them (Reinhold, 1989, p. 1). It was not until November 1989—2½ years after it began—that all the evidence had been presented. Jurors—the 12 who were left after six others had dropped out because of a stroke, emergency gall-bladder surgery, chronic back pain, personal problems, and threat of a lost job promotion—faced dealing with more than 60,000 pages of the court record, 1000 exhibits, and the testimony of 124 witnesses.

Peggy McMartin Buckey

Because of the drawn-out nature of the case, some of the nine children who testified were vague on the details of the charges. Most had been 5 or 6 years old when the alleged acts occurred; they testified five or six years later.

Deliberations began in early November 1989 and stretched into the new year and the new decade. Finally, on January 18, 1990, the judge announced the jury's verdict that the defendants were not guilty, on most of the counts. For some of the charges against Raymond Buckey, the jury could not agree on a verdict; hence a mistrial was declared. Subsequently, Buckey was retried on some of these charges, and the second jury found him not guilty on all counts.

(3) Does the physical separation of the defendant and the child witness (that is, not permitting the defendant to be present) create an impression for the jury that the defendant is "dangerous"? As of now, we lack any scientific evidence about either the benefits or the harms of changing the procedures for child witnesses in the courtroom.

How Effective Are Juvenile Courts?

Believing that children should be treated differently than adults, the Illinois legislature, in 1899, adopted a law creating a new and separate court—the world's first juvenile court— "to resolve legal problems concerning dependent, neglected, and delinquent children" (Ryerson, 1978, p. 3). During the next two decades all but three other states followed suit in seeking to "decriminalize" many youthful misbehaviors. These legislative acts were, at the same time, both conservative and optimistic— conservative because they were developed partly to control the masses of poor and immigrant people moving to the cities and optimistic because they believed that wayward youths could be reclaimed and go on to lead orderly and productive lives (Ryerson, 1978). From the beginning, the juvenile court idea was built on a philosophy of rehabilitation. It recognized that the defects that produced juvenile delinquency resulted as much from the environment as from the child; therefore the child should not be treated as a criminal (Bortner, 1984). At the same time, the system reflected a *nurturant* conception of the rights of children, as described earlier in this chapter.

The distinction between neglected and delinquent children became blurred; probation, rather than institutionalization, became the preferred disposition for child offenders; courtroom procedures were informal and lacked the adversarial nature of adult courts. The public

elected juvenile court judges who, it was hoped, were imbued with humanistic, legalistic, and sympathetic skills that would inspire trust from their youthful clients (Olson-Raymer, 1984). It was assumed that these offenders had a "smoldering ambition" to be good and that they had the potential and the desire to be productive citizens (Ryerson, 1978). Juvenile delinquents, the juvenile court movement assumed, needed only good role models.

In these early interventions, visits and informal counseling by the probation officer constituted the entire rehabilitation effort. Most probation officers did not have any relevant training or skills. "Constructive friendship" between the probation officer and the juvenile offender was seen as the important quality in their relationship. Thus the first two decades of this century saw the height of naive confidence in juvenile rehabilitation.

But the era of good feeling was brief. Criticism by newspapers, especially over charges of carelessness and neglect by probation officers, led to investigations by elected officials. Toward the end of World War I, in 1918, the public became increasingly concerned over the rising crime rate by adults, and public support of ameliorative efforts for juvenile offenders suffered as a result.

The system wasn't working as planned. In many states the staff of probation officers was too small to maintain frequent contact with the children. Officers had as many as 150 cases each and were unable to make home visits as often as every three months. The courts often adopted assembly-line operations in which cases were disposed of in less than ten minutes (Krisberg, 1989). The futility and frustration of working within such a system are eloquently evoked in Peter Prescott's description of New York City's Family Court (Prescott, 1981).

Many of the children in this system continued their delinquent behavior. Recidivism rates ranged from 30% to 88%. A 1934 study by sociologists Sheldon and Eleanor Glueck, reported in *One Thousand Delinquents* (1934), evaluated the conduct of delinquent boys during the five years after their treatment in juvenile court. More than 85% continued to break the law; they were arrested, on an average, between three and four times. The Gluecks concluded that these programs had very little effect in preventing recidivism.

By the late 1960s, Americans had lost faith in the system (Ryerson, 1978). The 1967 report of the President's Commission on Law Enforcement and the Administration of Justice concluded that juvenile courts couldn't work, because "delinquency is not so much an act of individual deviancy as a pattern of behavior which is induced by a multitude of pervasive societal influences well beyond the reach of actions by any judge, probation officer, correctional counselor, or psychiatrist" (quoted in Ryerson, 1978, p. 147).

A number of Supreme Court decisions in the late 1960s criticized juvenile court procedures; *In re Gault* (1967), described in Chapter 9, is one example, in which the Court made clear that juveniles, too, were entitled to due process. These decisions insisted that adolescents be provided regular trial procedures to ensure that an accurate determination of the facts is made, even if juveniles ultimately receive "treatment" rather than "punishment."

Diversion Programs: The Response of the 1970s

Around 1970 the juvenile court system began to develop alternative methods, called "diversion programs," for dealing with delinquent adolescents. Although optimism about long-term benefits waned, the desire remained to provide less formal and less stigmatizing procedures. It was still believed that the formal labeling of

delinquents contributed to their subsequent delinquent actions (Schur, 1973).

Diversion is intended to find community-based, short-term alternatives for handling delinquent youth. As Bynum and Greene (1984) note, common to these programs is the idea that juvenile offenders are "turned aside" from formal entry into the criminal justice system but still are provided necessary services. Though motivated by humanitarian concerns, diversion programs were viewed as cost-effective and necessary means of alleviating the overburdened juvenile courts. Ironically, the juvenile court, which itself began as an informal way of diverting youth from the stigma of being labeled "offenders," had now become "the legalistic tribunal from which children are to be diverted" (Bullington, Sprowls, Katkin, & Phillips, 1978, p. 69).

Although juvenile diversion programs have mushroomed over the last 25 years, the accumulated research evidence indicates that these programs have not consistently succeeded in creating a meaningful alternative to formal court processing (Klein, 1979; Nietzel & Himelein, 1986). Despite a few exemplary projects involving the use of paraprofessionals and behavior modification techniques (see, for example, Davidson, Redner, Blakely, Mitchell, & Emshoff, 1987), the effectiveness of diversion has been disappointing; it has not lowered recidivism rates significantly. Critics of diversion point out that the police have broad discretion in determining who is diverted. Also, the adolescents who participate in diversion programs were described by one evaluator (Klein, 1975) as "cream puff" cases, or those young people who were not in immediate jeopardy. Another observer (Rojek, 1978) indicated that "a diversion project can become the dumping ground for marginal offenders" (p. 5), such as first offenders in nonserious crimes.

Inclusion of first offenders in relatively

minor crimes in diversion programs has been called "widening the net" (Bynum & Greene, 1984; Empey, 1982), individuals are brought under state control who would have been ignored before (Latessa, Travis, & Wilson, 1984). Morris (1976) views this "net widening" as a manifestation of the "inherent conservatism" of decisions by the criminal justice system; that is, when a new disposition is created that lies in between two other dispositions (for example, between incarceration and release), the clients for the new alternative are likely to be drawn from the less serious cases. (This situation can be observed in other criminal justice "reforms," such as pretrial release programs and police citation programs.)

Diversion programs have also been criticized for their failure to provide due process to youths. Juveniles may be coerced into entering counseling or treatment, with the threat that, if they fail to, they will have to face the juvenile court (Klein, Teilmann, Lincoln, & Labin-Rosensweig, 1976; Lieberg, 1971).

What does the future hold for the juvenile justice system? In 1989, about one out of every five persons arrested for a serious crime was younger than 18 (Maguire & Flanagan, 1991). More poverty, homelessness, and illicit drug use suggest a "sharp and sustained rise in violent youth crime in the next decade" (Krisberg, 1989, p. 912). Since World War II, studies have consistently found that more than two-thirds of the most serious juvenile crime is committed by only about 6% of the youths under age 18 (Jacoby, 1988). Some critics claim that diversion programs were designed "to deal with delinquents who stole hubcaps, not those who mug old ladies" (Kramer, 1988). So juvenile justice agencies—just like the adult courts—are getting tougher (Meddis, 1987). Longer detention terms and fixed sentences are recent developments (Shenon, 1986). At the same time, "individualized justice"—favoring discretion

over equality—has become the model in Massachusetts, Utah, and other states (Moore, 1987).

Along with getting tougher, juvenile courts are tightening their procedures. Even though the court still claims to seek the juvenile's "best interest," legal reforms have established more formal criteria for discretionary decisions, such as pretrial detention (Grisso, Tomkins, & Casey, 1988). Almost every state has revised its juvenile codes in the last 15 years.

Treating Juvenile Offenders as Adults

As it became clear that diversion programs had not fulfilled many of their goals and that they were not being responsive to the perceived increase in serious crime by youth, the resulting disenchantment increased pressure on the justice system to fulfill its crime-control role.

Some jurisdictions responded by putting young people in jail with adults, at least for temporary detention before a decision was made about prosecution. It is hard to get accurate figures on the extent of this reaction, but as of 1990 the number of juvenile offenders temporarily held in adult jails on an average day was about 2300, less than 1% of the total jail population. Although this figure is relatively low, the outcomes can still be tragic. A 15-year-old girl in California, charged with assaulting a police officer, hanged herself after four days of isolated detention in a local jail. In West Virginia a truant was murdered by an adult inmate; in Ohio a teenaged girl was raped by a guard (Press, 1985). The federal government took action to change this procedure; states ran the risk of losing their federal funds for law enforcement programs unless they established alternatives to adult jails for juveniles by the end of the 1980s.

Despite the fact that confinement of

juveniles in adult jails has led to abuses, society seems to support punitive actions toward young offenders. The media have increased our awareness of serious crimes by some youths, even though the overall rate of juvenile crime has apparently not increased. Headlines proclaim "7-year-old undergoes court hearing," "Boys, ages 6 and 8, caught after breaking into bank," "Children suspected in beating death." As stated earlier, in 1989 about 20% of all persons arrested for crimes in the United States were under the age of 18. A Justice Department study reported that chronic juvenile offenders commit 61% of all juvenile crimes (Meddis, 1984b). Compared with juvenile offenders 15 years earlier, these hard-core offenders are more violent, break the law at a younger age, and commit more crimes. "A 10-year-old is now like a 13-year-old used to be," states a sergeant in the Newark, New Jersey, Police Department's youth section; "and the 16-year-olds are going on 40" (quoted by Applebome, 1987, p. 8).

The U.S. Supreme Court upheld a New York State decision to lock up, before trial, those juveniles who present a "serious risk" of committing another offense before they are tried for the present one. Such "preventive detention" of juveniles has been approved, even granting the fact that the vast majority of them are later released on probation or dismissed. As Press (1984) notes, "The law wants to prevent youngsters from committing crimes while it goes about determining whether they already have." Justice Rehnquist, who wrote the majority opinion, did not seem concerned about what happened after the trial: "The final disposition of a case is largely irrelevant to the legality of a pretrial detention," he wrote (quoted in Press, 1984).

As society becomes more terrified of its young, it again asks the question: at what age should a suspected offender be tried as an adult? Harvard law professor Arthur Miller ob-

serves: "The pendulum is swinging in favor of making juveniles accountable as adults, for adult crimes, at an earlier age" (quoted in "Age of Accountability," 1981). In some states there is no age limit at all; it is theoretically possible to try a young child as an adult and sentence him or her to life imprisonment. In most states, however, adolescents over the age of 14 charged with serious offenses are eligible to be tried as adults.

But the rules are changing, and sometimes a single offense is enough to cause those changes. The stabbing and rape of two young girls in Vermont, described at the beginning of this chapter, caused the governor of Vermont to call an emergency session of the legislature to revise the state laws regarding the eligibility of children to be tried as adults. The resulting act, which passed unanimously, represented one of the harshest reactions to juvenile crime anywhere in the United States (Meyer, 1985). It stated that, if a child between the ages of 10 and 16 committed a serious crime, he or she could be tried and sentenced as an adult. Serious crimes included arson that caused death, assault and robbery with a dangerous weapon, assault and robbery causing bodily injury, aggravated assault, murder, manslaughter, kidnapping, maiming, sexual assault, and burglary of occupied residences (Meyer, 1985). Furthermore, for the crime of murder, there was no age limit at all. The new law was a radical departure from the previous provisions, which stated that no Vermont juvenile under the age of 16 could be tried for anything but delinquency.

If children who commit aggravated murder are tried as adults, can they be sentenced to death if they are found guilty? The Supreme Court has drawn a line between the ages of 15 and 16 as far as the constitutionality of death sentences is concerned. In the 1988 case of *Thompson* v. *Oklahoma*, the Court ruled that the Eighth Amendment to the U.S. Constitution prohibited the execution of a person who was under the age of 16 at the time of the offense. One year later, in the companion cases of *Stanford* v. *Kentucky* and *Wilkins* v. *Missouri*, the Court decided that executions of juveniles for crimes committed at 16 or 17 were legal. Age 16 is now the constitutional age of responsibility for purposes of capital punishment. Of the more than 2000 people on death row in mid-1989, 27 had committed murders when they were as young as 16.

RIGHTS OF MENTAL PATIENTS

All 50 states and the District of Columbia have laws that authorize the custody and restraint of persons who, as a result of mental illness, are a danger to themselves or others or who are so gravely disabled that they cannot care for themselves. This restraint is usually accomplished by compulsory commitment to a mental hospital. The courts also provide rules and safeguards for how these involuntary commitments are to be accomplished.

Many of these procedures were instituted in the last 20 years, in response to a feeling that, in the 1950s and 1960s, it was too easy to commit people to state psychiatric facilities. At that time, persons who were mentally ill could be involuntarily committed whenever the state believed they needed treatment. Beginning around 1970, commitment proceedings began to be reformed, resulting in more legal rights for the mentally ill to resist compulsory commitment. The standard for commitment changed from mere mental illness to mental illness that was associated with dangerousness or grave lack of ability to care for oneself. Ironically, today many people believe "it's too hard to get people in and much too easy

to get them out" of mental hospitals (Riechmann, 1985, p. 6). Mental health activists and patients' families feel that patients are often "dumped," without concern for their fate on the outside. Some of these people end up in the courts and jails after being on the streets (Teplin, 1984b). Although the legislative changes of the 1970s were intended to protect the rights of the mentally ill, an exclusive concern with rights can sometimes leave patients without adequate care, housing, or the effective psychiatric treatment that can be provided in some hospitals (Turkheimer & Parry, 1992; Wexler, 1992).

Three Types of Commitment Procedures

The laws permit three types of commitment: (1) commitment without a court order, (2) commitment by court order, and (3) outpatient commitment.

Commitment without a court order is the means by which most mental patients are initially admitted to hospitals (Ennis & Siegel, 1973); that is, detention is permitted under emergency or temporary commitment statutes. A police officer, a mental health professional, or sometimes any citizen can initiate involuntary detention of another person. Usually the cause is actual or anticipated harmful behavior by the patient— either against self (for example, attempted suicide) or against others. The examination is performed by a physician or a qualified mental health professional. A few states require approval by a judge before emergency detention can be implemented. But usually the decision is left in the hands of professionals; judges defer to their expertise, because the goal is to protect individuals incapable of taking care of themselves (Hiday & Suval, 1984).

On admission, patients are read their rights, much as criminal suspects are read their rights from a *Miranda* card (H. Goodman, 1982). Patients committed on an emergency basis are told that they can be detained for only a specified length of time, before a review takes place. This duration varies widely, from 24 hours in Texas to 20 days in New Jersey. Then a preliminary hearing must be held before the patient can be confined any longer.

Of course, a person may volunteer to enter a mental institution. But, while there, the patient may find that the hospital has instigated commitment proceedings to challenge or delay his or her release. Schwitzgebel and Schwitzgebel (1980) note: "In actual practice, 'voluntary' admission is seldom as benign as the formalities make it appear. Usually there is considerable pressure from relatives, civil authorities, and mental health personnel who are becoming worried or angry about a person's deviant behavior" (p. 8). A research program by David Rosenhan (1973), described in Box 17-5, illustrates the tendency for patients, once committed to the hospital, to be seen as deserving to be there, whether they really are or not.

The second type of commitment is through court order. The criteria necessary to obtain a formal civil commitment vary from state to state; in general, however, the person must be mentally ill and fulfill both of the following:

1. Be dangerous to self and others or so gravely disabled as to be unable to provide for his or her own basic needs.
2. Need treatment that is available in a setting no less restrictive than a hospital.

Although the criterion of "dangerousness" is the most often discussed standard and therefore is deemed the most important criterion for involuntary hospitalization, grave disability ap-

---

Box **17-5** | *Perpetuating Mistaken Diagnoses in the Mental Hospital*

In 1973 David Rosenhan tested the ability of psychiatric-hospital staff members to distinguish "normal" from "insane" behaviors. He and seven other normal persons gained admission to hospitals (in five states on both the East and West coasts) by complaining of hearing voices that repeated the word *one*. The pseudopatients were a psychology graduate student, three psychologists, a pediatrician, a psychiatrist, a painter, and a homemaker—three women and five men.

Seven were diagnosed as schizophrenic and one as manic-depressive. Immediately after being admitted, the pseudopatients stopped saying they heard voices. They gave false names and employment data, but otherwise they responded honestly to questions about their lives and tried to interact normally with the staff. It became apparent to them that a psychiatric label, once attached, distorted the staff's interpretations of patients' behavior. For example, the pseudopatients had been told to keep detailed notes about life in the wards. Members of the staff, in observing this behavior, concluded that they were obsessive-compulsive.

None of the pseudopatients was detected as such by the staff of any of the hospitals. In fact, the only ones who sometimes recognized the pseudopatients as normal were other patients. But the pseudopatients were eventually released. The hospital stays averaged 19 days, with a range of 7 days to 52 days. Each of the pseudopatients who had been diagnosed as schizophrenic was eventually discharged with the label of "schizophrenia in remission." Thus the diagnostic label stuck, despite changes in behavior.

pears to be the standard that determines most commitments (Turkheimer & Parry, 1992).

For a court order to be obtained, the concerned persons must petition the court for a professional examination of the supposedly ill person. A formal court hearing usually follows the examination. In most states the hearing is mandatory, and persons whose commitment is sought can call witnesses and have their lawyer cross-examine witnesses who testify against them.

In recent years a third type of commitment procedure, known as *outpatient commitment,* has been attempted. This procedure, which is available in almost all states, allows the state to commit a patient to mandatory treatment in an outpatient setting, such as a community mental health center, rather than in a hospital (Hiday & Goodman, 1982). Outpatient commitments often constitute conditional releases from a hospital; that is, formerly hospitalized patients are ordered to continue treatment in the community. There are several legal and clinical complications with this approach. For example, what should be done with patients who refuse medication? Are therapists treating these patients liable for any dangerous acts they might commit? And, most important, is effective, community-based treatment available?

Dangerousness

Dangerousness is one of the central constructs of mental health law. Determining whether a person is now or could in the future be dangerous is a question that underlies many decisions in our system of justice. For our purposes, we define dangerousness as involving acts of physical violence or aggression by one person against another; verbal threats and destruction of property are not included in this definition.

Dangerousness is a major justification for involuntarily committing the mentally ill to hospitals. As we saw in Chapter 2 when we discussed the *Tarasoff* case, dangerousness is the basis for requiring therapists to protect third parties from possible acts of violence against them by the patients of these therapists. In Chapter 16 we learned that dangerousness is the justification for hospitalizing defendants after they have been found not guilty by reason of insanity. Chapter 10 identified dangerousness as a reason why bail could be denied to certain defendants. And, as you will learn in Chapter 18, some states use future dangerousness as one factor a jury can consider when deciding whether to sentence a convicted murderer to life in prison or death by execution.

Difficulties in Assessing Dangerousness

Can mental health experts accurately assess a person's present dangerousness and then predict whether that person will be dangerous in the future? Is mental illness a sign that a person will be dangerous? Do certain types of mental illness make a person more prone to dangerous conduct? These questions have been examined extensively by researchers for more than three decades, and they are at the heart of many real-life cases. For example, should the mental health professionals who treated John Hinckley in the past have predicted that he posed a danger to President Reagan? What about Jeffrey Dahmer? Was his brutal behavior predictable, given his early psychological problems?

The consensus of researchers has been that mental illness is not linked to a risk of violence. Moreover, leading scholars like John Monahan of the University of Virginia have traditionally concluded that clinicians cannot predict future dangerousness with any acceptable degree of accuracy. The following summary of this research is typical: "In one study after another, the same conclusion emerges: for every correct prediction of violence, there are numerous incorrect predictions" (Pfohl, 1984). Another common summary of the research on clinicians' ability to predict dangerousness is that these predictions are wrong in two out of every three cases.

Many factors work together to lower the accuracy of predictions of dangerousness. The base rate of dangerous behavior is generally very low, so clinicians are being asked to predict a phenomenon that rarely occurs. The clinical assessments of persons suspected of being dangerous are usually conducted in hospitals or prisons, whereas the environment where dangerousness is likely to occur is "on the streets." The predictions have often been for long-term dangerousness, which is harder to predict than dangerousness over a shorter time frame (e.g., two weeks). As a result of these and other difficulties, mental health professionals have yet to prove that they have any special ability beyond that of the average person to predict future violence (Litwack & Schlesinger, 1987).

However, if we examine clinicians' ability to predict dangerous behavior on a short-term basis, particularly when they are familiar with whether a person has a history of prior violence or has stated an intention to behave violently, we find that predictions can be made more accurately (Klassen & O'Connor, 1988). Thus, reasonable accuracy in predictions can be expected under the following conditions: (1) the predictions are for the short-term future; (2) they are made for environmental settings for which the clinician has data about the person's past behavior; (3) they are based on a knowledge of the person's history of past violent behavior; and (4) they are made for individuals belonging to groups with relatively high base rates of violence (Litwack & Schlesinger, 1987; Monahan, 1984).

As accustomed as psychologists have become to claiming that mental illness and violence are not associated, recent evidence suggests that this opinion may, in fact, be wrong. Monahan himself has revised his stance on this issue. Whereas he once dismissed any link between mental illness and violence, he now believes that a small, but reliable, connection exists. After reviewing recent studies that surveyed the prevalence of violent behavior among mentally ill people in the community and that measured levels of mental illness among violent citizens, Monahan (1992) concluded: " . . . there appears to be a relationship between mental disorder and violent behavior. Mental disorder may be a robust and significant risk factor for the occurrence of violence . . . " (p. 519).

Specific Rights of Mental Patients

As part of the increased concern with protecting the civil liberties of mentally ill and retarded persons, mental patients have been provided a number of specific rights, either by statute or by court decisions.

Youngberg v. *Romeo* (1982) involved Nicholas Romeo, a profoundly retarded 33-year-old man who was involuntarily committed to the Pennhurst (PA) State Hospital after his father died and his mother was unable to care for him. Over the next few years he was repeatedly injured, both by his own actions and by those of other patients reacting to his violence. As a consequence, he was restrained in a hospital bed. Dissatisfied with the conditions at Pennhurst, Romeo's mother filed suit, alleging that the state was violating his rights under the Due Process Clause of the Fourteenth Amendment by not keeping him in a safe environment and by not training him within his abilities. Ultimately the case reached the Supreme Court, which held that involuntarily committed patients have the following rights as a matter of Substantive Due Process under the U.S. Constitution:

- Adequate food, shelter, and clothing.
- Adequate medical care.
- A safe environment.
- Freedom from restraint, unless restraint is necessary for the protection of the patient or of others.
- Such training as may be required to ensure these rights. The Court's opinion made it clear that courts ordinarily should defer to the decisions of trained professional staff. Lower court cases since *Romeo* have held that decisions made by professionals in accord with professional standards will be upheld (*United States* v. *Charters*, 1988).

The rights listed above provide a constitutional "floor," below which a state cannot legally fall. Some federal courts (e.g., *Wyatt* v. *Stickney*, 1971) have listed other specific rights, but these specifics are not constitutionally required. In addition, most states provide certain rights by statute, among them:

- the right to an individual treatment plan, and the right to participate in the formulation of the plan;
- the right to refuse treatment (including medication), unless the treatment is necessary to protect the patient or others from harm;
- the right to receive visitors;
- the right to receive payment for work done for the hospital; and
- the right to be free from unreasonable use of seclusion and restraint [Kentucky Revised Statutes 202A.191, 1982].

When a mental patient refuses medication that a physician believes is beneficial, a fundamental question of personal autonomy is raised. Should society "help" the patient against her or his will? Should the patient be forced to take the medication? Based on concerns about the numerous side effects of many psychoactive drugs and also based on concerns about respecting patients' rights to privacy and to make autonomous decisions about their own bodies, two federal district courts—one in Massachusetts (*Rogers* v. *Okin*, 1979) and one in New Jersey (*Rennie* v. *Klein*, 1978)—held that mentally ill patients did have the right to refuse medications, even if these medications were likely to be beneficial. However, this right to refuse was held not to be absolute. A patient's desire to not be medicated could be overridden in three general situations: (1) if the patient was behaving dangerously toward self or others, (2) if the patient was so ill as to be unable to make a competent decision about treatment, or (3) if there was an emergency that, according to a physician, made forced medication necessary. In the 1990 case of *Washington* v. *Harper*, the Supreme Court held that a mentally ill prisoner could not be medicated against his will *unless* it was determined, by the application of professional standards, that the medication was necessary for safety reasons.

Moreover, the U.S. Supreme Court has refused to hold that mentally ill patients have a constitutional right to refuse all treatment. Instead, it has used a doctrine of deferring to the professional judgment of physicians who are treating the patient. In *Youngberg* v. *Romeo* the Court held that honoring the rights of patients cannot be used to unnecessarily restrict the professional judgment of treating physicians. Some states still allow patients a right to refuse treatment; but the availability of numerous ways to override a patient's refusal converts this right into more of a right to object to treatment and have the medical necessity of the treatment reviewed (Brooks, 1986). In reality, few patients refuse medication over a long period of time (Appelbaum & Hoge, 1986), and those who persistently refuse typically will have their decisions ultimately overridden (Godard, Bloom, Williams, & Faulkner, 1986).

Other Issues Involving Mentally Ill or Retarded Persons

As part of the movement in the early 1980s to "deinstitutionalize" the mentally ill and the retarded, patients were often transferred to houses in residential neighborhoods. But some cities established ordinances that required special zoning permits for such group homes; Cleburne, Texas, was one such city. In fact, it established obstacles to the creation of group homes for the "feeble-minded" (to quote the Cleburne ordinance) in neighborhoods where other multiple-person dwellings were permitted. In the case of *Cleburne Living Center, Inc. v. City of Cleburne, Texas* (1985), the Supreme Court ruled in favor of the retarded. The Court stated that cities cannot pass an ordinance requiring a special permit for a home for retarded men and women just because of community opposition and "irrational prejudice" (Melton & Garrison, 1987).

Turning from civil rights to criminal rights, the Supreme Court in 1989 considered a Texas decision to execute a murderer who was mentally retarded. Johnny Paul Penry had suffered brain damage since birth; as an adult he had an IQ of about 60, with the mental functioning of a 7-year-old (Greenhouse, 1989c). He was convicted in 1980 of raping a woman in her home and stabbing her to death; Penry was 22 when the crimes were committed. The Supreme Court ruled, in a 5-to-4 decision, that Penry's death sentence had been imposed in error because the jury had been limited by Texas law from adequately considering his intellectual deficit as a mitigating circumstance. But the majority opinion did not find that the execution of a retarded person was "categorically prohibited" by the Eighth Amendment of the U.S. Constitution. Therefore Penry could be sentenced to death again in a new proceeding. Some states, however, have passed laws forbidding the execution of a mentally retarded person.

RIGHTS OF PRISONERS

It wasn't until the 19th century that the use of prisons became widespread. Imprisonment was seen as a deterrent to criminal activity; it was considered to be more humane than whipping or other forms of corporal punishment (Rudovsky, 1973). A penitentiary, as the word implies, was intended to serve as a place for reflection in solitude, leading to repentance and redemption. But in actuality it became a vehicle for punishment.

Prison administrators had absolutely free rein to abuse their inmates as they wished. There were no "prisoners' rights"; in 1871 a judge in Virginia explicitly stated that prisoners had no more rights than did slaves (*Ruffin v. Commonwealth*, 1871). Although that opinion seemed harsh to some judges even at that time, the courts deferred to the supposed expertise and the tender mercies of prison officials and mostly maintained a "hands-off" policy, considering conditions within prisons to be off limits to their scrutiny (Bronstein, 1980).

But word began to spread about abuses—including, as Bronstein (1980, p. 20) notes, "abuses of the cruelest sort: physical brutality, gross medical neglect, the silence rules, racial discrimination, kangaroo courts for disciplinary matters, incredible tortures . . . , chain gangs, bread and water diets and worse, economic exploitation by the convict lease system . . . , along with meaningless and brutally hard work."

Slowly the policy of neglect was replaced by a judicial attitude that sought to eliminate the major abuses suffered by prisoners. Yet there remain relatively few decisions involving prisoners' rights. According to Rudovsky (1973, pp. 13–14), the courts make the following assumptions.

1. Lawful incarceration necessarily deprives prisoners of certain rights and privileges that they would enjoy in a free society.
2. Convicts do not lose all their civil rights; certain fundamental rights remain.
3. Prison officials are vested with broad discretion, and, unless constitutional or other fundamental rights are involved, the federal courts are reluctant to interfere in internal operations of prison discipline. Even as recently as 1979, the sweeping decision by the Supreme Court in the pivotal *Bell* v. *Wolfish* case has been interpreted as saying that prison management should be left to corrections officials (Singer, 1980).

Due-Process Rights

Elaboration of the first point in the preceding list comes from a consideration of the limits on normal due-process rights. It was not until 1974, in the case of *Wolff* v. *McDonnell*, that a prisoner charged with a serious disciplinary infraction was given the right to call witnesses and present documentary evidence in his or her defense at the disciplinary hearing. The court granted the prisoner no right to cross-examine witnesses, but prison officials had the discretion to permit this if they so chose. Moreover, it was held that the disciplinary committee may consider material in the inmate's file other than that which is relevant to the case (for example, the inmate's past crimes or prior conduct).

The courts have made only general statements regarding which due-process rights prisoners have. These include pallid comments like the following: facts in a prison disciplinary hearing should be "rationally determined," and the prisoner should be "afforded a reasonable opportunity to explain his actions." In the 1990 case of *Washington* v. *Harper*, the Supreme Court also held that prisoners were entitled to due-process protection against forcible administration of psychoactive medication. Only after it has been determined that the drug is medically appropriate and essential to ensuring the safety of the prisoner or the safety of others can it be administered against the will of the prisoner.

Cruel and Unusual Punishment

Like the rest of us, prisoners have the absolute right to be free from cruel and unusual punishment, under the Eighth Amendment. But it has been very difficult to persuade the courts to act when faced "with anything less than barbaric prison conditions" (Bronstein, 1980, p. 26). The courts appear to use three principal tests to determine violations of prisoners' rights to be free from cruel and unusual punishment (Rudovsky, 1973): (1) whether the punishment shocks the general conscience of a civilized society, (2) whether the punishment is unnecessarily cruel, and (3) whether the punishment goes beyond legitimate penal aims.

What conditions, then, amount to "cruel and unusual punishment"? In an Arkansas case the courts concluded that these conditions exist whenever prison officials cannot protect convicts from being seriously injured, sexually assaulted, or killed while in prison. More recently, focus has been on the totality of conditions in the prison. In a Pennsylvania case the courts ruled that general conditions could be so cumulative in their effect that they qualify as "cruel and unusual punishment"—overcrowdedness, wet and rat-infested cells, insufficient medical treatment, and random beatings by guards. Solitary confinement, in and of itself, is not "cruel and unusual"; nor is the deprivation of opportunities for sexual intercourse. However, prison guards are not allowed to use excessive force to hurt prisoners; the Supreme Court ruled in *Hudson* v. *McMillian* (1992) that to do so violates the Eighth Amendment's ban against cruel and unusual punishment. In an Alabama case, the court also labeled as cruel and unusual punishment any "prison conditions [that] are so debilitating that they necessarily deprive inmates of any opportunity to rehabilitate themselves or even maintain skills already possessed" (quoted in Bronstein, 1980, p. 27).

Rights to Free Communication

The law is unclear on whether prisoners have rights to free communication. The greatest degree of freedom involves correspondence with the courts, counsel, and government officials. But most prisons continue to screen and sometimes censor all outgoing and incoming mail. The Supreme Court has approved regulations of the Federal Bureau of Prisons that permit wardens to censor publications that "may lead to the use of physical violence" or that contain explicit homosexual material (Greenhouse, 1989b). Courts have also ruled that incoming mail can be inspected for drugs, weapons, and contraband.

Yet the courts have ruled that prisons cannot censor outgoing mail just because it criticizes prison conditions or contains factually inaccurate statements. In addition, the prison has no right to "protect" the public from vulgar or insulting letters from convicts. And prisoners must be told which letters written to them were kept from them.

However, prisoners cannot write to "just anybody." Usually there is an approved list of correspondents for each prisoner. A Rhode Island court decision that greatly expanded prisoners' rights to free communication at the same time upheld a prison regulation that limited correspondence (aside from mail to attorneys, religious figures, and government officials) to one letter per day. A Virginia court ruled that correspondence between prisoners in different institutions in the same prison system may be prohibited (*Laurence* v. *Davis*, 1975). Suits challenging these rulings have been successful only when the courts have agreed to apply the judicial test of "clear and present danger"—that is, would prison discipline or security be threatened if prisoners were allowed to possess the material in question?

An inmate's right to communicate by mail is especially important because the Supreme Court, in several decisions, has ruled that prison officials may bar interviews between convicts and the media. In fact, in 1989 the Court said that prison officials are not required to explain why they bar an inmate from having any visitors.

Religious Rights

Citizens in the United States are guaranteed free exercise of their religious beliefs. But prisoners experience restrictions even with regard to the most widely practiced religions. If religious exercises could disrupt security, safety, or prison discipline, the courts have upheld limitations on them. (Generally, though, traditional religious exercises are allowed.)

The courts have consistently supported the religious rights of Black Muslim prisoners. However, some literature—for example, the *Muhammad Speaks* newspaper or Elijah Muhammad's book—has been restricted by some prison officials, who claim a clear and present danger of breach of prison security or discipline. The dietary restrictions of Muslims have not always been honored.

Other Rights

The courts have consistently condemned racial segregation and discrimination, but, in special situations in which violence appears imminent, they have allowed temporary separation of the races.

The essential political rights secured by the First Amendment—free speech, association, assembly, and belief—have been granted little breathing space in prison (Bronstein, 1980). The very nature of imprisonment, it is claimed, justifies such restrictions. Rights to privacy and freedom to dress as one wishes are also restricted. Prisoners may be searched at any time, although the courts discourage arbitrary and capricious searches. A few of the regulations against long hair, beards, and mustaches have been relaxed. For example, for Native Americans, religious principles can take precedence over rules that require haircuts. Rigid requirements with regard to uniform appearance have generally been defended by prison officials as necessary health and safety precautions, but they also deprive prisoners of their sense of identity and serve to enforce regimentation in the prison (Bronstein, 1980).

SUMMARY

Certain groups in our society deserve special rights or protections. For centuries, children were treated simply as the property of their parents. During the last two decades, the separable rights of children have been scrutinized. Two conceptions of children's rights can be distinguished: the nurturance orientation stresses children's right to be provided benefits by society; the self-determination orientation emphasizes children's freedom to make their own choices. Measurements of attitudes toward these two conceptions show that they are independent of each other. A person may advocate only one type of "children's rights," both, or neither.

In a divorce, a judge must rule on the custody of minor children. Recently "the best interests of the child" have come to the forefront in custody decisions. Many states have implemented joint-custody arrangements; however, psychological evaluations of these arrangements indicate that the form of custody may not be as important for the child's adjustment as the level of conflict that persists between the divorced parents, regardless of who is awarded custody.

When children have been called to be witnesses in court, there has been great concern about their potential for inaccuracy. Recent psychological research suggests that children's ability to remember is better than assumed, as long as the task does not require complex organizational skills. Another reason for denying children the right to testify is the fear that it will add to whatever trauma they experienced as victims of or witnesses to violent crimes. Some states have adopted laws that permit the closed-circuit one-way televising of the testimony in private settings or the shielding of the child witness from the defendant.

Children are not only victims but are sometimes offenders. In the early 1900s, the legal system developed special juvenile courts in order to decriminalize the behaviors of juvenile lawbreakers. These courts embodied a desire to rehabilitate rather than punish; they employed probation officers to make home visits. But the juvenile court procedure collapsed under the weight of its task and changing conceptions about the nature of children.

More recently, diversion programs have been developed to provide juvenile offenders with necessary counseling services while keeping them free of the criminal justice system's usual procedures. Program evaluation indicates that this innovation has produced mostly disappointing outcomes and has had the unexpected effect of "widening the net" in the sense of bringing under state control a group of juveniles who otherwise would have been ignored.

Increasingly, states are responding to juvenile crime by treating children as adults in the legal system. Vermont lowered to 10 the age at which a child charged with a serious crime can be tried and sentenced as an adult. The Supreme Court has approved "preventive detention" of juvenile defendants. It also established age 16 as the lower limit for the death penalty.

Persons who are considered gravely disabled or dangerous to themselves or others can be temporarily committed to a state mental hospital against their will, but they have the right to a hearing shortly thereafter to determine whether they should be retained. After being hospitalized, some patients may continue on a form of commitment known as outpatient commitment. Long-term predictions of dangerousness cannot be made with any acceptable degree of accuracy, but there is a moderate association between mental illness and dangerous behavior.

Patients in state mental hospitals have the right to individualized treatment, a limited right to refuse medication, and rights regarding their personal activities and behavior.

In two recent decisions, the Supreme Court has made more explicit the rights of mentally retarded persons who are under the supervision of the state. First, those in public institutions have rights to personal safety and freedom from bodily restraints and to training to develop needed skills. Second, a city may not prevent the establishment of group homes (residences for small numbers of the retarded) in neighborhoods where other multiple-person dwellings exist (such as nursing homes or fraternity houses).

Convicted prisoners have fewer rights than other institutionalized persons. The courts have more or less assumed that their incarceration deprives them of certain rights. They do retain some rights to due process, the right to avoid "cruel and unusual punishment," and the right to express religious beliefs. But they may be searched at any time, their mail may be opened and curtailed, and their preferences in dress and grooming may be denied.

18

Punishment and Sentencing

As noted in Chapter 5, no other industrialized country has violent crime rates comparable to those of the United States. What can be done about crime? How should we respond to individual criminals? At present, state and federal prisons in the United States contain almost 700,000 convicted lawbreakers, and another 400,000 are confined in local jails. The rate at which the United States incarcerates criminals has doubled in just the past ten years. Is more imprisonment the solution to America's crime problem?

RESPONSES TO CRIME: THE ISSUE OF CRIME CONTROL

Chapter 1 described Packer's (1964) two models of the criminal justice system: the due-process model and the crime-control model. These models differ in their views of punishment. The crime-control model, which Packer believes has dominated the thinking of police officers, prosecutors, and many judges, sees the sole aim of law enforcement to be the apprehension and punishment of criminals. Its major purpose is to punish offenders so that they will not repeat the offense and so that others will be deterred from similar acts.

Punishment of criminals, whether by community supervision, fines, or imprisonment, can have several purposes. At least seven different goals have been identified (see, e.g., Greenberg & Ruback, 1984):

1. *General deterrence.* The punishment of one offender and the publicity given to it are assumed to discourage other potential lawbreakers. Some advocates of the death penalty, for example, believe that fear of death may be our strongest motivation; hence the death penalty should serve the function of general deterrence of severe crime.

2. *Individual deterrence.* Punishment of the offender is assumed to keep that person from committing other crimes in the future. Some theories assume that criminals lack internal inhibitors; hence, punitive sanctions must be used to teach offenders that their behavior will be controlled—if not by them, then by society.

3. *Incapacitation.* If a convicted offender is sent to prison, society can feel safe and confident while the felon is confined there. One influential position (Wilson, 1975) sees incapacitation as functioning to age the criminal—a desirable goal, given that many more crimes are committed by the young than by the old and that the rate of offending declines as offenders grow older.

4. *Retribution.* Society believes that offenders should not benefit from their crimes; rather, they should receive their "just deserts." This is the moral cornerstone of punishment: that it should be delivered to people who deserve it as a consequence of their misdeeds.

5. *Moral outrage.* Punishment has the effect of giving society a means of catharsis and relief from the feelings of frustration, hurt, loss, and anger that result from being victims of crime; what emerges is a sense of satisfaction that offenders have paid for what they have done to others.

6. *Rehabilitation.* One hope in sentencing has always been that offenders will recognize the error of their ways and develop new skills, values, and lifestyles so that they can return to normal life and become law abiding. Rehabilitation as a goal received a boost from an influential book by the psychiatrist Karl Menninger (1966), *The Crime of Punishment*, which proposed that criminals are capable of change if they are placed in humane prisons. However, the data generally tend to indicate that most

attempts at correctional rehabilitation have not been very effective.

7. *Restitution.* Wrongdoers should compensate victims for their damages and losses. Typical statutes now require the judge, in imposing a sentence, to consider requiring defendants to pay for victims' out-of-pocket expenses, property damage, and other monetary losses. Restitution is often a condition of probation.

Ironically, despite the original purpose of prisons as vehicles for rehabilitation and despite the variety of goals they more recently have been expected to accomplish, most prisons are of one type, called "punitive/custodial" (Cressey, 1965). As detailed in Chapter 17, they deny prisoners certain rights and many comforts and hence are punitive. Authority is centralized, communication is formalized, and rules are strictly maintained. (In contrast, only a few prisons embody qualities of Cressey's other type, the treatment-oriented prison.) A further irony is that the original purpose of prisons included the goal of creating a controlled environment that would separate the offender from corrupting influences of the real world. In fact, prisons often present inmates with enriched opportunities to learn new criminal behaviors and attitudes from one another. Given this state of affairs, it is worthwhile to examine the processes that occur after a lawbreaker has been convicted of a crime, to understand the assumptions behind the system of assigning punishments.

SENTENCING: IMPOSSIBLE CHOICES

The sentencing of a convicted criminal lies at the very center of society's efforts to ensure public order. The sentence serves the functions of both punishment and deterrence. The fine paid and/or the time served, in the best of worlds, may facilitate rehabilitation; but even if rehabilitation does not occur, society will have one fewer lawbreaker to worry about for the duration of any prison sentence that is ordered. Hoffman and Stone-Meierhoefer go so far as to state: "Next to the determination of guilt or innocence, a determination waived by a substantial proportion of defendants who plead guilty (around 90%), the sentencing decision is probably the most important decision made about the criminal defendant in the entire process" (1979, p. 241).

The irreconcilable dilemmas introduced at the beginning of this book are reflected in the sentencing process. In many jurisdictions the judge has vast discretion to determine both the type of punishment and its duration. Until recently, for any particular crime, federal judges could "impose a fine, a period of probation, a suspended sentence, any period of imprisonment up to the statutory maximum for the offense, or some combination of the above" (Hoffman & Stone-Meierhoefer, 1979, p. 241). Judges can employ all kinds of innovative punishments; some of these are illustrated in Box 18-1.

Discretion Justified as a Value

Discretion allows judges to capitalize on their perceptions of the crime, the criminal, and the circumstances so that their decisions can "serve, within limits set by law, that elusive concept of justice which the law in its wisdom refuses to define" (Gaylin, 1974, p. 67). The enormous individual differences in crimes, criminals, and circumstances justify individually tailored sentences for each case. Some judges become known for their tough sentences. In Dade County, Florida, Circuit Judge Ellen J. Morphonios is known as "Maximum Morphonios." After sentencing one offender to

1698 years—the maximum possible based on his many, many violations, including armed robbery—she told him not to worry, that he probably wouldn't serve even half that time.

In a highly publicized trial in 1985, three top officials of Film Recovery Systems, Inc., of Elk Grove Village, Illinois, were found guilty of causing the death of an employee who had died two years earlier after inhaling poisonous cyanide fumes inside the firm's plant. At the trial, the prosecution presented testimony that the three employers had not provided warnings of the dangers; on the contrary, some skull-and-crossbones warning signs had been scraped off the cyanide drums, apparently at the instructions of the defendants. The outcome of this trial was noteworthy because the prosecution brought murder charges against the three plant managers, and the jury found them guilty of that crime, rather than of manslaughter, the expected verdict. Given that the defendants were convicted of murder, the judge sentenced them to prison terms of 25 years each: "All the defendants are going to pay for it harshly," said Judge Ronald J. B. Banks as he announced the sentences. The defendants' attorney called the punishment "outrageous," but it illustrates the degree of discretion given to judges.

But judicial discretion can also result in leniency. It is people's perception of "discretion" that has made it one of the main targets of the conservative movement's intensive efforts to tighten and toughen sentencing standards. One New York State judge, Bruce Wright, has been nicknamed "Turn 'Em Loose Bruce" because of his bail setting of suspects. Here are some other recent examples of what appear to be lenient or inconsistent sentences:

Box **18-1** | *Innovative Sentences: Clever, Cute, or Cruel?*

Local and municipal judges still have wide discretion in the punishments they give. Here are some examples of innovative punishments:

1. A judge in Sarasota County, Florida, has required drunk drivers to place a bumper sticker saying "Convicted DUI" on their cars if they wish to drive the cars to work.
2. A circuit court judge in South Dakota sentenced convicted cattle rustlers to shovel manure for a week.
3. A construction manager who was an avid golfer was convicted of diverting $300,000 in materi-al and labor from a California building project in order to build a house near the famous Pebble Beach golf course. The judge ruled that for nine months he had to go to a busy public golf course and schedule tee-off times for other golfers. He was not allowed to play himself and was incarcerated except during working hours (Neff, 1987).
4. "David Wayte of Whittier, California, was ordered to spend six months at his grandmother's home for failing to register for the draft. The judge decided on probation and house arrest to *prevent* Wayte from doing public service, noting that he was already a volunteer at a school for the disabled and at a soup kitchen and shelter for the homeless. 'I'm punishing you by *not* allowing you to perform such service,' the judge explained" (Miller, 1987, p. 2).
5. The punishment that dentist Michael Koplik received for sexually abusing a heavily sedated female patient was to provide free treatment for six AIDS patients who had been rejected by other dentists (Sachs, 1989).

In Grand Rapids, Michigan, a man shot his ex-wife (a local judge) to death in the corridor outside her office and then exchanged gunfire with two police officers. Neither the police officers nor the man was injured, and the man surrendered. He was later found guilty of "provocation manslaughter" (not murder) of his ex-wife and attempted murder of the policemen. For the killing of the judge he received a sentence of 10 to 15 years, whereas his shooting at the police without harming them led to two *life terms* (Warren, 1989).

In another example, James J. Kilpatrick (1983), a conservative newspaper columnist, criticized what he called "an appalling decision by a softhearted federal judge in Los Angeles" (p. A-21). A mob boss convicted of extortion was given only a one-year sentence, in a community correctional unit. Even with that, the judge gave the convicted felon his freedom during daylight hours; he had to spend only his evenings restricted within the walls of the community center.

According to public opinion polls, most Americans believe that judges are too lenient in their sentencing of convicted criminals (Flanagan, McGarrell, & Brown, 1985). But the polls may not tell the whole story. When asked to recommend sentences for specific cases after they have learned some details about the crime and the offender, laypersons actually prefer sentences that are sometimes more lenient than the required minimum sentences for certain crimes (Diamond & Stalans, 1989; Stalans & Diamond, 1990). This discrepancy between general perceptions and specific sentencing preferences may be due to the fact that, when asked about sentences in general, the public typically imagines crimes and criminals that are much more severe and dangerous than the cases that are actually prosecuted.

A 1988 survey carried out by the Bureau of Justice Statistics found that, of offenders convicted of serious felonies (including murder, rape, robbery, aggravated assault, drug crimes, and burglary), 69% were incarcerated, 30% were placed on probation, and 1% received some other type of sentence. Incarceration rates were highest for defendants convicted of murder (95%), robbery (89%), and rape (86%). Public attitudes may account for some of the accelerated growth in imprisonment in the United States. As of 1990 the rate at which this country incarcerates its criminals is about 455 inmates per 100,000 population, double the incarceration rate of 1980 and triple the rate of 1970.

Sentencing Disparity and the Quest for Equal Treatment

Sentencing disparity is the label that critics use to condemn the practice of sentencing similar defendants in a dissimilar fashion. Disparity occurs as a by-product of the desire to individualize sentences. The predominant sentencing guidelines in the 1970s and early 1980s, which had been set up to allow very individualized sentences, provided little guidance to judges on exactly which defendants should be fined, which should be given probation, and which should be given short or long sentences. As a result, judges were free to use wide personal discretion in their sentencing of defendants. The inevitable result was disparate sentences.

Many critics consider *equality* to be a more desirable aspiration for allocation of punishments. Equality as a guideline not only restricts the tender-hearted judge, it checks the merciless one as well. It also reinforces our society's long tradition of equal treatment by the law.

Truth versus Conflict Resolution in the Sentencing Process

The dilemma between truth and conflict resolution as goals of society, (introduced in Chapter 1) is also manifested by decisions to distribute punishments. Truth as a value is exemplified in every sentencing decision that reflects a thorough examination of all relevant facts and conditions. An ideal is that every sentence be the most appropriate one for everybody involved. But searching for a "truthful" (that is, valid) punishment takes time and energy—and often more of these than the system can provide. Pressure results from the many decisions that must be made; if thorough consideration causes delays (as it often will), a backlog will emerge, and everyone—including unsentenced criminals—will suffer. So it is important to make sure that the system moves forward efficiently in achieving its goal of processing cases.

Furthermore, financial considerations often obstruct fair or "truthful" sentences, and compromises have to emerge. Most prisons are already overcrowded; construction of new facilities is too costly to pass the approval of many state legislatures. Assuming that approximately 700,000 inmates are incarcerated in federal and state prisons and that the total federal and state expenditures for corrections are about $14 billion per year, we can calculate that the annual cost of incarcerating one inmate, as of the early 1990s, has reached approximately $20,000. Citizens' support for more and longer prison sentences may erode when they realize how much they will have to pay for them.

In a 1989 public opinion study by the Public Agenda Foundation (Doble & Klein, 1989), the researchers found that citizens, after being informed about prison costs and alternative sentences, changed their views of imprisonment as the only adequate punishment for crime. The researchers selected a cross-section of 422 Alabama residents and had them complete a detailed questionnaire, indicating their preferred "sentences"—either prison or probation—in 23 hypothetical cases ranging from shoplifting to rape and armed robbery. The participants then watched a brief videotape that discussed prison costs and overcrowding in Alabama and presented five alternatives to incarceration: strict probation, strict probation plus restitution, strict probation plus community service, house arrest, and "boot camp." The video presented arguments for and against these alternatives.

After watching the video, participants convened in groups to discuss how the alternatives would work for various types of offenders. The subjects then filled out a second questionnaire for the 23 hypothetical cases, selecting sentences from the original two options (probation and prison) and the five "alternative sentences." Attitudes had changed dramatically. On the initial questionnaire a majority of participants would have sent 18 of the 23 defendants to prison; after the video and discussion, they would have sentenced only 4 of the 23 to prison. However, after learning of the alternatives, respondents would have imposed restrictions greater than straight probation on 18 of the 19 defendants not sent to prison. The participants favored sentences that required defendants to take active responsibility for their actions; thus, restitution and community service were preferred over house arrest or strict probation.

DETERMINANTS OF SENTENCING—RELEVANT AND IRRELEVANT

Punishment, to be morally acceptable, should be consistent with the seriousness of the crime. And, in the most general sense, this consistency occurs: graver crimes earn harsher punishments. But there is still much "error" in the system; in statistical terms, the relationship between seriousness of crime and severity of punishment shows a positive correlation but not an extremely high one.

Factors other than seriousness of crime influence sentencing. Should they? What is relevant and what is irrelevant in determining punishment? Should we take into account a criminal's past history—the fact that he was deprived as a child, always hungry, abused, and denied opportunities to go to school or to look for work? Or a criminal's past record? Her age? Her appearance? It should be irrelevant whether a defendant convicted of burglary is a man or a woman (Dane & Wrightsman, 1982), but Nagel (1969) found sentences to be more lenient for women than for men when the crime was grand larceny or burglary.

A survey of the sentences of more than 10,500 felony defendants in Los Angeles found that male judges gave more lenient punishments to women than to men, especially when the defendants were nonwhite (Associated Press, 1984). Even though women plead guilty and are convicted at about the same rate as men, they are more likely to receive suspended sentences and less likely to be incarcerated. "Judges . . . treat women more leniently than men because they do not want to subject the supposedly physically weaker sex to the harsh conditions of prison," concluded the authors of the survey, John Gruhel, Susan Welch, and Cassia Spohn, political scientists at the University of Nebraska (quoted by Associated Press, 1984). Judges apparently also give women offenders lighter punishments because they assume that many women are the sole care providers of young children and that placing them in jail may leave the children homeless. However, when we control for other factors, such the offender's past criminal record and the seriousness of the crime, a good deal of the leniency toward women disappears.

What about characteristics of the victim, including the victim's race? Green (1961) found

that black offenders with black victims got the mildest penalties, with half as many penitentiary sentences and four times the number of probations as either black/white or white/white offender/victim combinations. In Georgia a 1989 *Atlanta Journal-Constitution* study concluded that, throughout two-thirds of Georgia, black men were at least twice as likely to go to jail as whites convicted of the same offense (Anderson, 1990). We will consider the race of the victim again later in this chapter, in the section on the death penalty.

Straightforward demographic characteristics such as the race or socioeconomic status of the victim often show inconsistent relationships with severity of sentence. But these influences should not be cavalierly disregarded; as Dane and Wrightsman (1982) note, their effects are often indirect but real. For example, special characteristics of the victim may create anger toward the offender or sympathy toward the victim. Austin, Walster, and Utne (1976) found that more suffering by the victim led to more severe sentences. Related findings are reported in Box 18-2.

DISPARITIES IN JUDGES' SENTENCES

As indicated earlier, the majority of sentencing decisions are made by judges. It has always been assumed that judges will reflect the values of the society they represent. Likewise, it has been assumed that, when a judge's "values differ from those defined by law, he (or she) would, as a judge, serve the interests of the law over his personal interests" (Gaylin, 1974, p. 7). But to do so may generate great internal conflict and stress (Watson, 1989). Do judges conform to the requirements of the law, or do their own values enter in? One way to approach this question is to determine how serious the problem is. What is the extent of disparity in sentences for the same crime given by different judges?

Some findings lead us to conclude that by the early 1970s the disparity in sentencing had reached an appalling extreme. Variations in sentencing practices among the states are inevitable because the 50 state legislatures will view certain crimes differently. For example, the mandatory minimum jail sentence for a person convicted of a third drunk-driving offense in Indiana is 5 days; the same offense committed in Utah carries a mandatory minimum sentence of 720 days (Maguire & Flanagan, 1991). Variations occur even within the same state. Lunden (1957) found one judge in Iowa who gave ten times more suspended sentences than did his colleagues. Judge Marvin Frankel has written

---

Box 18-2 | Should the Age of the Victim Affect the Crime Sentence?

The same crime is committed in the same state at the same time, except that in one instance the victim is a child and in the other, an adult. Should the convicted criminals receive the same sentences?

According to a Department of Justice study, people who commit crimes against children go to prison less often and for shorter terms than other criminals, even though they are convicted more frequently for those crimes. Only 8% of people arrested for child-related felonies were sentenced to prison for more than a year, whereas 12% of those arrested for similar crimes involving adults were.

The differences were most extreme in sex offense cases, in which 65% of those arrested for sexual assaults against children were convicted, compared with 54% of those arrested for sexual assaults against adults. But, despite the higher conviction rate, only 13% of the child-related charges brought prison terms of more than a year, whereas 17% of the other sexual assaults did. The study was based on data on sentences over a period of two years (1981 and 1982) in four states (California, New York, Ohio, and Pennsylvania).

It is unclear whether the differences in outcome are a result of differences in the relationships between offenders and victims, differences in the severity of crimes against children and adults, or other factors. But it is possible that a double standard exists in sentencing.

The percentages for the dispositions of the types of cases, based on age of the victim, are shown in the table below.

Outcomes for Persons Charged with Crimes against Children and Crimes against Adults (percentages)

	Prosecuted (%)	Convicted (%)	Convicted but no prison sentence (suspended sentence or probation) (%)	Prison sentence of 1 year or more (%)
Charged with a crime against a child	93	64	40	8
Charged with a similar crime, victim of any age	90	57	26	12

that the situation as it once existed was "a wild array of sentencing judgments without any semblance of the consistency demanded by the ideal of equal justice" (1972, p. 5).

Are claims of unfair sentencing justified? Science, as a way of gaining knowledge, can help answer this question by comparing different judges' reactions to the same case. Austin and Williams (1977) asked Virginia district court judges attending an educational workshop to respond to the same hypothetical cases by recommending a verdict and sentence. For example, in one case the judges read:

> Debbie Jones, 18 years of age, appears in court. She was apprehended with her boyfriend in the apartment of an acquaintance of theirs. There were seven boys and girls present. Seven roaches, or butts, were found, none in Debbie's hands, and ten unused marijuana cigarettes were found in a paper bag on the coffee table.
>
> Debbie is charged with "Possession of Marijuana." Is she guilty or not guilty? As charged or what?
>
> Debbie has no previous record. She attends high school regularly as a senior. She does not appear particularly apologetic for her alleged use of marijuana, but neither does she appear rebellious against the "establishment." Her father, in court with her, is branch manager of a national manufacturer of duplicating equipment.
>
> Punishment?

Judges' reactions on this case varied greatly, as the following summary shows:

Verdicts:
Not guilty: 29 judges
Guilty: 18 judges

Sentences (based on the 18 judges ruling "guilty"):
Probation: 8 judges
Fine: 4 judges
Fine plus probation: 3 judges
Jail term: 3 judges

The lack of consensus on both the verdict and the sentence is apparent. It is paradoxical that the data for this striking illustration of sentencing disparity were gathered at a judicial workshop "designed, among other things, as a forum for judges and 'experts' to discuss the complexities of sentencing because a number of observers have called for such workshops as one way to reduce sentencing disparity" (Austin & Utne, 1977, pp. 173–174).

Sometimes differences in sentencing are justified on the ground that they reflect the norms and feelings of the community. A humorous example is provided by Judge Edward Lumbard:

> A visitor to a Texas court was amazed to hear the judge impose a suspended sentence where a man has pleaded guilty to manslaughter. A few minutes later the same judge sentenced a man who pleaded guilty to stealing a horse and gave him life imprisonment. When the judge was asked about the disparity of the two sentences, he replied, "Well, down here there is some men who need killin', but there ain't no horses that need stealin'!" [quoted in Gaylin, 1974, p. 8].

POSSIBLE SOURCES OF BIAS IN JUDGES

Judges are human. When latitude exists in the punishments they may give, their backgrounds and personal characteristics may influence their decisions (Hogarth, 1971). They may possess prejudices for or against certain groups—racial minorities, war resisters, homosexuals. A Dallas judge told a reporter that he was giving a lighter sentence to a murderer because the victims were "queers." A judge in Jackson County, Missouri, said in court that he would like to shoot people who vandalize automobiles "in the head . . . [so] they can't testify" (Blakeman, 1988, p. A1). Both judges later apologized; the Dallas judge was censured by the Texas State Commission on Judicial

Conduct. This section evaluates some qualities of judges that might affect their decisions.

The Judge's Age and Experience

How does a judge's experience affect his or her sentencing behavior? Are new judges more lenient? Or harsher? Harold Rothwax, the judge who presided in the Joel Steinberg child-killing case, used to see the defendant as the victim. Now he sees the victim as twice the victim, victimized first by the crime and again by the legal process (Rosenbaum, 1989). The following paragraphs reflect another judge's experience. Seymour Wishman, in *Confessions of a Criminal Lawyer*, writes:

I knew Judge Mangione well. Twelve years earlier I had been prosecuting in his court when he was first assigned to handle criminal cases. He had asked me for a list of all the cases I most frequently relied on so that he could read them and be prepared for the issues that came up in the course of the trials. I had given him a long list, and he had read all the cases by the following day. I remembered how hard he had worked in those early trials to be fair to defendants, not only in making sure he had conducted fair trials, but also in sentencing those who had been convicted. About 11 years after Judge Mangione had started handling criminal trials, a client of mine had pleaded guilty to a charge of possessing marijuana with the intention of distributing it. My client was a 19-year-old college student studying painting who had gotten caught doing something stupid; it had been his first problem with the law, and from the way the young man's hand shook, it was clear he wasn't going to get into any trouble again. The D.A. wouldn't offer a plea bargain guaranteeing that the boy wouldn't go to jail, but it was inconceivable to me that Mangione would send him away. He did.

After the sentencing, I went to see the judge in his chambers. "Judge, I can't believe what you did with that boy today. They'll rip him to pieces in jail. . . . "

"Seymour, I felt I had to do it. I've been giving young people breaks for years now, and they laugh at me. The crime rate only gets worse. We've got to do something."

To my mind, the sentence had been grossly unfair. That afternoon, as I talked to the judge, it was clear to me that he had undergone a dramatic change since I first met him. He must have been hardened by the constant exposure to so many vicious criminals and to all the atrocities they had committed. He must have felt impotent over the years to do anything that would have any appreciable effect on the violence that appeared in his courtroom. From earlier conversations, I also knew of another aspect in his reaction to the defendants brought before him—he felt personally betrayed by the false promises of the many who had said that if they had just one more break, they would not get in trouble again.

After an extended conversation in the judge's chambers, he agreed to re-sentence my client if I supplied affidavits from his college indicating that the school officials would exercise some supervisory control over the boy. It took about a week to get those affidavits. By the time my client had been re-sentenced to probation, he had been terrorized by the other inmates and lost 10 pounds [1981b, pp. 107–108].

But not all judges respond the way Judge Mangione has. Some gain trust over time and become more lenient in their sentencing. It is impossible to make a general statement about the effects of amount of judicial experience on sentencing. Perhaps older judges are *selectively* punitive; "that is, they impose harsher sanctions on certain offenders with whom, because of their age, they are least able to sympathize. Drug offenders are the most obvious possibility" (Myers, 1988, p. 654).

Previous Employment as a District Attorney

Judges who have been district attorneys may maintain their sympathy for the prosecution, and some research finds them to be selectively more punitive than judges who have not been prosecutors (Myers, 1988). Seymour Wishman writes: "What juries don't know is that many judges were once prosecutors and that they sometimes forget that it is no longer their duty to get convictions. A number of judges—admittedly fewer than a majority—want to 'beat' defense lawyers and are much more dangerous and difficult to deal with than prosecutors" (1981b, pp. 206–207).

Wishman writes further: "I remember talking to a judge in his chambers after a long trial that had just ended with the acquittal of my client. 'Well, Seymour, you put up a good fight. I guess you're entitled to win,' the judge said to me. 'But I just hate to lose.' He regarded the acquittal as a personal loss!" (1981b, p. 210).

Political Party Membership

Nagel (1962) found that a judge's political affiliation could be deduced from his or her sentencing behavior. In his study of the California supreme court, Nagel found that the Democratic judges' decisions favored the defense 85% of the time, whereas Republicans favored the defense only 18% of the time. When Rose Bird, a Democrat, was chief justice of the California supreme court, she received unfavorable publicity for her appellate decisions that reversed several convictions and death sentences. However, there is little evidence that trial judges' decisions are substantially correlated with their political affiliation.

The Judge's Philosophy about the Purposes of the Penalty

How would a given judge describe the objective of a sentence in a specific case? Austin and Utne (1977) speak of the judge's "theory of punishment." They ask: "Should the offender be punished to deter crime in general? To deter

the specific offense for which he or she was convicted? To establish equity? To gain retribution for society and the victim? To rehabilitate the offender?" (p. 168). Judges' views on these matters certainly can affect their sentencing decisions (Gottfredson, Gottfredson, & Conly, 1989).

Some judges give more severe sentences in order to punish the offender for lying on the stand as well as for committing the initial crime. Paul A. Bilzerian, a Florida investor who was one of the most successful corporate raiders of the 1980s, was sentenced to four years in prison and fined $1.5 million for conspiracy to violate securities laws. Federal Judge Robert Ward stated that his sentence was stiff in part because he believed that Bilzerian had perjured himself when he testified in his own defense. "I do believe that if Mr. Bilzerian had not testified at all at the trial, his sentence would not be what it was," the judge said (quoted by Eichenwald, 1989, p. 29).

THE SENTENCING PROCESS

The procedure used in most courts for sentencing has several components. The judge receives a file on the offender, prepared by the probation officer. It contains the probation officer's written report on the case, the offender's personal history, the offender's prior convictions (if any), and a number of documents describing various procedures (for example, the date of the arraignment, the formal indictment). The judge reviews the file before the sentencing hearing.

The Sentencing Hearing

At the hearing, recommendations for a sentence are presented to the judge by the district attorney and by the attorney representing the offender. The judge has at hand the probation officer's recommendation. The judge may ask the offender questions and will usually permit the offender to make a statement.

Two social psychologists, Ebbe Ebbesen and Vladimir Konecni (1981), observed more than 400 sentencing hearings in San Diego in 1976 and 1977 in order to determine which factors seemed to influence judges' decisions. (Chapter 10 reviewed these researchers' work on the determinants of bail setting by judges.)

Very few of the sentencing hearings in San Diego lasted more than *five minutes*. The average percentages of time spent by participants in the hearing were as follows:

Judge	42% of the time
District attorney	13%
Defense attorney	38%
Offender	3%
Probation officer	3%

The average length of utterance, *in seconds*, for each participant, was:

Judge	18 seconds
District attorney	10 seconds
Defense attorney	19 seconds
Offender	26 seconds
Probation officer	8 seconds

Usually anything said by the offender came at the end of the hearing, when the judge asked the offender if he or she wanted to make a statement.

What Predicts the Sentence?

In Ebbesen and Konecni's sample, four factors accounted for almost all the systematic variations among sentences:

1. Type of crime.
2. Extent of the offender's past record.
3. Status of the offender between arrest and conviction—that is, whether the offender

was released on his or her own recognizance, freed on bail, held in jail, or originally held in jail and then released on bail.
4. Probation officer's sentence recommendation The judge's sentence agreed with the probation officer's recommendation in more than 84% of the cases. When they disagreed, the judge was more lenient 10% of the time and more severe 6% of the time. There was little variation in the frequency with which different judges agreed with the probation officer's recommendations. Over the eight judges who supplied most of the data for this study, the range was from 93% to 75%, with a median of 87% agreement with the recommendation. Another, more recent, study in New Zealand found similar levels of agreement, with judges agreeing with the probation officer's recommendation 77% of the time (Rush & Robertson, 1987).

Ebbesen and Konecni conclude that sentencing works this way: The probation officer's recommendation is determined by the prior record, the seriousness of the current crime, and the offender's present status. An extensive past criminal record strongly increases the likelihood that a severe sentence will be recommended. The probation officer incorporates these factors into his or her recommendation; that is one reason why the judge's agreement with this recommendation is so high.

Sentencing Disparity among the San Diego Judges

Inconsistency in sentencing decisions is one of the major concerns of the judicial process. What evidence for inconsistency is there among the judges in the San Diego study?

These judges showed considerable variation in the rate at which they imposed prison sentences: from 9% for one judge to 33% for another. But Ebbesen and Konecni conclude that this disparity is due in large part (if not completely) to the fact that the probation officers varied the rate at which they recommended prison sentences across judges. They write:

> If true disparity (different sentences for identical cases) does exist, there is considerable evidence that its cause may rest in the decision strategies of the probation officers rather than the strategies of the judges. All of the judges seem to follow the same basic decision rule, impose the sentence that the probation officer recommends and occasionally moderate it by the offender's status.
>
> Evidence that the probation officers did not, to a large degree, consider who the judge was in reaching their recommendations comes from the fact that we were able to explain most of the variation in their recommendations with crime, prior records, and status. Apparently the differential recommendation rates reflect the fact that different judges tend to be exposed to different kinds of cases [1981, pp. 445–446].

Thus, in the study of the San Diego judges, there is little indication of "individualizing justice," or fitting the punishment to the individual criminal. Defense attorneys' efforts to advocate leniency because of "good character" or "mitigating circumstances" seemed to be a waste of time. The psychologists' systematic observations corroborate individual attorneys' impressions. "When a judge comes out on the bench, he (or she) generally has the specific sentence already formulated," says one attorney (quoted by Kurtz, 1990, p. 25). Billionaire hotel owner Leona Helmsley had her attorney plead for mercy at her sentencing hearing, but the judge sentenced her to four years in prison. And only minutes later, copies of the judge's remarks were sent to the press room, implying that he had decided on the sentence before all the histrionics (Kurtz, 1990).

THE DEATH PENALTY: THE ULTIMATE PUNISHMENT

In 1976, in the case of *Gregg* v. *Georgia*, the Supreme Court reinstituted the possibility of the death penalty. Previously, in the case of *Furman* v. *Georgia* (1972), the Court had in effect abolished the death penalty throughout the United States on the ground that, as it had been administered in the mid-1960s, it constituted "cruel and unusual punishment." After the *Furman* case, state legislatures revised their death penalty laws to answer the Court's concern that capital punishment was being applied in an arbitrary and discriminatory fashion due to the "unbridled discretion" in sentencing given to juries.

In order to address this concern, the states passed statutes that narrowed and guided the capital-sentencing discretion of juries. First, they made only certain crimes eligible for the death penalty. If a defendant is charged with one of these crimes, the trial is conducted in two phases. The jury decides the guilt or innocence of the defendant in the first phase. If the defendant is found guilty, the second, or sentencing, phase of the trial is held. During this phase the jury (in a few states, the judge, not the jury, makes the decision at the sentencing phase) hears evidence of *aggravating factors* (facts that argue for a death sentence) and *mitigating factors* (facts that argue for a sentence less than death). Specific aggravating and mitigating factors are listed in the statutes, but a jury is not limited to those factors in its deliberations. Before reaching a sentencing decision, the jurors hear instructions from the judge on how they are to weight the aggravating and mitigating factors. Generally, the jury cannot vote for a sentence of death unless it finds at least one aggravating factor to be present. However, even if it finds one or more aggravating circumstances to be present, it may still, after considering the mitigating factors, return a sentence of less than death.

Since its 1976 ruling allowing these guided-discretion statutes, the Supreme Court has issued several other opinions that have refined death penalty trial proceedings. The Court has paid particular attention to the way the penalty phase is conducted and the manner by which capital juries are impaneled and then reach their decisions (Costanzo & Costanzo, 1992; Luginbuhl, 1992). Box 18-3 lists several of the most important Supreme Court decisions regarding death penalty litigation.

Following the *Gregg* decision, state after state began setting execution dates for many of the hundreds of convicts who had been sentenced to death (Bedau, 1977). The first to be executed, on January 17, 1977, was Gary Gilmore, in Utah; in fact, he was the first person to die by court order in the United States in nearly ten years. Since Gilmore, more than 190 others have been executed.

As of June 1992, about 2600 inmates resided on the various "death rows" of the 36 states that permit the death penalty; there are almost 300 in Florida alone (Kaplan & Wright, 1990). The number of prisoners executed increased steadily during the first half of the 1980s, from 1 in 1981 to 2 in 1982, 5 in 1983, 21 in 1984, 18 in 1985, and 18 in 1986. It reached a peak in 1987, with 25; 11 people were executed in 1988 and 16 in 1989. During 1990, 23 convicts were executed, and 21 were put to death in 1992. Texas has executed more than 50 men in the past decade, the most of any state. Since 1976 only one woman has been executed, but more than 40 women are on death rows across the country. More than half of the prisoners who have been executed since 1977 have been white, more than a third have been black, and fewer than 10% have been Hispanics or Native Americans.

How many of these people were innocent of a capital crime we cannot say with precision; all we can say with confidence is that some executed defendants surely were. Hugo Adam Bedau, a philosopher at Tufts University, and Michael L. Radelet, of the University of Florida, conclude that at least 25 innocent persons have been executed in the United States since 1900. Some who were sentenced to death received reprieves. For example, Johnny Ross was sentenced for rape in 1975 in Louisiana but was released in 1981 when it was shown that his blood type did not match that of the rapist. Robert Henry McDowell was a North Carolina black man sentenced to death for the murder of a 4-year-old white girl. He received a stay of his execution only days before it was scheduled, when the victim's mother implicated the victim's stepfather. The conviction was reversed. Edgar Labat and Clinton Poret, two black men, were sentenced to death in Louisiana in 1953 for raping a white woman. After a dozen stays of execution and 16 years on death row, they were released because prosecution witnesses' testimony unraveled, alibi witnesses came forward, and evidence showed that one defendant had been beaten into confessing.

In 1992 Roger Dale Coleman was executed by the state of Virginia for the brutal rape and slaying of his sister-in-law. To the last, Coleman maintained his innocence. What is disturbing about the Coleman case is that courts refused to consider evidence, discovered after the trial, pointing to Coleman's innocence—because Coleman's attorneys failed to file a motion on time! What is unusual about the case is that, in the week before his death, Coleman became a media celebrity—appearing on the cover of *Time* magazine (under the headline "This Man May Be Innocent") and participating in extraordinary live interviews on CNN's *Larry King Live* and NBC's *Today* show.

Reasons for the Death Penalty

More than three-fourths of U.S. citizens support the death penalty; the percentage has increased in recent years, reflecting a national shift toward Packer's crime-control model (Walker, 1985). The U.S. Congress, in 1988, provided for the death penalty in federal crimes involving drug-related killings.

Many reasons have been advanced for endorsing the irrevocable penalty of death. While mayor of New York City, Ed Koch contended that the death penalty "affirms life." By failing to execute murderers, he said, we "signal a lessened regard for the value of the victim's life" (quoted in Bruck, 1985, p. 20). Capital punishment is thus seen as the only means we have of doing justice in response to heinous crimes. Koch could be labeled a retributivist (Foley, 1983), in that he is interested primarily in justice. Koch has written: "A truly civilized society need not shrink from imposing capital punishment as long as its procedures for determining guilt and passing sentence are constitutional and just" (1985, p. 21).

Michael Foley (1983), a retributivist him-

Box **18-3** | *Death Penalty Trials: The Supreme Court's Views*

Because it is the ultimate punishment a society can deliver, because of its enormous symbolic importance, and because of the impassioned rhetoric it inspires in both advocates and opponents, the death penalty has received special scrutiny from the Supreme Court in the past three decades. The Court has reviewed and regulated the procedures and outcomes of capital trials very closely, suggesting the view that society may tolerate the death penalty only when its use is carefully monitored. Along with the cases of *Wither-* *spoon*, *Witt*, and *Lockhart*, which are discussed at length in the text, the following Supreme Court cases have helped define what is acceptable and what is not in death penalty litigation across the United States.

Case:

1. *Lockett v. Ohio* (1978)   The jury is allowed to consider as a mitigating factor any aspect of the defendant's background or the offense that the defendant introduces.

2. *Payne v. Tennessee* (1991)   The jury is allowed to consider evidence about the impact a crime had on the victim before it reaches a sentencing decision.

3. *Mu'Min v. Virginia* (1991)   A judge does not have to ask prospective jurors about the content of the pretrial publicity to which they have been exposed.

4. *McCleskey v. Kemp* (1987)   A disparity in death sentences linked to racial differences of murder victims does not make the death penalty unconstitutional.

5. *Enmund v. Florida* (1982); *Tison v. Arizona* (1987)   If a defendant commits a felony in the course of which a murder is committed by another defendant, the first defendant cannot be sentenced to death if he or she did not kill or intend that killing or lethal force would take place (*Enmund*). However, if this defendant's participation in the crimes was major or the defendant showed a "reckless indifference to the value of human life," the defendant could be sentenced to death (*Tison*).

6. *Ford v. Wainwright* (1986)   A defendant sentenced to death must be competent before his or her execution can be carried out.

self, distinguishes between retribution and deterrence as reasons for the death penalty. Following the philosophy of Immanuel Kant, he believes that people should be treated as ends in themselves. But "if we use a criminal as an example to deter others from criminal activity, we are using that person as a means to an end" (Foley, 1983, p. 16).

Most justifications for the death penalty reflect value choices and thus extend beyond the capacity of empirical research findings to prove or disprove them. But a major reason for capital punishment held by the public—if not a reason given by experts—is the belief that it deters others from performing criminal acts. A *USA Today* poll ("USA Snapshots," 1984) asked "Does the death penalty deter crime?" Among respondents, 68% said yes, 18% said no, 10% were not sure, and 4% had no opinion.

With respect to this justification, empirical evidence *is* relevant, and a variety of empirical approaches have been used to evaluate the deterrence value of the death penalty. As Table 18-1 shows, these methods and findings consistently lead to a conclusion that the death penalty does not affect the incidence rate for crimes of violence.

The Future of the Death Penalty

Whether to extract the ultimate punishment of death for serious crimes has troubled judges, philosophers, theologians, and social scientists for centuries. The future of capital punishment is enmeshed in the dilemmas introduced in Chapter 1. The principle of the social good demands that we ask what we, as a society, want. We have the right to expect our government to provide us with safety and protection; yet we need to demonstrate a respect for human life as best we can. As Foley (1983) observes, an absolute moratorium on killing would seem to violate an optimal balance in these goals; for example, it may be necessary to kill a sniper if we are convinced that he will continue to kill people. But capital punishment is not the same as killing in self-defense, and society must ask whether the death penalty achieves the social good.

Does the death penalty achieve the goal of equal treatment before the law? About a fourth of the states, plus the District of Columbia, do not permit it, and vastly different rates of execution occur in those states that do. Discretion, rather than equality, seems to be the operating value; but it is discretion run amok, because the death penalty is administered in only a minority of eligible cases, and its determinants often seem inconsistent and unpredictable. There are dramatic regional differences in the application of the penalty; 20 of 21 executions in 1984 took place in Southern states. Furthermore, some of the decisions seem prejudicial; for instance, the victims of intentional homicide are equally divided between blacks and whites, and yet the chances of a death sentence are much greater for criminals who kill whites than those who kill blacks.

For example, the Supreme Court refused to overturn the death sentence of a Utah man who claimed that the jury that had decided his case was racially biased. The appellant and another man (since executed) were charged with entering an Ogden store in 1974, forcing five people to drink liquid drain cleaner, and then shooting three of them. During the trial a juror handed a bailiff a drawing of a man on a gallows with the inscription "Hang the niggers" (Beissert, 1988).

As another example, in Missouri, within a two-year period, two state troopers were killed in separate but similar incidents. (Both were killed during routine traffic checks.) Each defendant was found guilty of murder. David Tate, a white man, was sentenced to life in prison; Jerome Mallett, a black man, was given the death penalty.

Table 18-1 *Arguments for and against the Death Penalty as a Deterrent*

Arguments favoring the death penalty:
1. The death penalty accomplishes general deterrence.
2. "Potential murderers" who committed other crimes report they did not carry a gun out of fear of capital punishment.
3. Abolishing capital punishment would increase the homicide rate.
4. Execution of a criminal, if highly publicized, has at least a short-term deterrence effect.
5. Murderers are dangerous individuals, and allowing them to live increases the risk to inmates and prison guards; that is, they will kill in prison because they have nothing to lose.

Response by abolitionists to each of the preceding arguments:
1. Most homicides are emotional, spontaneous acts, not premeditated ones. Among premeditated murders, many offenders are convinced that they can escape detection. Hence many murderers do not consider the consequences of their act. Furthermore, a study of 110 nations by Dane Archer (1984) finds that the death penalty does not deter homicidal criminals (Wilkes, 1987).
2. Careful comparisons of states with and without the death penalty reflect no differences in homicide rates (Sellin, 1968).
3. Abolition or reintroduction of the death penalty has no effect on established trends in homicide rates, regardless of whether rates are increasing or decreasing (Lempert, 1981; Zeisel, 1976).
4. No empirical evidence exists for this conclusion. If anything, the opposite happens. In 1984 Florida executed eight men, the most of any state. Whereas nationally in 1984 the homicide rate declined, in Florida it actually rose by 5.1% (Bruck, 1985).
5. Ellison and Buckhout (1981) conclude that the evidence is "overwhelmingly against" this view, "as murderers generally make the best prisoners while incarcerated and are the least likely of all classes of offenders to return to crime once (if ever) released" (p. 274). Furthermore, most homicides in prisons are committed by those serving sentences for crimes other than murder.

Source: Baum (1985).

A recent appeal, *McCleskey* v. *Kemp* (1987), caused the Supreme Court to consider racial differences in sentencing. At issue was the question of whether the death penalty discriminated against blacks—or, more specifically, whether it discriminated against persons who murdered whites. Warren McCleskey was a black man who had been convicted of a 1978 armed robbery and the murder of a white police officer who had responded to an alarm while the robbery was in progress. McCleskey was sentenced to die in Georgia's electric chair. With the assistance of the NAACP Legal Defense and Educational Fund, he challenged the constitutionality of the death penalty on the ground that it was administered in a racially discriminatory manner in Georgia. In the words of one of his attorneys, "When you kill the organist at the Methodist Church, who is white, you're going to get the death penalty, but if you kill the black Baptist organist, the likelihood is that it will be plea-bargained down to a life sentence" (quoted in Noble, 1987, p. 7).

McCleskey's appeal contained a very detailed analysis of the race of the offender and the victim for 2000 murder and manslaughter convictions in Georgia from 1973 to 1979. David Baldus, a law professor at the University of Iowa, concluded in his survey that those who killed whites were 11 times more likely to receive the death penalty than those who killed blacks (Baldus, Pulaski, & Woodworth, 1983).

In Georgia, juries (in line with the Supreme Court guidelines we discussed earlier) must weigh aggravating and mitigating circumstances before deciding to sentence a convicted murderer to death rather than life in prison. Aggravating circumstances would include killing a police officer, killing for hire, killing that is especially cruel, or killing that is committed during other lawbreaking activities. Mitigating circumstances could include a defendant's mental illness or voluntary intoxication at the time of the offense. Anticipating the argument that some murders were typically more heinous than others, Baldus identified in his analysis 230 aggravating or mitigating factors. Then he eliminated cases in which extreme violence or other aggravating circumstances virtually ensured the death penalty. He also eliminated those in which overwhelming mitigating circumstances almost guaranteed a life sentence. For the remaining cases—which permitted the greatest jury discretion—he found that defendants were about four times more likely to be sentenced to death if their victims were white.

Despite the mass of statistical evidence, the Supreme Court upheld McCleskey's death sentence. The Court's majority opinion found no proof of arbitrary dispensation of justice (prohibited by the Eighth Amendment) or of deliberate racial prejudice in this specific case. Justice Lewis Powell, in the majority opinion, wrote that discretion is bound to lead to disparities, so statistical disparities were not proof enough. Powell noted: "At most, the Baldus study indicates a discrepancy that appears to correlate with race."

Four Supreme Court justices vigorously dissented, however; they wrote: "Race casts a large shadow on the capital sentencing process" and asked why statistical evidence—which is acceptable for attacking discrimination in employment—was not relevant in McCleskey's appeal (Lacayo, 1987a).

It is very unlikely that the Supreme Court will reject the death penalty in the near future. We have seen, with regard to the issue of deterrence as a justification for the death penalty, that social science has found no solid evidence to support this claim. However, the Supreme Court, in its 1976 decision reinstituting the capital punishment provision, concluded that

for many potential murderers the possibility of execution "is undoubtedly a significant deterrence." This discrepancy illustrates the sometimes-stark conflict between legal assumptions and social science observations.

Finally, regarding the dilemma between truth and stability as goals of law enforcement, the controversy over the propriety of capital punishment is again illustrative. Community standards often support capital punishment because society demands a sense of final justice after a heinous crime has been committed; the cathartic effect of learning that a murderer has himself been executed cannot be denied. For example, Morris Odell Mason was electrocuted in Virginia in 1985. He had been convicted of raping and murdering two elderly women, raping a 12-year-old girl, and maiming her 13-year-old sister. But Mason was a retarded black man with an IQ of 66 who had been diagnosed on three occasions as suffering from paranoid schizophrenia. He was found guilty of acts committed only *after* he had vainly pleaded with the state to be taken off the streets and put back into custody (Wicker, 1985). Was Morris Mason so clearly responsible for his behavior that it was appropriate for the state to kill him? Or would detention in a state hospital for the criminally insane have been more just? In a similar case, Justice Sandra Day O'Connor's majority opinion stated: "There is insufficient evidence of a national consensus against executing mentally retarded people convicted of capital offenses for us to conclude that it is categorically prohibited by the Eighth Amendment."

SENTENCING BY JURY

Who should do the sentencing? This, too, is an unresolved issue among the states. In most states, sentencing decisions are made by the trial judge, except in capital cases, for which juries usually decide the sentence. A few states give the jury responsibility for allocating other punishments. (This is true only when there has been a trial; if the offender has pleaded guilty before the trial, the judge determines the sentence.) The jury's power to sentence originated in colonial times. Most colonists remembered the abuses they had suffered from judges in Great Britain during the religious and political persecutions (Cilwick, 1984). Jury sentencing was one process by which the community could participate directly in criminal justice proceedings. But over the decades this power has eroded. Even in the states that still give juries the sentencing decision, there are limitations. In Texas, defendants can choose either the judge or the jury to sentence them. In Missouri and Oklahoma, judges have the responsibility for sentencing of repeat felons who have been convicted by juries.

Momentum is building in some of these states to abolish jury sentencing. It is believed that juries shield offenders from long sentences; in addition, juries may not be privy to detrimental information about the defendant's past record, especially if he or she has not taken the stand. Another concern is that juries are not fully informed about the liberal opportunities for parole. If jurors sentence a defendant to 20 years in prison, they may assume he or she will serve that long; in actuality, between parole and "good behavior" options, the defendant probably will serve less than half that long. And different juries may give inconsistent sentences to separate offenders who collaborated in the same crime, even when each collaborator played an equally serious part in the crime. In Kansas City, Missouri, several years ago, three codefendants were each found guilty of rape and sodomy by different juries; one was sentenced to life imprisonment, the second received a 25-year prison term, and the third, 10 years (Cilwick, 1984).

One remedy for these problems is to give juries more information about defendants before they impose a sentence. Some states with jury sentencing have developed "truth-in-sentencing" laws in which a bifurcated trial, similar to those used in capital cases, is employed. The jury first decides the guilt or innocence of the defendant. If the defendant is convicted, the jury then hears additional evidence about the defendant's past in a second phase of the trial. It then decides the sentence.

The Sentence of Death

When jurors are given the opportunity to advocate the ultimate punishment, it is legitimate to ask about their attitudes toward punishment generally and toward capital punishment specifically. Are some prospective jurors so hostile that they want to severely punish any suspect of a major crime? Are others so fearful of being victimized themselves that they would vote for the death penalty regardless of the weight of the evidence? Ironically, the law has been much more concerned about those potential jurors who are opposed to the death penalty than about those who, because of their own personal beliefs, might apply it even when it would be much too harsh a penalty. Until 1968, persons who indicated having any "scruples" against the death penalty were routinely prohibited from sitting as jurors in trials for capital crimes (Haney, 1984). In this sense, "scruples" means moral reservations or hesitancy because of conscientious feelings.

In 1968, in the case of *Witherspoon* v. *Illinois,* the U.S. Supreme Court concluded that having "scruples" was too broad a guideline, because it excluded too many people from jury service. In the *Witherspoon* decision, the Court restricted the standard of exclusions to unequivocal opposition of the sort that would prevent a juror from ever considering the death penalty, regardless of the crime. (This distinction is illustrated by the attitude survey questions in Box 18-4.)

Death Qualification and "Death-Qualified" Jurors

The procedure of *death qualification* occurs during the voir dire portion of a capital trial, when jurors are questioned about their beliefs regarding the death penalty. If, on the basis of their answers, jurors indicate extreme beliefs about the death penalty, they may be excused "for cause"—that is, dismissed from serving in that case. The procedures and standards for determining which jurors should be excused for cause in capital trials have undergone substantial changes in the past 25 years. These changes began with the *Witherspoon* case.

Witherspoon limited the reasons jurors could be excused for cause to the following two situations: (1) those prospective jurors who indicated that they would automatically vote against imposing capital punishment, without regard to any evidence they might hear at the trial, should be excluded; and (2) those prospective jurors who indicated that their beliefs about capital punishment would prevent them from making an impartial decision about the defendant's guilt should be excused for cause. As a result of this standard, most defendants facing the death penalty have been convicted and sentenced to die by these special "death-qualified" juries. Such decisions remain suspect because of the nature of the juries that rendered them: "in capital trials, unlike other criminal cases, the issue of guilt and innocence is decided exclusively by jurors who have stated a willingness to impose a death sentence" (W. C. Thompson, 1989, p. 185).

When William C. Witherspoon appealed his conviction and death sentence to the Supreme

---

Box **18-4** | *Reactions to Voting for the Death Penalty*

Jurow's (1971) Capital Punishment Attitude Questionnaire contained a section in which respondents were to assume that they were "on a jury to determine the sentence for a defendant who has already been convicted of a very serious crime." Then they were asked to choose among the following five answers:

1. I could not vote for the death penalty regardless of the facts and circumstances of the case.
2. There are some kinds of cases in which I know I could not vote

for the death penalty even if the law allowed me to, but others in which I would be willing to consider voting for it.
3. I would consider all the penalties provided by the law and the facts and circumstances of the particular case.
4. I would usually vote for the death penalty in a case when the law allows me to.
5. I would always vote for the death penalty in a case when the law allows me to.

Option 1 resembles the criteri-

on established in *Witherspoon* v. *Illinois* for exclusion of prospective jurors. Fitzgerald and Ellsworth (1984) found that about one-sixth of their respondents would be eliminated from jury service because they chose Option 1.

Before *Witherspoon*, a general "scruples" question was used, such as "Do you have any conscientious scruples that would cause you to hesitate about sentencing the defendant to death?" Under that rule, an even higher percentage was excluded.

Court, he did so on the ground that the jury selection procedures were so arranged that "such a jury must necessarily be biased in favor of conviction" (*Witherspoon* v. *Illinois*, 1968, p. 516). But the jury selection procedures had other problems; early in the voir dire of Witherspoon's trial, the presiding judge had said: "Let's get those conscientious objectors out of the way without wasting any time on them." In rapid succession, 47 members of the venire were successfully challenged for cause on the basis of their attitudes toward the death penalty.

To support his claims of bias, Mr. Witherspoon presented three unpublished studies showing that those jurors who survived the selection regarding attitudes about the death penalty were biased toward the *guilt* of the defendants; that is, they were not representative of all prospective jurors with regard to a verdict, which should be made independently of the later decision regarding punishment. But the Supreme Court balked; the data, it concluded, were "too fragmentary and tentative . . . to establish that jurors not opposed to the death penalty tend to favor the prosecution in the determination of guilt" (p. 527). So, with respect to the claim that the selection procedure had affected the verdict, Mr. Witherspoon lost his appeal; his conviction was upheld.

But on his claim that the sentencing procedure was inappropriate, Mr. Witherspoon won. The Supreme Court wrote: "It is self-evident that, in its role as arbiter of the punishment to be imposed, this jury fell woefully short of that impartiality to which the petitioner was entitled under the Sixth and Fourteenth Amendments" (p. 518). The Court agreed that excluding all jurors with any scruples about the death penalty produced a jury that was unfairly biased against the defendant in the penalty phase of the trial.

However, the Supreme Court left open the question of the conviction-proneness of death-qualified jurors, and from 1968 to 1980 the lower courts followed suit. They refused to consider the applicability of newer, better-designed social science studies on the topic (Gross, 1984). It was not until 1985 that the U.S. Supreme Court considered the issue again.

The first major development since the *Witherspoon* decision was an appeal to the California supreme court (*Hovey* v. *Superior Court*, 1980). As we noted, the previous decision had allowed two types of prospective jurors to be excused for cause: (1) those unequivocally against the death penalty in any case and (2) those who could not be fair and impartial in determining a capital defendant's guilt or innocence. The logic behind these exclusions was understandable: jurors must be willing and able to follow the law and to apply their judgment to the evidence (Gross, 1984).

The petitioner in *Hovey* argued: "Prospective jurors, who would automatically vote against death at the *penalty* phase, cannot constitutionally be excused from sitting at the *guilt* phase, if they can be fair and impartial at that phase." Hovey forced the California court to face two constitutional issues: (1) Are death-qualified juries prone to convict? (2) Are they less than representative? (Specifically, do they include fewer blacks and women?)

The brief prepared for Hovey's appeal reported several new empirical studies that had been conducted in 1979 but were not published until 1984, in a special issue of the journal *Law and Human Behavior*. Employing a better methodology than the earlier unpublished studies described in Witherspoon's brief, these studies produced results that were consistent with one another and with the earlier studies that the Supreme Court had disregarded; they showed that death-qualified jurors were conviction-prone (Gross, 1984).

Phoebe Ellsworth (then at Stanford University) and her colleagues were the authors of this integrated set of empirical studies that consistently demonstrated the effect of death qualification on verdicts as well as sentences. In the first study, Fitzgerald and Ellsworth (1984) surveyed a random sample of 811 eligible jurors in Alameda County, California, in April 1979. A total of 64% favored the death penalty (37% did so "strongly"). Another 17% said they could never vote to impose the death penalty and thus were excludable under the *Witherspoon* decision. This group included a higher percentage of the blacks than of the whites (25% in contrast to 15%) and more of the women than of the men (21% in contrast to 13%). Twice as many Democrats as Republicans were excluded.

The 17% representing the "excludables" may be higher than in other parts of the country. Palladino and his colleagues (1986) found in a telephone interview of a sample of prospective jurors in southern Indiana that only 9% would qualify as "Witherspoon excludables." This study found that, *if* the jury's vote is a recommendation to the judge, as it is in Indiana, a greater percentage of prospective jurors will be willing to vote for the death penalty. However, this study, like the one in California, found that a greater percentage of women (12%) than of men (4%), as well as a greater percentage of blacks than of whites, were "excludables." Another study (Luginbuhl & Middendorf, 1988), using North Carolina jurors, found 10% strongly opposed to the death penalty, with the same race and gender differences as the previous two studies.

In contrast, the remaining death-qualified jurors were more prone to favor the prosecutor's viewpoint, more likely to mistrust criminal defendants and their counsel, more in sympathy with a punitive approach toward offenders, and more concerned with crime control than with due process (see Chapter 1 for Packer's distinction between these two orientations toward the criminal process).

In a follow-up study, Cowan, Thompson, and Ellsworth (1984) showed a 2½-hour videotape of a murder trial reenactment to 288 mock jurors who were either death qualified or excludable, using the *Witherspoon* ruling. (Thirty of the 288 were excludable.) These adults were divided into juries. About half of the juries were composed entirely of death-qualified jurors; the others contained from two to four excludables, with the majority being death qualified. Three-fourths of the death-qualified jurors found the defendant guilty; only 53% of the excludables did. The "mixed" juries took a more serious approach to their deliberation task; they were more critical of witnesses and better able to remember the evidence.

Ellsworth, Bukaty, Cowan, and Thompson (1984) predicted that those persons who were excluded from jury service on capital cases because they opposed the death penalty would be more likely to accept an insanity defense in a homicide case than death-qualified subjects would. This prediction was confirmed when the insanity defense was based on a diagnosis of schizophrenia caused by nonorganic factors (that is, no brain damage). When organic disorders (epilepsy or mental retardation) were given as the causes of the purported insanity, death-qualified jurors were as likely as the excludables to find the defendant insane.

In a final study, Thompson, Cowan, Ellsworth, and Harrington (1984) studied why death-qualified jurors voted guilty more often than excludable jurors. The researchers found that the death-qualified jurors tend "to interpret evidence in a way more favorable to the prosecution and less favorable to the defense" (p. 104). The two groups expressed different kinds of regret over making a mistaken decision; death-qualified jurors were more upset about acquitting a guilty defendant, whereas excludables were more disturbed about convicting an innocent one.

But the California supreme court did not provide relief to Hovey. The court was concerned with a category of jurors not yet mentioned: those who would *always* vote to impose the death penalty in every capital case, regardless of the weight of the evidence. Such persons, if they exist, can be thought of as "automatic death penalty jurors" or, more colloquially, "hanging jurors." In California this type of prospective juror, who is the mirror-opposite of the juror irrevocably opposed to capital punishment, is also excluded from juries in capital cases, but none of the empirical studies identified this group. Frankly, the researchers considered the number of people with such attitudes to be too small to be of any practical importance. Ironically, the court expressed concern about excluding the same end of the continuum of prospective jurors that initiated our discussion of this topic—those who are ready to sentence a defendant to death no matter what the evidence is. Thus the court concluded that, because of this omission, the studies had made the wrong comparisons; that is, the death-qualified jury that they had described was not the *true* "California death-qualified jury" from which automatic death penalty jurors are excluded. The court acknowledged that this latter group may exist only "in theory," but the burden of proof was on the petitioner, Hovey, to show why excluding this type of juror would not offset the effects of excluding those who would never consider voting for the death penalty under any circumstances. So Hovey's appeal was denied.

The courts remained sensitive to possible implications of the use of death-qualified jurors, even though they have not prohibited the procedure. For example, in the case of *Grigsby* v. *Mabry* (1980), the court raised the concern that prosecutors may ask for the death penalty before trial in order to get a death-qualified jury, knowing full well that such a jury is more likely to convict. In the Grigsby trial, as soon as the prosecutor obtained a "guilty" verdict, he withdrew his request for the death penalty.

In 1985 the U.S. Supreme Court (in the case of *Wainwright* v. *Witt*) changed the standard for death-qualifying jurors and broadened its acceptance of death-qualified juries. By a 7-to-2 vote, it reinstated the death sentence of convicted Florida child killer Johnny Paul Witt; it overturned an 11th U.S. Circuit Court of Appeals decision that itself had thrown out Witt's sentence because one potential juror had been improperly dismissed for having doubts about capital punishment. Justice William H. Rehnquist, writing for the majority, stated that it was not necessary to show with "unmistakable clarity" that a juror has "automatic" opposition to the death penalty in order to exclude the prospective juror. Instead, Rehnquist wrote, a judge may bar the prospective juror on the basis of his or her decision that the juror's views would "prevent or substantially impair the performance of his duties as a juror in accordance with his instructions and his oath." Furthermore, he stated: "We do not think . . . a defendant is entitled to a legal presumption or standard that allows jurors to be seated who quite likely will be biased in his favor." The *Witt* standard will increase the percentage of prospective jurors who are excludable (Neises & Dillehay, 1987) beyond the previous estimates of 9% to 29%. A thorough review estimates that as many as 40% may be excluded (W. C. Thompson, 1989).

Reflecting his mistrust of social science methodology, Justice Rehnquist commented: "Determinations of juror bias cannot be reduced to question-and-answer sessions which obtain results in the manner of catechism." He added that a trial judge should have broad discretion in deciding which prospective jurors may be seated for capital cases, because the judge is able to observe each juror closely and is in a position to analyze whether jurors are trying to hide their true feelings. Justice Rehnquist is more sanguine about the ability of judges to detect deception than social scientists are on the basis of their findings from empirical studies. But in the conflict between the two, Justice Rehnquist's decision is the law as it applies to the acceptability of death-qualified jurors—despite the opinions of the social scientists and of some of his Supreme Court colleagues. Justice William Brennan, in a written dissent, reflected the conclusions of the social science research, that the ruling will lead to "a jury biased against the defendant, at least with respect to penalty."

For social scientists who hoped that their empirical findings would influence the courts, the decision in the case of *Lockhart* v. *McCree* (1986; Bersoff, 1987), decided by the Supreme Court in May 1986, seemed to be the final nail in the coffin. Ardia McCree was an Arkansas man who had been convicted of robbery and murder. At his trial the judge had excluded eight prospective jurors who said that they could not under any circumstances impose a death sentence (Taylor, 1986). As Bersoff (1987) notes, three decades of social science research have shown that the absence of jurors with such scruples results in a jury that is conviction-prone. The APA submitted an *amicus curiae* brief in support of Mr. McCree's position, which abstracted and critiqued the methodology and major empirical findings of the relevant research on the conviction-proneness and unrepresentativeness of death-qualified jurors.

But, in spite of this concerted effort, the Supreme Court, in a 6-to-3 vote, held that the jury in Mr. McCree's trial was not an improper one. Chief Justice Rehnquist wrote the majority opinion. On the issue of unrepresentativeness of death-qualified juries, he noted that the only requirement was to have representative jury *panels*

or venires. Exclusion of groups who were "defined solely in terms of shared attitudes" was not improper; these were not cognizable groups.

Furthermore, the majority rejected as "illogical and hopelessly impractical" the claim that death-qualified juries were less than neutral. An impartial jury, Justice Rehnquist wrote, "consists of nothing more than jurors who will conscientiously apply the law and find the facts"; he noted that Mr. McCree had conceded that each of the jurors who convicted him met that test. So the Supreme Court reversed the appellate decision and upheld the state's use of a death-qualified jury for the decision at the guilt/innocence phase; the defendant had argued for two juries: a guilt/innocence jury that was not death qualified and, if necessary, a penalty jury that was death qualified.

In effect, the majority opinion dismissed 30 years of research as irrelevant (W. C. Thompson, 1989). The conflict between social science and the law was never more sharply represented than in the majority opinion's final view:

> We will assume for purposes of this opinion that the studies are both methodologically valid and adequate to establish that "death-qualification" in fact produces juries somewhat more "conviction-prone" than "non-death-qualified juries." We hold, nonetheless, that the Constitution does not prohibit the states from "death-qualifying" juries in capital cases [p. 1764].

To summarize, many social scientists who have studied death qualification are concerned about recent Supreme Court decisions because they condone trial juries that are slanted toward both conviction and capital punishment. Although a few scholars question whether the evidence linking death penalty beliefs and conviction-proneness is strong (Elliott, 1991), the consensus is that death qualification disadvantages defendants (Ellsworth, 1991) and that alternative approaches to impaneling juries in capital cases could probably overcome these disadvantages (Cox & Tanford, 1989).

If, during the voir dire, a prospective juror were to state that he or she would automatically vote *for* the death penalty if the defendant were found guilty, this prospective juror also should be excluded by the judge. But in an Oklahoma case (*Ross* v. *Oklahoma*, 1988), the judge refused to exclude such a man. The jury in the trial convicted Ross, and he was sentenced to death. In responding to Ross's appeal, the Supreme Court, in a 5-to-4 vote, upheld the conviction and the death sentence. Justice Rehnquist wrote that it was true that the trial judge had erred, but this error had not deprived Ross of an impartial jury because his attorney later excluded this man from the jury by using one of the defense's peremptory challenges (Taylor, 1988a). The minority or dissenting opinion—surely consistent with the reaction of many social scientists—said that the defendant's rights had been violated; his attorney had been forced to use one of the limited number of peremptory challenges to dismiss someone who should have been dismissed for cause.

REVISIONS OF THE SENTENCING PROCEDURE

Concern over the disparity in sentences across the country has led to reactions both from the court system and from legislatures. We will now review some of these revisions.

Sentencing Councils

One arrangement used by some courts to reduce inconsistency in sentences is the sentencing council. In this procedure, the presiding judge, before imposing a sentence, meets with several colleagues to discuss what sentences they would impose if they were presiding over the case.

Diamond and Zeisel (1975) evaluated this innovation, studying federal courts in Chicago and New York. In each court the use of the council reduced sentencing disparity. In New York the disparity was reduced from 45% to 41%, and in Chicago from 37% to 33%.

Fixed, or Determinate, Sentencing

One contributor to sentencing disparity is the broadness of possible sentences that have been available for many crimes. A convicted robber may be sentenced to "1 to 20 years." A "life sentence" might mean 15 actual years in prison, taking into account "good behavior" and parole. In this so-called indeterminate sentencing procedure, it's highly uncertain how long offenders will really serve. With indeterminate sentencing the judge's influence actually becomes superseded by the later decisions of correctional and parole authorities (Miller, 1989).

About a decade and a half ago, some states began to tighten their sentencing guidelines. Maine, in 1976, was the first; several others have followed. Political conservatives spearheaded the movement, but liberals often joined the cause because they saw the use of determinate sentences as a way to reform the sentencing inequities that granted privileges to some offenders (Hamm, 1989). Many inmate groups have also supported fixed sentencing, because they have seen the vagueness of indeterminate sentencing used as a weapon to keep "uncooperative" offenders in prison longer than their peers. George Jackson, one of the "Soledad Brothers" associated with Angela Davis, was held in prison for 11 years for a $70 gas station robbery because, according to his partisans, he refused to soft-pedal political militancy whenever he appeared before a parole board.

Furthermore, inmates find it demoralizing to have no fixed release date. The certain expectation of being freed at a known time in the future provides a reference point around which they can orient their lives. Some inmates also contend that indeterminate sentences are inconsistent with the concept of "paying one's debt to society": they see more fairness in a system of definite and uniform sentences for particular crimes. One additional effect of determinate sentencing may be increased plea bargaining, because the defendant knows what he or she is going to get if convicted on a particular charge.

Alternative Sentencing, Based on Accountability

On recommendations from its Sentencing Reform Commission, the state of Delaware recently reformed its sentencing policies. The new system confronted one of the major limitations of previous procedures: the rigid choice of either sending the offender to prison or putting him or her on probation. The Delaware plan offers a sentencing judge a range of sanctions over ten "levels of accountability." This system is based on the belief that an offender should be sentenced to the least restrictive (and least costly) sanction available consistent with public safety (duPont, 1985).

In Delaware's system, Level 1 reflects unsupervised probation; Level 10 is maximum-security imprisonment. Between these extremes a full range of alternatives exist, each with a different degree of restrictiveness. Within each level, different degrees of control and accountability are specified. These include the offender's relative freedom of action within the community, the amount of supervision provided, and the privileges to be withheld. Another innovation is that the system provides for a range of possible financial sanctions to be imposed,

including compensation to victims. With this flexible system the state is able to control the offender's choice of job, place of residence, right to drive, right to drink, right to travel, and even right to make telephone calls. As Georgia and Florida have done, Delaware has added probation fees to its new sentencing procedures. A fee of $10–$50 per month is charged to those offenders released on probation, to help offset the costs of their supervision. Like the sanctions, the probation fee is increased if more supervision is required. Table 18-2 specifies the procedures and restrictions available under each level.

In an article reviewing the new sentencing procedures, Pierre S. duPont IV (1985), then governor of Delaware, offered two examples:

> First, let's take a drug offender with a minimal prior record but unstable employment record. He might be sentenced in Level 2 to supervised probation for two years, with restrictions on his place of residence, his association with certain individuals, and/or his right to visit high-drug/crime locations, and we might charge him a $10-per-month fee to offset some of the costs of keeping him straight.
>
> If he observes these conditions for the first year of his probation, he could move down the sanctions scale into Level 1. This level involves unsupervised probation and levies no fees, but holds out the possibility of certain restrictions on mobility and personal associations to minimize the chance of the offender slipping back into the drug scene and its associated crime. If our hypothetical drug offender violates the terms of his probation, he could be moved on to Level 3, with heightened supervision, a curfew, and an increased monthly fee. Thus, the offender has a clear incentive to comply with his sentence. And, equally important, the sentencing judge has available options other than prison when probation is violated. Having and using these options will increase the certainty of appropriate punishment.
>
> The second example is near the other end of

the offense spectrum. This time our hypothetical offender is a twice-convicted armed robber. He was sentenced to 20 years, with the sentence to begin at Level 10, or a maximum-security prison. After serving two years, and adhering to all the rules, the man might be moved to Level 9, a medium-security facility, where he might be able to take advantage of expanded rehabilitative programs.

Two years later, with continued good behavior, the offender again could move down the scale, this time to a minimum-security facility with still greater opportunities for rehabilitation. By the same token if the prisoner's action at Level 9 was disruptive and uncooperative, he could be returned to Level 10.

Later, at a parole hearing, some appropriate program at Level 6 might be selected instead of releasing the offender to fuller freedom in the streets or leaving him in prison [pp. 3–4].

The Delaware program reflects the psychological principles of Skinnerian behaviorism. Responses by the offender are either rewarded or punished, on the contingent basis of whether they facilitate or inhibit the prisoner's progress toward rehabilitation. This diversified program also reflects the realities of most offenders. Although the term *offender*, for most of us, conjures up the image of murderer or rapist,

Table 18-2   *Delaware's Ten-Level Sentencing Guidelines*

Restrictions	Level 1	Level 2	Level 3	Level 4
Mobility in the community	100% (unrestricted)	100% (unrestricted)	90% (restricted 0–10 hours/week)	80% (restricted 10–30 hours/week)
Amount of supervision	None	Monthly written report	1–2 face-to-face/month; 1–2 weekly phone contact	3–6 face-to-face/month; weekly phone contact
Privileges withheld or special conditions	100% (same as prior conviction)	100% (same as prior conviction)	1–2 privileges withheld	1–4 privileges withheld
Financial obligations	Fine, court costs may be applied (0- to 2-day fine)	Fine, court costs, restitution; probation (supervisory fee may be applied; 1- to 3-day fine)	Same (increase probation fee by $5–10/month; 2- to 4-day fine)	Same (increase probation fee by $5–10/month; 3- to 5-day fine)
Examples (Note: many other scenarios could be constructed meeting the requirements at each level)	$50 fine, court costs; 6 months' unsupervised probation	$50 fine, court costs, restitution; 6 months' supervised probation; $10 monthly fee; written report	Fine, court costs, restitution; 1 year probation; weekend community service; no drinking	Weekend community service or mandatory treatment 5 hours/day; $30/month probation fee; no drinking; no out-of-state trips

Source: DuPont, (1985).

Delaware found that only 21% of its present population of offenders fell within levels 9 or 10. The vast majority of offenders—70%—fell within levels 1, 2, and 3, with only 10% in the middle levels. (Most of these were in some sort of alcohol- or drug-abuse program.)

The Comprehensive Crime Control Act of 1984 and Federal Sentencing Guidelines

At the urging of President Reagan, the U.S. Congress passed the Comprehensive Crime Control Act of 1984. This law has had a massive effect on sentences in federal courts, as well as on the federal prisons.

The act established a U.S. Sentencing Commission, which developed formal sentencing guidelines for federal judges to follow (U. S. Sentencing Commission, 1987). These guidelines were intended to achieve three goals: (1) *honest* sentences whereby the sentence imposed closely matches the sentence actually served; (2) *uniform* sentences whereby similar offenses earn similar punishment; and

Level 5	Level 6	Level 7	Level 8	Level 9	Level 10
60% (restricted 30–40 hours/week)	30% (restricted 50–100 hours/week)	20% (restricted 100–140 hours/week)	10% (90% of time incarcerated)	Incarcerated	Incarcerated
2–6 face-to-face/week; daily phone contact; weekly written reports	Daily phone contact; daily face-to-face; weekly written reports	Daily on-site supervision 8–16 hours/day	Daily on-site supervision 24 hours/day	Daily on-site supervision 24 hours/day	Daily on-site supervision 24 hours/day
1–7 privileges withheld	1–10 privileges withheld	1–12 privileges withheld	5–15 privileges withheld	15–19 privileges withheld	20 or more privileges withheld
Same (pay partial cost of food/lodging/supervision fee; 4- to 7-day fine)	Same as Level 5 (8- to 10-day fine)	Same as Level 5 (11- to 12-day fine)	Fine, court costs, restitution payable upon release to Level 7 or lower (12- to 15-day fine)	Same as Level 8	Same as Level 8
Mandatory rehabilitation skills program 8 hours/day; restitution; $40/month probation fee; no drinking; curfew	Work release; pay portion of food/lodging; restitution; no kitchen privileges outside mealtimes; no drinking; no sex; weekends home	Residential treatment program; pay portion of program costs; limited privileges	Minimum-security prison	Medium-security prison	Maximum-security prison

(3) *proportionate* sentences whereby more serious offenses are punished with more severe penalties. Under this system, later approved by Congress, sentences were classified into 43 levels based on the coordination of two main factors:

1. The severity of the crime, based not just on the formal charges, but also on the real harm that resulted from the offense.
2. Offender characteristics, which include prior criminal history; health, emotional stability, and employment history; and the role of the offender in the current offense. Possible sentences for each level cover a relatively narrow range. For example, a first offender who commits an armed robbery and takes $20,000 can expect a sentence of 46 to 57 months (Jacoby, 1989).

The act permits federal judges to depart from a guideline sentence when they find special aggravating or mitigating circumstances. However, the act also requires judges to explain, in writing, any sentence of theirs that deviates from the limits of these guidelines. Recent data indicate that the major reason why judges hand out more severe sentences than prescribed by the guidelines is that the offender had an unusually extensive criminal history; the major reason for shorter sentences is that the offender assists the government in its prosecution of another offender (Maguire & Flanagan, 1991). Both prosecutors and defendants are permitted to appeal sentences that deviate from the standards.

The act also provided that, after five years, parole in federal prisons would be abolished completely. Until recently about four out of every five prisoners were eligible for parole after serving one-third of their sentences. This provision further establishes the fixed-sentence concept. Moreover, the act specified that good behavior in prison could earn only a 15% reduction in time served on a sentence—

much less than what past practices had allowed.

Although the procedures in this act are far-reaching, it should be remembered that they apply only to federal courts and federal prisons; 95% of violent crimes in the United States are prosecuted under the jurisdiction of individual states. Furthermore, some judges have criticized what they see as the restrictive nature of the sentencing guidelines; these judges would prefer to make the mandatory guidelines into advisory ones (Coyle, 1990). For example, a federal district judge in San Francisco told a jury that was about to deliberate in a crack-cocaine case about the sentence the defendant would receive if convicted. Judges almost never tell the jury the potential sentence for fear it will affect the verdict, but this judge said the jury should know because he had no sentencing discretion (Labaton, 1989).

The Comprehensive Crime Control Act of 1984 is clearly a sign of the times. Along with the Anti-Drug Abuse Act of 1986, which requires prison sentences for certain offenders, it will ensure that the federal prison population will continue to grow and that the average prison term for violent offenders will lengthen (Block & Rhodes, 1989).

A recent study by the Sentencing Commission found that in 2324 cases (25% of the sentences imposed from the initiation of the guidelines on November 1, 1987, through March 31, 1989), 82% fell within the prescribed guidelines. Only 3% were more severe than the guidelines, 9% were more lenient, and about 6% received credit for providing the government "substantial assistance" in other prosecutions. The apparent uniformity may be misleading, however, because plea bargaining before a conviction can still lead to differing sentences for the same real offense (Collora, 1990). Many observers believe that the guidelines unintentionally have given more power to prosecuting attorneys by pushing plea bargaining to the fore (Chambers, 1990).

SUMMARY

The allocation of punishments is second only to the determination of guilt or innocence in its importance to the criminal defendant. The sentencing process raises again the conflicts that permeate a psychological approach to the legal system. Until recently, judges (and, in some states, juries) have been allocated very broad discretion in sentencing. Some judges are much more severe than the norm; others, more lenient. Discretion is both a laudable goal and an undesirable opportunity for the manifestation of personal biases. In recent years, concern over sentencing disparity has led to greater use of determinate sentencing and tighter controls over judicial discretion in sentencing.

Determinants of the sentence can be divided into relevant and irrelevant factors. For example, seriousness of the crime is a relevant factor, and there is a general relationship between it and the severity of the punishment. But a number of other, less relevant, aspects also are related to severity of sentence, such as the race and gender of the offender and of the victim.

Possible sources of bias in judges' sentencing decisions include their age and experience. Although time served on the bench would seem to have an influence on most judges, no discernible pattern emerges; length of service does not make all judges either more severe or more lenient. However, judges who were previously prosecuting attorneys tend to be harsher in their sentencing, and Republican judges are more severe than Democrats.

The sentencing hearing is usually a brief, routinized procedure. A survey of judges in San Diego found that, in more than 80% of the decisions, the judge administered a punishment in keeping with the recommendations of the probation officer. Factors that predicted the sentence include (1) type of crime, (2) extent of the offender's past record, (3) status of the offender between arrest and conviction, and (4) the aforementioned recommendation by the probation officer.

When the trial jury is allowed to do the sentencing (as is permitted in several states), a particular concern arises over crimes that may carry the death penalty. Jurors who oppose the death penalty regardless of the nature of the crime or the circumstances of the case are excluded from both the guilt phase and the sentencing phase of capital trials. Social science research has shown that the remaining jurors—called "death-qualified" jurors—are not only unrepresentative of the entire population of potential jurors (fewer women and blacks) but also conviction-prone. But the Supreme Court has not been responsive to these findings.

Concern over sentencing disparity has led to several revisions. Some jurisdictions have used sentencing councils, in which the presiding judge consults with several colleagues before making a decision. Such peer review has the effect of reducing disparity by about 10%. Determinate, or fixed, sentencing has become common over the last decade; it narrows the range of possible sentences for a particular crime. Delaware has adopted a ten-level series of punishments that has built-in modifications based on the offender's behavior. The Comprehensive Crime Control Act of 1984 abolished parole in federal prisons (implemented as of 1989) and required federal judges to follow stricter guidelines for sentencing.

Chapter 19

The Appellate Process and the Supreme Court

Treatment of guilty defendants within the legal system does not end when they are sentenced to a prison term or to probation. To protect the rights of those who may have been convicted unjustly, society grants any defendant the opportunity to appeal a verdict to a higher level of courts. Appeals are also possible in virtually every civil suit.

As in earlier steps in the legal process, a conflict of values occurs as appeals are pursued. One goal is *equality* before the law—that is, to administer justice consistently and fairly. But appellate courts also try to be sensitive to individual differences in what at first appear to be similar cases. Appellate courts recognize that judges and juries can make errors. The appellate procedure is used to correct mistakes that substantially impair the fairness of trials; it also helps promote a level of consistency in trial procedures.

REASONS WHY APPELLATE COURTS WILL OVERTURN A DECISION

When a decision is appealed to a higher court, the appellate judges read the "record" (a transcript of the trial proceedings), the "pleadings" (motions and accompanying documents filed by the attorneys), and the "briefs" (written arguments—which are rarely brief—from both sides about the issues on appeal) and then decide whether to overturn the original trial decision or let it stand. If a verdict in a criminal trial is overturned, or *reversed*, the appeals court will either order a retrial or order the charges thrown out. In reviewing the decision in a civil case, an appellate court can let the decision stand, reverse it (that is, rule in favor of the side that lost rather than

the side that won), or make some other changes in the decision. One possible opinion in either civil or criminal appeals is that certain evidence should not have been admitted or certain instructions should not have been given; hence a new trial is ordered.

Why do decisions get overturned? At a most basic level, the task of appellate judges is to discover whether a legal error occurred that had a significant effect on the outcome of the trial (such errors are called "reversible errors"). Three different examples of legal errors are illustrated in the next sections.

The Trial Judge Has Made a Mistake That Could Have Affected the Outcome of the Trial

Judges are human, and they can misapply the law, sometimes to the detriment of a litigant. (Litigants who appeal a loss at their trial then become *appellants*.) Judges can also make decisions about the way a trial is conducted that adversely affect the litigant's chance to have an impartial trial.

For example, as we discussed in Chapter 10, more than 30 years ago a prominent physician in Cleveland, Ohio, Sam Sheppard, was charged with the brutal murder of his wife. The Cleveland newspapers gave massive publicity to the case, with sensationalistic headlines and gory photographs. In effect, they convicted Sheppard before a trial was ever held. Certainly it would have been appropriate for the judge to move the trial to another jurisdiction, but he refused. Despite protesting his innocence, Sheppard was convicted by the jury and sentenced to prison. Many years later, while Sheppard was still incarcerated, the lawyer F. Lee Bailey was able to get an appeals court to conclude that Sheppard had not received a fair trial due to the inflammatory pretrial publicity and the one-sided coverage of the case. Sheppard was therefore entitled to be tried anew. In this second trial, the jury found him not guilty.

More recently, the U.S. Circuit Court of Appeals for the Ninth Circuit overturned the espionage conviction of Richard W. Miller, the first FBI agent ever found guilty of spying (Bishop, 1989). The court ruled that the trial judge had made a mistake when he admitted into evidence extensive testimony about Miller's having failed several polygraph examinations. Miller could be retried, without the inclusion of such evidence. In both the Sheppard and Miller cases the appellate court believed that the trial judge's errors could have affected the outcome of the trial.

Generally decisions will not be reversed unless the appellant can establish that the error affected the outcome of the trial. If the prosecution improperly introduced hearsay evidence, for example, the appellate court will first ask "So what?" If the answer is that the evidence was unimportant, the decision will not be reversed; the appellate court might describe the admission of the evidence as "harmless error." Occasionally, however, the claim is that a defendant was denied the right to a fair trial, and that the decision should be reversed, because the error occurred at a stage at which it was impossible to demonstrate whether it impacted the ultimate decision. In Louisiana in the early 1970s, women were placed in the jury pool only if they asked to be—a situation resulting in jury pools with very few women. Billy Taylor, a male, complained about this practice. He claimed that to be tried before an all-male jury would deny him the right to a jury drawn from a fair cross-section of the community. The trial judge denied his motion to discharge the jury panel, Taylor was tried and convicted, and he appealed ultimately to the U.S. Supreme Court. The Court agreed with Taylor's contention and reversed his conviction, ordering a new trial,

even though it was impossible for Taylor to prove that the outcome would have been different if he had been tried before a constitutionally selected jury (*Taylor* v. *Louisiana*, 1975).

There are other instances in which convictions have been reversed even though it was not clear that the error contributed to the outcome. Take the case of Willie DeCoster. DeCoster was arrested as he stood at the desk of his transient hotel in Washington, DC, and was immediately identified by the crime victim as one of the robbers who had held him up a few minutes before.

The victim had been accosted by three men in a parking lot about 6:00 P.M. that day. One of the accomplices held him from behind, and another stood in front of him with a knife. The third, whom the victim identified as DeCoster, went through his pockets, removing a wallet containing $110.

Two police officers came on the scene as the crime was in progress. They chased the men; one of them caught a man named Eley, who had a straight razor in his pocket. The two other robbers split up; one ran into the hotel where the police found DeCoster at the desk. When searched, DeCoster had neither the stolen wallet nor any weapons.

Later, the circumstances got more complicated. Between the time of the robbery and the trial, the victim was in a critical automobile accident that led to lapses in his memory and limitations to his eyesight. At the trial the victim was not able to identify DeCoster or the straight razor taken from Eley.

Also at the trial, DeCoster testified that, on the afternoon of the robbery, he had met the victim for the first time at a bar near the parking lot where the robbery occurred. However, he claimed that at about 6:00 P.M., after having several drinks with the victim, he returned to his hotel, only to be arrested. The alleged accomplice, Eley, testified that he had seen

DeCoster and the victim drinking together the day of the crime, but he also said that he saw them fighting in the parking lot when the police arrived.

The jury found DeCoster guilty of aiding and abetting an armed robbery and an assault with a dangerous weapon. He was sentenced to two to eight years on each count.

After DeCoster challenged his conviction, the circuit court of appeals in Washington, DC, concluded that "several events and circumstances suggest that [DeCoster] may have been denied his Sixth Amendment right to the effective assistance of counsel" (*United States* v. *DeCoster*, 1973, p. 1199). Consider what DeCoster's court-appointed attorney did and did not do:

1. DeCoster could not raise bail before the trial, but he was accepted by the Black Man's Development Center, a kind of halfway house that would supervise his custody. Although he was approved for the halfway house on October 12, his attorney did not request a review of his custody situation until November 9, and even then the lawyer failed to mention the halfway-house arrangement and filed his review request in the wrong court! On November 13, DeCoster complained to the judge. Finally, on December 8, the attorney filed the motion in the appropriate court, and DeCoster was released to the development center—almost two months after he should have been.

2. DeCoster's lawyer was not prepared to go to trial. As the trial began, the following exchange took place between the judge and the attorney:

COURT: All right, are you ready for trial? If you are, can you give the names and addresses [of your alibi witnesses] to the prosecutor?

DEFENSE: No, at the present time I am not. . . .

COURT: Well, are you here for trial?

DEFENSE: I am here for trial, but if the court pleases, under the statute we have 20 days.

COURT: Are you asking for a continuance?

DEFENSE: I would ask for a four- or five-day continuance for this trial, which might give me an opportunity to give the prosecutor what we can in response to this notice.

COURT: Well, you did announce ready for trial, . . . and if you are going to rely on an alibi, then you must know the witnesses you are going to use as alibi witnesses. You announced "ready." . . . It seems to me that if you have your witnesses ready for trial there seems to be no reason why you shouldn't be able to give the names of the people you intend to call as alibi witnesses at this time.

DEFENSE: We will proceed without alibi witnesses. We will consider we don't have any alibi witnesses.

COURT: You will not rely on an alibi defense?

DEFENSE: That is correct [from *United States* v. *DeCoster*, 1973, p. 1200].

Although this excerpt is brief, it reflects unpreparedness, disorganization, and poor judgment by DeCoster's attorney. But matters were only to get worse.

3. DeCoster's attorney waived a jury trial; apparently he was unaware that that action meant his client would be tried by the same judge who had presided over the trials in which DeCoster's two alleged accomplices had already been found guilty. He apparently was unaware of the tendency for juries to render more lenient verdicts than do judges (as described in Chapter 12), and he failed to do his homework about the previous trials of the presiding judge.

4. When DeCoster asked his attorney to subpoena his two alleged accomplices—that is, to order them to appear at the trial as witnesses—the attorney responded that he had thought of calling them but "we have no address for them" (p. 1200). DeCoster responded that both were easy to locate; one of the men was currently in the District of Columbia jail, having been convicted for this self-same attempted robbery, and the other man had been placed on probation because of his involvement in this crime, by the same judge presiding over DeCoster's trial. But the attorney never called this latter witness.

5. DeCoster complained to the presiding judge, first by letter and then orally at the opening of the trial, that he was dissatisfied with his appointed counsel. On the latter occasion he pleaded: "Your honor, I feel that this case should be continued [that is, delayed] because . . . I can't get proper representation that I should be getting" (p. 1200). The trial judge denied his request.

6. The defense attorney called only two witnesses, DeCoster and one of the alleged accomplices. The latter contradicted DeCoster on a fundamental point; during direct examination by DeCoster's attorney, this witness placed De-Coster at the scene of the crime and testified that DeCoster had been engaged in a fight with the victim at the time when DeCoster had testified he was at his hotel. This major contradiction stripped the defense of its believability.

Although appeals courts don't pass judgment on the tactical decisions made by defense attorneys, they will review a conviction if the defendants have been denied the effective assistance of counsel. In ruling that DeCoster's new attorney could file a motion for a new trial, the appeals court established a landmark ruling: that defendants are not just entitled to something more than no counsel at all; they are entitled to *reasonably competent counsel.*

DeCoster's appeal was considered two more times by the District of Columbia Circuit Court. Ultimately, in 1979, the court upheld his conviction, concluding that DeCoster had failed to show that his counsel's inadequacies affected the outcome of his trial.

Legal Ambiguities Need to Be Settled So That the Law Remains Consistent

Any judgment by an appellate court deals not only with a particular dispute but also with an interpretation of the legal issues involved in the dispute. With the thousands of laws in existence, varying interpretations can be placed on them by different judges. The conviction of Lyn Nofziger, a close adviser to President Reagan, was overturned on the ground that the law under which he was convicted was ambiguous (Tolchin, 1989). Further, as new laws are passed, they may create unintended and unanticipated contradictions with previous laws still on the books. A major function of the appellate process is to settle ambiguities so that the application of the law is as consistent as possible. At times this action leads to a reversal of a lower court's decision; on first appearance, the courts seem to be inconsistent, even though the basic rationale for the reversal is to follow a fundamental principle. The lawsuit by a former Miss Wyoming against *Penthouse* magazine is an example.

Kimerli Pring brought a libel suit against the magazine, claiming that she had been defamed by a story in *Penthouse* that detailed the sexual exploits of a Miss Wyoming during the Miss America contest. She asked for $100 million in damages, and a jury awarded her $26.5 million. The trial judge later reduced the award to $12.5 million in punitive damages and $1.5 million in actual damages.

But lawyers for *Penthouse* challenged the award, claiming that the First Amendment's right of free speech protected such stories, especially since this particular article described events that would be impossible in real life and thus could not be libelous.

The appeals court (the Tenth U.S. Circuit Court of Appeals) overturned the jury verdict, concluding that the First Amendment applied even to "crude" literature like this and that that principle superseded any claims to defamation. The appeals court described the story as "a gross, unpleasant, crude, distorted attempt to ridicule the Miss America contest and contestants. It has no redeeming features whatever." But, the court ruled, the First Amendment's umbrella is not restricted to simply the socially desirable:

> The First Amendment is not limited to ideas, statements, or positions which are accepted, which are not outrageous, which are decent and popular, which are constructive or have some redeeming element. Although a story may be repugnant in the extreme to an ordinary reader, and we have encountered no difficulty in placing this story in such a category, the typical standards and doctrines under the First Amendment must nevertheless be applied.

The Law Needs to Be Changed

Occasionally, appellate courts decide that the law needs to be changed, and a case is appealed that provides an opportunity to make the needed change. The appellate courts in each state can change the judge-made law of that state (the "common law"), and the U.S. Supreme Court can change federal judge-made law. Often judicial changes are the result of interpretations or reinterpretations of state or federal constitutional provisions. The following are some examples in which appellate courts have changed the law:

• A father was rendered a paraplegic in an auto accident, and his children sued the insurer for loss of "consortium" (companionship, parental guidance, etc.). The appellate court recognized the "cause of action" (the legitimacy of the claim), thereby changing the law in the state (*Farley v. Progressive Casualty Co.,* Ohio 1992).

• A convicted felon serving a prison sentence was permitted to reside in a privately operated halfway house. While there, he left the premises, broke into the home of a woman, and raped and murdered her. The victim's estate sued the operator of the halfway house. The claim was dismissed by the trial court but reinstated by the appellate court, which held that the operator of such a facility must exercise reasonable supervision over the prisoners (*Dudley v. Offender Aid and Restoration,* Virginia 1991).

• A married couple allowed two 16-year-old girls to drink at their home. The girls left by car, a crash ensued, and the passenger was killed. Her mother sued the couple at whose home the girls drank. The appellate court held that the "hosts" (the couple) could be liable for a death caused by a teenage driver who had been served alcohol. This decision changed the law in Illinois (*Cravens v. Inman,* Illinois 1991).

• Thirty years ago state legislatures were grossly disproportioned; typically, rural voters had more legislators than their numbers warranted. The U.S. Supreme Court had consistently ruled that the makeup of state legislatures was a "political question," which could not be determined by the courts. Then, in a decision that was to dramatically change American politics, the Supreme Court ruled that it could decide the issue after all, and it held that the Due Process Clause of the Fourteenth Amendment requires equal representation, a concept then known as "one man, one vote" (in today's terminology it is "one person, one vote") (*Baker v. Carr,* 1962).

Limits of the Appellate Courts

As the preceding examples illustrate, much of the concern of appellate courts is with the procedural propriety of legal proceedings. Did the judge apply the law correctly? Were the proper safeguards included? If a judge rejects a motion by an attorney—perhaps a motion to include something specific in the judge's instructions to the jury, or a request for a change of venue, or an objection to a particular bit of testimony by an opposing witness—the appeals court's task is to rule on the appropriateness of this procedure.

Appellate courts also concern themselves with substantive issues. They may be asked to rule whether the weight of evidence supported a given verdict. The appeal by Douglas Williams, described below, furnishes an example of a state supreme court's reversal of a jury's guilty verdict because the court concluded that the evidence was insufficient to justify a conviction. (Ordinarily, appeals courts do not reexamine witnesses; rather, they rely on the transcript of the trial plus the oral arguments and written briefs by the appellant and the appellee.)

Kay Simmons (not her real name), a senior at Augusta High School in Butler County, Kansas, was looking forward to her graduation, only three weeks away. She worked part-time at a restaurant in Augusta, a town of 6000 people 20 miles from Wichita. When she got off work about 10:00 P.M. on May 8, 1979 (a Wednesday), she stopped to buy cigarettes at a gas station and then drove to the apartment of her boyfriend, Mike Roberts. When she arrived at about 10:15 or 10:20, Mike was not there; he was not to arrive home from work until about 1:30 A.M.

A woman named Bonnie Daniels and her young sons lived in the apartment below Roberts's, which was on the second floor of a fourplex apartment building. Bonnie noted when Kay arrived and heard Kay enter the boyfriend's apartment. Around 11:00 P.M., Bonnie heard the sound of something falling on the floor above her, but—regrettably—she didn't investigate. When Mike Roberts arrived home about $2\frac{1}{2}$ hours later, he found the door to his apartment unlocked and the apartment dark. Worried about what was going on, he quickly entered and discovered Kay's nude body on the bed; her throat had been cut and she was dead.

After a police investigation, two men were arrested and charged with rape, aggravated burglary, and the murder of Kay Simmons. The suspects, Allen R. Jordan and Douglas L. Williams, along with their women friends and two children, lived in the second-floor apartment across from Mike Roberts. Both men were well known in this small community as troublemakers. Rape was included as one of the charges because an examination of the victim's vagina showed the presence of semen.

Extensive circumstantial evidence existed against the suspects, although no one other than the victim witnessed the crimes. More important, some direct evidence implicated Jordan; Kay's eyeglasses were found beside her body on the bed, and crime-lab analyses positively identified his fingerprints on the eyeglasses. When confronted by the police, Jordan conceded that he had spoken to Kay outside but insisted that he then returned to his apartment.

Jordan had been convicted of robbery and was currently on parole. He had also been accused of the rape and sexual abuse of a 14-year-old girl but was never prosecuted because the victim was unwilling to testify. Needless to say, Jordan was familiar to the authorities.

Why did the police arrest *two* men? Because of the manner in which Kay's body was lying, with her arms parallel to her sides, the police speculated that one man had held her down while the other slashed her throat. In addition, nothing indicated that Kay had struggled, further implying multiple attackers. The autopsy showed an abrasion on the victim's left shoulder, which the police thought might have been caused by a metal watch band. Jordan wore no wristwatch, but Williams did—one with a metal band. Since Williams had been with Jordan earlier in the evening, he was a likely candidate for the other attacker.

Separate juries tried Jordan and Williams and found each guilty—Jordan for rape, aggravated burglary, and felony murder; Williams for felony murder and aggravated burglary. Both appealed their convictions. The aftermath of Williams's appeal provides us with more insight than is customary about the jury and its deliberations.

Williams protested that the evidence presented at his trial was insufficient to support his conviction. His testimony was consistent with Jordan's but only up to a point. They both agreed that sometime between 10:00 and 10:15 P.M. Jordan had shouted to Kay from inside the apartment and then left to talk to her. When he returned a few minutes later, Williams claimed, Jordan made a comment "about how good looking the girl was next door; that he would sure like to get in her pants." According to Williams, Jordan then said that he was returning next door, at which point Williams lay down on the couch and fell asleep. He didn't know when Jordan returned, waking up only when their women friends came home, about midnight. Another factor that strengthened Williams's appeal was the prosecutor's failure to introduce evidence about the victim's shoulder bruise or Williams's metal wristwatch. Although the police had speculated that these were linked, the coroner did not mention this injury when he testified about the wounds. In short, *from the evidence presented at the trial*, the jury had no grounds on which to conclude that Williams was even at the scene of the crime.

The prosecutor based his case against Williams on the inference that a second person must have been present to restrain the victim and that Williams was the logical party. The jury accepted this logic—perhaps because of the defendant's reputation in this small community—and convicted Williams. But the supreme court of Kansas ruled that there was insufficient evidence against Williams and set him free. (In criminal law, jury convictions can be overturned but acquittals cannot.)

Was Williams guilty? The trial jury believed he was. The appellate court said: not on the grounds presented at the trial. It may be that Williams escaped conviction only because the prosecutor failed to do his job effectively. But what is interesting about this case is that we know the jury strayed beyond the evidence in convicting Williams. Ordinarily, we would have no way of knowing whether a jury's verdict was tied to the evidence. At no point are jurors required to justify their actions. Their deliberations are off limits, not just to the media and snooping social scientists but even to the judge. However, in this case, when the verdict was overturned, several outraged jurors revealed the reasons for their verdict. Two jurors wrote letters of protest to the Kansas supreme court. A portion of one of these follows:

I am writing not only as a concerned citizen but also as a responsible adult. I was selected as a juror in December of 1979 in Butler County, Kansas, and thus served during the murder case of [Kay L. Simmons].

I speak for myself but I feel the other jurors would agree that much consideration went into the final decision in finding Douglas Williams guilty. We looked at every piece of evidence and listened to every witness with our utmost attention. We were in court for many days and hours. . . . Believe me, the facts were on my mind 24 hours a day even after the trial. It was a very emotional experience, but I was and I AM very confident that our decision was giving Williams justice.

I understand that you believe there was no evidence. (1) Both Jordan and Williams were heard shouting out the window to Miss [Simmons] about "how they'd like to get in her pants." Later two figures were seen heading for the apartment. (2) Williams's semen stain. (3) It was proven to us that two people had to commit the murder. According to the blood splatters, someone held her arms while another person slit her throat. (4) Douglas Williams had no eyewitnesses as to his whereabouts at the time of the murder. (5) The cigarette butts. All of the above plus other miscellaneous witnesses were enough for me to make a responsible decision concerning another adult's life. . . .

I am for capital punishment. The prisons are crowded and as taxpayers we are paying the criminal's bills. The present judicial system is just a big joke. . . .

Although this is a sincere letter from a concerned juror, the basis for the juror's conclusion *cannot be found in the evidence.* Regarding claim 1, there is no testimony that *Williams* said anything about the victim's allure. Nor was it proven that Williams or anyone else had been seen heading toward the neighboring apartment. Regarding claim 2, laboratory analyses of Williams's blood revealed that it was type A, whereas the semen in the victim's vagina came from a person with type-O blood. (Jordan was type O.)

With respect to claim 3, the prosecution reasoned that two persons must have committed the murder because there were no signs of a struggle. This is not evidence in the legal sense of the word. Likewise, the absence of eyewitnesses who could provide Williams an alibi (claim 4) is not proof that he was lying when he claimed he was asleep. Defendants do not have to show alibis to prove that they are innocent;

the prosecution must prove that they are guilty, at least to a degree beyond reasonable doubt. But this juror's use of claim 4 implies that, in her mind, an accused is guilty until proven innocent. The fifth piece of "evidence" proposed by the juror, the "cigarette butts," is circumstantial at best and certainly not enough to convict Williams.

Thus an appellate court can reverse a conviction if it concludes that evidence presented at the trial did not warrant that verdict.

FEDERAL COURTS AND STATE COURTS

As Baum (1985) observes, it is not correct, strictly speaking, to refer to a single court system in the United States. The court system is divided into a federal system and a separate system for each state. Most cases heard in federal courts fall into three categories:

1. Criminal and civil cases that arise from violations of federal laws, including the Constitution.
2. All cases to which the U.S. government is a party.
3. Certain civil suits. If a civil suit involves citizens in different states and the amount in question is sizable, either party can bring the case to federal court rather than to a state court (Baum, 1985).

State courts handle many more cases than do the federal courts; in a recent year about 240,000 cases were brought to federal court, whereas 2.7 million came to the trial courts of a single state, California.

Even though the two court systems are separate organizationally, they do interact. The federal courts may refer issues back to state courts for resolution or clarification. Chapter 17 described the case of *DeShaney* v. *Winnebago County* (1989), in which the U.S. Supreme Court found that public officials did not have a duty to rescue a child from privately inflicted harm. A year later the Supreme Court tossed the same issue back to the lower courts (in a case involving a school principal's failure to prevent a teacher from sexually abusing a student). One of the Supreme Court's important roles " . . . is to engage other courts in a continuing dialogue on what the law is and what it should be. Through the discourse, the law develops" (Greenhouse, 1989a, p. 14).

All states have at least one level of appellate courts. If there is only one level (the situation in about one-third of the states), it is usually called the state supreme court. The remaining states have two levels, an intermediate-level appellate court as well as a state supreme court.

Federal courts are structured differently. For the 94 district courts throughout the United States and its territories, there are currently 575 federal trial judgeships (although Chief Justice Rehnquist has requested 59 more, because the criminal caseload of these judges has increased more than 25% since 1984). Moving beyond the trial level, there are 12 circuit courts of appeals. These were established by Congress in 1891, to reduce delays at the Supreme Court level. The District of Columbia accounts for one circuit; each of the other circuits covers three or more states. Currently there are 168 federal appellate judgeships, with 16 more requested. Appeals of decisions made by one of these circuit courts of appeals are directed to the U.S. Supreme Court. Howard (1981) concluded, from a sample of three circuit courts, that 30% of the losing parties in the federal courts of appeals took their cases to the Supreme Court.

THE SUPREME COURT

The U.S. Supreme Court is, of course, the final appeal body. It can choose to review decisions by lower federal courts and any decisions by state courts that involve a federal statute or some provision of the U.S. Constitution. In contrast to English courts, which do not have the power to declare an act of Parliament unconstitutional, U.S. courts have the right to decide whether legislation passed by Congress meets the "presumption of constitutionality" (Rehnquist, 1987). Disputes between states can be resolved only by the Supreme Court. It intervenes to settle new or unresolved questions of constitutional law or federal statutory law or because it wishes to change (or confirm) earlier decisions on these subjects, including decisions by the executive and legislative branches of government, as well as court decisions.

Despite the importance of the Supreme Court, the public seems to know little about its procedures or personnel. In one survey, when asked to name the Chief Justice, only 9% of 1005 randomly selected adults were able to name Justice Rehnquist; 6% gave other names, and 85% did not know (Morin, 1989). Only 29% could name even one of the nine Supreme Court justices; Sandra Day O'Connor was most frequently named. In contrast, 54% were able to give the name of the judge on the television show *The People's Court* (Judge Wapner).

How Much Discretion Does the Supreme Court Have?

The Supreme Court has tremendous discretion. For example, it can rule on any state's action that impinges on a provision of the U.S. Constitution. Who decides whether an action contradicts the Constitution? The Supreme Court does, and its decision remains the law of the land, unless the U.S. Congress passes some legislation that directly supersedes it. For example, in *Brown* v. *Board of Education* (1954), the U.S. Supreme Court outlawed segregated public schools, even though public education had always been (and still is) a matter administered by the individual states. Some critics of this decision, to this day, maintain that it was inappropriate (see Box 19-1). But the Supreme Court is literally the judge of such matters.

The Court also chooses which cases it will consider. In its annual term of October to June or July, it usually receives 4000–5000 appeals. But it chooses to hear only a small percentage— around 150–160, and in recent years that num-

ber has been declining. It has complete discretion to act on only those that it considers the most significant and to disregard the rest. (Box 19-2 lists a few of the significant decisions made by the Court in the last 25 years.) The Court may avoid difficult cases or those that arouse the emotions of the public. From 1973 to 1976 the Burger Court agreed to hear only 1 of 35 cases appealed on the basis of a claimed violation of the *Miranda* rule. In addition, the Supreme Court does not issue a full opinion for all the cases it chooses to hear.

The Court also has discretion over the breadth or narrowness of each decision it makes—that is, whether the decision is restricted to a specific example or has wide applicabili-

---

Box **19-1**   *Criticisms of the* **Brown** *v.* **Board of Education** *Decision*

Criticisms by political conservatives of the Warren Court's decision abound. One, by L. Brent Bozell, focuses on the inappropriateness of federal court intervention:

In May, 1954, the country was very far from having made up its mind on the question of segregated schools. It was divided in its practices in this matter because it was still profoundly divided in its beliefs. No hard constitutional consensus had been reached, or was likely to be reached in the foreseeable future. Therefore neither side, neither the "integrationists" nor the "segregationists," insofar as they were then identified

as distinct groups, could realistically hope for the adoption of a constitutional amendment— a provision, that is, of the fixed constitution—that would embody its views and make them thenceforth the supreme and uniform law of the land. In this situation, the Supreme Court, visibly moved by the ideology of equality, took matters into its own hands and sought to impose upon the country a uniform solution to the problem of mixing the races in the public schools. The court not only decided that the Negro plaintiffs in the *Brown* case were entitled to admission to white schools. It also, the following year, ordered a staged desegregation of

public schools throughout the land, an order the judicial system itself proceeded to administer. And that was not all: although the claim had been implicit in the logic of the *Brown* opinion, the Warren Court, in 1958, formally proclaimed that its own views about segregated schools—or on any other subject for that matter—were binding on other public authorities in the country's political system. In the Little Rock school case of *Cooper* v. *Aaron*, the Supreme Court, for the first time, entered its own explicit claim to judicial supremacy [Bozell, 1966, pp. 32–33].

ty. In fact, it can decide which issues of a particular case it wants to address. In *Mapp* v. *Ohio* (1961) it took a case brought to it because of an obscenity charge but used the case to make a monumental decision regarding illegal search and seizure by the police (described in Chapter 9).

The issue of how "activist" the Supreme Court is will be described shortly. It is sufficient at this point to note that at times the Supreme Court has been accused of "running and hiding"—of avoiding the opportunity to make a sweeping pronouncement when it would have been in the best interests of the country to have done so.

But the Supreme Court does not have complete discretion. It cannot decide to resolve a controversy simply on its own initiative; justices cannot overrule just any decision they find distasteful or unlawful. The Court is limited to responding only on those matters that come before it for action (the 4000–5000 annual appeals). As Baum (1985) notes: "The court does not face legal questions in the abstract. Rather, the court addresses those questions in the pro-

cess of settling specific controversies between parties ('litigants') that bring cases to it" (p. 3).

The Supreme Court and Activism

Supreme courts differ in the breadth of action reflected in their decisions. Some make broader decisions; others limit their applicability. A court that tends to make wide-ranging decisions is called an "activist" court, and the thrust for this orientation lies in the justices' view of the Supreme Court as an agent of change. Baum (1985) observes that "one key element of the concept is the court's willingness to make significant changes in public policy, particularly in policies established by other institutions" (p. 5).

Activist judges usually defend their position by claiming that they are protecting fundamental values, such as liberty, equality, or justice. Activist judges may be either conservative or liberal in their political orientation; what distinguishes these two types is not their desire to bring about change but, rather, the choice of values they advocate (Lerner, 1987; Wilson,

---

Box **19-2** | *Significant Decisions by the Supreme Court*

In major cases heard by the Supreme Court in the past 25 years, the following important policy-relevant decisions were made:

1. In *Roe* v. *Wade* (1973) the Supreme Court severely limited the power of the states to prohibit abortions. But in a 1992 decision, *Planned Parenthood* v. *Casey*, the Court granted states

the right to place some restrictions on abortions.

2. The Court first abolished the death penalty statutes of most states but later approved a new set of capital-punishment guidelines.

3. Pivotal in the process that led President Nixon to resign was the Court's unanimous decision in *United States* v. *Nixon* (1974)

that the president could not use executive privilege as a justification not to turn over records to a federal court.

4. Prayers were banned at public-school graduation ceremonies because the Court ruled that they violated the First Amendment.

1987). William Rehnquist, currently the Chief Justice of the United States and a political conservative, sees the Court as playing an active role in social policy. For example, in 1988 he spearheaded a decision by the Court to reconsider whether members of minority groups have the right to sue private parties for racial discrimination; the decision by the Court to rehear arguments dealt with an issue that neither side had contested in a previous decision (Taylor, 1988a).

Many of the issues that come before the Supreme Court involve conflicts between liberal and conservative positions (Rohde & Spaeth, 1976); therefore, values play a primary role in the decisions. A psychological analysis of determinants of court decisions reveals several categories of values that can be distinguished:

1. *Freedom.* This includes civil liberties cases, involving both procedural matters, such as the rights of criminal defendants, and substantive ones, such as freedom of personal expression. The "flag-burning" issue of 1989 is one example. Liberals favor the open expression of these rights; conservatives are more likely to favor restrictions on them.
2. *Equality.* This category includes issues that derive from claims of discrimination under the Fourteenth Amendment and other provisions of the law. Liberals tend to be very sensitive to these claims, whereas conservatives are less sympathetic.
3. *Economic regulation.* How much should the government—especially the federal government—monitor and control private business—such as railroads, airlines, utility companies, manufacturers of children's clothing, chemical companies, and so forth? This value has also been referred to as "New Dealism" (Rohde & Spaeth, 1976), because much of this government regulation had its advent in the administration of President Franklin D. Roosevelt. Liberals generally favor government regulation, although their position is often complex; conservatives prefer a laissez faire approach in which private industry is "regulated" by the forces of free-market economics.
4. *Property rights versus personal rights.* Should a restaurant owner have the right to prohibit a certain group of people (blacks, people with beards, people without shoes) from eating at that restaurant? Conservatives place great value on property rights; liberals value these rights less strongly.
5. *States' rights versus federal governmental intervention.* Another issue that overlaps with the preceding ones is conservatives' insistence on the rights of individual states to determine their own policies without supervision or intervention by the federal government. Liberals are more likely to advocate oversight controls by the federal government.

Opposite to judicial activism is the doctrine of restraint. The distinguished former Supreme Court Justice Felix Frankfurter, an advocate of restraint, argued that the Court should minimize its interference with the policies of the other branches of the federal government. He believed it should endeavor to avoid constitutional questions whenever feasible and dodge controversy when practical.

Activism is a controversial orientation. Baum (1985) lists three major criticisms of the Court's making policy-oriented activist decisions:

1. The Supreme Court is a relatively undemocratic institution; its members are not elected by the populace, and they come from a rather limited stratum of society. (The "unrepresentativeness" of Supreme Court judges is apparent on some demographic grounds; recently all the justices have been lawyers, and all

were male until Sandra Day O'Connor was appointed by President Reagan. Only two have been members of a racial minority group, the former justice Thurgood Marshall and current justice Clarence Thomas. No Jew has sat on the Supreme Court since 1969, when Abe Fortas resigned (Margolick, 1989b). Among all the Supreme Court justices since the beginning of the Court in 1789, there have been only five divorces—three involving Justice William O. Douglas.)

2. Activism is risky because the Court is vulnerable to attack when it takes controversial positions. Recent decisions about school prayer and abortion are vivid examples.

3. "It is unwise because courts lack the capacity to make effective policy choices" (p. 5). For example, the Court can do only so much with the 150 cases for which it annually provides full opinions. In contrast, reports Baum, the federal administrative agencies publish about the same number of regulations *each week* as the Supreme Court issues in a year.

Additionally, the Court is limited in its impact by the actions of other policy-making bodies. Ordinarily, the legislative or the executive branch can have further say on the policies that the Court has addressed.

No Supreme Court justice would advocate activism in all cases; restraint is supported in some situations. Yet the activism/restraint dimension can be used to classify and understand the behavior of judges.

The Basis for Supreme Court Justices' Decisions

Justices realize that the Supreme Court is the "court of last resort," and they normally make their rulings with great care. The process of forming a judicial opinion is laid bare, especially when the judges face a "hard case"—that is, one in which precedents from past law would lead to one outcome and the judges' values or other central determinants would lead to another.

Supreme Court judges are not completely immune from pressures of public opinion and certain constituencies. It is true that they are free from the threat of being voted out of office for making unpopular decisions. Their jobs are for life, and their salaries of $153,600 per year (chief justice: $160,000) provide a modicum of financial security. Nevertheless, social and political factors can significantly affect their decisions. For example, when considering the *Webster* case on restrictions of abortions in 1989, the Supreme Court received more than 40,000 letters, and 300,000 people marched in support of women's rights. In the spring of 1992, when *Planned Parenthood* v. *Casey* was being considered, some 750,000 pro-choice supporters rallied on the Washington Mall in favor of abortion rights legislation, on the assumption that the Court would use *Casey* to overrule *Roe* v. *Wade*.

Justices are aware of public opinion; they know the acceptance of their decisions rests in part with the public. "Never for a very long period is the court out of touch with the populace," states Thomas G. Krattenmaker, associate dean of the Georgetown University law school; "they are always sensitive to what they perceive to be the shared values of Americans" (quoted in Rubin, 1989, p. 7A). Some justices also have a personal investment in the popularity of their actions. Justice William O. Douglas was discussed as a possible vice-presidential candidate in the 1940s and apparently had some ambitions for the presidency. Some of his colleagues felt that his ambitiousness affected his judicial decisions (Lash, 1975). Additionally, public opinion is considered a valid criterion for the interpretation of some constitutional amendments. Baum (1985) uses the example of the Eighth Amendment's prohibition of "cruel and unusual punishments"; justices on both sides have cited public opinion surveys in support of their interpretations of this amendment when making decisions about capital punishment (*Gregg* v. *Georgia*, 1976).

Justices' decisions are subtly but significantly influenced by the opinions of two more specific groups: the mass media and the legal community (Baum, 1985). Justices are sensitive to criticism by the press, and they are aware of the media's role in communicating their opinions to the public. In at least one decision, *Richmond Newspapers, Inc.* v. *Virginia* (1980), the Court's decision was affected by severe media criticism of a related decision it had made a year earlier (Lewis, 1981). (These decisions dealt with the right of the media to have information about jurors, including their names and addresses, during the trial and access to jurors after the trial.)

The legal profession is especially important to the justices because it serves as a reference group (Baum, 1985). Judges interact socially with other lawyers. More relevant to their professional activity, articles in law reviews are useful in forming their decisions.

Benjamin Cardozo (1921), a Supreme Court justice from 1932 to 1938, wrote a book-length classification of factors that determine an individual judge's ruling. He identified three main factors, as follows:

The Use of a Rule or Analogy and the Use of Precedents.

Some judges ask: How does this case resemble past cases? What principle or rule applies? By studying rulings in previous cases, the judge may see something analogous in the case at hand.

In such an approach, the place of precedent is central. As noted in Chapter 1, justices continually reaffirm the legal doctrine of *stare decisis* ("let the decision stand"). Many are reluctant to overturn precedents—that is, to take

completely new directions. Especially with regard to traditional topics, such as property and contracts, British and U.S. law developed "primarily through the aggregation of judicial decisions rather than through constitutions and statutes, and the only law to be interpreted was precedent" (Baum, 1985, p. 123).

Evolution. Cardozo notes that, often, precedents can be found to support both sides of a case. For that and other reasons, justices rely on other factors for their decisions. For example, they recognize that society changes, and these changes may make precedents inappropriate. According to the Congressional Research Service (1982), the Court overruled precedent in 75 decisions between 1961 and 1980. To varying degrees, judges acknowledge that law and society interact and that a purpose of the law is to meet the needs of society (Kadish & Kadish, 1971). As our characteristic ways of behaving change, new interpretations of the law are needed.

An example is the case of *Javins* v. *First National Realty Corporation* (1970). Ethel Javins was among several tenants in Washington, DC, who were threatened with eviction from their apartments for failure to pay their rent. They all lived in the same three-building complex called Clifton Terrace, in the northwest part of the city. The tenants admitted that they had not paid their rent because the landlord (First National Realty Corporation) had not corrected numerous violations of the housing regulations. The tenants estimated that there were approximately 1500 violations in the three-building complex. The landlord sued Javins for nonpayment of rent. When the local court heard this case, the trial judge refused to examine Javins's claims of proof and entered a verdict in favor of the landlord. The judge relied on property law, which was the traditional way the legal system approached such a claim.

However, the assumption of landlord/tenant law, derived from property law and going back to feudal times, is that a lease primarily conveys to a tenant the use of land. Nowadays, such an assumption may continue to be reasonable with regard to some leases, such as those involving farmland or commercial property (*Javins*, 1970, p. 1074); in such instances the value of the lease to the tenant is the land itself. But the contemporary United States is not primarily an agrarian society; for modern apartment dwellers the value of the lease is that it gives them a place to live. As Judge J. Skelly Wright, a strong proponent of judicial activism and author of the appeals court's opinion, commented:

> The city dweller who seeks to lease an apartment on the third floor of a tenement has little interest in the land 30 or 40 feet below, or even in the bare right to possession within the four walls of his apartment. When American city dwellers, both rich and poor, seek "shelter" today, they seek a well-known package of goods and services—a package which includes not merely walls and ceilings, but also adequate heat, light and ventilation, serviceable plumbing facilities, secure windows and doors, proper sanitation, and proper maintenance [*Javins*, 1970, p. 1074].

Thus the circuit court of appeals concluded that the old rules of property law governing leases are the wrong standard for today's transactions. The more modern precepts of contract law are more appropriate, because contract law has evolved to a point that sellers (or landlords, in this case) are seen to have a responsibility for the quality of goods and services through *implied warranties* of fitness and adequacy. In contract law, without any special agreement, the law holds a warrant that, when merchants offer their goods for sale or lease, those goods are fit for the ordinary purposes for which such goods are used and are of at least reasonably average quality. Lately the courts have begun to hold developers of real estate responsible for the quality of their products. Judge Wright concluded that such warranties applied to renters, too—that landlords have the obligation to keep their premises in a habitable condition. Thus contract law, especially the housing regulations of the District of Columbia, is applicable.

The circuit court of appeals ordered a new trial, in which Javins would be given the opportunity to prove that the alleged housing-code violations constituted a breach of the landlord's warranty.

"Sociological" Concerns.   Justice Cardozo's third major determinant of judges' decisions in hard cases was what he called "sociological concerns." By this he meant an awareness of changes in predominant values in American society that demand reinterpretations of the laws. For example, only recently was a right articulated for physically disabled people to have access to public buildings. Previously the disabled were left to their own devices to climb long flights of stairs, for example, in order to do the business (buy license plates, pay taxes, change deeds) required of them by law. The Americans with Disabilities Act, effective in 1992, expanded these rights to the area of employment by requiring employers to modify the workplace to make reasonable accommodations for disabled workers.

Several years ago, in an interview on the television program *60 Minutes*, a Dallas attorney proposed that manufacturers of handguns should be required to award damages to anyone injured by a handgun, whether as a result of a crime or an accident. This proposal may seem preposterous to some readers. But a court of appeals in Maryland has ruled unanimously that crime victims in that state can sue the makers, distributors, and sellers of those small, cheap handguns called "Saturday night specials." The judge who wrote the opinion stated that the maker or the seller of a "Saturday night special" knows, or ought to know, that the product's principal use is for criminal activity.

How does the Court become aware of "sociological concerns"? In addition to sources that influence all of us—mass media, literature, public debate—the Supreme Court also uses social science data to become informed about social issues and questions of a general psychological nature (Monahan & Walker, 1991). As we discussed in Chapter 1, psychologists have often filed *amicus curiae* briefs that summarize psychological research and social science perspectives relevant to specific issues in litigation (Acker, 1990). How successful are such briefs in influencing the Court's decisions?

On the one hand, citations to social science research in Supreme Court decisions appear to be increasing. In recent years the American Psychological Association has submitted *amicus* briefs on a broad spectrum of decisions, including the frequency and nature of certain sexual behaviors (*Bowers* v. *Hardwick*, 1986), sex stereotyping in employment (*Price-Waterhouse* v. *Hopkins*, 1989), death qualification of jurors (*Lockhart* v. *McCree*, 1986), and the psychological effects on children of testifying in court in the presence of a defendant charged with abuse of the child (*Kentucky* v. *Stincer*, 1987; *Maryland* v. *Craig*, 1990).

On the other hand, if we measure effectiveness in terms of "winning" decisions, the outcomes of several of the cases in which the APA has submitted briefs have been discouraging. Some scholars view this track record as further evidence that the Supreme Court is immune to any social science data that run counter to the results it prefers, but others suggest that psychology should become "less preoccupied with asserting its opinion on the legal question and basing its definition of success on the Court's adoption of those views" (Grisso & Saks, 1991, p. 210). From this perspective, psychology

should avoid advocating ultimate opinions about the Constitution in appeal briefs, just as individual psychologists are often urged not to give expert testimony about ultimate legal questions in trials.

A Contrasting View. Justice Cardozo's rather traditional view emphasized that decisions are dictated by the state of the law. Another prominent judge, Jerome Frank, strongly disagreed with Justice Cardozo. Cardozo's analysis may apply in the abstract, Frank stated; "In theory, the judge begins with some rule or principle of law as his premise, applies this premise to the facts, and thus arrives at his decision" (1930, p. 101). But this analysis does not describe the way judges actually decide cases.

> Since the judge is a human being and since no human being in his normal thinking processes arrives at decisions (except in dealing with a limited number of simple situations) by the route of any such syllogistic reasoning, it is fair to assume that the judge, merely by putting on the judicial ermine, will not acquire so artificial a method of reasoning. Judicial judgments, like other judgments, doubtless, in most cases, are worked out backward from conclusions tentatively formulated [1930, p. 101].

A psychologist would support Judge Frank's analysis more than Justice Cardozo's. A person's values—even a judge's—color that person's perception of the facts and hence influence his or her judgments. This is neither right nor wrong, good nor bad; it is simply inevitable. (We have to look no further than a comparison of decisions by the Warren Court and the Burger Court, a matter first described in Chapter 9 but approached from a different perspective here.)

However, Frank's conclusion can be extended too far. First, as Baum (1985) reminds us, occasionally justices will note that their judicial decisions do not reflect their personal views. Supreme Court Justices Harry Blackmun and

Potter Stewart both have voted to uphold laws endorsing capital punishment. But Blackmun expressed his "distaste, antipathy, and, indeed, abhorrence, for the death penalty" (*Furman* v. *Georgia,* 1972, p. 405), and Stewart said "If I were a legislator, I wouldn't even vote for it" (Reynolds, 1984).

Second, justices do not always line up in expected ways. Even though some patterns of votes are predictable from justices' positions on a conservative/liberal dimension (see Table 19-1), some alliances of strange bedfellows appear. A recent example includes three justices—Sandra Day O'Connor, Anthony Kennedy, and David Souter—appointed by presidents Reagan and Bush. All three justices were predicted to be consistent conservatives who would join the Court's two arch-conservatives, Antonin Scalia and William Rehnquist, along with newcomer Clarence Thomas, to produce a dramatic turn to the political right in Court opinions on civil rights, criminal law, First Amendment rights, and social issues. But the three justices have not behaved as expected. Instead, they have often teamed up to form a moderate, pragmatic center for the Court that produces cautious decisions, often affirming precedents that conservatives assumed (and hoped) would be abandoned. Three decisions in 1992 illustrate the influence of the O'Connor/Kennedy/Souter center; in each of these cases, the three justices joined in the majority opinion.

1. *Lee* v. *Weisman.* By a 5–4 vote, the Court ruled that prayers at public-school graduations violated the First Amendment, which prohibits the state from establishing a religion.
2. *Planned Parenthood* v. *Casey.* A 5–4 majority reaffirmed the basic holding of *Roe* v. *Wade* that a woman has a constitutional right to an abortion, but it allowed the states to restrict abortion rights as long as the restric-

tions do not constitute a substantial obstacle to a woman seeking an abortion.
3. *Wright* v. *West.* By a vote of 6–3, the Court rejected a proposal by the Bush administration to restrict the ability of federal judges to review and reevaluate the trials of criminal defendants in state courts.

Justices' values may change over time. Among contemporary justices, Harry Blackmun has reflected a shift in values over the last 15 years. Appointed by President Nixon in 1970, he was a Minnesota boyhood friend of Chief Justice Burger and the best man at Burger's wedding; hence journalists dubbed them the "Minnesota Twins." But gradually, over the decade of the 1970s, Blackmun moved toward the center of the political spectrum, and by 1980 he was joining Justice William Brennan in opinions more than he joined Chief Justice Burger. During the 1981 and 1982 terms, Blackmun and Burger supported the same opinion in 60% of the cases, whereas he agreed with the two liberals, Brennan and Marshall, 75% and 71% of the time (*The Supreme Court,* 1983). Blackmun told a reporter that one of his goals was to prevent the Court "from plunging rapidly to the right" (Jenkins, 1983). In the 1988–1989 term, Blackmun voted the same way that Chief Justice Rehnquist did only 54% of the time.

Changing Values and the Supreme Court

During the 1950s and 1960s the Warren Court was an activist one. It often stretched or ignored precedents. Chief Justice Earl Warren was not a legal technician. His favorite question to attorneys presenting their arguments before the Supreme Court was "But is it fair?" The most important consideration to Warren was equality.

As Republican presidents Nixon and Ford

Table 19-1 Scalogram of Supreme Court Justices' Votes in Cases Involving "Freedom" Issues, in the 1982 Term

Cases[a]	Justices[b]									Liberal votes
	Ma	Br	St	Bl	Po	Wh	Bu	O'C	Re	
74- 297	+	+	+	+	+	+	+	+	−	8
75- 295	+	+	+	+	+	+	+	+	−	8
75- 903	+	+	+	+	+	+	+	−	−	7
74- 430	+	+	−	+	+	+	+	+	−	7
74- 250	+	+	−	+	+	−	+	−	+	6
76- 687	+	+	+	+	+	−	+	−	−	6
77- 180	+	+	+	+	−	+	+	−	−	6
75- 229	+	+	+	−	+	+	−	−	−	5
74- 823	+	+	+	+	−	+	−	−	−	5
77- 637	+	+	+	+	+	−	−	−	−	5
75- 547	+	+	+	+	−	−	+	−	−	5
74- 646	+	+	+	+	−	−	−	−	−	4
74- 675	+	+	+	+	−	−	−	−	−	4
75- 708	+	+	+	+	−	−	−	−	−	4
76- 733	+	+	+	+	−	−	−	−	−	4
77- 694	+	+	+	+	−	−	−	−	−	4
77- 721	+	+	+	+	−	−	−	−	−	4
77- 405	+	+	+	+	−	−	−	−	−	4
77-1171	+	+	+	+	−	−	−	−	−	4
74- 794	+	+	+	−	+	−	−	−	−	4
74- 3	+	+	+	−	−	−	−	−	−	3
75- 813	+	+	+	−	−	−	−	−	−	3
76- 527	+	+	+	−	−	−	−	−	−	3
77- 22	+	+	+	−	−	−	−	−	−	3
77-1003	+	+	+	−	−	−	−	−	−	3
77-1019	+	+	+	−	−	−	−	−	−	3
77-1201	+	+	+	−	−	−	−	−	−	3
77-1267	+	+	+	−	−	−	−	−	−	3
77-1275	+	+	+	−	−	−	−	−	−	3
77- 614	+	−	−	+	−	+	−	−	−	3
77-1090	+	+	−	+	−	−	−	−	−	3
77-1134	+	+	−	+	−	−	−	−	−	3
77- 987	+	+	−	−	−	−	−	−	−	2
74- 748	+	−	+	−	−	−	−	−	−	2
74- 535	+	−	+	−	−	−	−	−	−	2
74- 12	+	−	−	−	−	−	−	−	−	1
74- 21	+	−	−	−	−	−	−	−	−	1
76- 143	−	−	+	−	−	−	−	−	−	1
Liberal votes	37	32	30	21	9	8	8	3	1	

[a]Numbers are volumes and pages of case citations in *Supreme Court Reports, Lawyers' Edition.*

[b]Ma = Marshall, Br = Brennan, St = Stevens, Bl = Blackmun, Po = Powell, Wh = White, Bu = Burger, O'C = O'Connor, Re = Rehnquist.

Note: Cases were included if the Court decided issues of procedural due process or substantive civil liberties, except equal protection, by nonunanimous vote; cases dealing with remedies for rights violations are excluded. Liberal votes are designated +; conservative votes, −. Boldface line divides justices into two groups according to conventional rules of scalogram analysis; − signs to left of line and + signs to right may be interpreted as votes inconsistent with ideological ordering of justices.

Source: Baum (1985, Fig. 4-1, p. 138).

began to appoint justices in the early 1970s, observers expected a decidedly conservative court to emerge. But the Burger Court was harder to characterize; one collection of articles about it was subtitled *The Counter-Revolution That Wasn't* (Blasi, 1982). Its decisions were often inconsistent, and some people questioned whether Burger provided the intellectual leadership or vision necessary to reflect a value-consistent orientation in the Court's actions.

Two Court observers, Fiss and Krauthammer (1982), argued that, even before his promotion to chief justice, William Rehnquist was leading the Court to many of its decisions. Rehnquist and Burger agreed on 80% of the cases for which full opinions were issued. When a chief justice is in the majority on a decision, he has the privilege of deciding whether he wants to author the majority opinion or, if not, who will write it. Burger consistently chose Rehnquist. In fact, Rehnquist wrote the opinion for the Court in almost all the important cases in which he was in the majority (Fiss & Krauthammer, 1982).

The Supreme Court as a Decision-Making Group

Recall that, of the 4000 or more cases (called "petitions for certiorari") submitted to the Supreme Court each term, the court will choose to hear fewer than 200. At least four of the nine justices must vote to hear a case (the "rule of four"). Chief Justice Rehnquist estimates that between 1000 and 2000 of the petitions each year are "patently without merit" (1987, p. 264). However, any justice can request discussion of a petition, in hopes that four of the justices will vote to hear the case.

If the Supreme Court agrees to hear a case, it is scheduled for written and oral arguments. Written arguments, called legal briefs, are filed with the Court and are available to the public. Oral arguments are presented in the Supreme Court's massive courtroom, with only 30 minutes usually allowed to each side. Rarely will additional time be given (Rehnquist, 1987). Rule 44 of the Supreme Court states: "Oral argument should undertake to emphasize and clarify the written argument appearing in the briefs theretofore filed. The court looks with disfavor on any oral argument that is read from a prepared text" (Stern & Gressman, 1962, p. 564).

An attorney presenting an oral argument before the Supreme Court can find the experience disconcerting. Justices can interrupt at any time—and often do—to ask the attorney penetrating or intemperate questions about the case or to offer their observations. The judges can even argue among themselves, as the attorney stands helplessly out of the line of fire. In a 1982 death penalty case, Justices William Rehnquist and Thurgood Marshall clashed. After Rehnquist pushed the point that it would be cheaper for the court system to execute a prisoner than to imprison him for a long period, Justice Marshall sarcastically interjected "Well, it would be cheaper just to shoot him when you arrested him, wouldn't it?" (Barbash, 1983). Discussions between justices can even get off the subject at hand; in 1982 Rehnquist and Justice John Paul Stevens disagreed about the position played by Hall of Fame baseball player Kiki Cuyler (Mann, 1983).

Do oral arguments have any influence? After all, the justices have previously read extensive briefs and reviewed relevant decisions; they have probably discussed the case with their law clerks. Despite all this prior activity, oral arguments are not simply a formality. According to Chief Justice Rehnquist, "I think that in a significant minority of the cases in which I have heard oral arguments, I have left the bench feeling different about the case than I did when I came on the bench. The change is seldom a full 180-degree swing, and I find it is most likely to occur in cases involving areas of law with which I am least familiar" (1987, p. 176).

A few days after having heard oral arguments, the Supreme Court meets to discuss the case and take an initial vote. During these conferences, the chief justice introduces the cases and offers his view of each. The other justices then speak in order of seniority on the Supreme Court. If the group's position is not clear, a vote is taken. One reason why Chief Justice Rehnquist believes that the discussion at the case conferences does not often change a justice's opinion is that each justice has been dealing with the case extensively through several stages (1987, p. 295). After the majority is identified, one of the justices is selected to write the majority opinion. As indicated earlier, the chief justice, if in the majority, can assign himself or someone else to do so. If the chief justice is not in the majority, the most senior of the justices in the majority assigns the opinion.

Preparing these opinion drafts is time consuming. Former Justice Powell has written: "For the most part, perhaps as much as 90% of the time, we function as nine small independent law firms" ("What the justices are saying," 1976, p. 1454). The designated justice circulates his or her opinion draft. Others may write dissents (or separate concurrences), and these are all circulated, too. Many drafts may be prepared, as "opinion and reasoning may be changed to accommodate other members of a potential majority or win over wavering justices" (Woodward & Armstrong, 1979, p. 3). A greater attempt to persuade others occurs here than in the prior vote-taking meeting. So the minority may even become the majority. Eventually the decision is announced.

As in any groups that must form an opinion or take action, many pressures operate during this judicial process, including pressures toward uniformity and opinion change. Baum (1985) observes:

> Once that opinion is completed and circulated, it often becomes a focus of negotiation. Ordinarily the assigned justice wishes to obtain the support of as many colleagues as possible for the opinion. The writer will seek to convince justices in the minority to change positions, and it also may be necessary to discourage allies in conference from leaving the fold [p. 115].

Sometimes the debate becomes intense and bitter.

Justices differ in how much they try to persuade their colleagues. Some (William O. Douglas was an example) have been uninterested in exerting influence, but others (Harlan Stone, Hugo L. Black, Felix Frankfurter) have been described as "evangelists" and "active proselytizers" (Douglas, 1980). They also differ in their skills at negotiation and persuasion. John Harlan, even as a conservative on the liberal Warren Court, was still influential because of his exceptional skills as a legal craftsperson (Baum, 1985).

As in all endeavors, one's personality affects one's ability to influence. A person who gets along with colleagues, who is likable and skilled in interpersonal relations, as Justice Rehnquist is, gains influence as a result. In contrast, Justice James McReynolds (who served from 1914 to 1941) alienated his colleagues with his unpleasantness, especially with his manner of noting on their written opinions "This statement makes me sick" (Pusey, 1951). In this respect, Felix Frankfurter is an especially poignant example, as noted by Baum (1985):

> Frankfurter came to the court in 1939 expecting to play a major leadership role, and he made great efforts to influence his colleagues. He gave special energy to courting new colleagues. But these efforts suffered for his arrogance and his tendency to lecture to his colleagues. His messages to other

justices during the decision-making process included an abundance of statements like the following: "And so, please, Mr. Jackson, do find time to read, if you have not already read, the chapter on Presumption in J. B. Thayer's Preliminary Treatise." "I would like to ask you to read or reread in cold blood the following cases." He also reacted sarcastically to opinions with which he disagreed. Frankfurter unintentionally alienated several colleagues with his behavior, and his influence within the court was fairly limited [p. 148].

Leadership style of the chief justice at the case conferences can influence the quality of discussion and outcomes. The most extensive contrast between chief justices in this century was that between Charles Evans Hughes and Harlan Stone (Baum, 1985). Chief Justice Hughes, who according to Frankfurter "radiated authority," exercised tight control on discussions and limited the time devoted to each case. Stone, who replaced Hughes in 1941, opted for a more open discussion, which led to longer and more acrimonious conferences. In choices like this there are always trade-offs between efficiency and thorough consideration.

SUMMARY

All convicted felons have the right to appeal their convictions. Losing parties in civil suits also can appeal. Appellate courts may overturn a judge's or a jury's decision for several reasons, including the following:

1. The trial judge made a mistake.
2. Legal ambiguities need to be settled.
3. The law needs to be changed.

Appellate courts are primarily concerned with procedural matters, such as the judge's decisions about appropriate laws. However, they can overrule a guilty verdict if they conclude that it was not warranted by the evidence, but they do so very cautiously.

The U.S. Supreme Court is the ultimate appeal body. It has extensive discretion in which cases it chooses to hear. Over the years, the Court has sometimes been activist, making wide-ranging decisions that affect government policies; at other times it has advocated restraint. Supreme Court justices' opinions are affected by the rule of analogy, or precedents; by evolution of society; and by sociological concerns. The values of the justices also explain some of the variation in their votes on particular cases.

As a decision-making group the Supreme Court is rife for the pressures that operate on any group that must form an opinion or take action.

Glossary

ABA American Bar Association; a recognized group of professional attorneys in the United States.

ACLU American Civil Liberties Union; a recognized group of attorneys and others committed to protecting the civil liberties of individuals.

acquittal A finding of not guilty in a criminal trial. The finding can be made by a judge or by a jury, and the judge can direct an order for acquittal if there is insufficient evidence to convict.

adjudication A decision, judgment, or decree resolving a controversy, handed down by a court.

aggravating circumstances Conditions that make a criminal act more serious—for example, to knowingly create a risk of death or serious injury to other persons as well as to the victim.

ALI American Law Institute.

alternative dispute resolution Any legal mechanism used to settle a conflict without going to court.

amicus curiae "Friend of the court"; someone not a party to the action (that is, not the defendant or plaintiff). Most often seen when filing a brief to argue a particular point.

APA American Psychological Association; a recognized group of professional psychologists.

appeal Process by which a trial order or judgment is reviewed by a higher court. At the first appeal the defendant has an automatic right of review and normally a right of counsel. Thereafter, both are discretionary (that is, the appellate court may decide which cases to review and whether counsel is necessary).

arbitration A form of alternative dispute resolution in which a neutral third party develops a resolution to which the disputing parties are bound.

arraignment A court appearance at which the defendant is informed of the pending charge and enters a plea.

Batson decision A ruling that, if the criminal defendant is black and if the prosecutor uses peremptory challenges to strike blacks as jurors, the prosecutor must provide reasons other than race for the decision to strike these particular prospective jurors.

belief in a just world Belief that justice exists in the world and people get what they deserve.

bias Human predisposition to make interpretations based on past experiences.

bifurcated trials A separation of a trial into different phases to try separate legal issues.

Brawner rule Also known as the ALI rule; states that a defendant is not responsible for criminal conduct when, as a result of mental disease or defect, he or she lacks substantial capacity either to appreciate the criminality (wrongfulness) of the conduct or to conform his or her conduct to the requirements of the law.

brief The written appellate argument filed by counsel for one of the parties.

burn-out Syndrome that is found to occur in people who work with other people; symptoms

468

include emotional exhaustion, depersonalization, and reduced personal accomplishment.

capital offense Crime for which the death penalty can be imposed.

capital punishment Sentence of death for a crime or crimes.

case law Law made by rulings in individual cases.

challenge for cause Occurs when individuals are interviewed during the jury selection process. If the judge agrees that there is justification for an attorney's claim of bias, a juror may be excused for cause. Also, a judge may excuse a panelist for cause without a request to do so from either attorney.

chemical castration Use of injections of a female hormone into male rapists as a method of lowering the sex drive.

civil procedure Legal action in which one party (the plaintiff) brings a claim against another (the defendant) for an alleged wrong.

closing statement Summation of evidence, made by an attorney at the end of a trial.

cognizable group A group of persons, usually defined by demographic characteristics such as race or gender, who are assumed to possess some shared beliefs or values.

common law Generally refers to the "judge-made" law (case law or decision law). Originating in England, the common law meant the rulings of judges based on tradition and custom. These rulings became the law common to the land. Common law is distinguished from statutes (laws enacted by legislatures).

community-based policing A policy that increases direct police/citizen contacts within a neighborhood so as to improve police/citizen relationships.

competence to stand trial Sufficient ability to understand the legal proceedings in which one is involved and to consult with one's attorney.

confabulation One effect of hypnosis, in which the subject adds false information to accurate recollections.

confession Any incriminating evidence offered by a defendant. Many different legal considerations affect the validity of a confession: due process, right to counsel, self-incrimination, and so on.

consultant Role of a psychologist in which he or she advises policy makers of relevant data or research findings.

context reinstatement Procedure to aid witnesses in recalling memories that may have been repressed because of trauma.

contraband Articles that the law prohibits a person from possessing, importing, or exporting.

corporal punishment Punishment inflicted on the body of a person; physical punishment.

crime-control model Point of view that emphasizes procedures that detect suspects and prosecute defendants.

criminal procedure Legal action in which the city, county, state, or federal district (the prosecutor) prosecutes an individual or individuals for breaking ordinances or laws. The defendant is represented by defense counsel.

criminal profiling Use of psychological principles as a crime investigation technique to guide police toward suspects who possess certain personal characteristics as revealed by the way a crime was committed.

criminology The study of crime and criminal behavior.

cruel and unusual punishment Sentence considered outlandish or extremely severe, based on three principal tests: (1) whether the punishment shocks the general conscience of a civilized society, (2) whether the punishment is unnecessarily cruel, and (3) whether the punishment goes beyond legitimate penal aims.

death-qualified jury Jury panel that excludes persons whose attitudes about capital punishment would prevent them from performing their sworn duty as jurors.

defendant In either a civil or a criminal procedure, the individual charged with wrongdoing.

deferred prosecution A procedure whereby offenders (usually first-time offenders) who admit their guilt are placed on probation and the charges against them are dismissed if they successfully complete probation.

Depo-Provera A drug that decreases levels of testosterone and is sometimes used to decrease sexual arousal in sexually aggressive offenders.

deposition Witness's pretrial statement given under oath.

determinate sentencing Provision of strict limits for the sentences that judges can give for particular crimes.

differential association Learning-theory approach that asserts that criminal behavior is the result of socialization into a system of values that is conducive to violations of the law.

diminished capacity Variation of the insanity defense that is applicable if the defendant (in the words of the law) lacks the ability to "meaningfully premeditate the crime."

discovery Procedure in which the attorney for one side seeks to become aware of the materials being used by the other side to form its case.

discretion Application of judgment to temper a response after having weighed the circumstances.

docket Official list of cases to be tried in court.

double jeopardy Second prosecution for the same offense. Prohibited by the Fifth Amendment.

due process Assurance found in the Fifth and Fourteenth Amendments that the defendant receives a trial that is fundamentally fair.

***Durham* rule** States that an accused is not criminally responsible if his or her unlawful conduct was the product of mental disease or defect.

entrapment Defense used by criminal defendants, claiming that the government used procedures to encourage criminal activity in otherwise law-abiding persons.

evidence Statements, documents, and items included in the legal record of a trial; these, and these alone, are to be considered by the jury in reaching a verdict.

exclusionary rule Principle ruling as off limits any material that was obtained illegally.

expert witness Someone who possesses special knowledge about the subject matter of a legal proceeding—knowledge that the average juror does not have.

fact finder Person (judge) or persons (jurors) who weigh the evidence in a trial and make a determination regarding the verdict.

felony Grave crime; a crime for which the punishment in federal law may be death or imprisonment for more than one year.

focal concerns theory Theory that relates the criminal activities of lower-class gangs to their need to achieve those ends that are most culturally valued through the simplest possible means.

forensic psychologists Psychologists who specialize in the evaluation and treatment of persons under court jurisdiction, consultation with litigators, provision of expert psychological testimony, or evaluation of psychological services within the legal system.

genetic fingerprinting Use of DNA to determine identification of an individual lawbreaker.

grand jury Group of citizens receiving evidence in closed proceedings and deciding whether to issue an indictment against any individuals. In most jurisdictions the defendant has no right to present his or her side in grand jury deliberations.

guilty but mentally ill A finding that a defendant has a mental illness but is still legally guilty for the crimes charged.

habeas corpus After direct appeals have been exhausted, the defendant may petition the trial court claiming that his or her continued detention is unlawful. If sufficient basis exists, the government may be asked to establish the legality of the detention.

hypermnesia One effect of hypnosis, in which the subject remembers more material than when he or she was not hypnotized.

hypnotically induced testimony Use of hypnosis to aid the recollection of victims or witnesses.

immunity Prosecution's promise not to prosecute a defendant if she or he agrees to make a statement at another's trial.

impeach To cross-examine a witness with the purpose of calling into question his or her credibility or reliability.

implicit personality theory A person's preconceptions about how certain attributes are related to one another and to behavior.

indictment Accusation issued by a grand jury charging the defendant with criminal conduct.

inquisitorial approach Procedure used in Europe, in which questioning is the sole responsibility of the presiding judge.

insanity A legal term for a mental disease or defect that, if proved to be present at the time a person committed a criminal act, can result in the person being found not criminally responsible for this act.

involuntary commitment Detention of an individual in a mental hospital without his or her consent; usually requires that the individual be considered dangerous to self or others or be gravely disabled.

irresistible impulse test States that the accused may be capable of distinguishing between right and wrong, but that he or she was not impelled to commit the act by an irresistible impulse.

joint custody A legal outcome in which divorcing parents share or divide various decision-making and control responsibilities for their children.

jurisdiction Authority of the court to exert its power over persons or matters within a certain geographical area.

jurisprudence System or body of law; the science or philosophy of law; the course of court decisions.

jury nullification Option for the jury that allows it to disregard both the law and the evidence and acquit the defendant if the jury believes an acquittal is justified.

leading question An attorney's question to a witness that suggests to the witness what the answer should be.

macho personality constellation Ideology consisting of (1) calloused sexual attitudes toward women, (2) a conception that violence is manly, and (3) a view of danger as exciting.

McNaughton rule States that, in order to establish a defense on the grounds of insanity, it must be proved that at the time of committing the act the accused was laboring under such a defect of reason, from a disease of the mind, as not to know the nature and quality of the act he was committing, or, if he did know it, that he did not know what he was doing was wrong.

mediation A form of alternative dispute resolution in which a neutral third party helps the disputing parties agree on a resolution to their conflict.

memory hardening A process sometimes associated with hypnotically aided recall whereby a subject transforms a belief or expectation into a "memory" that he or she is convinced is accurate.

mens rea Mental state accompanying a forbidden act.

mercy killing Killing of an individual for compassionate or altruistic motives.

Miranda warning Statement by police officer to suspect, informing the suspect of his or her rights to avoid self-incrimination.

misdemeanor Crime less serious than a felony.

mitigating circumstances Factors such as age, mental capacity, motivations, or duress that lessen the degree of guilt in a criminal offense and thus the nature of the punishment.

motion in limine A legal request for a judge to make a pretrial ruling on some matter of law expected to arise at the trial.

opening statements Not part of the evidence, these orations made by the lawyers on each side give an overview of the evidence that will be presented.

orienting response A pattern of greater physiological responsiveness when a person perceives a meaningful stimulus; used in the Guilty Knowledge approach to polygraphy.

outpatient commitment A procedure for requiring a severely mentally ill person who is also dangerous or gravely disabled to receive treatment in the community.

parens patriae The parent-like role of guardian assumed by the state to protect the interests of persons with disability.

parole After being imprisoned, the defendant may be freed before the normal release date, conditional on adherence to certain rules. If any of the rules are broken, the government will move to have the defendant's parole revoked.

per curiam opinion "By the court"; an opinion stating the decision of all the judges and not signed by any particular judge.

peremptory challenge Opportunity to exclude a certain number of potential jurors from the eventual jury without having to give any reasons; their number, determined in advance by the judge, varies from one jurisdiction to another.

perjury Lying on the witness stand.

petit jury Panel of 6 to 12 individuals selected to hear evidence and act as fact finders in a trial.

plea Statement of "guilty" or "not guilty" made by the defendant in the trial.

plea bargain In exchange for the defendant's promise to forego a trial, the government may promise to charge the defendant with a lesser crime or to ask the judge for a lesser sentence. When the "bargain" is reached, the defendant pleads guilty and no trial is held.

polygraph "Lie detector"; an instrument for recording variations in several physiological functions.

precedent Decision in an earlier case that is used as a model, authority, or example for deciding a case before the court in which the facts and issues are similar.

preliminary hearing Hearing before a magistrate to determine if there is sufficient evidence to justify a trial. The defendant is entitled to be represented by counsel.

preponderance of the evidence Standard for a verdict in a civil suit; the evidence for one side outweighs that of the other by even a small margin.

preventive bail Use of bail to incarcerate a defendant before trial, used if the defendant is considered dangerous. (Also called *preventive detention*.)

probable cause Reasonable ground for believing that a crime has been committed or that the person committed a crime. Probable cause is required to support the issuance of a search warrant or arrest warrant.

probation In lieu of a sentence of imprisonment, the judge can suspend sentence and free the defendant on condition that the defendant adhere to certain rules. If the defendant breaks any of the rules, the government will move to revoke probation.

probative Serving to prove; being certified as genuine or valid.

proof beyond a reasonable doubt Standard of proof in criminal cases. Unless the prosecution proves the defendant committed each element of the stated offense(s) beyond a reasonable doubt, the defendant must be found not guilty.

prosecutor Attorney who represents the government in a criminal procedure.

psychopathy A long-term pattern of unsocialized or criminal behavior by a person who feels little guilt about such conduct.

public defender Attorney appointed by the court to represent a defendant when the defendant cannot afford counsel.

rape trauma syndrome A collection of behaviors or symptoms that are common aftereffects of rape.

rebuttal Presentation of evidence to counter or disprove facts previously introduced by the adverse party.

recusal Practice of judges disqualifying themselves from participating or voting because of a possible conflict of interest or prejudice.

redirect questioning Questioning by the original attorney that follows the opposing counsel's cross-examination.

remand To send back to a lower court. A higher court can remand a case to a lower court with instructions to carry out certain orders.

rule of law Legal principle, recognized by authorities and used as a guide in deciding cases.

schema Mental structure that aids in the processing and interpretation of information.

scientific jury selection Systematic selection of jurors using the methods of social science to assess the characteristics of the pool of possible jurors by conducting surveys and demographic studies and using systematic ratings.

sentencing disparity Tendency of different judges to administer a variety of penalties for the same crime.

sentencing guidelines A system for ensuring more uniform criminal sentences by fixing sentences into one of several levels determined by the severity of the crime and the prior history of the defendant.

sequester Process of keeping juries secluded from influence outside the courtroom.

settlement negotiation In civil cases, the pretrial process whereby plaintiffs and defendants agree to an outcome that ends their legal disagreement.

"sleeper effect" Effect from a persuasive act that does not appear right away but does appear later.

stare decisis To stand on the decisions of the past. A principle that holds that courts and judges should follow prior decisions and judicial rulings in the interest of predictability, fairness, and certainty.

statute Law or act passed by a legislature (including Congress).

stipulation Condition, requirement, or item specified in a legal instrument.

Stockholm syndrome Feelings of dependency and

emotional closeness that hostages sometimes develop toward their kidnappers in prolonged hostage situations.

summary jury trial Brief presentation of both sides of a case, usually lasting only one day, in which a jury renders a verdict that is only advisory to the judge.

suppression hearing Hearing before a judge in which one of the attorneys argues that certain evidence should not be admitted at trial.

tabula rasa Literally "blank slate," the unbiased condition under which jurors are assumed to begin a trial.

Tarasoff **decision** Court decision that specified that psychotherapists have a "duty to protect" third parties.

team policing A policy of less centralized decision making within police organizations.

unconscious transference Generation of a memory that is based on the recall of several past occurrences, so that an innocent person may be confused with an offender.

venire Panel of prospective jurors drawn from a large list.

venue Place (district, county) where a portion of the crime took place and where the trial can be held.

verdict Decision of the judge or jury after hearing and considering the evidence.

voir dire Process by which the judge and/or attorneys ask potential jurors questions and attempt to uncover any biases.

waiver Defendant may wish to give up (or waive) his or her rights. For instance, after receiving *Miranda* warnings, the defendant may choose to confess without the presence of a lawyer.

warrant Order issued by a judicial official authorizing the bearer to arrest a particular individual or search a described place for enumerated items. A warrant is issued on a showing of probable cause that an individual has committed a described crime or that evidence of criminal activity will be found at the designated location.

weapons effect When confronted by an armed attacker, the victim's tendency to focus attention on the weapon and fail to notice other stimuli.

Witherspoon **excludables** Those prospective jurors who are so opposed to the death penalty that they never could give that sentence, regardless of the heinousness of the crime.

Yerkes-Dodson law Psychological law stating that increased stress lowers eyewitnesses' accuracy.

References

Abel, R. (1989). *American lawyers.* New York: Oxford University Press.

Abram, K. M., & Teplin, L. A. (1991). Co-occurring disorders among mentally ill jail detainees: Implications for public policy. *American Psychologist, 46,* 1036–1045.

Acker, J. R. (1990). Social science in Supreme Court criminal cases and briefs: The actual and potential contribution of social scientists as amici curiae. *Law and Human Behavior, 14,* 25–42.

Adler, F. (1973). Socioeconomic factors influencing jury verdicts. *New York University Review of Law and Social Change, 3,* 1–10.

Adorno, T., Frenkel-Brunswik, E., Levinson, D., & Sanford, N. (1950). *The authoritarian personality.* New York: Harper & Row.

Age of accountability. (1981, December 14). *Time,* 80.

Ake v. Oklahoma, 105 S.Ct. 977 (1985).

Alexander, F., & Healy, W. (1935). *Roots of crime.* New York: Knopf.

Alexander, J. (Ed.). (1963). *A brief narration of the case and trial of John Peter Zenger.* Boston: Little, Brown.

Alexander, S. (1979). *Anyone's daughter.* New York: Viking.

Alker, H. R., Jr., Hosticka, C., & Mitchell, M. (1976). Jury selection as a biased social process. *Law and Society Review, 11,* 9–41.

Alkus, S., & Padesky, C. (1983). Special problems of police officers: Stress-related issues and interventions. *Counseling Psychologist, 11,* 55–64.

Alschuler, A. W. (1968). The prosecutor's role in plea bargaining. *University of Chicago Law Review, 36,* 50–112.

Ambuel, B., & Rappaport, J. (1992). Developmental trends in adolescents' psychological and legal competence to consent to abortion. *Law and Human Behavior, 16,* 129–154.

American Bar Association (1978). *Standards relating to the administration of criminal justice, fair trial and free press.* Chicago: Author.

American Bar Association (1979). *Approval of law schools: American Bar Association standards and rules of procedure, as amended, 1979.* Chicago: Author.

American Bar Association (1989). *ABA Criminal Justice Mental Health Standards.* Washington, DC: Author.

American Friends Service Committee (1972). *Struggle for justice.* New York: Hill & Wang.

American Psychiatric Association (1982). APA statement on the insanity defense. *American Journal of Psychiatry, 140,* 681–688.

American Psychological Association (1990). Ethical principles of psychologists. *American Psychologist, 45,* 390–395.

American Psychological Association (1992). Ethical principles of psychologists and code of conduct. *American Psychologist, 47,* 1597–1611.

Anderson, D. (1988). *Crimes of justice.* New York: Times Books.

Anderson, G. (1990). Sentencing, race & rapport. *America,* 508.

Apodaca, Cooper, and Madden v. Oregon, 32 L. Ed. 2d 184 (1972).

Appelbaum, P. S., & Hoge, S. K. (1986). The right to refuse treatment: What the research reveals. *Behavioral Sciences and the Law, 4,* 279–292.

Applebome, P. (1987, February 3). Juvenile crime: The offenders are younger and the offenses more serious. *New York Times,* 8.

Archer, D. (with Gartner, R.). (1984). *Violence and crime in cross-national perspective.* New Haven, CT: Yale University Press.

Arens, R., Granfield, D. D., & Susman, J. (1965). Jurors, jury charges, and insanity. *Catholic University Law Review, 14,* 1–29.

Arens, R., & Susman, J. (1966). Judges, jury charges, and insanity. *Howard Law Journal, 12,* 1–34.

Ares, C. E., Rankin, A., & Sturz, H. (1963). The Manhattan bail project: An interim report on the use of pre-trial parole. *New York University Law Review, 38,* 67–95.

Argersinger v. Hamlin, 407 U.S. 25 (1972).

Aries, P. (1962). *Centuries of childhood.* New York: Random House.

Arnold, M. (1974, May 5). How Mitchell-Stans jury reached acquittal verdict. *New York Times,* 1.

Arnold, S., & Gold, A. (1978–1979). The use of a public opinion poll on a change of venue application. *Criminal Law Quarterly, 21,* 445–464.

Asch, S. E. (1956). Studies of independence and submission to group pressure: I. A minority of one against a unanimous majority. *Psychological Monographs, 70* (Whole No. 417).

Ashcraft v. Tennessee, 322 U.S. 143 (1944).

Associated Press (1982, August 29). Juries tough on media in libel suits. *Kansas City Times*, A5.

Associated Press (1984, November 23). Judicial leniency toward women found. *Kansas City Times*, A15.

Associated Press (1985, May 19). Date rape common, new study indicates. *Kansas City Star*, A10.

Associated Press (1988, January 13). Former Kansas woman identifies man in attack. *Kansas City Times*, B5.

Astin, A. W. (1984). Prelaw students: A national profile. *Journal of Legal Education*, 34, 73–85.

Attorney General's Commission on Pornography. (1986, July). *Final report*. Washington, DC: U.S. Department of Justice.

Auerbach, C. A. (1984). Legal education and some of its discontents. *Journal of Legal Education*, 34, 43–72.

Austin, W. (1980). Friendship and fairness: Effects of type of relationship and task performance on choice of distribution rules. *Personality and Social Psychology Bulletin*, 6, 402–408.

Austin, W., & Utne, M. K. (1977). Sentencing: Discretion and justice in judicial decision-making. In B. D. Sales (Ed.), *Psychology in the legal process*. (pp. 163–194). New York: Spectrum.

Austin, W., Walster, E., & Utne, M. K. (1976). Equity and the law: The effect of a harmdoer's "suffering in the act" on liking and assigned punishment. In L. Berkowitz & E. Walster (Eds.), *Advances in experimental social psychology* (Vol. 9, pp. 163–190). Orlando, FL: Academic Press.

Austin, W., & Williams, T. (1977). A survey of judges' responses to simulated legal cases: A research note on sentencing disparity. *Journal of Criminal Law and Criminology*, 68, 306–310.

Babcock, B. A. (1975). Voir dire: Preserving "its wonderful power." *Stanford Law Review*, 27, 545–566.

Backster, C. (1974). The anticlimax dampening concept. *Polygraph*, 3, 28–50.

Bailey, F. L. (1985, January 25). Justice must be served for defendants, too. *USA Today*, 12A.

Bailey, F. L., & Rothblatt, H. B. (1985). *Successful techniques for criminal trials* (2nd ed.). Rochester, NY: Lawyers Cooperative.

Bakan, D. (1966). *The duality of human existence*. Chicago: Rand McNally.

Baker, L. (1983). *Miranda: Crime, law, and politics*. New York: Atheneum.

Baker v. Carr, 369 U.S. 186 (1962).

Baldus, D., Pulaski, C., & Woodworth, G. (1983). Comparative review of death sentences: An empirical study of the Georgia experience. *Journal of Criminal Law and Criminology*, 74, 661–753.

Baldwin, J., & McConville, M. (1979). *Jury trials*. London: Oxford University Press.

Baldwin, J., & McConville, M. (1980). Does the composition of an English jury affect its verdict? *Judicature*, 64, 133–139.

Bales, J. (1988a, June). Child abuse prevention efficacy called in doubt. *APA Monitor*, 27.

Bales, J. (1988b, June). New laws limiting duty to protect. *APA Monitor*, 18.

Ballew v. Georgia, 435 U.S. 223 (1978).

Bandura, A. (1973). *Aggression: A social learning analysis*. Englewood Cliffs, NJ: Prentice-Hall.

Bandura, A. (1976). Social learning analysis of aggression. In E. Ribes-Inesta & A. Bandura (Eds.), *Analysis of delinquency and aggression* (pp. 203–232). Hillsdale, NJ: Erlbaum.

Bandura, A. (1977). *Social learning theory*. Englewood Cliffs, NJ: Prentice-Hall.

Bandura, A. (1986). *Social foundations of thought and action: A social cognitive theory*. Englewood Cliffs, NJ: Prentice-Hall.

Barbaree, H. E., & Marshall, W. L. (1991). The role of male sexual arousal in rape: Six models. *Journal of Consulting and Clinical Psychology*, 59, 621–630.

Barbash, F. (1983, December 5). Brennan, Marshall keep vigil against death penalty. *Washington Post*, A10.

Bard, M. (1969). Family intervention police teams as a community mental health resource. *Journal of Criminal Law, Criminology, and Police Science*, 60, 24.

Bard, M., & Berkowitz, B. (1967). Training police as specialists in family crisis intervention: A community psychology action program. *Community Mental Health Journal*, 3, 209–215.

Barker v. Wingo, 407 U.S. 514 (1972).

Barnett, N., & Feild, H. S. (1977). Sex differences in attitudes toward rape. *Journal of College Student Personnel*, 18, 93–96.

Barr, W. (1992, March). Comments by the Attorney General of the United States. Speech delivered at the University of Kansas, Lawrence.

Bart, P. B. (1981). A study of women who both were raped and avoided rape. *Journal of Social Issues*, 37(4), 123–137.

Bartlett, F. C. (1932). *Remembering: A study in experimental and social psychology*. New York: Cambridge University Press.

Bartol, C. (1983). *Psychology and American law*. Belmont, CA: Wadsworth.

Bartol, C. R. (1991). Predictive validation of the MMPI for small-town police officers who fail. *Professional Psychology: Research and Practice*, 22, 127–132.

Bates, R., & Whitehead, G. (1990). Do something different. *American Bar Association Journal*, 78, 78.

Batson v. Kentucky, 476 U.S. 79 (1986).

Baum, L. (1985). *The Supreme Court* (2nd ed.). Washington, DC: Congressional Quarterly.

Bayles, F. (1984, May 7). Law professor has a taste for controversial cases. *Lawrence Journal-World*, 16.

Beach, B. H. (1983, January 31). Out of the mouths of babes. *Time*, 58.

Beck, A. (1987, July 25). Recruits graduate to police duties. *Lawrence Journal-World*, 3A.

Beck, M. (1989, March 13). We need drastic measures. *Newsweek*, 21.

Becker, B. C. (1980, December). Jury nullification: Can a jury be trusted? *Trial*, 37, 58–59.

Bedau, H. A. (1977). *The courts, the constitution, and capital punishment*. Lexington, MA: Lexington Books.

Begam, R. (1977). Voir dire: The attorney's job. *Trial*, 13, 3.

Beiser, E. N. (1973). Are juries representative? *Judicature*, 57, 194–199.

Beissert, W. (1988, March 1). Stateline. *USA Today*, 9A.

Belkin, L. (1988, June 10). Expert witness is unfazed by "Dr. Death" label. *New York Times*, 23.

Bell v. Wolfish, 99 S.Ct. 1861 (1979).

Belli, M. (1954). *Modern trials*. Indianapolis: Bobbs-Merrill.

Belmont, J. M., & Butterfield, E. C. (1969). The relations of short-term memory to development and intelligence. In L. P. Lipsitt & H. W. Reese (Eds.), *Advances in child development and behavior* (Vol. 4, pp. 30–82). Orlando, FL: Academic Press.

Beneke, T. (1982). *Men on rape*. New York: St. Martin's Press.

Benenson, R. (1984, July 29). Practice of law a growth industry. *Kansas City Star*, F4.

Benner, A. W. (1986). Psychological screening of police applicants. In J. T. Reese & H. A. Goldstein (Eds.), *Psychological services for law enforcement* (pp. 11–20). Washington, DC: U. S. Government Printing Office.

Ben-Shakhar, G., Bar-Hillel, M., & Lieblich, I. (1986). Trial by polygraph: Scientific and juridical issues in lie detection. *Behavioral Sciences and the Law, 4,* 459–479.

Benton, A. A. (1971). Productivity, distributive justice, and bargaining among children. *Journal of Personality and Social Psychology, 18,* 68–78.

Berk, L. E. (1991). *Child development* (2nd ed.). Boston: Allyn & Bacon.

Berkemer v. McCarty, 468 U.S. 420 (1984).

Berliner, L., & Barbieri, M. K. (1984). The testimony of the child victim of sexual assault. *Journal of Social Issues, 40*(2), 125–137.

Berman, L. M., & Osborne, Y. H. (1987). Attorney's referrals for competency to stand trial evaluations: Comparisons of referred and nonreferred clients. *Behavioral Sciences and the Law, 5,* 373–380.

Bermant, G. (1977). *Conduct of the voir dire examination: Practices and opinions of federal district judges.* Washington, DC: Federal Judicial Center.

Bermant, G. (1982). *Jury selection procedures in United States district courts.* Washington, DC: Federal Judicial Center.

Bermant, G. (1985). Issues in trial management: Conducting the voir dire examination. In S. M. Kassin & L. S. Wrightsman (Eds.), *The psychology of evidence and trial procedure* (pp. 298–322). Newbury Park, CA: Sage.

Bermant, G., & Shapard, J. (1978). *The voir dire examination, juror challenges, and adversary advocacy.* Washington, DC: Federal Judicial Center.

Bernays, A. (1983, March 27). The passionate somnambulist. *New York Times Book Review, 13,* 31.

Bersoff, D. N. (1987). Social science data and the Supreme Court: Lockhart as a case in point. *American Psychologist, 42,* 52–58.

Betts v. Brady, 316 U.S. 455 (1942).

Beutler, L. E., Storm, A., Kirkish, P., Scogin, F., & Gaines, J. A. (1985). Parameters in the prediction of police officer performance. *Professional Psychology: Research and Practice, 16,* 324–335.

Bevan, W. (1991). Contemporary psychology: A tour inside the onion. *American Psychologist, 46,* 475–483.

Beyer, H. A. (1974, September). *The child's right to refuse mental health treatment.* Paper presented at the meeting of the American Psychological Association, New Orleans.

Binder, A. (1988). Juvenile delinquency. In M. R. Rosenzweig & L. W. Porter (Eds.), *Annual review of psychology* (pp. 253–282). Palo Alto, CA: Annual Reviews.

Bishop, K. (1989, April 26). FBI agent's conviction is reversed. *New York Times,* 11.

Bishop, K. (1990, January 17). Laws aim to turn off ear-splitting "boom" cars. *New York Times,* 10.

Bittner, E. (1967). Police discretion in emergency apprehension of mentally ill persons. *Social Problems, 14,* 278–292.

Bjorklund, D. F., & Green, B. L. (1992). The adaptive nature of cognitive immaturity. *American Psychologist. 47,* 46–54.

Black, D. (1972). The boundaries of legal sociology. *Yale Law Journal, 81,* 1086–1100.

Black, D. (1976). *The behavior of law.* Orlando, FL: Academic Press.

Blader, J. C., & Marshall, W. L. (1989). Is assessment of sexual arousal in rapists worthwhile? A critique of current methods and the development of a response compatibility approach. *Clinical Psychology Review, 9,* 569–587.

Blakeman, K. (1988, January 16). Baker says he regrets remark about vandals. *Kansas City Times,* A1, A16.

Blasi, V. (Ed.) (1982). *The Burger Court: The counter-revolution that wasn't.* New Haven, CT: Yale University Press.

Blau, T. H. (1986). Deadly force: Psychosocial factors and objective. In J. T. Reese & H. A. Goldstein (Eds.), *Psychological services for law enforcement* (pp. 315–334). Washington, DC: U.S. Government Printing Office.

Blauner, R. (1972). *Racial oppression in America.* New York: Harper & Row.

Block, M. K., & Rhodes, W. M. (1989). Forecasting the impact of the Federal Sentencing Guidelines. *Behavioral Sciences and the Law, 7,* 51–72.

Blum, A. (1989, July 24). Experts: How good are they? *National Law Journal, 1,* 38.

Blum, A. (1990, January 8). "Raiders" at 20 look forward. *National Law Journal,* 24–25.

Blum, D. (1986). *Bad karma: A true story of obsession and murder.* New York: Jove Books.

Blunk, R., & Sales, B. (1977). Persuasion during the voir dire. In B. Sales (Ed.), *Psychology in the legal process* (pp. 39–58). New York: Spectrum.

Boehnert, C. (1989). Characteristics of successful and unsuccessful insanity pleas. *Law and Human Behavior, 13,* 31–40.

Bolton, B. (1985). Review of Inwald Personality Inventory. In J. V. Mitchell (Ed.), *The ninth mental measurement yearbook* (pp. 711–713). Lincoln: Buros Institute of Mental Measurements, University of Nebraska.

Bonnie, R., & Slobogin, C. (1980). The role of mental health professionals in the criminal process: The case for informed speculation. *Virginia Law Review, 66,* 427–522.

Bonsignore v. The city of New York, 521 F.Supp. 394 (1981).

Bordenkircher v. Hayes, 434 U.S. 357, 363 (1978).

Borgida, E. (1980). Evidentiary reform of rape laws: A psycholegal approach. In P. D. Lipsitt & B. D. Sales (Eds.), *New directions in psycholegal research* (pp. 171–197). New York: Litton.

Borgida, E. (1981). Legal reform of rape laws. In L. Bickman (Ed.), *Applied social psychology annual* (Vol. 2, pp. 211–241). Newbury Park, CA: Sage.

Borgida, E., & Brekke, N. (1985). Psycholegal research on rape trials. In A. Burgess (Ed.), *Research handbook on rape and sexual assault* (pp. 313–342). New York: Garland.

Borgida, E., & Park, R. (1988). The entrapment defense: Juror comprehension and decision making. *Law and Human Behavior, 12,* 19–40.

Bortner, M. A. (1984). *Inside a juvenile court: The tarnished ideal of individualized justice.* New York: New York University Press.

Boswell, J. (1989). *The kindness of strangers: The abandonment of children in Western Europe from late antiquity to the Renaissance.* New York: Pantheon Books.

Bothwell, R. K., Brigham, J. C., & Malpass, R. S. (1989). Cross-racial identification. *Personality and Social Psychology Bulletin, 15,* 19–25.

Bothwell, R. K., Deffenbacher, K. A., & Brigham, J. C. (1987). Correlation of eyewitness accuracy and confidence: Optimality hypothesis revised. *Journal of Applied Psychology, 72,* 691–695.

Boulding, K. E. (1975). Truth or power. *Science, 190,* 423.

Bower, B. (1984, October 6). Not popular by reason of insanity. *Science News, 126,* 218–219.

Bowers v. Hardwick, 106 S.Ct. 2841 (1986).

Bowlby, J. (1949). In *Why delinquency?* Report of the conference on the scientific study of juvenile delinquency. London: National Association for Mental Health.

Bowlby, J. (1953). *Child care and the growth of love.* Baltimore: Penguin.

Bowlby, J., & Salter-Ainsworth, M. D. (1965). *Child care and the growth of love.* London: Penguin.

Bozell, L. B. (1966). *The Warren revolution.* New Rochelle, NY: Arlington House.

Brady v. Maryland, 373 U.S. 83 (1963).

Brady v. United States, 397 U.S. 742 (1970).

Bram v. United States, 168 U.S. 532 (1897).

Bramel, D. (1969). Determinants of beliefs about other people. In J. Mills (Ed.), *Experimental social psychology.* New York: Macmillan.

Branch v. State, 40 Cr.L. Rpts. (BNA) 2215 (Ala. 1986).

Brandon, R., & Davies, C. (1973). *Wrongful imprisonment.* London: Allen & Unwin.

Branscombe, N. R., & Weir, J. A. (1989, May). *Observers' attributions in a rape case as a function of the victim's resistance.* Paper presented at the meetings of the Midwestern Psychological Association, Chicago.

Bransford, J. D., & Johnson, M. D. (1972). Contextual prerequisites for understanding: Some investigations of comprehension and recall. *Journal of Verbal Learning and Verbal Behavior, 11,* 717–726.

Bray, R. M., & Noble, A. M. (1978). Authoritarianism and decisions of mock juries: Evidence of jury bias and group polarization. *Journal of Personality and Social Psychology, 36,* 1424–1430.

Brehm, J. W. (1966). *A theory of psychological reactance.* Orlando, FL: Academic Press.

Brewer, W. F., & Nakamura, G. V. (1984). The nature and function of schemas. In R. S. Wyer & T. K. Srull (Eds.), *Handbook of social cognition* (Vol. 1). Hillsdale, NJ: Erlbaum.

Brewer v. Williams, 430 U.S. 387 (1977).

Briere, J., & Malamuth, N. M. (1983). Self-reported likelihood of sexually aggressive behavior: Attitudinal versus sexual explanation. *Journal of Research in Personality, 17,* 315–323.

Brigham, J. C. (1988, August). Expert testimony on future dangerousness in capital cases. *APA Monitor, 26.*

Brigham, J. C. (1989, August). *Assessing the fairness of police lineups.* Paper presented at the meeting of the American Psychological Association, New Orleans.

Brigham, J. C., & Bothwell, R. K. (1983). The ability of prospective jurors to estimate the accuracy of eyewitness identifications. *Law and Human Behavior, 7,* 19–30.

Brill, S. (1978, March 14). When lawyers help villains. *Esquire, 21.*

Brill, S. (1984, December). Inside the DeLorean jury room. *American Lawyer, 1,* 93–105.

Broeder, D. W. (1959). The University of Chicago jury project. *Nebraska Law Review, 38,* 744–760.

Broeder, D. W. (1965). Voir dire examinations: An empirical study. *Southern California Law Review, 38,* 503–528.

Bronstein, A. J. (1980). Prisoners' rights: A history. In G. P. Alpert (Ed.), *Legal rights of prisoners* (pp. 19–45). Newbury Park, CA: Sage.

Brooks, A. (1986). Law and antipsychotic medications. *Behavioral Sciences and the Law, 4,* 247–264.

Brown, E. L., Deffenbacher, K. A., & Sturgill, W. (1977). Memory for faces and the circumstances of encounter. *Journal of Applied Psychology, 62,* 311–318.

Brown v. Board of Education, 347 U.S. 483 (1954).

Brown v. Mississippi, 297 U.S. 278 (1936).

Brownmiller, S. (1975). *Against our will: Rape, women, and men.* New York: Simon & Schuster.

Bruck, D. (1985, May 20). The death penalty: An exchange. *New Republic,* 20–21.

Bryan, W. J. (1971). *The chosen ones.* New York: Vantage Press.

Buckhout, R. (1974). Eyewitness testimony. *Scientific American, 231,* 23–31.

Buckhout, R. (1975). Nearly 2000 witnesses can be wrong. *Social Action and the Law, 2,* 7.

Buckhout, R. (1983). Psychologist v. the judge: Expert testimony on identification. *Social Action and the Law, 9*(3), 67–76.

Buie, J. (1988, November). Joint custody advantages doubted. *APA Monitor, 25.*

Buie, J. (1989, March). Jury clears therapist in duty-to-protect case. *APA Monitor, 20.*

Bulkley, J. (1988). Legal proceedings, reforms, and emerging issues in child sexual abuse cases. *Behavioral Sciences and the Law, 6,* 153–180.

Bullington, B., Sprowls, J., Katkin, D., & Phillips, M. (1978). Diversionary juvenile justice. *Crime and Delinquency, 24,* 54–71.

Burger, W. B. (1982). Isn't there a better way? *American Bar Association Journal, 68,* 274–277.

Burgess, A. W., & Holmstrom, L. L. (1974). *Rape: Victims of crisis.* Bowie, MA: Robert J. Brady.

Burgess, A. W., & Holmstrom, L. L. (1979). Rape: Sexual disruption and recovery. *American Journal of Orthopsychiatry, 49,* 648–657.

Burnet v. Coronado Oil and Gas Co., 285 U.S. 393, 406, 52 S.Ct. 443, 447, 76 L.Ed. 815 (1932).

Burt, M. R. (1980). Cultural myths and supports for rape. *Journal of Personality and Social Psychology, 38,* 217–230.

Burt, R., & Morris, N. (1972). A proposal for the abolition of the incompetency plea. *University of Chicago Law Review, 40,* 66–95.

Buss, A. H. (1966). *Psychopathology.* New York: Wiley.

Byczynski, L. (1987, December 29). Is joint custody better? *Kansas City Times,* A1, A4.

Bynum, T. S., & Greene, J. R. (1984). How wide the net? Probing the boundaries of the juvenile court. In S. H. Decker (Ed.), *Juvenile justice policy: Analyzing trends and outcomes* (pp. 129–143). Newbury Park, CA: Sage.

Calhoun, K., Atkeson, B., & Resick, P. (1982). A longitudinal examination of fear reactions in victims of rape. *Journal of Counseling Psychology, 29,* 656–661.

California v. Acevedo, 111 S.Ct. 1982 (1991).

California v. Byers, 402 U.S. 424 (1971).

California v. Ciraola, 476 U.S. 207 (1986).

California v. Greenwood, 108 S.Ct. 1625 (1988).

Callahan, V. A., McGreevey, M. A., Cirincione, C., & Steadman, H. J. (1992). Measuring the effects of the guilty but mentally ill (GBMI) verdict: Georgia's 1982 GBMI reform. *Law and Human Behavior, 16,* 447–462.

Campbell, D. T. (1969). Reforms as experiments. *American Psychologist, 24,* 409–429.

Caprino, M. (1989, May 7). Employers use tests to head off work force problems. *Lawrence Journal-World,* 11D.

Cardozo, B. N. (1921). *The nature of the judicial process.* New Haven, CT: Yale University Press.

Carey v. Population Services International, 431 U.S. 678 (1976).

Carlson, H., Thayer, R. E., & Germann, A. C. (1971). Social attitudes and personality differences among members of two kinds of police departments (innovative vs. traditional) and students. *Journal of Criminal Law, Criminology, and Police Science, 62,* 564–567.

Carroll, J. S., Kerr, N. L., Alfini, J. J., Weaver, F. M., MacCoun, R. J., & Feldman, V. (1986). Free press and fair trial: The role of behavioral research. *Law and Human Behavior, 10,* 187–201.

Casper, J. D. (1972). *American criminal justice: The defendant's perspective.* Englewood Cliffs, NJ: Prentice-Hall.

Casper, J. D., Benedict, K., & Kelly, J. R. (1988). Cognitions, attitudes, and decision-making in search and seizure cases. *Journal of Applied Social Psychology, 18,* 93–113.

Cavoukian, A., & Heslegrave, R. J. (1980). The admissibility of polygraph evidence in court. *Law and Human Behavior, 4,* 117–131.

Ceci, S. J., Ross, D. F., & Toglia, M. P. (1987). Age differences in suggestibility: Narrowing the uncertainties. In S. J. Ceci, M. P. Toglia, & D. F. Ross (Eds.), *Children's eyewitness memory.* New York: Springer-Verlag.

Ceci, S. J., Toglia, D. F., & Ross, M. P. (1988). On remembering . . . more or less: A trace strength interpretation of developmental differences in suggestibility. *Journal of Experimental Psychology: General, 117,* 201–203.

Chambers, M. (1990, January 22). Sentencing by secret committee? *National Law Journal,* 13–14.

Chambliss, W. J. (1984). The saints and the roughnecks. In W. J. Chambliss (Ed.), *Criminal law in action* (2nd ed., pp. 126–135). New York: Wiley.

Chambliss, W. J., & Seidman, R. B. (1971). *Law, order, and power.* Reading, MA: Addison-Wesley.

Chappell, D. (1989). Sexual criminal violence. In N. A. Weiner & M. E. Wolfgang (Eds.), *Pathways to criminal violence* (pp. 68–108). Newbury Park, CA: Sage.

Charles, M. T. (1986). *Policing the streets.* Springfield, IL: Charles C Thomas.

Chevigny, P. (1969). *Police power: Police abuse in New York City.* New York: Vintage Books.

Chi, M. T. H., Glaser, R., & Farr, M. J. (Eds.) (1988). *The nature of expertise.* Hillsdale, NJ: Erlbaum.

Chodorow, N. (1978). *The reproduction of mothering: Psychoanalysis and the sociology of gender.* Berkeley: University of California Press.

Christiansen, K. O. (1977a). A preliminary study of criminality among twins. In S. A. Mednick & K. O. Christiansen (Eds.), *Biosocial bases of criminal behavior.* New York: Wiley.

Christiansen, K. O. (1977b). A review of studies of criminality among twins. In S. A. Mednick & K. O. Christiansen (Eds.), *Biosocial bases of criminal behavior.* New York: Wiley.

Christie, R. (1976). Probability v. precedence: The social psychology of jury selection. In G. Bermant, C. Nemeth, & N. Vidmar (Eds.), *Psychology and the law: Research frontiers* (pp. 265–281). Lexington, MA: Lexington Books.

Cilwick, T. (1984, September 17). Deliberations begin: Should state abolish sentencing by jury? *Kansas City Times,* A1, A5.

Clancy, P. (1987, July 22). Cops battle stress; "I'm hurting . . . " *USA Today,* 1A–2A.

Clark, L. D. (1975). *The grand jury: The use and abuse of political power.* New York: Quadrangle Books.

Clark, R. V. G., & Heal, K. H. (1979, January). Police effectiveness in dealing with crime: Some current British research. *Police Journal,* 24–41.

Clarke, E. (1975). The selection of juries, qualifications for service, and the right to challenge. In N. Walker (Ed.), *The British jury system.* Cambridge, England: Institute of Criminology, Cambridge University.

Cleburne Living Center, Inc. v. City of Cleburne, Texas, 52 L.W. 2515, 726 F.3d 191 (1985).

Cloward, R. A., & Ohlin, L. E. (1960). *Delinquency and opportunity: A theory of delinquent gangs.* New York: Free Press.

Coblentz, W. K. (1983, June 27). A glut of lawyers. *Newsweek,* 17.

Cochran, P. A. (1971). A situational approach to the study of police-Negro relations. *Sociological Quarterly, 12,* 232–237.

Cohen, A. K. (1955). *Delinquent boys: The culture of the gang.* Glencoe, IL: Free Press.

Cohen, L. J. (1986). The role of evidential weight in criminal proof. *Boston University Law Review, 66,* 635–649.

Cohen, M. I., Spodak, M. K., Silver, S. B., & Williams, K. (1988). Predicting outcome of insanity acquittees released to the community. *Behavioral Sciences and the Law, 6,* 515–530.

Cohen, R. L., & Harnick, M. A. (1980). The susceptibility of child witnesses to suggestion. *Law and Human Behavior, 4,* 201–210.

Cohn, A., & Udolf, R. (1979). *The criminal justice system and its psychology.* New York: Van Nostrand Reinhold.

Cohn, E. S., Carlson, S. J., & White, S. O. (1984). *Legal development and its effect on legal attitudes and behaviors: Moral development versus legal context explanations.* Unpublished manuscript, University of New Hampshire.

Cohn, E. S., & White, S. O. (1990). *Legal socialization: A study of norms and rules.* New York: Springer-Verlag.

Colby, A., Kohlberg, L., & collaborators (1987). *The measurement of moral judgment, Vol. 1: Theoretical foundations and research validation.* Cambridge, England: Cambridge University Press.

Colby, A., Kohlberg, L., Gibbs, J., & Lieberman, M. (1983). A longitudinal study of moral judgment. *Monographs of the Society for Research in Child Development, 48*(1–2, Serial No. 200).

Coleman, C. (1984, July 25). Local troublemakers keep bonding agent in the bail business. *University Daily Kansan,* 1, 5.

Collora, M. A. (1990, January 22). Sentencing guidelines: Commission's goal of uniformity is still elusive after one year. *National Law Journal,* 15–16.

Colorado v. Connelly, 107 S.Ct. 515 (1986).

Colorado v. Spring, 479 U.S. 564 (1987).

Comment (1968). Anxiety and the first semester of law school. *Wisconsin Law Review, 1968,* 1201–1218.

Committee on Ethical Guidelines for Forensic Psychologists. (1991). Specialty guidelines for forensic psychologists. *Law and Human Behavior, 15,* 655–665.

Commonwealth v. Wall, 606 A.2d 449 (Pa. 1992).

Conger, R. (1980). Juvenile delinquency: Behavior restraint or behavior facilitation? In T. Hirschi & M. Gottfredson (Eds.), *Understanding crime: Current theory and research* (pp. 131–142). Newbury Park, CA: Sage.

Congressional Research Service. (1982). *The Constitution of the United States America: Analysis and interpretation.* Washington, DC: U.S. Government Printing Office.

Conn, J. H. (1981). The myth of coercion through hypnosis: A brief communication. *International Journal of Clinical and Experimental Hypnosis, 29,* 95–100.

Constantini, E., & King, J. (1980). The partial juror: Correlates and causes of prejudgment. *Law and Society Review, 15,* 9–40.

Cook, S. W. (1984, August). *Participation by social scientists in litigation regarding school desegregation: Past contributions and future opportunities.* Paper presented at the meetings of the American Psychological Association, Toronto.

Cooper v. Aaron, 358 U.S. 1 (1958).

Cornish, D. B., & Clarke, R. V. (1986). *The reasoning criminal: Rational choice perspectives on offending.* New York: Springer.

Cornish, W. R. (1968). *The jury.* London: Allen Lane.

Cortes, J. B. (1972). *Delinquency and crime: A biopsychosocial approach.* New York: Seminar Press.

Coser, L. A. (1974). *Greedy institutions: Patterns of undivided commitment.* New York: Free Press.

Costanzo, M., & Costanzo, S. (1992). Jury decision making in the capital penalty phase: Legal assumptions, empirical findings, and a research agenda. *Law and Human Behavior, 16,* 185–202.

Cowan, C. L., Thompson, W. C., & Ellsworth, P. C. (1984). The effects of death qualification on jurors' predispositions to convict and on the quality of deliberation. *Law and Human Behavior, 8,* 53–79.

Cowley, G. (1988, December 26). Of pain and progress. *Newsweek,* 50–59.

Cox, G. D. (1989, June 26). Trial by ordeal. *National Law Journal,* 1, 42–43.

Cox, M., & Tanford, S. (1989). An alternative method of capital jury selection. *Law and Human Behavior, 13,* 167–184.

Coy v. Iowa, 108 S.Ct. 2798 (1988).

Coyle, M. (1990, February 12). Proposals on courts debated. *National Law Journal,* 1, 27.

Crano, W. D., & Messe, L. A. (1982). *Social psychology: Principles and themes of interpersonal behavior.* Pacific Grove, CA: Brooks/Cole.

Cravens v. Inman, 586 N.P. NE 2d 367 (Ill. App. 1991).

Cressey, D. R. (1965). Prison organization. In J. G. March (Ed.), *Handbook of organizations.* Skokie, IL: Rand McNally.

Cressey, D. R. (1979). Fifty years of criminology. *Pacific Sociology Review, 22,* 457–480.

Cutler, B. L. (1989, June). Reasonable suspicion and investigative detention. *APA Monitor,* 28.

Cutler, B. L. (1990). Introduction: The status of scientific jury selection in psychology and law. *Forensic Reports, 3,* 227–232.

Cutler, B. L., & Penrod, S. D. (1988). Improving the reliability of eyewitness identification: Lineup construction and presentation. *Journal of Applied Psychology, 73,* 281–290.

Cutler, B. L., Penrod, S. D., & Dexter, H. R. (1989). The eyewitness, the expert psychologist, and the jury. *Law and Human Behavior, 13,* 311–332.

Cutler, B. L., Penrod, S. D., & Dexter, H. R. (1990). Juror sensitivity to eyewitness identification evidence. *Law and Human Behavior, 14,* 185–192.

Cutler, B. L., Penrod, S. D., & Stuve, T. E. (1988). Juror decision making in eyewitness identification cases. *Law and Human Behavior, 12,* 41–55.

D'Agostino, C. (1986). Police psychological services: Ethical issues. In J. T. Reese & H. A. Goldstein (Eds.), *Psychological services for law enforcement* (pp. 241–248). Washington, DC: U.S. Government Printing Office.

Dane, F. C., & Wrightsman, L. S. (1982). Effects of defendants' and victims' characteristics on jurors' verdicts. In N. L. Kerr & R. Bray (Eds.) *Psychology of the courtroom* (pp. 83–115). Orlando, FL: Academic Press.

Davidson, W. S., Redner, R., Blakely, C. H., Mitchell, C. M., & Emshoff, J. G. (1987). Diversion of offenders: An experimental comparison. *Journal of Consulting and Clinical Psychology, 55,* 68–75.

Davis, L. V. (1985). Female and male voices in social work. *Social Work, 30*(2), 106–113.

Davis, M. J. (1985, September 16). Too many lawyers? *Lawrence Journal-World,* 1, 5.

Davis v. North Carolina, 384 U.S. 737 (1966).

Dawes, R. M., Faust, D., & Meehl, P. E. (1989). Clinical versus actuarial judgment. *Science, 243,* 1668–1674.

Deitchman, M. A., Kennedy, W. A., & Beckham, J. C. (1991). Self-selection factors in the participation of mental health professionals in competency for execution evaluations. *Law and Human Behavior, 15,* 287–303.

Deitz, S. R., Blackwell, K. T., Daley, P. C., & Bentley, B. J. (1982).

Measurement of empathy toward rape victims and rapists. *Journal of Personality and Social Psychology, 43,* 372–384.

Deitz, S. R., Littman, M., & Bentley, B. J. (1984). Attribution of responsibility for rape: The influence of observer empathy, victim resistance, and victim attractiveness. *Sex Roles, 10,* 261–280.

Deitz, S. R., Russell, S. A., & Hammes, K. M. (1989, August). *Who's on trial?: Information processing by jurors in rape cases.* Paper presented at meetings of the American Psychological Association, New Orleans.

Dennis v. *United States,* 384 U.S. 855 (1966).

Dershowitz, A. (1982). *The best defense.* New York: Random House.

DeShaney v. *Winnebago County,* 109 S.Ct. 998 (1989).

Deutsch, M. (1975). Equity, equality, and need: What determines which value will be used as the basis for distributive justice? *Journal of Social Issues, 31*(3), 137–149.

Dexter, N. R., & Cutler, B. L. (1991). *In search of the fair jury: Does extended voir dire remedy the prejudicial effects of pretrial publicity?* Paper presented as part of a Symposium (Gary Moran, Chair) at the Meetings of the American Psychological Association, San Francisco.

Diamond, B. L. (1980). Inherent problems in the use of pretrial hypnosis on a prospective witness. *California Law Review, 68,* 313–349.

Diamond, S. S., & Stalans, L. J. (1989). The myth of judicial leniency in sentencing. *Behavioral Sciences and the Law, 7,* 73–89.

Diamond, S. S., & Zeisel, H. (1975). Sentencing councils: A study in sentence disparity and its reduction. *University of Chicago Law Review, 43,* 109–149.

Dietz, P. E., & Reese, J. T. (1986). The perils of police psychology: 10 strategies for minimizing role conflicts when providing mental health services and consultation to law enforcement agencies. *Behavioral Sciences and the Law, 4,* 385–400.

DiLalla, L. F., & Gottesman, I. I. (1991). Biological and genetic contributors to violence—Widom's untold tale. *Psychological Bulletin, 109,* 125–129.

Dillehay, R. C., & Nietzel, M. T. (1980). Conceptualizing mock jury/juror research: Critique and illustrations. In K. S. Larsen (Ed.), *Social psychology: Crisis or failure.* Monmouth, OR: Institute for Theoretical History.

Dillehay, R. C., & Nietzel, M. T. (1985). Juror experience and jury verdicts. *Law and Human Behavior, 9,* 179–191.

Dinges, J., & Landau, S. (1980). *Assassination on Embassy Row.* New York: McGraw-Hill.

Doble, J., & Klein, J. (1989). *Punishing criminals: The public's view: An Alabama survey.* New York: Edna McConnell Clark Foundation.

Donnerstein, E. (1982). Erotica and human aggression. In R. G. Green & E. Donnerstein (Eds.), *Aggression: Theoretical and empirical views.* Orlando, FL: Academic Press.

Donnerstein, E., & Berkowitz, L. (1981). Victim reactions in aggressive erotic films as a factor in violence against women. *Journal of Personality and Social Psychology, 41,* 710–724.

Doren, D. M. (1987). *Understanding and treating the psychopath.* New York: Wiley.

Dornstein, M. (1988). Pay equity evaluations of occupations and their bases. *Journal of Applied Social Psychology, 18,* 905–924.

Douglas, J. E., Ressler, R. K., Burgess, A. W., & Hartman, C. R. (1986). Criminal profiling from crime scene analysis. *Behavioral Sciences and the Law, 4,* 401–421.

Douglas, W. O. (1980). *The Court years 1939–1975: The autobiography of William O. Douglas.* New York: Random House.

Dowd, M. (1983, September 5). Rape: The sexual weapon. *Time,* 27–29.

Drucker, M., & Goldstein, G. (1983). A mental health consultation program to the police. *Psychiatric Hospital, 14,* 225–228.

Dubrow, M. (1984, April 4). Escorts become attackers in date rape. *USA Today,* 3D.

Dudley v. *Offender Aid and Restoration,* 41 S.E.2d 878 (Va. 1991).

Dugdale, R. (1877). *The Jukes: A study in crime, pauperism, and heredity.* New York: Putnam.

Duncan, E. M., Whitney, P., & Kunen, S. (1982). Integration of visual and verbal information in children's memories. *Child Development, 53,* 1215–1223.

Duncan, S., & Kravitz, M. (1979). *Police stress—A selected bibliography.* Washington, DC: Superintendent of Documents.

Duncan v. *Louisiana,* 391 U.S. 145 (1968).

Duning, C., & Hanchette, J. (1985, March 28). Don't shoot, Court tells police. *USA Today,* 2A.

duPont, P. S. IV (1985, January). Expanding sentencing options: A governor's perspective. *Research in brief.* Washington, DC: National Institute of Justice.

Durham v. *United States,* 214 F.2d 862 (1954).

Dusky v. *United States,* 362 U.S. 402 (1960).

Dutton, D. G. (1987). The criminal justice response to wife assault. *Law and Human Behavior, 11,* 189–206.

Dywan, J., & Bowers, K. S. (1983). The use of hypnosis to enhance recall. *Science, 222,* 184–185.

Ebbesen, E. B., & Konecni, V. J. (1975). Decision making and information integration in the courts: The setting of bail. *Journal of Personality and Social Psychology, 32,* 805–821.

Ebbesen, E. B., & Konecni, V. J. (1981). The process of sentencing adult felons: A causal analysis of judicial decision. In B. D. Sales (Ed.), *The trial process* (pp. 413–458). New York: Plenum.

Eckholm, E. (1985, July 4). Stockholm syndrome: Hostages' reactions. *Lawrence Journal-World,* 6.

Edmonson v. *Leesville Concrete Co.,* 111 S.Ct. 2077 (1991).

Edwards v. *Arizona,* 451 U.S. 477 (1981).

Egeth, H. E., & McCloskey, M. (1984). Expert testimony about eyewitness behavior. In G. L. Wells & E. F. Loftus (Eds.), *Eyewitness testimony: Psychological perspectives* (pp. 283–303). New York: Cambridge University Press.

Eichenwald, K. (1989, September 28). Bilzerian gets four years in jail, stiffest in stock crackdown. *New York Times,* 29, 36.

Ekman, P. (1985). *Telling lies.* New York: W. W. Norton.

Ekman, P., & O'Sullivan, M. (1991). Who can catch a liar? *American Psychologist, 46,* 899–912.

Elliott, D. S. (1988, August). *Is there a common etiology for multiple problems in youth?* Paper presented at meetings of the American Psychological Association, Atlanta.

Elliott, G. C., & Meeker, B. F. (1986). Achieving fairness in the face of competing concerns: The different effects of individual and group characteristics. *Journal of Personality and Social Psychology, 50,* 754–760.

Elliott, R. (1991). Social science data and the APA: The *Lockhart* brief as a case in point. *Law and Human Behavior, 15*, 59–76.

Ellis, E. (1983). A review of empirical rape research: Victim reactions and response to treatment. *Clinical Psychology Review, 3*, 473–490.

Ellis, L. (1989). *Theories of rape: Inquiries into the causes of sexual aggression.* New York: Hemisphere.

Ellis, L. (1991). A synthesized (biosocial) theory of rape. *Journal of Consulting and Clinical Psychology, 59*, 631–642.

Ellison, K., & Buckhout, R. (1981). *Psychology and criminal justice.* New York: Harper & Row.

Ellsworth, P. C. (1991). To tell what we know or wait for Godot? *Law and Human Behavior, 15*, 77–90.

Ellsworth, P. C., Bukaty, R. M., Cowan, C. L., & Thompson, W. C. (1984). The death-qualified jury and the defense of insanity. *Law and Human Behavior, 8*, 81–93.

Elwork, A., Sales, B. D., & Alfini, J. J. (1977). Juridic decisions: In ignorance of the law or in light of it? *Law and Human Behavior, 1*, 163–189.

Elwork, A., Sales, B. D., & Suggs, D. (1981). The trial: A research review. In B. D. Sales (Ed.), *The trial process* (pp. 1–68). New York: Plenum.

Emery, R. E., & Wyer, M. M. (1987). Divorce mediation. *American Psychologist, 42*, 472–480.

Empey, L. T. (1982). *American delinquency: Its meaning and construction.* Belmont, CA: Wadsworth.

Enmund v. Florida, 458 U.S. (1932).

Ennis, B., & Siegel, L. (1973). *The rights of mental patients.* New York: Avon.

Eron, L. D., & Redmount, R. S. (1957). The effect of legal education on attitudes. *Journal of Legal Education, 9*, 431–443.

Escobedo v. Illinois, 378 U.S. 478 (1964).

Estrich, S. (1987). *Real rape.* Cambridge, MA: Harvard University Press.

Etzioni, A. (1974a, September). On the scientific manipulation of juries. *Human Behavior*, 10–11.

Etzioni, A. (1974b, May 26). Science: Threatening the jury trial. *Washington Post*, C3.

Ewing, C. P. (1991). Preventive detention and execution: The constitutionality of punishing future crimes. *Law and Human Behavior, 15*, 139–164.

Eysenck, H. J. (1964). *Crime and personality.* Boston: Houghton Mifflin.

Eysenck, H. J., & Gudjonsson, G. H. (1989). *The causes and cures of criminality.* New York: Plenum.

Eysenck, H. J., & Gudjonsson, G. H. (1991). Crime, personality, and punishment. *Contemporary Psychology, 36*, 575–577.

Fare v. Michael C., 21 Cal. 3d 471, 519 P.2d 7 (1979).

Farley v. Progressive Casualty Co., WL 32111 (Ohio App. 6 Dist. 1992).

Farmer, M. W. (1976). Jury composition challenges. *Law and Psychology Review, 2*, 45–74.

Farson, R. (1974). *Birthrights.* New York: Macmillan.

Feeley, M. M. (1983). *Court reform on trial.* New York: Basic Books.

Feild, H. S. (1978a). Attitudes toward rape: A comparative analysis of police, rapists, crisis counselors, and citizens. *Journal of Personality and Social Psychology, 36*, 156–179.

Feild, H. S. (1978b). Juror background characteristics and attitudes toward rape: Correlates of jurors' decisions in rape trials. *Law and Human Behavior, 2*, 73–93.

Feild, H. S. (1979). Rape trials and jurors' decisions: A psycholegal analysis of the effects of victim, defendant, and case characteristics. *Law and Human Behavior, 3*, 261–284.

Feild, H. S., & Barnett, N. J. (1978). Simulated jury trials: Students vs. "real" people as jurors. *Journal of Social Psychology, 104*, 287–293.

Feild, H. S., & Bienen, L. B. (1980). *Jurors and rape: A study in psychology and law.* Lexington, MA: Heath.

Feldman, M. P. (1977). *Criminal behavior: A psychological analysis.* New York: Wiley.

Feldman-Summers, S., & Ashworth, C. D. (1981). Factors related to intentions to report a rape. *Journal of Social Issues, 37*(4), 71–92.

Feldman-Summers, S., Gordon, P. E., & Meagher, J. R. (1979). The impact of rape on sexual satisfaction. *Journal of Abnormal Psychology, 88*, 101–105.

Fenster, G. A., & Locke, B. (1973). Neuroticism among policemen: An examination of police personality. *Journal of Applied Psychology, 57*, 358–359.

Fentiman, L. (1986). Whose right is it anyway? Rethinking competency to stand trial in light of the synthetically sane insanity defendant. *University of Miami Law Review, 40*, 1109–1169.

Feretta v. California, 422 U.S. 806 (1975).

Ferri, E. (1917). *Criminal sociology.* Translated by Joseph I. Kelley & John Lisle. Boston: Little, Brown.

Feshbach, S., & Malamuth, N. (1978, November). Sex and aggression: Proving the link. *Psychology Today, 12*, 110–112.

Finkel, N. J. (1989). The Insanity Defense Reform Act of 1984: Much ado about nothing. *Behavioral Sciences and the Law, 7*, 403–419.

Finkel, N. J. (1991). The insanity defense: A comparison of verdict schemas. *Law and Human Behavior, 15*, 533–556.

Fischer, P. J., & Breakey, W. R. (1991). The epidemiology of alcohol, drug, and mental disorders among homeless persons. *American Psychologist, 46*, 1115–1128.

Fisher, R. P., & Quigley, K. L. (1989, August). *The cognitive interview, person description, and person recognition.* Paper presented at the meeting of the American Psychological Association, New Orleans.

Fiske, S. T., Bersoff, D. N., Borgida, E., Deaux, K, & Heilman, M. E. (1991). Social science research on trial: Use of sex stereotyping research in *Price Waterhouse v. Hopkins. American Psychologist, 46*, 1049–1060.

Fiss, O., & Krauthammer, C. (1982, March 10). The Rehnquist court. *New Republic*, 14–21.

Fitzgerald, R., & Ellsworth, P. C. (1984). Due process vs. crime control: Death qualification and jury attitudes. *Law and Human Behavior, 8*, 31–51.

Flanagan, T. J., McGarrell, E. F., & Brown, E. J. (1985). Public perceptions of the criminal courts: The role of demographic and related attitudinal variables. *Journal of Research in Crime and Delinquency, 22*, 66–82.

Flango, V. E. (1980). Would jurors do a better job if they could take notes? *Judicature, 63*(9), 436–443.

Florida v. Bostick, 501 U.S. (1991).

Florida v. Jimeno, 111 S.Ct. 1801 (1991).

Foley, M. (1983). Confessions of a retributivist. *Social Action and the Law, 9*(1), 16–17.

Footlick, J. (1978, May 8). Insanity on trial. *Newsweek,* 108–112.

Ford v. Wainwright, 477 U.S. 399 (1986).

Forsyth, D. J. (1990). *An introduction to group dynamics* (2nd ed.). Pacific Grove, CA: Brooks/Cole.

Foucha v. Louisiana, 112 S.Ct. 1780 (1992).

Fox, S. G., & Walters, H. A. (1986). The impact of general versus specific expert testimony and eyewitness confidence upon mock juror judgment. *Law and Human Behavior, 10,* 215–228.

Frank, J. (1930). *Law and the modern mind.* New York: Coward: McCann.

Frank, J. (1949). *Courts on trial.* Princeton, NJ: Princeton University Press.

Frankel, M. E. (1972). *Criminal sentences.* New York: Hill & Wang.

Frankel, M. E., & Naftalis, G. P. (1977). *The grand jury: An institution on trial.* New York: Hill & Wang.

Frazier, P., & Borgida, E. (1985). Rape trauma syndrome evidence in court. *American Psychologist, 40,* 984–993.

Frazier, P., & Borgida, E. (1992). Rape trauma syndrome: A review of case law and psychological research. *Law and Human Behavior, 16,* 293–311.

Freed, D., & Landis, F. S. (1980). *Death in Washington: The murder of Orlando Letelier.* Westport, CT: Lawrence Hill.

Freedman, J. L. (1984). Effect of television violence on aggressiveness. *Psychological Bulletin, 96,* 227–246.

Freedman, J. L. (1986). Television violence and aggression: A rejoinder. *Psychological Bulletin, 100,* 372–378.

Frendak v. United States, 408 A.2d 364 (D.C. 1979).

Freud, S. (1961). *The complete psychological works of Sigmund Freud* (Vol. 19). London: Hogarth.

Friedrich, W. N., Belike, R. L., & Urguiza, A. J. (1987). Children from sexually abusive families: A behavioral comparison. *Journal of Interpersonal Violence. 2,* 391–402.

Friedrich, W. N., Beilke, R. L., & Urquiza, A. J. (1988). Behavior problems in young sexually abused boys. *Journal of Pediatric Psychology, 11,* 1–12.

Friedrich-Cofer, L., & Huston, A. C. (1986). Television violence and aggression: A rejoinder. *Psychological Bulletin, 100,* 364–371.

Fromm, E. (1956). *The art of loving.* New York: Harper & Row.

Frye v. United States, 293 F. 1013, 34 A.L.R. 145 (D.C. Cir. 1923).

Fulero, S. M. (1987). The role of behavioral research in the free press/free trial controversy: Another view. *Law and Human Behavior, 11,* 259–264.

Fulero, S. M. (1988, August). *Eyewitness expert testimony: An overview and annotated bibliography, 1931–1988.* Paper presented at the meeting of the American Psychological Association, Atlanta.

Fulero, S. M., & Finkel, N. J. (1991). Barring ultimate issue testimony: An "insane" rule? *Law and Human Behavior, 15,* 495–508.

Fulero, S. M., & Penrod, S. D. (1990). Attorney jury selection folklore: What do they think and how can psychologists help? *Forensic Reports, 3,* 233–259.

Furman v. Georgia, 408 U.S. 238 (1972).

Fyfe, J. J. (1982). Blind justice: Police shootings in Memphis. *Journal of Criminal Law and Criminology, 73,* 707–722.

Fyfe, J. J. (1988). Police shooting: Environment and license. In J. E. Scott & T. Hirschi (Eds.), *Controversial issues in crime and justice* (pp. 79–94). Newbury Park, CA: Sage.

Gallup Organization. (1989, June 23). A jury of one's peers. *Lawrence Journal-World,* 1B.

Gannett Co. v. DePasquale, 443 U.S. 368 (1979).

Garofalo, R. (1914). *Criminology.* Translated by Robert W. Millar. Boston: Little, Brown.

Gavey, N. (1991). Sexual victimization prevalence among New Zealand University students. *Journal of Consulting and Clinical Psychology, 59,* 464–466.

Gaylin, W. (1974). *Partial justice: A study of bias in sentencing.* New York: Vintage Books.

Gaylin, W. (1982). *The killing of Bonnie Garland: A question of justice.* New York: Simon & Schuster.

Gayoso, A., Cutler, B. L., & Moran, G. (in press). Assessing the value of social scientists as trial consultants: A consumer research approach. *Forensic Reports.*

Gee, E. G., & Jackson, D. W. (1977). Bridging the gap: Legal education and lawyer competency. *Brigham Young University Law Review,* 695–990.

Geis, G., & Monahan, J. (1976). The social ecology of violence. In T. Lickona (Ed.), *Moral development and behavior: Theory, research, and social issues* (pp. 342–356). New York: Holt, Rinehart, & Winston.

Geiselman, R. E., Fisher, R. P., MacKinnon, D. P., & Holland, H. L. (1985). Eyewitness memory enhancement in the police interview. *Journal of Applied Psychology, 70,* 401–412.

Gelles, R. J., & Cornell, C. P. (1985). *Intimate violence in families.* Newbury Park, CA: Sage.

Georgia v. McCollum, 112 S.Ct. 2348 (1992).

Gerbasi, K. C., Zuckerman, M., & Reis, H. T. (1977). Justice needs a new blindfold: A review of mock jury research. *Psychological Bulletin, 84,* 323–345.

Gershman, B. L. (1982). Abscam, the judiciary, and the ethics of entrapment. *Yale Law Journal, 91,* 1565–1591.

Gerstein v. Pugh, 420 U.S. 103 (1975).

Gideon v. Wainwright, 372 U.S. 335 (1963).

Gillen, J. (1946). *The Wisconsin prisoner: Studies in crimogenesis.* Madison: University of Wisconsin Press.

Gillers, S., & Dorsen, N. (1989). *Regulations of lawyers.* Boston: Little, Brown.

Gilligan, C. (1977). In a different voice: Women's conceptions of the self and of morality. *Harvard Educational Review, 47,* 481–517.

Gilligan, C. (1982). *In a different voice: Psychological theory and women's development.* Cambridge, MA: Harvard University Press.

Gilligan, C. (1988). Adolescent development reconsidered. In C. Gilligan, J. V. Ward, & J. McL. Taylor (Eds.), *Mapping the moral domain.* Cambridge, MA: Harvard University Press, vii–xxxix.

Gilligan, C., Ward, J. V., & Taylor, J. McL. (Eds.). (1988). *Mapping the moral domain.* Cambridge, MA: Harvard University Press.

Gist, R. M., & Perry, J. D. (1985). Perspectives on negotiation in local jurisdictions, Part 1: A different typology of situations. *FBI Law Enforcement Bulletin, 54*(11), 21.

Glaberson, W. (1989, February 1). Challenge for jurors. *New York Times,* 46.

Glaser, R., & Chi, M. T. H. (1988). Overview. In M. T. H. Chi, R. Glaser, & M. J. Farr (Eds.), *The nature of expertise* (pp. xv–xxvii). Hillsdale, NJ: Erlbaum.

Gleick, J. (1978, August 21). Getting away with murder. *New Times,* 21–27.

Glueck, S., & Glueck, E. (1934). *One thousand delinquents.* Cambridge, MA: Harvard University Press.

Glueck, S., & Glueck, E. (1950). *Unraveling juvenile delinquency.* Cambridge, MA: Harvard University Press.

Glueck, S., & Glueck, E. (1956). *Physique and delinquency.* New York: Harper & Row.

Godard, S. L., Bloom, J. D., Williams, M. H., & Faulkner, L. R. (1986). The right to refuse treatment in Oregon: A two-year statewide experience. *Behavioral Sciences and the Law, 4,* 293–304.

Goddard, H. (1916). *The Kallilak family: A study in the heredity of feeblemindedness.* New York: Macmillan.

Godschalx, S. M. (1984). Effect of a mental health education program upon police officers. *Research in Nursing and Health, 7,* 111–117.

Goldfarb, R. L. (1965). *Ransom.* New York: Harper & Row.

Golding, S. L., Roesch, R., & Schreiber, J. (1984). Assessment and conceptualization of competency to stand trial: Preliminary data on the Interdisciplinary Fitness Interview. *Law and Human Behavior, 8,* 321–334.

Goldkamp, J. S., & Gottfredson, M. R. (1979). Bail decision making and pretrial detention. *Law and Human Behavior, 3,* 227–249.

Goldkamp, J. S., & Gottfredson, M. R. (1988). Guidelines for bail and pretrial release in three urban courts. (Unpublished Final Report).

Goldstein, T. (1988a, January 15). No straight A's for the law schools. *New York Times,* 10.

Goldstein, T. (1988b, February 12). Women in the law aren't yet equal partners. *New York Times,* 14.

Goleman, D. (1984, November 13). Studies judge youths to be as believable in court as adults. *Kansas City Times,* B5, B7.

Goleman, D. (1987, April 7). The bully: New research depicts a paranoid, lifelong loser. *New York Times,* 19, 23.

Goodman, E. (1983, October 18). Real men may be the only ones to cry. *Lawrence Journal-World,* 5.

Goodman, E. (1989, May 22). Murdered women seen as somehow asking for it. *Kansas City Times,* A9.

Goodman, G. S. (1984a). Children's testimony in historical perspective. *Journal of Social Issues, 40*(2), 9–31.

Goodman, G. S. (1984b). The child witness: An introduction. *Journal of Social Issues, 40*(2), 1–7.

Goodman, G. S., Aman, C., & Hirschman, J. (1987). Child sexual and physical abuse: Children's testimony. In S. J. Ceci, M. P. Toglia, & D. F. Ross (Eds.), *Children's eyewitness testimony.* New York: Springer-Verlag.

Goodman, G. S., Golding, J. M., & Haith, M. M. (1984). Jurors' reactions to child witnesses. *Journal of Social Issues, 40*(2), 139–156.

Goodman, G. S., & Hahn, A. (1987). Evaluating eyewitness testimony. In I. B. Weiner & A. K. Hess (Eds.), *Handbook of forensic psychology* (pp. 258–292). New York: Wiley.

Goodman, G. S., & Helgeson, V. S. (1986). Child sexual assault: Children's memory and the law. *University of Miami Law Review, 40,* 181–208.

Goodman, G. S., & Reed, R. S. (1986). Age differences in eyewitness testimony. *Law and Human Behavior, 10,* 317–332.

Goodman, H. (1982, August 9). Mental patients' rights clash with public's desire for safety. *Kansas City Times,* A1, A4.

Gordon, R. A. (1986, August). *IQ commensurability of black-white differences in crime and delinquency.* Paper presented at the meeting of the American Psychological Association, Washington, DC.

Gorenstein, G. W., & Ellsworth, P. C. (1980). Effect of choosing an incorrect photograph on a later identification by an eyewitness. *Journal of Applied Psychology, 65,* 616–622.

Gorer, G. (1955). Modification of national character: The role of police in England. *Journal of Social Issues, 11*(2), 24–32.

Gorman, C. (1989, January 23). Honestly, can we trust you? *Time,* 44.

Gottfredson, D. M., Gottfredson, S. D., & Conly, C. H. (1989). Stakes and risks: Incapacitative intent in sentencing decisions. *Behavioral Sciences and the Law, 7,* 91–106.

Gottfredson, L. (1986, August). *IQ versus training: Job performance and black-white occupational inequality.* Paper presented at the meeting of the American Psychological Association, Washington, DC.

Grady v. Corbin, 495 U.S. 508 (1990).

Gravitz, M. A. (1983). An early case of investigative hypnosis: A brief communication. *International Journal of Clinical and Experimental Hypnosis, 31,* 224–226.

Green, E. (1961). *Judicial attitudes in sentencing.* London: Macmillan.

Green, S. (1984). Victim-offender reconciliation program: A review of the concept. *Social Action and the Law, 10*(2), 43–52.

Greenberg, M. S., & Ruback, R. B. (1984). *Social psychology of the criminal justice system.* Pacific Grove, CA: Brooks/Cole.

Greenberger, M. D., & Connor, K. (1991). Parental notice and consent for abortion: Out of step with family law principles and policies. *Family Planning Perspectives, 23,* 31–35.

Greene, E. (1986). Forensic hypnosis to lift amnesia: The jury is still out. *Behavioral Sciences and the Law, 4,* 65–72.

Greene, E. (1988). Judge's instruction on eyewitness testimony: Evaluation and revision. *Journal of Applied Social Psychology, 18,* 252–276.

Greenhouse, L. (1989a, February 23). Court says state intervention in child abuse isn't mandate. *New York Times,* 1.

Greenhouse, L. (1989b, May 16). New limits put on inmates' reading. *New York Times,* 8.

Greenhouse, L. (1989c, June 27). Death sentences against retarded and young upheld. *New York Times,* 1, 10.

Greenwood, P. W., & Petersilia, J. (1976). *The criminal investigation process.* Washington, DC: Law Enforcement Assistance Administration.

Gregg v. Georgia, 428 U.S. 153 (1976).

Gregory, W. L., Mowen, J. C., & Linder, D. E. (1978). Social psychology and plea bargaining: Applications, methodology, and theory. *Journal of Personality and Social Psychology, 36,* 1521–1530.

Griffin v. Wisconsin, 107 S.Ct. 3164 (1987).

Grigsby v. Mabry, 483 F.Supp. 1372 (E.D. Ark. 1980). Modified and remanded, 637 F.2d 525 (8th Cir. 1980).

Grisso, T. (1981). *Juveniles' waivers of rights: Legal and psychological competence.* New York: Plenum.

Grisso, T. (1985, November). Judicial notebook. *APA Monitor, 21.*

Grisso, T. (1986). *Evaluating competencies: Forensic assessments and instruments.* New York: Plenum.

Grisso, T., & Saks, M. J. (1991). Psychology's influence on constitutional interpretation: A comment on how to succeed. *Law and Human Behavior, 15,* 205–211.

Grisso, T., & Siegel, S. K. (1986). Assessment of competency to stand criminal trial. In W. J. Curran, A. L. McGarry, & S. A. Shah (Eds.), *Forensic psychiatry and psychology* (pp. 145–165). Philadelphia: F. A. Davis.

Grisso, T., Tomkins, A., & Casey, P. (1988). Psychosocial concepts in juvenile law. *Law and Human Behavior, 12,* 403–437.

Gross, S. R. (1984). Determining the neutrality of death-qualified juries: Judicial appraisal of empirical data. *Law and Human Behavior, 8,* 7–30.

Groth, A. N., with Birnbaum, H. J. (1979). *Men who rape.* New York: Plenum.

Grych, J. H., & Fincham, F. D. (1992). Interventions for children of divorce: Toward greater integration of research and action. *Psychological Bulletin, 111,* 434–454.

Guastello, S. J., & Rieke, M. L. (1991). A review and critique of honesty test research. *Behavioral Sciences and the Law, 9,* 501–523.

Gunter, G. (1985, January 25). Voices across the USA. *USA Today,* 12A.

Haley v. Ohio, 332 U.S. 596 (1948).

Hall, D. F., Loftus, E. F., & Tousignant, J. P. (1984). Postevent information and changes in recollection for a natural event. In G. L. Wells & E. F. Loftus (Eds.) *Eyewitness testimony: Psychological perspectives* (pp. 124–141). New York: Cambridge University Press.

Hall, G. C. N. (1990). Prediction of sexual aggression. *Clinical Psychology Review, 10,* 229–245.

Hall, G. C. N., & Hirschman, R. (1991). Toward a theory of sexual aggression: A quadripartite model. *Journal of Consulting and Clinical Psychology, 59,* 662–669.

Hall, G. C. N., & Proctor, W. C. (1987). Criminological predictors of recidivism in a sexual offender population. *Journal of Consulting and Clinical Psychology, 55,* 111–112.

Hamilton, D. L., Katz, L. B., & Leirer, V. O. (1980). Cognitive representation of personality impressions: Organizational processes in first impression formation. *Journal of Personality and Social Psychology, 39,* 1050–1063.

Hamm, M. S. (1989). The conscience and convenience of sentencing reform in Indiana. *Behavioral Sciences and the Law, 7,* 107–126.

Handman, L. R. (1977). Underrepresentation of economic groups on federal juries. *Boston University Law Review, 57*(1), 198–224.

Haney, C. (1984). Editor's introduction. *Law and Human Behavior, 8,* 1–6.

Haney, C. (1991). The Fourteenth Amendment and symbolic legality: Let them eat due process. *Law and Human Behavior, 15,* 183–204.

Hanley, R. (1989, May 26). New Jersey town shattered by sex assault on girl, 17. *New York Times,* 11.

Hans, V. P. (1982). Jury selection in two cultures: A psychological perspective. *Current Psychological Reviews, 2,* 283–300.

Hans, V. P. (1988, November). Confronting the accused. *APA Monitor, 35.*

Hans, V. P. (1992). Judgments of justice. *Psychological Science, 3,* 218–220.

Hans, V. P., & Slater, D. (1983). John Hinckley, Jr., and the insanity defense: The public's verdict. *Public Opinion Quarterly, 47,* 202–212.

Hans, V. P., & Vidmar, N. (1982). Jury selection. In N. L. Kerr & R. M. Bray (Eds.), *The psychology of the courtroom* (pp. 39–82). Orlando, FL: Academic Press.

Hans, V. P., & Vidmar, N. (1986). *Judging the jury.* New York: Plenum.

Harding v. State (of Maryland), 5 Md.App. 230, 246 A.2d 302 (1968), 252 Md. 731, Cert. denied, 395 U.S. 949, 89 S.Ct. 2030, 23 L.Ed.2d 468 (1969).

Hare, R. D., Hart, S. D., & Harpur, T. J. (1991). Psychopathy and the DSM-IV criteria for Antisocial Personality Disorder. *Journal of Abnormal Psychology, 100,* 391–398.

Hare, R. D., & McPherson, L. M. (1984). Violent and aggressive behavior by criminal psychopaths. *International Journal of Law and Psychiatry, 7,* 35–50.

Harmelin v. Michigan, 111 S.Ct. 2680 (1991).

Harper, T. (1984, April 29). State rape laws see decade of change. *Lawrence Journal-World,* 1B.

Harris v. New York, 401 U.S. 222 (1971).

Harvey, J. H., & Smith, W. P. (1977). *Social psychology: An attributional approach.* St. Louis: Mosby.

Hastie, R. (1980). *From eyewitness testimony to beyond reasonable doubt.* Unpublished manuscript, Harvard University.

Hastie, R., Penrod, S. D., & Pennington, N. (1983). *Inside the jury.* Cambridge, MA: Harvard University Press.

Haugaard, J. J. (1988). Judicial determination of children's competency to testify: Should it be abandoned? *Professional Psychology, 19,* 102–107.

Haugaard, J. J., Reppucci, N. D., Laird, J., & Nauful, T. (1991). Children's definitions of the truth and their competency as witnesses in legal proceedings. *Law and Human Behavior, 15,* 253–272.

Hawrish, E., & Tate, E. (1974–1975). Determinants of jury selection. *Saskatchewan Law Review, 30,* 285–292.

Hazelwood, R. R., & Douglas, J. E. (1980). The lust murderer. *FBI Law Enforcement Bulletin, 49*(4), 18–22.

Heilbrun, K. S. (1987). The assessment of competency for execution: An overview. *Behavioral Sciences and the Law, 5,* 383–396.

Heilbrun, K. S. (1992). The role of psychological testing in forensic assessment. *Law and Human Behavior, 16,* 257–272.

Heilbrun, K. S., Heilbrun, P., & Griffin, N. (1988). Comparing females acquitted by reason of insanity, convicted, and civilly committed in Florida: 1977–1984. *Law and Human Behavior, 12*, 295–312.

Hepburn, J. R. (1980). The objective reality of evidence and the utility of systematic jury selection. *Law and Human Behavior, 4*, 89–102.

Herzfeld, C. (1988, March 7). "L.A. Law" popularity may be rubbing off. *Kansas City Star*, 3A.

Heuer, L., & Penrod, S. (1988). Increasing jurors' participation in trials: A field experiment with jury notetaking and question asking. *Law and Human Behavior, 12*, 231–262.

Heuer, L., & Penrod, S. (1989). Instructing jurors: A field experiment with written and preliminary instructions. *Law and Human Behavior, 13*, 409–430.

Heumann, M. (1978). *Plea bargaining*. Chicago: University of Chicago Press.

Heussanstamm, F. K. (1975). Bumper stickers and the cops. In D. J. Steffensmeier & R. M. Terry (Eds.), *Examining deviance experimentally: Selected readings*, pp. 251–255. Port Washington, NY: Alfred.

Hiatt, D., & Hargrave, G. E. (1988). Predicting job performance problems with psychological screening. *Journal of Police Science and Administration, 16*, 122–125.

Hibbard, W. S., & Worring, R. W. (1981). *Forensic hypnosis*. Springfield, IL.: Charles C Thomas.

Hiday, V. A., & Goodman, R. R. (1982). The least restrictive alternative to involuntary hospitalization, outpatient commitment: Its use and effectiveness. *Journal of Psychiatry and Law, 10*, 81–96.

Hiday, V. A., & Suval, E. M. (1984). Dangerousness of the mentally ill and inebriates in civil commitment. In L. A. Teplin (Ed.), *Mental health and criminal justice* (pp. 227–250). Newbury Park, CA: Sage.

Himelein, M. J., Nietzel, M. T., & Dillehay, R. C. (1991). Effects of prior juror experience on jury sentencing. *Behavioral Sciences and the Law, 9*, 97–106.

Hindelang, M. J., & Davis, B. L. (1977). Forcible rape in the United States: A statistical profile. In D. Chappell, R. Geis, & G. Geis (Eds.), *Forcible rape: The crime, the victim, and the offender* (pp. 87–114). New York: Columbia University Press.

Hirschi, T. (1969). *Causes of delinquency*. Berkeley: University of California Press.

Hirschi, T. (1978). Causes and prevention of juvenile delinquency. In H. M. Johnson (Ed.), *Social systems and legal process*. San Francisco: Jossey-Bass.

Hoffman, L. R. (1965). Group problem solving. In L. Berkowitz (Ed.), *Advances in experimental social psychology* (Vol. 2, pp. 99–127). Orlando, FL: Academic Press.

Hoffman, P. B., & Stone-Meierhoefer, B. (1979). Application of guidelines to sentencing. In L. E. Abt & I. R. Stuart (Eds.), *Social psychology and discretionary law* (pp. 241–258). New York: Van Nostrand.

Hogan, R. (1971). Personality characteristics of highly rated policemen. *Personnel Psychology, 24*, 679–686.

Hogarth, J. (1971). *Sentencing as a human process*. Toronto: University of Toronto Press.

Holland v. Illinois, 493 U.S. 474 (1990).

Holloway v. United States, 326 U.S. 687 (1945).

Holmes, D. S. (1991). *Abnormal psychology*. New York: Harper.

Holmes, R. M., & DeBurger, J. (1988). *Serial murder*. Newbury Park, CA: Sage.

Holt, J. (1974, October). Free the children: They need room to grow. *Psychology Today, 38*, 133–137.

Hooton, E. A. (1939). *Crime and the man*. Cambridge, MA: Harvard University Press.

Hopt v. Utah, 110 U.S. 574 (1884).

Horgan, D. D. (1988, August). *The ethics of unexpected advocacy*. Paper presented at the meeting of the American Psychological Association, Atlanta.

Horowitz, I. A. (1980). Juror selection: A comparison of two methods in several criminal cases. *Journal of Applied Social Psychology, 10*, 86–99.

Horowitz, I. A. (1985). The effect of jury nullification instructions on verdicts and jury functioning in criminal trials. *Law and Human Behavior, 9*, 25–36.

Horowitz, I. A., & Bordens, K. S. (1990). An experimental investigation of procedural issues in complex tort trials. *Law and Human Behavior, 14*, 269–286.

Horowitz, I. A., & Willging, T. E. (1984). *The psychology of law*. Boston: Little, Brown.

Hosch, H. M., Beck, E. L., & McIntyre, P. (1980). Influence of expert testimony regarding eyewitness accuracy on jury decisions. *Law and Human Behavior, 4*, 287–296.

Hostetler, A. J. (1988, June). Indictment, Congress send message on fraud. *APA Monitor*, 5.

Houlden, P. (1981). Impact of procedural modifications on evaluations of plea bargaining. *Law and Society Review, 15*, 267–292.

Hovey v. Superior Court (of California), 28 Cal.3d 1 (1980).

Howard, J. W., Jr. (1981). *Courts of appeals in the federal judicial system: A study of the second, fifth, and District of Columbia circuits*. Princeton, NJ: Princeton University Press.

Howard, R. C., & Clark, C. R. (1985). When courts and experts disagree: Discordance between insanity recommendations and adjudications. *Law and Human Behavior, 9*, 385–395.

Hudson v. McMillian, 112 S.Ct. 995 (1992).

Huesmann, L. R., Eron, L. D., & Yarmel, P. W. (1987). Intellectual functioning and aggression. *Journal of Personality and Social Psychology, 52*, 232–240.

Hvistendahl, J. (1979). The effect of placement of biasing information. *Journalism Quarterly, 56*, 863–865.

Hyman, H. M., & Tarrant, C. M. (1975). Aspects of American trial jury history. In R. J. Simon (Ed.), *The jury system in America: A critical overview* (pp. 21–44). Newbury Park, CA: Sage.

Illinois v. Lafayette, 462 U.S. 640 (1983).

Illinois v. Perkins, 110 S.Ct. 2394 (1990).

In re Gault, 387 U.S. 1, 87 S.Ct. 1428 (1967).

Inwald, R. E. (1986). Issues and guidelines for mental health professionals conducting pre-employment psychological screening programs in law enforcement agencies. In J. T. Reese & H. A. Goldstein (Eds.), *Psychological services for law enforcement* (pp. 47–50). Washington, DC: U.S. Government Printing Office.

Inwald, R. E., Knadz, H., & Shusman, E. (1983). *Inwald Personality Inventory Manual.* New York: Hilson Research.

Irvin v. Dowd, 366 U.S. 717 (1961).

Irwin, J. (1970). *The felon.* Englewood Cliffs, NJ: Prentice-Hall.

Jack, D., & Jack, R. (1988). Women lawyers: Archetype and alternatives. In C. Gilligan, J. V. Ward, & J. McL. Taylor (Eds.), *Mapping the moral domain* (pp. 263–288). Cambridge, MA: Harvard University Press.

Jackson, S. E., & Maslach, C. (1982). After-effects of job-related stress: Families as victims. *Journal of Occupational Behavior, 3,* 63–77.

Jackson, S. E., & Schuler, R. S. (1983, March–April). Preventing employee burnout. *Personnel,* 58–68.

Jackson v. Denno, 378 U.S. 368 (1964).

Jackson v. Indiana, 406 U.S. 715 (1972).

Jacobson v. United States, 112 S.Ct. 1535 (1992).

Jacoby, S. (1988, April 10). Children without remorse. *New York Times Book Review,* 9, 11.

Jacoby, T. (1988, July 18). Fighting crime by the rules. *Newsweek,* 53.

Jacoby, T. (1989, January 30). An end to judicial roulette. *Newsweek,* 76.

James, R. (1959). Status and competence of juries. *American Journal of Sociology, 64,* 563–570.

Janis, I. L. (1982). *Groupthink: Psychological studies of policy decisions and fiascoes* (2nd ed.). Boston: Houghton Mifflin.

Javins v. First National Realty Corporation, 428 F.2d 1071 (1970).

Jeffers, H. P. (1991). *Who killed Precious?* New York: Pharos Books.

Jenkins, J. A. (1983, February 20). A candid talk with Justice Blackmun. *New York Times Magazine,* 20.

Johnson, J., & Kamlani, R. (1991, August 26). Do we have too many lawyers? *Time, 138,* 54–55.

Johnson, M. K., & Foley, M.A. (1984). Differentiating fact from fantasy: The reliability of children's memory. *Journal of Social Issues, 40*(2), 33–50.

Johnson v. Louisiana, 32 L.Ed.2d 152 (1972).

Johnson v. Zerbst, 304 U.S. 458 (1938).

Jones, A. (1989, June 18). The whole town was molested. *New York Times Book Review,* 12–13.

Jones, D.P.H. (1985). *Reliable and fictitious accounts of sexual abuse in children.* Paper presented at the Seventh National Conference on Child Abuse and Neglect, Chicago.

Jones, E. E., & Goethals, G. R. (1971). *Order effects in impression formation: Attribution context and the nature of the entity.* Morristown, NJ: General Learning Press.

Jones, E. E., & Harris, V. A. (1967). The attribution of attitudes. *Journal of Experimental Social Psychology, 3,* 1–24.

Jones, E. E., & Nisbett, R. (1971). *The actor and the observer: Divergent perceptions of the causes of behavior.* Morristown, NJ: General Learning Press.

Josephson, M. (n. d.). *How to avoid the first year trauma.* Privately published.

Jurow, G. (1971). New data on the effect of a death-qualified jury on the guilt determination process. *Harvard Law Review, 84,* 567–611.

Kadish, M. R., & Kadish, S. H. (1971). The institutionalization of conflict: Jury acquittals. *Journal of Social Issues, 27*(2), 199–218.

Kagehiro, D. K., Taylor, R. B., & Harland, A. T. (1991). Reasonable expectation of privacy and third-party consent searches. *Law and Human Behavior, 15,* 121–138.

Kagehiro, D. K., Taylor, R. B., Laufer, W. S., & Harland, A. T. (1991). Hindsight bias and third-party consentors to warrantless police searches. *Law and Human Behavior, 15,* 305–314.

Kagehiro, D. K., & Werner, C. M. (1977, May). *Effects of authoritarianism and inadmissibility of evidence on jurors' verdicts.* Paper presented at the meeting of the Midwestern Psychological Association, Chicago.

Kahn, A., Nelson, R. E., & Gaeddert, W. P. (1980). Sex of subject and sex composition of the group as determinants of reward allocations. *Journal of Personality and Social Psychology, 38,* 737–750.

Kairys, D. (1972). Juror selection: The law, a mathematical method of analysis, and a case study. *American Criminal Law Review, 10,* 771–806.

Kairys, D., Kadane, B., & Lehoczky, P. (1977). Jury representativeness: A mandate for multiple source lists. *California Law Review, 65,* 776–827.

Kalven, H., & Zeisel, H. (1966). *The American jury.* Boston: Little, Brown.

Kamisar, Y. (1988, March 16). The Gideon case 25 years later. *New York Times,* 27.

Kamisar, Y., LaFave, W. R., & Israel, J. (1986). *Basic criminal procedure: Cases, comments and questions.* St. Paul, MN: West.

Kanin, E. (1957). Male aggression in dating-courtship situations. *American Journal of Sociology, 63,* 197–204.

Kanin, E. (1971). Sexually aggressive college males. *Journal of College Student Personnel, 12*(2), 107–110.

Kaplan, D. A., & Wright, L. (1990, February 19). Breaking the death barrier. *Newsweek,* 72–73.

Kaplan, J. (1972). A legal look at prosocial behavior: What can happen for failing to help or trying to help. *Journal of Social Issues, 28*(3), 218–226.

Karmen, A. (1984). *Crime victims: An introduction to victimology.* Pacific Grove, CA: Brooks/Cole.

Kassen, D., & O'Connor, W. (1988). Crime, inpatient admissions, and violence among male mental patients. *International Journal of Law and Psychiatry, 11,* 305–312.

Kassin, S. M. (1984). Eyewitness identification: Victims versus bystanders. *Journal of Applied Social Psychology, 14,* 519–529.

Kassin, S. M. (1985, August). *Juries and the doctrine of entrapment.* Paper presented at the meeting of the American Psychological Association, Los Angeles.

Kassin, S. M., Ellsworth, P. C., & Smith, V. L. (1989). The "general acceptance" of psychological research on eyewitness testimony: A survey of the experts. *American Psychologist, 44,* 1089–1098.

Kassin, S. M., & McNall, K. (1991). Police interrogations and confessions: Communicating promises and threats by pragmatic implication. *Law and Human Behavior, 15,* 233–251.

Kassin, S. M., Reddy, M. E., & Tulloch, W. F. (1990). Juror interpretations of ambiguous evidence: The need for cognition, presentation order, and persuasion. *Law and Human Behavior, 14,* 43–56.

Kassin, S. M., & Wrightsman, L. S. (1979). On the requirement of proof: The timing of judicial instructions and mock juror verdicts. *Journal of Personality and Social Psychology, 37,* 1877–1887.

Kassin, S. M., & Wrightsman, L. S. (1980). Prior confessions and mock jury verdicts. *Journal of Applied Social Psychology, 10,* 133–146.

Kassin, S. M., & Wrightsman, L. S. (1981). Coerced confessions, judicial instruction, and mock juror verdicts. *Journal of Applied Social Psychology, 11,* 489–506.

Kassin, S. M., & Wrightsman, L. S. (1983). The construction and validation of a juror bias scale. *Journal of Research in Personality, 17,* 423–441.

Kassin, S. M., & Wrightsman, L. S. (1985). Confession evidence. In S. M. Kassin & L. S. Wrightsman (Eds.), *The psychology of evidence and trial procedure* (pp. 67–94). Newbury Park, CA: Sage.

Kassin, S. M., & Wrightsman, L. S. (1988). *The American jury on trial: Psychological perspectives.* New York: Hemisphere.

Katz, J. (1988). *Seductions of crime.* New York: Basic Books.

Katz, L. (1987). *Bad acts and guilty minds.* Chicago: University of Chicago Press.

Kaul, D. (1989, May 4). Young woman jogger in Central Park was not behaving bravely. *Kansas City Times,* A15.

Kayle, H. S. (1989, February). Jude Deveraux: Velvet author. *Inside Books,* 67–69.

Keeton, R. E. (1973). *Trial tactics and methods* (2nd ed.). Boston: Little, Brown.

Kelley, H. H. (1971). *Attribution in social interaction.* Morristown, NJ: General Learning Press.

Kelling, G., et al. (1974). *The Kansas City Preventive Patrol Experiment: A summary report.* Washington, DC: Police Foundation.

Kennedy, L. (1985). *The airman and the carpenter: The Lindbergh kidnapping and the framing of Richard Hauptmann.* New York: Viking.

Kent, D. A., & Eisenberg, T. (1972). The selection and promotion of police officers: A selected review of recent literature. *Police Chief, 39,* 20–29.

Kentucky v. *Stincer,* 482 U.S. 730 (1987).

Kerlinger, F. N. (1958). Progressivism and traditionalism: Basic factors of educational attitudes. *Journal of Social Psychology, 48,* 111–135.

Kerlinger, F. N. (1961). Factor invariance in the measurement of attitudes toward education. *Educational and Psychological Measurement, 21,* 273–285.

Kerlinger, F. N. (1967). Social attitudes and their criterial referents: A structural theory. *Psychological Review, 74,* 110–122.

Kerper, H. B. (1972). *Introduction to the criminal justice system.* St. Paul, MN: West.

Kerr, N., Kramer, G. P., Carroll, J. S., & Alfini, J. J. (1991). On the effectiveness of voir dire in criminal cases with prejudicial pretrial publicity: An empirical study. *American Law Review, 40,* 665–701.

Ketterman, T., & Kravitz, M. (1978). *Police crisis intervention: A selected biography.* Washington, DC: U.S. Government Printing Office.

Kiesler, C. A. (1982). Public and professional myths about mental hospitalization: An empirical reassessment of policy-related beliefs. *American Psychologist, 37,* 1323–1339.

Kilpatrick, D., Best, C., & Veronen, L. (1984, August). *Mental health consequences of criminal victimization: A random community survey.* Paper presented at the meeting of the American Psychological Association, Toronto.

Kilpatrick, D. G., Resick, P., & Veronen, L. (1981). Effects of a rape experience: A longitudinal study. *Journal of Social Issues, 37*(4), 105–112.

Kilpatrick, J. J. (1983, December 1). Justice officials are fuming over "wrist slap" in porn extortion case. *Kansas City Times,* A21.

Kilpatrick, J. J. (1985, March 12). Let the states set speed. *Kansas City Times,* A15.

King, H. E., & Webb, C. (1981). Rape crisis centers: Progress and problems. *Journal of Social Issues, 37*(4), 93–104.

Kingson, J. A. (1988, August 8). Women in the law say path is limited by "mommy track." *New York Times,* 1, 8.

Kipnis, K. (1979). Plea bargaining: A critic's rejoinder. *Law and Society Review, 13,* 555–564.

Kirby, C. (1976). Three years of adjustment: Where your ideals go. *Juris Doctor, 6,* 34–43.

Kircher, J. C., Horowitz, S. W., & Raskin, D. C. (1988). Meta-analysis of mock crime studies of the control question polygraph technique. *Law and Human Behavior, 12,* 79–90.

Kitsuse, J. I., & Dietrick, D. C. (1959). Delinquent boys: A critique. *American Sociological Review, 24,* 208–215.

Klassen, D., & O'Connor, W. A. (1988). A prospective study of predictors of violence in adult male mental health admissions. *Law and Human Behavior, 12,* 143–158.

Klein, M. W. (1975). *Alternative dispositions for juvenile offenders.* Los Angeles: University of Southern California Press.

Klein, M. W. (1979). Deinstitutionalization and diversion of juvenile offenders: A litany of impediments. In N. Morris & M. Tonry (Eds.), *Crime and justice: An annual review of research* (pp. 145–201). Chicago: University of Chicago Press.

Klein, M. W., Teilmann, K. S., Lincoln, J. A, & Labin-Rosensweig, S. (1976). The explosion in police diversion programs: Evaluating the structural dimensions of a social fad. In M. W. Klein (Ed.), *The juvenile justice system* (pp. 101–120). Newbury Park, CA: Sage.

Kleinberg, H. (1989, January 29). It's tough to have sympathy for Bundy. *Lawrence Journal-World,* 5A.

Kleinmuntz, B., & Szucko, J. J. (1984). Lie detection in ancient and modern times: A call for contemporary scientific study. *American Psychologist, 39,* 766–776.

Kline, M., Tschann, J. M., Johnston, J. R., & Wallerstein, J. S. (1989). Children's adjustment in joint and sole custody families. *Developmental Psychology, 25,* 430–438.

Kline, M. V. (1983). *Forensic hypnosis: Clinical tactics in the courtroom.* Springfield, IL: Charles C Thomas.

Klyver, N. (1986). LAPD's peer counseling program after three years. In J. T. Reese & H. A. Goldstein (Eds.), *Psychological services for law enforcement* (pp. 121–136). Washington, DC: U.S. Government Printing Office.

Koch, E. I. (1985, May 20). The death penalty: An exchange. *New Republic,* 21.

Kohlberg, L. (1958). *The development of modes of thinking and choices in years 10 to 16.* Unpublished doctoral dissertation, University of Chicago.

Kohlberg, L. (1963). The development of children's orientations toward a moral order: I. Sequence in the development of moral thought. *Vita Humana, 6,* 11–33.

Kohlberg, L. (1973). Stages and aging in moral development: Some speculations. *Gerontologist, 13,* 497–502.

Kohlberg, L. (1981). *The philosophy of moral development.* San Francisco: Harper & Row.

Konecni, V. J., & Ebbesen, E. B. (1986). Courtroom testimony by psychologists on eyewitness identification issues: Critical notes and reflections. *Law and Human Behavior, 10,* 117–126.

Koss, M. P. (1985). The hidden rape victim: Personality, attitudes and situational characteristics. *Psychology of Women Quarterly, 9,* 193–212.

Koss, M. P., & Leonard, K. E. (1984). Sexually aggressive men: Empirical findings and theoretical implications. In N. Malamuth & E. Donnerstein (Eds.), *Pornography and sexual aggression.* Orlando, FL: Academic Press.

Koss, M. P., & Oros, C. (1982). Sexual experiences survey: A research instrument investigating sexual aggression and victimization. *Journal of Consulting and Clinical Psychology, 50,* 455–457.

Kramer, G. P., Kerr, N. L., & Carroll, J. S. (1990). Pretrial publicity, judicial remedies, and jury bias. *Law and Human Behavior, 14,* 409–438.

Kramer, R. (1988). *At a tender age: Violent youth and juvenile justice.* New York: Holt.

Kramer, T. H., Buckhout, R., & Eugenio, P. (1990). Weapon focus, arousal, and eyewitness memory: Attention must be paid. *Law and Human Behavior, 14,* 167–184.

Kranz, H. (1936). *Lebenschicksale krimineller Zwillinge.* Berlin: Springer-Verlag OHG.

Kranz, H. (1937). Untersuchungen an Zwillingen in Furosorgeerjiehungsanstalten. Z. *Induktive Abstammungs-Vererbungslehre, 73,* 508–512.

Kraske, S., & Kaut, S. (1989, January 22). Ten notorious brothers. *Kansas City Star,* 1B.

Krisberg, B. (1989). Kids in court. *Contemporary Psychology, 34,* 911–912.

Kroger, W. S., & Douce, R. G. (1980). Forensic use of hypnosis. *American Journal of Clinical Hypnosis, 23,* 86–93.

Kunen, J. (1983). *"How can you defend those people?" The making of a criminal lawyer.* New York: Random House.

Kunen, J. S., Mathison, D., Brown, S. A., & Nugent, T. (1989, July 17). Frustrated grand jurors say it was no accident Ted Kennedy got off easy. *People,* 34–36.

Kurtz, H. (1988, December 5–11). Take a number, cop a plea. *Washington Post National Weekly Edition,* 9–10.

Kurtz, H. (1990, January 22–28). And above all, be humble . . . *Washington Post National Weekly Edition,* 25.

Kutchinski, B. (1988, June). *Pornography and sexual violence: The criminological evidence from aggregated data in several countries.* Paper presented at the Fourteenth International Congress on Law and Mental Health, Montreal.

Labaton, S. (1989, December 29). New tactics in the war on drugs tilt scales of justice off balance. *New York Times,* 1, 14.

Laboratory for Community Psychiatry (1974). *Competency to stand trial and mental illness.* Northvale, NJ: Jason Aronson.

LaBuy, W. J. (1963). *Jury instructions in federal criminal cases.* St. Paul, MN: West.

Lacayo, R. (1986, August 11). Rattling the gilded cage. *Time,* 39.

Lacayo, R. (1987a, May 4). Clearing a path to the chair. *Time,* 80.

Lacayo, R. (1987b, June 8). First the sentence, then the trial. *Time,* 69.

Lacayo, R. (1989, May 29). Our bulging prisons. *Time,* 28–31.

LaFave, W. (1965). *Arrest: The decision to take a suspect into custody.* Boston: Little, Brown.

Lamar, J. V. (1989, February 6). "I deserve punishment." *Time,* 34.

Lane, I. M., & Messe, L. A. (1971). Equity and the distribution of rewards. *Journal of Personality and Social Psychology, 20,* 1–17.

Langbein, J. H. (1978). Torture and plea bargaining. *University of Chicago Law Review, 46,* 12–13.

Lange, J. (1929). *Verbrechen als Schiskal.* Leipzig: Georg Thieme.

Langer, E. J., & Abelson, R. P. (1974). A patient by any other name . . . : Clinical group differences in labeling bias. *Journal of Consulting and Clinical Psychology, 42,* 4–9.

Largen, M. A. (1988). Rape-law reform: An analysis. In A. W. Burgess (Ed.), *Rape and sexual assault* (Vol. 2). New York: Garland.

Larson, J. A. (1932). *Lying and its detection.* Chicago: University of Chicago Press.

Lash, J. P. (Ed.) (1975). *From the diaries of Felix Frankfurter.* New York: W. W. Norton.

Latessa, E. J., Travis, L. F. III, & Wilson, G. P. (1984). Juvenile diversion: Factors related to decision making and outcome. In S. H. Decker (Ed.), *Juvenile justice policy: Analyzing trends and outcomes* (pp. 145–165). Newbury Park, CA: Sage.

Laurence, J. R., & Perry, C. (1983). Forensic hypnosis in the late nineteenth century. *International Journal of Clinical and Experimental Hypnosis, 31,* 266–283.

Laurence v. Davis, 401 F.Supp. 1023 (W.D. Va. 1975).

Lawrence, J. (1984, May 23). Child's fear affects testimony on abuse. *Lawrence Journal-World,* 12.

Lawrence, R. (1984). Checking the allure of increased conviction rates: The admissibility of expert testimony on rape trauma syndrome in criminal proceedings. *University of Virginia Law Review, 70,* 1657–1704.

Leary, W. E. (1988, November 15). Novel methods unlock witnesses' memories. *New York Times,* 23.

Lee, F. (1985, May 16). Women are put "on trial" in rape cases. *USA Today,* 1A.

Lee, F. R. (1989, May 22). Bad crack, waiting witnesses, low pay—A prosecutor's day. *New York Times,* 14.

Lee v. Weisman, 112 S.Ct. 2649 (1992).

Leech, E. (1985, April 10). Backers say videotaping spares abused child from court trauma. *Kansas City Times,* A1, A11.

Lefkowitz, J. (1975). Psychological attributes of policemen: A review of research and opinion. *Journal of Social Issues, 31*(1), 3–26.

Lego v. Twomey, 404 U.S. 477 (1972).

Lemert, E. M. (1951). *Social pathology.* New York: McGraw-Hill.

Lemert, E. M. (1972). *Human deviance, social problems, and social control* (2nd ed.). Englewood Cliffs, NJ: Prentice-Hall.

Lempert, R. (1972). Law school grading: An experiment with pass-fail. *Journal of Legal Education, 24,* 251–308.

Lempert, R. O. (1981). Desert and deterrence: An assessment of the moral bases of the case for capital punishment. *Michigan Law Review, 79,* 1177-1231.

Lerner, M. (1987, September 14 and 21). Bork's progress. *New Republic,* 18-20.

Lerner, M. J. (1970). The desire for justice and reactions to victims. In J. Macaulay & L. Berkowitz (Eds.), *Altruism and helping behavior* (pp. 205-229). Orlando, FL: Academic Press.

Lerner, M. J. (1974). Social psychology of justice and interpersonal attraction. In T. L. Huston (Ed.), *Foundations of interpersonal attraction* (pp. 331-351). Orlando, FL: Academic Press.

Lerner, M. J. (1977). The justice motive in social behavior: Some hypotheses as to its origins and forms. *Journal of Personality, 45,* 1-52.

Lerner, M. J. (1980). *The belief in a just world: A fundamental delusion.* New York: Plenum.

Lerner, M. J., & Simmons, C. H. (1966). The observer's reaction to the "innocent victim": Compassion or rejection? *Journal of Personality and Social Psychology, 4,* 203-210.

Lester, D., Babcock, S. D., Cassissi, J. P., & Brunetta, M. (1980). Hiring despite the psychologists' objections. *Criminal Justice and Behavior, 7,* 41-49.

Leventhal, G. S. (1976). The distribution of rewards and resources in groups and organizations. In L. Berkowitz & E. Walster (Eds.), *Advances in experimental social psychology* (Vol. 9). Orlando, FL: Academic Press.

Leventhal, G. S., & Lane, D. W. (1970). Sex, age and equity behavior. *Journal of Personality and Social Psychology, 15,* 312-316.

Levin, H. (1970). Psychologist to the powerless. In F. F. Korten, S. W. Cook, & J. I. Lacy (Eds.), *Psychology and the problems of society* (pp. 121-127). Washington, DC: American Psychological Association.

Levin, J., & Fox, J. A. (1985). *Mass murder.* New York: Plenum.

Levine, A. G., & Schweber-Koren, C. (1976). Jury selection in Erie County: Changing a sexist system. *Law and Society Review, 11,* 43-55.

Levine, F. J., & Tapp, J. L. (1977). The dialectic of legal socialization in community and school. In J. L. Tapp & F. L. Levine (Eds.), *Law, justice, and the individual in society* (pp. 163-182). New York: Holt, Rinehart, & Winston

Levine, M., & Battistoni, L. (1991). The corroboration requirement in child sex abuse cases. *Behavioral Sciences and the Law, 9,* 21-32.

LeVine, R. (1959). Gusii sex offenses: A study in social control. *American Anthropologist, 61,* 965-990.

Levinger, G. (1966). Marital dissatisfaction among divorce applicants. *American Journal of Orthopsychiatry, 36,* 803-807.

Levy, R. J. (1967). Predicting police failures. *Journal of Criminal Law, Criminology, and Police Science, 58,* 265-276.

Lewis, A. (1981). A public right to know about public institutions. In P. B. Kurland & G. Casper (Eds.), *The Supreme Court Review 1980.* Chicago: University of Chicago Press.

Lewis, A. (1984, November 16). Rights won by "unworthy" are won for all. *Kansas City Times,* A17.

Lewis, N. A. (1982, March 10). Justice O'Connor's first six months. *New Republic,* 17.

Leyton, E. (1986). *Compulsive killers.* New York: New York University Press.

Lichtenstein, A. (1985). Polls, public opinion, pre-trial publicity and the prosecution of Bernhard H. Goetz. *Social Action and the Law, 10,* 95-102.

Lieberg, L. (1971). *Project Crossroads: Final report to the Manpower Administration, U.S. Department of Labor.* Washington, DC: U.S. Government Printing Office.

Lilly, J. R., Cullen, F. T., & Ball, R. A. (1989). *Criminological theory: Context and consequences.* Newbury Park, CA: Sage.

Lind, E. A. (1975). The exercise of information influence in legal advocacy. *Journal of Applied Social Psychology, 5,* 127-143.

Lind, E. A. (1982). The psychology of courtroom procedure. In N. L. Kerr & R. M. Bray (Eds.), *Psychology in the courtroom* (pp. 13-37). Orlando, FL: Academic Press.

Lind, E. A., Erickson, B. E., Friedland, N., & Dickenberger, M. (1978). Reactions to procedural models for adjudicative conflict resolution. *Journal of Conflict Resolution, 22,* 318-341.

Lind, E. A., Thibaut, J., & Walker, L. (1973). Discovery and presentation of evidence in adversary and nonadversary proceedings. *Michigan Law Review, 71,* 1129-1144.

Lind, E. A., & Tyler, T. R. (1988). *The social psychology of procedural justice.* New York: Plenum.

Lindberg, M. A. (1980). Is knowledge base development a necessary and sufficient condition for memory development? *Journal of Experimental Child Psychology, 30,* 401-410.

Lindsay, R. C. L., Wells, G. L., & O'Connor, F. J. (1989). Mock-juror belief of accurate and inaccurate eyewitnesses: A replication and extension. *Law and Human Behavior, 13,* 333-340.

Lindsey, R. (1979). *The falcon and the snowman: A true story of friendship and espionage.* New York: Pocket Books.

Lindsey, R. (1983). *The flight of the falcon.* New York: Pocket Books.

Lingle, J. H., & Ostrom, T. M. (1981). Principles of memory and cognition in attitude formation. In R. E. Petty, T. M. Ostrom, & T. C. Brock (Eds.). *Cognitive responses in persuasion.* Hillsdale, NJ: Erlbaum.

Linz, D., Donnerstein, E., & Penrod, S. (1984). The effects of long-term exposure to filmed violence against women. *Journal of Communications, 34,* 130-147.

Linz, D., Donnerstein, E., & Penrod, S. (1987a). Sexual violence in the mass media: Social psychological implications. In P. Shaver & C. Hendrick (Eds.), *Sex and gender* (pp. 95-123). Newbury Park, CA: Sage.

Linz, D., Donnerstein, E., & Penrod, S. (1987b). The findings and recommendations of the Attorney General's Commission on Pornography: Do the psychological facts fit the political fury? *American Psychologist, 42,* 946-953.

Linz, D., Donnerstein, E., & Penrod, S. (1988). Effects of long-term exposure to violent and sexually degrading depictions of women. *Journal of Personality and Social Psychology, 55,* 758-768.

Lipset, S. M., & Ladd, E. C., Jr. (1970). . . . And what professors think. *Psychology Today, 4*(6), 49-51.

Lipsitt, P. D., Lelos, D., & McGarry, A. L. (1971). Competency for trial: A screening instrument. *American Journal of Psychiatry, 128,* 105-109.

Lipton, J. P. (1977). On the psychology of eyewitness testimony. *Journal of Applied Psychology, 62,* 90-95.

Little v. Armontrout, 835 F.2d 1240 (8th Cir. 1987).

Litwack, T. R., & Schlesinger, L. B. (1987). Assessing and predicting violence: Research, law and applications. In I. B. Weiner & A. K. Hess (Eds.), *Handbook of forensic psychology* (pp. 205–257). New York: Wiley.

Lockett v. Ohio, 438 U.S. 586 (1978).

Lockhart v. McCree, 106 S.Ct. 1758 (1986).

Loftus, E. F. (1974). Reconstructing memory: The incredible witness. *Psychology Today, 8,* 116–119.

Loftus, E. F. (1975). Leading questions and the eyewitness report. *Cognitive Psychology, 7,* 560–572.

Loftus, E. F. (1979). *Eyewitness testimony.* Cambridge, MA: Harvard University Press.

Loftus, E. F. (1980). Impact of expert psychological testimony on the unreliability of eyewitness identification. *Journal of Applied Psychology, 65,* 9–15.

Loftus, E. F. (1983). Silence is not golden. *American Psychologist, 38,* 564–572.

Loftus, E. F. (1984). Expert testimony on the eyewitness. In G. L. Wells & E. F. Loftus (Eds.), *Eyewitness testimony: Psychological perspectives* (pp. 273–282). New York: Cambridge University Press.

Loftus, E. F., & Davies, G. M. (1984). Distortions in the memory of children. *Journal of Social Issues, 40*(2), 51–67.

Loftus, E. F., Loftus, G. R., & Messo, J. (1987). Some facts about "weapons focus." *Law and Human Behavior, 11,* 55–62.

Loftus, E. F., & Palmer, J. C. (1974). Reconstruction of automobile destruction: An example of the interaction between language and memory. *Journal of Verbal Learning and Verbal Behavior, 13,* 585–589.

Loftus, E. F., & Schneider, N. G. (1987). "Behold with strange surprise": Judicial reactions to expert testimony concerning eyewitness reliability. *UMKC Law Review, 56,* 1–45.

Loftus, E. F., & Wagenaar, W. (1990). Ten cases of eyewitness identification: Logical and procedural problems. *Journal of Criminal Justice, 18,* 291–305.

Loftus, E. F., & Zanni, G. (1975). Eyewitness testimony: The influence of the wording of a question. *Bulletin of the Psychonomic Society, 5,* 86–88.

Loh, W. D. (1981). What has reform of rape legislation wrought? *Journal of Social Issues, 37*(4), 28–52.

Loh, W. D. (1984). *Social research in the judicial process.* Newbury Park, CA: Sage.

Lohr, S. (1987, November 30). For crime detection, "genetic fingerprinting." *New York Times, 5.*

Lombroso, C. (1876). *L' Uomo Delinquente.* Milan: Hoepli.

Longino, H. E. (1980). Pornography, oppression, and freedom: A closer look. In L. Lederer (Ed.), *Take back the night: Women on pornography.* New York: William Morrow.

Loomis, S. D. (1965). EEG abnormalities as a correlate of behavior in adolescent male delinquents. *American Journal of Psychiatry, 121,* 1003.

Lott, B., Reilly, M. E., & Howard, D. R. (1982). Sexual assault and harassment: A campus community case study. *Signs: Journal of Women in Culture and Society, 8,* 296–319.

Love, A., & Childers, J. (1963). *Listen to leaders in law.* New York: Holt, Rinehart & Winston.

Loving, N., & Quirk, M. (1982). Spouse abuse: The need for new law enforcement responses. *FBI Law Enforcement Bulletin, 51,* 10–16.

Lowe, R. H., & Wittig, M. A. (Eds.). (1989). Approaching pay equity through comparable worth (special issue). *Journal of Social Issues, 45*(4), 11–246.

Luginbuhl, J. (1992). Comprehension of judges' instructions in the penalty phase of a capital trial: Focus on mitigating circumstances. *Law and Human Behavior, 16,* 203–218.

Luginbuhl, J., & Middendorf, K. (1988). Death penalty beliefs and jurors' responses to aggravating and mitigating circumstances in capital trials. *Law and Human Behavior, 12,* 263–281.

Lunde, D. T., & Morgan, J. (1980). *The die song: A journey into the mind of a mass murderer.* New York: W. W. Norton.

Lunden, W. A. (1957). *The courts and other criminal justice in Iowa.* Ames: Iowa State University Press.

Luus, C. A. E., & Wells, G. L. (1991). Eyewitness identification and the selection of distracters for lineups. *Law and Human Behavior, 15,* 43–57.

Lykken, D. T. (1981). *A tremor in the blood: Uses and abuses of the lie detector.* New York: McGraw-Hill.

Lykken, D. T. (1985). The probity of the polygraph. In S. M. Kassin & L. S. Wrightsman (Eds.), *The psychology of evidence and trial procedure* (pp. 95–123). Newbury Park, CA: Sage.

Maass, A., Brigham, J. C., & West, S. G. (1985). Testifying on eyewitness reliability: Expert advice is not always persuasive. *Journal of Applied Social Psychology, 15,* 207–229.

Maass, A., & Köhnken, G. (1989). Eyewitness identification: Simulating the "Weapon Effect." *Law and Human Behavior, 13,* 397–408.

MacAndrew, C., & Edgerton, R. B. (1969). *Drunken comportment: A social explanation.* Chicago: Aldine.

Macauley, W. A., & Heubel, E. J. (1981). Achieving representative juries: A system that works. *Judicature, 65*(3), 126–135.

MacCoun, R. J., & Tyler, T. R. (1988). The basis of citizens' perceptions of the criminal jury: Procedural fairness, accuracy, and efficiency. *Law and Human Behavior, 12,* 333–352.

Maeder, T. (1985). *Crime and madness: The origins and evolution of the insanity defense.* New York: Harper & Row.

Maguire, K., & Flanagan, T. J. (Eds.) (1991). *Sourcebook of criminal justice.* Washington, DC: U.S. Department of Justice, Bureau of Justice Statistics.

Major, B., McFarlin, D. B., & Gagnon, D. (1984). Overworked and underpaid: On the nature of gender differences in personal entitlement. *Journal of Personality and Social Psychology, 47,* 1399–1412.

Malamuth, N. M. (1981). Rape proclivity among males. *Journal of Social Issues, 37*(4), 138–157.

Malamuth, N. M. (1989). Distinguishing between the Surgeon General's personal views and the consensus reached at his workshop on pornography. *American Psychologist, 44,* 580.

Malamuth, N. M., & Donnerstein, E. (1982). The effects of aggressive-pornographic mass media stimuli. In L. Berkowitz (Ed.), *Advances in experimental social psychology* (Vol. 15). Orlando, FL: Academic Press.

Malcolm, A. H. (1989, June 12). FBI opening door to wide use of genetic tests in solving crimes. *New York Times,* 1, 14.

Malpass, R. S., & Devine, P. G. (1984). Research on suggestion in lineups and photospreads. In G. L. Wells & E. F. Loftus (Eds.), *Eyewitness testimony: Psychological perspectives* (pp. 64–91). New York: Cambridge University Press.

Mankoff, M. (1971). Societal reaction and career deviance: A critical analysis. *Sociological Quarterly, 12,* 204–218.

Mann, J. (1983, September). Year-end salute. *American Lawyer,* 94.

Manson v. Braithwaite, 432 U.S. 98 (1977).

Mapp v. Ohio, 367 U.S. 643 (1961).

Margolick, D. (1984, August 17). A case for DeLorean. *New York Times,* B6.

Margolick, D. (1989a, February 10). Alienated lawyers seeking counsel in making the transition to other careers. *New York Times,* 25.

Margolick, D. (1989b, December 22). Jews on the Supreme Court: Were they different and why are there none now? *New York Times,* 28.

Marin, B. V., Holmes, D. L., Guth, M., & Kovac, P. (1979). The potential of children as eyewitnesses: A comparison of children and adults on eyewitness tasks. *Law and Human Behavior, 3,* 295–304.

Marolla, J., & Scully, D. (1982). *Attitudes toward women, violence, and rape: A comparison of convicted rapists and other felons.* Rockville, MD: National Institute of Mental Health.

Marshall, J. (1968). *Intention in law and society.* New York: Minerva.

Marshall, W. L., Jones, R., Ward, T., Johnston, P., & Barbaree, H. E. (1991). Treatment outcome with sex offenders. *Clinical Psychology Review, 11,* 465–485.

Maryland v. Craig, 110 S.Ct. 3157 (1990).

Maslach, C., & Jackson, S. E. (1984). Burnout in organizational settings. In S. Oskamp (Ed.), *Applied social psychology annual* (pp. 133–154). Newbury Park, CA: Sage.

Massoni v. State Highway Commission, 214 Kan. 844, 522 P.2d 973 (1974).

Mathes, W. C., & Devitt, E. J. (1965). *Federal jury practice and instructions.* St. Paul, MN: West.

Matthews, A. (1970). Observations on police policy and procedures for emergency detention of the mentally ill. *Journal of Criminal Law, Criminology, and Police Science, 61,* 283–295.

Maurer, A. (Chair). (1974, March). *A bill of rights for children.* Ann Arbor, MI: Committee on Children's Rights, Society for the Psychological Study of Social Issues.

McCleskey v. Kemp, 107 S.Ct. 1756 (1987).

McCloskey, M., & Egeth, H. (1983). What can a psychologist tell a jury? *American Psychologist, 38,* 550–563.

McCloskey, M., Egeth, H., & McKenna, J. (1986). The experimental psychologist in court: The ethics of expert testimony. *Law and Human Behavior, 10,* 1–13.

McConahay, J. B. (1978). Jury size, decision rule, and the null hypothesis. *Contemporary Psychology, 23,* 171–172.

McConahay, J. B., Mullin, C., & Frederick, J. (1977). The uses of social science in trials with political and racial overtones: The trial of Joan Little. *Law and Contemporary Problems, 41,* 205–229.

McCord, W. (1982). *The psychopath and milieu therapy: A longitudinal study.* Orlando, FL: Academic Press.

McLaurin v. Oklahoma State Regents for Higher Education, 339 U.S. 637 (1950).

McManis, M. J. (1986). Post shooting trauma: Demographics of professional support. In J. T. Reese & H. A. Goldstein (Eds.), *Psychological services for law enforcement* (pp. 361–364). Washington, DC: U.S. Government Printing Office.

Meddis, S. (1984a, August 27). Victims rate judges low in crime cases. *USA Today,* 2A.

Meddis, S. (1984b, December 29). Repeat juvenile offenders now a more violent breed. *USA Today,* 2A.

Meddis, S. (1987, August 3). USA gets tougher on juveniles. *USA Today,* 3A.

Meddis, S., & Kelley, J. (1985, April 8). Crime drops but fear on rise. *USA Today,* 1A.

Mednick, S. A., & Christiansen, K. O. (1977). *Biosocial bases of criminal behavior.* New York: Gardner Press.

Mednick, S. A., Gabrielli, W. F., Jr., & Hutchings, B. (1984). Genetic factors in the etiology of criminal behavior. In S. A. Mednick, T. E. Moffitt, & S. A. Stack (Eds.), *The causes of crime: New biological approaches* (pp. 74–91). Cambridge, England: Cambridge University Press.

Melani, L., & Fodaski, L. (1974). The psychology of the rapist and his victim. In New York Radical Feminists (Eds.), *Rape: The first sourcebook for women* (pp. 82–93). New York: New American Library.

Melton, G. B. (1981). Children's competency to testify. *Law and Human Behavior, 5,* 73–83.

Melton, G. B. (1987). Legal regulation of adolescent abortion: Unintended effects. *American Psychologist, 42,* 79–83.

Melton, G. B. (1990). Law, science, and humanity: The normative foundation of social science in law. *Law and Human Behavior, 14,* 315–332.

Melton, G. B. (1991). Psychology in the law: Why we do what we do. *Law and Human Behavior, 15,* 328–330.

Melton, G. B., Bulkley, J. A., & Wulkan, D. (1985). Competency of children as witnesses. In J. A. Bulkley (Ed.). *Child sexual abuse and the law* (pp. 125–145). Washington, DC: American Bar Association.

Melton, G. B., & Garrison, E. G. (1987). Fear, prejudice, and neglect: Discrimination against mentally disabled persons. *American Psychologist, 42,* 1007–1026.

Melton, G. B., Petrila, J., Poythress, N. G., & Slobogin, C. (1987). *Psychological evaluations for the courts.* New York: Guilford Press.

Melton, G. B., & Russo, N. F. (1987). Adolescent abortion: Psychological perspectives on public policy. *American Psychologist, 42,* 69–72.

Melton, G. B., & Thompson, R. A. (1987). Getting out of a rut: Detours to less traveled paths in child-witness research. In S. J. Ceci, M. P. Toglia, & D. F. Ross (Eds.), *Children's eyewitness testimony.* New York: Springer-Verlag.

Melton, G. B., Weithorn, L. A., & Slobogin, C. (1985). *Community mental health centers and the courts: An evaluation of community-based forensic services.* Lincoln: University of Nebraska Press.

Menninger, K. (1966). *The crime of punishment.* New York: Viking.

Merton, R. K. (1968). *Social theory and social structure.* New York: Free Press.

Meyer, P. (1982). *The Yale murder*. New York: Empire Books.

Meyer, P. (1985). *Death of innocence: A case of murder in Vermont*. New York: Putnam's.

Milgram, S. (1963). Behavioral study of obedience. *Journal of Abnormal and Social Psychology, 67*, 371–378.

Miller, A. (1988, April 25). Stress on the job. *Newsweek*, 40–45.

Miller, G. R., & Boster, F. J. (1977). Three images of a trial: Their implications for psychological research. In B. D. Sales (Ed.), *Psychology in the legal process* (pp. 19–38). New York: Spectrum.

Miller, M. (1989). Guidelines are not enough: The need for written sentencing options. *Behavioral Sciences and the Law, 7*, 3–24.

Miller, P. V. (1967). Personality differences and student survival in law school. *Journal of Legal Education, 19*, 460–467.

Miller, T. (1987, March). *Plumber's Friend*, (42), 2.

Miller, W. B. (1958). Lower-class culture as a generating milieu of gang delinquency. *Journal of Social Issues, 14*, 5–19.

Mills, K. (1983, September 19). Some lawyers alter tactics as more women take seats on juries. *Kansas City Times*, A1.

Mills, M. C., & Stratton, J. G. (1982). MMPI and the prediction of job performance. *FBI Law Enforcement Bulletin, 51*, 10–15.

Mills, R. B., McDevitt, R. J., & Tonkin, S. (1966). Situational tests in metropolitan police recruit selection. *Journal of Criminal Law, Criminology, and Police Science, 57*, 99–104.

Miranda v. Arizona, 384 U.S. 486 (1966).

Mitchell, H. E., & Byrne, D. (1972, May). *Minimizing the influence of irrelevant factors in the courtroom: The defendant's character, judge's instructions, and authoritarianism*. Paper presented at the meeting of the Midwestern Psychological Association, Cleveland.

Mitchell, P. (1976). *Act of love: The killing of George Zygmanik*. New York: Knopf.

Mitford, J. (1974). *Kind and usual punishment: The prison business*. New York: Vintage Books.

Moffitt, T. E., & Mednick S. A. (1988). *Biological contributions to crime causation*. New York: Martinus Nijhoff.

Moffitt, T. E., & Silva, P. A. (1988). IQ and delinquency: A direct test of the differential detection hypothesis. *Journal of Abnormal Psychology, 97*, 330–333.

Monahan, J. (1975a, April). *Abolishing the indeterminate sentence*. Testimony before the California Select Committee on Penal Institutions, Sacramento.

Monahan, J. (1975b). The prediction of violence. In D. Chappell & J. Monahan (Eds.), *Violence and criminal justice* (pp. 15–31). Lexington, MA: Lexington Books.

Monahan, J. (1977). Community psychology and public policy: The promise and the pitfalls. In B. D. Sales (Ed.), *Psychology in the legal process* (pp. 197–213). New York: Spectrum.

Monahan, J. (1984). The prediction of violent behavior: Toward a second generation of theory and practice. *American Journal of Psychiatry, 141*, 10–15.

Monahan, J. (1992). Mental disorder and violent behavior: Perceptions and evidence. *American Psychologist, 47*, 511–521.

Monahan, J., & Cummings, L. (1975). The prediction of dangerousness as a function of its perceived consequences. *Journal of Criminal Justice, 2*, 239–242.

Monahan, J., & Walker, L. (1990). *Social sciences in law: Cases and materials* (2nd ed). Westbury, NY: Foundation Press.

Monahan, J., & Walker, J. (1991). Judicial use of social science research. *Law and Human Behavior, 15*, 571–584.

Moore, M. H. (1987). *From children to citizens. Vol. 1: The mandate for juvenile justice*. New York: Springer-Verlag.

Moran, G., & Comfort, J. C. (1982). Scientific juror selection: Sex as a moderator of demographic and personality predictors of impaneled felony juror behavior. *Journal of Personality and Social Psychology, 43*, 1052–1063.

Moran, G., & Cutler, B. L. (1991). The prejudicial impact of pretrial publicity. *Journal of Applied Social Psychology, 21*, 345–367.

Moran, G., Cutler, B. L., & Loftus, E. F. (1990). Jury selection in major controlled substance trials: The need for extended voir dire. *Forensic Reports, 3*, 331–348.

Morin, R. (1989, June 26–July 2). The case for TV in the highest court. *Washington Post National Weekly Edition*, 37.

Morris, N. (1976). *The future of imprisonment*. Chicago: University of Chicago Press.

Morris, P., & Heal, K. (1981). *Crime control and the police: A review of research*. London: Home Office Research Study No. 67.

Morris, R. A. (1989). The admissibility of evidence derived from hypnosis and polygraphy. In D. C. Raskin (Ed.), *Psychological methods in criminal investigation and evidence* (pp. 333–353). New York: Springer.

Morse, S. J. (1978). Law and mental health professionals: The limits of expertise. *Professional Psychology, 9*, 389–399.

Mosher, D. L., & Anderson, R. D. (1986). Macho personality, sexual aggression, and reactions to guided imagery of realistic rape. *Journal of Research in Personality, 20*, 77–94.

Mosher, D. L., & Sirkin, M. (1984). Measuring a macho personality constellation. *Journal of Research on Personality, 18*, 150–163.

Moss, D. (1988). Self helpers on the increase. *American Bar Association Journal, 76*, 40.

Moss, D. (1991). Lawyer personality. *American Bar Association Journal, 79*, 34.

Mossman, D. (1987). Assessing and restoring competency to be executed: Should psychiatrists participate? *Behavioral Sciences and the Law, 5*, 397–410.

Mossman, K. (1973, May). Jury selection: An expert's view. *Psychology Today*, 78–79.

Muehlenhard, C. L., & Linton, M. A. (1987). Date rape and sexual aggression in dating situations: Incidence and risk factors. *Journal of Counseling Psychology, 34*, 186–196.

Muir, W. K., Jr. (1977). *Police: Streetcorner politicians*. Chicago: University of Chicago Press.

Mu'Min v. Virginia, 111 S.Ct 1899 (1991).

Munsterberg, H. (1908). *On the witness stand*. New York: Doubleday, Page.

Murphy v. Florida, 421 U.S. 794 (1965).

Myers, M. A. (1988). Sentencing behavior of judges. *Criminology, 26*, 649–675.

Nagel, R. (1989, April 24). The no-bail solution. *New Republic*, 13–14.

Nagel, S. (1962). Judicial backgrounds and criminal cases. *Journal of Criminal Law, Criminology, and Police Science, 53*, 333–339.

Nagel, S. (1969). *The legal process from a behavioral perspective*. Pacific Grove, CA: Brooks/Cole.

Narby, D. J., Cutler, B. L., & Moran, G. (in press). A meta-analysis of the association between authoritarianism and jurors' perceptions of defendant culpability. *Journal of Applied Psychology*.

National Advisory Commission on Criminal Justice Standards and Goals (1973). *Corrections*. Washington, DC: U.S. Government Printing Office.

Nebraska Press Association v. Stuart, 427 U.S. 539 (1976).

Neff, C. (1987, April 8). Scorecard. *Sports Illustrated*, 28.

Neil v. Biggers, 409 U.S. 188 (1972).

Neises, M. L., & Dillehay, R. C. (1987). Death qualification and conviction proneness: *Witt* and *Witherspoon* compared. *Behavioral Sciences and the Law*, 5, 479–494.

Neisser, U. (1976). *Cognition and reality: Principles and implications of cognitive psychology*. San Francisco: W. H. Freeman.

Neisser, U. (1979). The control of information pickup in selective looking. In A.D. Pick (Ed.), *Perception and its development: A tribute to Eleanor Gibson* (pp. 201–219). Hillsdale, NY: Erlbaum.

Nettler, G. (1974). *Explaining crime*. New York: McGraw-Hill.

Neubauer, D. W. (1988). *America's courts and the criminal justice system* (3rd ed.). Pacific Grove, CA: Brooks/Cole.

New Jersey v. T.L.O., 469 U.S. 325 (1985).

New York Radical Feminists (Eds.) (1974). *Rape: The first sourcebook for women*. New York: New American Library.

New York v. Burger, 107 S.Ct. 2636 (1987).

New York v. Quarles, 467 U.S. 649 (1984).

Nicholson, R. A., Briggs, S. R., & Robertson, H. C. (1988). Instruments for assessing competency to stand trial: How do they work? *Professional Psychology: Research and Practice*, 19, 383–394.

Nicholson, R. A., & Kugler, K. E. (1991). Competent and incompetent criminal defendants: A quantitative review of comparative research. *Psychological Bulletin*, 109, 355–370.

Nicholson, R. A., Norwood, S., & Enyart, C. (1991). Characteristics and outcomes of insanity acquittees in Oklahoma. *Behavioral Sciences and the Law*, 9, 487–500.

Nicholson, R. A., Robertson, H., Johnson, W., & Jensen, G. (1988). A comparison of instruments for assessing competency to stand trial. *Law and Human Behavior*, 12, 313–321.

Niederhoffer, A. (1967). *Behind the shield: The police in urban society*. New York: Anchor Books.

Nielsen, J. R. (1984, June 11). The flaw in our law schools. *Newsweek*, 15.

Nietzel, M. T. (1979). *Crime and its modification: A social learning perspective*. New York: Pergamon Press.

Nietzel, M. T., & Dade, J. (1973). Bail reform as an example of a community psychology intervention in the criminal justice system. *American Journal of Community Psychology*, 1, 238–247.

Nietzel, M. T., & Dillehay, R. C. (1982). The effects of variations in voir dire procedures in capital murder trials. *Law and Human Behavior*, 6, 1–13.

Nietzel, M. T., & Dillehay, R. C. (1986). *Psychological consultation in the courtrooms*. New York: Pergamon Press.

Nietzel, M. T., & Himelein, M. J. (1986). Prevention of crime and delinquency. In B. A. Edelstein & L. Michelson (Eds.), *Handbook of prevention* (pp. 195–222). New York: Plenum.

Nix, C. (1987, July 9). 1000 new officers graduate to New York City streets. *New York Times*, 15.

Nix v. Williams, 467 U.S. 431 (1984).

Nizer, L. (1961). *My life in court*. New York: Pyramid.

(No author). (1987, August 3). West Virginia bar claims attorney billed a 75–hour day. *National Law Journal*, 13.

Nobile, P. (1989, July). The making of a monster. *Playboy*, 41–45.

Noble, K. B. (1987, March 23). High court to decide whether death penalty discriminates against blacks. *New York Times*, 7.

Nordheimer, J. (1989, January 25). Bundy is put to death in Florida, closing murder cases across U.S. *New York Times*, 1, 11.

North Carolina v. Butler, 441 U.S. 369 (1979).

Office of Technology Assessment (1983). *Scientific validity of polygraph testing: A research review and evaluation*. Washington, DC: U.S. Government Printing Office.

Ogloff, J. R. P. (1991). A comparison of insanity defense standards on juror decision making. *Law and Human Behavior*, 15, 509–532.

Olczak, P. V., Kaplan, M. F., & Penrod, S. (1991). Attorneys' lay psychology and its effectiveness in selecting jurors: Three empirical studies. *Journal of Social Behavior and Personality*, 6, 431–452.

Oliver v. United States, 466 U.S. 170 (1984).

Olsen, J. (1989). *"Doc": The rape of the town of Lovell*. New York: Atheneum.

Olson-Raymer, G. (1984). National juvenile justice policy: Myth or reality? In S. H. Decker (Ed.), *Juvenile justice policy: Analyzing trends and outcomes* (pp. 19–57). Newbury Park, CA: Sage.

Olweus, D. (1987). Testosterone and adrenaline: Aggressive antisocial behavior in normal adolescent males. In S. A. Mednick, T. E. Moffitt, & S. A. Stack (Eds.), *The causes of crime: New biological approaches* (pp. 263–282). Cambridge, England: Cambridge University Press.

Oregon v. Bradshaw, 462 U.S. 1039 (1983).

O'Reilly, J., & Sales, B. D. (1987). Privacy for the institutionalized mentally ill: Are court-ordered standards effective? *Law and Human Behavior*, 11, 41–53.

Orne, M. T. (1979). The use and misuse of hypnosis in court. *International Journal of Clinical and Experimental Hypnosis*, 27, 311–341.

Orne, M. T., Soskis, D. A., Dinges, D. F., & Orne, E. C. (1984). Hypnotically induced testimony. In G. L. Wells & E. F. Loftus (Eds.), *Eyewitness testimony: Psychological perspectives* (pp. 171–213). New York: Cambridge University Press.

O'Rourke, T. E., Penrod, S. D., Cutler, B. L., & Stuve, T. E. (1989). The external validity of eyewitness identification research: Generalizing across subject populations. *Law and Human Behavior*, 13, 385–396.

Ostroff, R. (1983, February 3). Legal, ethical problems abound in film. *Kansas City Times*, B3.

Ostrov, E. (1986). Police/law enforcement and psychology. *Behavioral Sciences and the Law*, 4, 353–370.

Otto, R. K., Heilbrun, K., & Grisso, T. (1990). Training and career options in psychology and law. *Behavioral Sciences and the Law*, 8, 217–231.

Packer, H. L. (1964). Two models of the criminal process. *University of Pennsylvania Law Review*, 113, 1–68.

Padawer-Singer, A. M., & Barton, A. H. (1975). The impact of pretrial publicity on jurors' verdicts. In R. J. Simon (Ed.), *The jury system in America: A critical overview* (pp. 123–139). Newbury Park, CA: Sage.

Padawer-Singer, A. M., Singer, A., & Singer, R. (1974). Voir dire by two lawyers: An essential safeguard. *Judicature, 57,* 386–391.

Page, S. (1989). Misrepresentation of pornography research: Psychology's role. *American Psychologist, 44,* 578–580.

Palladino, J. J., van Giesen, S., Emerson, R., Pitzer, T., Price, T., Crowe, G., & Fisher, R. (1986, May). *Effects of death qualification on attitudes and demographics of the potential juror pool.* Paper presented at the meeting of the Midwestern Psychological Association, Chicago.

Pasewark, R. A., Bieber, S., Bosten, K. J., Kiser, M., & Steadman, H. J. (1982). Criminal recidivism among insanity acquittees. *International Journal of Law and Psychiatry, 5,* 365–374.

Pasewark, R. A., & Pantle, M. L. (1981). Opinions about the insanity plea. *Journal of Forensic Psychology, 8,* 63.

Pate, A., & Kelling, G. (1980). *Police patrol research: The lessons.* Unpublished paper cited by Skolnick & Bayley, 1986.

Patterson, G. R. (1982). *Coercive family process.* Eugene, OR: Castalia.

Patterson, G. R. (1986). Performance models for antisocial boys. *American Psychologist, 41,* 432–444.

Patton, M. J. (1968). The student, the situation, and performance during the first year of law school. *Journal of Legal Education, 21,* 10–51.

Patton v. Yount, 467 U.S. 1025 (1984).

Payne v. Tennessee, 498 U.S. 21 (1991).

Pearce, J. B., & Snortum, J. R. (1983). Police effectiveness in handling disturbance calls: An evaluation of crisis intervention training. *Criminal Justice and Behavior, 10,* 71–92.

Pearl, D., Bouthilet, L., & Lazar, J. (Eds.). (1982). *Television and behavior: Ten years of scientific progress and implications for the eighties.* (Vols. 1 and 2). Washington, DC: U.S. Government Printing Office.

Penn, S. (1985, April 22). Offenders face victims in program that's an alternative to jail. *Kansas City Times,* B2.

Pennington, N., & Hastie, R. (1986). Evidence evaluation in complex decision-making. *Journal of Personality and Social Psychology, 51,* 242–258.

Pennington, N., & Hastie, R. (1988). Explanation-based decision making: Effects of memory structure on judgment. *Journal of Experimental Psychology: Learning, Memory, and Cognition, 14,* 521–533.

Penrod, S. D. (1979). *Study of attorney and "scientific" jury selection models.* Unpublished doctoral dissertation, Harvard University.

Penrod, S. D. (1990). Predictors of jury decision making in criminal and civil cases: A field experiment. *Forensic Reports, 3,* 261–278.

Penrod, S. D., Loftus, E. F., & Winkler, J. (1982). The reliability of eyewitness testimony: A psychological perspective. In N. L. Kerr & R. M. Bray (Eds.), *The psychology of the courtroom* (pp. 119–168). Orlando, FL: Academic Press.

People v. Ebanks, 117 Cal. 652; 49 P. 1049; 40 LAR 269 (1897).

People v. Hughes, 453 N.E.2d 484 (N.Y. App. 1983).

People (of California) v. Shirley, 641 P.2d 775 (Cal. 1982). Cert. denied, 408 U.S.

People v. Worthington, 105 Cal. 167; 38 P.2d 689 (1894).

Pepinsky, H. E. (1975). Police decision-making. In D. M. Gottfred-

son (Ed.), *Decision-making in the criminal-justice system: Reviews and essays.* Washington, DC: U.S. Government Printing Office.

Perez v. State, 94 S.W. 1036 (Tex. Crim. App. 1906).

Perlin, M. L. (1992). Fatal assumption: A critical evaluation of the role of counsel in mental disability cases. *Law and Human Behavior, 16,* 39–60.

Perry, N. W., & Teply, L. L. (1985). Interviewing, counseling, and in-court examination of children: Practical approaches for attorneys. *Creighton Law Review, 18,* 1369–1426.

Perry, N. W., & Wrightsman, L. S. (1991). *Children as eyewitnesses in court.* Newbury Park, CA: Sage.

Petrella, R. C., & Poythress, N. G. (1983). The quality of forensic evaluations: An interdisciplinary study. *Journal of Consulting and Clinical Psychology, 51,* 76–85.

Pfohl, S. J. (1984). Predicting dangerousness: A social deconstruction of psychiatric reality. In L. A. Teplin (Ed.), *Mental health and criminal justice* (pp. 201–225). Newbury Park, CA: Sage.

Pfohl, S. J. (1985). *Images of deviance and social control: A sociological history.* New York: McGraw-Hill.

Phares, E. J. (1976). *Locus of control in personality.* Morristown, NJ: General Learning Press.

Phares, E. J., & Wilson, K. G. (1972). Responsibility attribution: Role of outcome severity, situational ambiguity, and internal-external control. *Journal of Personality, 40,* 392–406.

Phillips, D. A. (1979). *The great Texas murder trials: A compelling account of the sensational T. Cullen Davis case.* New York: Macmillan.

Phillips, S. (1977). *No heroes, no villains: The story of a murder trial.* New York: Random House.

Pinizzotto, A. J., & Finkel, N. J. (1990). Criminal personality profiling: An outcome and process study. *Law and Human Behavior, 14,* 215–234.

Pipkin, R. M. (1982). Moonlighting in law school: A multischool study of part-time employment of full-time students. *American Bar Foundation Research Journal, 1982*(4), 1109–1162.

Pitt, D. E. (1989, January 13). After New York test, most new sergeants in police are white. *New York Times,* 1, 26.

Planned Parenthood v. Casey, 112 S.Ct. 2791 (1992).

Platt, J. J., & Prout, M. F. (1987). Cognitive-behavioral theory and interventions for crime and delinquency. In E. K. Morris & C. J. Braukmann (Eds.), *Behavioral approaches to crime and delinquency: A handbook of application, research, and concepts* (pp. 477–497). New York: Plenum.

Platz, S. J., & Hosch, H. M. (1988). Cross-racial ethnic eyewitness identification: A field study. *Journal of Applied Social Psychology, 18,* 972–984.

Plessy v. Ferguson, 163 U.S. 537 (1896).

Poland, J. M. (1978). Police selection methods and the prediction of police performance. *Journal of Police Science and Administration, 6,* 374–393.

Police Foundation (1981). *The Newark foot patrol experiment.* Washington, DC: Author.

Pollock, A. (1977). The use of public opinion polls to obtain changes of venue and continuance in criminal trials. *Criminal Justice Journal, 1,* 269–288.

Porter, B. (1983). Mind hunters. *Psychology Today, 17,* 44–52.

Post, C. G. (1963). *An introduction to the law*. Englewood Cliffs, NJ: Prentice-Hall.

Powell, D. D. (1981). Race, rank, and police discretion. *Journal of Police Science and Administration, 9*, 383–389.

Powers v. Ohio, 111 S.Ct. 1364 (1991).

Poythress, N. (1982). Concerning reform in expert testimony. *Law and Human Behavior, 6*, 39–43.

Prentky, R. A., & Knight, R. A. (1991). Identifying critical dimensions for discriminating among rapists. *Journal of Consulting and Clinical Psychology, 59*, 643–661.

Prescott, P. S. (1981). *The child savers: Juvenile justice observed*. New York: Knopf.

President's Commission on Law Enforcement and Administration of Justice (1967). *Toward a just America*. Washington, DC: U.S. Government Printing Office.

Press, A. (1983a, January 10). Divorce American style. *Newsweek*, 42–48.

Press, A. (1983b, February 28). "The Verdict": A legal opinion. *Newsweek*, 51.

Press, A. (1984, June 18). Juveniles: A hold action. *Newsweek*, 84.

Press, A. (1985, May 27). When children go to jail. *Newsweek*, 87, 89.

Press, A. (1988, May 2). Helping the cops and jails. *Newsweek*, 67.

Prettyman, E. B. (1960). Jury instructions—First or last? *American Bar Association Journal, 46*, 1066.

Price-Waterhouse v. Hopkins, 109 S.Ct. 1775 (1989).

Pruitt, D. G. (1987, December). Solutions; not winners. *Psychology Today*, 58–62.

Pryor, J. B., McDaniel, M. A., & Kott-Russo, T. (1986). The influence of the level of schema abstractness upon the processing of social information. *Journal of Experimental Social Psychology, 22*, 312–327.

Pusey, M. J. (1951). *Charles Evans Hughes*. New York: Macmillan.

Putnam, W. H. (1979). Hypnosis and distortions in eyewitness memory. *International Journal of Clinical and Experimental Hypnosis, 27*(4), 437–448.

Pyszczynski, T., Greenberg, J., Mack, D., & Wrightsman, L. S. (1981). Opening statements in a jury trial: The effect of promising more than the evidence can show. *Journal of Applied Social Psychology, 11*, 434–444.

Pyszczynski, T., & Wrightsman, L. S. (1981). The effects of opening statements on mock jurors' verdicts in a simulated criminal trial. *Journal of Applied Social Psychology, 11*, 301–313.

Quay, H. C. (1965). *Personality and delinquency*. In H. C. Quay (Ed.), *Juvenile delinquency*. Princeton, NJ: Van Nostrand.

Quinn, K. M. (1988). The credibility of children's allegations of sexual abuse. *Behavioral Sciences and the Law, 6*, 181–200.

Quinsey, V. L. (1984). Sexual aggression: Studies of offenders against women. In D. Weisstub (Ed.), *Law and mental health: International perspectives* (Vol. 1, pp. 84–121). New York: Pergamon Press.

Quinsey, V. L., Chaplin, T. C., Maguire, A., & Upfold, D. (1987). The behavioral treatment of rapists and child molesters. In E. K. Morris & C. J. Braukman (Eds.), *Behavioral approaches to crime and delinquency: A handbook of applications, research, and concepts*. New York: Plenum.

Rakas v. Illinois, 439 U.S. 128 (1978).

Randolph, J. J., Hicks, T., & Mason, D. (1981). The competency screening test: A replication and extension. *Criminal Justice and Behavior, 8*, 471–482.

Rappaport, J. (1981). In praise of paradox: A social policy of empowerment over prevention. *American Journal of Community Psychology, 9*, 1–25.

Rappaport, J. (1987). Terms of empowerment/exemplars of prevention: Toward a theory of community psychology. *American Journal of Community Psychology, 15*, 121–144.

Raskin, D. C. (1982). The scientific basis of polygraph techniques and their uses in the judicial process. In A. Trankell (Ed.), *Reconstructing the past: The role of psychologists in criminal trials* (pp. 317–371). Stockholm: Norstedt and Soners.

Raskin D. C. (1989). *Psychological methods in criminal investigation and evidence*. New York: Springer.

Reck v. Pate, 367 U.S. 433 (1961).

Reckless, W. C. (1961). *The crime problem*. New York: Appleton-Century-Crofts.

Reckless, W. C. (1967). *The crime problem* (4th ed.). New York: Meredith.

Reeves, R. (1989, June 25). Busybodies have plenty to report. *Kansas City Star*, 5D.

Rehnquist, W. H. (1987). *The Supreme Court: How it was, how it is*. New York: William Morrow.

Reid, J. E., & Inbau, F. E. (1966). *Truth and deception: The polygraph ("lie-detector") technique*. Baltimore: Williams & Wilkins.

Reid, S. T. (1976). *Crime and criminology*. Hinsdale, IL: Dryden Press.

Reinhold, R. (1989, July 27). Long child molestation trial viewed as system run amok. *New York Times*, 1, 8.

Reis, H., & Jackson, L. (1981). Sex differences in reward allocation: Subjects, partners and tasks. *Journal of Personality and Social Psychology, 40*, 465–478.

Reiser, M. (1980). *Handbook of investigative hypnosis*. Los Angeles: LEHI.

Reiser, M., & Geiger, S. (1984). Police officer as victim. *Professional Psychology: Research and Practice, 15*, 315–323.

Reiser, M., & Klyver, N. (1987). Consulting with police. In I. B. Weiner & A. K. Hess (Eds.), *Handbook of forensic psychology* (pp. 437–459). New York: Wiley.

Reiser, M., & Nielson, M. (1980). Investigative hypnosis: A developing specialty. *American Journal of Clinical Hypnosis, 23*, 75–83.

Reiss, A. J., Jr. (1971). *The police and the public*. New Haven, CT: Yale University Press.

Reiss, I. L. (1986). *Journey into sexuality: An exploratory voyage*. Englewood Cliffs, NJ: Prentice-Hall.

Rembar, C. (1980). *The law of the land*. New York: Simon & Schuster.

Rennie v. Klein, 462 F.Supp. 1131 (D.N.J. 1978).

Rensberger, B. (1988, August 29–September 4). New findings on the crime rate of urban black youths. *Washington Post National Weekly Edition*, 39.

Reppucci, N. D. (1984). The wisdom of Solomon: Issues in child custody determination. In N. D. Reppucci, L. A. Weithorn, E. P. Mulvey, & J. Monahan (Eds.), *Children, mental health, and the law* (pp. 59–78). Newbury Park, CA: Sage.

Reppucci, N. D., & Haugaard, J. J. (1989). Prevention of child sexual abuse: Myth or reality. *American Psychologist, 44,* 1266–1275.

Ressler, R. K., Burgess, A. W., & Douglas, J. E. (1988). *Sexual homicide: Patterns and motives.* Lexington, MA: Lexington Books.

Reynolds, B. (1984, January 10). It's best to be judge—not a philosopher. *USA Today,* 9A.

Ribes-Inesta, E., & Bandura, A. (Eds.) (1976). *Analysis of delinquency and aggression.* Hillsdale, NJ: Erlbaum.

Richmond Newspapers, Inc. v. Virginia, 448 U.S. 555 (1980).

Rideau v. Louisiana, 373 U.S. 723 (1963).

Rider, A. O. (1980). The firesetter: A psychological profile. *FBI Law Enforcement Bulletin, 49,* 1–23.

Riechmann, J. (1985, May 21). Mental illness: Parents of deranged children suffer private tragedies. *Lawrence Journal-World,* 6.

Riggins v. Nevada, 112 S.Ct. 1810 (1992).

Ring, K. (1971). *Let's get started: An appeal to what's left in psychology.* Unpublished manuscript, University of Connecticut.

Ritter, M. (1985, February 10). Hypnosis questioned as courtroom tool. *Lawrence Journal-World,* 10A.

Riverside County v. McLaughlin, 111 S.Ct. 1661 (1991).

Rizzo v. Goode, 420 U.S. 663 (1976).

Roberts, C. F., & Golding, S. L. (1991). The social construction of criminal responsibility and insanity. *Law and Human Behavior, 15,* 349–376.

Roberts, C. F., Golding, S. L., & Fincham, F. D. (1987). Implicit theories of criminal responsibility: Decision making and the insanity defense. *Law and Human Behavior, 11,* 207–232.

Robinson, P. (1982, June 9). Criminals and victims. *New Republic,* 37–38.

Rock v. Arkansas, 107 S.Ct. 2704 (1987).

Rodham, H. (1973). Children under the law. *Harvard Educational Review, 43,* 487–514.

Roe v. Wade, 410 U.S. 113 (1973).

Roesch, R., & Golding, S. L. (1980). *Competency to stand trial.* Urbana: University of Illinois Press.

Roesch, R., & Golding, S. L. (1987). Defining and assessing competence to stand trial. In I. Weiner & A. Hess (Eds.), *Handbook of forensic psychology* (pp. 378–394). New York: Wiley.

Rogers, C. M., & Wrightsman, L. S. (1978). Attitudes toward children's rights: Nurturance or self-determination? *Journal of Social Issues, 34*(2), 59–68.

Rogers, R. (1986). *Conducting insanity evaluations.* New York: Van Nostrand.

Rogers, R. (1988). *Clinical assessment of malingering and deception.* New York: Guilford Press.

Rogers, R., & Ewing, C. P. (1989). Ultimate opinion proscriptions: A cosmetic fix and a plea for empiricism. *Law and Human Behavior, 13,* 357–374.

Rogers, R., Gillis, J. R., Dickens, S. E., & Bagby, R. M. (1991). Standardized assessment of malingering: Validation of the structured interview of reported symptoms. *Psychological Assessment: A Journal of Clinical and Consulting Psychology, 3,* 89–96.

Rogers v. Okin, 478 F.Supp. 1342, 1369 (Mass. 1979).

Rohde, D. W., & Spaeth, H. J. (1976). *Supreme Court decision making.* San Francisco: W. H. Freeman.

Rojek, D. G. (1978). *Evaluation of status offender project, Pima County, Arizona.* Tucson: University of Arizona Press.

Rollings, H. E., & Blascovich, J. (1977). The case of Patricia Hearst: Pretrial publicity and opinion. *Journal of Communication, 27,* 58–65.

Rosenbaum, R. (1989, June). Rothwax: Here comes the judge. *Vanity Fair,* 120–123, 180–186.

Rosenbaum, R. (1990, May). Travels with Dr. Death. *Vanity Fair,* 140–147, 166–174.

Rosenhan, D. L. (1973). On being sane in insane places. *Science, 179,* 250–258.

Rosenthal, D. (1970). *Genetic theory and abnormal behavior.* New York: McGraw-Hill.

Ross, J. (1983). The overlooked expert in rape prosecutions. *Toledo Law Review, 14,* 707–734.

Ross v. Oklahoma, 108 S.Ct. 2273 (1988).

Ross v. United States, 102 S.Ct. 444 (1982).

Rotter, J. B. (1966). Generalized expectancies for internal versus external control of reinforcement. *Psychological Monographs, 80*(1, Whole No. 609).

Rouse v. Cameron, 373 F.2d 451 (1966).

Rowland, J. (1985). *The ultimate violation.* New York: Doubleday.

Royko, M. (1989, May 26). Should granny be in slammer? *Kansas City Times,* A17.

Rubin, J. H. (1989, March 12). How much does public opinion sway court? *Lawrence Journal-World,* 7A.

Rubin, Z., & Peplau, L. A. (1975). Who believes in a just world? *Journal of Social Issues, 31*(3), 65–90.

Rubinstein, M. L., Clarke, S. H., & White, T. J. (1980). *Alaska bans plea bargaining.* Washington, DC: National Institute of Justice, U.S. Department of Justice.

Rudovsky, D. (1973). *The rights of prisoners.* New York: Richard A. Baron.

Ruffin v. Commonwealth, 62 Va. (21 Gratt) 790 (1871).

Runda, J. (1991). *Personal affidavit filed with authors.* Lexington: University of Kentucky Press.

Rusbult, C. E., Lowery, D., Hubbard, M. L., Maravankin, O. J., & Neises, M. (1988). Impact of employee mobility and employee performance on the allocation of rewards under conditions of constraint. *Journal of Personality and Social Psychology, 54,* 605–615.

Rush, C., & Robertson, J. (1987). Presentence reports: The utility of information to the sentencing decision. *Law and Human Behavior, 11,* 147–155.

Russell, D. E. H. (1975). *The politics of rape.* New York: Stein & Day.

Russell, D. E. H. (1984). *Sexual exploitation: Rape, child sexual abuse, and workplace harassment.* Newbury Park, CA: Sage.

Rust v. Sullivan, 111 S.Ct. 1759 (1991).

Ryerson, E. (1978). *The best-laid plans: America's juvenile court experiment.* New York: Hill & Wang.

Sachs, A. (1989, September 11). Doing the crime, not the time. *Time,* 81.

Sacks, A. M. (1984). Legal education and the changing role of lawyers in dispute resolution. *Journal of Legal Education, 34,* 237–244.

Saks, M. J. (1976). The limits of scientific jury selection. *Jurimetrics Journal, 17*, 3–22.

Saks, M. J. (1977). *Jury verdicts: The role of group size and social decision rule.* Lexington, MA: Lexington Books.

Saks, M. J., & Kidd, R. F. (1986). Human information processing and adjudication: Trial by heuristics. In H. R. Arkes & K. P. Hammond (Eds.), *Judgment and decision making: An interdisciplinary reader* (pp. 213–242). Cambridge, England: Cambridge University Press.

Saks, M. J., & Ostrom, T. M. (1975). Jury size and consensus requirements: The laws of probability vs. the laws of the land. *Journal of Contemporary Law, 1*, 163–173.

Sales, B. D., & Hafemeister, T. (1984). Empiricism and legal policy on the insanity defense. In L. A. Teplin (Ed.), *Mental health and criminal justice* (pp. 253–278). Newbury Park, CA: Sage.

Samenow, S. E. (1984). *Inside the criminal mind.* New York: Times Books.

Sampson, E. E. (1975). On justice as equality. *Journal of Social Issues, 31*(3), 45–64.

Sanday, P. R. (1981). The socio-cultural context of rape: A cross-cultural study. *Journal of Social Issues, 37*(4), 5–27.

Sander, F. E. A. (1984). Alternative dispute resolution in the law school curriculum. *Journal of Legal Education, 34*, 229–236.

Sanders, A. L. (1989, September 18). Opening the door to kids. *Time,* 75.

Santobello v. New York, 404 U.S. 257 (1971).

Saxe, L. (1991). Lying: Thoughts of an applied social psychologist. *American Psychologist, 46*, 409–415.

Saxe, L., Dougherty, D., & Cross, T. (1985). The validity of polygraph testing: Scientific analysis and public controversy. *American Psychologist, 40*, 355–366.

Saxe, L., & Fine, M. (1981). *Social experiments: Methods for design and evaluation.* Newbury Park, CA: Sage.

Scheflin, A. (1972). Jury nullification: The right to say no. *Southern California Law Review, 45*, 168–226.

Scheflin, A. W., & Shapiro, J. L. (1989). *Trance on trial.* New York: Guilford Press.

Scheflin, A. W., & Van Dyke, J. (1980). Jury nullification: The contours of a controversy. *Law and Contemporary Problems, 4*, 52–115.

Schlossberg, H., & Freeman, L. (1974). *Psychologists with a gun.* New York: Coward, McCann, & Geoghegan.

Schretlen, D., Wilkins, S. S., Van Gorp, W. G., & Bobholz, J. H. (1992). Cross-validation of a psychological test battery to detect faked insanity. *Psychological Assessment, 4*, 77–83.

Schuller, R. A., & Vidmar, N. (1992). Battered woman syndrome evidence in the courtroom: A review of the literature. *Law and Human Behavior, 16*, 273–291.

Schulman, J., Shaver, P., Colman, R., Emrich, B., & Christie, R. (1973, May). Recipe for a jury. *Psychology Today,* 37–44, 77–84.

Schulsinger, F. (1972). Psychopathy, heredity, and environment. In L. Erlenmayer-Kimling (Ed.), *International Journal of Mental Health, 1,* 190.

Schur, E. M. (1973). *Radical non-intervention: Rethinking the delinquency problem.* Englewood Cliffs, NJ: Prentice-Hall.

Schwartz, H. (Ed.). (1988). *The Burger years: Rights and wrongs in the Supreme Court 1969–1986.* New York: Viking.

Schwitzgebel, R. L., & Schwitzgebel, R. K. (1980). *Law and psychological practice.* New York: Wiley.

Scroggs, J. R. (1976). Penalties for rape as a function of victim provocativeness, damage, and resistance. *Journal of Applied Social Psychology, 6*, 360–368.

Seedman, A. A., & Hellman, P. (1974). *Chief!* New York: Arthur Fields.

Seligmann, J. (1984, April 9). The date who rapes. *Newsweek,* 91–92.

Sellin, T. (1968). *Capital punishment.* New York: United Nations Publications.

Serrill, M. S. (1984, September 17). Breaking the spell of hypnosis. *Time,* 62.

Sessions, W. (1989, April 27). *Law and public service.* Invited address, University of Kansas, Lawrence.

Sheehan, P. W., & Tilden, J. (1983). Effects of suggestibility and hypnosis on accurate and distorted retrieval from memory. *Journal of Experimental Psychology: Learning, Memory, and Cognition, 9*, 283–293.

Sheldon, W. H. (1942). *The varieties of temperament: A psychology of constitutional differences.* New York: Harper & Row.

Sheldon, W. H. (1949). *Varieties of delinquent youth: An introduction to constitutional psychiatry.* New York: Harper & Row.

Sheley, J. F. (1985). *America's "crime problem": An introduction to criminology.* Belmont, CA: Wadsworth.

Shenon, P. (1986, August 29). U.S. report on youth crime urges fixed sentencing plan. *New York Times,* 1, 12.

Sheppard, B. H., & Vidmar, N. (1980). Adversary pretrial procedures and testimonial evidence: Effects of lawyer's role and Machiavellianism. *Journal of Personality and Social Psychology, 39*, 320–332.

Sheppard, B. H., & Vidmar, N. (1983, June). *Is it fair to worry about fairness?* Paper presented at the Law and Society Association Meeting, Denver, Colorado.

Sheppard v. Maxwell, 384 U.S. 333 (1966).

Sherman v. United States, 356 U.S. 369 (1958).

Siegal, L. J., Sullivan, D. C., & Greene, J. R. (1974). Decision games applied to police decision making: An explanatory study of information usage. *Journal of Criminal Justice, 2*, 131–146.

Siegel, A. M., & Elwork, A. (1990). Treating incompetence to stand trial. *Law and Human Behavior, 14*, 57–65.

Silberman, C. E. (1978). *Criminal justice, criminal violence.* New York: Random House.

Silkwood v. Kerr-McGee Corp., 78 L.Ed.2d 443 (1984).

Simon, R. J. (1966). Murders, juries, and the press: Does sensational reporting lead to verdicts of guilty? *Trans/Action, 3*, 40–42.

Simon, R. J. (1967). *The jury and the defense of insanity.* Boston: Little, Brown.

Singer, R. (1980). The *Wolfish* case: Has the *Bell* tolled for prisoner litigation in the federal courts? In G. L. Alpert (Ed.), *Legal rights of prisoners* (pp. 67–111). Newbury Park, CA: Sage.

Skafte, D. (1985). *Child custody evaluations: A practical guide.* Newbury Park, CA: Sage.

Skolnick, J. H. (1975). *Justice without trial: Law enforcement in a democratic society* (2nd ed.). New York: Wiley.

Skolnick, J. H., & Bayley, D. H. (1986). *The new blue line: Police innovation in six American cities.* New York: Free Press.

Slater, D., & Hans, V. P. (1984). Public opinion of forensic psychiatry following the Hinckley verdict. *American Journal of Psychiatry, 141,* 675–679.

Slobogin, C. (1984). Dangerousness and expertise. *University of Pennsylvania Law Review, 133,* 97–117.

Slobogin, C., & Schumacher, J. E. (in press). Rating the intrusiveness of law enforcement searches and seizures. *Law and Human Behavior, 17.*

Small, M. A. (1991). The normative foundation of social science in law revisited: A reply to Melton. *Law and Human Behavior, 15,* 325–328.

Smith, L., & Malandro, L. (1986). *Courtroom communication strategies.* New York: Kluwer.

Smith, M. C. (1983). Hypnotic memory enhancement of witnesses: Does it work? *Psychological Bulletin, 94,* 387–407.

Smith, W. P. (1987). Conflict and negotiation: Trends and emerging issues. *Journal of Applied Social Psychology, 17,* 641–677.

Smith, V. L. (1990). The feasibility and utility of pretrial instruction in the substantive law: A survey of judges. *Law and Human Behavior, 14,* 235–248.

Smith v. United States, 148 F.2d 665 (1929).

Snarey, J. R. (1985). Cross-cultural universality of social-moral development: A critical review of Kohlbergian research. *Psychological Bulletin, 97,* 202–232.

Solomon, R. M., & Horn, J. M. (1986). Post-shooting traumatic reactions: A pilot study. In J. T. Reese & H. A. Goldstein (Eds.), *Psychological services for law enforcement* (pp. 383–394). Washington, DC: U.S. Government Printing Office.

Sony Corp. of America v. Universal City Studios, 78 L.Ed.2d 574 (1984).

Soskis, D. A., & Van Zandt, C. R. (1986). Hostage negotiation: Law enforcement's most effective nonlethal weapon. *Behavioral Sciences and the Law, 4,* 423–436.

South Dakota v. Neville, 459 U.S. 553 (1983).

Spanos, N. P., Gwynn, M. I., Comer, S. L., Baltruweit, W. J., & de Groh, M. (1989). Are hypnotically induced pseudomemories resistant to cross-examination? *Law and Human Behavior, 13*(3), 271–289.

Spanos, N. P., Quigley, C. A., Gwynn, M. I., Glatt, R. L., & Perlini, A. H. (1991). Hypnotic interrogation, pretrial preparation, and witness testimony during direct and cross-examination. *Law and Human Behavior, 15*(6), 639–653.

Sparf and Hansen v. United States, 156 U.S. 51 (1895).

Spence, G., & Polk, A. (1982). *Gerry Spence: Gunning for justice.* New York: Doubleday.

Sperling, D. (1985, March 1). Trauma of rape continues without therapy. *USA Today,* 3A.

Spielberger, C. D. (Ed.) (1979). *Police selection and evaluation: Issues and techniques.* Washington, DC: Hemisphere.

Spielberger, C. D., Spaulding, H. C., & Ward, J. C. (1978). *Selecting effective law enforcement officers: The Florida police standards research project.* Tampa, FL: Human Resources Institute.

Spielberger, C. D., Westberry, L. G., Grier, K. S., & Greenfield, G. (1980). *The police stress survey: Sources of stress in law enforcement.* Tampa, FL: Human Resources Institute.

Spindler-Cruden, K. (1983, March 11). Joint custody a solution, but it's rough, parents say. *Kansas City Times,* C1, C2.

Spivak, J. (1989, January 22). Lawyer hired for retarded Missouri inmate. *Kansas City Star,* 6B.

Stalans, L. J., & Diamond, S. S. (1990). Formation and change in lay evaluations of criminal sentencing: Misperception and discontent. *Law and Human Behavior, 14,* 199–214.

Standish, F. (1984, January 31). Child abuser sentenced to treatment. *Lawrence Journal-World,* 8.

Stanford v. Kentucky, 492 U.S. 361 (1989).

State v. Collins, 464 A.2d 1028 (Md. App. 1983).

State v. Gray, 51 ALB Law J., 241 (1895); 39 P. 1050 (1895).

State v. Hayes, 389 A.2d 1379 (1978).

State v. Johnson, 133 Wisc.2d 307, 395 N.W.2d 176 (1986).

State [of Kansas] v. Brown, 430 P.2d 499 (1982).

State [of Kansas] v. Warren, 635 P.2d 1236 (1981).

State [of Minnesota] v. Mack, 292 N.W.2d 764 (Minn. 1980).

State [of New Jersey] v. Hurd, 432 A.2d 86 (N.J. 1981).

Steadman, H. J. (1979). *Beating a rap? Defendants found incompetent to stand trial.* Chicago: University of Chicago Press.

Steadman, H. J., & Braff, J. (1983). Defendants not guilty by reason of insanity. In J. Monahan & H. J. Steadman (Eds.), *Mentally disordered offenders: Perspectives from law and social science.* New York: Plenum.

Steadman, H. J., Keitner, L., Braff, J., & Arvanites, T. M. (1983). Factors associated with a successful insanity plea. *American Journal of Psychiatry, 140,* 401–405.

Steadman, H. J., Monahan, J., Hartstone, E., Davis, S. K., & Robbins, P. C. (1982). Mentally disordered offenders: A national survey of patients and facilities. *Law and Human Behavior, 6,* 31–38.

Steadman, H. J., Rosenstein, M. J., MacAskill, R. L., & Manderscheid, R. W. (1988). A profile of mentally disordered offenders admitted to inpatient psychiatric services in the United States. *Law and Human Behavior, 12,* 91–99.

Steele, W. W., Jr. (1971). A comparison of attitudes of freshman and senior law students. *Journal of Legal Education, 23,* 318–321.

Steinman, S. (1981). The experience of children in a joint-custody arrangement: A report of a study. *American Journal of Orthopsychiatry, 51,* 403–414.

Steinmetz, S. K., & Straus, M. (1974). *Violence in the family.* New York: Harper & Row.

Stern, R. L., & Gressman, E. (1962). *Supreme Court practice* (3rd ed.). Washington, DC: Bureau of National Affairs.

Stevens, R. (1973). Law schools and law students. *Virginia Law Review, 59,* 551–707.

Strasser, F. (1989, June 26). Look-alikes win in court. *National Law Journal,* 63.

Strauder v. West Virginia, 100 U.S. 303 (1880).

Straus, M. (1980). A sociological perspective on the causes of family violence. In M. R. Green (Ed.), *Violence and the family* (pp. 7–31). Boulder, CO: Westview.

Strodtbeck, F., James, R., & Hawkins, C. (1957). Social status in jury deliberations. *American Sociological Review, 22,* 713–718.

Strodtbeck, F., & Lipinski, R. M. (1985). Becoming first among equals: Moral considerations in jury foreman selection. *Journal of Personality and Social Psychology, 49,* 927–936.

Strodtbeck, F., & Mann, R. (1956). Sex role differentiation in jury deliberations. *American Sociological Review, 19,* 3–11.

Sue, S., Smith, R. E., & Caldwell, C. (1973). Effects of inadmissible evidence on the decisions of simulated jurors: A moral dilemma. *Journal of Applied Social Psychology, 3,* 345–353.

Sue, S., Smith, R. E., & Gilbert, R. (1974). Biasing effect of pretrial publicity on judicial decisions. *Journal of Criminal Justice, 2,* 163–171.

Sue, S., Smith, R. E., & Pedroza, G. (1975). Authoritarianism, pretrial publicity, and awareness of bias in simulated jurors. *Psychological Reports, 37,* 1299–1302.

Supreme Court, 1982 term (1983). *Harvard Law Review, 97,* 304.

Surgeon General's Scientific Advisory Committee on Television and Social Behavior (1972). *Television and growing up: The impact of televised violence.* Washington, DC: U.S. Government Printing Office.

Susman, D. (1992). *Effects of three different legal standards on psychologists' determinations of competency for execution.* Unpublished Doctoral Dissertation. University of Kentucky, Lexington.

Sutherland, E. H. (1947). *Principles of criminology* (4th ed.). Philadelphia: Lippincott.

Sutherland, E. H., & Cressey, D. R. (1974). *Principles of criminology* (9th ed.). New York: Lippincott.

Swain v. Alabama, 380 U.S. 202 (1965).

Swartz, J. D. (1985). Review of Inwald Personality Inventory. In J. V. Mitchell (Ed.), *The ninth mental measurements yearbook* (pp. 711–713). Lincoln: Buros Institute of Mental Measurements, University of Nebraska.

Sweatt v. Painter, 210 S.W. 2d 442 (1947), 339 U.S. 629 (1950).

Tanford, J. A. (1990). The law and psychology of jury instructions. *Nebraska Law Review, 69,* 71–111.

Tans, M. D., & Chaffee, S. H. (1966). Pretrial publicity and juror prejudice. *Journalism Quarterly, 43,* 647–654.

Tapp, J. L., & Levine, F. J. (1970). Persuasion to virtue: A preliminary statement. *Law and Society Review, 4,* 565–582.

Tapp, J. L., & Levine, F. J. (1974). Legal socialization: Strategies for an ethical legality. *Stanford Law Review, 24,* 1–72.

Tarasoff v. Regents of the University of California, 17 Cal.3d 425, 551 P.2d 334, 131 Cal.Rptr. 14 (1976).

Taubman, B. (1988). *The preppy murder trial.* New York: St. Martin's Press.

Taylor, S., Jr. (1986, May 6). Justices reject broad challenge in capital cases. *New York Times,* 1, 12.

Taylor, S., Jr. (1987a, May 27). Court backs law letting U.S. widen pretrial jailing. *New York Times,* 1, 8–9.

Taylor, S., Jr. (1987b, June 16). Justices, 5–4, bar impact evidence in death hearings. *New York Times,* 1, 5.

Taylor, S., Jr. (1987c, June 23). Some hypnosis-enhanced testimony is upheld. *New York Times,* 12.

Taylor, S., Jr. (1988a, April 26). Court, 5–4, votes to restudy rights in minority suits. *New York Times,* 1, 11.

Taylor, S., Jr. (1988b, June 16). Court reaffirms limits in questioning of suspects. *New York Times,* 9.

Taylor, S., Jr. (1988c, June 23). Rulings curb protection in white-collar crimes. *New York Times,* 11.

Taylor, S. E., & Crocker, J. (1981). Schematic bases of social information processing. In E. T. Higgins, C. P. Herman, & M. P. Zanna (Eds.), *Social cognition: The Ontario symposium* (Vol. 1). Hillsdale, NJ: Erlbaum.

Taylor v. Louisiana, 419 U.S. 522 (1975).

Teahan, J. E. (1975a). Role playing and group experience to facilitate attitude and value changes among black and white police officers. *Journal of Social Issues, 31*(1), 35–46.

Teahan, J. E. (1975b). A longitudinal study of attitude shifts among black and white police officers. *Journal of Social Issues, 31*(1), 47–56.

Teplin, L. A. (1984a). Editor's introduction. In L. A. Teplin (Ed.), *Mental health and criminal justice* (pp. 13–17). Newbury Park, CA: Sage.

Teplin, L. A. (1984b). The criminalization of the mentally ill: Speculation in search of data. In L. A. Teplin (Ed.), *Mental health and criminal justice* (pp. 63–85). Newbury Park, CA: Sage.

Terman, L. M. (1917). A trial of mental and pedagogical tests in a civil service examination for policemen and firemen. *Journal of Applied Psychology, 1,* 17–29.

Terry v. Ohio, 391 U.S. 1 (1968).

Thibaut, J., & Walker, L. (1975). *Procedural justice: A psychological analysis.* Hillsdale, NJ: Erlbaum.

Thibaut, J., Walker, L., & Lind, E. A. (1972). Adversary presentation and bias in legal decision making. *Harvard Law Review, 86,* 386–401.

Thielens, W. (1980). *The socialization of law students: A case study in three parts.* New York: Arno Press.

Thomas, E. (1991). *The man to see.* Boston: Little, Brown.

Thompson, J. (1984, February 2). Case thrusts Wichita into national debate over drug for rapists. *Kansas City Times,* A1, A14.

Thompson, M. (1989, April 3). Misprint. *New Republic,* 14–15.

Thompson, W. C. (1989). Death qualification after *Wainwright v. Witt* and *Lockhart v. McCree. Law and Human Behavior, 13,* 185–215.

Thompson, W. C., Cowan, C. L., Ellsworth, P. C., & Harrington, J. C. (1984). Death penalty attitudes and conviction proneness: The translation of attitudes into verdicts. *Law and Human Behavior, 8,* 95–113.

Thompson, W. C., Fong, G. T., & Rosenhan, D. L. (1981). Inadmissible evidence and juror verdicts. *Journal of Personality and Social Psychology, 40,* 453–463.

Thompson, W. C., & Ford, S. (1989). DNA typing: Acceptance and weight of the new genetic identification tests. *Virginia Law Review, 75,* 45–108.

Thompson v. Oklahoma, 487 U.S. 815 (1988).

Tinterow, M. M. (1970). *Foundations of hypnosis: Franz Mesmer to Freud.* Springfield, IL: Charles C Thomas.

Tison v. Arizona, 481 U.S. 137 (1987).

Tolchin, M. (1989, June 28). Court overturns guilty verdict in Nofziger case. *New York Times,* 1.

Tomkins, A. J. (1988a, April). Mandating the use of alternative dispute resolution procedures. *APA Monitor,* 28.

Tomkins, A. J. (1988b, October). Using social science evidence to prove discrimination. *APA Monitor,* 40.

Tooley, V., Brigham, J. C., Maass, A., & Bothwell, R. K. (1987). Facial recognition: Weapon effect and attentional focus. *Journal of Applied Social Psychology, 17,* 845–859.

Toplikar, D. (1984, December 9). Court ruling won't alter local procedure on drunken drivers. *Lawrence Journal-World,* 6A.

Torry, S., & Lawrence, B. H. (1989, March 13–19). Free agents in the legal big leagues. *Washington Post National Weekly Edition,* 11.

Toufexis, A. (1989, February 6). The lasting worlds of divorce. *Time,* 61.

Toulmin, S. (1990). *Cosmopolis: The hidden agenda of modernity.* New York: Free Press.

Townsend v. Swain, 372 U.S. 293 (1963).

Trubek, D. M., Sarat, A., Felstiner, W. L. F., Kritzer, H. M., & Grossman, J. B. (1983). The costs of ordinary litigation. *U.C.L.A. Law Review, 31,* 72–127.

Turkheimer, E., & Parry, C. D. H. (1992). Why the gap? Practice and policy in civil commitment hearings. *American Psychologist, 47,* 646–655.

Turkington, C. (1985, April). Psychiatric help ruled to be defendant right. *APA Monitor,* 2.

Turow, S. (1977). *ONE L.* New York: Putnam's.

Udolf, R. (1983). *Forensic hypnosis: Psychological and legal aspects.* Lexington, MA: Heath.

Underwager, R., & Wakefield, H. (1992). Poor psychology produces poor law. *Law and Human Behavior, 16,* 233–243.

Underwood, R. H., & Fortune, W. H. (1988). *Trial ethics.* Boston: Little, Brown.

United States Bureau of the Census (1990). *Statistical Abstract of the United States: 1990 (10th edition).* Washington, DC: U.S. Government Printing Office.

United States Sentencing Commission (1987). *Sentencing guidelines and policy statements.* Washington, DC: U.S. Government Printing Office.

United States v. Burr, 24 F.Cas. 49 (D.Va. 1807).

United States v. Charters, 863 F.2d. 302 4th Cir. (1988).

United States v. DeCoster, 487 F.2d 1197 (1973).

United States v. Dellinger, 475 F.2d 340, 368 (7th Cir. 1972).

United States v. Dougherty, 473 F.2d 1113, 1130–1137 (D.C. Cir. 1972).

United States v. Leon, 468 U.S. 897 (1984).

United States v. Masthers, 549 F.2d 721 (D.C. Cir. 1976).

United States v. Miller, 425 U.S. 431 (1976).

United States v. Montoya de Hernandez, 105 S.Ct. 3304 (1985).

United States v. Nixon, 418 U.S. 683 (1974).

United States v. Payner, 447 U.S. 727 (1980).

United States v. Robinson, 414 U.S. 218 (1973).

United States v. Ross, 456 U.S. 798 (1982).

United States v. Salerno, 481 U.S. 739 (1987).

United States v. Sokolow, 109 S.Ct. 1581 (1989).

United States v. Telfaire, 469 F.2d 552 (D.C. Cir. 1972).

United States v. Wade, 388 U.S. 218 (1967).

Urbom, W. K. (1982). Toward better treatment of jurors by judges. *Nebraska Law Review, 61,* 409–427.

USA snapshots: Capital punishment. (1984, June 25). *USA Today,* 1A.

Uviller, H. R. (1988). *Tempered zeal: A Columbia law professor's year on the streets with the New York City police.* New York: Contemporary Books.

Van Dyke, J. (1970). The jury as a political institution. *Catholic Law Review, 16,* 224–270.

Van Dyke, J. (1977). *Jury selection procedures.* Cambridge, MA: Ballinger.

Veronen, L. J., Kilpatrick, D. G., & Resick, P. A. (1979). Treatment of fear and anxiety in rape victims: Implications for the criminal justice system. In W. H. Parsonage (Ed.), *Perspectives on victimology.* Newbury Park, CA: Sage.

Vidmar, N. (1992). Commentary: Procedural justice and alternative dispute resolution. *Psychological Science, 3,* 2224–2228.

Vidmar, N., & Judson, J. (1981). The use of social sciences in a change of venue application. *Canadian Bar Review, 59,* 76–102.

Villasenor, V. (1977). *Jury: The people vs. Juan Corona.* Boston: Little, Brown.

Vinacke, W. E. (1959). Sex roles in a three-person game. *Sociometry, 22,* 343–360.

Vinson, D. E., & Anthony, P. K. (1985). *Social science research methods for litigation.* Charlottesville, VA: Michie.

Vise, D. A. (1989, August 7–13). Using a Mafia law to bust high-flying stockbrokers. *Washington Post National Weekly Edition,* 20.

Visher, C. A. (1987). Juror decision making: The importance of evidence. *Law and Human Behavior, 11,* 1–18.

Wadden, T. A., & Anderton, C. H. (1982). The clinical use of hypnosis. *Psychological Bulletin, 91,* 215–243.

Waggett, G. J. (1989, May 27). Let's stop turning rapists into heroes. *TV Guide,* 10–11.

Wainright v. Witt, 53 L.W. 4108 (1985).

Wald, M., Ayres, R., Hess, D. W., Schantz, M., & Whitebread, C. H. (1967). Interrogations in New Haven: The impact of *Miranda. Yale Law Journal, 76,* 1519–1648.

Walker, L. (1979). *The battered woman.* New York: Harper & Row.

Walker, L. (1984). Sex differences in the development of moral reasoning: A critical review. *Child Development, 55,* 677–691.

Walker, L., La Tour, S., Lind, E. A., & Thibaut, J. (1974). Reactions of participants and observers to modes of adjudication. *Journal of Applied Social Psychology, 4,* 295–310.

Walker, S. (1982, October). What have civil liberties ever done for crime victims? Plenty! *ACJS [Academy of Criminal Justice Sciences] Today,* 4–5.

Walker, S. (1985). *Sense and nonsense about crime: A policy guide.* Pacific Grove, CA: Brooks/Cole.

Walker, W. (1989, February 19). In cold DNA. *New York Times Book Review,* 11.

Wall, P. M. (1965). *Eyewitness identification in criminal cases.* Springfield, IL: Charles C Thomas.

Wallerstein, J. S., & Blakeslee, S. (1989). *Second changes: Men, women, and children a decade after divorce.* New York: Ticknor & Fields.

Walster, E., Walster, G. W., & Berscheid, E. (1978). *Equity: Theory and research.* Boston: Allyn & Bacon.

Wambaugh, J. (1989). *The blooding.* New York: William Morrow.

Warner, T. D. (1987). *The effects of judge's instructions and expert testimony on jurors' reactions to an eyewitness.* Unpublished doctoral dissertation, University of Kansas.

Warren, L. (1989, October). If only. . . . *Grand Rapids Magazine,* 24–28, 61–62.

Warshaw, R. (1988). *I never called it rape.* New York: Harper & Row.

Washington v. Harper, 494 U.S. 210 (1990).

Watson, A. S. (1989). Some psychological aspects of the trial judge's decision-making. *Law Quadrangle Notes, 33*(2), 36–40.

Watts, B. L., Messe, L. A., & Vallacher, R. R. (1982). Toward understanding sex differences in reward allocation: Agency, communion and reward distribution behavior. *Sex Roles, 8,* 1175–1187.

Wayte v. United States, 105 S.Ct. 1524 (1985).

Webster v. Reproductive Health Services, 109 S.Ct. 3040 (1989).

Weiner, B. A. (1986). Confidentiality and the legal issues raised by the psychological evaluations. In J. T. Reese & H.A. Goldstein (Eds.), *Psychological services for law enforcement* (pp. 97–104). Washington, DC: U.S. Government Printing Office.

Weir, J. A., & Branscombe, N. R. (1989). *Discriminating self-reported males who are prone-to-rape from those without such a proclivity.* Unpublished manuscript, University of Kansas.

Weir, J. A., Willis, C. E., & Wrightsman, L. S. (1989). *Reactions of jurors to rape victims on the witness stand.* Paper presented at the meeting of the American Psychological Association, New Orleans.

Weir, J. A., & Wrightsman, L. S. (1990). The determinants of mock jurors' verdicts in a rape case. *Journal of Applied Social Psychology, 20,* 901–919.

Weld, H. P., & Danzig, E. R. (1940). A study of the way in which a verdict is reached by a jury. *American Journal of Psychology, 53,* 518–536.

Wells, G. (in press). What do we know about eyewitness identification? *American Psychologist.*

Wells, G. L. (1980). Asymmetric attributions for compliance: Reward vs. punishment. *Journal of Experimental Social Psychology, 16,* 47–60.

Wells, G. L. (1984). A reanalysis of the expert testimony issue. In G. L. Wells & E. F. Loftus (Eds.), *Eyewitness testimony: Psychological perspectives* (pp. 304–314). New York: Cambridge University Press.

Wells, G. L. (1992). Naked statistical evidence of liability: Is subjective probability enough? *Journal of Personality and Social Psychology, 62,* 739–752.

Wells, G. L., & Lindsay, R. C. L. (1980). On estimating the diagnosticity of eyewitness nonidentifications. *Psychological Bulletin, 88,* 776–784.

Wells, G. L., Lindsay, R. C. L., & Ferguson, T. J. (1979). Accuracy, confidence, and juror perceptions in eyewitness identification. *Journal of Applied Psychology, 64,* 440–448.

Wells, G. L., & Loftus, E. F. (1984). Eyewitness research: Then and now. In G. L. Wells & E. F. Loftus (Eds.). *Eyewitness testimony: Psychological perspectives* (pp. 1–11). New York: Cambridge University Press.

Wells, G. L., Miene, P. K., & Wrightsman, L. S. (1985). The timing of the defense opening statement: Don't wait until the evidence is in. *Journal of Applied Social Psychology, 15,* 758–772.

Wells, G. L., & Murray, D. M. (1983). What can psychology say about the *Neil v. Biggers* criteria for judging eyewitness accuracy? *Journal of Applied Psychology, 68,* 347–362.

Westley, W. A. (1970). *Violence and the police: A sociological study of law, custom, and morality.* Cambridge, MA: MIT Press.

Wetter, M., Baer, R., Berry, D., Smith, G., & Larsen, L. (1992). Sensitivity of MMPI-2 validity scales to random responding and malingering. *Psychological Assessment, 4,* 369–374.

Wexler, D. B. (1992). Putting mental health into mental health law: Therapeutic jurisprudence. *Law and Human Behavior, 16,* 27–38.

Whalen v. United States, 346 F.2d 812 (1965).

What the justices are saying. (1976, November). *American Bar Association Journal, 62,* 1454–1456.

Wheeler v. United States, 159 U.S. 523 (1895).

Whipple, S. B. (1937). *The trial of Bruno Richard Hauptmann.* New York: Doubleday.

White, J. W., Lawrence, P. S., Biggerstaff, C., & Grubb, T. D. (1985). Factors of stress among police officers. *Criminal Justice and Behavior, 12,* 111–128.

White, J. W., Scott, L. P., Biggerstaff, C., & Grubb, T. D. (1985). Factors of stress among police officers. *Criminal Justice and Behavior, 12,* 111–128.

Wicker, T. (1985, June 28). Gnawing doubt—if those who are executed may prove to be innocent. *Lawrence Journal-World,* 4.

Wiener, R. L., Wiener, A. T. F., & Grisso, T. (1989). Empathy and biased assimilation of testimonies in cases of alleged rape. *Law and Human Behavior, 13,* 343–356.

Wigmore, J. H. (1970). *Evidence* (Vol. 3). (Revised by J. H. Chadbourn). Boston: Little, Brown. (Originally published in 1940.)

Wilcox, B. (1987). Pornography, social science, and politics: When research and ideology collide. *American Psychologist, 42,* 941–943.

Wildman, R. W. II, Batchelor, E. S., Thompson, L., Nelson, F. R., Moore, J. T., Patterson, M. E., & de Laosa, M. (1978). *The Georgia Court Competency Test: An attempt to develop a rapid, quantitative measure of fitness for trial.* Unpublished manuscript, Forensic Services Division, Central State Hospital, Milledgeville, GA.

Wilkes, J. (1987, June). Murder in mind. *Psychology Today,* 26–32.

Wilkins v. Missouri, 492 U.S. 361 (1989).

Will, G. (1984, January 22). Fitting laws to dynamic society likened to trousers on 10-year-old. *Lawrence Journal-World,* 6.

Will, G. (1987, June 21). Narrowing truths provided by victim-impact statement. *Lawrence Journal-World,* 5A.

Willging, T. E., & Dunn, T. G. (1982). The moral development of the law student: Theory and data on legal education. *Journal of Legal Education, 31,* 306–358.

Williams, G. R. (1984). Using simulation exercises for negotiation and other dispute resolution courses. *Journal of Legal Education, 34,* 307–314.

Williams, W., & Miller, K. S. (1981). The processing and disposition of incompetent mentally ill offenders. *Law and Human Behavior, 5,* 245–261.

Williams v. Florida, 399 U.S. 78 (1970).

Wilson, J. Q. (1975). *Thinking about crime.* New York: Basic Books.

Wilson, J. Q. (1978). *Varieties of police behavior* (2nd ed.). Cambridge, MA: Harvard University Press.

Wilson, J. Q. (1987, September 14). Political power and the picking of judges. *Washington Post National Weekly Edition*, 29.

Wilson, J. Q., & Herrnstein, R. (1985). *Crime and human nature*. New York: Simon & Schuster.

Wilson, J. Q., & Kelling, G. L. (1989, April 24). Beating criminals to the punch. *New York Times*, 23.

Wilson, L., Greene, E., & Loftus, E. F. (1986). Beliefs about forensic hypnosis. *International Journal of Clinical and Experimental Hypnosis*, 34, 110–121.

Wilson v. United States, 391 F.2d. 460 (1968).

Wilt, G., Bannon, J., Breedlove, R., Sandker, D., & Michaelson, S. (1977). *Domestic violence and the police—Studies in Detroit and Kansas City*. Washington, DC: Police Foundation.

Winslade, W. J., & Ross, J. W. (1983). *The insanity plea*. New York: Scribner's.

Winters v. Miller, 466 F.2d 65 (1971), cert. denied, 404 U.S. 985.

Wishman, S. (1981a, November 9). A lawyer's guilty secrets. *Newsweek*, 25.

Wishman, S. (1981b). *Confessions of a criminal lawyer*. New York: Times Books.

Witherspoon v. Illinois, 391 U.S. 510, 88 S.Ct. 1770, 20 L.Ed.2d 776 (1968).

Witkin, H. A., Mednick, S. A., Schulsinger, F., Bakkestrom, E., Christiansen, K. O., Goodenough, D. R., Hirschhorn, K., Lundstean, C., Owen, D. R., Philip, J., Rubin, D. B., & Stocking, M. (1976). XYY and XXY men: Criminality and aggression. *Science*, 193, 547–555.

Wolf, S., & Montgomery, D. A. (1977). Effects of inadmissible evidence and level of judicial admonishment to disregard on the judgments of mock jurors. *Journal of Applied Social Psychology*, 7, 205–219.

Wolff v. McDonnell, 418 U.S. 539 (1974).

Wolfgang, M. (1958). *Patterns in criminal homicide*. New York: Wiley.

Woocher, F. D. (1986). Legal principles governing expert testimony by experimental psychologists. *Law and Human Behavior*, 10, 47–61.

Woodward, B., & Armstrong, S. (1979). *The brethren: Inside the Supreme Court*. New York: Simon & Schuster.

Woodward, K. K., & Uehling, M. D. (1985, January 14). The hardest question. *Newsweek*, 29.

Woody, R. H. (1977). Psychologists in child custody. In B. D. Sales (Ed.), *Psychology and the legal process* (pp. 249–267). New York: Plenum.

Work, C. P. (1985, January 21). The good times roll for "expert witnesses." *U.S. News & World Report*, 65–66.

Worsfold, V. L. (1974). A philosophical justification for children's rights. *Harvard Educational Review*, 44, 142–157.

Wright, W. (1983). *The von Bülow affair*. New York: Delacorte Press.

Wright v. West, 112 S.Ct. 2482 (1992).

Wrightsman, L. S. (1989, May). *Application of the expert-novice distinction to decision making by judges versus juries*. Paper presented at meetings of the Midwestern Psychological Association, Chicago.

Wyatt, G. E., Guthrie, D., & Notgrass, C. M. (1992). Differential effects of women's child sexual abuse and subsequent sexual revictimization. *Journal of Consulting and Clinical Psychology*, 60, 167–173.

Wyatt v. Stickney, 325 F.Supp. 781 (1971).

Yegidis, B. L. (1986). Date rape and other forced sexual encounters among college students. *Journal of Sex Education and Therapy*, 12, 51–54.

Yochelson, S., & Samenow, S. E. (1976). *The criminal personality (Vol. 1): A profile for change*. New York: Jason Aronson.

Youngberg v. Romeo, 457 U.S. 307 (1982).

Zajonc, R. B., & McIntosh, D. N. (1992). Emotions research: Some promising questions and some questionable promises. *Psychological Science*, 3, 70–74.

Zebrowitz, L. A., & McDonald, S. M. (1991). The impact of litigants' baby-facedness and attractiveness on adjudications in small claims courts. *Law and Human Behavior*, 15, 603–624.

Zeisel, H. (1971). . . . And then there were none: The diminution of the federal jury. *University of Chicago Law Review*, 38, 710–724.

Zeisel, H. (1976). The deterrent effect of the death penalty: Facts and faiths. *Supreme Court Review*, 317–343.

Zeisel, H., & Diamond, S. S. (1976). The jury selection in the Mitchell-Stans conspiracy trial. *American Bar Foundation Research Journal*, 1976(1), 151–174.

Zeisel, H., & Diamond, S. S. (1978). The effect of peremptory challenges on jury and verdict: An experiment in a federal district court. *Stanford Law Review*, 30, 491–529.

Zelig, M., & Beidleman, W. B. (1981). The investigative use of hypnosis: A word of caution. *International Journal of Clinical and Experimental Hypnosis*, 29, 401–412.

Zimbardo, P. G. (1970). The human choice: Individuation, reason, and order versus deindividuation, impulse, and chaos. In W. J. Arnold & D. Levine (Eds.), *Nebraska Symposium on Motivation, 1969*. Lincoln: University of Nebraska Press.

Zimring, F. E. (1982). *The changing legal world of adolescence*. New York: Free Press.

Ziskin, J., & Faust, D. (1988). *Coping with psychiatric and psychological testimony* (4th ed., Vols 1–3). Marina del Rey, CA: Law and Psychology Press.

Author Index

Subject Index

CREDITS

This page constitutes an extension of the copyright page.

We have made every effort to trace the ownership of all copyrighted material and to secure permission from copyright holders. In the event of any question arising as to the use of any material, we will be pleased to make necessary corrections in future printings.

32, Box 2-1 reprinted from Page 205, Chapter 11, in *Psychology in the Legal Process,* by Bruce D. Sales (Ed.). Copyright 1977, Spectrum Publications, Inc., Jamaica, New York.

74, Box 4-2 and quote from *ONE L* by Scott Turow. Copyright © 1977 by Scott Turow. Reprinted by permission of Farrar, Straus & Giroux, Inc.

98, Table 5-2 from "Genetic Factors in the Etiology of Criminal Behavior," by S. A. Mednick, W. F. Gabrielli, Jr., and B. Hutchings. In *The Causes of Crime: New Biological Approaches,* by T. E. Mednick, S. A. Moffitt, and S. A. Stack (Eds.), pp. 74–91. Copyright © 1984 by Cambridge University Press.

202, Box 9-2 adapted from *Psychology and Criminal Justice,* by Katherine W. Ellison and Robert Buckhout. Copyright © 1981 by Katherine W. Ellison and Robert Buckhout. Reprinted by permission of HarperCollins Publishers.

229, Table 10-1 from "Decision Making and Information Integration in the Courts," by E. B. Ebbesen and V. J. Konecni, *Journal of Personality and Social Psychology, 32,* pp. 805–821. Copyright © 1975 by the American Psychological Association. Adapted by permission.

254, Box 11-3 from "Competency for Trial: A Screening Instrument," by P. D. Lipsitt, D. Lelos, and A. L. McGarry. In *American Journal of Psychiatry, 128,* pp. 105–109. Copyright © 1971 by the American Psychiatric Association.

256–257, Box 11-4 from *Competency to Stand Trial and Mental Illness,* by the Laboratory for Community Psychiatry. Copyright © 1974 by Jason Aronson.

384, quotes reprinted with permission of Charles Scribner's Sons, an imprint of Macmillan Publishing Company, from *The Insanity Plea,* by William J. Winslade and Judith Ross. Copyright ©1983 William J. Winslade and Judith Wilson Ross.

432, Table 18-1 and quotes in Chapter 18 from *The Supreme Court,* 2nd Ed., by L. Baum. Copyright © 1985 by Congressional Quarterly. Reprinted by permission.

PHOTOS

10, 88, 102, 203, 204, 268, 269, 280, 293, 373, 382, 383, 400, 401, AP/Wide World Photos; **301,** U.S. Library of Congress.

TO THE OWNER OF THIS BOOK:

We hope that you have found *Psychology and the Legal System, Third Edition,* useful. So that this book can be improved in a future edition, would you take the time to complete this sheet and return it? Thank you.

School and address: _____

Department: _____

Instructor's name: _____

_____

1. What I like most about this book is: _____

_____

2. What I like least about this book is: _____

_____

_____

3. My general reaction to this book is: _____

_____

4. The name of the course in which I used this book is: _____

_____

5. Were all of the chapters of the book assigned for you to read? _____

   If not, which ones weren't? _____

6. In the space below, or on a separate sheet of paper, please write specific suggestions for improving this book and anything else you'd care to share about your experience in using the book.

_____

_____

_____

_____

_____

_____

_____